Lecture Notes in Computer Science   10108

Commenced Publication in 1973
Founding and Former Series Editors:
Gerhard Goos, Juris Hartmanis, and Jan van Leeuwen

More information about this series at http://www.springer.com/series/7409

Lecture Notes in Computer Science   10108

Commenced Publication in 1973
Founding and Former Series Editors:
Gerhard Goos, Juris Hartmanis, and Jan van Leeuwen

More information about this series at http://www.springer.com/series/7409

Ting-Ting Wu · Rosella Gennari
Yueh-Min Huang · Haoran Xie
Yiwei Cao (Eds.)

Emerging Technologies for Education

First International Symposium, SETE 2016
Held in Conjunction with ICWL 2016
Rome, Italy, October 26–29, 2016
Revised Selected Papers

 Springer

Editors
Ting-Ting Wu
National Yunlin University of Science and
   Technology
Yunlin
Taiwan

Rosella Gennari
Free University of Bozen-Bolzano
Rome
Italy

Yueh-Min Huang
National Cheng-Kung University
Tainan
Taiwan

Haoran Xie
The Education University of Hong Kong
Hong Kong
Hong Kong

Yiwei Cao
MC Information Multimedia
   Communication AG
Saarbrücken
Germany

ISSN 0302-9743   ISSN 1611-3349   (electronic)
Lecture Notes in Computer Science
ISBN 978-3-319-52835-9   ISBN 978-3-319-52836-6   (eBook)
DOI 10.1007/978-3-319-52836-6

Library of Congress Control Number: 2016963603

LNCS Sublibrary: SL3 – Information Systems and Applications, incl. Internet/Web, and HCI

Printed on acid-free paper

This Springer imprint is published by Springer Nature
The registered company is Springer International Publishing AG
The registered company address is: Gewerbestrasse 11, 6330 Cham, Switzerland

Ting-Ting Wu · Rosella Gennari
Yueh-Min Huang · Haoran Xie
Yiwei Cao (Eds.)

Emerging Technologies for Education

First International Symposium, SETE 2016
Held in Conjunction with ICWL 2016
Rome, Italy, October 26–29, 2016
Revised Selected Papers

 Springer

Editors
Ting-Ting Wu
National Yunlin University of Science and
   Technology
Yunlin
Taiwan

Rosella Gennari
Free University of Bozen-Bolzano
Rome
Italy

Yueh-Min Huang
National Cheng-Kung University
Tainan
Taiwan

Haoran Xie
The Education University of Hong Kong
Hong Kong
Hong Kong

Yiwei Cao
MC Information Multimedia
   Communication AG
Saarbrücken
Germany

ISSN 0302-9743   ISSN 1611-3349 (electronic)
Lecture Notes in Computer Science
ISBN 978-3-319-52835-9   ISBN 978-3-319-52836-6 (eBook)
DOI 10.1007/978-3-319-52836-6

Library of Congress Control Number: 2016963603

LNCS Sublibrary: SL3 – Information Systems and Applications, incl. Internet/Web, and HCI

Printed on acid-free paper

This Springer imprint is published by Springer Nature
The registered company is Springer International Publishing AG
The registered company address is: Gewerbestrasse 11, 6330 Cham, Switzerland

Preface

SETE 2016 was the first Annual International Symposium on Emerging Technologies for Education held in conjunction with ICWL 2016 and organized by the Hong Kong Web Society. SETE is open to the public for organizing a workshop or a track so as to achieve diversity in the symposium. Fueled by ICT technologies, the e-learning environment in the education sector has become more innovative than ever before. Diversified emerging technologies containing various software and hardware components provide the underlying infrastructure creating enormous potential educational applications incorporated by proper learning strategies. Moreover, these prevalent technologies might also lead to changes in the educational environment as well as in learning performance. Moreover, new paradigms are also emerging with the purpose of bringing these innovations to a level where they are widely accepted and sustainable. Therefore, this symposium aims to be a meeting point for researchers, educationists, and practitioners to discuss state-of-the-art and in-progress research, exchange ideas, and share experiences about emerging technologies for education. This symposium attempts to provide opportunities for the cross-fertilization of knowledge and ideas from researchers in diverse fields that make up this interdisciplinary research area. We hope that the implications of the findings of each work presented at this symposium can be used to improve the development of educational environments.

This year's conference was located in Rome, the vibrant capital of Italy, which stands on the ancient trading routes between North and South. This strategic position has made Rome a hotspot where many cultures have met, battled, traded, and exchanged knowledge.

This year we received 139 submissions from 12 countries worldwide. After a rigorous double-blind review process, 81 papers were selected as full/short papers, yielding an acceptance rate of 59%. These contributions cover the latest findings in various areas, such as: emerging technologies for open access to education and learning; emerging technologies-supported personalized and adaptive learning; emerging technologies for the design, model, and framework of learning systems; emerging technologies support for intelligent tutoring; emerging technologies support for game-based and joyful learning; emerging technologies-enhanced language learning; emerging technologies-supported big data analytics in education; emerging technologies-supported collaborative learning; emerging technologies of pedagogical issues; emerging technologies for affective learning; and emerging technologies for tangible learning.

Moreover, SETE 2016 featured three distinguished keynote presentations and eight workshops, complementing the main conference areas and covering a wide range of topics including: active ageing and digital inclusion; emerging technologies for language learning; online adaptive learning techniques and applications; social and personal computing for Web-supported learning communities; user modeling for Web-based learning; peer review, peer assessment, and self-assessment in education;

technology-enhanced language learning; and the applications of information and communication technologies in adult and continuing education.

We would like to thank the entire Organizing Committee and especially the organization co-chairs, Yueh-Min Huang and Rosella Gennari, for their efforts and time spent to ensure the success of the conference. We would also like to express our gratitude to the Program Committee members for their timely and helpful reviews. And last but not least, we would like to thank all the authors for their contribution in maintaining a high-quality conference – we count on your continual support to play a significant role in the Web-based learning community in the future.

September 2016

Yueh-Min Huang
Rosella Gennari
Yiwei Cao
Haoran Xie
Ting-Ting Wu

Organization

Conference Co-chairs

Yueh-Min Huang   National Cheng-Kung University, Taiwan
Rosella Gennari   Free University of Bozen-Bolzano, Italy

Program Co-chairs

Yiwei Cao   MC Information Multimedia Communication AG,
     Germany
Haoran Xie   The Education University of Hong Kong, Hong Kong,
     SAR China
Ting-Ting Wu   National Yunlin University of Science and Technology,
     Taiwan

Program Committee

Dimitra Anastasiou   Luxembourg Institute of Science and Technology,
     Luxembourg
Gautam Biswas   Vanderbilt University, USA
Yi Cai   South China University of Technology, China
Chi-Cheng Chang   National Taiwan Normal University, Taiwan
Gabriella Dodero   Free University of Bozen-Bolzano, Italy
Vincenzo Del Fatto   Free University of Bozen-Bolzano, Italy
Tianyong Hao   Guangdong University of Foreign Studies, China
Rong-Huai Huang   Beijing Normal University, China
Tristan E. Johnson   Northeastern University, USA
Kinshuk   University of North Texas, USA
Ming-Chi Liu   National Cheng Kung University, Taiwan
Tzu-Chien Liu   National Central University, Taiwan
Tania Di Mascio   University of L'Aquila, Italy
Alessandra Melonio   Free University of Bozen-Bolzano, Italy
Hiroaki Ogata   Kyushu University, Japan
Yanghui Rao   Sun Yat-sen University, China
Demetrios G. Sampson   Curtin University, Australia
Frode Eika Sandnes   Oslo and Akershus University College
     of Applied Sciences, Norway
Michael Spector   University of North Texas, USA
Daniel Spikol   Malmo University, Sweden
Andreja Istenic Starcic   University of Ljubljana, Slovenia
Yao-Ting Sung   National Taiwan Normal University, Taiwan

Pierpaolo Vittorini	University of L'Aquila, Italy
Dan Wang	Caritas Institute of Higher Education, Hong Kong, SAR China
Fu Lee Wang	Caritas Institute of Higher Education, Hong Kong, SAR China
Tak-Lam Wong	The Hong Kong Institute of Education, Hong Kong, SAR China
Zhenguo Yang	City University of Hong Kong, Hong Kong, SAR China
Neil Yen	University of Aizu, Japan
Chengjiu Yin	Kyushu University, Japan
Matej Zajc	University of Ljubljana, Slovenia
Yunhui Zhuang	City University of Hong Kong, Hong Kong, SAR China
Di Zou	The Hong Kong Polytechnic University, Hong Kong, SAR China

Main Organizer

Co-organizers

Contents

Emerging Technologies Enhanced Language Learning

Emerging Technologies Supported Innovative Learning

Workshop on Active Ageing and Digital Inclusion

Workshop on Emerging Technologies for Language Learning

Workshop on Online Adaptive Learning Techniques and Applications

Workshop on Social and Personal Computing for Web-Supported Learning Communities

Workshop on User Modeling for Web-Based Learning

Workshop on Peer Review, Peer Assessment, and Self-assessment in Education

**Workshop on the Applications of Information and Communication
Technologies in Adult and Continuing Education**

Emerging Technologies Support for Game-Based and Joyful Learning

The Analysis of Incidental Learning in the Affinity Spaces of a Smartphone Game "*Neko Atsume*"

Toru Fujimoto[1(✉)] and Christopher Michael Yap[2]

[1] The University of Tokyo, Tokyo, Japan
tfujimt@he.u-tokyo.ac.jp
[2] Nara Institute of Science and Technology, Nara, Japan
christopher-y@is.naist.jp

Abstract. This study investigated the player community of the smartphone game *Neko Atsume: Kitty Collector* in terms of incidental learning. The game attracts both gamers and non-gamers alike with its simple and unique game design that facilitates emergent narrative among the users even though the game does not offer any in-game communication means. The researchers conducted an international user survey to understand the game experience of the users. The result of the user survey revealed how users were engaged in social communication enhanced by game play.

Keywords: *Neko Atsume* · Affinity spaces · Incidental learning · Emergent narrative · Game-based learning

1 Introduction

The recent advancement of digital game technologies has extended the pervasive world of online game environments, such as Massive Multiplayer Online games (MMO) and social games on mobile phone, where millions of players can play the same game at the same time.

Since most popular game titles usually require players to play very long hours to be skilled and complete, the more players engage in a game, the more they have to dedicate vast amounts of their time to it. While such a trait is not unusual for games (and may even be considered normal for any kind of hobby/recreational activity), online games and recent social games have been notorious for causing players to lose control in the management of their social lives and for causing some players to become isolated from their friends and family.

Recent researches and practices on the use of the positive aspect of videogames, such as educational values in the classroom, various potentials for healthcare needs, and the social impact of game-based advocacy [1, 2], tell us that videogames are not just a playful tool for leisure or definitely not a social problem, but they could also provide players with an engaging learning environment in a non-educational setting. For instance, players communicate with each other to share knowledge to play better, achieve goals, and collaborate to build resources in the game world. There is a

© Springer International Publishing AG 2017
T.-T. Wu et al. (Eds.): SETE 2016, LNCS 10108, pp. 3–13, 2017.
DOI: 10.1007/978-3-319-52836-6_1

tremendous amount of so-called "user-created content" widespread on the internet, including game guides for beginners, walk-throughs, strategy guides, solutions, and maps to learn how to move on to accomplish a specific task in the game. Even in simple casual games for mobile phones, players learn from each other through interaction and knowledge construction activities.

In this present study, we investigated the player community of "*Neko Atsume: Kitty Collector*" as a case for this research since this game offers a great example of how a simple single player online game can create rich affinity spaces that facilitate incidental learning in the player community during their game play. *Neko Atsume* is a good example to focus on in terms of learning technologies since it is on a ubiquitous mobile platform which is easy to patch remotely. With a user survey and theoretical analysis of the game design, this study described the nature of user communities built through playing a game and analyzed how incidental learning occurs in game play.

2 Theoretical Background

2.1 Affinity Spaces

As noted, there are a wide variety of wikis, blogs, and posts on social media such as Twitter and Facebook provided by players. Games with such user-created resources work as systems in which players learn and collaborate through social interactions. Gee called such online environments "affinity spaces," a set of places where people can affiliate with others based on shared activities, interests and goals [3]. The key features which characterize affinity spaces include (1) openness to any participant, (2) sharing of the common spaces by players, regardless of their experience, (3) the creation and extension of spaces by the players, (4) the availability of multiple routes of participation, and (5) the creation and sharing of relevant knowledge among players.

While the notion of affinity spaces provides an analytical lens to look at how people interact and learn from each other socially in online environments, previous researches are concerned primarily with the rich and complex game environments that require players to explore vast game worlds and improve their skills to overcome difficult challenges in the game, such as MMOs and Real Time Strategy games [4]. Since it is uncertain if the concept of affinity spaces can be applicable for the simple, less challenging single player games with no in-game social interaction, it is beneficial for those who are interested in affinity spaces to study single player online games with features that are different from the previous researches on affinity spaces to articulate the elements of this concept.

2.2 Incidental Learning

The nature of the learning that occurs in affinity spaces is fundamentally incidental. Incidental learning is defined as unintentional or unplanned learning that results from other activities [5]. It is characterized as informal, situated and contextually embedded. The concept is similar to informal learning, but it particularly focuses on the nature of unintentionality in unplanned situations. Incidental learning is likely to occur when a learner is motivated to do the activity regardless of the type of activity that might be. Formal instruction is not necessary to facilitate this type of learning. Providing a fun activity that the learner is willing to participate in is more important. While conducting the activity, meaningful knowledge of the activity will be learned during the process. To design such a learning environment, it is important to find things that are inherently fun and to understand those things that learners naturally want to learn [6]. Therefore it is worthwhile to study game players who are having fun with their favorite games and to understand what kind of knowledge is learned during their game play.

2.3   Emergent Narrative

We applied the concept of emergent narrative as a theoretical framework to analyze the game design of *Neko Atsume* to articulate the mechanism of how and why players are driven to interact with other players. Emergent narrative refers to a narrative or story which is not found inherently within the game software itself, but instead coalesces *after* human players have interacted with the game [7]. Like emergence in other disciplines such as in philosophy [8], computer science [9], and biology [10], emergent narrative is both unintended and irreducible to its constituent parts. In other words, one can never truly predict the emergence of the narrative, even if you have a full understanding of the pieces which led to the emergent product. Thusly, emergent narrative can be thought of as a highly-subjective player interpretation of the actual, objective events and objects of the game. Like incidental learning, the phenomenon of emergent narrative is unintended (by the game designers) and is akin to a surprising side-effect stemming from the inherently engaging design of the game itself. By tracing the trajectory of players' narrative construction, we can have a better understanding on the relationship between game design and the interaction of players.

3   Research Field

"*Neko Atsume*" is a free to play, cat collecting smartphone game application for Android and iPhone produced by Hit-Point Inc., a game development company based in Kyoto, Japan [11]. In the game, players purchase foods and goods for cats, and place them in the yard to attract a variety of cats (Fig. 1).

The players can simply watch them or take photos of them. The cats randomly leave silver or gold fish after leaving the yard. They occasionally give players mementos as a token of appreciation. Since its release in October 2014, the number of downloads has increased rapidly, and counts over 13 million downloads in January 2016.

Neko Atsume's originality in game design is recognized in the game industry internationally. The game was awarded the best game design of CEDEC AWARDS 2015 by Computer Entertainment Association in Japan [12]. Game Spot awarded *Neko Atsume* the Top 5 Mobile Games of 2015 [13]. Though the game was originally released only in Japanese, it became popular even for players who could not read Japanese because of its simplicity and playability [14]. When Hit-Point released the

Fig. 1. Screenshot of *"Neko Atsume"* ©HIT-POINT

English version in October 2015, the game extended its popularity to a worldwide audience with its English title *"Neko Atsume: Kitty Collector"*.

The main features of *Neko Atsume* we considered as unique game design elements are as follows:

– Free-to-play: While players can spend real money for in-game money (gold fish) to purchase foods and items, it is not necessary in order to fully enjoy the game.
– Interaction: While other online games usually have in-game interaction with other players as well as instant feedback to the player's action, *Neko Atsume* does not have these features. Players communicate outside the game world with social media services such as Twitter and Facebook. The game also requires players to close the game window and wait for a few minutes to see the response to their action in the game.
– Sharing: The game offers a function for taking photos of cats and sharing that image via Twitter. Screenshots taken in the game can also be easily shared via Instagram or other image sharing social networking services.
– Goals: Although there are some forms of achievement such as completing the cat and memento collections, there are no ultimate goals in *Neko Atsume*.
– Non-narrative: The game provides very little narrative context, dialog, cinematic scenes, plot, or anything that is normally associated with a narrative.

4   Method

To understand what kind of activities players are conducting and what elements facilitate the player participation during their play of *Neko Atsume*, we conducted an exploratory Internet survey to gain perspective on players' activities outside of the game. We conducted an exploratory Internet search by keyword *"Neko Atsume"*, and "ねこあつめ" in Japanese during December 2015 to January 2016.

After the exploratory survey, we carried out an online questionnaire to the players to understand how players are engaged in the game and what they think about their play experience. The questionnaire was constructed using a commercial online survey system offered by SurveyMonkey. We recruited the survey participants with advertisements on several social networking services including Facebook groups, Reddit, and Twitter. The questionnaire consisted of 8 questions regarding participants' profile (e.g. age, gender, education level, and nationality), 14 questions regarding how they play the game (e.g. language, interaction with others, progress, how they start playing, time length of play), and 20 questions regarding their impressions and feelings about the game (e.g. favorite cats, what they like about the game, and how they feel about the cats and features). This player survey was conducted from April 1 to May 10, 2016. We focused on reporting the aspects of incidental learning in this paper.

5   Result and Discussion

5.1   Proportion of *Neko Atsume's* Affinity Spaces

The Internet search resulted in massive user conversation data and user-generated contents in terms of *Neko Atsume* on various news articles, personal websites, and social media postings. The researchers carefully examined the data and irrelevant data was excluded from the data pool. The table below shows the various types of data collected (Table 1).

Table 1. Collected Data

Media	Collected data
Twitter	5178 tweets (during 2016/1/29-2/2)
Facebook	88 pages/groups (16 Fan pages, 51 closed & 21 open groups)
Official application download page (Google Play, App Store)	More than 300 comments (during 2015/12-2016/1 on GooglePlay download page)
Instagram	More than 300 image files (129,747 hits in total)
Tumblr	More than 300 posts
YouTube	More than 100 video posts
Soundcloud	56 audio files (as of 2016/1/30)
Other relevant data collected	Personal blogs, summary websites, news media articles

The data was categorized based on the content included and types of information shared in the posts by the researchers. The table below shows the examples of categories (Table 2). While there also exists detailed practical information to play efficiently, such as game walkthroughs, hints and tips just as for other popular games, the majority of user-generated content is non-practical information which is not useful in terms of achieving the game's goals. This is unusual for games with complex game contents with difficult challenges. In the affinity spaces built around such complex

Table 2. Amount of collected data

Category	Content
Sharing updates	Sharing latest official announcements, related events and products
Sharing feelings	Posting images of cats to express feelings how cute/funny they are
Sharing achievements	Posting images of cats to show achievements (e.g. find a new cat/obtain a memento). Comments by others expressing how they feel
Sharing narratives	Posting images of cats to describe how they interpret the situation. Comments how others felt the narrative and add one's interpretation to the post
Sharing creative play	Posting screenshots to share the results of arranging goods in a unique way (e.g. arranging goods to create a funny image)
Q&A	Trouble shooting questions and asking solutions to experienced players by novice players
Requests to publisher	Comments on the technical problems and requests to improve the game application
Derivative works	Posting user-created funny images by modifying the screenshots taken from the game, and artwork using the game characters

games, players typically interact with other players to share knowledge and techniques to be skillful and achieve game objectives faster. Since *Neko Atsume* does not contain such game goals and challenging objectives, players do not need to exchange such practical information.

5.2   Players' Recognition on Incidental Learning

A total of 1067 individuals from all over the world completed the survey. More than three quarters of the respondents were female (78.2%). The largest age group was age 25 to 34 (32.6%), and the group of age 18 to 24 followed (29.8%). More than half of the respondents live in the United States (54.6%), and Japan (13.9%) was the second largest group. While the population may reflect the main players of the game based on its language availability (English and Japanese), it is noted that this proportion of respondent population does not necessarily reflect the actual proportion of the player population of *Neko Atsume*.

While nearly half of the respondents (48.1%) are casual gamers or non-gamers who do not play videogames other than *Neko Atsume*, most of them play *Neko Atsume* almost every day (85.7%). About two-thirds of them have played the game for more than three months (67.9%), and typically play less than 30 min a day (65.9%). The result indicated that *Neko Atsume* attracts not only gamers, but occasional gamers as well.

To look into the nature of how incidental learning occurs in the game play, we asked the respondents if they recognized the game play as a learning activity with the question, "By playing "*Neko Atsume*", do you find out or learn something new?" This question intended to evoke respondents' self-reflection and associating their game play with learning. As a result, about one third of the entire respondents (33.8%) have noticed that they actually learned something new from playing the game.

In order to understand the context of the response, we have conducted a qualitative coding and analysis of the free-answer question "If you answered 'agree' to the question above, what did you find out or learn from 'Neko Atsume'? Please describe your thoughts." The result indicated that one third of the respondents consider they learned about cat behavior or knowledge about cats (34.4%). When the players interact with virtual cats with items and foods in the game world, they are exposed to such kinds of information which are relevant to the game activity. While playing the game, they are likely to be driven by curiosity to find out more, simply for fun. Such a process leads them to the state of incidental learning.

There were players who were not familiar with the vocabulary used in the game. In such cases, the game offered them an opportunity to acquire new knowledge on language such as the name of Japanese furniture, foods, and cat toys. About one fifth of them recognized this type of learning (20.1%). Beyond the knowledge explicitly included in the game world, some respondents found they learned cultural matters through game play (23.8%).

The table below exhibits some examples of comments by respondents that elaborated their thoughts on what they learned in the game for each category (Table 3).

Table 3. Example of comments

Category	Comments
Language	*"Some Japanese things like kotatsus, cat coat colours, a few Japanese words like akage/ginger, a few English words too like nihilistic"* (ID:148)
Reflection/lesson	*"there are more cat lovers in this world then I thought. I have loved cats for a long time and the fact you guys were able to capture their feelings and actions so well in this game make me so happy...."* (ID:122)
Cultural matters	*"...learned about behavior culture, become interested in some artists, paintings and ultimately been more interested reading books from behavior authors"* (ID:008)
Cat behavior	*"learn to study cats' behavior and learn more about Japanese cats from facebook"* (ID:020)
Design	*"Idle games have their place in gaming world and they don't have to be complicated. Something simple like this has its own charm too"* (ID:216)

5.3   Analysis on Player-Side Emergent Narrative

Players of Neko Atsume also seem to share their game experience in terms of narrative context, even though the game does not have many elements of challenge, achievement, or dialog like other popular games. To articulate the mechanism of how and why players are driven to interact with other players in sharing narratives, we investigated how players interact with the game content in terms of emergent narrative. As previously mentioned, aside from the single-adjective descriptors provided by each cat's respective dossier ("capricious," "shy," "sensitive," etc.) (Fig. 2 (left)), *Neko Atsume* is considerably bereft of conventional narrative. This characteristic lack of narrative traits within the game is also highlighted by the fact that the player herself is unable to directly interact with or influence the cats of *Neko Atsume*.

Fig. 2. (Left) The cat dossier for "Marshmallow." (right) "How do you think is the cat is feeling" ©HIT-POINT

Despite the lack of conventional narrative, survey respondents indicated that they crafted their own subjective narrative contexts for the cats. For example, regarding the question "How do you think is the cat is feeling? Please briefly describe your answer below" (Fig. 2 (right)), some respondents offered particularly context-laden answers. While no concrete narrative descriptions of the depicted situations were provided by the game, respondents still associated the images with various emotional and psychological states, with some respondents even crafting specific reasons and situations as to why the cats were portrayed thusly.

In response to the image, interpretive responses ranged from the objectively literal (*"This cat is staring mysteriously off into the distance. I don't know what, if anything, it's feeling."*), the personal (*"Upset with me?/Annoyed with the player/Shunning me"*), the negative (*"pissed off at the humans for something"*), to the context-specific (*"Someday. Someday I will reach my goal. But not today."*). One particularly intriguing Japanese response was the single word *"たそがれている"* (which, loosely translated, means something akin to *"reflecting on the twilight of one's own life (after having peaked)"*). Despite the wide range of interpretations of the images, the actual game provides no direct context for any of the portrayals of the cats in the game. It merely provides images.

If the seemingly random creation of narrative context is occurring despite the absence of conventional narrative in the game itself, this begs the question about where that narrative experience may be coming from. Based on both the ludic structure and aesthetic content of the game as well as the varying interpretive responses from the survey, it can be said that narrative context in *Neko Atsume* does not inherently come *from Neko Atsume* per se, but is instead potentially *created out of* a player's interaction with *Neko Atsume*. The narrative experience is something that coalesces within the mind of the player (extraneous to the literal game software). In this way, it can be contended that the narrative experience of *Neko Atsume* constitutes a kind of *player-side emergent narrative* phenomenon, where game narrative is not pre-hardcoded into the game by the developers, but rather, through strategically-ambiguous cues, the narrative experience is *emergently* inspired by the game design [15].

In making the above observation, it is also important to note that the game by itself may not be intentionally attempting to tell narratives. Despite this, the sharing of emergent narratives among players in online communities constitutes a helpful means of understanding and observing the role of game design with respect to encouraging certain kinds of player activity. In particular, the observations seem to suggest that the design of this game seems to naturally play upon a player's need for meaning or context. The survey responses seem to indicate that players are willfully associating and creating their own narrative contexts out of the game and (perhaps even unconsciously) projecting those contexts onto the cat characters of the game, and it is this narrative experience which is essentially emergent. This is akin to one of the main player activities noticed in the survey, which was the sharing of narrative, where an overt lack of information in the game design has accidentally inspired curiosity in the players of *Neko Atsume*.

6 Conclusion

The results of the player survey indicated that *Neko Atsume* enhances player's incidental learning in some sense through its game design. The sharing of narratives by players in the affinity space of *Neko Atsume* is largely influenced by the lack of conventional narrative provided by the game. As it is considered that the primary importance of game-based learning is to prepare for future learning [16], even if the game play is not directly relevant to educational purposes, such knowledge learned incidentally by playing entertainment games may potentially help players to perform better in other practical contexts in the future. In the case of *Neko Atsume* while players are driven to conduct playful activities offered in the game, they become curious about ambiguous information and consequently, inspired to gain more information to understand the context. Although it may not apply to every player, engaged players tend to learn more information than the game provides and they become knowledgeable in the relevant knowledge, in this case, knowledge about cats and Japanese culture.

If we consider making use of the strength of this game educationally, it can be used by educators as a potentially effective classroom activity for aiding in group discussion, critical dialog, and perhaps even public speaking. For example, a specific potential use case could be that discussing the cats of *Neko Atsume* could serve as writing prompts in creative writing classes or workshops on extemporaneous speech. Furthermore, *Neko Atsume*'s premise of attracting cats to the player's yard for the sake of observing them is ethically-neutral, thereby avoiding many of the moral issues related to conventional games which employ violence as a game mechanic. Unlike many games where player progress is predicated on competition or a measure of player skill (strategic or otherwise), *Neko Atsume* is a game which all players/students can enjoy and "successfully play" regardless of skill level.

In such educational activities, it is not necessary to learn everything in order to meet an educational purpose from a game. It is not the most effective direction for educators to teach everything through game play. Rather, it is important to embed reflective activities around the game play which encourage students to want to play and learn on their own.

In terms of the limits of the scope of this research, it should also be noted that this study is still a preliminary effort which will require further qualification in order to solidify our claims regarding the potential for incidental learning, affinity spaces, and emergent narrative in casual mobile games such as *Neko Atsume*. This game is but one example in a genre that is becoming increasingly widespread in the modern world, and while it is a good example of incidental learning, more work needs to be done to see if the same kinds of phenomenon can be observed in other such games. Furthermore, all games do have a natural tendency to lose player attraction over time. However, games like *Neko Atsume*, which are updated remotely, can potentially counter such a loss of interest by adding content via software patches.

Though this study is still in its initial phases, subsequent efforts for this research will continue to investigate how the design of *Neko Atsume* further inspires incidental learning to take place in affinity spaces, as well as the depth of narrative interpretation *Neko Atsume* evokes within its player base, which can be potentially evident in the game's affinity spaces. Furthermore, it will be important to investigate any potential synergistic links between incidental learning and emergent narrative phenomenon in (and perhaps out of) affinity spaces as well.

References

1. Steinkuehler, C., Squire, K.: Videogames and learning. In: Sawyer, R.K. (ed.) Cambridge Handbook of the Learning Sciences, 2nd edn. Cambridge University Press, New York (2014)
2. Klopfer, E., Osterweil, S., Salen, K.: Moving Learning Games Forward: Obstacles, Opportunities & Openness. MIT The Education Arcade, Cambridge (2009)
3. Gee, J.P.: Situated Language and Learning: A Critique of Traditional Schooling. Routledge, London (2004)
4. Gee, J., Hayes, E.: Nurturing affinity spaces and game-based learning. In: Steinkuehler, C., Squire, K., Barab, S.A. (eds.) Games, Learning, and Society: Learning and Meaning in the Digital Age, pp. 129–153. Cambridge University Press, Cambridge (2012)
5. Kerka, S.: Incidental learning. trends and issues alert no. 18. http://eric.ed.gov/?q=%E2% 80%9DIncidental+learning%E2%80%9D+Kerka&id=ED446234 (2000). Accessed 30 May 2016
6. Schank, R.C., Cleary, C.: Engines for Education, pp. 95–105. Lawrence Erlbaum Associates Publishers, Hillsdale (1995)
7. Louchart, S.: Emergent narrative: towards a narrative theory of virtual reality. University of Salford (2007)
8. Lewes, G.H.: Problems of Life and Mind (First Series), vol. 2. Trübner, London (1875)
9. Forrest, S.: Emergent computation: self-organizing, collective, and cooperative phenomena in natural and artificial computing networks: introduction to the proceedings of the ninth annual CNLS conference. Phys. D Nonlinear Phenom. **42**(1), 1–11 (1990)
10. Oparin, A.I.: The Origin of Life. Courier Dover Publications, Dover (2003)
11. Hit-Point: Neko Atsume: kitty collector. http://hpmobile.jp/games/neko/ (2014). Accessed 30 Jan 2016
12. CESA: CEDEC awards recipients. http://cedec.cesa.or.jp/2015/event/awards_prize.html (2015). Accessed 30 Jan 2016

13. Game Spot: Top 5 mobile games the best mobile games of 2015. http://www.gamespot.com/articles/the-best-mobile-games-of-2015/1100-6432488/ (2015). Accessed 30 Jan 2016
14. Bradley, R.: Why am i obsessed with a cellphone game about collecting cats? The New York Times Magazine. http://www.nytimes.com/2016/02/18/magazine/why-am-i-obsessed-with-a-cellphone-game-about-collecting-cats.html (2016). Accessed 30 Jan 2016
15. Yap, C.M.: Conceptualizing player-side emergence in interactive games: between hard-coded software and the human mind in papers, please and gone home. Int. J. Gaming Comput. Mediated Simul. 7(3), 1–21 (2015)
16. Schwartz, D.L., Martin, T.: Inventing to prepare for learning: the hidden efficiency of original student production in statistics instruction. Cogn. Instr. 22, 129–184 (2004)

Exploring the Factors that Influence
the Intention to Play a Color Mixing Game

Yong-Ming Huang[1(✉)], Chia-Sui Wang[2], Tien-Chi Huang[3],
and Chia-Chen Chen[4]

[1] Department of Applied Informatics and Multimedia,
Chia Nan University of Pharmacy and Science, Tainan, Taiwan, R.O.C.
ym.huang.tw@gmail.com
[2] Department of Information Management,
Chia Nan University of Pharmacy and Science, Tainan, Taiwan, R.O.C.
lcwang@mail.chna.edu.tw
[3] Department of Information Management,
National Taichung Universityof Science and Technology,
Taichung, Taiwan, R.O.C.
tchuang@nutc.edu.tw
[4] Department of Management Information Systems,
National Chung Hsing University, Taichung, Taiwan, R.O.C.
emily@nchu.edu.tw

Abstract. Color mixing is viewed as one of the most important stages with regard to learning colors, and digital games have been identified as a useful means for encouraging students in learning. However, little effort has been devoted to using digital games to assist students in learning color mixing. To remedy this deficiency, this study developed a color mixing game and further explored the subjects' perspectives on the game. More specifically, the technology acceptance model was employed to develop a questionnaire to collect the subjects' opinions about the game, through which the decisive factors behind the subjects' intention to play the game can be analyzed. The questionnaire delivered two significant results. First, the subjects' perceived ease of playing influenced their attitude toward playing through the mediation of perceived usefulness. Second, the subjects' perceived usefulness influenced their intention to play through the mediation of attitude toward playing. The mediation of perceived usefulness and attitude toward playing implied that both ways of influence were indirect.

1 Introduction

Color mixing is one of the most important stages in relation to learning colors. It is a process of creating a specific color by mixing primary colors [1, 2]. More specifically, color mixing can be achieved through additive and subtractive methods. The additive color mixing is to overlap spotlights in a dark space, in which its primary colors include red, green, and blue [1]. The subtractive color mixing is to use white light to illuminate colored filters from behind, in which its primary colors are cyan, magenta, and yellow [1]. In general, the subtractive color mixing is implemented by using paints and

© Springer International Publishing AG 2017
T.-T. Wu et al. (Eds.): SETE 2016, LNCS 10108, pp. 14–20, 2017.
DOI: 10.1007/978-3-319-52836-6_2

pigments. This means that the study of the subtractive color mixing is more difficult than the additive one, for the latter depends simply on overlapping spotlights [2]. Thus, developing a sound approach to assist students in learning subtractive color mixing has become a vital issue.

However, this issue has received surprisingly little scholarly attention. In fact, only a few studies focused on how to help students learn color mixing, and they mainly suggested using computer technologies to achieve this goal. For example, Lányi et al. developed a computer-based color education system to support students in learning color mixing [3]. Lányi et al. claimed that the system they proposed is more competent than traditional teaching material in helping students make color experiments and simulate color mixing. Similarly, Perge and Zichar also developed a piece of interactive software for students to learn color mixing. Overall, both studies used computer technologies to simulate color mixing, so that students can directly try to mix two different colors rather than spend time on using spotlights or paints.

The system and software proposed by the foregoing studies might had been useful for learning color mixing, but they are rather outdated for today's learning contexts due to technological advances. With the advances in multimedia technologies, digital games have been regarded as a promising tool for enhancing students' learning motivation [4, 5]. These studies showed digital games as competent to create congenial learning contexts that are more attractive than traditional ones, so as to increase students' learning motivation. They also indicated that such type of games can provide students with an immersive experience, which may in turn increase their motivation to overcome the challenges and accomplish the missions assigned by the games [6, 7]. As a result, digital games have attracted considerable attention in recent times.

To facilitate students' learning of color mixing, we designed a color mixing game, a smartphone App that students can play anytime and anywhere. To explore the subjects' perspectives on the game, this study conducted an experiment based on the technology acceptance model (TAM) [8, 9], and also developed a questionnaire accordingly to collect related data. Finally, we carried out a series of analyses to examine the research model and drew conclusions about the analyses.

2 Research Design

2.1 Research Model and Hypotheses

Figure 1 shows the research model adapted from the TAM [8, 9]. Five hypotheses are formulated accordingly and explicated below.

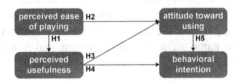

Fig. 1. Research model.

TAM is a popular model which has been widely used to explore users' perspectives on technologies. Davis et al. proposed this four-construct model to explore the decisive factors behind users' intention to use technologies. The four constructs include perceived ease of use, perceived usefulness, attitude toward using, and behavioral intention. Perceived ease of use is defined as "the degree to which a person believes that using a particular system would be free from effort" [8]. Perceived usefulness is defined as "the degree to which a person believes that using a particular system would enhance his or her job performance" [8]. Attitude toward using refers to the degree to which a person prefers a particular system [10]. Behavioral intention refers to the degree to which a person is willing to use a particular system [10]. Based on these definitions, Davis et al. further formulated the following hypotheses to explore the relationships among these constructs, so as to identify the determinants of users' intention to use technologies. First, perceived ease of use has a positive and significant influence on perceived usefulness and attitude toward using. Second, perceived usefulness has a positive and significant influence on attitude toward using and behavioral intention. Third, attitude toward using has a positive and significant influence on behavioral intention [8, 9]. This means that the TAM is an effective tool for explaining or predicting the degree to which the subjects accept or reject the proposed mobile game, through which we can measure the value of this new technology. In this study, perceived ease of use and attitude toward using were respectively replaced by perceived ease of playing and attitude toward playing, since the technology employed is a mobile game. Accordingly, this study formulated the following five hypotheses:

H1. Perceived ease of playing has a positive and significant effect on perceived usefulness.
H2. Perceived ease of playing has a positive and significant effect on attitude toward playing.
H3. Perceived usefulness has a positive and significant effect on attitude toward playing.
H4. Perceived usefulness has a positive and significant effect on behavioral intention.
H5. Attitude toward playing has a positive and significant effect on behavioral intention.

2.2   Color Mixing Game

Figure 2 illustrates the color mixing game which takes on the form of a puzzle game. The player is asked to mix three primary colors to create a specific color within a limited amount of time. The three primary colors are presented in the form of bubbles that will burst over time. In the game scene, the color in the transparent pot changes randomly. To inform the player of the mission objective, a hexagram of colors is shown in the upper left of the game scene. The arrangement makes this game particularly suitable for learning color mixing.

Fig. 2. The color mixing game. (Color figure online)

2.3 Measurement and Data Collection

To collect the data on the subjects' perspectives on the proposed mobile game, a structured questionnaire was developed on the basis of an extensive review of previous studies [8, 9, 11]. The questionnaire includes four constructs, namely perceived ease of playing, perceived usefulness, attitude toward playing, and behavioral intention. The final questionnaire was distributed to the subjects who were asked to indicate their level of agreement with the statements using a five-point Likert scale.

The subjects who volunteered to participate in this study were 205 college students. They firstly learned to play the mobile game under our instruction. Then they played the game on their own for 30 min after knowing how to play it. Finally, they were required to fill in the questionnaire, from which the validity of the research model and hypotheses can be examined.

3 Results

This study employed the partial least squares approach to analyze the questionnaire data, and applied the SmartPLS 3.0 software to perform the approach, which includes the measurement model and the structural one.

3.1 Measurement Model

The measurement model was examined by using the reliability of the measures as well as the convergent and discriminant validities. The reliability of the measures was evaluated by composite reliability and Cronbach's alpha. In general, the minimum acceptable value of composite reliability is 0.7 and that of Cronbach's alpha is 0.6 [12]. The convergent validity was assessed by the average variance extracted (AVE) whose value is required to exceed the standard minimum threshold of 0.5 [12]. The discriminant validity was assessed by the square root of the AVE and the latent variable correlations. Each construct's square root of the AVE must exceed its correlation coefficient with other constructs in the model [13]. Tables 1 and 2 indicate that the results delivered by the measurement model are significant and acceptable, because all the values meet the required minimum standards.

Table 1. The reliability and convergent validity of the measurement model.

Construct	Reliability of measure		Convergent validity
	Composite reliability	Cronbach's alpha	AVE
Perceived ease of playing	0.94	0.91	0.85
Perceived usefulness	0.96	0.93	0.88
Attitude toward using	0.96	0.94	0.89
Behavioral intention	0.97	0.95	0.95

Table 2. The discriminant validity of the measurement model.

Construct	Discriminant validity				
	Latent variable correlations				
		1	2	3	4
Perceived ease of playing	1	0.92			
Perceived usefulness	2	0.72	0.94		
Attitude toward using	3	0.63	0.88	0.94	
Behavioral intention	4	0.57	0.80	0.87	0.97

3.2 Structural Model

Based on the path coefficients and the R^2 values, the structural model was employed to test the hypotheses formulated in this study [14]. The path coefficients served as the indicator for the statistical significance of the hypotheses, and the R^2 values indicated the model's ability in explaining the variation in the dependent variables. Figure 3 demonstrates the results delivered by the structural model, which highlighted the rejection of H2 and H4, and confirmed the other three hypotheses.

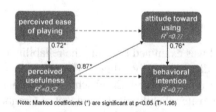

Note: Marked coefficients (*) are significant at p<0.05 (T>1.96)

Fig. 3. The results of the structural model.

4 Conclusion

Learning colors is important, because colors are all around us, performing stimulating, expressive, cultural, and symbolic functions that greatly embellish our quotidian existence. Color mixing is one of the most important stages for learning colors. In this study, we developed a color mixing game to help students learn color mixing. We also applied the TAM to design a questionnaire, through which we gathered the data on the subjects' opinions about the game. The results delivered by the questionnaire suggested that (1) the subjects' perceived ease of playing had a positive and significant influence on their perceived usefulness rather than on their attitude toward playing; (2) the subjects' perceived usefulness had a positive and significant influence on their attitude toward playing rather than on their behavioral intention; and (3) the subjects' attitude toward playing had a positive and significant influence on their behavioral intention. The research findings revealed that the subjects' perceived usefulness was a significant mediating factor between their perceived ease of paying and attitude toward playing, and the subjects' attitude toward playing is the most important factor behind their intention to play the color mixing game.

Acknowledgements. We would like to express special thanks to Ms. Ting-Ying Du, Ms. Li-Rong Weng, Mr. Lun Hong, Ms. Yi-Jing Huang, and Mr. Wei-Long Chen who provided effective technical support to implement the color mixing game. The authors also would like to thank the Ministry of Science and Technology of the Republic of China, Taiwan, for financially supporting this research under Contract No. MOST 103-2511-S-041-002-MY3.

References

1. Perge, E., Zichar, M.: Computer assisted method for cognitive improvement of color aptitude. In: Proceedings of 6th IEEE International Conference on Cognitive Infocommunications, Gyor, Hungary (2015)
2. Holtzschue, L.: Understanding Color. Wiley, Hoboken (2011)
3. Lányi, C.S., Kosztyán, Z., Kránicz, B., Schanda, J., Navvab, M.: Using multimedia interactive e-teaching in color science. LEUKOS **4**(1), 71–82 (2007)
4. Chen, N.S., Hwang, G.J.: Transforming the classrooms: innovative digital game- based learning designs and applications. Educ. Technol. Res. Dev. **62**(2), 125–128 (2014)
5. Huang, Y.M., Huang, Y.M.: A scaffolding strategy to develop handheld sensor- based vocabulary games for improving students' learning motivation and performance. Educ. Technol. Res. Dev. **63**(5), 691–708 (2015)
6. Cagiltay, N.E.: Teaching software engineering by means of computer-game development: challenges and opportunities. Br. J. Educ. Technol. **38**(3), 405–415 (2007)
7. Kinzie, M.B., Joseph, D.R.D.: Gender differences in game activity preferences of middle school children: implications for educational game design. Educ. Technol. Res. Dev. **56**(5–6), 643–663 (2008)
8. Davis, F.D.: Perceived usefulness, perceived ease of use and user acceptance of information technology. MIS Q. **13**(3), 319–340 (1989)
9. Davis, F.D., Bagozzi, R.P., Warshaw, P.R.: User acceptance of computer technology: a comparison of two theoretical models. Manage. Sci. **35**(8), 982–1003 (1989)
10. Fishbein, M., Azjen, I.: Belief, Attitude, Intention and Behavior: An Introduction to Theory and Research. Addison-Wesley, Reading (1975)
11. Hong, J.C., Hwang, M.Y., Chen, Y.J., Lin, P.H., Huang, Y.T., Cheng, H.Y., Lee, C.C.: Using the saliency-based model to design a digital archaeological game to motivate players' intention to visit the digital archives of Taiwan's natural science museum. Comput. Educ. **66**, 74–82 (2013)

12. Hair, J.F., Black, W.C., Babin, B.J., Anderson, R.E., Tatham, R.L.: Multivariate Data Analysis, 6th edn. Prentice-Hall, New Jersey (2006)
13. Fornell, C., Larcker, D.F.: Evaluating structural equation models with unobservable variables and measurement error. J. Mark. Res. **18**(1), 39–50 (1981)
14. Chin, W.W., Newsted, P.R.: Structural equation modeling analysis with small samples using partial least squares. In: Hoyle, R. (ed.) Statistical Strategies for Small Sample Research, pp. 307–341. Sage Publications, California (1999)

Imitating a Hot Puzzle Game for English Vocabulary Exercise in E-book System

Tien-Wen Sung[1(✉)] and Ting-Ting Wu[2]

[1] Fujian Provincial Key Laboratory of Big Data Mining and Applications,
College of Information Science and Engineering,
Fujian University of Technology, Fuzhou, China
twsung@fjut.edu.cn
[2] Graduate School of Technological and Vocational Education,
National Yunlin University of Science and Technology, Douliou, Taiwan
ttwu@yuntech.edu.tw

Abstract. Pure memorization of English words are usually uninteresting and provides limited help to the improvement of English proficiency. This paper imitates the popular block elimination puzzle game of Candy Crush Saga to develop a similar mobile game about English vocabulary elimination. The proposed puzzle game in this paper is used as an integrated tool with an e-book reading system and is utilized for vocabulary practices and examinations. The design and implementation of the proposed tablet-based mobile game aims to make English vocabulary learning more interesting and motivated. The purpose is to provide a game-based tool for English as a Second Language (ESL) learners to improve their English learning efficiency.

Keywords: Puzzle game · English vocabulary · E-book · English learning

1 Introduction

In recent years, the mobile APPs of block elimination puzzle games are continuously popular with mobile device users. Among these APPs, Candy Crush Saga is the favorite one and has drawn much attention from the public in its different versions on the platforms of Facebook, iOS, Android, and Windows. This condition motivates the study in this paper to imitate the Candy Crush Saga and develop a similar puzzle game for English learning. Many students usually feel learning or memorizing English vocabulary is uninteresting and dull. Therefore the motivation of this study is to design and implement a puzzle game about eliminating letters of English words to provide students with a motive and to stimulate their enthusiasms for learning English vocabulary. The prototype system developed in this study is an assistant subsystem to our previous study of English learning e-book system. The vocabulary game is used as a practice or an examination tool after English article reading to help learners memorizing English words. The objective is to develop and integrate a game-based learning tool into the previously proposed e-book reading system, and then to facilitate English vocabulary learning and improve the English learning efficiency for ESL (English as a Second Language) learners.

© Springer International Publishing AG 2017
T.-T. Wu et al. (Eds.): SETE 2016, LNCS 10108, pp. 21–26, 2017.
DOI: 10.1007/978-3-319-52836-6_3

2 Literatures

Computer and information technologies have been applied to facilitate the English learning in many cases [1, 2]. Digital game-based learning is one of the learning models. Although digital game-based learning can provide a relaxed and joyful learning environment, the key point should be also focused on the learning contents and corresponding presentation designs. In other words, the learning game should help learners to effectively acquire the expected knowledge and achieve the learning objective. The purpose of the game is used to reduce the misgivings and promote the motivations in learning [3]. There has been many explorations and researches regarding digital game-based learning and the integration of amusements and learning processes has gained advantages for learning in many domains [4, 5]. It is also generally accepted that game-based English learning for ESL learners can increase their interesting and motivations and reduce their anxiety during learning. The study of VocaWord game [6] was utilized for ESL students playing a vocabulary learning and practicing game in English classes at university level. It obtained a result of that the experimental group doubles the vocabulary improvement rate of the control group. A computer game was also developed in the study [7] for ESL learners learning English words. The results also demonstrated the improvement of learners' motivations and the reduction of learning misgivings. Then a better learning performance by using the game was also obtained. The study [8] applied game-based learning to English courses in an elementary school. The experiment indicated that the approach can quicken the learning progress and facilitate the meaning understanding of English words. The study [9] utilized the BONE game in English learning and explored the reactions of ESL learners. The learners gave positive results and indicated that they are fond of that kind of learning method. According to the popularity of mobile devices and the advances of wireless and mobile technologies, mobile learning approaches for English learners [10, 11] also can be utilized. This paper imitates the hot block elimination game, Candy Crush Saga, and develops a mobile puzzle game for English vocabulary learning.

3 System Designs

The vocabulary elimination puzzle game in this paper was developed for mobile tablets. This is due to the integration need for previous English e-book reading system on tablet. The system architecture is shown in Fig. 1. Learners play the game by executing the APP installed on the mobile device. The teacher uses a web browser as a learning management system (LMS) client to query users' learning information or configure the parameters of the game. The APP or browser communicates with an application server (game server and LMS server) through a wired or wireless network environment. The game server or LMS server connects to e-book material or learning portfolio database for necessary accesses. This system was established by a three-tier architecture, namely presentation tier, application tier, and data tier. The game server transmits the playing parameters of a game, the set of English words picked from e-book articles, and the quotas of special assistance tools to the learner client. The data of learner portfolio, such as information about operations and playing scores, generated by the client APP will be transmitted to and recorded on the portfolio database for further usages of statistical analyses or teacher queries. This can provide the teacher to well know the learning progresses and results of learners. It also can provide the parameters to determine the set of words from the English e-books for the game. In addition, an external dictionary provided by a third-party service is necessary for translation between English and Chinese in the puzzle game. HTTP requests will be send from game server to the dictionary server to obtain essential translation data.

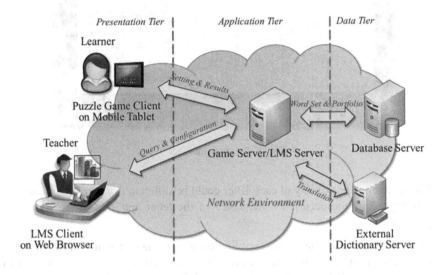

Fig. 1. System architecture

The interface of the vocabulary elimination game in learner client APP is shown in Fig. 2. The system will give words one by one and learners should draw a line on the screen by indicating each letter of the word in sequence. Once the action is completed, the letters will disappear and the learner will gain corresponding points or a special function tool of word elimination. To pass each stage of the game, learners must finish a set of words in a given limited time. If the learner do not complete the action in the given period, the system will prompt the answer by highlighting the letters. This can help users to learn those words that they are not familiar with. However the system will generate a corresponding record for this situation into the learner portfolio. Regarding to the arrangement of letters on screen, the system will automatically check whether there exists a sequence of letters before the learner beginning to find the answer. If not, the letters appeared on the screen will be appropriately rearranged. In fact, there has several designs to reduce the necessary rearrangement of letters:

1. Most of existing block elimination games use square blocks. The letter blocks in this study are hexagonal, thus each block has six adjacent blocks. This can increase the success of connecting a sequence of word letters.
2. During the progress of playing game, sometimes special function tools will be presented in the blocks to facilitate the success of word eliminations. For example, a universal block, which can be treated as any English letters.

Fig. 2. Learner interface

3. The occurrence probability of each letter could be different from the other letters. It will depend on the occurrence frequency of the letter appeared in the set of the given words.

In regard to the selection of the set of English words, the system uses a combination of four decision strategies with respective assigned weights ($\omega_1, \omega_2, \omega_3$, and ω_4) to determine the vocabulary item set which will be given in the game. They are content-based set (S_1), difficulty-based set (S_2), portfolio-based set (S_3), and assignment-based set (S_4). For each vocabulary item $v \in S = S_1 \cup S_2 \cup S_3 \cup S_4$, the occurrence probability of v is as follows, where $\omega_1 + \omega_2 + \omega_3 + \omega_4 = 1$.

$$p(v) = \left(\sum_{i=1}^{4} f_i(v) \right) \cdot \frac{1}{|S|} \qquad (1)$$

$$f_i(v) = \begin{cases} \omega_i, & \text{if } v \in S_i \\ 0, & \text{otherwise} \end{cases} \qquad (2)$$

Moreover, four playing modes was designed in the game to provide different exercises for learning English vocabulary. The 'English to English' and 'Chinese to English' modes give English and Chinese respectively and ask the learner to complete the spelling in English. The 'Text Mode' and 'Voice Mode' give words by showing and enunciating methods respectively. Furthermore, to add interest to the game, special function tools are provided in the game:

1. Star block: a universal block and can be treated as any one of the 26 letters.
2. Bomb block: used to make one block and its 6 adjacent blocks disappeared.
3. Bolt block: make the blocks on a vertical line all disappeared.

4. Heart block: let users get one more chance to retry current stage with timer reinstated.
5. Hammer block: use to make an indicated block disappeared.

4 Evaluation of System Acceptance

The practicality of an application system will influence the intention of learners in using the system, hence it affects the learning effectiveness. This study performs a survey of system acceptance by a questionnaire for the evaluation of students' perceptions of the learning game. The questionnaire is based on the Likert 5-point scale ranging from 5 (strongly agree) to 1 (strongly disagree). There were 52 participants asked to fill out the copies of the questionnaire. A total of 52 copies were recycled and among the recycled ones, 48 are valid with an effective rate of 92.3%. Table 1 shows the result of the survey of students' perceptions of the learning game. In general, the result presents that the learners gave the positive feedbacks of system acceptance and indicated that the elimination puzzle game for English vocabulary is useful and positively affect their learning. The evaluation currently is a preliminary, and further experiments and evaluations are in progress for the advanced larger-scale research of this English learning puzzle game.

Table 1. Summary of students' perceptions of the learning game.

Question statements	Strongly agree → Strongly disagree					Mean
	5	4	3	2	1	
The game attracts me	25.0%	54.2%	14.6%	4.2%	2.1%	3.96
The instructions are clear	14.6%	37.5%	27.1%	16.7%	4.2%	3.42
The interface is friendly and well designed	18.8%	35.4%	22.9%	18.8%	4.2%	3.46
The game helps me deepen understanding	37.5%	52.1%	8.3%	2.1%	0.0%	4.25
The game helps me improve English listening	27.1%	45.8%	22.9%	2.1%	2.1%	3.94
The game helps me learn English words	31.3%	47.9%	16.7%	4.2%	0.0%	4.06
The game helps me improve English ability	27.1%	43.8%	25.0%	2.1%	2.1%	3.92
The game increases my learning interest	33.3%	41.7%	16.7%	4.2%	4.2%	3.96
The game is good to be an exercise tool	45.8%	22.9%	25.0%	4.2%	2.1%	4.06
The game is good to be an examination tool	27.1%	31.3%	18.8%	14.6%	8.3%	3.54

5 Conclusion

Since block elimination games have been the most popular puzzle games on mobile APPs, this paper proposed a preliminary English vocabulary elimination puzzle game for ESL learners. The game was integrated into the previously developed English e-book reading system and is used as an exercise or examination tool for learning English when learners finish their reading activities. The game was expected to help learners to easily practice and memorize the English words with higher interest and motivation, and accordingly achieve an effective English learning. After the survey of students' perceptions of the learning game, the students gave feedbacks and positively indicated that it is useful and interesting for vocabulary practices and English learning. Finally, the in-progress advanced research and its details of widely evaluation and analysis will be proposed in the future.

Acknowledgments. This work is supported in part by Fujian Provincial Key Laboratory of Big Data Mining and Applications, Fujian University of Technology, China and supported in part by Ministry of Science and Technology, Taiwan under grant MOST 103-2511-S-224-004-MY3, MOST 104-2511-S-224-003-MY3, and MOST 105-2628-S-224-001-MY3.

References

1. Wu, T.T., Sung, T.W., Huang, Y.M., Yang, C.S., Yang, J.T.: Ubiquitous English-reading learning system with dynamic personalized guidance of learning portfolio. Educ. Technol. Soc. **14**(4), 164–180 (2011)
2. Hsu, C.K., Hwang, G.J., Chang, C.K.: An automatic caption filtering and partial hiding approach to improving the English listening comprehension of EFL students. Educ. Technol. Soc. **17**(2), 270–283 (2014)
3. Lee, Y.Y., Cheon, J., Key, S.: Learners' perceptions of video games for second/foreign language learning. In: Proceedings of the International Conference of Society for Information Technology and Teacher Education, Las Vegas, USA (2008)
4. Shih, J.L., Shih, B.J., Shih, C.C., Su, H.Y., Chuang, C.W.: The influence of collaboration styles to children's cognitive performance in digital problem-solving game "William Adventure": a comparative case study. Comput. Educ. **55**(3), 982–993 (2010)
5. Vos, N., Van der Meijden, H., Denessen, E.: Effects of constructing versus playing an educational game on student motivation and deep learning strategy use. Comput. Educ. **56**(1), 127–137 (2011)
6. Uzun, L., Cetinavci, U.R., Korkmaz, S., Salihoglu, U.M.: Developing and applying a foreign language vocabulary learning and practice game: the effect of VocaWord. Digital Culture Education **5**(1), 48–70 (2013)
7. Smith, G.G., Li, M., Drobisz, J., Park, H.R., Kim, D., Smith, S.D.: Play games or study? Computer games in eBooks to learn English vocabulary. Comput. Educ. **69**, 274–286 (2013)
8. Chou, M.H.: Assessing English vocabulary and enhancing young English as a Foreign Language (EFL) learners' motivation through games, songs, and stories. Educ. 3–13: Int. J. Prim. Elementary Early Years Educ. **42**(3), 284–297 (2014)
9. Chen, H.J., Yang, T.Y.: The impact of adventure video games on foreign language learning and the perceptions of learners. Interact. Learn. Environ. **21**(2), 129–141 (2013)
10. Wu, T.T., Sung, T.W., Huang, Y.M., Yang, C.S.: Location awareness mobile situated English reading learning system. J. Internet Technol. **11**(7), 923–934 (2010)
11. Hwang, W.Y., Chen, S.L., Shadiev, R., Huang, Y.M., Chen, C.Y.: Improving English as a foreign language writing in elementary schools using mobile devices in familiar situational contexts. Comput. Assist. Lang. Learn. **27**(5), 359–378 (2014)

Coding, the New Literacy: Thinking-Oriented Programing Learning e-Book

Tien-Chi Huang[1], Vera Yu Shu[2(✉)], Chia-Chen Chen[3],
and Yu-Lin Jeng[4]

[1] National Taichung University of Science and Technology, Taichung, Taiwan
tchuang@nutc.edu.tw
[2] National Changhua University of Education, Changhua, Taiwan
vera.yushu@gmail.com
[3] National Chung Hsing University, Taichung, Taiwan
emily@nchu.edu.tw
[4] Southern Taiwan University of Science and Technology, Tainan, Taiwan
jackjeng@mail.stust.edu.tw

Abstract. We learned in interviews of this study that schools education plays an important role in the coding education. Traditional teaching model of one to many conducted in a computer classroom resulted in many students giving up because lacking of personal assistance and guidance which makes it difficult for beginners to understand the abstract programming languages. Critical thinking skill emphasizes on logical training the most, therefore it is quite an ideal teaching technique for coding training. This study explores the key elements in studying coding based on interviews and literatures, and further develops an innovative web-based system called JACT that integrating critical thinking into coding. In particular, this study aims to use the web-based system to help beginners to start from thinking, understand programming languages, and enhance their motives and performance in studying coding.

Keywords: Programming · e-book · Critical thinking

1 Introduction

"Programming is the new literacy" Prensky [4]. After the advent of the information age, coding has become an emerging capacity. In response to this wave, many countries have begun to take root by education. For example, the originate country of Skype, Estonia, is one of the first countries going comprehensive e-formalization. It has started to teach some of their elementary students programming language since 2012. British government, in September 2014, facilitated "coding" into course outlines in elementary and middle schools to train children the logic to write programming language, attempting to build United Kingdom as an information big power.

Coding, is based on programming languages to generate codes in order to create certain tasks, such as to develop a system, website, APP, or to construct databases. When coding beginners manage to understand the execution of coding process and construct problem-solving solutions, they often deal with complicated and abstract

© Springer International Publishing AG 2017
T.-T. Wu et al. (Eds.): SETE 2016, LNCS 10108, pp. 27–33, 2017.
DOI: 10.1007/978-3-319-52836-6_4

syntax and commands, which makes learning coding a difficult and complicated task (Kelleher and Pausch, 2005). Thus, in light of the course above, learning programing and coding are tasks requiring high level of thinking skills. From the observation in actual courses, researchers find that many learners consider coding difficult because they know how but do not know why, or the make logical errors. According to above, coding requires higher thinking skills.

If coding is the creative output language, critical thinking skill is the most needed input ability in this era of information explosion. Critical thinking is crucial when facing an abundant of information, which includes "how to think", "the ability to rationally decide what to do and what to believe", and "the intention to use this type of thinking. Critical thinking is an important ability for judgement (Ennis, 1987; Howe and Warren, 1989; Schafersman, 1991). Norris and Ennis (1989) concluded three abilities and one strategy for critical thinking, respectively clarification, basic support, inference, and interactive debate with strategies. For teaching of critical thinking, Paul summarized a 4-facets instruction method [3] that cultivates critical thinking, respectively: provide opportunity to discover and think, guide learners to explore different ideas, ask learners their reasons and explore the certainty, and keep trying, trial-and-error.

In addition to the coding skills, as coding engineers, their problem identification and problem solving skills are very important. Shafto stated that coding helps students to express problem-solving methods in correct and logical way [7]. Valente also pointed out repeated cycle of "description, implantation, reflection and debug" during coding is the most effective thinking training for students [8] (Deek, Kimmel and McHugh, 1998). Engineers can use different language logic to express the same objective when programming, which is in turn a process of exploring. In other words, critical thinking skill plays an indispensable role in learning coding.

Coding education in Taiwan has paid minimal attention on thinking skills; and courses are often carried out in a computer classroom. The learning process requires large amount of debugging, modification, and executions, which highly depend on guidance which is usually insufficient in tradition one-to-many classroom. Therefore, students often give up learning because lacking of adequate individual assistance. Yet this condition is beyond a teacher's power to change. Fortunately, E-learning is able to compensate for this limitation. Online learning platform and e-books create individualized, repeated, and introductory materials to help beginners learn coding. Accordingly, this study uses the framework of learning critical thinking to develop a jQuery web-based learning system.

2   Interview

To explore the crucial element of a well-designed coding learning platform, this study adopts semi-open interviews to understand the learning process and difficulties in coding. Participants are 6 information domain graduated students from a national university in taiwan. The average age of participants is 21 and they all acquire coding skills. The interview questions are as follows:

Please describe how you first start coding.

- Please describe the difficulties you, as a coding beginner, encountered. And how did you solve these difficulties?
- In your opinion, what kind of thinking ability is required for coding?
- Do you know anyone who is amotivation or give up on coding?
- In opinion, what caused such situation?
- What features or functionalities do you think a good programming-assisted learning system should possess?

3 Results and Conclusions

3.1 About the Learning Process of Learning Programing

Programming language is the language of future, and also one that intimidating lots of beginners. According to field observation and interviews, this study concludes the following views on coding learning:

1. Abstractness makes it difficult to start: coding is quite abstract. Different programming languages such as C ++, Java, and Ruby have their own (to a certain extent of unique) operating instructions and logic. Students also expressed that "(I) encountered great frustration during learning process and had no sense of achievement," "it cannot boost more motivation when facing pure logical knowledge."
2. Should be included in curriculum: all participants came into contact with coding because of school curriculum. Therefore, include coding into formal or informal curriculum allows more learners to have the opportunity to learn coding.
3. The importance of logical thinking: all participants agreed that the logic of programming language is the most likely difficulty encountered by beginners. It is also the most likely reason why beginners give up. Students expressed: "(I) fail to transfer ideas into logic programming language," "(you) will think it is impossible in human's thinking but programming will not," "the structure of programming language is so abstract and difficult to learn," most trouble of coding came from "not fully understanding" the "structure." In other words, it is absolutely necessary to teach students the logic and the meaning of programming languages. Logic, deduction, and inference are important skills in critical thinking.
4. The importance of observation: observation is also an important strategy in learning coding. Participants expressed that "if I have the ability to observe how people think, I can understand why the writer writes such codes and I can write in this way."
5. The importance of thinking ability: "Having good thinking ability allows me to modify errors or write more sophisticated code to optimize coding". When coding with one programming language, different structure of codes could reach the same execution result. However, different sructures means different levels of efficiency or completeness. If one couldn't code adaptively, the overall efficiency will not improve.

6. Reification and scaffolding: abstract logic is one of the reasons why coding is difficult. Hence, reifications the abstract concept could help beginners understand the codes and the structure. Moreover, "examples" help program writers in efficient debugging.
7. ARCS-oriented: participants expressed that the sense of accomplishment encourages them in learning coding. "The greatest sense of achievement in coding is the outcome," "students became amotivation when encountering a great deal of frustration." Some students expressed that "most programming language class is abstract and boring; it cannot motivates us," "(we) need more interesting teaching materials to arouse our interesting in learning," "(requiring) life-relevant examples." All these opinions highlight the importance of attention and relevance.

3.2   Proposing the JACT System

Elements of coding learning process mentioned above highlight that the critical thinking plays an important role. Accordingly, this study develops a web-based coding learning system called JACT (jQuery and critical system) that integrating critical thinking into coding. Its structure adopts responsive web design, which allows learners to access to learning environment of this system with any mobile devices and situation. The system architecture is shown in Fig. 1.

In the system, the learners could use four learning tools designed by the system. The tools and instructions are designed according to Paul's critical thinking teaching steps [6]. Learners organize and analyze the key point of the questions they try to solve. In the reflection note for solving the questions, learners strengthen their express and logic. Finally the learning exhort, according to the coding cycle proposed by Valente [8], guides learners to write jQuery language. Through debugging, learners train their self- adjustment, correction, and judging abilities.

The function and purpose of the four learning tools (Fig. 2) are illustrated as follows:

Reading and analyses. Provide articles related to learning topics allows learners to discover the key points via article analysis. Learners are required to record the key points they discovered in learning notes in order to practice the analysis ability.

Keyword Search. Keyword search enhances learners' skills to use of keyword. By searching with adequate key words, students have to distinguish the importance of the concepts.

Personifying Situational Dialogue. We develop videos with situational dialogue; the conversation contents are personified functions or proper nouns of jQuery. The videos allow learners to explore differences in concept and clarify reasons, enhancing their understanding of programming language.

Different Perspective. Provide codes that are written with certain logic and ask learners to try to write with a different logic. Train learners to think from different perspective.

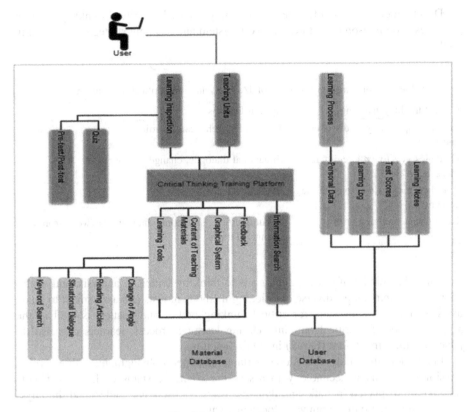

Fig. 1. System architecture

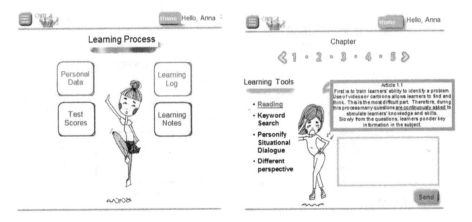

Fig. 2. Login screen and the content and learning tools of jQuery (translation)

Development of system features of this study is based on critical thinking teaching strategies. Comparison of features of JACT system and teaching strategies is shown in Table 1:

Table 1. Comparison of features of JACT System and critical thinking training

Critical thinking teaching	System features
Provide opportunity to discover and think	Keyword search, reading article
Guide learners to explore different ideas	Situational dialogue, change of angle
Ask their reasons and explore the certainty	Reading article
Keep trying, trial-and-error	Reading article, situational dialogue, keyword search, change of angle

Since the spindle of critical thinking is to think by criticism, analysis, and evaluation, this system adopts diverse questioning methods in tests and assessment to guide users to think. A subsystem for critical thinking pretest and posttest is built as the assessment tool for critical thinking. During learning process, learners can also do jQuery Achievement Test (Fig. 3) in JQuiz function.

In addition, this study also adopts portable electroencephalography with emerging physiological sensing technology to assess the cognitive status of learners. Charts (Fig. 4) are displayed in static and dynamic ways, so users can understand the physiological information of brainwave for their focus.

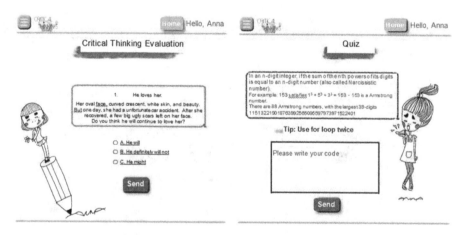

Fig. 3. Pretest/posttest and jQuiz of critical thinking

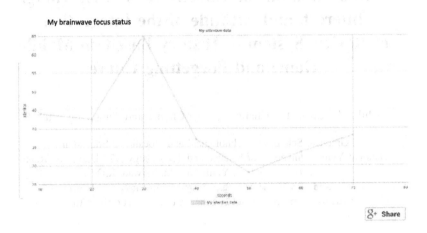

Fig. 4. Focus level line chart

In summary, this study adopts semi-open interviews to explore the eight elements of learning coding and developed a set of web-based coding learning system called JACT that is critical thinking oriented. In follow-up studies, we will further conduct the empirical research on critical thinking skills and brainwave focus.

References

1. Shafto, S.A.: Programming for learning in mathematics and science. ACM SIGCSE Bull. **18**(1), 296–302 (1986)
2. Valente, J.A.: Logo as a window into the mind. Logo Update **4**(1), 1–4 (1995)
3. Li, J.F., Liu, G.Z.: On training of critical thinking. J. Northwest Normal Univ. (Soc. Sci.) **43**(3), 63–67 (2006)
4. Prensky, Marc. Programming Is the New Literacy (2008). http://www.edutopia.org/literacy-computer-programmingon2016/7/1

Exploration on the Effectiveness of Learning, Interest, and Attitude of the Integration of Review System of History Based on Mobile Game and Forgetting Curve

Chih Wei Chao, Lei Chang, An-Chi Cheng, and Ting-Ting Wu[(⊠)]

Graduate School of Technological and Vocational Education,
National Yunlin University of Science and Technology, 123 University Road,
Section 3, Douliou, Yunlin 64002, Taiwan, R.O.C.
bluejit23@gmail.com, zegxiazhang@gmail.com,
koufukutenshi@gmail.com, ttwu@yuntech.edu.tw

Abstract. According to Ebbinghaus' forgetting curve theory, memory is unreliable and a substantial amount of information is lost immediately after learning. Therefore, this study constructed a review system based on mobile gaming, which was provided to students as a review tool within 20 min of completing a history lesson. The aim of this study was to enhance student effectiveness, attitude, and interest. The research tool included three exams and questionnaires regarding learning attitude and learning interest. The learning scores did not exhibit significant differences between the control and the experimental group; however, the mean for the experimental group was greater than that for the control group. Moreover, learning attitude and interest were significantly different between the two groups.

Keywords: Forgetting curve · History · Digital-game based learning

1 Introduction

Courses provided during primary education in a 12-year public education system aim to cultivate students' basic knowledge and abilities while deepening their sense of learning. Students are expected to care about local events and recognize and embrace cultural diversity. Numerous fields of social studies exist, among which history, involving rich changes and influences, explores the origin of culture from an objective perspective [1]. Current studies focus largely on major subjects such as Chinese, English, and mathematics. By contrast, the current study centered on history courses and attempted to emphasize the overall importance of social studies in education. Moreover, this study applied information technology to strengthen students' motivation to study.

Changes in information technology have engendered changes in traditional learning environments. With the rapid development of information technology, the acquisition, application, and communication of information have undergone tremendous changes [2]. Furthermore, information technology is currently widely incorporated into general

© Springer International Publishing AG 2017
T.-T. Wu et al. (Eds.): SETE 2016, LNCS 10108, pp. 34–42, 2017.
DOI: 10.1007/978-3-319-52836-6_5

learning [3]. Educational environments complemented by information technology are commonly available. The increasing popularity of wireless technology and mobile devices has propelled mobile learning [4].

Among diversified learning environments, digital game-based learning approaches engender enjoyment during learning. Specifically, gaming can enhance enjoyment and enthusiasm during the learning process. Game-based learning attracts learners and generates motivation. As students advance in games, more problem-solving skills are "unlocked." Students not only achieve learning goals and strengthen their confidence, but also experience an increased desire to learn more and obtain a sense of satisfaction and achievement. Hence, joyful learning leads to positive attitudes. Game-based learning therefore generates more motivation than traditional learning environments [5].

Games are rich in media properties, integrating animation, text, sound, video, and other related content [6]. Game design focuses on a student-centered education module and integrates learning content. The principal goal is to improve student problem-solving abilities [7]. As students pass gateways, they achieve learning goals; deepen their learning impressions; and enhance their interest, effectiveness, and attitude toward learning. Learning attitude refers to enthusiasm, initiative, and a strong recognition of content. Learning attitudes have shifted from passive learning in the past to systems that involve searching for relevant course content. Increased learning interest results from the combination of gaming and social studies courses, which enhances student interest in course content, engenders different forms of media, offers diversified and lively learning environments, and improves previous learning models.

The objective of the current study was to enhance student effectiveness, attitude, and interest toward learning. To study effectiveness, this study adopted the forgetting curve proposed by Hermann Ebbinghaus. This curve asserts that the 20 min after learning is the period wherein people forget the most information. To strengthen student memory, a game-based review system designed by this study was introduced within the 20 min of information input. A tablet was added to the teaching materials. The games generated excitement and stimulation and enhanced learner attitude and interest.

The practical mobile devices can complement the lack of a traditional learning environment, encouraging student confidence and active participation in the learning process [8]. Our system combines gaming and review questions, and implement in the tablet device. The purpose of the system is to provide an alternative to traditional review methods. Student attitude and interest were assessed following their use of our game- based review system.

2   Literature Review

2.1   Digital-Game Based Learning

Game-based learning introduces game and software into a learning environment to help students gain knowledge and enhance ability. Problem solving and challenges within games can provide learners with context and atmosphere to facilitate the achievement of goals [9].

In the game-based learning system, design elements included goals, conditions and rules, outcome, and impact on player [10]. The following conditions must be met to immerse students in the game:

(1) The game should incorporate appropriate goals and objects, and the subject of each game should be clear.
(2) Real-time feedback should be provided to enable students to promptly evaluate their learning outcomes as they progress.
(3) Rules should be coherent so that learners can be compliant to and understand the organization and content of the game, thus enabling them to effectively realize their learning goals.
(4) Students should progress in a logical, step-by-step manner in the game to enable them adapt to the learning context.
(5) Interest in learning should be enhanced by combining the game with the course.
(6) The sound, animation, and visuals of the game should attract attention.
(7) Student motivation should be maintained.
(8) The game should be designed to adapt to individual progress, create a competitive and comparative learning atmosphere, and generate a "survival-of-the-fittest" mentality. This can consequently increase their engagement in learning and motivation to promote their interest. Concurrently, the students can focus on the learning context, thus enhancing their attitude toward the social studies.

2.2   Forgetting Curve

The learning process comprises two parts: retention and forgetting [11]. Forgetting rates vary individually. Forgetting refers to a loss of knowledge after the input of information [12]. In this study, the measured forgetting rate was extremely fast. Table 1 shows Ebbinghaus' forgetting curve, indicating that the forgetting rate slowed over time. Therefore, this study introduced the review system within 20 min of learning to prolong students' memory and enhance learning effectiveness.

Table 1. Ebbinghaus' forgetting curve

After learning	Memory retention	Memory left
Learning Just finished	100%	0%
20 min	58%	42%
1 h	44%	56%
9 h	36%	64%
1 day	34%	66%
2 days	28%	72%
6 days	25%	75%
31 days	21%	79%

3   Method

This study investigated the learning outcome, interest, and attitude of students after using a game-based review system following study. In contrast to traditional assessment methods, this study applied a digital game-based review system and Ebbinghaus' forgetting curve, and introduced the system within 20 min after information input, a period during which students had the fastest forgetting rate. Review of the course content helped students prolong their memory and enhance their academic achievement.

3.1   Participant

Two classes of fourth-grade primary school students served as the subjects. A total of 44 students were grouped according to classroom, wherein a class of 21 students constituted the experimental group and another class of 23 students constituted the control group.

For the experimental group, the game-based review system was introduced in addition to traditional review methods, whereas for the control group, students reviewed material along with a teacher's oral explanation, as in traditional methods. The average student age was 10. Both classes were taught by the same teacher, who had 10 years of experience teaching social studies.

3.2   The Design of Game

The game is entitled "Rescue the Princess." The prince must advance through multiple levels, duel with the boss, and ultimately save the princess. At the beginning of each level, the plot and procedure are explained (Fig. 1). The engaging game scenarios attract students to the game. Students can advance at personalized speeds to complete the game.

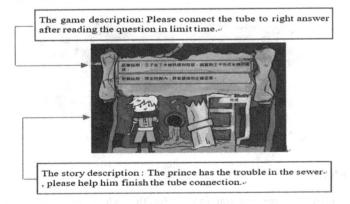

Fig. 1. The description of the story and explanation the operation at the beginning of level.

The game contains five levels (Fig. 2), all of which were designed to enhance student memory of what was previously taught. Level 1 requires students to read questions and guide the prince to the answer using a pipeline jigsaw within a limited time. Students can organize their own routes to the destination to increase their ability of diverse thinking. Most Level 2 questions are multiple choice. Students must flip cards to answer, and. numerous cards appear below the questions. Students are required to find and flip two identical cards to derive the answer. The answer card is then automatically transferred to the answer box. This level was designed so that students can experience a variety of stimulating factors and improve both their memory and their ability to distinguish. For Level 3, guests are invited to join. Students must pass the answers on top to the guests to solve their issues. Students must read and answer the questions quickly, thereby becoming excited and engaged in the game. Level 4 contains multiple choice questions. After reading the questions, students must shoot balloons with answers inside. For Level 5, the prince must answer questions accurately to gain the opportunity to challenge the boss. Otherwise, the prince is attacked by the boss.

The game emphasizes the function of reviewing. When students provide incorrect answers, the game displays additional content related to the question. Students can then circle the relevant answers manually, and then restart the game. The manual circle function enables students to gain memory points through reading and manual operations in the reviewing part.

Regarding learning content, level records, operations, and other relevant student records are recorded in a system log in detail.

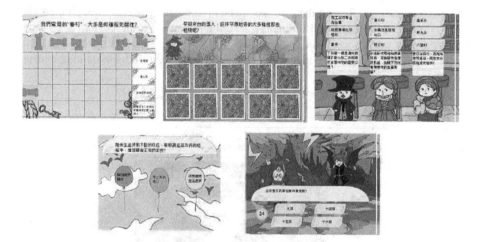

Fig. 2. The five levels in the game based review system.

3.3   Procedure

This study utilized course material from a fourth-grade history class. The content included two lessons. Games were designed to correspond to each lesson. Figure 3 shows the experiment content. The experimental and control groups received a pretest questionnaire regarding interest and attitude before the experiment began. Prior to being taught the first unit, the game and relevant operations were explained to the experimental group. The teacher then taught Lesson 1 for 100 min. Within 20 min following the lecture, the control group reviewed the lesson with their teacher; in the same period, the game was introduced to the experimental group. The game had three levels. A test on Lesson 1 began after the review. The steps for Lesson 2 were similar to those for Lesson 1; however, the models of two of the three levels were different. A posttest was taken in the 9th week. Finally, a posttest questionnaire about interest and attitude of learning was distributed. Throughout the experiment, the teacher and the programmer were available to the students to provide timely assistance.

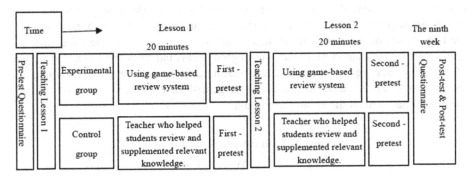

Fig. 3. Experiment procedure

3.4 Assessment Tools

The research tool was self-designed game review software. It included a game map that allowed learners to progress step-by-step through the learning course modules. Every level had questions related to each lesson. Supplementary questions were incorporated into the levels to enable students to succeed and review areas they have made mistakes in or were unfamiliar with, thus improving their knowledge of the relevant topic. In addition, the experiment contained three tests: first pretest, second pretest, and posttest. All questions were in multiple choice. The game employed choice questions, matching questions, and linking games. All test questions were designed by the aforementioned history teacher.

The questionnaires on learning attitude and learning interest were quoted from Hwang and Chang (2011) [13]. The questionnaire regarding learning attitude contained eight questions, which were about learning attitude and the significance of learning. The questionnaire regarding learning interest contained four questions, focusing on the student interest in the course material.

4 Result

4.1 Learning Achievement

Study effectiveness analysis was based on the first pretest, second pretest, and posttest scores of the experimental and the control groups. All the three tests entailed employing an independent sample t test to calculate the learning differences between the two groups; statistical significance was set at $p < 0.05$. Table 2 displays the scores of the experimental group (M = 61.43, SD = 28.202) and the control group (M = 64.78, SD = 27.858). The average score of the experimental group was lower than that of the control group. Moreover, no significant difference was observed between the two groups ($p = 0.374$). This is because students in the experimental group exhibited different behavior patterns and experienced a greater change in the learning model than the control group did. Hence, the results of the first pretest for the experimental group were low. In the second pretest and posttest, although the scores of the two classes were similar, the average scores of the two tests of the experimental group were higher than those of the control group. This indicates that the introduction of the tablet game significantly improved student academic performance. According to the posttest results, students provided with the game-based review system had retained more information than the control group did.

Table 2. Learning achievement result

	Group	N	Mean	Std. Deviation	t	p
First-pretest	Experimental	21	61.43	28.202	−.397	.374
	Control	23	64.78	27.858		
Second-pretest	Experimental	21	60.48	23.817	.329	.372
	Control	23	58.26	28.492		
Post-test	Experimental	21	75.62	17.107	.562	.2885
	Control	23	72.78	16.368		

4.2 Learning Attitude

Prior to the experiment, the two classes showed no significant differences regarding learning attitude. Before the introduction of the game-based learning approach, the two classes had the same attitude toward the study of social studies ($p = 0.202$, $t = -3.97$). Table 3 indicates that after the experiment, the two classes' learning attitudes had

Table 3. Learning attitude result

	Group	N	Mean	Std. Deviation	t	p
Pre-test	Experimental	21	4.97	0.689	0.842	0.202
	Control	23	4.74	1.035		
Post-test	Experimental	21	4.95	0.736	1.996	0.026[a]
	Control	23	4.46	0.88		

[a]$p < 0.05$

significant differences ($p = 0.026$). In the research environment, because of less employment of relevant devices in the teaching environment, the game and tablet were used in teaching. The questionnaire on learning attitude contained eight questions, and its Cronbach's α value was 0.817.

4.3   Learning Interest

In the pretest, the experimental group (M = 4.6, SD = 1.065) and the control group (M = 4.13, SD = 0.859) did not exhibit any significant differences in terms of learning interest levels ($p = 0.54$). However, subsequent interest level assessments revealed that the scores of the experimental group (M = 4.75, SD = 1.092) and those of the control group (M = 4.05, SD = 1.081) were significantly different ($p = 0.02$). The application of the proposed game-based review software enhanced student fondness for the courses and intensified their interest. The questionnaire regarding learning interest contained four questions, and its Cronbach's α value was 0.875 (Table 4).

Table 4. Learning interest result

	Group	N	Mean	Std. Deviation	t	p
Pre-test	Experimental	21	4.6	1.065	1.641	0.54
	Control	23	4.13	0.859		
Post-test	Experimental	21	4.75	1.092	2.12	0.02[a]
	Control	23	4.05	1.081		

[a]$p < 0.05$

5   Conclusion

Although the scores of the first pretest, second pretest, and posttest of the experimental group and control group did not reach significance, the average scores of the first pretest and second pretest of the experimental group were higher than those of the control group because of the introduction of the review system. The system combined game levels with questions and provided additional review functions following incorrect answers. Students could read content related to the incorrectly answered question and manually circle keywords to retain the information. Additionally, the introduction of mobile devices and gamed-based review software improved student learning attitude. As the students advanced in the game, they expressed desire to learn the content of the level to pass it, which enhanced their awareness of goals and initiative and provided them with a unique learning experience. The multimedia features of the implemented game-based review software improved learning interest. Students were happy about what they learned, and their interest and willingness to learn increased. Students exhibited enthusiasm and devoted time to the course, thereby enhancing their learning effectiveness and attitude. Future studies can examine behavior and motivation to conduct more in-depth research and discussions to serve as reference for scholars in the relevant fields.

Acknowledgements. This work was supported in part by the Ministry of Science and Technology (MOST), Taiwan, ROC, under Grant MOST 103-2511-S-224-004-MY3, MOST 104-2511-S-224-003-MY3, and MOST 105-2628-S-224-001-MY3.

References

1. Yu, Z., Yu, W.H., Fan, X., Wang, X.: An exploration of computer game-based instruction in the "world history" class in secondary education: a comparative study in China. PLoS One **9**, 5 (2013)
2. Wu, T.T.: English reading e-book system integrating grouping and guided reading mechanisms based on the analysis of learning portfolios. J. Internet Technol. **17**(2), 231–241 (2016)
3. Park, S.Y., Nam, M.W., Cha, S.B.: University students' behavioral intention to use mobile learning: evaluating the technology acceptance model. Br. J. Educ. Technol. **43**(4), 592–605 (2012)
4. Wu, T.T., Huang, Y.M., Chao, H.C., Park, J.H.: Personlized English reading sequencing based on learning portfolio analysis. Inf. Sci. **257**, 248–263 (2014)
5. Chen, C.H., Law, V.: Scaffolding individual and collaborative game-based learning in learning performance and intrinsic motivation. Comput. Hum. Behav. **55**, 1201–1212 (2016)
6. Angeli, C., Tsaggari, A.: Examining the effects of learning in dyads with computer-based multimedia on third-grade students' performance in history. Comput. Educ. **92–93**, 171–180 (2016)
7. Hwang, G.J., Yang, L.H., Wang, S.Y.: A concept map-embedded educational computer game for improving students' learning performance in natural science courses. Comput. Educ. **69**, 121–130 (2013)
8. Wu, T.T.: Using smart mobile devices in social-network-based health education practice: a learning behavior analysis. Nurse Educ. Today **34**, 958–963 (2014)
9. Qian, M., Clark, K.: Game-based learning and 21st century skills: a review of recent research. Comput. Hum. Behav. **63**, 50–58 (2016)
10. Hainey, T., Westera, W., Connolly, T.M., Boyle, L., Baxter, G., Beeby, R.B., Soflano, M.: Students' attitudes toward playing games and using games in education: comparing Scotland and the Netherlands. Comput. Educ. **69**, 474–484 (2013)
11. Prensky, M.: Digital natives, digital immigrants part 1. Horiz. **9**(5), 1–6 (2001)
12. Miao, Y.: Mobile learning against forgetting. In: The Second International Conference on Next Generation Mobile Applications, Services, and Technologies, pp. 241–246. IEEE Press, Cardiff (2008)
13. Wang, Z., Li, H., Liu, F.: The design of mobile learning English word memory management software function module. In: 2014 International Conference of Educational Innovation through Technology, pp. 49–53. IEEE Press, Brisbane (2014)
14. Hwang, G.J., Chang, H.F.: A formative assessment-based mobile learning approach to improving the learning attitudes and achievements of students. Comput. Educ. **56**(1), 1023–1031 (2011)

Emerging Technologies of Design, Model and Framework of Learning Systems

The Effect of 635 Brainstorming
on the Creativity of Programming Design

Tzone-I Wang[(⊠)] and Po-Ching Chang

Department of Engineering Science,
National Cheng Kung University, Tainan, Taiwan
wti535@mail.ncku.edu.tw

Abstract. This study develops a methodology that joins the creative problem-solving mode and the 635 brainstorming method to help students developing innovative software applications. To verify the effectiveness of the methodology, two experiments were conducted, with 52 participants who takes a programming design course. In the first experiment, participant groups receive some open data on a subject, with which they go through the procedure of the methodology and decide their final applications. In the second one they receive a problem with clear specs, with which they go through the experiment. At the divergent thinking stage, the experimental group uses the 635 brainstorming method to discuss their ideas while the control group uses just simple discussions. The results show the experimental group performs significantly better in almost all the creative indexes and can confirm the corporative brainstorming method, in this study, can help boosting team creativity to create innovative and valuable applications.

Keywords: Team Creativity · 635 Brainstorming method · Programming design

1 Introduction

Creativity has been recognized as one of the important abilities for programmers in developing software applications, especially innovative applications for such a fast changing world. Innovative applications can help companies establishing competitive advantages. To build mid-to-large systems requires team works. Today, team collaboration is a common operational model in enterprises [1]. To develop innovative applications, one of a company's educational trainings must focus on how to improve team creativity [2]. Many researchers believe that users must master collaborative learning skills, because the interaction between users can promote the exchange of knowledge and ideas, and achieve knowledge sharing [3, 4]. For recent e-learning environment, Computer Supported Collaborative Learning (CSCL) platforms support a

This study is supported by the National Science Council (now Ministry Of Science and Technology) of Taiwan under the project contract No.: NSC 102-2511-S-006-017-MY3 an MOST 104-2511-S-006-009.

© Springer International Publishing AG 2017
T.-T. Wu et al. (Eds.): SETE 2016, LNCS 10108, pp. 45–51, 2017.
DOI: 10.1007/978-3-319-52836-6_6

more convenient way for learners to exchange knowledge in a learning group [5]. It has been recognized that collaborative learning is an effective method for stimulating and boosting team creativity of team works [6]. The core of team creativity consists of creativity from team members, a problem solving oriented environment, techniques and activities for stimulating creativity, and altitude for creation and adventure [7]. That is, to boost team creativity, members have to do divergent thinking together for creating new ideas, to have mutual discussion on these ideas, and to do convergent thinking together on the ideas and reach a consensus on a final product, which should be useful [8]. For such a purpose, a CSCL platform should support tools for boosting team creativity in various kinds of situations, for example, in helping users on agitating their minds and finding out creative and valuable applications, or on seeking innovative and effective solutions for a specific application topic.

This study builds a CSCL programming system and established a methodology that combines creative problem-solving mode with the 635 brainstorming method [9, 10] to help learners achieving exchanges in knowledge and ideas, and stirring up creativity to develop innovative applications or software.

2 Methodology and Materials

The online CSCL programming system designed in this study harnesses a methodology that operates in accordance with the creative problem solving (CPS) mode [11], which forces the learners to perform the "Generating Ideas" first phase that is followed by the "Planning for Actions" second phase. In the "Generating Ideas" phase, learners a corporative brainstorming method to help their team generating as many ideas as possible. After that, all the team members start to discuss and decide on a rating standard, by which, they anonymously give score to every idea ever generated. All the ideas are then sorted by their averaged scores to help the team members converging and reaching consensus for their programming goal, which, in this study, will be the final application developed by the team.

In the "Planning for Actions" phase, team members discuss the processes and the methods for programming, write down virtual codes for the application, and translate the virtual codes into C++ statements to complete the applications. Fig 1. Summarizes the operation of the methodology designed in this study.

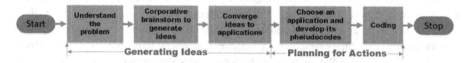

Fig. 1. The operation of the methodology

2.1 Creativity Assessment

There are four scales: fluency, flexibility, originality, and elaboration, evaluated for the creativity in the original Torrance Tests of Creative Thinking (TTCT) [12]. The TTCT uses verbal and figural tests for evaluations. This study is to assess the effectiveness of corporative brainstorm 635 method on students' creative programming design. The original TTCT verbal and figural tests seem inappropriate. In this study, the number of ideas generated in the brainstorming stage are eventually classified as potential software applications, and are tightly related to innovation and form the basis for creativity assessment. Thus, the TTCT indexes, in this study, are adapted by redefining the first three scales based on the number of ideas generated as:

Fluency: the total number of ideas after merging extended or modified ideas, i.e. if idea B is extended from idea A or idea C is modified from A, they are counted as AB or AC only.

Flexibility: the total number of categories of ideas formed in a team, i.e. the number of potential applications, classified by programming experts,

Originality: how unique an application is among all the applications generated by all the teams? A formula is established for this scale in this study by the experts. This scale is measured by programming experts too.

The study ignores the fourth elaboration scale because the theme focus on whether students can, via the brainstorming tool, generate more creative potential applications and every of them counts, irrelevant to its detail. Two additional scales other than those in the TTCT's are evaluated in this study, the applicability and innovativeness of the final chosen application by each team. These are assessed by programming experts. All the assessments given by the experts will be tested by Kendall coefficient of concordance to test the consistency of the evaluations.

2.2 The CSCL Platform

This study constructs an online Computer-Supported Corporative Learning (CSCL) e-platform with several corporative divergent thinking tools that operate in compliance with the creative problem-solving mode. Major components are a Corporative Brain-storming Module, an Idea Converging Module, and a Coding Module, now providing a C++ programming environment. This study uses its 635 brainstorming method to help members of a team to inspire their creativity before writing program codes.

3   Experiments and results

To verify the effectiveness of the proposed methodology, this study conducted two experiments, which recruited 52 freshmen who enrolled in a programming course of a national university in Southern Taiwan. All the participants are grouped into 13 teams based on the results of a prior knowledge pre-test which includes two activities, the test of their prior knowledge on programming and a creative self-efficacy measurement with 22 items [13]. They are then evenly divided into an experimental group (7 teams) and a control group (6 teams). The ANOVA test on the prior knowledge pre-test between the two groups confirms that the two groups are evenly distributed. The ANOVA test on creative self-efficacy measurement on each member of the two groups also confirms that the two groups have no significant difference on producing ideas from a topic before the experiments.

3.1   Experimental Process

Two kinds of experiments are conducted; all the participants in the first experiment get some open data about the historical sites in an ancient city, on which, they discuss and decide their final applications; while in the second experiment, they get a specific problem from the UVa Online Judge problem pool with clear specs, and, according to which, they develop their applications [14]. At the creative thinking stage, the teams in the experimental group use the 635 brainstorming method to create their ideas, while the ones in the control group brainstorm using only online group discussions. After the thinking stage, every team has to sort the ideas, choose the best one as their application, write down some virtual codes, and implement it into C++ codes.

3.2   Results and Discussion

Analysis on the results of the experiments are for both divergent thinking and program design. For divergent thinking in the first experiments, results depicted in Fig. 2 shows the experimental group is significantly better than the control group in fluency and originality, but not in flexibility, though still better. Both the flexibility and originality are classified and measured by three experts. The Kendall coefficient of concordance of both scales are 0.853 and 0.794 that confirms the high consistency among the ratings.

Creativity Scales	group	No. of Teams	Average	STD	F	p-value
fluency	Experimental	7	32.29	3.546	6.795	0.024* (<0.05)
	Control	6	24.33	7.146		
flexibility	Experimental	7	21.047	2.067	4.049	0.069
	Control	6	16.888	5.022		
Originality	Experimental	7	14.754	1.791	5.459	0.039*(<0.05)
	Control	6	11.149	3.615		

Fig. 2. ANOVA tests on the three creativity scales for the first experiment

The ANOVA tests on the two additional scales, i.e. the applicability and innovativeness of the final chosen application, for the first experiment are assessed by the same three experts. The Kendall coefficient of concordance of both scales are 0.752 and 0.704 that confirm the high consistency among the ratings. The results in Fig. 3 shows the experimental group is not significantly better than the control group in these two scales.

Creativity Scales	group	No. of Teams	Average	STD	F	p-value
applicability	Experimental	7	7.10	1.197	0.422	0.529
	Control	6	7.56	1.361		
innovativeness	Experimental	7	14.754	1.791	5.459	0.240
	Control	6	11.149	3.615		

Fig. 3. ANOVA tests on the applicability and innovativeness scales for the first experiment

By analyzing the records of ideas generations, it is noted that when using 635 brainstorming method, most of the participants generate their ideas by modifying or extending from other members'. This might explain why the categories of ideas generated by the experimental group do not have superior numbers to the control group. For divergent thinking in the second experiment, which gives participants an application with clearly specified requirements the experimental group performs significantly better in fluency, flexibility, and originality than the control group.

For divergent thinking in the second experiments, the results depicted in Fig. 4 show the experimental group, performs significantly better than the control group in all the three scales. The Kendall coefficient of concordance of flexibility and originality scales are 0.940 and 0.928 that confirms the high consistency among the ratings. For the second experiment, the two scales, i.e. the applicability and innovativeness of the application, are not evaluated for the specifications of the application is given in the first place.

Creativity Scales	group	No. of Teams	Average	STD	F	p-value
fluency	Experimental	6	11.166	2.136	29.580	0.000*** (<0.001)
	Control	7	4.428	2.299		
flexibility	Experimental	6	8.055	1.781	11.665	0.006** (<0.01)
	Control	7	4.285	2.138		
Originality	Experimental	6	14.910	4.306	13.500	0.004** (<0.01)
	Control	7	6.516	3.931		

Fig. 4. ANOVA tests on the three creativity scales for the second experiment

4   Conclusion

The methodology established in this study is compliance with the creative problem solving mode, and is to use creative thinking tools to help group learners, by stimulating ideas and sharing and knowledge, developing innovative applications or software. Two experiments are conducted, with the experimental group using the 635 brainstorming method and the control group using online discussion tool to perform divergent thinking. The first experiment requires the participant teams to create innovative applications form some open data, while the second one from an UVa problem with clear specs. The results confirm the effectiveness of this proposed methodology in creative application design, as shown in Table 1, which can draw the following conclusions in this study:

Table 1. What the experiments confirm in this study

Subject from Creativity scales	Open data	UVa Online Judge problem with Clear specifications
fluency	significant	significant
flexibility	not significant	significant
originality	significant	significant
Application applicability	not significant	
Application innovativeness	not significant	

1. On the fluency and the originality scales of divergent thinking, in both experiments, the experimental group performs significantly better than the control group.
2. On the flexibility scale of divergent thinking, in the first experiment that uses open data subject, the experimental group performs better but not to a significant extend than the control group. In the second experiment that uses subject with clear specification, the experimental group performs significantly better than the control group.
3. On the application applicability and innovativeness, the experimental group does not perform significantly better than the control group in both experiments.

References

1. Waller, M.J.: The timing of adaptive group responses to nonroutine events. Acad. Manage. J. **42**(2), 127–137 (1999)
2. Fagan, M.H.: The influence of creative style and climate on software development team creativity: an exploratory study. J. Comput. Inf. Syst. **44**(3), 73–80 (2004)
3. Su, A.Y., Yang, S.J., Hwang, W.-Y., Zhang, J.: A Web 2.0-based collaborative annotation system for enhancing knowledge sharing in collaborative learning environments. Comput. Educ. **55**(2), 752–766 (2010)
4. Roger, T., Johnson, D.W.: An overview of cooperative learning. In: Thousand, J., Villa, A., Nevin, A. (eds.) Creativity and collaborative learning. Brookes Press, Baltimore (1994)
5. Falloon, G., Khoo, E.: Exploring young students' talk in iPad-supported collaborative learning environments. Comput. Educ. **77**, 13–28 (2014)
6. Drucker, P.: Innovation and Entrepreneurship. Routledge, UK (2014)
7. Bonneau, G.A., Amegan, S.: Evaluating community creativity and innovation: Methodological proposal and reflexions. J. Creative Behav. **33**(3), 208–219 (1999)

8. Leonard, D., Swap, W.: When Sparks Fly: Igniting Creativity in Groups. Harvard Business School Press, Boston (1999)
9. Rohrbach, B.: Kreativ nach Regeln – Methode 635, eine neue Technik zum Lösen von Problemen. (Creative by rules - Method 635, a new technique for solving problems). Absatzwirtschaft, vol. 12, pp. 53–73 (1969)
10. Paulus, P.B., Yang, H.-C.: Idea generation in groups: a basis for creativity in organizations. Organ. Behav. Hum. Decis. Process. **82**(1), 76–87 (2000)
11. Osborn, A.: Applied Imagination: Principles and Procedures of Creative Problem Solving. Creative Education Foundation Press, Amherst (1953/2001)
12. Torrance, E.: Predictive validity of the torrance tests of creative thinking. J. Creative Behav. **6**(4), 236–262 (1972)
13. Tierney, P., Farmer, S.M.: Creative self-efficacy: its potential antecedents and relationship to creative performance. Acad. Manage. J. **45**(6), 1137–1148 (2002)
14. The UVa Online Judge. https://uva.onlinejudge.org/

Exploring the Development of Engineering Design in an Integrative Robotic STEM Program

Yu-Kai Chen[✉] and Chi-Cheng Chang

Department of Technology Application and Human Resource Development,
National Taiwan Normal University, Taipei, Taiwan
frank.kai6812@gmail.com, samchang@ntnu.edu.tw

Abstract. The present study intends to propose an interdisciplinary program that is based on integrative STEM approach and further to explore the development of engineering design in the program. The participants are 29 graduate and university students who take an optional course 'Robotics' in an university in Taiwan. Data collections include the groups' research notes and interviews from selected groups. The result reveals that the participants could perform most of the engineering design practices, however, they have insufficient practices on the meta-cognitive dimensions. In addition, the factors that affect the participants' engineering design are also revealed. Some suggestions that are beneficial in developing the engineering design are proposed in this study.

Keywords: Engineering design · Robot · STEM

1 Introduction

Developing the engineering design has been viewed as an important factor that affects individuals' learning effects of engineering education (Apedoe et al. 2008; Dym et al. 2005; Hynes et al. 2011; Silva et al. 2015). The traditional engineering curricula in universities tend to provide a step-by-step learning process that infrequently emphasizes on engineering design practices. This may cause that although students have some subject knowledge, they lack the abilities to apply it in new design situations (Silva et al. 2015). In this study, we intend to propose an interdisciplinary program that is based on integrative STEM approach and further to explore the development of engineering design in the program.

2 Engineering Design

This section documents the rationale for the position of engineering design within the robotic STEM program. Engineering design could be viewed as the mechanisms that bridge an engineer's intention and product production. Typically, engineers' cognitive practices include: (1) clarifying and articulate the needs, (2) creating a design to meet the needs, and (3) implementing the design (Bailey et al. 2006). In this study,

© Springer International Publishing AG 2017
T.-T. Wu et al. (Eds.): SETE 2016, LNCS 10108, pp. 52–57, 2017.
DOI: 10.1007/978-3-319-52836-6_7

we propose eight dimensions by literatures reviewing to present the constructs of engineering design including: (1) problem definition, (2) gather information, (3) generate ideas, (4) modeling, (5) feasibility analysis, (6) evaluation, (7) decision, and (8) communication (Atman et al. 2007; Denson 2011; Lloyd 2013; Silva et al. 2015).

3   Methodology

3.1   Participants

This study was held in an university in Taipei, Taiwan. The participants were 29 graduate and university students who take an optional course 'Robotics' and most of the university participants lack prior experiences before taking the course. The participants were divided into seven groups.

3.2   Instructional Design of Robotic STEM Program

The instructional components of the robotic program include robot mechanism design, robot motion analysis, robot dynamics, trajectory generation, robot control, and group competition. To meet the components above mentioned, the framework of the robotic STEM program, including five particular tasks with related engineering design activities, is shown in Table 1.

Table 1. Framework of the robotic STEM program

	Description of task	Engineering design activities
Task 1	1.1 Robot-mechanism design Design and fabricate the chassis of a wheel-robot	a. Problem definition
		b. Gather information
		c. Generate ideas
		d. Modeling
		e. Feasibility analysis
		f. Evaluation
		g. Decision
		h. Communication
	1.2 Test the sensors	b. Gather information
		e. Feasibility analysis
	1.3 Programming	b. Gather information
		c. Generate ideas
Task 2	2.1 Trajectory generation and testing	a. Problem definition
		b. Gather information
		d. Modeling
		e. Feasibility analysis
		g. Decision
		h. Communication

(*continued*)

Table 1. (*continued*)

	Description of task	Engineering design activities
Task 3	3.1 Robot mechanism design	a. Problem definition
		b. Gather information
		c. Generate ideas
		d. Modeling
		e. Feasibility analysis
		f. Evaluation
		g. Decision
		h. Communication
	3.2 Evaluation	a. Problem definition
		e. Feasibility analysis
Task 4	4.1 Robot motion control and analysis	a. Problem definition
		d. Modeling
		e. Feasibility analysis
		g. Decision
		h. Communication
Task 5	5.1 Group competition	h. Communication

3.3 Data Collection and Analysis

Each group's research notes were firstly collected and were analyzed by engineering design coding schema shown in Table 2 (revised from Atmen et al. 2007). There were two groups of students (G5 and G6) interviewed and randomly selected from the groups that were willing to share their feelings toward the program. The strategy for data analysis was to combine various data in order to produce the research proposals.

4 Results

Table 3 shows the status of the participants' engineering design practices. The state in Table 3 means the accounts of individual group's performances. For example, once the G1 perform a behavior related to problem definition, we account 1 for the perform. In light of the results in Table 3, we propose some insights as follows. Firstly, most of the groups performed most of engineering design practices during the program implementation. It reveals that the robotic STEM program provides the students opportunities to perform the critical engineering design practices. However, as shown in Table 3, we found that students perform more engineering design practices on 'generate ideas' and 'modeling' dimensions, but less on 'feasibility analysis' and 'evaluation' dimensions. It reveals the weak abilities of students on metacognition.

In addition, some specific features of the participants' engineering design practices are revealed. For example, we found that prior experience and classroom understanding are critical factors that affect the quality of students' engineering design. Furthermore, the graduate group performed more elaborate engineering design practices than the university group's.

Table 2. Coding schema of engineering design

Engineering design activities	Engineering design practices
a. Problem definition	1. Defining what the problem really is 2. Identifying constraints and criteria 3. Rereading or questioning the problem statement
b. Gather information	1. Searching for and recalling information beyond that provided 2. Searching for and collecting information needed to solve the problem
c. Generate ideas	1. Listing different alternatives 2. Developing potential solutions (or parts of potential solutions) to the problem
d. Modeling	1. Describing and detailing how to build the solution (or parts of the solutions) to the problem 2. Fitting the initial solution concepts in the design to the problem 3. Estimating or calculating the measurements
e. Feasibility analysis	1. Verifying and assessing on a possible or planned solution to the problem in workability 2. Determining whether a solution (or solution element) meets the constraints and criteria
f. Evaluation	1. Comparing two (or more) solutions to the problem on a particular dimension (or set of dimensions) 2. Making judgments about one alternative relative to another
g. Decision	1. Selecting one idea or solution to the problem (or parts of the problem) from those considered alternatives
h. Communication	1. Communicating the design elements in writing (e.g., sketches, diagrams, lists) 2. Oral reporting or defining the design solution to others

Table 3. Status of the participants' engineering design practices

	G1	G2	G3	G4	G5	G6	G7
Problem definition	7	7	3	11	10	10	3
a1	3	2	2	4	5	4	2
a2	3	3	1	4	3	4	1
a3	1	2	0	3	2	2	0
Gather information	4	5	3	6	7	6	3
b1	2	2	2	4	4	1	0
b2	2	3	1	2	3	5	3
Generate ideas	18	15	22	25	30	20	5
c1	9	6	10	13	16	12	4
c2	9	9	12	12	14	8	1
Modeling	30	35	22	23	41	30	26
d1	7	8	6	8	10	5	4
d2	8	8	8	8	10	7	15

(*continued*)

Table 3. (*continued*)

	G1	G2	G3	G4	G5	G6	G7
d3	15	19	8	7	21	18	7
Feasibility analysis	3	4	3	3	5	13	2
e1	1	3	2	2	3	5	2
e2	2	1	1	1	2	8	0
Evaluation	4	6	6	4	10	8	6
f1	1	2	3	2	3	2	2
f2	2	3	1	1	3	3	1
f3	1	1	2	1	4	3	3
Decision	2	3	3	5	6	4	3
Communication	5	7	7	5	9	10	6
h1	2	4	4	3	6	6	2
h2	3	3	3	2	3	4	4

5 Conclusion

The present study aims to propose an interdisciplinary program that is based on integrative STEM approach and further to explore the development of engineering design in the program. The students could perform most of the engineering design practices, however, they have insufficient practices on the metacognitive dimensions. In addition, we also reveal some factors that affect students' engineering design. In light of the results, we propose some instructional suggestions for developing engineering design.

References

Apedoe, X., Reynolds, B., Ellefson, M., Schunn, C.: Bringing engineering design into high school science classrooms: The heating/cooling unit. J. Sci. Educ. Technol. **17**(5), 454–465 (2008)

Atman, C.J., Adams, R.S., Cardella, M.E., Turns, J., Mosborg, S., Saleem, J.: Engineering design processes: A comparison of students and expert practitioners. J. Eng. Educ. **96**(4), 359–379 (2007)

Bailey, R., Szabo, Z.: Assessing engineering design process knowledge. Int. J. Eng. Educ. **22**(3), 508–518 (2006)

Denson, C.D.: Building a Framework for Engineering Design Experiences in STEM: A Synthesis. National Center for Engineering and Technology Education (2011)

Dym, C.L., Agogino, A.M., Eris, O., Frey, D.D., Leifer, L.J.: Engineering design thinking, teaching, and learning. J. Eng. Educ. **94**(1), 103–120 (2005)

Hynes, M., Portsmore, M., Dare, E., Milto, E., Rogers, C., Hammer, D.: Infusing engineering design into high school STEM courses. National Center for Engineering and Technology Education (2011)

Lloyd, P.: Embedded creativity: teaching design thinking via distance education. Int. J. Technol. Des. Educ. **23**(3), 749–765 (2013)

Silva, A., Fontul, M., Henriques, E.: Teaching design in the first years of a traditional mechanical engineering degree: methods, issues and future perspectives. Eur. J. Eng. Educ. **40**(1), 1–13 (2015)

Increasing the Learning Performance via Augmented Reality Technology

A Case Study of Digital Image Processing Course

ChinLun Lai[1](✉) and YuFang Chu[2]

[1] Department of Communication Engineering,
Oriental Institute of Technology, Taipei, Taiwan
fo001@mail.oit.edu.tw
[2] Education Resources and Publishing Center,
National Academy for Educational Research, Taipei, Taiwan
yufang@mail.naer.edu.tw

Abstract. In this paper, an innovative teaching model to reinforce the teaching performance of teachers and the learning performance is proposed. Based on the digital image processing courses, an interactive teaching method containing immediate image retrieval, visual analysis and processing, imaging control, theoretical narration, and the extensive applications using AR technology and wearable devices is designed. This method converts the mode from teacher's traditional theoretical lectures and the student's passive learning behaviors into immediate and dynamic operations, immersive observations; changing combinations; and bi-directional interactions, exchanges, and discussions. It is expected that this method can improve student's interest and motivation in learning and help them comprehensively understand the abstract concepts of course content and technology theories, as well as the skill in practical application, through real-time and immersive surrounding observations and interactive interface operations, thereby can enhance the learning performance.

Keywords: Augmented reality · Engineering education · Digital image processing · Wearable device · Video analysis

1 Introduction

Augmented reality (AR) refers to the integration of real-world objects with virtual graphics or images and the rendering of these composite images on electronic displays. Therefore, AR is a type of technology that emphasizes the interaction between the real and virtual worlds. The development of AR began in the 1900s. It has since been expanded into the medical, industrial, and entertainment domains amidst the advancements in computer technology. Although viewing the effects of AR requires the use of specialized devices, technological improvement has made these devices smarter and easier to use, which consequently enhances the convenience and broadens the application of AR. One of the popular examples is the game 'Pokemon Go'.

© Springer International Publishing AG 2017
T.-T. Wu et al. (Eds.): SETE 2016, LNCS 10108, pp. 58–64, 2017.
DOI: 10.1007/978-3-319-52836-6_8

AR is particularly useful for abstract explanation since it deed present the phenomena processing or events observing. Therefore, it can be applied in the education domain to facilitate learners in observing 3D objects and animation created for AR and learning the occurrence of phenomena, thereby achieving learning objectives through AR field observations [1–9]. AR contains several features and affordances thus can be served as attributes for learning aids. (1) It can render course content in 3D to help students develop and understand 3D spatial concepts, such as producing a 3D representation of 2D plants revolving around the image of the sun. (2) Specific scenarios can be incorporated into collaborative learning, where students can engage in indoor/outdoor scenario-based AR learning using mobile devices, as well as cooperation and interaction through information retrieval and analysis. (3) It provides immediate sensory feedback thus the students can immersive themselves in AR and gain immediate feedback through human-machine interaction. (4) It facilitates the digital visualization of invisible objects. AR can virtually represent objects that students cannot see with the naked eyes, such as chemical molecules within a 3D space to highlight molecular arrangement. (5) It links classroom lessons with outdoor learning. For example, AR can link campus environments with science material when teaching campus flora and fauna.

On the other hand, AR combines physical objects with virtual graphics and then presented as an operable interface on a display to help students transcend original sensory learning methods and impart understanding of the knowledge and information both in quality and quantity. In course learning, the physical and microscopic elements of multi-dimensional and special learning processes can become interchangeable through design, such as zooming into a crystal structure to present its molecular arrangement. To explain in further detail, AR can serve as an auxiliary tool to enhance the practical, cognitive, and affective domains of learning. In terms of the practical domain, AR provides a way for hands-on learning, facilitating scientific comprehension through result observation of the real-time operation. In terms of the cognitive domain, the association of macroscopic, microscopic, and symbolic scales; the operation of abstract expressions; and the integration of time and space through AR can be employed to build scientific models to facilitate comprehension. In terms of the affective domain, collective learning using mobile technology can promote peer interaction and communication and stimulate positive attitudes and interest towards course learning.

In the recent years, some novel concepts are proposed to enhance the teaching, training, and learning performance in a diversity fields and courses by using the AR technique as well as the mobile devices [10–12]. Some of the important advantages of using these tools include: (1) It increases the learning interest, especially for those courses with profound theory or taught by teacher's lectures only. (2) It makes the students comprehend the course contents more quickly and deeply by live scene observation. (3) It significantly reduces the time for a learner from beginner to profession. For example, in the field of digital image processing, there are thousands basic image processing functions should be practiced and acquainted for the beginner where such process may takes several months to years. After that, it is possible for them to make the correct decision in which processes they should take once a live image processing problem occurs. The aforementioned learning process is necessary for a learner who interests in image processing and the related advanced techniques such as computer vision or pattern recognition. However, it takes a long time to familiar with the basic image processing functions by studying, programming, and experiments, thus know how to apply them correctly for the corresponding cases. By the help of App aids, learner can be experienced quickly by observing the real-time captured images and the corresponding processing results at the same time, thus understand the effect of operating image processing function.

Accordingly, this paper try to proposes an innovative teaching model as well as teaching aid system to reinforce the teaching performance of teachers and the learning performance of students. Based on digital image processing courses, an interactive teaching method containing immediate image retrieval, visual analysis and processing, imaging control, theoretical narration, and the extensive applications using AR technology and wearable devices is designed. This method converts the mode from teacher's traditional theoretical lectures and the student's passive learning behaviors into immediate and dynamic operations, immersive observations; changing combinations; and bi-directional interactions, exchanges, and discussions. It is expected that this method can improve student's interest and motivation in learning and help them comprehensively understand the abstract concepts of course content and technology theories, as well as the skill in practical application, through real-time and immersive surrounding observations and interactive interface operations, thereby can enhance the learning performance.

2 The Research Methodology

To achieve the aforementioned objectives, a course APP for mobile devices will be designed and implemented. The APP can be used in conjunction with Google Card-Board to achieve a more immersive experience. An interactive interface will be de signed for the APP to control different display modes, providing learners with different selections and operations. Such modes include the instant scene mode, which displays real-world images using the camera on the mobile device; operation processing mode, which displays images processed through video processing; and tile display mode, which displays the original image and the processed image simultaneously.

In the initial App design, there are 20 popular image processing functions, among the digital image processing techniques such as listed in Tables 1 and 2, will be implemented for users to select and use, including thresholding, edge extraction, color coordinate conversion, high/low pass filters, contrast adjustment, median filter, spectrum space conversion, and morphological processing, among numerous others. Some of the implemented processes are similar to running the MATLAB programs in desktop PC as shown in Figs. 1 and 2, where educators largely adopt abstract introductions to impart these basic theories. They may also provide experiential courses to enable learners to write their own programs or operate existing applications, thereby presenting images before and after processing and facilitating learners understand theories of processing functions. The proposed interactive APP enables learners to capture images of the real world using the cameras on their devices, and then selecting a processing function to view processing outcomes immediately. The ability to dynamically change operating parameters, observing images change before and after

Table 1. Some popular basic image processing functions and its descriptions (MATLAB Image enhancement and deblurring)

imadjust	Adjust image intensity values or colormap
imcontrast	Adjust Contrast tool
imsharpen	Sharpen image using unsharp masking
histeq	Enhance contrast using histogram equalization
adapthisteq	Contrast-limited adaptive histogram equalization (CLAHE)
imhistmatch	Adjust histogram of image to match N-bin histogram of reference image
decorrstretch	Apply decorrelation stretch to multichannel image
stretchlim	Find limits to contrast stretch image
intlut	Convert integer values using lookup table
imnoise	Add noise to image
deconvblind	Deblur image using blind deconvolution
deconvlucy	Deblur image using Lucy-Richardson method
deconvreg	Deblur image using regularized filter
deconvwnr	Deblur image using Wiener filter
edgetaper	Taper discontinuities along image edges
otf2psf	Convert optical transfer function to point-spread function

the processing, and analyzing numerical differences allows learners to gain a greater understanding of the various functions in different display mode such as shown in Figs. 3 and 4. Moreover, the application of real-world images and content enhances the liveliness of learning. Learners are more able to resonate with the content, thus

Table 2. Cont., Some popular basic image processing functions and its descriptions (MATLAB Image transforms)

bwdist	Distance transform of binary image
bwdistgeodesic	Geodesic distance transform of binary image
graydist	Gray-weighted distance transform of grayscale image
hough	Hough transform
dct2	2-D discrete cosine transform
dctmtx	Discrete cosine transform matrix
fan2para	Convert fan-beam projections to parallel-beam
fanbeam	Fan-beam transform
idct2	2-D inverse discrete cosine transform
ifanbeam	Inverse fan-beam transform
iradon	Inverse Radon transform
para2fan	Convert parallel-beam projections to fan-beam
radon	Radon transform
fft2	2-D fast Fourier transform
fftshift	Shift zero-frequency component to center of spectrum
ifft2	2-D inverse fast Fourier transform
ifftshift	Inverse FFT shift

```
Write a M-File function to provide Contrast stretching (Basic gray-
level transformations.)
function [y]=contraststretch1(varargin)
aa=varargin{1};
[m n]=size(aa);
a=im2double(aa);
sum=0
for i=1:1:m
  for j=1:1:n
num=sum+a(i,j);
end
end
sum
pro=m*n;
level=sum/pro;(varargin)
S = 1./(1+(level./a).^2)
mat2gray(S)
y=S
Output:
a=imread('cam.bmp')
imshow(a)
b=contraststretch(a)
imshow(b)
```

Fig:Original image   Fig after contrast stretching

Fig. 1. Matlab script example of image enhancement processing

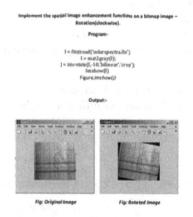

```
Implement the spatial image enhancement functions on a bitmap image –
Rotation(clockwise).

Program-

I = fitstread('solarspectra.fts');
I = mat2gray(I);
J = imrotate(I,-10,'bilinear','crop');
imshow(J)
Figure,imshow(J)

Output:-
```

Fig: Original Image   Fig: Rotated Image

Fig. 2. Matlab script example of image rotation processing

Fig. 3. Display Type I: mobile device

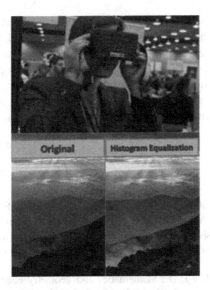

Fig. 4. Display Type II: AR device

increasing their learning motivations and interests. In future, an infinite number of image processing functions can be added into the teaching APP. Adjustment to the operations or displays modes can also be made depending on course content to reinforce extended application capabilities, thereby expanding the applicability of the proposed APP in different professional courses.

3   Conclusions

Currently, teachers primarily used slides, animation, video examples, journals, and books as teaching materials for science and technology subjects. Interactive technology device is seldom applied in science and technology teaching. Thus, learning performance relies heavily on students' learning motivation and their ability to comprehend abstract concepts. Appropriate implementation of technology applications can embody the abstract of theories hence effectively attract the interest of students and enhance their understanding of figurative expressions. Among various technological applications, wearable devices and applications for course teaching should be widely developed and promoted including 3D structure imaging, AR experiment operation and training, interactive comparative observations, and instantaneous operation and display. The present study investigated a teaching method and teaching aids which use the AR technology in designing the course aids App to try to improve the teaching/learning performance. However, implementation of the App needs cooperation of interdisciplinary experts including course teacher, image processing engineer, and the App designer/programmer. It is expected that after empirical research test in the teaching scene once the App is completed, the innovative teaching method/aids will be proved to satisfy the aforementioned teaching resource requirements and achieve learning performance goals. That is, the experiment results will be applied to field courses test to collect feedback data from students thus to verify the effect of the proposed teaching method. Moreover, the method proposed in the present study can be extended to other professional subjects. Future scholars endeavoring to develop of similar teaching materials should invite more teachers to provide their teaching needs, which would facilitate developers in creating teaching aids that meet site demands and enhance teaching content and learning materials, thereby improving learning performance.

References

1. Lee, K.: Augmented reality in education and training. TechTrends **56**(2), 13–21 (2012)
2. Zhung, S.-K.: Design an Augmented Reality Teaching System with Concept Mapping Technique. Master thesis of Industrial Design of National Cheng Kung University (2006)
3. Azuma, R.T.: A survey of augmented reality. Presence: Teleoperators Virtual Environ. **6**(4), 355–385 (1997)
4. Kaufmann, H., Schmalstieg, D.: Mathematics and geometry education with collaborative augmented reality. Comput. Graph. **27**(3), 339–345 (2003)
5. van Krevelen, D.W.F., Poelman, R.: A survey of augmented reality technologies, applications and limitations. Int. J. Virtual Reality **9**(2), 1 (2010)
6. Dunleavy, M., Dede, C., Mitchell, R.: Affordances and limitations of immersive participatory augmented reality simulations for teaching and learning. J. Sci. Educ. Technol. **18**(1), 7–22 (2009)
7. Liarokapis, F., et al.: Web3D and augmented reality to support engineering education. World Trans. Eng. Technol. Educ. **3**(1), 11–14 (2004)
8. Schmalstieg, D., et al.: The studierstube augmented reality project. Presence: Teleoperators Virtual Environ. **11**(1), 33–54 (2002)
9. Starner, T., et al.: Augmented reality through wearable computing. Presence: Teleoperators Virtual Environ. **6**(4), 386–398 (1997)
10. Gogula, S.K., Gogula, S.D., Puranam, C.: Augmented reality in enhancing qualitative education. Int. J. Comput. Appl. **132**(14), 41–45 (2015)
11. Parmar, D., Pelmahale, K., Kothwade, R., Badgujar, P.: Augmented reality system for engineering graphics. Int. J. Adv. Res. Comput. Commun. Eng. **4**(10), 327–330 (2015)
12. Onime, C., Abiona, O.: 3D mobile augmented reality interface for laboratory experiments. Int. J. Commun. Netw. Syst. Sci. **9**, 67–76 (2016)

A Conceptual Framework Over Contextual Analysis of Concept Learning Within Human-Machine Interplays

Farshad Badie[(✉)]

Center for Linguistics, Aalborg University,
Rendsburggade 14, 9000 Aalborg, Denmark
badie@id.aau.dk

Abstract. This research provides a contextual description concerning existential and structural analysis of 'Relations' between human beings and machines. Subsequently, it will focus on conceptual and epistemological analysis of (i) my own semantics-based framework [for human meaning construction] and of (ii) a well-structured machine concept learning framework. Accordingly, I will, semantically and epistemologically, focus on linking those two frameworks for logical analysis of concept learning in the context of human-machine interrelationships. It will be demonstrated that the proposed framework provides a supportive structure over the described contextualisation of 'relations' between human beings and machines within concept learning processes.

1 Introduction and Motivation

Machine Learning as a subfield of Artificial Intelligence and Computer Science works on creating and developing appropriate procedures and techniques that allow machines to improve the productivity of their performances concerning a given goal, see [16]. Regarding [16], a machine program is said to learn from an experience if (*i*) there is a set of tasks for machine, (*ii*) there is a machine's performance measure, and (*iii*) the machine's performance at those tasks, as measured, improves with its experiences. *Concept Learning* as a paradigm of machine learning has been structured over a set of theories and methodologies that focus on a kind of task in which a machine is trained [by a human being] in order to classify things (objects). Additionally, regarding *Concept Training*, the human being [as the trainer] shows the sets of example and non-example objects to the machine. Subsequently, the main machine's task is a type of simplification. Actually, the machine compares the given thing with the provided examples. Thus, a characteristic feature of most concept learning approaches is the use of background knowledge. In concept learning with background knowledge, a machine, with regard to the given set of training examples and background knowledge, focuses on hypothesis generation. According to [13, 14], machine concept learning approaches lead to the construction of concepts (classes). The concept learning problems are tackled as a search through a space of candidate descriptions in the reference representation guided by exemplars of the target concepts. Also, the same algorithms can be adapted to solve the ontological problems. Note that these ontological problems

© Springer International Publishing AG 2017
T.-T. Wu et al. (Eds.): SETE 2016, LNCS 10108, pp. 65–74, 2017.
DOI: 10.1007/978-3-319-52836-6_9

are defined over the usage of ontologies in information and computer sciences. According to [8], an ontology in information sciences is a formal and explicit specification of a shared conceptualisation on a domain of interest.

It shall be emphasised that the central focus of this research is on conceptual and epistemological issues of the expressions 'concept', 'concept learning' and 'concept training' within human-machine interplays. So, I will need to be careful with these terms. In this research I will focus on epistemological analysis of concept learning while I will claim that "Machine Concept Learning approaches tackle to provide comprehensible logical representations for (*i*) describing human beings' constructed concepts and (*ii*) describing the interrelationships between the constructed concepts after having been transformed (from humans' minds into machines' knowledge bases and ontological descriptions)". In [4] I have focused on conceptual analysis of concept representation in the context of human-machine interactions. This paper has provided a conceptual and epistemological junction between human beings' minds and machines' knowledge bases [and ontological descriptions]. In [5] I have offered a description saying that the word 'learning' in machine learning has been utilised as a binary predicate with the word 'machine'. 'Learning' as a binary predicate has been asserted (with regard to the language of descriptive logics) and has been described to be a role that is being performed by a machine. Thus, the act (role) of learning for a machine could be interpreted as a reflection (or mirroring) of the [human] learning phenomenon in machines. This research has been built on the basis of [5, 6]. So, I will—conceptually and epistemologically—summarise their conclusions in the framework of concept learning and in the context of human-machine interrelationships. Subsequently, I will show that they can provide a contextual description concerning existential analysis of 'relations' between human beings and machines. Later on, I will focus on conceptual analysis of my own semantics-based framework [for meaning construction by human beings] and a well-structured machine concept learning framework and on their junctions. Accordingly it will be shown that this framework provides a supportive structure underpinning the described contextualisation of 'relations' between human beings and machines within concept learning processes.

2   Background of Thought

First, I shall take up the notion of 'concept' and integrate it into my line of thought. The term 'concept' is an especially intricate term in philosophy, linguistics, psychology, epistemology, cybernetics and computer sciences. In my approach, concept has been understood to be, on the one hand, a linkage between a human's mental images of parts of reality, and, on the other hand, a human's linguistic expressions and statements concerning those images, see [9]. In machine concept training approaches, a concept is transformed into a [logically] equivalent form in order to be represented and be expressed in machines' knowledge bases and ontological descriptions. For instance, relying on descriptive logical approaches concepts can be reflected, and, subsequently, be represented in the form of 'entities' and as the classes of objects, see [1, 10, 11]. Regarding my research in [6], human beings refine their constructed concepts into various conceptions that are representable in the form of hypotheses. Accordingly, the represented hypotheses could become corresponding to distinct entities or to their essential attributes, features, characteristics and properties. A hypothesis[1] is a supposition or proposed explanation made on the basis of limited evidence as a starting point for further investigation. So, this supposition is capable of describing the multiple theories based on terminologies and in the form of world descriptions for a particular technical application and within the domain of interest. Consequently, the hypotheses created over the defined and analysed terminologies support inferential and reasoning processes and satisfy multiple conditions for definitions of truth with regard to interpretation functions.

This article focuses on [5] that has been structured over Predicate Logic (PL), see [15]. PL has supported me in the formal semantic[2] analysis of the term 'relationships' within human-machine interplays. Consequently, the conclusions supported my thoughts about the HowNess of establishing a formal semantics concerning human-machine interactions. Based on Predicate Logic and focusing on Description Logics (see [1]) a unary predicate is supposed to be logically equivalent to a concept. Relying on descriptive logical approaches we can translate a unary predicate into a concept in order to employ it in concept expression (so-called *concept learning*) processes. Furthermore, according to the aforementioned characteristics of hypotheses, a concept can be logically described by a hypothesis, see [13, 16]. Regarding [16], a hypothesis—as a logical description of a concept—arises during a machine learning process. It is a tentative explanation of 'why the objects are members (or non members) of the concepts'. Conceptually and logically, the hypotheses focus on describing the predicates. Then, they are expected to describe the same attributes, characteristics and properties. In my opinion, the outcomes of

i. providing a strong logical description for amalgamation of mental representations of a thing's linguistic expressions and its other mental images in the form of hypotheses,
ii. analysing the supportive inferential processes on those hypothesis, and
iii. focusing on world descriptions using generated hypotheses relying on defined terminologies

could determine the applications of predicates, and, subsequently, the applications of terms and statements.

---

[1] See http://www.oxforddictionaries.com/definition/english/hypothesis.

[2] Semantics is the study of the meanings, and the relation of signs to the objects to which the signs are applicable. In formal languages semantics is the study and analysis of the meanings of symbols and signifiers. Semantics focuses on the relationships between the signifiers of any language. In fact, the formal semantics employs the products of the human beings' interpretations in order to produce meanings.

3 Formal Semantic Analysis

The following axioms in PL focus on defining the outcomes of my interpretations, which will be employed for formal semantic analysis of relationships between 'human' an 'machine':

a. The terms 'human' and 'machine' are constant symbols.
b. The most significant unary predicates in the formalism are `Learner` and `Trainer`. According to this interpretation, `Learner(machine)` and `Trainer(human)` represent two world descriptions over unary predicates. They represent the facts that the machine is a learner and the human is a trainer respectively.
c. Considering the unary predicates `Learner` and `Trainer`, the binary predicates `TrainerOf` and `LearnerOf` can be defined. Consequently, `TrainerOf(human, machine)` and `LearnerOf(machine, human)` are two world descriptions over binary predicates. For instance, the relation `TrainerOf(human, machine)` describes that the human is the trainer of the machine.
d. The functions `trainer(machine)` and `learner(human)` can be defined in order to represent the 'trainer of machine' and the 'learner of human' respectively.

Based on these four axioms, we may conclude that:

$$
\begin{aligned}
&\texttt{TrainerOf(human,machine)} \rightarrow \\
&[\ (\texttt{trainer(machine)} \rightarrow \texttt{human}\ )\ \&\ (\ \texttt{human} \rightarrow \\
&\qquad\qquad \texttt{trainer(machine)}\ )\ ] \\
&\qquad\qquad\qquad \text{AND} \\
&[\ (\ \texttt{trainer(machine)} \rightarrow \texttt{human}\ )\ \&\ (\ \texttt{human} \rightarrow \\
&\qquad\qquad \texttt{trainer(machine)}\ )\ ] \rightarrow \\
&\qquad \texttt{TrainerOf(human,machine)}.
\end{aligned}
$$

This logical term is structurally equal to:

$$
\begin{aligned}
&\texttt{Relation} \rightarrow \\
&[\ (\ \texttt{function} \rightarrow \texttt{constant}\ )\ \&\ (\ \texttt{constant} \rightarrow \texttt{function}\ )\ ] \\
&\qquad\qquad\qquad \text{AND} \\
&[\ (\ \texttt{function} \rightarrow \texttt{constant}\ )\ \&\ (\ \texttt{constant} \rightarrow \texttt{function}\ )\ ] \\
&\qquad\qquad \rightarrow \\
&\qquad \texttt{Relation}.
\end{aligned}
$$

Obviously, this logical description (let me name it *RFC*) has been structured over four fundamentals: (1) The `training` relationship between human and machine (from human into machine), (2) The `learning` relationship between machine and human (from machine into human), (3) The iterative loops between human and machine (from human into machine and then from machine into human), and (4) The iterative loops between machine and human (from machine into human and then from human into machine). Therefore, the formal semantics of training-learning relationship in the context of human-machine interactions is definable and analysable over two constructive bi-conditions:

I. Indicating the existence of the 'iterative loops between human and machine' from the 'training relation between human and machine'. Inversely, indicating the truth (or the existence) of the 'training relationship between human and machine' from the 'iterative loops between human and machine'.

II. Indicating the existence of the 'iterative loops between machine and human' from the 'learning relation between machine and human'. Inversely, indicating the truth (or the existence) of the 'learning relationship between machine and human' from the 'iterative loops between machine and human'.

According to the deduced results, the following is valid:

I. The process of machine training (as a relation between human and machine) supports the interrelationships between 'the act and the process of training' and 'the machine (as the learner)', and inversely, the interrelationships between 'the act of training' and 'the machine (as the learner)' support the machine training (as a relation between human and machine).

II. The process of machine learning (as a relation between machine and human) supports the interrelationships between 'the act and the process of learning' and 'the human (as the trainer)', and inversely, the interrelationships between 'the act and the process of learning' and 'the human (as the trainer)' support the machine learning (as a relation between machine and human).

More specifically, by taking 'concepts' into consideration and limiting the 'Learning' task to 'Concept Learning', we can come up with the following consequences:

A. The concept training relations (from human into machine) support the interrelationships between 'the act and the process of concept training' and 'the machine (as the learner)'. Subsequently, interrelationships between 'the act and the process of concept training' and 'the machine (as the learner)' support the concept training relations (from human into machine).

B. The concept learning relations (from machine into human) support the interrelationships between 'the act and the process of concept learning' and 'the human (as the trainer)'. Subsequently, the interrelationships between 'the act and the process of concept learning' and 'the human (as the trainer)' support the concept learning relations (from machine into human).

Proposition. The combination of A and B provides a contextual description concerning existential analysis of 'relations' between human beings and machines. This contextual description has been supported by the fact that the formal semantics of 'relations' between human beings and machines is describable over six components (i.e., two constants, two functions and two relations) as can be seen in the logical description *RFC*.

4   A Conceptual Framework

The central focus of this section is on building and analysing a conceptual framework over the proposed contextual and conceptual analysis of 'relations' between human beings and machines. This framework expresses "the junction of humans' meaning construction processes and machines' concept learning over humans' constructed concepts". This framework provides a supportive structure over the described contextualisation of 're- lations' between human beings and machines within concept learning processes. It has been built over the separated components [a] and [b]. The component [b] represents the process of concept learning (by machine) and the component [a] represents the process of meaning construction (by human being). It shall be claimed that the interrelationships between a human being (as a trainer) and a machine (as a learner) could be represented as the reflection of [a] in [b], and as the conformation of [b] on [a]. In [6] I have focused on logical characterisation of 'reflection' and 'conformation' transformations.

4.1   Component [b]: Concept Learning by Machine

As mentioned, a very important and determinative feature belonging typically to all machine concept learning approaches is using background knowledge. Generally, the background knowledge could be classified as concept descriptions in knowledge bases and in ontological descriptions. However, there are strong dependencies between concept descriptions and ontological descriptions. For instance, in semantics-based technologies the background knowledge could be categorised as (*i*) Ontology Lan- guages (e.g., OWL[3]) that represent specified knowledge about various things and objects, (*ii*) internal knowledge bases, (*iii*) Question-Answering and querying end- points [that focus on querying a knowledge base using the querying languages (e.g., SPARQL[4])], and (*iv*) the collection of the interrelated datasets (e.g., Linked Data[5]). [12] has focused on analysing a successful component-based framework[6] for concept learning in Description Logics and in OWL. The architecture of this component-based framework has been structured over four components. Actually, besides the 'Knowl- edge Source' component (see Fig. 1), the 'Machine Learning Problem' component (e.g., definitions of atomic concepts by more specified descriptions, providing sub- sumption and equality axioms in terminological knowledge, providing positive and negative examples of classes of objects), the 'Machine Learning Algorithm' compo- nent, and the 'Reasoning System' component are related to each other, see Fig. 1. I shall stress that the architecture of this framework could clarify what ingredients (as the building blocks) are effective within concept learning processes and how those ingredients could be connected to each other. You will see the interconnections of this Framework and my developed Framework in the next section.

4.2   Component [a]: Meaning Construction by Human Being

For analysing meaning construction and production, I rely on my own semantics-based framework, see [2, 3, 7]. I shall start with this conception that "a human being, before

---

[3] www.w3.org/2001/sw/wiki/OWL.

[4] www.w3.org/wiki/SparqlEndpoints.

[5] www.w3.org/standards/semanticweb/data.

[6] http://dl-learner.org/development/architecture/.

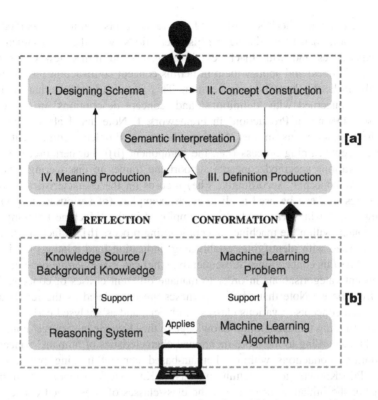

Fig. 1. A conceptual framework for concept learning within human-machine interplays

becoming a trainer of a machine, is the developer of her/his personal conceptions (of her/his constructed concepts) over the individual designed schemata[7] (or mental objects)", see 'Designing Schema' in Framework 1. Schemata are cohesive, repeatable action sequence possessing component actions that are tightly interconnected and governed by a core meaning, see [17]. In my semantic approach, schemata (or mental objects) support humans in constructing their own concepts [and in linking their mental images of the world and their linguistic expressions]. Furthermore, schemata support humans (who are the trainers of machines) in developing their constructed concepts and in producing their own conceptions in order to employ them in generating hypotheses, see 'Concept Construction' in Framework 1. The constructed concepts provide strong backbones for humans' semantic interpretation and meaning construction processes within their concept training. I shall claim that the most significant importance of the proposed contextual and conceptual description of concept learning [and concept training] regarding interrelationships between humans and machines is that "they have been analysed over schemata-based conceptualisations and conceptual representations". Considering my researches in [2, 3, 7], the trainer needs to employ inductive

---

[7] See   http://plato.stanford.edu/entries/schema/   and   http://global.britannica.com/topic/schema-cognitive.

rules in order to expand her/his constructed general concepts into more specified ones. Additionally, a human being during her/his interactions (with the environment, with her/his experiences and with machines) investigates and forms new concepts (or reforms the old ones) and applies them in her/his concept construction processes, and accordingly, in her/his hypotheses generation. This fact clearly shows that the trainer has become concerned with 'definitions' and 'concept descriptions' in his training process, see 'Definition Production' in Framework 1. Note that I already have discussed these descriptions in the 'Machine Learning Problem' component within machine concept learning process (i.e., the component **[b]**). Furthermore, the generalisation of various specified concepts support the trainer in discovering [and constructing] new concepts. Accordingly, s(he) focuses on the characteristics, attributes and properties that can be used to distinguish exemplars (of various concepts) from non-exemplars. Again, these products are employed in the 'Machine Learning Problem' component within the machine concept learning process **[b]**. In fact, the trainer is highly concerned with identifying, establishing, indicating [and relating] the induced examples of her/his conceptions. Subsequently, s(he) can make her/his personal labels of the concept categorisations in order to manage different classes of concepts in the form of hypotheses. Note that these hypotheses are considered as the reflections of her/his created concepts in various classes of objects, and as analysed earlier, they are used in constructing the background knowledge in the 'Knowledge Source' component (see Fig. 1). According to the afore-mentioned characteristics of humans' conceptions and definition productions within schemata-based concept training processes, the sequence 'PriorKnowledge → Definition → New Knowledge' supports the trainer in searching for the initiative meanings of the class/classes of constructed concepts and their relationships, see 'Meaning Production' in Framework 1. It's only possible by means of semantic interpretations, see 'Semantic Interpretation' in Framework 1. From the logical point of view, the interpretation of a defined constructed concept is a function. This function has turned a definition into a meaning. The Interpretation functions operate the trainer's definitions over her/his constructed concepts. Therefore, the interpretations 'activate' the meanings of her/his constructed concept. Consequently, the productions have made appropriate backgrounds for verifying the personally found meanings based on personal defined constructed concepts. I shall stress that "a meaning would be given a better shape after checking the balanced definitions based on personal constructed concepts". So, there could be a number of loops between Definitions and Meanings. Methodologically, meanings are the supportive backbones for providing meaningful conceptual structures. The meaningful conceptual structures are all personally organised based on individual constructed concepts and definitions. On the other hand, the meaningful conceptual structures could induce more developed meanings on higher conceptual levels [and after more experience within interaction with environment, self and the machine]. The produced meanings could be employed in developing the individual schemata through higher levels of conceptions.

5   Conclusions

Concept Learning as a paradigm of machine learning has been structured over a set of theories and methodologies that focus on a kind of task, in which machines are trained [by human beings] in order to classify various things (objects). A characteristic feature of most concept learning approaches is the use of background knowledge. In concept learning with background knowledge, a machine, with regard to the given set of training examples and background knowledge, focuses on hypothesis generation. Through the lenses of logics and relying on descriptive logical approaches, the machine concept learning paradigm tackles to provide comprehensible logical representations in order to (a) describe humans' constructed concepts, and (b) describe the interrelationships between the constructed concepts after having been transformed (from humans' minds into machines' knowledge bases and ontological descriptions). The central focus of this research has been to conceptual and epistemological issues of the expressions 'concept', 'concept learning' and 'concept training' within human-machine interplays. Regarding my previous researches on (i) concept representation analysis in the context of human-machine interactions, (ii) conceptual analysis of concept representation in the context of human-machine interactions, (iii) epistemological junctions between human beings' minds and machines' knowledge bases [and ontological descriptions], and (iv) meaning construction over humans' constructed concepts, I have initiated this research with the conception that "a human being, before becoming a trainer of a machine, is the developer of her/his personal conceptions over her/his designed schemata". This research has provided a contextual description concerning existential and structural analysis of 'Relations' between human beings and machines. It has been suggested that the most significant importance of provided contextual [and conceptual] description of concept learning [and concept training] regarding the interrelationships between humans and machines, has been established over schemata-based conceptualisations and conceptual representations. Subsequently, I have focused on, conceptual and epistemological, analysis of (i) my own semantics-based framework [meaning construction] over individual constructed concepts, and of (ii) a well-structured component-based machine concept learning framework that works over Description Logics and within ontological languages. Accordingly, I have focused on linking those two frameworks for logical analysis of concept learning in the context of human-machine interrelationships. It has been demonstrated that the proposed framework provides a supportive structure over the described contextualisation of 'relations' between human beings and machines within concept learning processes. This research has formed a building block of my PhD research, which is dealing with Semantic Analysis of Constructivist Concept Leaning.

References

1. Baader, F., Calvanese, D., McGuinness, D., Nardi, D., Patel-Schneider, P.: The Description Logic Handbook: Theory, Implementation and Applications. Cambridge University Press, New York (2010)

2. Badie, F.: A semantic basis for meaning construction in constructivist interactions. In: Proceedings of 12th International Conference on Cognition and Exploratory Learning in Digital Age, Ireland (2015)
3. Badie, F.: Towards a semantics based framework for meaning construction in constructivist interactions. In: Proceedings of 8th Annual International Conference of Education, Research and Innovation, Spain (2015)
4. Badie, F.: Concept representation analysis in the context of human-machine interactions. In: Proceedings of 14th International Conference on e-Society, Portugal (2016)
5. Badie, F.: Logical characterisation of concept transformations from human into machine relying on predicate logic. In: Ninth International Conference on Advances in Computer-Human Interactions (ACHI), International Journal on Advances in Intelligent systems, Italy (2016)
6. Badie, F.: Towards semantic analysis of training-learning relationships within human-machine interactions. In: Ninth International Conference on Advances in Computer-Human Interactions (ACHI), International Journal on Advances in Intelligent systems, Italy (2016)
7. Badie, F.: A conceptual framework for knowledge creation based on constructed meanings within mentor-learner conversations. In: Uskov, V.L., Howlett, R.J., Jain, L.C. (eds.). SIST, vol. 59, pp. 167–177Springer, Heidelberg (2016). doi:10.1007/978-3-319-39690-3_15
8. Gangemi, A., Presutti, V.: Handbook of ontologies, 2 edn. In: Staab, R., Studer, S. (eds.) Springer, Berlin (2009)
9. Götzsche, H.: Deviational Syntactic Structures. Bloomsbury Academic, London/New Delhi/New York/Sydney (2013)
10. Hitzler, P., Krötzsch, M., Parsia, B., Patel-Schneider, P., Rudolph, S.: OWL 2 Web Ontology Language: Primer, Latest version (2009)
11. Hitzler, P., Krötzsch, M., Rudolph, S.: Foundations of Semantic Web Technologies. Chapman & Hall/CRC Textbooks in Computing (2009)
12. Lehmann, J.: DL-learner: learning concepts in description logics. J. Mach. Learn. Res. (JMLR) **10**, 2639–2642 (2009)
13. Lehmann, J.: Learning OWL Class Expressions. Leipziger Beiträge zur Informatik (2010)
14. Lehmann, J., Fanizzi, N., Bühmann, L., d'Amato, C.: Concept Learning, in 'Perspectives on Ontology Learning, pp. 71–91. AKA/IOS Press (2014)
15. Mendelson, E.: Introduction to Mathematical Logic, 3 edn. Chapman and Hall (1987)
16. Mitchell, T.: Machine learning, in Machine Learning, Kluwer Academic Publishers. Mach. Learn. J. **78**(1–2), 203–250 (1997)
17. Piaget, J., Cook, M.T.: The origins of Intelligence in Children. International University Press, New York (1952)

An Intelligent Concept Map for e-book via Automatic Keyword Extraction

Chin-Feng Lai[1](✉), Chun-Wei Tsai[2], Shih-Yeh Chen[1],
Ren-Hung Hwang[3], and Chu-Sing Yang[4]

[1] Department of Engineering Science,
National Cheng Kung University, Tainan, Taiwan
cinfon@ieee.org, me.ya404@gmail.com
[2] Department of Computer Science and Information Engineering,
National Ilan University, Yilan, Taiwan
cwtsai@niu.edu.tw
[3] Department of Computer Science and Information Engineering,
National Chung Cheng University, Chaiyi, Taiwan
rhhwang@cs.ccu.edu.tw
[4] Department of Electrical Engineering,
National Cheng Kung University, Tainan, Taiwan
csyang@ee.ncku.edu.tw

Abstract. The advance of internet technologies and digital information systems has played a critical role in the development of modern education. In particular, several innovative information technologies and products have witnessed the changes of learning behaviors in recent years. Among them, how to use e-books to improve the learning performance of audience has become a promising research topic because it can be used to automatically record the reading behaviors of audience. In this way, we can provide personalized information to the audience. Generally speaking, an e-book can typically be regarded as a product of a book after it is digitized, because modern information technologies make it possible for an e-book abundant in multimedia contents than does a textbook. In Taiwan, the ministry of education encourages instructors to try new teaching methods, strategies, devices, and even environments to enhance the learning motivation of students. Using handheld devices, mobile applications, and e-books to support the learning of elementary students has become a popular research topic. In this study, we will present a novel e-book system that integrates two different technologies to enhance the learning performance of an e-book, which are: (1) information retrieval to understand the contents to the e-book system, and (2) concept map to provide knowledge to the audience. Before building a concept map, the proposed system has to extract the keywords from the e-book and to understand their relationships. To evaluate the performance of the proposed algorithm, a sixth grade class of 61 students in Taiwan are used as a test. In this study, all of the students, never learned these materials before, are divided into two groups. Experimental results show that the proposed e-book system with keyword concept map can significantly improve the learning performance of students compared to the traditional e-book in terms of both the scores received after learning and the results of satisfaction questionnaire on learning, practising, and system satisfaction.

Keywords: e-book · Concept map · Information retrieval

© Springer International Publishing AG 2017
T.-T. Wu et al. (Eds.): SETE 2016, LNCS 10108, pp. 75–85, 2017.
DOI: 10.1007/978-3-319-52836-6_10

1 Introduction

With the advance of information technology (IT), many things around us have been changed. Although not every change caused by IT makes our daily life better, the original idea behind these changes is to provide humans a more convenient life. The e-book [16] can typically be regarded as a product of IT; it can also be regarded as a product of book that has been digitized and that is composed of many kinds of digitized contents. For example, many modern online magazines or books, such as Times (see also http://time.com/magazine/), provide not only many simple ways for their audience to find the related information of the 100 most influential people in the world they elected but also many interactive ways to see the relevant multimedia contents. Such kinds of contents can typically be read by using modern interactive digital devices, e.g., desktop computers, smart phones, or tablets. According to our observations, the interactive interface of e-books make it possible to provide many more possibilities than just the digital contents to the audience. This means that having the images, audios, and other interactive multimedia contents displayed in this way, e-book is capable of playing the role of training students while at the same time providing a platform to help students exchange their ideas. It is just like the epitome of an e-learning platform. In brief, e-book can provide abundant multimedia contents to the audience (users) that are simply impossible for the paper-book. That is why the development of e-book has included a variety of multimedia products in one book [12].

Experience shows that reading an e-book still is not exactly the same as reading a paper-book [16]. This means that this new kind of learning material contains not only text and images, it may also contain audios, videos, and information available on the Internet. One of the important advantages of an e-book is that it can be read by using interactive digital devices (e.g., desktop computers, cell phones, or tablets); therefore, the audience is able to find the information they need quickly. However, although reading a traditional e-book is quite similar to reading a paper-book in the sense that it is to be read page by page, which makes it not easy for the audience to grasp the overall structure of such a book. In addition to displaying the contents of a paper-book in digital format on a computer or an e-book reader [11], several recent studies [7, 9] have attempted to improve the learning performance of the audience. For example, Li et al. [9] presented an integrated solution that combines the reading guidance module and annotation map of an e-book to discuss the impact of that kind of system on college students. Another interesting example is that the learning behaviours of the audience reading an e-book can be observed to provide more needed contents from their cognition styles, e.g., browsing patterns, navigation facilities, and annotation patterns [7].

An intelligent e-book system, which integrates the information technologies (i.e., information retrieval module) and the education technologies (i.e., concept map module) to provide a better e-book solution, will be presented in this paper. The information retrieval module in such an e-book system plays the role of finding out the important keywords of the learning contents in the e-book based on the term frequency-inverse document frequency (TF-IDF) [2] to automatically calculate the importance and similarity of keywords between different sections of the e-book to provide the similarity information of keywords in different sections to the concept map module. Since the concept map [15] for education can be used to organize and construct the knowledge, computer assisted instruction, or directed learning tool, the concept map technologies will be used in this study to build a map to make it easy for the audience to recognize the content structure of the e-book to help them find out the needed contents quickly. With information retrieval and concept map technologies at hand, the proposed e-book system can build a concept map with several keywords to describe the content structure of an e-book. Each keyword in the concept map is associated with a hyperlink to the relevant context; thus, the audience can easily jump to the section they are interested. Equipped with the keyword concept map and the hyperlink, we expect that the learning achievement of the reader can be raised. The main contributions of this study can be summarized as follows:

– We provide an intelligent e-book system by integrating the information and education technologies together.
– The proposed e-book system provides a better way to teach students, which in turn significantly improves their learning performance.

The remainder of this paper is organized as follows. Section 2 gives a brief introduction to the electronic book, concept map, data mining, machine learning and information retrieval technologies that will be used in the proposed system. Section 3 begins with the basic idea of the proposed system and then explains how it works. Section 3 presents the experimental results to show the performance of the proposed e-book system. The conclusion and future works are drawn in Sect. 5.

2   Related Work

Since the traditional e-books are usually read page by page, that makes it tough for the readers to grasp the overall structure of such a book and its basic ideas. Thus, the proposed e-book system is aimed to make it easy for the readers to understand most, if not all, of the things in the book very quickly, by using the keywords of the contents (i.e., concept map) in the book when reading it the very first time. This work, of course, will confront the dilemma stating that finding out applicable keywords to represent the consents in a book is a pretty difficult job. To solve this problem, the proposed system uses the term frequency-inverse document frequency (TF-IDF) to calculate the frequency of words appearing in different sections or subsections. With this information, the proposed system can then automatically select particular keywords to represent the contents of different sections. The readers (e.g., students) can then easily find out the needed information or contents very quickly. To achieve these goals, this study adopts the so-called concept map and some intelligent technologies (e.g., data mining, machine learning, and information retrieval technologies). Therefore, Sect. 2.1 begins with a brief introduction to the electronic book, followed by an introduction to the concept map and intelligent methods in Sects. 2.2 and 2.3, respectively.

2.1 Electronic Book

Personal computers (PC) have been with us for almost a half century while most of the things around us have also been digitized in these years. Today, most, if not all, of the information are created as digital file or stored in an information system. It is expected that, sooner or later, we will digitize all the books we need. A well known example is the google book (https://books.google.com/) which shows the impact e-books may bring to us. A simple way to create e-books is to display the contents of traditional paper-books in a digital format. Although the idea of e-books is not new, there exists no definition that is universally accepted. For this reason, Vassiliou et al. [13] attempted to define the e-books from different perspectives, such as developments, technologies, markets, and characteristics. Cox [4] also pointed out the main challenges and opportunities of e-books today. In addition to transforming the contents (from traditional paper-book to e-book), several new distinguishing features (e.g., multimedia contents or dynamic annotations) make them even more interesting. In brief, an e-book owns the characteristics of a PC for which a traditional paper-book does not have. Therefore, an e-book makes it possible to provide readers a book that is abundant in contents instead of just linear contents and that contains links to all kinds of information systems, such as e-learning systems.

Many researchers, be it in academia or government, are also interested in another research topic of e-book; that is, will the paper-books disappear (Velde and Ernst [14]) in the foreseeable future? Since paper-books and e-books each have pros and cons, they are simply not able to supersede each other. Put it in another way, although more and more students use e-books or online books to get the information they need, paper-books are still widely used in getting the information too. Some recent studies claimed that not only students but also their parents would like to learn the knowledge from the paper-books, not the e-books [16]. There still exist discussions and questions about the e-books. For example, one of the main questions is that most of the e-books are displayed on LCD and tablet, they might hurt the eyes of children if they are used too much. However, because the reading behavior of e-books can be stored in an information system, which can be very useful for improving the learning performance (e.g., changing the reading behavior for particular students), the discussion of paper-books vs. e-books is still on going. Since e-books may provide a solution to the problem of how to improve the learning performance of reading, we will focus on the development of a more useful e-book system to make it easy for the students to catch and thus understand the ideas embedded in the contents of a book as quickly as possible.

2.2 Concept Map

In this study, we use the so-called concept map to create an e-book system so as to provide students a simple map to understand the content structure of a book so that the students will not get stuck on the excessive contents of a book. In other words, most students are incapable of handling all the concepts and keywords given in a page at the same time. This is simply because we cannot memorize nor understand too many things within a short time, especially when these things are not displayed in a systematic way that would help humans either memorize or understand the things. For modern education, how to improve the learning performance of students has become an important research topic, especially in a learning environment with computers. Mindtool (Jonassen et al. [8]) is one of the well-known solutions that can be used: (1) to show to the students the kinds of situations they are in, (2) to support the students to organize the knowledge, and (3) to integrate the knowledge. According to the study described in [1], the approaches taken by mindtools for education can typically be divided into five categories viz (1) database mindtools, (2) graph mindtools, (3) concept mapping, (4) search Internet mindtools, and (5) visualization mindtools. In brief, the basic idea behind the concept map is to create a figure to display the "relationships" between the "concepts" embedded in the contents of a book. This graphical tool is typically used to help us organize and structure the knowledge so that it can be easily recognized. More precisely, "concepts" and "relationships" can be used, respectively, as the keyword of nodes and the path between nodes to display the overall structure of the contents.

It is easy to imagine that a concept map can be used for not only traditional paper-books but also e-books. In other words, all we have to do is to make it digital. For this reason, a digital concept map is needed in this study. Of course, the advantage of digital concept map can be found in several recent studies (Hwang et al. [6, 17]). Of course, these studies have shown that the digital concept map can significantly improve the learning performance of students by using the concept map technologies. In [17], in addition to the concept map, a realtime assessment and feedback was integrated into the education system to improve the learning performance of students. According to these observations, this study will use the keywords and pictures to represent the contents of each section to make it easy for the students to catch the structure and contents of a book very quickly. Thus, students can then go to the section that they are interested to find out the information they need when they use the e-book system we propose herein.

2.3 Intelligent Methods

To automatically extract the keywords that can be used to represent the contents of each section, the very thing we need is the so-called information retrieval [2]. Among the technologies of information retrieval, the preprocessing (e.g., stopwords and stemming) and keyword finding, (e.g., term frequency-inverse document frequency; TFIDF) are the technologies we need to employ. The stopwords and stemming technology plays the role of filtering out the redundant words and converting all the words to their word stems, respectively. The TFIDF technology in such a system plays the role of understanding the importance of the keywords so that we can use it pick keywords to represent the contents in different parts of a book.

The data mining technologies [5] are used in such kinds of researches for content analysis. This means that they can be used to find out the relationships between the contents of the book, classify the student behaviors on e-books, or even recommend the possible good learning paths for students. Compared to the data mining technologies, machine learning [10] technologies can also provide many possibilities for enhancing the learning performance of education. In such kind of e-book system, machine learning typically plays the role of finding a better solution for the data mining or information retrieval problems of the e-book system. For example, neural network algorithms (a machine learning method) can be used to provide appropriate weights for the relationships between the contents.

In summary, the technologies of data mining, machine learning, and information retrieval employed in this study can be regarded as intelligent methods that are capable of analyzing the contents of a book, understanding the learning behaviors of students, or even fine-tuning the e-book system to provide more suitable contents to the students. For this reason, intelligent methods employed in this study will be used in several modules of the proposed e-book system. In the next section, we will explain how to use them to enhance the value of the proposed e-book system.

3 The Proposed System

In this section, we will turn our discussion to the proposed system. We begin with the basic idea behind the design of such a system, which is followed by the discussion on the user interface to explain how to use it to learn new knowledge.

3.1 The System Design

As shown in Fig. 1, the proposed system can be divided into four layers. In addition to the input layer (i.e., input module) and the output layer (i.e., display module), the proposed system also contains the preprocessing layer (i.e., preprocessing module), and information retrieval layer (i.e., TFIDF, concept map, and data mining modules). Although readers (or students) are not part of the proposed system, we still have to record their reading behaviours to improve the performance of the proposed e-book system. Because this study is aimed to design an intelligent e-book system, by using the keyword concept map for improving the learning performance of students; the feedback of the students is also the main consideration of this study.

Generally speaking, the input module of the proposed system plays the role of loading the contents to the system and then splitting them by sections. As shown in Fig. 1, each circle can be regarded as the contents of a section in the book. Different circles represent contents in different sections. After that, the proposed system will use the stopwords and stemming methods to extract the keywords from the contents by sections. More precisely, the small black circles in the prepossessing layer of Fig. 1 represent the keywords which are extracted from Sect. 1 of the book. Since there is still plenty of room to improve the accuracy of these methods, especially when the contents are not in English, we may need experts (e.g., teachers) to fine-tune the results of this module from time to time. TFIDF, concept map, and data mining modules are in the information retrieval layer of the proposed system. TFIDF plays the role of computing the importance of the keywords in terms of similarities and relationships between these keywords. The information will then be used to select the most applicable keywords to represent the contents of each section. Based on these results, the concept map module can construct the concept map for the book and use a simple way to display the

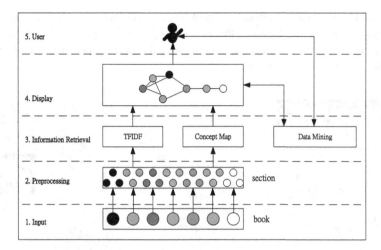

Fig. 1. System design.

structure of the contents. The data mining module plays the role of analyzing the results of the modules of information retrieval and user reading behaviors. For example, the association rule methods in this module can be used to understand the reading order (sequence) of the sections so that a student can understand the contents as quickly as possible or quicker than the other students. By using this information, we can then give suggestions to the other students so that they may read the book in different ways so as to speed up its understanding of the contents of the book. The display and user modules are designed to take into account all the information together. The display module typically plays the role of showing to the reader (student) concepts that are composed of keywords as nodes and their relationships as paths. When readers use the concept and move on to a different section to learn the knowledge, the user module plays the role of recording their reading behaviors. Therefore, the proposed algorithm can use the data mining technologies to further understand the behavior of students and provide suggestions to improve the learning behavior.

3.2   The Interface of the Proposed System

As shown in Fig. 2, the proposed e-book system is an extended work of [3], which was developed on the Android environment for smart phones and tablets. Although the interface of the proposed e-book system continues to use the results of [3], as shown in Fig. 2(a), the main difference is that the concept map of [3] is created by a teacher, but the concept map in the proposed e-book system is created by an intelligent system. Moreover, as shown in Fig. 2(b), we also provide a different kind of concept map for displaying the structure of the contents, i.e., by using photos to make it easier for the readers to understand the structure of the contents. Figure 2(c) shows that after displaying the concept map to the reader, the system will wait for the request from the reader to see if more detailed information is needed for any particular concept (i.e., node). If it is, then the proposed e-book system will show the needed information to the reader. In summary, based on this new concept map, the proposed system will be able to show the keyword concept map to improve the learning performance of readers when they use an e-book system.

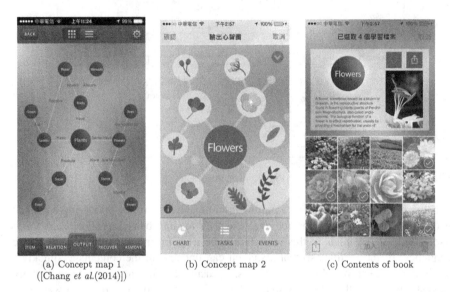

(a) Concept map 1
([Chang *et al.*(2014)])

(b) Concept map 2

(c) Contents of book

Fig. 2. Snapshot of the proposed e-book system.

4   Experimental Results

In addition to the development of a new e-book system, we also provide it to some sixth grade students in Taiwan to better understand its effects. In this section, we will first explain the participants and the experimental procedure used to evaluate the performance the proposed e-book system in Sect. 4.1. Then, Sect. 4.2 will compare the results of using and not using the proposed e-book system.

4.1   Participants and Experimental Procedure

To evaluate the performance of using the traditional e-book and the proposed e-book system, 61 students from a sixth grade class were involved in the experiment that are divided into two different groups. Also, all the students joining this experiment have not learned these materials before. The first group of students (G1) uses e-books with the keyword concept map while the second group of students (G2) uses e-books without the keyword concept map. G1 is the experimental group having 31 students while G2 is the control group having 30 students. To compare the learning performance of the students using e-books with and without keyword concept map, the experiment consists of five stages, namely, (1) using pre-test to understand the ability of students in these two groups, (2) providing a tutorial to explain this experiment, (3) providing e-book, with and without the keyword concept map, to the students, (4) using post-test to understand the ability of students in these two groups, and (5) using test after review to measure the learning performance of these two groups of students.

As shown in Fig. 3, for the purpose of comparing the results of the groups G1 and G2, the experimental procedure is composed of five stages. More precisely, teachers will let the students know how to use the e-book to learn the knowledge. Before and after using the e-book to learn the knowledge, we use the pre-test and post-test to understand the ability of all the students to further analyze the learning performance of these students.

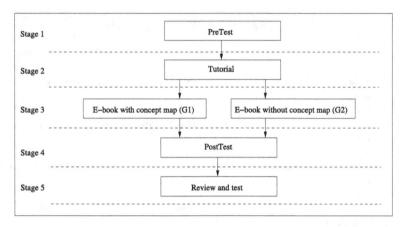

Fig. 3. Experimental procedure.

4.2 Results of Learning Performance

Table 1 shows that the results of pre-test, post-test, and test in all the procedures for the control and experimental groups. These results of pre-test further shows that the average score of students in the control group (G2) is better than that of the experimental group (G1). However, the results of post-test shows that after using the proposed e-book system with concept map, students in the experimental group (G1) get a better achievement than students in the control group (G2). The similar results shows up in another test after four days of post-test. This means that the learning performance of students using the e-book system with concept map is significantly better than those using the e-book system without concept map.

Table 1. Pre-test, Post-test, and Review test.

	Group	N	Mean.	Std.
Pre-test	1	31	66.84	12.461
	2	30	69.80	6.980
Post-test	1	31	81.68	10.849
	2	30	72.93	7.114
Review-test	1	31	83.13	10.874
	2	30	75.33	7.284

Table 2 also shows the independent sample t-test with confidence level 95% for these pre-tests, post-tests, and review-tests that further explains that the proposed e-book system with concept map can improve the learning performance of students very effectively from the perspective of statistics.

Table 2. Independent samples test.

		Levene's test for equality of variances		t-test for equality of means						
		F	Sig.	t	df	Sig.2T	M.D.	Std. E.D.	95% confidence interval of the difference	
									Low	Upper
Pre-test	Equal Variances assumed	16.932	0	−1.140	59	0.259	−2.961	2.598	−8.160	2.237
	Equal Variances not assumed			−1.150	47.447	0.256	−2.961	2.575	−8.141	2.218
Post-test	Equal Variances assumed	5.145	0.027	3.709	59	0	0.744	2.357	4.027	13.461
	Equal Variances not assumed			3.734	51.971	0	0.744	2.342	4.045	13.443
Review-test	Equal Variances assumed	6.430	0.014	3.278	59	0.002	7.796	2.378	3.038	12.554
	Equal Variances not assumed			3.229	52.576	0.002	7.796	2.363	3.056	12.536

N.B.: Sig. 2T indicates Sig. (2-tailed), M.D. indicates Mean Difference, and Std. E.D. indicates Std. Error Difference.

5   Conclusion

In this study, we proposed an e-book system with keyword and figure concept map to improve the learning performance of traditional e-book. Moreover, the proposed system adopted several information technologies (e.g., information retrieval) to make it do the wort either automatically or semi-automatically. Thus, it can reduce the loading of a teacher in developing this kind of material for teaching. The experimental results show that the proposed e-book system can significant improve the students' ability than students using an e-book system without concept map. In addition to the three tests mentioned, we also use satisfaction questionnaire to measure and understand the learning performance of students. The satisfaction questionnaire gives the similar results; that is, the achievement of students using the e-book with concept map is better than those using e-book without concept. In the future, the main focus of our study will be on the flexibility and user friendliness of the proposed e-book system because the development of this kind of learning behavior depends, to a large extent, on changing the learning style of the teachers and students. Moreover, the proposed system can also reduce the load of teacher in creating teaching materials for this kind of e-book system.

References

1. Averill, D.S.: Using mindtools in education. Technical report, Technological Horizons in Education Journal (2005)
2. Baeza-Yates, R.A., Ribeiro-Neto, B.: Modern Information Retrieval. Addison-Wesley Longman Publishing Co., Inc., Boston (1999)
3. Chang, D.W., Lai, C.F., Chen, S.Y., Huang, Y.M., Jeng, Y.L.: A concept maps oriented e-book content design system for evaluating learning performance. In: Proceedings of the Tenth International Conference on Intelligent Information Hiding and Multimedia Signal Processing, pp. 864–867 (2014)
4. Cox, J.: E-Books: challenges and opportunities. D-Lib Mag. **10**(10) (2004)
5. Fayyad, U.M., Piatetsky-Shapiro, G., Smyth, P.: From data mining to knowledge discovery in databases. AI Mag. **17**(3), 37–54 (1996)
6. Hwang, G.-J., Wu, P.-H., Ke, H.-R.: An interactive concept map approach to supporting mobile learning activities for natural science courses. Comput. Educ. **57**(4), 2272–2280 (2011)
7. Hwang, J.-P., Kinshuk, Huang, Y.-M.: Investigating e-book reading patterns: a human factors perspective. In: Proceedings of the IEEE 14th International Conference on Advanced Learning Technologies, pp. 104–108 (2014)
8. Jonassen, D.H., Carr, C., Yueh, H.-P.: Computers as mindtools for engaging learners in critical thinking. TechTrends **43**, 24–32 (1998)
9. Li, L., Fan, C., Huang, D., Chen, G.: The effects of the e-book system with the reading guidance and the annotation map on the reading performance of college students. Educ. Technol. Soc. **17**(1), 320–331 (2014)
10. Michie, D., Spiegelhalter, D.J., Taylor, C.C., Campbell, J. (eds.) Machine Learning, Neural and Statistical Classification. Ellis Horwood, Upper Saddle River (1994)
11. Rao, S.S.: Electronic books: a review and evaluation. Library Hi Tech **21**(1), 85–93 (2003)
12. Siegenthaler, E., Wurtz, P., Groner, R.: Improving the usability of e-book readers. J. Usability Stud. **6**(1), 3:25–3:38 (2010)
13. Vassiliou, M., Rowley, J.: Progressing the definition of "e-book". Library Hi Tech **26**(3), 355–368 (2008)
14. Velde, W., Ernst, O.: The future of eBooks? Will print disappear? An end-user perspective. Library Hi Tech **27**(4), 570–583 (2009)
15. Weinerth, K., Koenig, V., Brunner, M., Martin, R.: Concept maps: a useful and usable tool for computer-based knowledge assessment? A literature review with a focus on usability. Comput. Educ. **78**, 201–209 (2014)
16. Woody, W.D., Daniel, D.B., Baker, C.A.: E-books or textbooks: students prefer textbooks. Comput. Educ. **55**(3), 945–948 (2010)
17. Wu, P.-H., Hwang, G.-J., Milrad, M., Ke, H.-R., Huang, Y.-M.: An innovative concept map approach for improving students' learning performance with an instant feedback mechanism. Br. J. Educ. Technol. **43**(2), 217–232 (2012)

Using Mindtool-Based Collaborative Learning Approach for Higher Education to Support Concept Map Construction

Chia-Chen Chen[1], Yueh-Min Huang[2], Pei-Hsuan Lin[2(✉)],
Yu-Lin Jeng[3], Yong-Ming Huang[4], and Mu-Yen Chen[5]

[1] Department of Management Information Systems,
National Chung Hsing University, Taichung, Taiwan, R.O.C.
emily@nchu.edu.tw
[2] Department of Engineering Science, National Cheng Kung University,
Taichung, Taiwan, R.O.C.
{huang,n98054037}@ncku.edu.tw
[3] Department of Information Management,
Southern Taiwan University of Science and Technology, Tainan, Taiwan
jackjeng@mail.stust.edu.tw
[4] Department of Applied Informatics and Multimedia,
Chia Nan University of Pharmacy and Science, Tainan, Taiwan
ym.huang.tw@gmail.com
[5] Department of Information Management, National Taichung University
of Science and Technology, Taichung, Taiwan
im@nutc.edu.tw

Abstract. This study is based on cooperate Concept Map through Mindtool (Coggle) to increase students' motivation and can learn effectively. According to the Index of Learning Style (ILS) proposed by Felder and Soloman, this study discuss different learning style and teaching strategy impact students' academic achievement after they learning. The independent variable was teaching strategy from learning style, the dependent variable was academic achievement. The participants were 50 graduate students in Taichung. This research shows that (1) The knowledge can be acquired not only from the classroom educated by teacher, but also exploring voluntarily by learners themselves to enhance their experiential thinking and reflective thinking. (2) This study use rubric method to measure the impact of different learning style and teaching strategy to students' academic achievement. (3) In accordance with students' learning contents and views, teachers can provide supplemental materials and instructions and adjust teaching strategy.

Keywords: Concept mapping · Mindtool · E-learning · Learning style

1 Introduction

With the flourishing development of information technology in recent years, people's lifestyle is closely related to computers and the internet. With the increase in the frequency of use, the device efficacy and memory capacity have been improved. In

© Springer International Publishing AG 2017
T.-T. Wu et al. (Eds.): SETE 2016, LNCS 10108, pp. 86–96, 2017.
DOI: 10.1007/978-3-319-52836-6_11

Taiwan, the percentage of people having surfed the internet grows year by year, the way of study is learnt and transferred from classroom to Electronic Learning (E-learning). Following this trend, Ministry of Education continues to promote e-learning with the focus on Massive Open Online Course (MOOCs), mobile learning, e-learning partners, and self-learning sources, in accordance with different strategies and learning patterns. In Taiwanese academic research, discussions over e-learning are playing a leading role around the world, especially in instructional design, and the most of participants are university students in those research [1, 2]. Jonassen et al. [3] also pointed out that technology should serve as a tool that helps students learn proactively. The participants were 50 graduate students in Taichung City, Taiwan. In Taiwan, the undergraduate programs focus on the instruction in professional knowledge and skills, while the master programs aim to develop student's abilities to explore proactively, think independently, and grasp the key points of complicated concepts. According to Ministry of Education of Department of Statistics in 2016, in subjects of business and management, the average number of students in undergraduate programs is 6 times that in master programs. With a system of small classes, master programs combine a variety of learning styles, which helps explore the learning achievement of different instructional strategies.

The Concept Map gives explanations of themes in breadth and depth by horizontally dividing concepts into different branches and the concepts in different branches are spread out vertically based on subordination. Some studies showed that students improve their creativity and reflective thinking through Concept Map [4]. Vygotsky [5] pointed out that knowledge is generated by the interaction between classmates. In the conversation, students express different experiences and ideas. Mindtools visualize ideas through Concept Map, allowing students to compare the differences in ideas and experiences at once [6]. In course of learning, students have a certain pattern of receiving and dealing with information and messages, which belongs to a type of habit and preference [7]. The learning achievement of students will be improved by adjusting instructional strategies based on different learning styles.

The flourishing development of information technology has brought considerable inspiration to education. In the past, management courses were mainly held in classrooms. Professors instruct and explain knowledge through texts and figures in the textbooks. This way of learning is unilateral and rote. To achieve e-learning, teachers often integrate some model applications and presentations into instructions to deepen students' understanding of concepts and applications of management models. Nevertheless, students still lack abilities to grasp learning objectives and need a tool that helps them achieve effective learning. Based on Concept Map, the study explored learning achievement of students through Mindtool and their learning styles. For the purpose of the abovementioned motive, the study aimed to

1. Explore learning achievement of students with different learning styles through traditional instructions.
2. Explore learning achievement of students with different learning styles through Mindtool.

2 Related Works

2.1 E-learning

With the advance of information technology and popularity of computers and the internet, e-Learning refers to teaching and learning through digital media. Sarah et al. thought that e-learning allows learners to complete works effectively and independently according to their own progresses and paces. Robertson and Howells [8] applied e-learning to game design and found that students were more engaged in courses, intended to achieve better performance, and cooperated with each other better; Vos et al. [9] allowed six-grade students to design games through memory games on the websites and found that those who designed games in person had significant learning motives and use of in-depth strategies; Venkataraman and Sivakumar [10] integrated e-learning into teamwork and applied them together to higher education. The result showed that this way of learning was helpful to students and adaptive to learners with different educational backgrounds; Son and Jung [11] gave access to digital video learning system, allowing students with disabilities to learn at home and have a bilateral communication with teachers at the same time.

As these new technologies apply to higher education, students can understand the learning content and instructional implications more thoroughly. The applications are not limited to learning and teaching on the subjects, but also cover complicated technical skills required in the industry. Based on a student-oriented learning style, e-learning allows learners to learn, work, and make efforts proactively and flexibly [10, 12]. Management courses in universities belong to higher education, so the study aimed to help students achieve effective learning through e-learning.

2.2 Learning Style

The learning style is a process of memory, concentration, and internalization of new and difficult information or knowledge with the intrinsic property that is constant and stable and influenced by experience and the environment [13, 14]. Demirkan [15] also indicated that teachers should instruct knowledge and help students accumulate knowledge based on different learning styles and instructional strategies. After the term "learning style" came up, many different definitions were given. For example, Group Embedded Figures Test (GEFT) proposed by Witkin et al. [16] identified the personal preference for learning styles (Field Independent or Field Dependent) by asking learners to find the simple geometry embedded or hidden in a complicated image; Index of Learning Style (ILS) proposed by Felder and Soloman [17] focused on the understanding of learners' preferences for sensory receipt by exploring learners' awareness of messages and ways of dealing with them; and Experimental Learning Style proposed by Kolb [18] was divided into four learning patterns based on the preference for information receipt and way of dealing with information: Diverger, Converger, Assimilator, and Accommodator.

There are many domestic and foreign literatures on learning styles and learning achievement. For example, Davidson - Shivers, Nowlin and Lanouette [19] applied learning styles to the exploration of writing skills of university students and found that no significant difference in writing skills existed between students with different learning styles; Carmel-Gilfilen [20] studied the relationship between thinking and learning styles of 139 primary, advanced, and skilled interior design and architecture learners and found that no significant difference existed between learners at all levels; Demirkan [15] carried out the in-depth exploration of knowledge building of interior design and architecture students from the perspective of learning styles and found that a difference in learning styles existed in interior design students.

The study aimed to understand whether a difference in learning achievement exists in instructional strategies based on the application of different learning styles in course of learning. Therefore, the study adopted the classification of learning styles proposed by Felder and Soloman [17], as shown in Table 1, and focused on "Accustomed to memorizing pictures, tables and figures/accustomed to textual or verbal explanation" in "Visual" and "Verbal" types of learning styles.

Table 1. Learning styles by Felder and Soloman

Type	Learning Preference	Features
Active	Prefer transforming information into knowledge	1. Prefer dealing with external message through group discussion, active test, and explanation 2. Provide an opportunity for hands-on practice to achieve better learning achievement
Reflective		1. Prefer dealing with external message through reflective observations and thinking; prefer independent learning 2. Provide an opportunity to think over messages to achieve better learning achievement
Sensing	Prefer using senses	1. Prefer collecting messages through observations and feelings 2. Prefer specific materials and facts 3. Accustomed to solving problems through established procedures
Intuitive		1. Prefer collecting messages directly and unconsciously, such as thinking, illusions or instincts 2. Prefer principles, theories, and concepts
Visual	Prefer sensory information	Accustomed to memorizing pictures, tables and figures, flow charts, and physical objects
Verbal		Accustomed to textual or verbal explanation or discussions
Sequential	Prefer information presented in sequence	1. Accustomed to understanding messages through linear steps and solving problems through logic 2. Good at analyzing and solving a question with a single answer
Global		1. Accustomed to understanding messages through fragments or randomly 2. Understand messages in general to quickly solve complex problems

Source: Felder and Soloman [17]

2.3   Concept Map and Mindtool

Proposed by Novak and Gowin [21], the Concept Map is a group of linked concepts based on one theme. The Concept Map gives explanations of themes in breadth and depth by horizontally dividing concepts into different branches and the concepts in different branches are spread out vertically based on subordination. Some studies showed that students improve their creativity and reflective thinking through Concept Map [4]. Vygotsky [5] pointed out that knowledge is generated by the interaction between classmates. In the conversation, students express different experiences and ideas. Mindtools visualize ideas through Concept Map, allowing students to compare the differences in ideas and experiences [6]. Ideas generated in course of interactive learning are divided into experiential thinking and reflective thinking. Experiential thinking refers to ideas generated from some decisions and personal experiences in course of learning; reflective thinking refers to new ideas generated in course of learning that build the knowledge of the learning subject based on the comparison with the previous ideas. Such way of learning improves students' learning achievement and creativity. Therefore, it is every important to build knowledge and experience reflective thinking through peer interaction [22, 23]. Chu et al. [24] integrated computers and Concept Map and applied them to science courses in elementary schools to help students explain and organize knowledge collected; Schwendimann and Linn [25] also applied the Concept Map to biology courses in senior high schools to compare learning achievement based on different ways of instructions.

Among many learning tools, Mindtool is considered a useful way to help students explain and organize personal knowledge. Mindtool allows students to build knowledge and cultivate in-depth and advanced capabilities of critical thinking, creative thinking, and problem solving using computers. When using Mindtool, students have to maneuver complicated thinking skills to solve problems or demonstrate the knowledge [6, 26]. Hwang et al. [6] also integrated the Concept Map and Mindtool and applied them to the butterfly garden. The result showed that students preferred navigation in the ubiquitous learning environment and that the integration of Mindtool improved the interest in learning and learning motives; Yang et al. [27] applied Mindtool to the gas learning in chemistry courses in senior high schools through visualization of knowledge in order to strengthen students abilities to solve problems and learning achievement; Hou et al. [28] integrated Mindtool with project-based learning and spatial thinking and evaluated its effect. The result showed a positive attitude toward learning after use.

2.4   Rubrics

Assessment tools refer to the scale that assesses performances of certain assignments based on the criteria defined by experts and scholars. They are suitable to complicated learning assignments. In recent years, assessment tools become a trend because (1) they are easy to use and explain; (2) they help create clearer standards for performance measurement; (3) they provide students with more opinions on strengths and weaknesses; (4) the scoring scale supports learning; (5) the scoring scale supports skill development; (6) the scoring scale supports cognitive development; and (7) the scoring scale maintains good thinking [29, 30]. Ashton and Davies [31] allowed peers to evaluate each other using the assessment scale in the MOOC writing course; Wollenschlager et al. [32] explored teachers' correctness of opinions on students' performances and learning motives in the science course using the assessment scale.

2.5   Higher Education

According to the definition given in Encyclopedia Britannica, higher education refers to educational institutions higher than secondary education that grant the predetermined degree, diploma, or certificate after the completion of study. Higher education includes comprehensive universities and colleges, vocational institutions that provide preparatory courses in law, theology, medicine, business, music and art, teaching training schools, junior colleges and technical colleges. For most of higher educational institutions, the prerequisite is the completion of courses after secondary education, including undergraduate education, graduate programs and post-graduate courses.

The study designed the course in the advanced information management theory for the master program of business and management. The course aims to explore the management of information system (in an organization) and theoretical introductions to information management in order to help researchers understand the basic ideas of theoretical applications in aspects of technology, information system, management, and users. Technological applications include software and hardware related to computer science and communication sciences; the information system is divided into procedures, methods, and systems, with applications related to management science and systems engineering; management contains economy, strategies, finance, and marketing, with applications related to economics and management; and users consist of individuals, groups, organizations, and the society, with applications related to psychology and sociology.

The purpose of study on master programs is divided into two parts: Knowledge discovery and problem solving. Knowledge discovery refers to the discovery of new knowledge based on known facts or materials, while problem solving refers to the solution based on theories or causality derived from models. The difference between the two is that knowledge discovery does not necessarily involve in solving a specific problem but problem solving often involves in solving a specific problem through known knowledge [33]. Therefore, the study helped students cultivate capabilities of knowledge discovery and problem solving through Mindtool.

3   Research Design

The participants were 50 graduate students in Taichung City and carried out an 18-week experimental instruction. The experimental procedures are shown in Fig. 1. In the 1st week, teacher introduced the advanced information management course and Learning style classified; in the 2nd to 8th week, teacher used traditional written materials in the instruction; in the 9th week, teacher evaluated students' performances

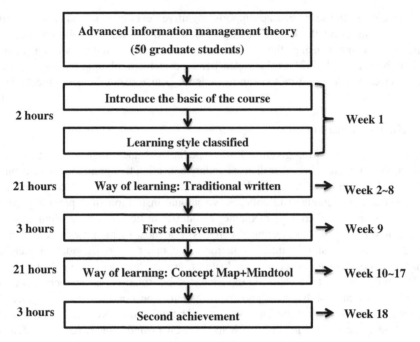

Fig. 1. Experimental procedures

in the first seven weeks using the rubrics; in the 10th to 17th week, the authors integrated the Concept Map and Mindtool into the instruction; in the 18th week, the author evaluated students' performances in the first seven weeks using the rubrics.

Last, the author explored the difference between students with the "Visual" type of learning style and those with the "Verbal" type of learning style and found that visual-type students were accustomed to memorizing pictures, tables and figures, flow charts, and physical objects, while verbal-type students were accustomed to textual or verbal explanation or discussions.

Based on different instructional strategies and learning styles, four learning types are classified, including "Visual-type students learn through texts", "Visual-type students learn through Mindtool", "Verbal-type students learn through texts", and "Verbal-type students learn through Mindtool" (as shown in Fig. 2). Students cultivated their capabilities of experiential thinking and reflective thinking by editing the learning content and expressing and reviewing ideas in a form of online group discussion.

Research tools adopted in the study include the learning style scale proposed by Felder and Soloman [17] and the assessment form made by the teacher. In course of Mindtool learning, the teacher gave related instructions to each group, including the model background, author, year, dimension (explanations for different dimensions), related literature (literature review of model applications), model derivative (relationship between models and explanations), and other (brainstorming), as shown in Fig. 3.

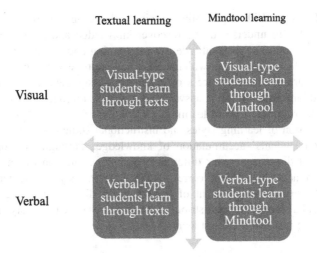

Textual learning   Mindtool learning

Visual   Visual-type students learn through texts   Visual-type students learn through Mindtool

Verbal   Verbal-type students learn through texts   Verbal-type students learn through Mindtool

Fig. 2. Four learning types

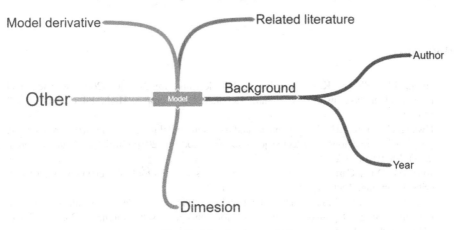

Fig. 3. Moodtool snapshot

4 Conclusion

The flourishing development of information technology has brought considerable inspiration to education. Based on the Concept Map, the study explored learning styles and learning achievement of students through Mindtool. The result is described as follows:

1. Students received the instruction through Mindtool based on the Concept Map different from texts and figures in the textbooks. This way of learning improved students' understanding of management models. The obtainment of knowledge was transformed from the passive instillation by teachers into proactive discovery

through Mindtool. With experiential learning rather than aimless conception, students were able to understand and discover knowledge and maneuver creativity, which further improved their attitude toward learning and learning achievement.

2. Collaborative learning together with materials can improve learning motives and the interest of learning. In the process of completing assignments, students collected and shared information and answered questions through discussion, which improved their attitude toward learning.

3. The combination of learning styles and instructional strategies had a considerable influence on students' accumulation of knowledge. Through the application of Mindtool and discussions over different ways of presentation of knowledge and messages in accordance with corresponding learning styles, the teacher could understand learning achievement of students with different learning styles. The teacher could also refer to the distribution and features of learning styles to provide more adaptive instructions for students.

Acknowledgements. The authors thank the support of Ministry of Science and Technology (MOST) of the Republic of China (ROC) to this research under Grant No. MOST 104-2511-S-005-003- and MOST 103-2622-S-005-001-CC3.

References

1. Hung, J.L., Zhang, K.: Examining mobile learning trends 2003–2008: a categorical meta-trend analysis using text mining techniques. J. Comput. High. Educ. **24**(1), 1–17 (2012)
2. Hwang, G.J., Wu, P.H.: Advancements and trends in digital game-based learning research: A review of publications in selected journals from 2001 to 2010. British J. Educ. Technol. **43**(1), E6–E10 (2012)
3. Jonassen, D.H., Carr, C., Yueh, H.P.: Computers as Mindtools for engaging learners in critical thinking. TechTrends **43**(2), 24–32 (1998)
4. Kao, G.Y.M., Lin, S.S.J., Sun, C.T.: Breaking concept boundaries to enhance creative potential: using integrated concept maps for conceptual self-awareness. Comput. Educ. **51**(4), 1718–1728 (2008)
5. Vygotsky, L.: Mind in society: the development of higher psychological process. Harvard University Press, Cambridge (1978)
6. Hwang, G.J., Shi, Y.R., Chu, H.C.: A concept map approach to developing collaborative Mindtools for context-aware ubiquitous learning. Br. J. Educ. Technol. **42**(5), 778–789 (2011)
7. Felder, R.M.: Learning and teaching styles in engineering education. Eng. Education **78**(7), 674–681 (1988)
8. Robertson, J., Howells, C.: Computer game design: opportunities for successful learning. Comput. Educ. **50**(2), 559–578 (2008)
9. Vos, N., van der Meijden, H., Denessen, E.: Effects of constructing versus playing an educational game on student motivation and deep learning strategy use. Comput. Educ. **56**(1), 127–137 (2011)

10. Venkataraman, S., Sivakumar, S.: Engaging students in group based learning through e-learning techniques in Higher Education System. Int. J. Emerg. Trends Sci. Technol. **2**(1), 1741–1746 (2015)
11. Son, Y.M., Jung, B.S.: Convergence development of video and E-learning system for education disabled students. J. Korea Convergence Soc. **6**(4), 113–119 (2015)
12. Shopova, T.: E-learning in higher education environment. In: International Conference the Future of Education, Bulgaria (2012)
13. Dunn, R., Stevenson, J.M.: Teaching diverse college students to study with a learning-styles prescription. Coll. Student J. **31**, 333–339 (1997)
14. Rochford, R.A.: Assessing learning styles to improve the quality of performance of community college students in developmental writing programs: a pilot study. Community Coll. J. Res. Pract. **27**(8), 665–677 (2003)
15. Demirkan, H.: An inquiry into the learning-style and knowledge-building preferences of interior architecture students. Design Stud. **44**, 28–51 (2016)
16. Witkin, H.A., Oltman, P.K., Raskin, E., Karp, S.: A manual for the embedded figures test. Consulting Psychologists Press, California (1971)
17. Felder, R.M., Solomon, B.A.: Index of learning styles (1991). www.ncsu.edu/effective_teaching/ILSdir/ILS-a.htm. Accessed 10 Aug 2010, 2009
18. Kolb, D.A.: Experiential Learning: Experience as the Source of Learning and Development. Prentice-Hall, Englewood Cliffs (1984)
19. Davidson-Shivers, G.V., Nowlin, B., Lanouette, M.: Do multimedia lesson structure and learning styles influence undergraduate writing performance? Coll. Student J. **36**(1), 20–32 (2002)
20. Carmel-Gilfilen, C.: Uncovering pathways of design thinking and learning: inquiry on intellectual development and learning style preferences. J. Interior Des. **37**(3), 47–66 (2012)
21. Novak, J.D., Gowin, D.B.: Learning how to learn. Cambridge University Press, New York and Cambridge (1984)
22. Norman, D.A.: Things that make us smart: defending human attributes in the age of the machine. Reading. Addison-Wesley Publishing Co, MA (1993)
23. Burleson, W.: Developing creativity, motivation, and self-actualization with learning systems. Int. J. Hum.-Comput. Stud. **63**(4–5), 436–451 (2005)
24. Chu, H.C., Hwang, G.J., Liang, Y.R.: A cooperative computerized concept mapping approach to improving students' learning performance in web-based information-seeking activities. J. Comput. Educ. **1**(1), 19–33 (2014)
25. Schwendimann, B.A., Linn, M.C.: Comparing two forms of concept map critique activities to facilitate knowledge integration processes in evolution education. J. Res. Sci. Teach. **53**(1), 70–94 (2015)
26. Jonassen, D.H.: Computers as Mindtools for schools, engaging critical thinking. Prentice-Hall, Englewood Cliffs, NJ (1999)
27. Yang, K.J., Chu, H.C., Yang, K.H.: Using the augmented reality technique to develop visualization Mindtools for chemical inquiry-based activities. Advanced Applied Informatics, pp. 354–357 (2015)
28. Hou, H.T., Yu, T.F., Wu, Y.X., Sung, Y.T., Chang, K.E.: Development and evaluation of a web map mind tool environment with the theory of spatial thinking and project-based learning strategy. Br. J. Educ. Technol. **47**(2), 390–402 (2016)
29. Andrade, H.G.: Using rubrics to promote thinking and learning. Educ. Leadersh. **57**(5), 13–18 (2000)
30. Mertler, C.A.: Designing scoring rubrics for your classroom. Pract. Assess. Res. Eval. **7**(25) (2001). http://PAREonline.net/getvn.asp?v=7&n=25. 15 June 2016

31. Ashton, S., Davies, R.S.: Using scaffolded rubrics to improve peer assessment in a MOOC writing course. Dist. Educ. **36**(3), 312–334 (2015)
32. Wollenschlager, M., Hattie, J., Machts, N., Moller, J., Harms, U.: What makes rubrics effective in teacher-feedback? Transparency of learning goals is not enough. Contemp. Educ. Psychol. **44–45**, 1–11 (2016)
33. Langley, P.W., Simon, H.A., Bradshaw, G.L., Zytkow, J.M.: Scientific Discovery: Computational Explorations of the Creative Processes. MIT Press (1987)

Construction of Efficient Cloud-Based Digital Course Learning Platform for Agricultural Worker

Jui-Hung Chang[1(✉)], Chien-Yuan Tseng[2], and Ren-Hung Hwang[3]

[1] Computer and Network Center, National Cheng Kung University,
Tainan City 701, Taiwan
changrh@mail.ncku.edu.tw
[2] Department of Computer Science and Information Engineering,
National Cheng Kung University, Tainan City 701, Taiwan
P76031488@mail.ncku.edu.tw
[3] Department of Computer Science and Information Engineering,
National Chung Cheng University, Chiayi, Taiwan
rhhwang@cs.ccu.edu.tw

Abstract. The trend of e-learning has become increasingly important. E-learning technically applies the advantages of features of the network, including no limitation to place and time, highly interactive, community impacts, and data analysis. Governments, educational institutions, companies and non-profit organizations have quickly established an eco-system to replace the traditional forms of teaching. How to use the ever-changing technology to enhance the manpower quality of government agencies and to help nurture talent is the objective of this study. Therefore, this study proposed a construction of efficient cloud architecture based digital course learning platform for agricultural workers. Through the proposed real-time streaming technology in this study, we can learn the network streaming traffic when videos are played. Furthermore, by employing the cloud architecture, the proposed method can optimize the efficiency of server resources via dynamic allocation and will contribute to a high-quality digital learning effect when users learn digital courses online.

Keywords: E-learning · Traditional teaching · Cloud architecture · Digital courses and Real-time streaming

1 Introduction

Government agencies enhance the manpower quality, pursue excellence and attach more importance to the nurturing of talents to keep up with the modern countries. Since agricultural research is an onerous task and the government agencies usually employ agricultural investigators and dispatch manpower where the personnel come from different counties and regions, it results in quality varies of personnel and high turnover. How to successfully and smoothly complete agricultural investigation and to improve work efficiency and enhance the value of data's application are of great importance to the nursing of agricultural manpower. The current practice is to organize

© Springer International Publishing AG 2017
T.-T. Wu et al. (Eds.): SETE 2016, LNCS 10108, pp. 97–106, 2017.
DOI: 10.1007/978-3-319-52836-6_12

trainings, workshops and working sessions on a regular basis and to provide the agricultural personnel appropriate capability development and in-service trainings. However, since the personnel come from different counties and regions, this will give rise to heavy burden on the human cost of training, it is an extremely significant topic to establish a set of digital course learning system meeting the attributes of agricultural investigators in order to enhance the effectiveness of learning and achieve better learning efficiency.

In recent years, cloud computing technology is increasingly advanced. The main characteristics [16] of cloud computing are on-demand self-service, broad network access, resource pooling, rapid elasticity and measured service. A rising number of researchers conducted tons of studies on cloud application in e-learning. Among them, Sultan and Weber noted that cloud computing could assist organizations in remote areas to construct various information services [17, 19], since these organizations did not need to spend time and manpower to build the basic software and hardware facilities. Rather, they could directly rent the cloud computing services to develop their teaching science and technology. Additionally, some scholars also discussed how to develop a cloud computing-based learning system suitable for cloud computing, by which the efficiency, availability and extendibility of the traditional learning systems could be improved [11, 12].

Digital courses are increasing and people tend to learn these courses through movies. Therefore, the data volume of calculation and storage is surging as well. How to store and process the immense data of digital learning films is a topic of research. Moreover, since the users are from different counties and regions, by constructing a digital course learning system platform for agricultural worker, the users can view the digital curriculum films constructed in this system via relevant vehicles for resolving the following problems:

- When the number of users viewing the digital course movies increases, the problem of how to enable the digital course learning platform to provide continuous and high resolution film play services is arising.
- When the amount of data increases in multiples each year, how to access and analyze more massive data is a research topic that cloud computing has always studied for many years.

[13] primarily studied the latest cloud-based developments in P2P, and the results show that in video streaming technology, the vast majority of digital learning systems use P2P technology. DVB-RCS [7] is an application which is based on satellite network and can provide interactive and multimedia applications. It can simultaneously transmit the stream fragments to users at any places at any time. Parts of digital course learning platforms use virtual machine technology [15] to allocate the server resources. This study proposed a digital course learning platform which can be constructed for realtime analysis of the data [9, 10]. When the users play the course videos, the relevant streaming data can be analyzed in a real-time manner. The analyzed data include the video format, video length, video resolution and video viewership, and the massive data are processed via the distributed architecture Spark streaming [6] in a real-time manner. Then, the streaming traffic of video played by the system's users in different regions is calculated. The efficiency of the system is adjusted in a real-time manner to

enable the users to have superior learning quality when watching the videos. This system platform sets up related Apache Mesos [5] for server resource allocation and adjustment. The related videos courses are mainly stored in the Hadoop Distributed File System (HDFS) [3], which is also equipped with a complete backup mechanism.

The contributions of this study are as follows:

- Since the users viewing the course videos are from different regions and the number of viewers is indefinite, through real-time analysis of streaming data, this study provides users with an efficient digital course learning platform which can improves the agricultural personnel's willingness to learn. Comparing with traditional digital learning platforms such as MOOCs and Youtube, this digital learning system dynamic adjustment cloud server recourse provides more effective and highly usability cloud server to users for watching videos in a non-stop environment.

- This study also provides a set of feasible cloud digital learning system and a highly efficient, flexible and extensible architecture of cloud digital courses. The system aims on agricultural trainees that are in the agricultural region, especially remote areas. In these areas, computer hardware equipments and network effectiveness are inferior to those in big cities. Thus, it leads to the difficulty of watching digital learning videos. This study provides a whole set of construction of cloud digital learning system. Related research parties can set up cloud servers at the remote areas. This will provide users in these areas a better learning environment because users can get access to the local cloud server via Global Positioning System (GPS).

The remainder of this paper is organized as follows: Sect. 2 is the literature review; Sect. 3 presents the architecture of digital learning system; Sect. 4 summarized conclusion and future works.

2 Related Work

Digital learning is gaining popularity. Large numbers of educational institutions in the world gradually adopt the teaching method of digital learning, but digital learning requires tons of hardware, software and maintenance resources, which many educational institutions cannot offer. The cloud technology lifts a ray of hope. MD. Anwar Hossain Masud and Xiaodi Huang proposed a framework to enable educational institutions to gain a detailed understanding of cloud technology and to gradually adopt it [14]. The study took into consideration the relevant policy issues and technological factors that the professional equipment may be located in foreign countries in order to make better use of the cloud computing technology. In conclusion, this study bolstered the educational institutions' confidence in applying the cloud technology to digital learning, and also mentioned that the future studies should focus on verification and common assessment. Utpal Jyoti Bora and Majidul Ahmed concentrated on introducing the influence of applying cloud technology to digital learning systems [18], including low cost (software, hardware, staff, and other expenses), quick and effective information transmission, safety, privacy, flexibility and availability. The cloud technology could reduce the time of building a digital learning system, and could enhance fault-tolerance, feasibility and even cooperation. The cloud technology regards these space and software resources as a service, while the traditional network-centered digital learning lacks many of the above features.

2.1 Cloud Computing

Hsu, Yang and Yu established a cloud-centered on-board system [9], analyzed the videos shot by the camera on the vehicle in a real-time manner, stored video data via HDFS and analyzed the data by integrating the environmental issues. Xiuqin LIN, Peng WANG and Bin WU proposed a log file analysis [20] through a cloud platform. By combining with Hadoop and Spark and coupled with Hive and Shark analysis tools, etc., this platform can analyze and process log in batch and the calculation in the memory is characterized by high stability and efficiency.

Introduction to Apache Hadoop. Apache Hadoop is a distributed system infrastructure developed by the Apache Software Foundation. The users could develop distributed programs even though they did not the distributed underlying details. They could take full advantage of computer clusters for high-speed operation and storage. Hadoop implemented a distributed file system (Hadoop Distributed File System), referred to as HDFS. HDFS was characterized by high fault tolerance, and was designed to be installed on in low-cost hardware and suitable for the applications of large data sets.

Introduction to Apache Spark. Apache Spark is an open source cluster computing framework developed by the AMPLab of the University of California, Berkeley. Compared with the MapReduce frame-work of Hadoop which would store the metadata into the disk after the tasks were fulfilled, Spark employed operation technology in memory. It could conduct analysis and operation in the memory when the data were not written to the hard disk. Its main feature was the inclusion of the distributed computing model of Resilient distributed Dataset (RDD).

Spark streaming was an extension of the Spark's core API and it had the features of extensibility, high throughput and fault tolerance for the processing of real-time data streaming. The data can be accessed from Kafka [4] and other sources, or calculated through the complex algorithms composed of by higher-order functions such as map and reduce. Finally, the processed data can be pushed to the file systems, databases and real-time dashboard.

Introduction to Apache Mesos. Apache Mesos is an open source software project and a cluster computer management tool, It can manage the CPU, memory, storage devices and other computing resources in the computer systems of data center.

Mesos [8] is a platform where the commodity cluster is shared in several diverse cluster computing frameworks. Mesos translates the data from each machine to subtly share resources. To support the complex processes of the current framework, it employs a distributed and two-layer scheduling mechanism. To put it simply, Mesos decides the amount of resources allocated to each framework, while each framework decides to accept which resources and agrees to implement which operation in those frameworks. The results find that Mesos can attain almost optimized data locality in a diverse framework in terms of sharing clusters.

2.2 Studies on Streaming Media

Streaming media is a technique that compresses a series of media information and delivers the information pieces by pieces instantly to the internet enabling users to watch online. This technique makes information packets sent like the flow of water in streams. The streaming media can deliver live videos or reserved videos. When the viewer watches a video, the video will be played immediately after user's computer accesses the delivered video. There will be no need to the user to download all of the files to play the videos.

Video quality is an important indicator to assess video transmission. Bit rate [1, 2] refers to the number of bit per second used to store media data, and is usually represented in bit/ s or bps, said even Mbit/s. The higher the bit rate is, the better the video quality is. For example, the video quality of a VCD (bit rate of 1Mbit/s) is often inferior to that of DVD (bit rate of 5Mbit/s). The video quality of HD is higher and its bit rate is up to 20Mbit/s. Take the bit rate of an image file as an example. It includes the bit rate of video and audio, that is, Video bit rate + Audio bit rate = total bit rate.

3 Digital Course Learning Platform for Agricultural Worker

This paper built a digital course learning platform whose architecture is shown in Fig. 1. The digital course learning platform is divided into four parts:

1. Real-time streaming analysis unit
2. Cloud server service unit

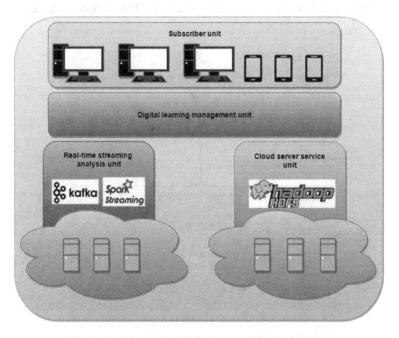

Fig. 1. Architecture of digital course learning platform

3. Digital learning management unit
4. Subscriber unit

This study constructed an efficient cloud architecture-based digital course learning platform for agricultural workers. By employing the real-time streaming technology, this study learned the network streaming traffic when videos are played, and used the cloud architecture to optimize the efficiency of server resources via dynamic allocation and to allowed users to enjoy high-quality digital learning effect when watching digital courses online. The relevant units will be detailed in the following chapter.

3.1   Cloud Server Service Unit

The cloud server service unit built in this study provides the access function of digital course videos and its architecture is presented in Fig. 2. Mesos cluster manages the allocation of hardware resources (including CPU and Memory) of the cluster computers. HDFS is a distributed storage system and can scatter and store the data on multiple nodes after the data are segmented. In order to enhance the efficiency of video data transmission, Video Channel, taking Hadoop cluster as the core of cloud operation, can access the videos. Apache ZooKeeper enables the distributed framework to realize software of high availability. When one Video Channel is interrupted, it will automatically switch to the other Video Channel. Hbase is a highly reliable and efficient distributed database system (NoSQL).

This study used the HDFS to store course videos. The video data were divided into different blocks and stored in different nodes. Each block, via the file storage mechanism of HDFS, was backed up into multiple copies. This method can maintain the

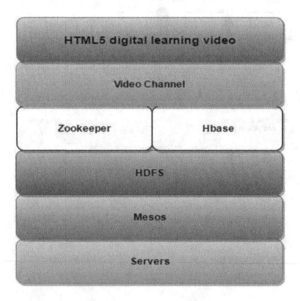

Fig. 2. Architecture of cloud server service unit

integrity of video data and enhance the efficiency of parallel access to videos. This study calculated in a real-time way the current network streaming traffic of the videos played. Mesos adopted specific schedule to dynamically allocate hardware resources in the Video Channel. To take Fig. 3 as an example, when the network streaming traffic of videos in the Video Channel increases (on the left of Fig. 3), accordingly, the server hardware resource utilization of the Video Channel will also rise (the blue block on the right of Fig. 3), thereby maximizing the server resource allocation. Finally, Hbase stored the real-time streaming data once every ten seconds, and the data encompass the network streaming traffic of the videos played, timestamp and which region the net-work streaming traffic comes from (latitude and longitude or IP) for more in-depth analysis.

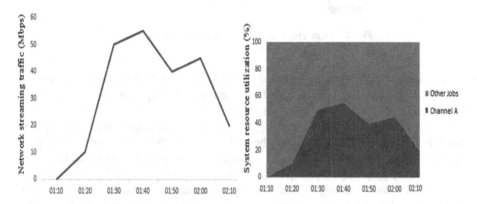

Fig. 3. Server resources dynamically adjusted with network streaming traffic

3.2 Real-Time Streaming Analysis Unit

The flow chart of the real-time streaming analysis unit of this study is shown in Fig. 4. The unit uses the distributed message reception-transmission system of Apache Kafka [4] to collect the information returned by different vehicles which include computer, cell phone, tablet. Required information is as follows:

1. Video play format
2. Video length
3. Number of real-time video viewers

Apache Kafka buffers the data and provides the data to the Spark Streaming operation. The goal of this unit is to calculate the all viewing streaming traffic. The formula of the video streaming traffic is as follows [2]:

Total flow of the video stream = Length of video file (in seconds) * Bit rate of video file (bit/s) * number of real-time video viewers.

This research uses the vehicles to get access to the length of the video and calculate the number of online watching viewers. Different video resolution corresponds to different Bit rate. The total flow of the stream video of the cloud digital learning system

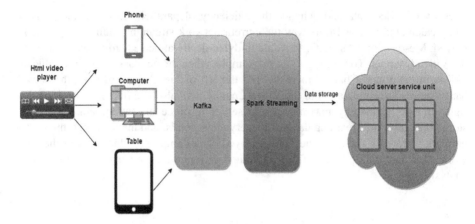

Fig. 4. Flow chart of real-time streaming analysis unit

can be gain by Spark Streaming method. It will be returned to the cloud server service unit which dynamically allocates hardware resources through specific schedule and Mesos, optimizing the efficiency of server resources.

The executive interface of the digital learning management unit is HyperText Markup Language 5 (HTML5), and the architecture of the unit is shown in Fig. 5. Specifically, the subscriber unit displays the basic data of teachers and students such as name, gender, age, address etc. Teachers use the teaching material unit to manage courses and upload teaching videos. The digital learning unit allows students to view the course videos while the streaming resources management unit is to display the number of real-time video viewers and network streaming traffic. This unit will show the video viewers and the volume of instant stream by graphs.

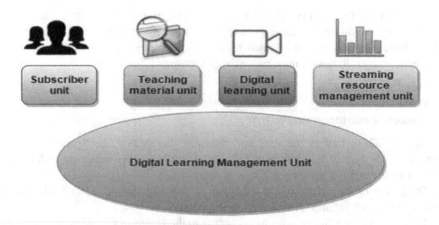

Fig. 5. Digital learning management unit

4   Conclusion and Future Works

This study puts forward a digital course learning platform for agricultural workers. When the relevant agricultural workers play the digital course learning videos, this system framework can provide real-time streaming analysis and return the operation results to the digital learning cloud platform to dynamically adjust the server resources. Therefore, agricultural workers can have access to high-quality learning of digital courses in any region. Apart from improving their learning willingness, they do not have to receive course training in a particular area, are not restricted by time and space and can repeatedly learn the abstruse professional agricultural investigation.

The future systems can offer more user return information for analysis. For instance, by referring to the address filled by the users in registration or analyzing the GPS latitude and longitude data during video viewing, users can link to the nearest servers and the time of network transmission can be reduced. In the future, the network streaming traffic of vehicle's playing videos recorded by Hbase once every ten seconds will also be employed. Currently, through calculating which areas (latitude and longitude or IP) have relatively high network streaming traffic, new servers can be constructed for the areas of relatively high network streaming traffic, hence allowing the users to enjoy high-quality learning effect of viewing digital courses online.

References

1. https://en.wikipedia.org/wiki/Bit_rate
2. https://en.wikipedia.org/wiki/Streaming_media
3. https://hadoop.apache.org/docs/r1.2.1/hdfs_design.html
4. http://kafka.apache.org/
5. http://mesos.apache.org/
6. http://spark.apache.org/streaming/
7. Adjei-Frimpong, B., Akom, K., Ntiamoah-Sarpong, K.: Implementation of E-learning using Digital Video Broadcasting-Return Channel Via Satellite (DVB-RCS) in Ghana International Journal of Science and Research (IJSR). ISSN (Online) 2319-7064
8. Hindman, B., Konwinski, A., Zaharia, M., Ghodsi, A., Joseph, A.D., Katz, R.H., Shenker, S. and Stoica, I.: A Platform for Fine-Grained Resource Sharing in the Data Center
9. Lin, C.-F., Yuan, S.-M., Leu, M.-C., Tsai, C.-T.: A framework for scalable cloud video recorder system in surveillance environment. In: Proceeding 9th International Conference Ubiquitous Intelligence & Computing and 9th International Conference on Autonomic & Trusted Computing (UIC/ATC), pp. 655–660, September 2012
10. Hsu, C.-Y., Yang, C.-A., Yu, L.-C., et al.: Development of a cloud-based service framework for energy conservation in a sustainable intelligent transportation system. Int. J. Prod. Econ. **164**, 454–461 (2015)
11. Dong, B., Zheng, Q., Qiao, M., Shu, J., Yang, J.: BlueSky cloud framework: an E-Learning framework embracing cloud computing. In: Jaatun, M.G., Zhao, G., Rong, C. (eds.) CloudCom 2009. LNCS, vol. 5931. Springer, Heidelberg (2009)
12. Dong, B., Zheng, Q., Yang, J., Li, H., Qiao, M.: An e-learning ecosystem based on cloud computing infrastructure. In: Proceedings of the IEEE International Conference on Advanced Learning Technologies, Riga, Latvia (2009b)

13. Ab Wahid, N.W.B., Jenni, K., Mandala, S., Supriyanto, E.: Review on cloud computing application in P2P video streaming. Procedia Comput. Sci. **50**, 185–190 (2015)
14. Masud, M.A.H., Huang, X.: A novel approach for adopting cloud-based E-learning system. In: 2012 IEEE/ACIS 11th International Conference on Computer and Information Science (2012)
15. Luo, M.-Y., Lin, S.-W.: From monolithic systems to a federated E-learning cloud system. In: IEEE International Conference on Cloud Engineering, San Francisco, California, USA (2013)
16. Mell, P., Grance, T.: The NIST definition of cloud computing. Technical report, National Institute of Standard and Technology (NIST), January 2011
17. Sultan, N.: Cloud computing for education: a new dawn? Int. J. Inf. Manage. **30**(2), 109–116 (2010)
18. Bora, U.J., Ahmed, M.: E-learning using cloud computing. Int. J. Sci. Modern Eng. (IJISME), **1**(2) (2013). ISSN: 2319-6386
19. Weber, A.S.: Cloud computing in education in the Middle East and North Africa (Mena) region: can barriers be overcome? In: Proceedings of the 7th International Scientific Conference eLSE - eLearning and Software for Education, Bucuresti, Romania (2011)
20. Lin, X., Wang, P., Wu, B.: Log analysis in cloud computing environment with hadoop and spark. In: Proceedings of IEEE IC-BNMT (2013)

Towards Semantic Analysis
of Mentoring-Learning Relationships
Within Constructivist Interactions

Farshad Badie[(⊠)]

Center for Linguistics, Aalborg University,
Rendsburggade 14, 9000 Aalborg, Denmark
badie@id.aau.dk

Abstract. The multilevel conversational exchanges between a mentor and a learner could be seen as a radical constructivist account of their comprehensions. The process of knowledge construction could be realised to have a significant importance in the context of mentor-learner interactions. The most important fundamental is that 'the conversational exchanges between mentors and learners ask questions and give answers concerning their individual conceptions, comprehensions and reasonings'. These questions and answers are the main building blocks of the 'Relations' between mentors and learners. In this article, I will employ Predicate Logic in order to focus on the relationships between learners and mentors. This research will—conceptually and logically—be concerned with [formal] semantic analysis of mentoring-learning relationships in the context of constructivist interactions. The conclusions will shed light on how a [formal] semantics for constructivist interactions is established.

1 Introduction

The multilevel interactions and conversational exchanges between a human being (as a mentor, trainer, teacher) and another human being (as a learner, student) could be seen as a radical constructivist account of their cognitions, realisations and comprehensions, see [17]. First, I shall draw your attention to some fundamentals that will clarify my conception of, and my way of thinking about, the use of the term 'learning' in this article. Relying on First-Order Predicate Logic (FOL), in the expression 'human learning', the word 'learning' has been utilised in the form of a predicate with the word 'human'. Thus, *learning* can describe something about a human being who is being discussed and interpreted. In other words, *learning* in *human learning* has been described—in the form of a predicate—to model a role that is being performed by a human being. I shall emphasise that I am fully aware of the basic principle in linguistic analysis that there is a fundamental difference between the phrase *human learning* and a sentence/clause like *the human is learning*. In fact, relying on linguistic analysis, assertions [and statements] can only be made by sentences (and not by phrases), but, since the central focus of this research is on logical analysis of the term 'human learning' and its formal semantics. According to the proposed logical conception, a *subject* could be related to *Human* by means of *Learning*. Through the lens of

© Springer International Publishing AG 2017
T.-T. Wu et al. (Eds.): SETE 2016, LNCS 10108, pp. 107–116, 2017.
DOI: 10.1007/978-3-319-52836-6_13

cognition, 'learning' as a human's act could be interpreted and explained from different perspectives. In this research *learning* is recognised as the act of [knowledge] construction. And the most central assumption of this research is 'considering learning as the activity of knowledge construction and as the developmental process of the constructed knowledge'. Knowledge construction (that is, a salient product of constructivist learning) could be realised to have a significant importance in the context of mentor-learner interactions and in their conversational exchanges; for more details about constructivist learning[1] see [9, 14, 16]. The most important fundamental is that 'the conversational exchanges between mentors and learners ask questions and give answers concerning their individual conceptions, comprehensions and reasonings'. In my opinion, these questions and answers are the main building blocks of the [constructivist] *Relations* between mentors and learners. In the following section i will be more specific about the concept of 'relation'. The processes of knowledge acquisition, knowledge construction and knowledge development could work illustratively, interpretively, instructively and heuristically in the framework of Conversation Theory (CT), which is conceived and elaborated by Gordon Pask, see [12, 13]. Pask's main premise is that reliable knowledge exists, and it evolves in action-grounded conversations, see [10]. Relying on CT and regarding my achievements in meaning construction, the framework of conversational learning is inherently a semantic model that accounts for the emergence of the domain of the learner's and of the mentor's constructed knowledge. *Semantics* as the study of the meanings can express how the produced meanings based upon learners' and mentors' constructed concepts could support them in constructing their universal knowledge. Furthermore, producing one's own understanding of world and developing it during the interaction could be said to be the most valuable product of a constructivist interaction. A constructivist interaction supports the mentor, and, subsequently, the learner, in exchanging their own conceptions (over their conceptualisations) with each other, and in discussing their own and the interlocutor's produced comprehensions.

In this article, the interactions will be analysed with respect to developmental processes[2] of humans' world constructions over their conceptions and concept constructions (I will explain more about concepts). I contemplate that the developmental processes of personal world constructions [by mentors and learners] provide supportive backbones for a semantic model that accounts for the meeting of their constructed knowledge. In this article, FOL will be employed in order to analyse the *relationships* between learners and mentors. Predicate Logic allows us to make arbitrarily specified relationships between different objects of the conversational learning system.

---

[1] Jean Piaget is the originator of the theory of constructivism. He argues that humans generate knowledge and meaning from an interaction between their experiences and their ideas, see [14, 15]. Piaget's developmental theory of learning contemplates that the constructivist learning is concerned with how a human being goes about constructing her/his individual knowledge structures. In philosophy of education, Constructivism as a theory and as an epistemology-based model focuses on knowledge construction in human beings' own cognitive apparatus.

[2] Developmental Processes of Learning could be seen as the product of Developmental Theory of Learning and Cognitive Development, see psychohawks.wordpress.com/2010/09/05/theories-of-cognitive-development-jean-piaget.

This research will—conceptually and logically—, be concerned with [formal] semantic analysis of mentoring-learning relationships in the context of constructivist interactions. The conclusions will shed light on how a [formal] semantics for constructivist interactions is established.

2 About Concepts

The notion of 'concept' is a very sensitive term that must be used with caution, but I assume the use of *concept* to be comprehensible in this context and in the following logical formalisms. Concepts play fundamental parts in the use of reasons and languages, see [18]. According to [6], a concept is an interrelationship between humans' mental images of [parts of] reality and their linguistic expressions (and descriptions). Also, my conceptual approaches in [1–3] are based on this theoretical notion of 'concept'. In this research I consider the collection of (i) mental images [of an object/phenomenon], (ii) linguistic expressions [about that object/phenomenon], and (iii) the interrelationships between (i) and (ii) as a conceptual entity and name it *Concept*. This article is tackling to propose a logical description of concept analysis in the context of mentor-learner interaction, so I shall propose that the concepts could be represented by hypotheses in order to correspond to a distinct entity or to its essential attributes, features and properties. Subsequently, assessed by logics, the entities determine the applications of terms and phrases, and can manifest themselves in the form of [unary] predicates (you will see about them in the next section). Therefore, FOL-based predicates could be employed in logical and formal analysis of this research's objectives.

3 Predicate Logic and Predication

Propositional Logic and its formulae[3] are constructed based on atomic objects. The statements involving atomic objects, and, subsequently, the statements involving non-atomic formulae could only be either true or false. Predicate Logic (as the logic of predication) is constructed over propositional logic by considering objects as the elements of sets, and by applying universal and existential quantifications (restrictions) on different objects, see [5, 11]. The fundamental symbols in Predicate Logic are divided into logical and non-logical symbols. The logical symbols are: Conjunction ($\land$), Disjunction ($\lor$), Negation ($\neg$), Implication ($\rightarrow$), Bi-conditional ($\longleftrightarrow$), Equality ($=$), Existential Restriction ($\exists$), Universal Restriction ($\forall$), Tautology ($\top$), Contradiction ($\bot$) and Parentheses. Any of the logical symbols have the same meaning in different contexts and conditions. This statement means that we are not allowed to interpret them and assign multiple values and definitions to them. Besides logical symbols, the non-logical symbols are interpreted and represented in the following forms (obviously, we need to interpret the non-logical symbols of a logical system in order to produce

---

[3] The logical relationships and rules expressed in Propositional Logic's symbols are known as Propositional Logic's Formulae.

meanings and to clarify what we mean by those symbols): (**A**) *Constant Symbols* (beginning with a lower-case letter): For instance, martin, apple, yellow, and п denote constants. (**B**) *Unary Predicates* (beginning with an upper-case letter): In P(a) and Q(b), P and Q denote unary predicates. Also, a and b are variables (multiple constant symbols) and are the instances of P and Q respectively. For example, Fruit (apple) denotes that "apple is a fruit". Also, one may claim that it denotes that "all apples are fruits". So, what it actually means is that a specific individual denoted by the constant apple is a Fruit and the individual 'apple' belongs to the set of fruits. As mentioned, the unary predicates could represent *concepts*. So, the unary predicate Fruit denotes a concept and the constant apple denotes an instance of the concept Fruit. (**C**) *Binary Predicates* or *Relations*: R(m, n) is a binary predicate and represents a relation between two variables m and n. For example, FatherOf (john, mary) can represent the fact that "John is the father of Mary". (**D**) *Function Symbols* (beginning with a lower-case letter): f(x) is a function that operates the variable x. For example, father(john) can represent the "father of john".

4 Conversational Learning Theory

According to [7, 8], Laurillard's framework can be interpreted as a learning theory and as a practical framework for designing educational and pedagogical environments. This framework includes four important components: (i) Mentor's concepts [and conceptions], (ii) Mentor's constructed learning environment [that produces the mentor's constructed world], (iii) Learner's concepts [and conceptions], and (iv) Learner's specific actions [that construct the learner's world]. Regarding Laurillard's framework, we need to consider different forms of communication and associated mental activities. The main constructors of the associated mental activities are discussion, adaptation, interaction, and reflection. In fact, relying on Pask's Conversation Theory and focusing on Laurillard's framework, there are four kinds of human activities that take place in different kinds of flows between the components of Laurillard's framework: (1) Discussion between the mentor and the learner [on their conceptions, descriptions, comprehensions and reasonings], (2) Adaptation of the learner's actions and of the mentor's constructed environment. There is a kind of adaptation of the learner's mental universe and of the mentor's mental universe, (3) Interactions between the learner and the environment that is defined by the mentor, and (4) Reflection of the learner's performance by both the mentor and the learner. I have illustrated the above-mentioned characteristics in the framework represented in Fig. 1. I have analysed meaning construction over this framework in [4]. In this framework, the learner and the mentor are incorporated. They converse and exchange their conceptions in order to construct and develop their knowledge. This framework provides a contextual ground for semantic analysis of mentor-learner interactions and relationships.

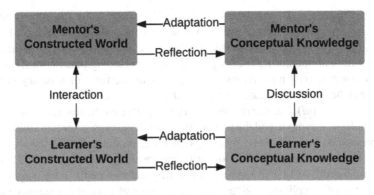

Fig. 1. The conversational learning framework

5   Semantic Analysis of Mentoring-Learning Relationships

This research aims at investigating where the formal semantics come from and when it appears within a relationship between a mentor and a learner. I shall draw your attention to four fundamental axioms that clarify what could be offered by the non-logical symbols within my formalism. Defining axioms is the most important prerequisite for bridging the gap between formalism and the meanings. (**1**) The symbols m and l denote mentor and learner respectively. They both represent constant symbols. (**2**) The atomic concepts in logical analysis of interactions between learner and mentor are *Learner* and *Mentor*. Transforming them into predication, the unary predicates Learner and Mentor are the fundamental unary predicates in the logical system. Also, Learner(l) and Mentor(m) represent two world descriptions over unary predicates. They demonstrate that the constant symbol l is an instance of the unary predicate Learner and the constant symbol m is an instance of the unary predicate Mentor. In other words, l is a Learner and m is a Mentor. (**3**) Considering the unary predicates Learner and Mentor, the binary predicates MentorOf and LearnerOf are definable. Consequently, MentorOf(m,l) and LearnerOf(l,m) are two world descriptions over relations that express the facts that "the individual m is the mentor of the individual l" and "the individual l is the learner of the individual m" respectively. These two world descriptions have described the most fundamental (atomic) relationships between two humans in the form of binary predications. (**4**) The functions mentor(l) and learner(m) are defined for representing the concepts of "the mentor of the individual l" and "the learner of the individual m" respectively. These functions are introduced in order to make a logical linkage between an individual and the role of her/his interlocutor. According to the proposed axioms, I shall claim that the binary predicate MentorOf(m,l), logically, implies that "the mentor of the individual l is (equality) the individual m". In fact, a world description over the relation between a mentor and a learner has supported the conclusion that there is an alignment between an agent (mentor or learner) and her/his role (mentoring or learning) for her/his interlocutor (learner or mentor). Let me focus on the mentor's perspective in order to provide the formal analysis:

MentorOf (m, 1) (*i*) ⇒ mentor (1) = m (*ii*). The equality (*ii*) is the product of interpretation and the binary predicate (*i*) describes the interpreted relation between mentor (1) and m. I shall claim that this equality is the root [and the origin] of the formal semantics within all mentoring-learning relationships including the relationships in the context of constructivist interactions. The equality in the form of a binary predicate describes that the meanings of mentor (1) and m are the same. Then we have: Equals (mentor (1) , m) (*iii*). Considering the binary predicate (*iii*), the function mentor (1) that is a non-logical symbol, and the person (individual) m that is a constant symbol, have been expressed to have the same meanings. Relying on commutative laws, mentor (1) = m and m = mentor (1) are logically and meaningfully equivalent. Therefore: Equals (m, mentor (1)) (*iv*). Accordingly, (*iii*) and (*iv*) are the conclusions of (*ii*). So, "the mentor of 1 implies m" and "m implies the mentor of 1" are the conclusions of "the mentor of 1 is m". Therefore: [mentor (1) = m] ⇒ [(mentor (1) → m) ∧ (m → mentor (1))] (*v*). The logical term (*v*) is inherently equal to: (function → constant) & (constant → function) (*vi*). I have already deduced that my central focus has been on the interrelationships between function symbols and constant symbols. Note that there is a bi-conditional relation between (*i*) and (*v*). Therefore: MentorOf (m, 1) ⟷ [(mentor (1) → m) ∧ (m → mentor (1))] (*vii*). Equivalently: MentorOf (m, 1) → [(mentor (1) → m) ∧ (m → mentor (1))] AND [(mentor (1) → m) ∧ (m → mentor (1))] → MentorOf (m, 1) (*viii*). The logical term (*viii*) is structurally equal to: Relation → [(function → constant) ∧ (constant → function)] AND [(function → constant) ∧ (constant → function)] → Relation (*ix*). In Fig. 2, this logical conclusion has been figured out. Regarding (*viii*) in the form of (*ix*), the logical system of (*i*) has been constructed over four fundamental relationships: **(a)** The mentoring relationships [from mentor into learner]. **(b)** The learning relationships [from learner into mentor]. **(c)** The iterative loops between mentor and learner (beginning from mentor into learner). **(d)** The iterative loops between learner and mentor (beginning from learner into mentor). Therefore, the formal semantics of mentoring-learning relationship in the context of mentor-learner conversational exchanges is definable over four constructive implications as follows (that are all extracted from *viii*).

Fig. 2. The general structure of the formal semantics within mentor and learner relationships

I. Implying (c) from (a). Formally: MentorOf(m,1) → [(mentor(1) → m) ∧ (m → mentor(1))] (*x*). It expresses: [(Mentoring Relation) → (Mentoring Function ⟷ Learner Constant)].

II. Implying (d) from (b). Formally: LearnerOf(1,m) → [(learner(m) 1) ∧ (1 → learner(m))] (*xi*). It expresses: [(Learning Relation) → (Learning Function ⟷ Mentor Constant)].

III. Implying (a) from (c). Formally: [(mentor(1) → m) ∧ (m → mentor(1))] → MentorOf(m,1) (*xii*). It expresses: [(Mentoring Function ⟷ Learner Constant) → (Mentoring Relation)].

IV. Implying (b) from (d). Formally: [(learner(m) → 1) ∧ (1 → learner(m))] → LearnerOf(1,m) (*xiii*). It expresses: [(Learning Function ⟷ Mentor Constant) → (Learning Relation)].

According to the deduced results, the unification of the following four items gives meaning (based on formal logic) to the relationship between mentor and learner, see Fig. 3. **(I)** The mentoring relations (from mentor into learner) support the interrelationships between 'the act of mentoring' and 'the learner'. **(II)** The learning relations (from learner into mentor) support the interrelationships between 'the act of learning' and 'the mentor'. **(III)** The interrelations between 'the act of mentoring' and 'the learner' support the mentoring relations (from mentor into learner). **(IV)** The interrelations between 'the act of learning' and 'the mentor' support the learning relations (from learner into mentor).

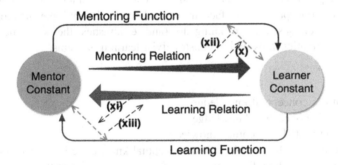

Fig. 3. Stablishing meaning in the relationship between mentor and learner

Consequently, by merging (I) and (III) and by merging (II) and (IV) and focusing on constructivist interactions, we have the following conceptual conclusions:

A. The constructivist mentoring relations (from mentor into learner) support the interrelationships between 'the act of constructivist mentoring' and 'the learner'. Subsequently, the interrelations between 'the act of constructivist mentoring' and 'the learner' support the constructivist mentoring relations (from mentor into learner). Taking the conversational learning framework into account, the constructivist mentoring relations are adapted [and provided] by the mentor's conceptual knowledge. Then the mentor's conceptual knowledge supports the interrelationships between 'the act of constructivist mentoring' and 'the learner'. Additionally, the interrelations between 'the act of constructivist mentoring' and 'the learner' support the mentor's conceptual knowledge.

B. The constructivist learning relations (from learner into mentor) support the interrelationships between 'the act of constructivist learning' and 'the mentor'. Subsequently, the interrelations between 'the act of constructivist learning' and 'the mentor' support the constructivist learning relations (from learner into mentor). Relying on the conversational learning framework, the constructivist learning relations (from learner into mentor) are adopted [and provided] by the learner's conceptual knowledge. Then, the learner's conceptual knowledge supports the interrelationships between 'the act of constructivist learning' and 'the mentor'. Moreover, the interrelationships between 'the act of constructivist learning' and 'the mentor' support the learner's conceptual knowledge.

Summary. The mentor's conceptual knowledge and the learner' conceptual knowledge are being transformed and exchanged during the constructivist interaction. Furthermore, conversational learning's main premise is that the reliable knowledge exists and evolves in action-grounded interactions and conversations. So, the discussions between the mentor's and the learner's conceptual knowledge make a balance in their united [and global] reliable conceptual knowledge. This reliable knowledge affects both A and B. Accordingly, A and B have interconnections with each other. The results of the interactions between A and B are reflected in reliable united conceptual knowledge. Regarding the proposed conceptual analysis, there are strong interrelationships between two classes of concepts. And in fact, in a broad sense, the multiple interconnections between these classes give meaning to (and establishes the semantics of) the mentor-learner relationships within constructivist learning systems.

Class 1

- The mentor's conceptual knowledge.
- The learner's conceptual knowledge.
- The reliable united conceptual knowledge.
- The adaptation of the reliable united conceptual knowledge in the mentor's world.
- The adaptation of the reliable united conceptual knowledge in the learner's world.

Class 2

- The reflection of the constructivist mentoring relations (from mentor into learner) in the reliable united conceptual knowledge, and, respectively, in the mentor's conceptual knowledge.
- The reflection of the interrelationships between 'the act of constructivist mentoring' and 'the learner' in the reliable united conceptual knowledge, and, respectively, in the mentor's conceptual knowledge.
- The reflection of the constructivist learning relations (from learner into mentor) in the reliable united conceptual knowledge, and, respectively, in the learner's conceptual knowledge.

- The reflection of the interrelationships between 'the act of constructivist learning' and 'the mentor' in the reliable united conceptual knowledge, and, respectively, in the learner's conceptual knowledge.

6   Conclusions

In the expressions *human learning* and *human mentoring*, the words 'learning' and 'mentoring' are utilised as binary predicates (roles) with the word 'human'. Knowledge construction as the most important objective of constructivist learning is a significant matter in the context of mentor-learner interactions. The most central focus of this article has been on 'Relations' between mentors and learners. I have focused on the process of knowledge construction in the framework of Conversation Theory (CT) and have assumed that conversational learning is inherently a semantic model to account for the emergence of the domain of the learner's and of the mentor's conceptual knowledge. The developmental processes of personal world constructions [by mentors and learners] provide supportive backbones for that semantic model. Furthermore, I have considered the fact that conversational learning could express how the produced meanings based upon constructed concepts could support mentor and learner in constructing their universal conceptual knowledge. In this article, Predicate Logic has been employed in order to provide a logical basis for relationships between learners and mentors. Relying on Predicate Logic, this research, conceptually and logically, has been concerned with semantic analysis of mentoring-learning relationships in the context of constructivist interactions. I have thought of the establishment of meaning (in a broad sense) in the relationships between mentors and learners. Taking the results into consideration and reconsidering the framework of constructivist conversational learning, it has been checked how the produced meanings could be related to the discussions between the mentors' and the learners' conceptual knowledge. Consequently, relying on the semantic ground of conversational learning framework, it has been realised that the produced meanings are interrelated in order to get reflected (mirrored) in the [mentor's and learner's] united conceptual knowledge. This research has formed a building block of my PhD research which is dealing with Semantic Analysis of Constructivist Concept Leaning.

References

1. Badie, F.: A Semantic basis for meaning construction in constructivist interactions. In: Proceedings of 12th International Conference on Cognition and Exploratory Learning in Digital Age, Ireland (2015)
2. Badie, F.: Towards a semantics based framework for meaning construction in constructivist interactions. In: Proceedings of 8th Annual International Conference of Education, Research and Innovation, Spain (2015)
3. Badie, F.: Concept representation analysis in the context of human-machine interactions. In: Proceedings of 14th International Conference on e-Society (ES), Portugal (2016)

4. Badie, F.: A conceptual framework for knowledge creation based on constructed meanings within mentor-learner conversations. In: Uskov, V.L., Howlett, R.J., Jain, L.C. (eds.). SIST, vol. 59, pp. 167–177. Springer, Heidelberg (2016). doi:10.1007/978-3-319-39690-3_15
5. Barwise, J.: Studies in Logic and the Foundations of Mathematics. North-Holland Publishing Company, Amsterdam (1977)
6. Götzsche, H.: Deviational Syntactic Structures. Bloomsbury Academic, London (2013)
7. Laurillard, D.M.: Rethinking University Teaching: A Framework for the Effective Use of Educational Technology. Routledge, London (1993)
8. Laurillard, D.M.: Rethinking University Teaching. A Conversational Framework for the Effective Use of Learning Technologies. Routledge, London (2002)
9. McGawand Peterson, P.: Constructivism and learning. In: International Encyclopaedia of Education, 3rd edn. Oxford, Elsevier (2007)
10. McIntyre Boyd, G.: Conversation theory. In: Handbook of Research on Educational Communications and Technology (2004)
11. Mendelson, E.: Introduction to Mathematical Logic, 3rd edn. Chapman and Hall, London (1987)
12. Pask, G.: Conversation, Cognition and Learning: A Cybernetic Theory and Methodology. Elsevier, New York (1975)
13. Pask, G.: Developments in conversation theory (part 1). Int. J. Man Mach. Stud. **13**, 357–411 (1980). Elsevier
14. Piaget, J.: Development and learning. In: Ripple, R.E., Rockcastle, V.N. (eds.) Piaget Rediscovered: A Report on the Conference of Cognitive Studies and Curriculum Development, Ithaca, NY, pp. 7–20. Cornell University (1964)
15. Piaget, J.: Six Psychological Studies. Random House, New York (1967)
16. Phillips, D.C.: The Good, the Bad, and the Ugly: The Many Faces of Constructivism. Educational Researcher, Washington, DC (1995)
17. Scott, B.: Conversation theory: a constructivist, dialogical approach to educational technology. Cybern. Hum. Knowing **8**(4), 1–25 (2001)
18. Simpson, J.A., Weiner, E.S.C.: The Oxford English Dictionary. Oxford University Press, Oxford (1989)

Using AHP to Critical Thinking Develop in Precision Measurement of Vocational College Students

Dyi-Cheng Chen[⊠], Ci-Syong You, Fu-Yuan Gao, and Bo-Yan Lai

Department of Industrial Education and Technology, National Changhua
University of Education, Changhua 500, Taiwan
dcchen@cc.ncue.edu.tw

Abstract. While critical thinking applications have been extensively investigated, the precision measurement for vocational college students is unexplored. First, this study collects the status of precision measurement in various countries, the scope of technical knowledge of Precision measurement and the relevant literature on critical thinking performance. Critical thinking has used in the generation of novel ideas for student. The three kinds of critical thinking were Intellectual traits, Element of thought, Intellectual standards. In addition, this study involves a quantitative and qualitative content analysis of relevant documents, textbooks and teaching objectives of precision measurement performance, which includes Intellectual traits, element of thought, Intellectual standards, in 3 hierarchies and 15 indexes. Second, this study assesses these criteria by employing the analytic hierarchy process (AHP) technique to solicit opinions from 11 experts by using questionnaires. Results show that intellectual traits, element of thought, intellectual standards have weights of 0.357%, 0.342%, 0.301%, respectively.

Keywords: Critical thinking · Precision measurement · Analytic hierarchy process (AHP)

1 Introduction

Teaching students how to think more productively, generate and evaluate ideas is vital in contemporary engineering education. Critical thinking is essential for modern creative engineers. The paper focuses on engineering students critical thinking, logic and analytical skills. Critical thinking is generally recognized as an important skill, and one that is a primary goal of higher education. Development of critical thinking skills is generally recognized as an important aspect of engineering education. Critical thinking is generally recognized as an important skill, and one that is a primary goal of higher education. However, there is surprisingly little in the literature regarding critical thinking in engineering [1]. Engineering students need to develop and apply critical

Dyi-Cheng Chen—SETE 2016.

T.-T. Wu et al. (Eds.): SETE 2016, LNCS 10108, pp. 117–122, 2017.
DOI: 10.1007/978-3-319-52836-6_14

thinking skills in doing their academic studies, solving various complicated problems that they face, and to evaluate the critical choices they will be forced to make as a result of the information explosion and other rapid technological changes. They can also learn to demonstrate habits of thinking behaviors in their daily and professional activities [2]. Many components are manufactured to very close dimensions. Therefore, a machinist cannot afford to make a mistake while measuring or machining workpieces. Once the piece has been machined, there is no turning back or adding on. It is, therefore, important for him to become familiar with precision measuring tools, instruments, and with the types of fits, allowances and tolerances required for his job.

2   Literature Review

2.1   Critical Thinking

Critical thinking figure prominently among the goals for education, whether one asks developers of curricula, educational researchers, parents, or employers. Although there are some quite diverse definitions of critical thinking nearly all emphasize the ability and tendency to gather, evaluate, and use information effectively [3]. Critical thinking is the art of analyzing and evaluating thinking with a view to improving it [4]. Critical thinkers routinely apply the intellectual standards to the elements of reasoning in order to develop intellectual traits. For students it is a critical thinking supplement to any textbook for any course. Faculty can use it to design instruction, assignments, and tests in any subject. Students can use it to improve their learning in any content area. Its generic skills apply to all subjects. For example, critical thinkers are clear as to the purpose at hand and the question at issue. They question information, conclusions, and points of view. They strive to be clear, accurate, precise, and relevant. They seek to think beneath the surface, to be logical, and fair. They apply these skills to their reading and writing as well as to their speaking and listening. They apply them in professional and personal life. The Fig. 1 shows the critical thinking of the architecture of this study [5].

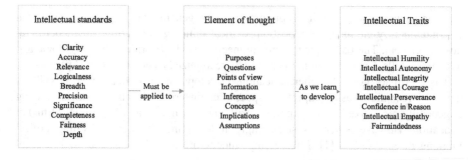

Fig. 1. Critical thinking of the architecture [5]

2.2   Precision Measurement

Precision closeness of agreement between indications or measured quantity values obtained replicate measurements on the same or similar objects under specified conditions. Measurement precision is usually expressed numerically by measures of imprecision, such as standard deviation, variance, or coefficient of variation under the specified conditions of measurement [6].

3   Research Method

3.1   Analytic Hierarchy Process

The Analytic Hierarchy Process (AHP), developed by Saaty [7], is an analytic logic that combines inductive and deductive methods. It is an effective decision-making method that reflects the process of decomposition, judgment, and the synthesis of decisive thinking in humans. The AHP primarily is utilized in the multiple-goal decision-making method. The AHP method maps complicated decision problems to a hierarchical diagram. With the resulting criteria hierarchy structure, eigenvectors can be calculated using a matrix of pair comparison of each criterion by a nominal scale. It can be used to represent and calculate the weights of each criterion in certain hierarchies and then organize them, creating a reference for decision analysis. The steps of analysis are as follows: (1) Describe and analyses the problem; (2) Determine structural hierarchical relationships; (3) Design and collect questionnaires; (4) Build a pairwise comparison matrix; (5) Calculate the maximal eigenvector of A (λmax) and the eigenvector (Wi); and (6) Perform a consistency test.

Next, in this study, a comparison matrix was developed by comparing pairs of criteria or alternatives. This pairwise comparison helps experts independently judge the contribution of each criterion to the objective. Following Saaty [7], the researcher assigned a single number drawn from the fundamental 1–9 scale of absolute numbers shown in Table 1 [8]. Pairwise comparison generally refers to any process of comparing entities in pairs to judge, which of each pair is preferred or has a greater amount of some quantitative property.

Table 1. The pairwise comparison scale.

Intensity of importance	Definition
1	Equal importance
3	Moderate importance
5	Strong importance
7	Very strong or demonstrated importance
9	Extreme importance
2, 4, 6, 8	Intermediate values between two adjacent judgments

4 Results and Discussion

The consistency test was used to screen effective questionnaires and control the reliability of the results. By using AHP pair-wise comparison, the relative weights of all criteria was obtained to construct the weight system and provide as a valuable reference for relevant units. Table 2 shows the comparison of relative weights for individual major criteria. In respect of the hierarchy of evaluation criteria, eleven experts from universities of Taiwan suggested that the most important three criteria were as follows: Intellectual traits (0.357), Element of thought (0.342), Intellectual standards (0.301).

Table 2. Weights of 3 major criteria

Major criteria	Weight	Order
Intellectual standards	0.301	3
Element of thought	0.342	2
Intellectual traits	0.357	1

Table 3 also shows the relative weight for individual sub-criteria under specific major criteria. Under the evaluation criterion of "Intellectual Standards", the experts suggest that the most important criterion was "Roundness measurement metrics" (0.225). Under the evaluation criterion of "Element of thought", the experts suggest that the most important criterion was "The importance of precision measuring tools for machining" (0.225). Under the evaluation criterion of "Intellectual traits", the experts suggest that the most important criterion was "Linear detection" (0.223). Table 4 is teaching objectives of precision measurement of based on critical thinking, including three Major criteria, 15 Sub-criteria for all teaching objectives.

Table 3. Weights of 15 sub-criteria

Major criteria	Sub-criteria	Relative weight	Order
Intellectual standards	Accuracy	0.210	2
	Length	0.181	4
	Angle of taper	0.180	5
	Roundness measurement metrics	0.225	1
	Contour	0.204	3
Element of thought	The basic conditions for precision measuring chamber	0.150	5
	The importance of precision measuring tools for machining	0.225	1
	Category of precision measuring tools	0.210	3
	Use and maintenance of measuring	0.201	4
	The importance of instrument calibration gauge	0.214	2
Intellectual traits	Statistical process control	0.191	4
	Gauge instrument calibration	0.205	2
	Measurement error	0.201	3
	Linear detection	0.223	1
	Tolerance and fit	0.180	5

Table 4. Teaching objectives

Major criteria	Sub-criteria	Teaching objectives
Intellectual standards	Accuracy	**Clarity** enables students to apply in Accuracy **Relevance** enables students to apply in Accuracy
	Length	**Logicalness** enables students to apply in length **Breadth** enables students to apply in length
	Angle of taper	**Precision** enables students to apply in Angle **Significance** enables students to apply in "Angle of taper"
	Roundness measurement metrics	**Completeness** enables students to apply in "Roundness measurement metrics"
	Contour	**Fairness** enables students to apply in "Contour"
Element of thought	The basic conditions for precision measuring chamber	**Purposes** enables students to apply in "The basic conditions for precision measuring chamber" **Questions** enables students to apply in "The basic conditions for precision measuring chamber"
	The importance of precision measuring tools for machining	**Points of view** enables students to apply in "The importance of precision measuring tools for machining" **Information** enables students to apply in The importance of precision measuring tools for machining"
	Category of precision measuring tools	**Inferences** enables students to apply in "Category of precision measuring tools" **Concepts** enables students to apply in "Category of precision measuring tools"
	Use and maintenance of measuring	**Implications** enables students to apply in "Use and maintenance of measuring"
	The importance of instrument calibration gauge	**Assumptions** enables students to apply in "The importance of instrument calibration gauge"
Intellectual traits	Statistical Process Control	**Intellectual Humility** enables students to apply in "Statistical Process Control" **Intellectual Autonomy** enables students to apply in "Statistical Process Control"
	Gauge instrument calibration	**Intellectual Integrity** enables students to apply in "Gauge instrument calibration" **Intellectual Courage** enables students to apply in "Gauge instrument calibration"

(continued)

Table 4. (*continued*)

Major criteria	Sub-criteria	Teaching objectives
	Measurement error	**Intellectual Perseverance** enables students to apply in "Measurement error" **Confidence** in Reason enables students to apply in "Measurement error"
	Linear detection	**Intellectual Empathy** enables students to apply in "Linear detection"
	Tolerance and fit	**Fair-mindedness** enables students to apply in "Tolerance and fit"

5 Conclusions

This study determined the industry-oriented most important three criteria were as follows: Intellectual traits (0.357), Element of thought (0.342), Intellectual standards (0.301). The researcher assigned a single number drawn from the fundamental 1–9 scale of absolute numbers. Although the priority of the precision measurement curriculum was thoroughly investigated in this study, the limitations should be addressed in future studies. This study was conducted with relatively small samples, especially of the precision measurement experts. This may have caused a sample selection bias problem. This study applied the AHP approach, and found it useful for a complicated precision measurement curriculum problem. The analytic hierarchy process can be applied to future studies on various critical thinking curriculum planning problems in educational.

References

1. Douglas, E.P.: Defining and measuring critical thinking in engineering. Procedia Soc. Behav. Sci. **56**, 153–159 (2012)
2. Kobzeva, N.: Scrabble as a tool for engineering students' critical thinking skills development. Procedia Soc. Behav. Sci. **182**, 369–374 (2015)
3. Beyer, B.K.: Critical Thinking. Phi Delta Kappa Educational Foundation, Bloomington (1995)
4. Paul, R., Elder, L.: Foundation for Critical Thinking, Sonoma university, Santa Rosa, CA (2007)
5. Paul, R., Elder, L.: The Miniature Guide to Critical Thinking Concepts and Tools. The Foundation for Critical Thinking, Tomales (2006)
6. JCGM: International vocabulary of metrology — Basic and general concepts and associated terms (VIM) (2008)
7. Saaty, T.L.: An exposition on the AHP in reply to the paper remarks on the analytic hierarchy process. Manage. Sci. **36**, 259–268 (1990)
8. Saaty, T.L.: Relative measurement and its generalization in decision making why pairwise comparisons are central in mathematics for the measurement of intangible factors the analytic hierarchy/network process. Revista de la Real Academia de Ciencias Exactas, Fisicas y Naturales. Serie A. Mathematics **102**, 251–318 (2008)

Using Summarization Technology
for Supporting Problem-Based Learning

Yu-Lin Jeng[1]([✉]), Yong-Ming Huang[2], and Tien-Chi Huang[3]

[1] Department of Information Management,
Southern Taiwan University of Science and Technology, Tainan, Taiwan
jackjeng@mail.stust.edu.tw
[2] Department of Applied Informatics and Multimedia,
Chia Nan University of Pharmacy and Science, Tainan, Taiwan
ym.huang.tw@gmail.com
[3] Department of Information Management,
National Taichung University of Science and Technology, Taichung, Taiwan
tchuang@nutc.edu.tw

Abstract. In this information explosion era, more and more users are experienced information overload issue. Text summarization technology provides short version of document for user to reduce information overload. In e-learning field, a lengthy learning materials may cause such issue so that learner cannot focus on the main concept of the course. In traditional problem-based learning (PBL) activity, panel discussion is the key process for learners to consolidate their knowledge and provide solutions of the problem. In order to accelerate the discussion process, this study proposes a summarization module for learners to obtain short version of learning materials. In this manner, learners can focus on the main learning concept in their discussion and practice the problem-solving skills.

Keywords: Text summarization · PBL · e-learning · Problem-solving

1 Introduction

There are lots amount of data on Internet which causes information overload issue in this digital era. Therefore, automatic text summarization has drawn substantial attention since it provides an approach to the information overload issue for users [9–11]. Readers are more interested in shorter versions of text documents than the lengthy versions. In e-learning field, there is a micro-learning strategy which tries to compress learning materials into small pieces for learners. It also avoid information overload for e-learning learners and promote their learning by learning small concept step by step. Learners use e-learning platform to read learning materials or to review important items of the course. In the same viewpoint, learners like to read short version of learning materials more than the full version of learning materials. Such learning approach is applicable to learners who need to review the course or get the main content quickly. In the panel discussion situation, learners provide ideas about a subject using their prior knowledge and get feedback from others. Sometimes, they need to look for information to support their argument and provide others sufficient knowledge.

© Springer International Publishing AG 2017
T.-T. Wu et al. (Eds.): SETE 2016, LNCS 10108, pp. 123–131, 2017.
DOI: 10.1007/978-3-319-52836-6_15

In this learning situation, learners should not waste too much time to read the entire learning materials to get the small piece of knowledge. It would be efficient for learners to receive summarized information in a panel discussion situation. In Problem-based Learning (PBL) process, panel discussion is a key phase in this learning activity. Therefore, in this study, we present a summarization learning module for learners to supporting the PBL learning activity. The proposed learning module provides summarized learning materials for learners so that they can focus on the discussion without spending too much time on reading text information. The research purposes includes:

- Does the tutor agree the summarized learning materials are generated appropriate?
- Does the proposed learning module help the process of PBL?
- Does the proposed learning module accelerate the discussion process?

The rest of the paper is organized as follows: Sect. 2 refers the related works, Sect. 3 describes the proposed system module. The questionnaire result and its discussion presented in Sect. 4. Finally, the conclusions for this study are summarized in Sect. 5.

2 Related Works

2.1 Problem-Based Learning

A problem based learning (PBL) approach is designed to solve open-ended problems/questions in groups of learners. PBL activity usually includes designing a problem, analyzing how to solve the problem, teaching the related knowledge for solving the problem, and helping the learners to consolidate the knowledge and then have the ability to solve similar problems [1]. According to the definition, PBL is a learning model which uses a practice example that actually exist to actually have a group discussion and solve the problem to achieve the purpose of autonomous learning [3, 4]. During the process of autonomous learning, learners not only solve problems, but also participate in the learning process of PBL for them to increase knowledge during problem-solving and discussion process. Problem-solving and discussion process is learners' use of prior knowledge, skills, concepts learned, and understanding to meet the needs of new contexts, reorganize the information they have, and develop new methods and apply them to new contexts to obtain a solution [4]. Therefore, problem-solving is a process. When learners cannot use prior knowledge and experiences to solve a new problem, they will recall the knowledge concepts that they have learned to further attempt to solve the problem. Therefore, it would be efficient if there is a system help learner recall the knowledge concepts by providing summarized important sentences in this process. During this process, if the connection between learners' knowledge acquisition and knowledge becomes high-level thinking and can be further applied to similar problems, such problem-solving process becomes a cognitive strategy that can guide cognitive behaviors. As a matter of fact, PBL is to train learners' abilities to face problems, understand them, and solve them. Such abilities enable learners to face other problems to be encountered in the future. Besides, PBL refers to learners' learning of how to identify problems, analyze them, and solve them through practices under the guidance of tutors. During the process of problem handling, learners learn necessary knowledge concepts on their own and understand the knowledge concepts in which they are deficient. The learning under such a model impresses learners more, and enables them to further develop relevant cognitive strategies to help them follow past problem-solving method to face and handle problems in the future. From the description above, in order to help learners to get into high-level thinking quickly, this research provides a summarization module for learner to acquire the important concepts of the learning materials in an efficient manner.

2.2 Micro-learning Strategy

Micro-learning is a learning strategy used for relatively micro-learning materials and learning activities [5]. The definition of "micro" includes the number of concepts covered in learning materials themselves and the length of lasting time of learning activities. Besides, micro-learning materials are also relatively easier to be obtained by learners using simple learning devices, such as smart handheld devices and tablet PC. Because the time of learning activities is shorter, it is convenient for learners to acquire knowledge and learning concepts. Therefore, the concepts of micro-learning have become more popular due to the rapid development of information technologies in recent years [6]. For example, learners can read micro-learning materials on mobile phone or tablet easily on the bus or train to get small learning concept quickly. Moreover, in this manner, learners can help teachers develop refined design and production of learning materials by responding each of learning materials. Consequently, it is important for learners to have feedback channel on each micro-learning materials. The concept of Micro-Content refers to the use of information technology presentation methods, such as subject of email, main title of webpage, cellular phone text content, and short Q&A, to describe a summarized form of a concept. Furthermore, combined with the concept of modern knowledge dissemination media of micro-learning materials can be expanded to various forms, such as WiKi, Blog, RSS, and Twitter. The composition content is more inclined to information concepts of fragmented concepts, loose structures, and instant reorganization of concepts. A micro-learning materials can be the content designed by teachers or refined teaching materials of more refined concept content decomposed from larger learning materials or themes by teachers according to concepts. In order to provide micro-learning materials and feedback channel for learners, this research proposes a summarization module to generate a smaller learning materials for learners in a PBL situation. The detailed description of this module is illustrated in Sect. 3.

2.3 Text Summarization

The huge volume of data available today on the Internet has become the information resource for everyone. However, it is hard for human to consume those data and retrieve useful information from it. Therefore, the purpose of text summarization is to teach automatic tool to understand, index, classify and present information of text documents. One solution for such purpose is using automatic text summarization (TS) techniques. TS focuses on getting the main context of documents and then provides summarized content for users. There are two main techniques which are Extractive and Abstractive approaches. In short, Extractive approach produces a set of the most significant sentences from the document. And Abstractive approach try to improve the coherence among sentences and may even produce new sentences for the document. Extractive methods are usually performed in three steps [7]: (1) Create an intermediate representation of the original text; (2) Sentence scoring; and (3) Selecting a summary consisting of several sentences. Among those steps, there are several scoring methods published in the research field.

In general, sentence scoring methods are classified according to three categories: Word-based Scoring, Sentence-based Scoring and Graph-based Scoring. In Word-based Scoring approach, each word in the document receives a score and the weight of each sentence is the sum of all scores of its constituent words. In Sentence-based Scoring approach, it analyzes the features of the sentence according to different cues or expressions in the document. In Graph-based Scoring approach, the score is generated by the relationship among sentences. For example, when a sentence refers to another sentence, it generates a link with an associated weight between these two sentences. The weights are used to generate the scores of the sentence. In [8], the author proposes a new summarization system that easily combines different sentence scoring methods in order to obtain the best summaries depending on the context. Therefore, we refer these researches and build a summarization module in the learning system for supporting discussion phase of a PBL activity.

3   Research Design

3.1   System Design

This research aims to build a web-based summarization module for learners to learn and search course materials in a PBL discussion. The proposed system module is developed as a supporting learning tool in a sequential PBL activity. Figure 1 shows the supporting process in a PBL activity. In the beginning of the PBL activity, tutor needs to define and develop a proper problem/question for learners to solve. The problem/question must have a certain degree of complexity and challenges, and there is enough information and clues to guide the learners to gather information and facilitate the participation of all learners. The second step is to initiate of PBL events which includes inquiring and investigating. Learners needs to define the problem range for the problem set in the previous step, discuss and develop strategies and solutions through group cooperation in order to explore and collect the question information. The last step is to provide the problem/question solution. Learners in a group will analyze and filter the data collected in the previous phase, and then verify the problem-solving strategies and summarize the correct solutions to the problem/question. In these three steps of PBL activity, the proposed summarization module will provide the learning support during the second step of process. In the second step, learners are supposed to discuss and collect data according to the problem/question. This module generates the summarized information from original learning materials for learners to get the knowledge quickly and promote discussion in a smooth manner.

Fig. 1. The proposed learning-support tool in a PBL activity

During the panel discussion in a PBL activity, the learners follow the pre-designed learning situations, prompting members of the group through discussion to criticize the way of learning materials content, in order to be able to integrate a solution to the problem. In this process, tutor can participate in timely discussions, to enhance learners learning a higher level of interactive discussion. Therefore, learners needs to think learning objectives, understand their skills, and develop learning objectives in a PBL discussion. The proposed learning supporting tool accelerates the data searching process and knowledge acquiring process so that learners can focus on the developing of the problem-solving strategies.

3.2   System Architecture

The system is deployed on Windows 7 platform. Tomcat software is responsible for web server communication and the summarization module is in charge of learning materials summarization service. In a PBL activity, tutor is responsible for providing the original learning materials and guiding the panel discussion. During the discussion, learners need to investigate the problem and to search/learn the knowledge related to the subject. However, if learners needs to read the entire learning materials, the discussion focus would be shifted and the learners cannot concentrate their attention on the problem itself. In the proposed system architecture, learners can get the summarization of learning materials in the system module using various learning devices interface including mobile phone, tablet and desktop computer. The detailed process of each component is shown in Fig. 2.

The proposed summarization module provides the function of compressing the original learning materials so that learners can get the main learning concept quickly in a PBL discussion process. In this manner, learners can be more focusing on the problem-solving discussion without wasting too much time on reading materials. In the design of PBL activity, learner must emphasize problem-based learning initiative to think learning objectives, understanding their skills, develop learning objectives and learning plans by themselves. Therefore, the proposed process offers much time for learners to think and to develop main learning outcomes.

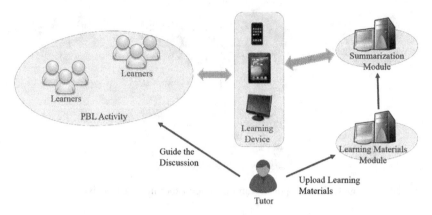

Fig. 2. The proposed system architecture for PBL activity

3.3   Using Example

The proposed system is designed to assist the discussion process of PBL activity and to obtain the learners' preference between the original learning materials and the summarization materials. Followings are the screenshots of the summarization module in different client interface. The interface provides the original learning materials and the summarization materials at the same time. Learners can choose one of them to read and then send their preference by clicking the 'Like' button. In this approach, the system can get the leaners' feedback about the quality of the summarization materials. The web-based and mobile interfaces show in Figs. 3 and 4.

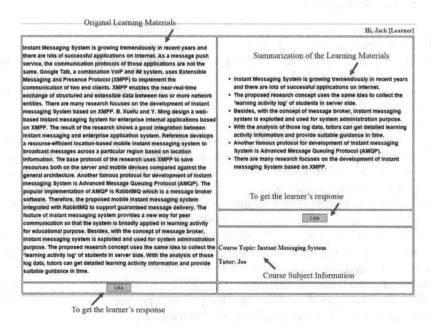

Fig. 3. Web-based interface of summarization module

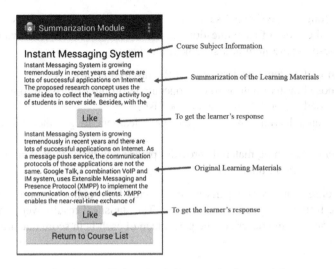

Fig. 4. Mobile interface of summarization module

Figure 3 is the web-based interface of summarization module. Learner chooses the learning subject in the system and then the learning materials will show on the left hand side of the browser. In the meantime, the proposed module generates the summarized document on the right hand side of the browser. Learner decides which learning materials is best fit for the learning situation and then send the 'Like' to the system.

Learner can also use the proposed system via mobile devices. Figure 4 is the mobile interface. The upside part presents the summarized document and the original learning materials show below it. There are also 'Like' buttons in the mobile learning interface.

4   Questionnaire Results and Discussions

In a PBL activity process, the most important stage is that learners need to understand the problem, propose questions related to the problem, search for useful learning materials, analyze possible solutions and conclude the learning results. In this stage, panel discussion provides an environment for learners to exchange their ideas and elaborate the learning information. Therefore, it would be valuable if the proposed system can help promote the discussion progress and enhance the discussion effectiveness.

Besides, we invite several experts to explore the proposed system and evaluate the effectiveness of the summarization module by replying questionnaires. A total of 15 experts who have strong academic backgrounds, research experience and professional in the area of PBL research were invited to participate in the experimental assessment. The response portion of each question in the questionnaire was designed using a 5-point Likert scale. Typically, an item in a Likert scale is given as a statement and the invited experts need to respond the statement using a scale from 1 to 5, in which 5 stands for "strongly agree" and 1 stands for "strongly disagree". The 5 level responses also stand for the score of each question thus we can calculate the mean value of each item. The questionnaire item and statement includes:

(1) The proposed system accelerates the PBL discussion process.
(2) The proposed system help learners concentrate on the discussion topic.
(3) The proposed methodology is good for PBL.
(4) The generated learning materials can help learners to get the subject concept quickly.
(5) The generated learning materials provides precise summarized content according to the original learning materials.

The responses data from experts were collected from online questionnaire system and it can be further analyzed and discussed. The statistical results were presented in Table 1. The 5th column describes the percentage of each item score that are greater or equal to 4.

Table 1. Questionnaire results

Item	Mean	Stand deviation	Variance	Score > = 4
1	4.267	0.799	0.638	80%
2	4.200	0.676	0.457	86.7%
3	4.467	0.834	0.695	80%
4	4.200	0.862	0.743	73.3%
5	4.067	0.799	0.638	73.3%

The responses to Item (1) and (2) indicate that the experts agree he proposed system can help learners focus on the discussion process during PBL. This reflects that the proposed system can be used for a learning assistant tool in PBL activity. The responses to Item (3) suggests the proposed methodology have positive effect on PBL activity. The responses to Item (4) and (5) indicate that the generated summarized learning materials do help learners to get the learning concept quickly. However, the summarized content needs to be generated more precisely to reflect the main concept of the learning materials.

5   Conclusions

The studies of text summarization technology keeps increasing in the research field. In a PBL activity, to help learners perform deep-thinking and discussion is important for tutor or an assistant information system. In this study, we build a summarization learning module embedded in a learning platform to support learner in their panel discussion process. With the help of the proposed learning module, learners can get the learning concept in an efficient way. There are several perspectives to evaluate the proposed learning process, we applied questionnaire approach to get experts' responses about this learning module and the enhanced learning process. The result shows positive opinions about the proposed learning module. However, the automatic summarized content need to be more precisely to reflect the main concept of the original learning materials. According to [8], different combinations of sentence scoring algorithms yield different results. They found that the best combinations of sentence scoring methods are for news, blogs and articles. In the future work, if the writing style of learning materials can be written in those format, the accuracy could be more precisely. Besides, we will evaluate the proposed learning module and the learning process by observing learners' learning outcome and feedback to consolidate the contribution of this study.

Acknowledgement. The authors would like to thank the Ministry of Science and Technology of the Republic of China, Taiwan, for financially supporting this research under Contract No. MOST 104-2511-S-218-006-.

References

1. Hou, X., Yang, H. B., Liu, J.B.: A problem-based teaching method in XML course. In: International Conference on Computer Science and Education, pp. 399–402 (2010)
2. Hung, W.: The nine-step process for designing PBL problems: application of the 3C3R model. Paper presented at the AERA 2006 Annual Meeting, San Francisco, CA (2006)
3. Hwang, G.J., Tseng, J.C.R., Hwang, G.H.: Diagnosing student learning problems based on historical assessment records. Innovations Educ. Teach. Int. **45**(1), 77–89 (2008)
4. Kahney, H.: Problem solving: Current Issues. Open University Press, Philadelphia (1993)
5. Hug, T., Lindner, M., Bruck, P.A.: Microlearning: emerging concepts, practices and technologies after e-learning. In: Proceedings of Microlearning, Innsbruck. Innsbruck University Press (2005)
6. Siemens, G.: Connectivism: a learning theory for the digital age (2004). http://www.elearnspace.org/Articles/connectivism.htm
7. Nenkova, A., McKeown, K.: A survey of text summarization techniques. In: Aggarwal, C. C., Zhai, C.X. (eds.) Mining Text Data, pp. 43–76. Springer, Heidelberg (2012)
8. Rafael, F., Frederico, F., Luciano, S.C., Rafael, D.L., Rinaldo, L., Gabriel, F., Steven, J.S., Luciano, F.: A context based text summarization system. In: IAPR International Workshop on Document Analysis Systems, pp. 66–70 (2014)
9. Anusha, B., Ashesh, K., Shivam, P., Sowmya, K.S.: A novel technique for efficient text document summarization as a service. In: Third International Conference on Advances in Computing and Communications, pp. 50–53 (2013)
10. Wu, K., Shi, P., Pan, D.: An approach to automatic summarization for chinese text based on the combination of spectral clustering and LexRank. In: 12th International Conference on Fuzzy Systems and Knowledge Discovery (FSKD), pp. 1350–1354 (2015)
11. Yang, G., Chen, N.S., Kinshuk, S.E., Anderson, T., Wen, D.: The effectiveness of automatic text summarization in mobile learning contexts. Comput. Educ. **68**, 233–243 (2013)

Emerging Technologies Supported Personalized and Adaptive Learning

Change Support to Maintain Quality in Learning Technology Systems

Claus Pahl[(⊠)]

Free University of Bozen-Bolzano, Bolzano, Italy
Claus.pahl@unibz.it

Abstract. The quality of learning technology systems can degrade over time due to changes in learners, content and the software environment. This might occur as long-term evolution of the system to adjust the system to environmental changes or as part of short-term adaptation in order to adapt to the learner behaviour and knowledge. We present a quality management framework for changing environments that integrates evolution and adaptation. The framework sees evolution and adaption as two incarnation of change. A key concept is the notion of feedback that causes quality goals such as learning achievement or learner experience to be changed or the need to adjust the system to maintain existing goals. The aim is to support instructors, course designer and platform support in understanding the interaction of evolution and adaptation and to help them in designing, modelling, running and maintaining learning technology systems in order to achieve and maintain the expected quality.

Keywords: Learning technology system · Quality management · Change

1 Introduction

Adaptive learning technology systems (LTS) [4, 5, 14] change in terms of their interaction with the user based on the user profile and her/his behaviour. Both content and the learning process (e.g., through the navigation structure of the interface) are possibly subject to adaption [1]. This adaptation aims at improving the user experience and resulting in better learner attainment and also acceptance [23]. In this situation, the user model is bound to change frequently, due to new knowledge acquired or learning problems being identified [10, 19, 21]. As a result, the content and interface might need to be changed to maintain quality. However, content and interface might also be changed for other reasons. Content simply changes because it needs to reflect reality, which of course changes. Interfaces (and the presentation of content) might need to change because the learner changes the device s/he is using. Furthermore, the platform of the LTS that delivers the content to the user might change due to organisational changes [17]. Change costs can often be prohibitive, limiting the maintainability of critical educational goals in LTS. In all cases there is a negative impact on quality goals such as a generally good user experience or the achievement of learning objectives through the LTS.

In all cases change occurs, either as short-term adaptation to the user or as a more long-term evolution of content or platform. Still, the goal remains to enable a good user experience and achieve the learning objectives set.

© Springer International Publishing AG 2017
T.-T. Wu et al. (Eds.): SETE 2016, LNCS 10108, pp. 135–142, 2017.
DOI: 10.1007/978-3-319-52836-6_16

We present a quality management framework for changing environments in which we integrated the evolution and adaptation dimensions and that also links the instructor, course developer and software engineer perspectives. We look at how change occurs, i.e., which are the drivers and how this effects an LTS and its quality goals. Change always happens. However, reacting to change can be costly if not planned. Not reacting can result in a deterioration of quality objectives.

The aim of the framework is to allow instructors, course designers and platform support people to understand factors causing change and consider how this impacts on course, delivery and platform quality. It should aid these different stakeholders in designing, modelling and managing LTS. At the core of the framework is the concept of a feedback loop that captures quality attributes, analyses these and feeds backs a reaction plan into the system in terms of content, interface or platform changes. This concept is often called a controller in automated (adaptive) systems, but shall here also be applied to human-involved evolution. We look at concrete situations where these change forms occur and how the framework captures these situation and helps to manage change.

2 Use Case and Experience

In order to illustrate the framework, we refer to the Interactive Database Learning Environment (IDLE) [3]. IDLE targets university students. It provides lectures, tutorials and labs as different modes of learning. Multi-media features include audio lectures, animations to support tutorials and lab features including integrated software tools such as diagram editors. Additionally, self-assessment features such as multiple-choice questions in quizzes are provided. In a programming lab, solutions are automatically analysed and a recommender suggest suitable further exercises and links to background material, depending on the correctness of the solutions submitted.

There are similar adaptive LTS. We picked our system here for illustration as we can refer to first-hand experience. And our experience includes dramatic degradations up to the full loss of functionality, but with proactive change, quality can even be improved.

This system has been used for more than 10 years, during which change occurred in various forms:

- content has been changed to improve it, but also to adapt to changes in the context (new technologies, standards, etc.)
- the platform has been changed to integrate new features, to adjust to new organisational platforms (e.g., migration of the university to Moodle) [22].

The goals was always to either improve the quality for the learner to adapt to changes in the environment in order to maintain existing quality.

The changes are enacted automatically, in which case we talk about adaptation. The programming lab is an example. Some major platform changes are clearly long-term evolution, involving humans (instructors and software developers). We have also developed techniques that allow a semi-automation of e.g. content change. For the quizzes, we use an ontology that captures domain knowledge and auto-generate questions from there [7, 11]. We have developed an ontology change framework that allows consistent changes through a set of standard operators [20].

3   Change Framework

Our framework essentially, which is a reflection of experience with LTS management including our own, stipulates that change is either short-term automated adaptivity or more long-term and more manual evolution, see Fig. 1.

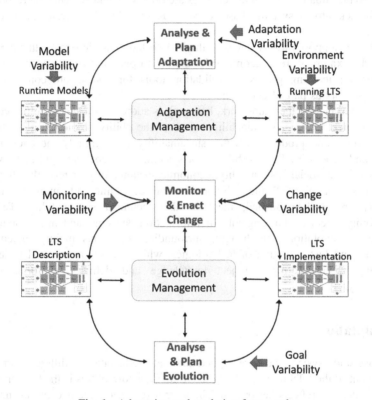

Fig. 1. Adaptation and evolution framework

- Evolution and adaptation cycles result in continuous change. Each of these two change forms is represented as a separate loop in the model.
- These continuous loops are structured in a feedback loop consisting of monitoring, situation analysis, planning and plan enactment stages.
- Stages are effected by variation points that signal what can actually change.
  That means that change happens and, through a monitoring mechanism that may be technical (a tool) or by observation by a human stakeholder, the varying concern is identified.
- Important are goals and goal changes and decision on how to evolve or adapt.
  Adaptation is concerned with the continuity of goals, i.e., making sure that the LTS satisfies the goals. Evolution deals typically with changing goals and the subsequent change of the LTS to reflect this.

The different parts of the loop are characterised by variability points that reflect a decision to be taken based on some uncertain situation [18]. The points are linked to changes in observed quality.

The loops are instantiations of what in adaptive systems is called the MAPE- K loop: **M**onitor the system under consideration, **A**nalyse the observed situation, **P**lan a response to the situation, e.g., if deficiencies are observed, and **E**xecute the response by feeding it back into the system – based on some **K**nowledge about system, environment and user.

Tools can support various stages of the MAPE loop and thus make this a relevant framework. Examples are a recommender engine to plan and enable adaptation, goal adaptation for learning processes, validation tools for courseware composition or change operators as part of evolution.

The importance of the framework, however, is addressing a sustainability concern. In an ecological context, sustainability refers to the ability of biological systems to remain diverse and productive. Thus, sustainability is essentially the endurance of systems and processes. Sustainability is a systemic concept that applies to various concerns such as social sustainability, economic sustainability or recently often environmental sustainability. While individual, social, economic and environmental sustainability are well-established, there is also technical sustainability. Technical sustainability refers to the longevity of information, systems, and infrastructure and their adequate evolution with changing surrounding conditions, mainly related to the continuous and fast evolution of technologies, which we see aggravated in learning technology where learners, subject knowledge and delivery platforms change continuously.

4   Adaptation

In our case study system, we have applied automated adaptation in different forms. The environment of the LTS induces changes. At the very core of this is the learner and the learner model that reflects her or him. The learner (or user) state is captures through a model containing general profile information and a reflection of the behaviour in the system in terms of what has been done (activity) and how successful this was (achievement of learning goals) [3]. Content can be adapted using the MAPE-K cycle (analyse, plan, enact). For instance, consider automated lab exercises and marking/assessment in the IDLE LTS [3].

– M: receive submitted learner solutions
– A: analyse the correctness of the solution
– P: derive a study recommendation
– E: create a new page with recommended exercises and background links

Another situation allowing for automated adaptation is technology-oriented related to device settings. Both content delivery, but also navigation (i.e., the learning process) can be adapted to technical settings. A very simple example is Web site responsiveness to the device it requests a page using HTML5 media queries, which can also be described in terms of MAPE-K (determine media/device type, analyse situation

(script/CSS) and enact the coded page settings through the browser). For the adaptive navigation, more advanced goal based process adaptation solutions exist [12]. General goal policies capture situations that would change the learning process. The goal policies can for instance captures device settings to adapt to these (cf., HTML5/CSS3 media queries).

5 Evolution

Evolution as a semi-automated process can happen in various ways. Firstly, *content* is changeable based on different variability conditions relating to the learner, the technical environment (user device) or the wider context. Secondly, the *platform* evolves by adding or changing features of the software platform.

An example for content change is content used in IDLE for the dynamic creation of content – although this applies to static delivery as well [6]. As we had a structured representation of content in IDLE, we applied in this case a semi-automated approach to content evolution. This instantiates the MAPE loop:

- monitor the correctness of content
- determine changes to content and analyse their impact (e.g., consistency)
- select change operator
- apply the selected operator

Another example is the integration of new features. This is an example of architectural evolution. As already apparent for the content evolution example, it is important that the important requirements, specifically concerning the learning objective remain satisfied. Validation instruments exist for the analysis and planning stages of the MAPE loop [9].

6 Discussion and Conclusions

we often adapt an LTS to the user, specifically the learner profile and behaviour in an LTS, but further change subjects and drivers should also be considered in a wider quality management solution – and whether they can be addressed automatically or manually.

We discussed a number of change techniques that we experienced with IDLE:

(i) a fully-automated content adaptation and recommendation system based on the user model (correctness of answers) or the environment (which device the learner uses), (ii) a semi-automated content evolution solution (which depending on the subject can change frequently) and (iii) (mostly) manual changes of the platform. The joint consideration of adaptation and change is beneficial as both are driven by quality-oriented goals that might either be addressed by adaptation or evolution.

They have been evaluated in terms of managing and maintaining LTS quality [3, 13, 17]. Adaptivity is proven to be beneficial [3]. Change needs to be addressed, e.g., as a system architecture concern in architecture evolution [2, 8, 16]. We have observed that without constant change, often quality degradation results [15].

Change occurs in LTS at content as well as platform level. Some changes are full automated and clearly part of the direct learner experience, others involve different stakeholders to change the system architecture every now and then. Targetted change management is important to maintain quality. In many environments, maintaining content is up to the instructor and no wider structures exist to manage LTS. The effort and costs associated to change are often prohibitive, resulting in a quality degradation if the change is not automated. Thus, building change in a structured way into a management plan for content and platform is crucial to maintain quality.

We argue that a holistic perspective is beneficial toward addressing a technical sustainability goal. Our change framework shows that in order to maintain learning goals, adaptation and evolution are linked, e.g., regarding content. In LTS, goals are often linked to the learner and learning experience. From a longterm perspective, also more technical, software-related goals and their change are important to maintain learning-oriented quality. For all stakeholders it is important that the feedback loop is considered. It asks to determine for instance the factors that impact on quality, identify and analyse their current situation and to create a change plan that can then be enacted.

We have illustrated a number of common change situations from our case study. In order to develop this change framework into a fully-fledged management solution for LTS [27], more solution patterns need to be collected in a more encompassing catalogue. We have been using change management methodologies for LTS for a while [17], for instance applied in the IDLE system development and maintenance. We have added here the evolution vs. adaptation distinction. More application to a variety of systems is necessary to further validate the empirical observations that have influence its definition so far. Another direction is the use of cloud computing for hosting and delivering LTS [24]. Many systems are built from scratch or migrated into the cloud [26]. Edge clouds are distributed architectures are also relevant as they allow to better integrate local devices and computation [25]. This also leads into considering any object or devices as a learning object. This context also requires further investigation. At least at the platform level, these allow better adaptivity, e.g., to manage the quality of experience.

However, the framework's main message is the importance of constant monitoring quality and react if necessary – be that automatically to user changes in adaptive systems or manually otherwise.

References

1. Gagne, R.M.: Instructional Technology: Foundations. Routledge, New York (2013)
2. Dawson, M., Al Saeed, I., Wright, J., Omar, M.: Technology enhanced learning with open source software for scientists and engineers. In: INTED2013 Proceedings, pp. 5583–5589 (2013)
3. Kenny, C., Pahl, C.: Intelligent and adaptive tutoring for active learning and training environments. Interact. Learn. Environ. J. **17**(2), 181–195 (2009)
4. Tseng, J.C., Chu, H.C., Hwang, G.J., Tsai, C.C.: Development of an adaptive learning system with two sources of personalization information. Comput. Educ. **51**(2), 776–786 (2008)

5. Brusilovsky, P., Karagiannidis, C., Sampson, D.: Layered evaluation of adaptive learning systems. Int. J. Continuing Eng. Educ. Life Long Learn. **14**(4–5), 402–421 (2004)
6. Javed, M., Abgaz, Y.M., Pahl, C.: A pattern-based framework of change operators for ontology evolution. In: Meersman, R., Herrero, P., Dillon, T. (eds.) OTM 2009. LNCS, vol. 5872, pp. 544–553. Springer, Heidelberg (2009). doi:10.1007/978-3-642-05290-3_68
7. Zablith, F., Antoniou, G., d'Aquin, M., Flouris, G., Kondylakis, H., Motta, E., Sabou, M.: Ontology evolution: a process-centric survey. Knowl. Eng. Rev. **30**(01), 45–75 (2015)
8. Pahl, C.: Architecture Solutions for e-Learning Systems. IGI Global, Hershey (2007)
9. Melia, M., Pahl, C.: Constraint-based validation of adaptive e-learning courseware. IEEE Trans. Learn. Technol. **2**(1), 37–49 (2009)
10. Murray, S., Ryan, J., Pahl, C.: A tool-mediated cognitive apprenticeship approach for a computer engineering course. In: 3rd IEEE International Conference on Advanced Learning Technologies (ICALT 2003), pp. 2–6 (2003)
11. Holohan, E., Melia, M., McMullen, D., Pahl, C.: The generation of e-learning exercise problems from subject ontologies. In: 6th International Conference on Advanced Learning Technologies (ICALT 2006), pp. 967–969 (2006)
12. Wang, M.X., Bandara, K.Y., Pahl, C.: Integrated constraint violation handling for dynamic service composition. In: IEEE International Conference on Services Computing (SCC 2009) (2009)
13. Lei, X., Pahl, C., Donnellan, D.: An evaluation technique for content interaction in web-based teaching and learning environments. In: 3rd IEEE International Conference on Advanced Learning Technologies, pp. 294–295 (2003)
14. Shi, L., Al Qudah, D., Qaffas, A., Cristea, Alexandra, I.: Topolor: a social personalized adaptive e-learning system. In: Carberry, S., Weibelzahl, S., Micarelli, A., Semeraro, G. (eds.) UMAP 2013. LNCS, vol. 7899, pp. 338–340. Springer, Heidelberg (2013). doi:10.1007/978-3-642-38844-6_32
15. Jamshidi, P., Ghafari, M., Aakash, A., Pahl, C.: A framework for classifying and comparing architecture-centric software evolution research. In: 17th European Conference on Software Maintenance and Reengineering (2013)
16. Ahmad, A., Jamshidi, P., Pahl, C.: Classification and comparison of architecture evolution reuse knowledge – a systematic review. J. Softw. Evol. Process **26**(7), 654–691 (2014)
17. Pahl, C.: The life and times of a learning technology system: the impact of change and evolution. Int. J. Web Based Learn. Teach. Technol. **8**(3), 24–41 (2013)
18. Weyns, D., Caporuscio, M., Vogel, B., Kurti, A.: Design for sustainability = runtime adaptation U evolution. In: Proceedings of the 1st International Workshop on Sustainable Architecture: Global Collaboration, Requirements, Analysis (SAGRA 2015), pp. 62:1–62:7 (2015)
19. Yang, T.C., Hwang, G.J., Yang, S.J.H.: Development of an adaptive learning system with multiple perspectives based on students? Learning styles and cognitive styles. Educ. Technol. Soc. **16**(4), 185–200 (2013)
20. Javed, M., Abgaz, Y.M., Pahl, C.: Ontology change management and identification of change patterns. J. Data Semant. **2**(2–3), 119–143 (2013)
21. Roca, J.C., Chiu, C.M., Martinez, F.J.: Understanding e-learning continuance intention: an extension of the technology acceptance model. Int. J. Hum. Comput. Stud. **64**(8), 683–696 (2006)
22. Raible, J., Bennett, L., Jowallah, R.: Factors influencing the selection of an adaptive learning technology within university and K-12. FDLA J. **1**(1), 1 (2014)
23. Cody-Allen, E., Kishore, R.: An extension of the UTAUT model with e-quality, trust, and satisfaction constructs. In: Proceedings of the 2006 ACM SIGMIS CPR Conference on Computer Personnel Research, pp. 82–89. ACM (2006)

24. Pahl, C., Xiong, H.: Migration to PaaS clouds – migration process and architectural concerns. In: 7th International Symposium on the Maintenance and Evolution of Service-Oriented and Cloud-Based Systems (MESOCA 2013). IEEE (2013)
25. Pahl, C., Lee, B.: Containers and clusters for edge cloud architectures – a technology review. In: 3rd International Conference on Future Internet of Things and Cloud (FiCloud 2015) (2015)
26. Pahl, C.: Containerization and the PaaS cloud. IEEE Cloud Comput. 2(3), 24–31 (2015)
27. Tseng, S.S., Su, J.M., Hwang, G.J., Hwang, G.H., Tsai, C.C., Tsai, C.J.: An object-oriented course framework for developing adaptive learning systems. Educ. Technol. Soc. 11(2), 171–191 (2008)

Smart, Innovative Teaching Supported by Decision Software – Case Study in Educational Institution

Hana Mohelska[⊠], Marcela Sokolova, and Vaclav Zubr

Faculty of Informatics and Management,
The University of Hradec Kralove, Hradec Kralove, Czech Republic
{hana.mohelska,marcela.sokolova,vaclav.zubr}@uhk.cz

Abstract. This article aims to describe the use of software Expert Choice and Criterium DecisionPlus in order to support the multi-criteria decision in education and to evaluate the added value of this innovation. Both decision-making software, solves the same problem of the case study. Firstly, the decision-making problem is de-fined, as well as the relevant criteria and possible alternative solutions. Based on the decision-making process and the output decisions are both software evaluated in terms of selected criteria. Students in the role of customers verify the quality of the two software tools and from which they elect a better alternative. Further-more, according to marketing metrics of Customer Perceived Value (CPV) is determined a value perceived by customers/students as the difference between the evaluation of the benefits, supply costs and perceived alternatives.

Keywords: Multi-criteria decision making · Decision support system software · Expert choice · Criterium DecisionPlus · Customer perceived value

1 Introduction

Tasks related to multi-criteria decision making are characterized by the selection process that is used to reach the ultimate decision, i.e. the choice between the specified finite set of n variants that are rated on the basis of m criteria. The objective is to select the best rated (optimal) variant according to the established criteria [6].

Variants (alternatives) are "specific decision options, the subject of the actual decision-making process; they are feasible and are not logical nonsense". [9] They must be selected with regard to their attainability and appropriateness in solving the given decision-making problem. The variants are then evaluated according to various criteria.

A criterion is "a viewpoint for evaluating (rating, valuation) variants, and it can be either qualitative or quantitative". [9] The criteria must be independent of each other and should cover all aspects of the selection. However, their number must not be so large that you lose clarity of the problem.

If the criteria-based rating of variants is quantified, the data can be organized into criterial matrix Y, represented by Fig. 1. Matrix columns correspond to the criteria

© Springer International Publishing AG 2017
T.-T. Wu et al. (Eds.): SETE 2016, LNCS 10108, pp. 143–152, 2017.
DOI: 10.1007/978-3-319-52836-6_17

while matrix rows correspond to the evaluated variants. Element yij expresses an evaluation of the i-th variant according to the j-th criterion. If all the criteria are not quantitative, then we have a criterion table. This table contains both numeric and verbal evaluations of variants [9].

$$Y = \begin{array}{c} \\ a_1 \\ a_2 \\ \ldots \\ a_m \end{array} \begin{array}{cccc} f_1 & f_2 & \ldots & f_n \\ \begin{pmatrix} y_{11} & y_{12} & \ldots & y_{1n} \\ y_{21} & y_{22} & \ldots & y_{2n} \\ \ldots & \ldots & \ldots & \ldots \\ y_{m1} & y_{m2} & \ldots & y_{mn} \end{pmatrix} \end{array}$$

Fig. 1. Criterial matrix Y [9]

Multi-criteria decision-making can be classified into two groups according to how the set of feasible variants is specified. [6] Tasks of multi-criteria evaluation of variants are referred to if the set of feasible variants is specified as a definitive list and the variants are evaluated according to individual criteria. On the other hand, tasks of multi-criteria programming (optimization) are referred to if the set of feasible variants is defined as a set of conditions that feasible decision alternatives must meet. In this case, the set of variants includes an infinite number of elements expressed by defining conditions and "rating individual variants occurs through individual test functions". [9] According to Brožová, special types of models include DEA (Data Envelopment Analysis) models and multi-criteria project management models [1].

The demandingness of decision-making process considerably increases with an increasing number of alternatives and criteria. Multi-criteria decision making can often exceed the decision maker's cognitive and rational (intellectual) limits. In such cases, it is desirable to use multi-criteria decision support software that brings a certain level of structuralization into unstructured or semi-structured decision problems, which enables us to effectively consider an otherwise too large number of alternatives and criteria, provides outputs calculated using a tested methodology and allows us to perform sensitivity analyses.

Software support for multi-criteria decision making is offered by Decision Support Systems. For their calculations, these systems use diverse computing methodologies, such as the Saaty's method of quantitative pairwise comparison or the Analytic Hierarchy Process method. Decision Support Systems can be used to select the business model of the core services and identify the implications for the business model of all the actors involved in the network [2].

A central question for the decision maker is which method of the broad spectrum of known or new methods and which software tool to support multi-criteria decision making should be used.

2 Methodology

The methodology of the paper is based on a literature overview; the methodology of the research is based on a survey. The paper stems from the theoretical bases described in the chapter entitled Introduction. It describes selected Decision Support Systems, hereinafter referred to as DSSs, which are process-based on the above literature sources with regard to the practical applicability of these systems in supporting decision making.

The case study was formulated with respect to its applicability in other sections that immediately follow and that to a large extend depend on it. The method of quantitative pairwise comparison by Saaty is used to determine the weights of the criteria. Partial rating of variants with respect to the criteria and the overall ranking was done based on the Analytic Hierarchy Process method, hereinafter referred to as AHP. The reason for choosing these methods was their use in selected software tools for supporting decisions on which the application part is based.

The case study was also used in Expert Choice and Criterium DecisionPlus tools, which were chosen due to their accessibility to the authors. Uniform data were entered into both pieces of software. In the case study were involved 121 master's degree students of the Faculty of Informatics and Management studying at University of Hradec Kralove. The survey was conducted in the two month period.

Students (acting the role of customers) tested the quality of both software tools, from which they chose the better alternative. Further, according to marketing metrics named CPV, was examined the value perceived by these students. This value was calculated as the difference between the evaluation of all benefits, supply costs and perceived alternatives.

3 Multi-criteria Decision-Making Under Certainty

When the decision maker has reliable information about the future state of the world, then he/she is making decisions under conditions of certainty [9].

3.1 Creation of Variants

One of the most important phases of decision problem solving is the creation of variants. The quality of created variants affects the quality of the final solution. Methods for creating variants can be divided into intuitive methods and systematic-analytical methods [3].

3.2 Criteria Selection

In determining criteria for evaluating individual variants, it is particularly important to consider objectives that the decision maker wants to achieve when solving the decision problem, "…because the evaluation criteria are mainly used for determining the degree of fulfilling these objectives through selected variants" [3].

In addition to general principles, the criteria should meet specific requirements that ensure their applicability in the next phase of the decision-making process. These requirements are: completeness, operationality, non-redundancy (non-overlapping), minimum range, independence [3, 5].

3.3 Methods for Determining the Weights of Criteria

In most methods of multi-criteria decision making, it is necessary to distinguish different criteria in terms of their significance. For this purpose, we can use numerical expression by employing the weights of criteria (sometimes also called significance coefficients), where the following applies: the more significant the criterion, the greater its weight. The weight of criterion Kj is indicated as vj, j = 1, 2, ..., n, where n is the number of all considered criteria. For comparing the weights of the criteria set by different methods, they are expressed in standard values (wj) which are calculated according to the relationship in Fig. 2. "Generally, the weight of any criterion is a value from the interval $\langle 0; 1 \rangle$ that reflects the relative importance of the respective criterion in comparison with other criteria". [9] Their sum is then equal to one [4].

$$w_j = \frac{v_j}{\sum_{k=1}^{n} v_k}, j = 1, 2, \dots, n$$

Fig. 2. A calculation of standard values for criteria weights w_j

3.4 Methods of Evaluating the Variants

Methods for making a multi-criteria evaluation, as well as simple methods used to determine the value of variants "pursue a certain additivation of criteria, not through converting into a common monetary criterion ... but through transforming the values of criteria into a dimensionless additive quantity" [3] known as the value, benefit, utility or rating of variants. This is useful for supporting such decision making processes by structuring and quantifying the preferences of decision makers or stakeholders [8].

4 Software Support for Multi-criteria Decision Making

There are two basic methods of software support for managerial decision making, and both are aimed at supporting senior management: [10]

- **MIS (Management Information System):** storage, sorting, updating and retrieving of information;
- **DSS (Decision Support Systems):** interactive applications of mathematical models.

4.1 DSS

DSS is an interactive, flexible and adaptable computer information system, specially developed to support solutions to non-structured management problems and improve the decision-making process. According to Plevný, DSS applications consist of the following subsystems: data management subsystems; model management subsystems; user interface subsystems; knowledge base subsystems [7].

The paper focuses on two software products for providing decision support, Expert Choice and Criterium DecisionPlus.

5 Case Study

5.1 Case Study Assignment

A certain e-shop that offers a wide range of goods wants to expand its selection of delivery services to include the ability to view and pick up the goods at the company's distribution center in order to acquire new customers, increase its market share and improve competitiveness in the sector. The company's responsible manager decided that the location of this distribution site would be judged according to the five criteria listed in Table 1.

Table 1. Criteria for evaluating the selection of the distribution site

	Criterion	Unit
K_1	Distance of the distribution site from warehouses (expressed as the average transport time from warehouses to the distribution site during rush hour)	Minutes
K_2	Availability of the distribution site for clients (expressed as a percentage of clients located at distances of less than a one- hour drive away)	%
K_3	Condition and equipment of the distribution site (necessity for its renovation, Internet and telephone connections, etc.	-
K_4	Area of the distribution site	m^2
K_5	Monthly rent	Thousands of CZK

(Source: self-created)

Most of the criteria are expressed numerically (K1, K2, K4, K5); only one criterion is qualitative (K3). To measure it, it is possible to use a three-level scale, where level A corresponds to the best condition and equipment at the distribution site, level B characterizes a partial fulfilment of the criterion and level C is used for distribution sites in poor condition or without the required equipment.

Five variants (denoted as M1, M2, M3, M4 and M5) entered the final assessment; they form a set of location variants. The characteristics of the set of variants for selecting the distribution site are presented in Table 2.

Table 2. The characteristics of the set of variants for selecting the distribution site

Criterion		Variant				
Name	Unit	M_1	M_2	M_3	M_4	M_5
K_1	Minutes	50	20	15	25	35
K_2	%	45	80	75	80	70
K_3	-	A	B	C	A	C
K_4	m^2	40	40	30	50	25
K_5	Thousands of CZK	16	11.5	10	15	13

(Source: self-created)

5.2 Determining the Criteria Weights

Criteria weights are determined according to Saaty's method of quantitative pairwise comparison and the point scale recommended by Saaty, with descriptors from Table 2 augmented by intermediate stages according to the recommendations [4].

The ranking of criteria corresponds to their significance. Values of Saaty's matrix of relative importances in Table 3 therefore correspond to the preferences of the decision maker. A partial rating of the variants with respect to the criteria in the given case study is based on Saaty's method (AHP) from the perspective of one expert.

Table 3. Determining criteria weights (Saaty's matrix)

Criterion	K_1	K_2	K_3	K_4	K_5	Geometrical mean	Weights
K_1	1	2	4	5	6	2.99	**0.41**
K_2	1/2	1	5	7	8	2.69	**0.37**
K_3	1/4	1/5	1	5	3	0.94	**0.13**
K_4	1/5	1/7	1/5	1	2	0.41	**0.06**
K_5	1/6	1/8	1/3	1/2	1	0.32	**0.04**
Sum:						7.35	1.00

(Source: self-created based on the methodology by [3, 9])

6 Results of the Survey

6.1 Overall Rating (The Ranking of Variants)

The overall rating of variants and thus their ranking pursuant to the AHP method was obtained as a weighted sum of partial ratings of variants with respect to individual criteria when using the criteria weights from Table 3.

Table 4 shows that the best rating pursuant to Saaty's AHP method belongs to the third variant M3; therefore, this method is recommended as the best variant for establishing the e-shop distribution site according to the given criteria.

Table 4. The overall rating of variants and their ranking when evaluating Saaty's matrix pursuant to a scale of 1–9

Variant	A partial rating with respect to the criteria					Sum	Ranking
	K_1	K_2	K_3	K_4	K_5		
M_1	0.0344	0.0311	0.3467	0.1886	0.0354	**0.0819**	**5.**
M_2	0.2463	0.3271	0.2065	0.1886	0.2712	**0.2686**	**2.**
M_3	0.4509	0.1937	0.0609	0.0684	0.4627	**0.2861**	**1.**
M_4	0.1669	0.3271	0.2850	0.5163	0.0765	**0.2560**	**3.**
M_5	0.1015	0.1211	0.1009	0.0380	0.1542	**0.1074**	**4.**
Criteria weights	0.4069	0.3653	0.1284	0.0556	0.0438		

(Source: self-created following [3])

6.2 Rating Criteria

In next sections, the chosen DSSs will be compared and assessed based on the following criteria: Options to enter criteria and alternatives; The spectrum of available methods; Output quality; Intuitiveness and user friendliness; Language; Price; Interoperability with other software programs.

7 Results of the Survey

7.1 The Solution in Expert Choice

The case study was solved using Expert Choice 2000. In addition to the afore-mentioned and described options, Expert Choice also offers many other options that will not be further discussed here due to the limited scope of this paper.

Determining Criteria Weights. Criteria weights can be entered after right-clicking over the goal and selecting the "Pairwise Assessement" option. Expert Choice then prompts the user to enter his/her preferences (Compare the relative preference with respect to: Goal: Selection of the distribution site) using a pairwise comparison of individual criteria, i.e. completion of the area above the main diagonal of Saaty's matrix.

Partial Rating of Variants with Respect to the Criteria. After obtaining the criteria weights, it is possible to start expressing preferences of variants with respect to individual criteria. This can be done by right-clicking over criterion K1 and selecting the "Pairwise Assessement" option, which redirects the user to a pairwise evaluation of variants with respect to criterion K1.

The Overall Rating of Variants and Their Ranking. The overall rating of alternatives can now be accessed via the top menu by selecting the "Synthesize" and then "With Respect to Goal" options.

When setting "Ideal mode", the software does not normalize the weights of individual criteria, but instead assigns the whole weight to the best alternative. In contrast, "Distributive mode" distributes the weights of individual criteria at a certain level. If a standardization of weights is desirable, the selection of "Distributive mode" may lead to another ranking of variants. While "Ideal mode" recommends variant M2 as the best one, "Distributive mode" offers variant M3. Expert Choice also offers a representation of details ranked by criteria or alternatives.

A Sensitivity Analysis. Expert Choice offers five options for performing sensitivity analyses by selecting "Sensitivity-Graphs" in the top menu and by choosing from among "Performance", "Dynamic", "Gradient", "Head-to-Head" and "2D".

The best evaluated variant is M3, which has the best partial evaluation for the most important K1 criterion and similarly also for criterion K5.

7.2   The Solution Using Criterium DecisionPlus

The case study was further solved using Criterium DecisionPlus 3.0 (CDP).

Model Creation. By default, CDP enters alternatives and criteria immediately after being started.

It is interesting that this software is specifically designed for brainstorming. First, "Goal" in the oval must be replaced with our goal. Then we can enter variants (M1 to M5) that can simply be written in a row in the right column under "Alternatives".

The window for entering criteria is adapted for brainstorming. Individual criteria (K1 to K5) can simply be inscribed in the white space around the goal.

Determining Criteria Weights. Before the actual model evaluation, within the top menu in the "Model" and "Technique-Alternatives" tabs, it is necessary to change the method from S.M.A.R.T. to AHP, which was used in Expert Choice and in the case study. This is due to the comparability of outputs from both pieces of software.

Criteria weights K1 to K5 can be set after indicating the goal and clicking on "Rate". The window named "AHP Rating – Direct Method" will then appear. For changing the method to pairwise comparisons, select "Method" and "Full Pairwise" in the window's upper menu.

Parting rating the variants with respect to criterion K1 can be done after clicking on K1 in the diagram or after its selection and clicking on "Rate" in the top menu.

The Overall Rating of Variants and Their Ranking. The overall rating of variants can be accessed via "Scores" in the top menu after opening the "AHP Decision Scores" window.

Ranking from the CDP output is consistent with that according to Expert Choice as well as according to the case study.

Sensitivity Analysis. CDP offers five options for performing a sensitivity analysis under "Analysis" in the top menu.

The "Contributions by Criteria" graph of the sensitivity analysis is very interesting. Columns represent the overall rating of alternatives and their colours quantify the contributions of individual criteria to the given result. Contributions of these criteria (K1 to K5) can be also visualized in separate graphs upon their selection from the "Criterion Name" drop down menu.

8   Discussion

Customer Perceived Value shows the difference between the evaluation of all benefits, supply costs and perceived alternatives. The study confirmed that from the majority of students (covered by 64.5%) preferred Expert Choice. In absolute terms, it means that 78 students (from the total number 121 students) chose the Expert Choice software. The results of the comparison between the two similar tools, which were implemented within the innovation of the educational process, are presented in the following text.

8.1   The Process of Creating a Model

The processes used to save and enter a file name as well as specifying the goal in the two pieces of software do not significantly differ.

For entering variants in EC, it is necessary to click on the "Add Alternative" icon; for entering criteria, the respective action must also first be activated by right-clicking on the goal.

Regarding the amount of entered alternatives and criteria, Expert Choice allows a virtually unlimited number, even in the student version. By contrast, the student version of Criterium DecisionPlus is limited to 20 elements, and this number includes the goal, criteria and alternatives. CDP refers to this limitation during leaving the brainstorming stage and changing over to the hierarchical model. The spectrum of methods and process of entering preferences.

Expert Choice provides three different interfaces to specify preferences, allowing the user to work with scales, horizontal coloured columns, or directly enter numeric values. Throughout the time of expressing preferences, the user can view Saaty's matrix. The outcome of the decision-making process is therefore immediately apparent without any necessity for calling the output.

In comparison with the EC software, which uses only the AHP method to determine the weights, the main menu of Criterium DecisionPlus enables the user to also select the S.M.A.R.T. method.

8.2   The Quality of Outputs

In their basic form, the outputs from both decision support tools include an overall rating of individual variants and a horizontal bar graph.

Both pieces of software enable ranking of alternatives pursuant to their names or the overall rating.

8.3   Sensitivity Analysis Options

EC provides five sensitivity analysis tools switchable among each other. CDP also offers five options of sensitivity analysis; only four of them, however, are available for the pairwise comparison method.

9   Conclusion

9.1   Intuitiveness and User Friendliness

CDP seems to be more user-friendly during the phase of creating the model. It offers a simple environment for brainstorming in which the decision maker can take bearings easily and intuitively even without any previous experience with this software.

On the other hand, EC software seems to be more user-friendly when expressing the decision maker's preferences and performing the model valuation.

In terms of outputs, the two compared decision support tools appear similar. Individual sensitivity analysis graphs are similar in many aspects. Sensitivity graphs in CDP are surrounded by various options for their adaptation and adjustment, while the controls for the graphs in EC are "hidden" in the top menu.

Acknowledgement. The paper was written with the support of the specific project grant "Determinants affecting job satisfaction" granted by the University of Hradec Králové, Czech Republic.

References

1. Brožová, H., Houska, M., Šubrt, T.: Modely pro vícekriteriální rozhodování, 1st edn., p. 172. Credit, Praha (2003)
2. Daas, D., Hurkmans, T., Overbeek, S., Bouwman, H.: Developing a decision support system for business model design. Electron. Markets **23**, 251–265 (2013)
3. Fotr, J., Švecová, L.: Manažerské rozhodování: postupy, metody a nástroje, 2nd edn., p. 474. Ekopress, Praha (2010)
4. Friebelová, J.: Vícekriteriální rozhodování za jistoty. Tvorba a softwarová podpora projektů (2009). http://www2.ef.jcu.cz/ ~ jfrieb/tspp/data/teorie/Vicekritko.pdf. Accessed 17 Aug 2015
5. Ho, W., Xu, X., Dey, P.K.: Multi-criteria decision making approaches for supplier evaluation and selection: a literature review. Eur. J. Oper. Res. **202**, 16–24 (2010)
6. Křupka, J., Kašparová, M., Máchová, R.: Rozhodovací procesy. Univerzita Pardubice, Pardubice (2012)
7. Plevný, M., Žižka, M.: Modelování a optimalizace v manažerském rozhodování, 2nd edn. Západočeská univerzita v Plzni, Plzeň (2010)
8. Reichert, P., Schuwirth, N., Langhans, S.: Constructing, evaluating and visualizing value and utility functions for decision support. Environ. Model Softw. **46**, 283–291 (2013)
9. Šubrt, T.: Ekonomicko-matematické metody, p. 351. Vydavatelství a nakladatelství Aleš Čeněk, Plzeň (2011)
10. Weiser, J.: Manažerské rozhodování. ISŠ Mladá Boleslav (2015). http://issmb.cz/DUM/V. 2%201/V.2%201.23.pdf. Accessed 17 Aug 2015

Computer Adaptive Learning Platform for Calculus

Shing-Lin Chang and Shu-Chen Cheng[✉]

Department of Computer Science and Information Engineering,
Southern Taiwan University of Science and Technology, Tainan, Taiwan
{slchang,kittyc}@stust.edu.tw

Abstract. We proposed the idea of establishing computer adaptive learning platform for Calculus. Students can do self-testing using the system any time after learning. Computerized adaptive testing (CAT) is used in the assessment of tests in this learning platform. The system gives students adaptive testing items to collect and to examine students' learning situation. After analyzing students' learning portfolio, the system sends the information to the teacher so that he realize the learning situations for every student at any time. This learning platform will be a great help when students' learning Calculus.

Keywords: Adaptive testing · Computer adaptive learning · Personalized learning

1 Introduction

In recent years, the use of smart phones and tablet computers have pervaded all levels of society, so developing auxiliary tutor platform applications on these devices has become very important and popular. As a teacher, knowing how to use these tools to improve students' effective learning, and interest and to give customized counseling is not only a responsibility but a duty. This is especially true for difficult subjects such as calculus. During the students' learning process, some abstract and difficult concepts may confuse some students, and sometimes students can't find the crux of the problem, and thus the teacher cannot give proper adaptive counseling. Thanks to science and technology, we can use a computer to establish a set of computerized adaptive calculus learning platforms, which can not only test what students have learned, but also give individual diagnosis according to students' learning conditions. In addition, it can give timely and appropriate data for assessing papers and study aids, including multi-media materials, visual materials, etc. This not only increases the effectiveness of student learning but also reduces the counseling load of teachers.

Purdue University in America has been implementing the course signal system [1], in which a competence bonus is at the core of enhancing student learning effectiveness. Purdue University provides an early warning mechanism of learning for college students, which is the course signal. Its operational concept is as follows: after every two to three week (set by the teacher) course, according to the information collected by online quizzes or teacher assessment carried out in the classroom, each student will receive a report that will clearly inform them of the professional knowledge that they

© Springer International Publishing AG 2017
T.-T. Wu et al. (Eds.): SETE 2016, LNCS 10108, pp. 153–162, 2017.
DOI: 10.1007/978-3-319-52836-6_18

failed to master. Thus students must seek counseling with teaching assistants to proceed to the next stage of learning. The teaching assistants should clearly know of specific students in need of counseling, and when the two sides meet, they will aim to clarify the relevant concepts in order to improve the effectiveness of counseling. The intelligent computerized adaptive learning platform we are going to establish uses computers to assist teaching, which not only meets the requirements of the course signal system, but will also provide students with adaptive teaching materials and exams, thus allowing students to do self-determination exercises in order to receive a competence bonus.

This paper mainly discusses how to establish the degree of difficulty of items and the students' testing performance in the general teaching method for those items.

2 Literature Reviews

2.1 Item Response Theory (IRT)

In this paper, we will use the "Rasch" model proposed by G. Rasch [2]:

$$p(\theta) = \frac{e^{\theta-b}}{1+e^{\theta-b}}$$

Curves drawn on the basis of these models are Item Characteristic Curves, or ICCs, in the sense which they describe the relationship between "the possibility of successfully answering a question" and "students' ability θ". Figure 1 is an example of the Rasch model, in which the students' ability θ can be from $-\infty$ to ∞, and the corresponding $p(\theta)$ is from 0 to 1. However, the value θ of is generally from -3 to 3, and when $p(\theta) = 0.5$ and $\theta = b$, it shows that the probability of students answering questions correctly can reach 50% when they reach a level of competence. Therefore, when the ICC curve moves to the right, it shows that the students should be more likely to answer the question correctly; that is to say, the value of b should be bigger. Therefore, the value of b can be used to determine the difficulty level of questions and to compare students' correctness rates.

2.2 Cognitive Diagnosis Model

After the United States passed the *No Child Left Behind Act* in 2001, psychometric and educational assessment experts have paid attention to cognitive diagnostic assessments (CDA). The main purpose of these assessments is to diagnose whether every skill or latent attribute is mastered by the test takers, and to allow teachers to provide adaptive remedial teaching or suggested learning directions based on the results of the survey. Therefore, the "cognitive diagnosis model" (CDM), of which CDA is a part, becomes very important, as the results of CDAs provided by the CDM can let teachers know whether learners are mastered in every skill or latent attribute. The CDM differs from IRT by providing only a broad potential competence and uses every vector $\alpha_i = \langle \alpha_{i1}, \alpha_{i2}, \cdots, \alpha_{iK} \rangle$ constituted by a cognitive attribute to show whether the student is

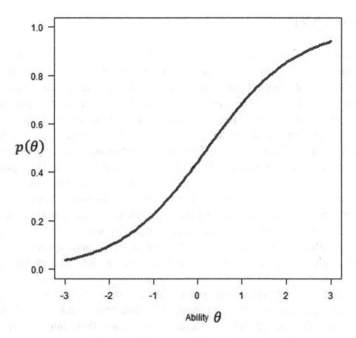

Fig. 1. ICC curve of Rasch model

mastered in that attribute, in which $\alpha_{ik} = 1$ means the student has mastered the cognitive attribute of k, otherwise it is 0. Implementation of most CDMs need the construction of Q-matrix [3], which is set by the teacher. The Q-matrix can be obtained from the cognitive attribute of each question, and after students are finished answering, cognitive concepts that students haven't master can be simply diagnosed through Q-matrix. The $Q = \left[q_{jk}\right]_{JK'}$ J is the number of items, and K is the number of attributes, in which $q_{jk} = 1$ and item j needs the cognitive attribute k, otherwise it will be 0. The most common models of CDMs are the DINA model (deterministic inputs; noisy "and" gate model) [4–6], the NIDA model (noisy inputs; deterministic "and" gate model) [4], G-DINA model [7], DINO model [8] and HO-DINA model [9], etc.

2.3 Question-Selecting Methods of Computerized Adaptive Testing

Due to the development of computer science and technology, computerized adaptive testing (CAT) has been widely used in the assessment of tests. Compared with traditional papers and pencil tests, CAT can accurately assess one or more of a student's areas of potential competence by asking fewer questions, so high efficiency is a major advantage of CAT. In order to more effectively apply and manage student competence, the cognitive diagnosis computerized adaptive testing (CD-CAT), developed by combining CAT and CDM, has become a new test mode and a very important research issue [10].

3   Research Method

The computerized adaptive calculus learning platform aims mainly at calculus courses. Its design elements are: (1) to be practical: it will establish a network platform for long-term use, so that students can truly enhance their knowledge and ability by using the platform, particularly for adaptive learning, and students can freely select a chapter or unit to learn. (2) to be easy to use: it will not be too troublesome for students. When presenting relevant content data, it will not delay or wait too long, which would be bad for impatient learners. There is also no limit on time or location, meaning that students can learn and take tests at any time. (3) to be wise: the system has an intelligent agents system function to keep abreast of student learning conditions. The system will pass information to the teacher or teaching assistants and students so that tutors and students can understand the current situation, and the counselor can counsel students timely and adaptively. The system may also make recommendations to students, and when learners have difficulty in some courses, the platform will give appropriate learning materials through intelligent agents. The development architecture of the system is shown in Fig. 2.

Here we will only introduce some parts of the general tests. We will first establish unit cognitive attributes by means of course content, then make the unit tests and empirically determine the difficulty of questions and collect them into the item bank of general tests, in which these questions have segments with the adaptive tests that the students practice by themselves. Finally, the teachers can make tests based on the course chapters or the content and the number of questions selected by the unit test. After the test, we can use the Rasch model, which shows students' answering

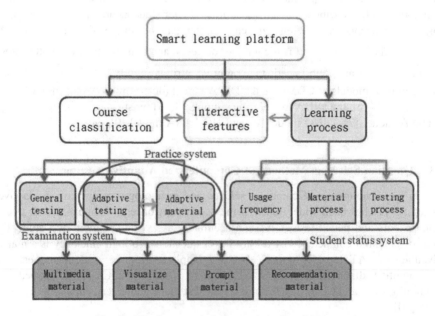

Fig. 2. The framework for smart learning platform

Table 1. Unit 3-2: Cognitive Operations of Derivative Computing

Attributes	Operational competence
1	Be able to do limit operation of e
2	Be able to do the derivative of logarithmic functions
3	Be able to do the derivative of exponential functions
4	Be able to do the limit operation of trigonometric functions
5	Be able to do the derivative of trigonometric functions
6	Be able to do the derivative of inverse trigonometric functions
7	Be able to do the derivative of hyperbolic and inverse hyperbolic functions
8	Realize higher order derivative and computing

conditions and teachers' cognition levels, to determine the difficulty of the questions. Take the example of unit 3-2, where we can see that in Table 1, the cognitive ability to be tested in the unit is 8 and a there is a total of 60 questions. 108 freshmen in the Information Engineering Department were surveyed, who were divided into four groups of about 27 persons. Each student had to complete 15 questions in one hour.

We designed the test questions in the following manner:

I3-2-1. If $f(x) = x^2|x|$, determine which of the following is wrong.

$$(1)f'(x) = \begin{cases} 3x^2, x \geq 0 \\ -3x^2, x < 0 \end{cases} \quad (2)f''(x) = \begin{cases} 6x, x \geq 0 \\ -6x, x < 0 \end{cases}$$

$$(3)f'''(x) = \begin{cases} 6, x \geq 0 \\ -6, x < 0 \end{cases} \quad (4)f^{(4)}(x) = 0, x \neq 0$$

Answer: 3 Attribute: 8 Difficulty: 2

I3-2-2. Find $f'(2)$ if $f(x) = xe^x$. (1) $2e^2$ (2) e^2 (3) $3e^2$ (4) $4e$
Answer: 3 Attribute: 3 Difficulty: 1

I3-2-3. Find $f'(2)$ if $f(x) = sin(x^3 + 2)$.
(1) sin 10 (2) 12 sin 10 (3) -12 cos 10 (4) 12 cos 10
Answer: 4 Attribute: 5 Difficulty: 1

I3-2-8. If $y = \sinh^{-1} 3x$,, find $\frac{dy}{dx}\big|_{x=1}$. (1) $-\frac{3}{\sqrt{10}}$ (2) $\frac{1}{\sqrt{10}}$ (3) $\frac{3}{\sqrt{10}}$ (4) $\frac{3}{\sqrt{8}}$
Answer: 3 Attribute: 7 Difficulty: 1

I3-2-9. Find y'' if $x^3 - y^3 = 1$. (1) $-\frac{2x}{y^5}$ (2) $\frac{2x}{y^5}$ (3) $-\frac{x^2}{y^2}$ (4) $\frac{x^2}{y^2}$
Answer: 1 Attribute: 8 Difficulty: 3

I3-2-10. Find f' (1) if $f(x) = e^{2x} \ln(x^3 + 1)$.
(1) $(2\ln 2 + 3)e^2$ (2) $(2\ln 2 + \frac{3}{2})e^2$ (3) e^2 (4) $(2\ln 2 + \frac{1}{2})e^2$
Answer: 2 Attribute: 2、3 Difficulty: 2

In each of the questions, we will give the corresponding cognitive attributes and degree of difficulty according to the type of question, and divide the difficulty into three levels. Difficulty 1 means basic questions that can be answered using equations. Difficulty 2 represents moderate questions that may have two or more concepts or computing elements. Difficulty 3 represents questions with higher difficulty.

Students with a prior competence score of 30% should be able to answer the questions correctly. Of course, the issue that we would like to explore is whether the cognitive difficulty of teachers is consistent with the answering results of students. We consider a correct percentage of 0–30% on all tests as a difficulty level of 3, indicating that the problem is more difficult by student results; 30% to 70% as moderate with a difficulty level of 2; and greater than 70% as easier with a difficulty level of 1. If a teacher thinks the degree of difficulty of one test is 3, but the students' results show 2 or 1, then the teachers may underestimate the competence of their students. A converse scenario would imply that teachers overestimate the competence of their students. If the difference between the two is 2, it shows a particular overestimation or underestimation that the difficulty level shall be adjusted.

In addition, we also used the Rasch model to compare students' correct rates, as shown in Fig. 3, ◆ shows the degree of difficulty of each question that students answered correctly, and there are only 6 questions with difficulty level of 1, with most being more difficult. ■ is used by the Rasch model to determine the value of item difficulty, and the observed value can be distinguished by student answer difficulty. A difficulty level of 1, b value is about -3 to -1; a difficulty level of 2, b value is about -1 to 1; and a difficulty level of 3, b value is about 1 to 3. The Rasch model allows us to objectively adjust the degree of difficulty, and it can be seen from Fig. 3 that unit 3-2 is more difficult.

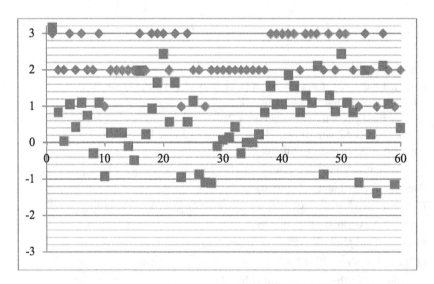

Fig. 3. To compare Rasch model and students' answer

We can also simultaneously estimate the value of θ the comprehensive ability of students via the Rasch model, but we will use matrix Q to determine whether the students mastered each cognitive attribute. The cognitive attributes of each group of 15

Table 2. Q-matrix for Unit 3-2

Item	Attribute							
3-2-	1	2	3	4	5	6	7	8
1	0	0	0	0	0	0	0	1
2	0	0	1	0	0	0	0	0
3	0	0	0	0	1	0	0	0
8	0	0	0	0	0	0	1	0
9	0	0	0	0	0	0	0	1
10	0	1	1	0	0	0	0	0
19	0	0	0	0	0	1	0	0
20	0	0	0	0	1	0	0	1
21	1	0	0	0	0	0	0	0
27	0	0	0	0	0	0	1	0
28	0	0	0	0	1	0	0	1
29	0	0	0	1	0	1	0	0
55	0	0	0	0	0	0	0	1
56	0	0	1	0	0	0	0	1
57	0	1	1	0	0	0	0	0

questions constitute a matrix formed by 0 or 1, in which 1 denotes questions containing cognitive attributes, and 0 means none. Take a group as an example, as shown in Q-matrix of 15×8 in Table 2. If a student answers items 2,3,9,19,21,28,55,56, and 57 correctly, then we use vector X to show that the value of the number of correct answers is 1, otherwise it is 0, and we can get X = [0 1 1 0 1 0 1 0 1 0 1 0 1 1 1]. And make Y = XQ, then Y = [1 1 3 0 2 1 0 4]; that is, learner answers several items of each cognitive attribute correctly. Each item contains one or more cognitive attributes, so we add each column of Q-matrix to obtain S = [1 2 4 1 3 2 2 6], that is, the number of times each cognitive attributes appear. Each corresponding to the elements of division of I and S: $Y./S = [1 \quad 1/2 \quad 3/4 \quad 0 \quad 2/3 \quad 1/2 \quad 0 \quad 2/3] = P$, that is, the probability of the value $P = [p_1 \quad p_2 \quad \cdots \quad p_8]$ of the learner answered correctly in each cognitive attribute. The higher the value p_i is, the more the students have mastered the cognitive attribute, and vice visa. For example, $p_1 = 1$, attribute 1 (Be able to do limit operations of e), then the student is mastered. However, $p_4 = p_7 = 0$, attribute 4 (Be able to do the limit operation of trigonometric functions), and attribute 7 (Be able to do the derivative of hyperbolic and inverse hyperbolic functions), then the student is not mastered, and needs to be receive adaptive tutoring or be introduced to learning materials.

4   Experimental Results

Currently we have completed the design on six modules, as shown in Table 3, according to student's correctness rates to distinguish the difficulty levels, with a total of 245 questions. Difficulty levels 3, 2, and 1 accounted for 12%, 41%, and 47% of the results respectively, with less difficult questions. Table 4 found that the average amount of students answering correctly was 45%, indicating that the subject as a whole should be rated as moderate. While assessing the degree of difficulty of the subject, we found that the teacher's assessment of each unit was usually lower than the students' measure of difficulty, representing that teachers overestimate the competence of students, with especially overvalued averages of about 7%, and one problem in particular was underestimated. Therefore, it is necessary to make adjustments on these topics in order to correspond to the degree of difficulty. On the whole, these questions are currently too difficult for the students. We can take the first test scores as a reference, because the first unit is the basic function, which is better able to reflect the original mathematical ability of students. There are three groups which are divided according to the students' abilities, in which the first 30% is the lower academic ability group, the 30% following is the high academic ability group, and the rest is the middle academic ability group. In our current assessment of teaching, we use the one-way ANOVA and Scheffe multiple

Table 3. Number of items and difficult levels in every unit

Unit	No. of skills	No. of items	Difficulty 3	Difficulty 2	Difficulty 1
1-1 Cognitive operations of essential functions	7	43	4	14	25
2-1 Cognitive operations of limit and continuity	8	50	9	20	21
3-1 Cognitive operations of basic concept of derivative	8	50	4	24	22
3-2 Cognitive operations of derivative operation	8	60	7	29	24
4-1 Cognitive operations of the first and second derivative test	8	22	2	8	12
4-2 Cognitive operations of applications of differentiation	8	20	4	5	11

Table 4. To compare correctness rate and special overestimated rate

Unit	Average correctness rate	Assessment difficulty by teacher	Difficulty by students answer	Special over-estimated rate	Need to adjust
1-1	54%	1.51	1.77	0.02	1
2-1	49%	1.76	2.04	0.08	4
3-1	50%	1.64	1.98	0.1	4
3-2	39%	1.72	2.28	0.08	6
4-1	45%	1.55	2.05	0	0
4-2	39%	1.65	2.25	0.15	3

Table 5. Group of students' ability

Test unit	Low ability group	Middle ability group	High ability group	Significant
1-1	27.92	55.35	76.77	0.000
2-1	36.04	47.67	58.49	0.000
3-1	36.00	49.31	64.89	0.000
3-2	22.71	34.09	47.10	0.000
4-1 + 4-2	28.79	40.57	46.32	0.003

comparison procedures to test the difference between the three groups. We found significant differences in the three groups of the quiz, with $p - value \approx 0.00$ showing that the current teaching method with general testing is the same as the competence performance of the three groups (Table 5).

5 Conclusion

When constructing computerized adaptive tests, we must first be able to work out the most appropriate difficulty level for each test item. In particular, we need artificial intelligence to compute the difficulty level automatically. It is not suitable for the teacher to do it manually for it not only wastes lots of labor, but also our research data shows that the level of difficulty determined by teachers is often higher than the actual cognitive load of the students tested. Therefore, the degree of difficulty of the questions should be determined by an automated system, and the results should be determined by theoretical questions in order to review the appropriateness of the degree of difficulty. Our current study of computerized adaptive Calculus learning platforms is still in progress, and when we construct complete adaptive materials, test questions and platform design, we believe they will help improve students' learning a lot. In the future, the Rasch model can be used to obtain a more accurate value for the degree of difficulty. Also, we can use the technology to build other courses adaptive learning platform, for example engineering mathematics, discrete mathematics, probability and statistics, and so on.

References

1. Purdue University's Course Signals (2015). http://www.itap.purdue.edu/studio/signals/
2. Rasch, G.: Probabilistic models for some intelligence and attainment tests. (Copenhagen, Danish Institute for Educational Research), expanded edition (1980) with foreword and afterword. B.D. Wright. The University of Chicago Press, Chicago (1960/1980)
3. Tatsuoka, K.K.: A probabilistic model for diagnosing misconceptions in the pattern classification approach. J. Educ. Stat. **10**, 55–73 (1985)
4. Junker, B.W., Sijtsma, K.: Cognitive assessment models with few assumptions, and connections with nonparametric item response theory. Appl. Psychol. Meas. **25**, 258–272 (2001)

5. de la Torre, J.: DINA model and parameter estimation: a didactic. J. Educ. Behav. Stat. **34**, 115–130 (2009)
6. von Davier, M.: The DINA model as a constrained general diagnostic model: two variants of a model equivalency. Br. J. Math. Stat. Psychol. **67**(1), 49–71 (2014)
7. de la Torre, J.: The generalized DINA model framework. Psychometrika **76**(2), 179–199 (2011)
8. Templin, J., Henson, R.: Measurement of psychological disorders using cognitive diagnosis models. Psychol. Methods **11**, 287–305 (2006)
9. de la Torre, J., Douglas, J.: Higher-order latent trait models for cognitive diagnosis. Psychometrika **69**(3), 333–353 (2004)
10. Huebner: Cognitive diagnostic computer adaptive assessments. J. Educ. Meas. **46**(3), 293–313 (2010)

Emerging Technologies of Pedagogical Issues

A Pathway into Computational Thinking in Primary Schools

Aleksandra Djurdjevic-Pahl[1], Claus Pahl[2(✉)], Ilenia Fronza[2],
and Nabil El Ioini[2]

[1] Independent Researcher and Instructor, Bolzano, Italy
[2] Free University of Bozen-Bolzano, Bolzano, Italy
claus.pahl@unibz.it

Abstract. Computing is a key skill that cannot be underestimated in todays digitalised world. Computing abilities enable humans of all ages and backgrounds to understand, create and manage computerised environments. Consequently, computing education becomes an important concern. For instance, the national curriculum in the UK states that a high-quality computing education equips pupils to use computational thinking and creativity to understand and change the world. Our aim is to support the early stages of computing education in primary schools. Our proposal is a pathway into Computing Education (CE) through Computational Thinking (CT), starting off from traditional mathematics curricula for primary schools. This is a first step, not involving concrete computer programming or ICT management, but develops the key skills of computational thinking such as logical reasoning or abstraction.

Keywords: Computational thinking · Mathematics · Primary schools

1 Introduction

Computing is a key skill that has a significant value in todays digitalised world. Computing abilities enable people of all ages and backgrounds to understand, create and manage computerised environments and the digital content in them. Consequently, computing education becomes a critical concern for our societies. The national curriculum in the UK states that "a high-quality computing education equips pupils to use computational thinking and creativity to understand and change the world"[1]. Computational thinking (CT) brings problem solving, design and understanding together in a way meaningful to computing. CT research can be considered at a formative stage. CT essentially started in 2006 after J. Wing's seminal article [23]. Two adopted definitions of CT are [1, 23]:

- a conceptual framework and a vocabulary for K-12 educators [14],
- an operational definition identifying concepts, practices and perspectives [4].

---

[1] https://www.gov.uk/government/publications/national-curriculum-in-england-computing-programmes-of-study/.

© Springer International Publishing AG 2017
T.-T. Wu et al. (Eds.): SETE 2016, LNCS 10108, pp. 165–175, 2017.
DOI: 10.1007/978-3-319-52836-6_19

More recently, more practical concerns such as the further development, promotion or assessment of CT are investigated. Still, there is no agreement regarding accepted CT techniques. What is still left unclear is the actual attainment of students in CT-based eduction, i.e., what do we expect students to know after participating in CT education [12] and how to assess this.

According to Wing, CT can be explained as"the thought processes involved in formulating a problem and expressing its solution(s) in such a way that a computer – human or machine – can effectively carry out". Thus, CT does not focus only on problem solving, but also on problem formulation. Our aim is to support the early stages of computing thinking with problem analysis, formulation and solving in primary schools [3, 5, 8, 9, 11, 20, 21]. Our proposal is a pathway into computing education through CT, starting off from traditional mathematics curricula for primary schools. Our approach is a first step that does not involve concrete computer programming or ICT management, but develops the key skills of computational thinking such as logical reasoning or abstraction.

2 Computational Thinking

Computational Thinking (CT) involves solving problems, designing systems, and understanding human behavior, by drawing on concepts fundamental to Computer Science [23]. The Computer Science Teachers Association (CSTA) and the International Society for Technology in Education (ISTE) suggested an operational definition of CT that provides a framework that aims at K-12 educators [14]. In 2012, an operational definition with three key dimensions includes [4].

- concepts (such as sequences, loops, and conditionals),
- practices (such as testing and reusing),
- perspectives (such as questioning and expressing).

Teachers and students should use an appropriate vocabulary to describe problems and solutions [2]. Students should learn to accept wrong solutions as part of a path for a positive result. Moreover, they should be encouraged to work as a team and to use decomposition, abstraction, negotiations, and consensus building. It is also important to stimulate interest in computational concerns.

Recent work on CT focused on tools to support CT [13]. Graphical programming environments are probably the most commonly used solution, since they allow an early experience of design and construction in a computing context, while avoiding syntax problems. Some recent research looks at CT assessment, i.e., how to evaluate the effectiveness of a CT curriculum by measuring what students have effectively learned [17, 22].

Some sample CT strategies and tools to teach and assess CT will now be described. Visual programming languages allow creating programs by manipulating graphical elements; the notation is usually based on diagrams or blocks to be joined between them [6]. Animation programs, for instance, show some aspects of program execution in an explicit form (e.g., the call stack) to illustrate the concept of execution. Moreover, visual simulation of programs allows students to learn how to read code, understand the flow in it and then trace it.

The state-of-the-art in CT research reveals shortcomings that would benefit from further mainly empirical research [13]:

- Grade and age-appropriate curricula for CT still need to be designed or improved [10]. Most of the studies have been conducted in an undergraduate context. Thus, more empirical work in the K-12 context is needed to understand the problems faced during the first computing experiences. We look at primary schools here, which have been neglected.
- Emphasis has been put on coding so far [7]. This has led instructors to focus on a small aspect of CT, thus neglecting its broader aims. We approach the subject from a mathematics baseline, also drawing in a variety of other areas.

While at secondary school level, coding can form part of the curriculum, at primary school level this opportunity is more restricted. While some programming tools like Scratch Junior exist (https://www.scratchjr.org/), more emphasis should be put here on the foundations that coding is based on. This is reflected in the community by an agreed set of CT capabilities. CT aims at capabilities that help with using computers to solve or model problems [1, 24], but can actually be learned without programming. Key capabilities are (see Fig. 1 for a visualisation): *algorithms*: making steps and rules; *logic and logical reasoning*: predicting and analysing; *decomposition*: breaking down into parts; *patterns*: spotting and using similarities; *abstraction*: removing unnecessary detail; *evaluation*: making judgements.

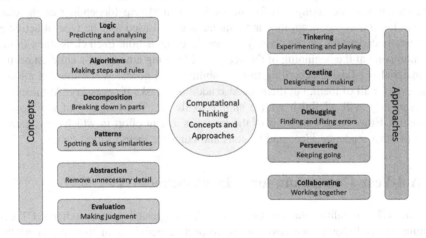

Fig. 1. CT Principles – concepts and approaches.

We show here a pathway into CT that builds these capabilities in a nonprogramming environment. This specifically provides an outline for 4-year curriculum for primary school children from year 1 onwards.

3 Thinking Outside the Box

We describe here a 4-year curriculum for primary school children that is based on our experience of developing and teaching this at a primary school. The material has been taught as a 1-hour per week extra-curricular activity called "Thinking Outside the Box" – a name that is meant to capture the idea of (computational) thinking in the broadest possible sense.

Thinking Outside the Box (TOtB) is a series of classes of mathematics grounded computational thinking activities designed to make pupils think. Generally, the activities are complementary to those being taught in traditional classroom activities and their aim is to help children develop logical thinking, acquire analytical and problem solving skills. The approach is however different.

In traditional primary school education, children often tend to develop a compartmentalized view of mathematics from a very early age. At the same time, they tend to develop a dislike for maths and logic. To avoid something like that happening as much as possible, we propose to use a much wider approach to maths and computational thinking through problem solving based on a dedicated set of materials. The tasks all focus on CT capabilities, but the wider context is in the area of art, language or science as much as is in the area of maths and computing, thus stressing the multi-disciplinary impact and relevance of CT.

A key aim is that children have to deduce themselves in an exploratory and discursive way, often as a group, what their tasks are, rather than being told what to do. For children who are taking part for the second or third year (depending on the class they are in), this is a concept they are familiar with and used to. The type of activities vary greatly depending on the class (year) and its composition. Each class starts from a common point at the beginning of the year and if layering amongst the children occurs, the material is adjusted according to their abilities and needs. While there is a basic, joint level for all of them, but there are also additional tasks if necessary. At the end of the year, they will all finish with a similar skills set. The majority of the work is individual. However, the analysis of the results is a joint effort in which they learn to listen to other students' ideas and reasons and compare them to their own.

4 A 4-Year Curriculum for Primary School CT

The core CT capabilities that are targeted by the suggested primary schools CT curriculum are as follows. We also list the respective activities in thematic areas that address them, cf. Fig. 2:

- abstraction (through arithmetic and spatial coordination)
- logical reasoning (through cryptography, and applied arts, language and nature-based problems)
- patterns (through geometry/symmetry and art)
- decomposition (through spatial coordination)
- algorithms (through cryptography, arithmetic and geometric puzzles)
- evaluation, which is one of the CT capabilities, is a cross-cutting concern.

	Arithmetic	Geometry	Cryptography	Spacial Coordination	Applied Problems
Abstraction	X			X	
Logic			X		X
Patterns		X			
Decomposition				X	
Algorithms	X	X	X		
Evaluation	X	X	X	X	X

Fig. 2. Concerns Mapping: Capabilities (abstraction etc.) addressed through Activities (arithmetric etc.).

While not involving computing per se, the aim is to introduce the children to problems that can be solved through computers and providing them with the core skills to program these computers. Thus, a further key objective is to draw on problems from a range of contexts: arts, languages, nature, maps and spaces.

This aims to bring the idea across that problems from a range of disciplines that can be solved through computational methods. At this early stage of a child's education, this broadness of application domains is more important than the coding/programming that is often seen as the core of CT.

We have associated CT capabilities with subjects suitable to teach them, see Fig. 2. These include standard tools like tangrams or pentaminos. We provide concrete activities around these subjects that involve tools (manipulative in Sect. 4.1) or other forms of exercises (non-manipulative in Sect. 4.2).

4.1   Manipulative Activities

Manipulative work aims to support logical thinking and spatial awareness (including eye-hand coordination). For the latter, objects from one-dimensional to three-dimensional (1D, 2D, 3D) are involved. We now outline the tools we used.

- 1D and 2D shapes: Tangrams are used with additionally created stencils, aiming at the analysis of space. Pentaminos are used, firstly, slotting given shapes into rectangles and, secondly, slotting free chosen shapes into any form. Tantrix^{TM} is a puzzle-based table geometry and strategy game.
- 3D shapes: Soma cubes are used in two ways: firstly, for beginners, to build 3D shapes based on 3D graphical presentations using given set of pieces and, secondly, for advanced learners, to build 3D shape based on 2D graphical presentation using given set of pieces. Katamino^{TM} and 3D Pentamino are used to enhance the 2D skills. This could involve building from 2D plans showing front/back/left/right/top aspects of the model. This can be done using any blocks including interlocking ones.
- LÜK^{TM} is a multi-purpose learning system (from mathematical to language to science and arts) that provides a self-learning approach with selfassessment and correction.

4.2 Non-manipulative Activities

Non-manipulative work is about exploring constitutional parts of CT – pattern, abstractions, decomposition – using, firstly, different application contexts: (i) art (painitngs/drawings by Kandinsky, Klee, Escher, etc.) and (ii) language (looking at the syntax and semantics) Secondly, more traditional technical subjects are used in the following way. (i) Science and humanities: geography for spatial awareness/map reading and coordinate finding; history to reason about time travel; astronomy with problems based on constellations or light speed; biology. (ii) Cryptography: using code crackers to explore the relationship between numbers, letters (or letter shapes and symbols) and ciphers. (iii) Technical drawing: including symmetry work (left, right, split left/right in the same picture (1 line)/up, down (1 line)/under angle (14 lines); drawing from perspective based on an existing drawing; scaling down or up based on existing drawings).

5 Curriculum by Year

We can map the core manipulative and non-manipulative activities onto a 4-year primary school curriculum. The proposal here is meant to complement a normal curriculum, in particular ongoing maths activities. It is aimed to expose pupils to principles of CT towards educating children to become computationally literate and competent, but also demonstrating topics from a multi-disciplinary context that CT is an ingredient of many other non-maths or non-computing subjects. We detail this now for each year (joining similar 3rd and 4th year).

1st Year activities. First year activities are divided into four areas to explore constitutional parts of maths such as pattern, abstractions, decomposition using:

- The **arithmetic** part includes work on different number puzzles and simple code crackers. The aim of both is to make the children feel comfortable with numbers, move them away from horizontal or vertical addition/subtraction, and to put numbers into a wider context, connecting them with language (letters, words) and art (shapes).
- **Logic reasoning** includes work on sequencing, pattern recognition and pattern prediction and covers art, language and nature. This part of the childrens activity includes often work with manipulative puzzles such as pentaminos and tangrams as well as the use of LÜK.
- **Spatial awareness**, basic map reading and coordinate finding.
- **Geometry** consists of one-line symmetry exercises. The idea behind these exercises is to train eye–hand coordination, fine motor movement and the use of rulers as part of a wider geometry and space concern.

2nd Year activities. Second year activities focus on four areas in particular: arithmetic, comprehension, logic reasoning and symmetry, because these are important for a better understanding of problems.

- **Arithmetic** work includes arithmetic puzzles in different forms as often as possible and combines them with logic reasoning and comprehension exercises where the children have to interpret the text and express it through numbers or the other way around. Introduction to different calculation strategies becomes another important aspect of their arithmetic work at this time.
- **Logic reasoning** includes further work on more complex sequencing, pattern recognition and pattern prediction and covers again art, language and nature. The children also continue to work with manipulative puzzles (pentaminos and tangrams) as well as LÜK.
- **Symmetry**. Image reproduction work consists from two parts: one-line symmetry exercises (which includes left-right, up-down and split (one-line) symmetry) and finishing partially fragmented/degraded image when only a rough outline is given (connecting dots to make an image) based on a smaller version of the original shown in the picture. The aim of these exercises was to work on their concentration, analysis of space and precision. This part of the childrens' work allows us to understand better how they see things around them and how they process the acquired visual information. In a group setting, this aids negotiation and consensus building.

3rd Year and 4th Year. As children in 3rd and 4th year are more advanced, their curricula differ less. The work with third and fourth year is done through a series of problem solving questions as it is a flexible way to explore a variety of topics. Using this platform, the classes explored numbers, patterns, space and change, but again in a wide context of language and art. In addition to this, the children were introduced to cryptography. This aims at exploring pattern, abstractions, decomposition:

- **Logic reasoning** includes further work with tangrams, pentaminos. The children are also introduced to the soma cube. Tasks include building 3D shapes based on 3D graphical presentations using a given set of pieces (in 3rd year) to build 3D shapes based on 2D graphical presentation using a given set of pieces (in 4th year). Another part focuses on cyphers. The children get encrypted tasks which they had to decipher. The clues to deciphering were either embedded in graphical presentations that accompanied the problem or were given at the end of the encrypted text.
- **Geometry** work includes four-line symmetry, finishing partially fragmented or degraded images when only an outline is given (connecting dots to make an image) based on a smaller version of the original shown in the picture.

6 Observations and Lessons Learned

These courses have been taught over a four-year period as extra-curricular activities in a primary school. One group per year, therefore four groups per academic school year. The average number of students per group was 12. The program was developed for children ranging from 6–9 years of age. The ratio of girls to boys on average was close to 50/50. Generally, classes were attended by children of all abilities, both groups with strong mathematical capabilities and those being weaker in the maths classes. One group has passed through all four stages during this process. The aim here was to foster an enjoyment in acquiring CT capabilities, without a pressure for good performance or even any awareness of being monitored and/or assessed in this process. The parents' reason to enrol their children ranged from initiating an interest and developing skills in the topic to supporting already existing interest.

The setting also left out an important aspect of education, which is the assessment. As this was taught to children who participated voluntarily and as this was not part of the standard curriculum (and thus not to be graded), no formal evaluation was carried out. Thus, attainment evaluation was not part of the course settings, but of course this might be a concern for courses fully integrated into a schools curriculum. However, CT assessment in general, beyond primary schools, remains a very immature area that requires more research, as we already noted in Sect. 2.

We looked, however, at the overall experience with factors such as engagement and joyfulness as the key evaluation criterion. Increasing confidence is another aspect. We also comment on progress and attainment evaluation.

The **childrens perception** is positive. All children liked the classes and found them great for the following reasons: (i) TOtB brought out a playful side of mathematical and computational topics by exploring patterns and numbers through pictures, letters, words and shapes for the youngest children, (ii) TOtB brought out a sense of adventure in trying to solve different tasks for the older children, (iii) they learnt that there is often more than one way to solve a problem and that by trying different approaches they can find quicker way to solve tasks. This is despite the fact that the classes did create intentional challenges:

- They (as a group) had to conclude themselves what the tasks were about, i.e., they were not told what to do.
- In order to solve tasks, they had to look/search for a pattern/(s) that would not be immediately obvious.
- They had to find connections between different things they would normally not connect, e.g. numbers, letters, shapes, etc.
- They had to be precise/accurate in what they do in order to solve the tasks.

In order to elicit some progress results, we asked for the **parents' perception** informally. The parents were very positive about the general impact of the course. A general observation they had was that children became more focused and quicker in solving tasks. This is confirmed by the **instructor's observations**:

- The children got increasingly more focused in what they were doing and were more quickly able to identify the approach and solve the problem.
- They were able to understand problems better by organising the information into smaller pieces/blocks.
- By understanding smaller blocks, they were able to understand better how these were interconnected into one whole.

Other observations relate to **long-term progress**. In each year/class, about 80% of children would continue with the classes in the following year.

- During any year, their general awareness increased, which resulted in noticeable progress in the childrens ability to understand the tasks given. As a consequence, they were able to solve the tasks quicker and more accurately.
- In particular first class pupils became more confident with not only the numerical aspect of maths, but also the language part as they were constantly encouraged to bring the two together. Working at this intersection of domains from the very beginning has been crucial for the progress they made.
- The strongest effect was observed in children who took part for all 4 years, as the classes were a medium-to-long-term project where children are systematically encouraged to think, ask questions and question what they find, analyse and make connections amongst the things that might not be at first glance related to one another and use what they find to solve problems.

Our wide approach and the variety of problems have made mathematical and computational concerns more interesting and less dry.

A limitation that applies to CT in general is the lack of reliable assessment methods. Specifically in the context of children progress and attainment are difficult to measure. Due to the lack of specifically non-intrusive methods, we have restrained from evaluating these concerns more formally than the qualitative assessment presented. Not using formal assessment also made monitoring systematically and adjusting material to the needs of the children more difficult.

7   Conclusions

Our main observation from our experience is that CT can be started from an early stage, beginning with the first year in primary school. As maths is an element in generally all curricula, we complement and expand on maths on a pathway into computational knowledge and skills towards computing education.

We see this as a pathway towards more computing (and in this sense programming) activities, but we left out early exposure to computers in order to deepen the core CT capabilities first. The emphasis has been on the core CT capabilities from algorithmic thinking and logic to evaluation, make available through a mix of arithmetric, geometry and space related, cryptographic and language related and applied problems.

It has also been an important objective to demonstrate that CT can be applied to non-maths and non-computing subjects, thus emphasising the relevance of CT beyond computing as a technical subject.

Assessment has already been discussed as an issue that needs further investigation [16]. Another direction is an online support system that allows children to interact and that adapts to their abilities [15, 18, 19].

References

1. Aho, A.V.: Computation and computational thinking. Comput. J. **55**(7), 832–835 (2012)
2. Barr, V., Stephenson, C.: Bringing computational thinking to K-12: what is Involved and what is the role of the computer science education community? ACM Inroads **2**(1), 48–54 (2011)
3. Berry, M.: Computational thinking in primary schools (2014). http://milesberry.net/03/computational-thinking-in-primaryschools/
4. Brennan, K., Resnick, M.: New frameworks for studying and assessing the development of computational thinking. In: 2012 Annual Meeting of the American Educational Research Association (AERA12), pp. 1–25 (2012)
5. Computing at School: Computational Thinking (2016). http://community.computingatschool.org.uk/resources/252
6. Charlton, P.: Computational thinking and computer science in schools (2012). https://www.lkldev.ioe.ac.uk/lklinnovation/wp-content/uploads/2013/01/Time-to-ReLoadWhatTheResearchSaysBriefing27April2012.pdf
7. Crow, D.: Why every child should learn to code (2014). http://www.theguardian.com/technology/2014/feb/07/
8. Computer Science Teachers Association – CSTA Computational Thinking Task Force: Computational Thinking Resources (2016). http://csta.acm.org/Curriculum/sub/CompThinking.html
9. Curzon, P., Dorling, M., Ng, T., Selby, C., Woollard, J.: Developing computational thinking in the classroom: a framework. in: computing at school (2014)
10. Fronza, I., El Ioini, N., Corral, L.: Students want to create apps: leveraging computational thinking to teach mobile software development. In: 16th Annual Conference on Information Technology Education (SIGITE 2015), pp. 21–26 (2015)
11. Google for education: exploring computational thinking (2016). www.google.com/edu/computational-thinking/index.html
12. Grover, S.: Systems of Assessments for deeper learning of Computational Thinking in K-12. In: Annual Meeting American Educational Research Association, pp. 1–9 (2015)
13. Grover, S., Pea, R.: Computational thinking in K-12: a review of the state of the field. Educ. Res. **42**(1), 38–43 (2013)
14. ISTE and CSTA: Computational Thinking – Teacher Resources (2nd edn.) (2011). http://csta.acm.org/Curriculum/sub/CompThinking.html
15. Kenny, C., Pahl, C.: Intelligent and adaptive tutoring for active learning and training environments. Interact. Learn. Environ. **17**(2), 181–195 (2009)
16. Holohan, E., Melia, M., McMullen, D., Pahl, C.: The generation of e-learning exercise problems from subject ontologies. In: 6th International Conference on Advanced Learning Technologies ICALT 2006, pp. 967–969 (2006)
17. Koh, K.H., Basawapatna, A., Bennett, V., Repenning, A.: Towards the automatic recognition of computational thinking for adaptive visual language learning. In: Symposium on Visual Languages and Human-Centric Computing (2010)
18. Pahl, C., Kenny, C.: Interactive correction and recommendation for computer language learning and training. IEEE Trans. Knowl. Data Eng. **21**(6), 854–866 (2009)
19. Murray, S., Ryan, J., Pahl, C.: A tool-mediated cognitive apprenticeship approach for a computer engineering course. In: 3rd IEEE International Conference on Advanced Learning Technologies ICALT 2003, pp. 2–6 (2003)

20. Mooney, A., Duffin, J., Naughton, T., Monahan, R., Power, J., Maguire, P.: PACT: an initiative to introduce computational thinking to second-level education in Ireland. In: International Conference on Engaging Pedagogy (2014)
21. Settle, A., Franke, B., Hansen, R., Spaltro, F., Jurisson, C., Rennert-May, C., Wildeman, B.: Infusing computational thinking into the middle and high-school curriculum. In: Conference on Innovation and Technology in Computer Science Education (2012)
22. Werner, L., Denner, J., Campe, S., Kawamoto, D.C.: The fairy performance assessment: measuring computational thinking in middle school. In: 43rd ACM Technical Symposium on Computer Science Education (SIGCSE12). 215–220 (2012)
23. Wing, J.M.: Computational Thinking. Comm. ACM **49**, 3 (2006)
24. Wing, J.M.: Computational thinking benefits society (2014). http://socialissues.cs.toronto.edu

Development and Evaluation of STEM Based Instructional Design: An Example of Quadcopter Course

Chih-Hung Lai and Chih-Ming Chu[✉]

Department of Computer Science and Information Engineering,
National Dong-Hwa University, Hualien 97401, Taiwan
richrichlai@gmail.com, cmchu817@gmail.com

Abstract. STEM is an acronym that refers to the academic disciplines of science, technology, engineering and mathematics. The term is typically used in schools to improve competitiveness in science and technology development. The purpose of this study is to develop instructional design based on 6E's STEM and investigates its impact on participants' knowledge. The participants were 48 junior high school students, and a quasi-experimental research design was employed. The course is about concept instruction and the assembly of quadcopters. The content of online discussion was analyzed through the quantitative content analysis and the lag sequential analysis. The experimental results indicated that the STEM based instructional design not only enhanced students' learning achievement, but also improved their discussion quality.

Keywords: STEM based instruction · 6E model · Quadcopter

1 Introduction

1.1 Background and Motivation

The quadcopter has been a very popular technology product. It was small size, light weight make it portable and convenient for personal use and commercial applications in aerial photography, movie shooting, field monitoring, terrain exploration and other missions. Most of the commercially available quadcopter were ready to go out of the box and can render the finished product from its existing features. Customized products and modifications were rare. The quadcopter instruction was lacking instructional design. The students' learning was fragmented and unable to create knowledge link. However, STEM was method of integrated learn, it seems to solve this problem.

In this study, students were allowed to purchase their own quadcopter materials and components to complete the hardware assembly. Students develop software modules for joystick and computer control. Students write interface to understand the principles of the actual control of quadcopter, and they complete a variety of practical applications. The quadcopter design principles involve science (fluid dynamics), technology (microprocessor systems, programming, electronics, automation), engineering (engineering design process, organization) and mathematics (calculus, measurements, angles, geometry, computing). These concepts were relevant and very suitable as

© Springer International Publishing AG 2017
T.-T. Wu et al. (Eds.): SETE 2016, LNCS 10108, pp. 176–191, 2017.
DOI: 10.1007/978-3-319-52836-6_20

STEM instructional design unit topics. STEM education ties the four topics of Science, Technology, Engineering and Mathematics into a single integrated educational experience. STEM aims to link all subject-related courses so that theory and implementation were combined to increase students' interest, and thus be able to obtain and use knowledge from real world situations and applications [1]. STEM aims to help teachers to teach and students to learn. Obstacles that students face with standard classroom instruction system that only describes scientific knowledge and theory based learning include: difficulty understanding the relevance, no application of coursework, preventing lateral thinking, and hindering cross-subject links. Providing students with math and opportunities for technological applications [2]. Sadaf, Newby and Ertmer [3] proposed to integrate concepts related to scientific principles and mathematical theory of learning with improved results and products. Despite STEM education's growing appeal, designing and conducting effective STEM courses was the reason why this study raises important points.

The idea behind STEM course instruction was the fusion of scientific inquiry, technologies, engineering and exploration of different disciplines of mathematical analysis. It uses science and technology to understand the structure and function of the natural world, and so it depends on current technologies and recent science developments and modern field tests to prove the laws, theories and principles of science [4, 5]. STEM provides a mathematical language of communication between science and technology. This integration of engineering technology and scientific discovery ultimately was how products needed by society were designed [6]. Over the last seven years, the US has reformed "innovation and instruction" with the Educate to Innovate initiatives, which has begun to set foundations of innovation and invention. The reformed programs emphasize the link between academic knowledge and practical technology through the integration of STEM focused applications with hands-on or project-based learning. This enables students to understand the tools and how to apply appropriate skills to solve real-world problems [7]. The Becker and Park [8] study found that with the emphasis on integration of STEM disciplines in instruction method, only mathematics or physics, as compared to other subjects, aroused students' interest in learning. Kirk Olson, vice president of TrendSights at Horizon Media has said "Science and math have always been core subjects. But the addition of technology and engineering makes STEM education feel current and critical." The US government and others have made a number of development-related investments in STEM education, the most ambitious and high-profile project belongs to STEM teacher training program, the STEM Master teacher Corps. This program was launched in 2012, and was expected to carefully select, recruit, train, and counsel 100,000 of the best domestic STEM teachers by 2021. It was hoped these STEM "seed" teachers, will improve students' self-management, systems analysis, problem solving, self-development and other interactive and communication skills [9, 10]. Also, according to the Bybee [11] study, in order to improve the country's competitiveness, the poor performance by US students in mathematics and science must be addressed by joining science, technology and engineering studies. In October 2015, US "Horizon Media" published the results of a web survey from a 3,000 person online research community in which 86% of those replying to the poll said knowing how to use a computer was "just as important as knowing how to read and write." 73% agreed that "in the future, all the best jobs will require knowledge of computer coding languages." 65% agreed that "most students would benefit more from learning a computer coding language than a foreign language." In the same year the US Congress passed the "STEM Education Act, 2015", the future of America's schools added programming language to the curriculum, so that it was no longer "mysterious" geek or "otaku" network technology. The Lindberg, Pinelli, and Batterson [12] concluded that the use of STEM instruction will enhance eight key students' abilities:

(1) Problem-solving and critical thinking skills.
(2) Reasoning, assessment and analysis.
(3) A closer relationship between high-level math and science, and the real world.
(4) Demonstrate the value of teamwork, cooperation and collaboration.
(5) Construction of language arts and communication skills.
(6) Improve the technological literacy.
(7) Foster creativity, ingenuity and innovation.
(8) Training organization, planning and time management skills.

The above shows that the world of education in advanced countries was changing as the legislation needed to make improvements and inject funds to cultivate and expand STEM education instructional human resources. In the face of this trend, we should proceed with the transformation of curriculum and in the instructional design of the STEM courses to enhance students' learning ability [13].

In the 1980s, the American Biological Sciences Curriculum Study (BSCS) developed the BSCS 5E Instruction Model for instruction. It included Engage, Explore, Explain, Elaborate, and Evaluate (E5). The instruction model has been widely discussed and applied [8, 10]. In the field of science and technology and engineering education, Barry [15] proposed the 6E instruction mode (description below). In this study, the 6E instruction model was used as the quadcopter STEM instructional reference design. Moreover, engineering design process in STEM instructional activities can be divided into nine steps: (1) Identify and define problem, (2) Research the need or problem, (3) Develop possible solutions, (4) Select the best possible solution, (5) Construct a prototype, (6) Test and evaluate the solution, (7) Communicate the solution, (8) Redesign, (9) Completion [16].

(1) Engage: To stimulate students curiosity, interest and investment. By questioning the students, the teachers connect the students prior experiences and knowledge to the key points of the unit. The questions hint to the design process and the overview of operating techniques. Questions also help to assess the ability of students and decide on instructional strategies. Students first outline of the main concepts of the unit, confirming the content, setting learning objectives, main points, materials and equipment.
(2) Explore: To provide opportunities for students to construct a learning experience. Teachers begin modeling, a concept introduced as COPA (Constraints, Optimization, Predictive and Analysis), and designing review process to guide students to use interrogation method of thinking and encouraging students to participate in discussions and group work. Students join the group discussions,

with modeling and predictive analysis (based on group information, project criteria and restrictions).

(3) Explain: Students explain what they have learned, and what can be improved. Teachers explain the system concept, design a review process, and through a cross-examination they guide students to do more in-depth analysis. They guide the discussion to clarify the concept of loss and error. They make sure that students learn concepts within a broader context. Students apply concepts related to the system, test principles and theories, model human values and system, develop programs, use design programs to explain the formation, and apply a variety of information and communication technologies.

(4) Engineer: Students will learn about nature, as applied to the artificial world. In order to obtain a deeper understanding, they will use the concepts, techniques, and attitudes applied to the main issue. The teacher introduces the concept of interactive design, suggests programs to guide students through inquiry based learning, provides the necessary resources for students to apply engineering solutions, and facilitates quality control. Students apply design concepts, principles and theories, and use resources by making decisions. The students use design, modeling, human values and systems development programs in accordance with program they co-designed to make tests and make improvements and control for quality.

(5) Enrich: To enable students to do more in-depth study and applied study on more complex issues. Teachers will provide resources for students to design concepts for new applications. Through questions, the students broaden their view and possible applications. Students learn the design process, and apply it to new situations. They then expand beyond project concepts to new situations and new applications, conduct research, keep an inventors log, and improve upon the original design.

(6) Evaluate: Students and teachers understand the effects of learning. Teachers measure students' knowledge needs and gaps. They confirm that students were learning in accordance with the curriculum standards by the use of formative assessment at each stage. Ratings and grades and evaluations provide feedback. The use of assessment tools raises the effectiveness of these programs. Engineering students must understand the concepts of design, modeling, and system resources to solve the problem. Complete assessments (formative and summative) confirm whether learning objectives were reached.

1.2 Objective

This study was based on using quadcopter, as a design for STEM instruction method. Its main purpose was as follows:

(1) The quadcopter serves as an example to explore the feasibility of designing suitable STEM instructional design.
(2) Through student online discussion message to examination the instructional design whether appropriate for learning of quadcopter.

2 Method

2.1 Participants

The participants were 48 students at junior high school. Students were divided into experimental and control groups according to the level of students' grades. Each level was subdivided into three groups of 8. The experimental group and control group met separately on different days. There were 5 days of 40 h quadcopter instruction. Teachers were the same for the all groups.

2.2 Research Design and Procedures

To understand the use of 6E STEM instruction method, whether helpful discussions quality and knowledge links of student groups. In this study, finish quadcopter as an example. This included their understanding of the principles of flight, fundamental of electrical, electronic components introduction, computer hardware assembly, computer program design, test flight, systems calibration, and flight safety etc. Both the experimental group and the control group were given the same 40 h of instruction. The experimental group of teachers enabled the students with the 6E STEM instruction (shown in Table 1), while the control group used lecture instruction method. The two

Table 1. 6E STEM instruction for produce quadcopter

6E	Engineering design	Teacher activity	Student activity	Instruction tools
		1.Collection course-related information 2.Prepare materials and tools 3.Grouping 4.Division of designers and schedule 5.Design Class list	1.Course-related information to the reading teacher	
Engage	1.Identify and define problem	1.Outline the course, the job description and performance goals 2.Explain groups and announcement group results 3.Introduce personnel division of tasks, lists, timelines and schedules 4.Show quadcopter related video to explain functions and	1.Division of labor, responsibilities and the completed list of related work schedules 2.Group discussion and questions	1.Course presentation file 2.Projector

(*continued*)

Table 1. (*continued*)

6E	Engineering design	Teacher activity	Student activity	Instruction tools
		to arouse students' curiosity and interest 5.Engage students with questions linked to the student's learning experience and prior knowledge 6.Point out the importance of this unit, and illustrate the design procedure and operating techniques, to assess the ability of students 7.Issue each group of students a list of all the necessary materials 8.Issue a list of goals, targets and objectives to the groups. These should be described in detail		
Explore	1.Research the need or problem	1.Introduce the principle of quadcopter 2.Guide the students to search the internet for the parts, the features, specifications and price 3.Guide students to explore related issues and information 4.Encourage students to participate in discussions and group work 5.Describe STEM content at every step	1.Before class, collect data related to quadcopter 2.Group discussion and questions	1.Course presentation file 2.Projector 3.Class list
Explain	1.Develop possible solutions 2.Select the best possible solution	1.Assess according to the mathematical theory and practice of science and technology. Guide students to think about how to choose the best system configuration	1.Through reading and discussion, be familiar with the mathematical theory and practical understanding of related science and technology	1.Course presentation file 2.Projector 3.Class list 4.The quadcopter hardware material

(*continued*)

Table 1. (*continued*)

6E	Engineering design	Teacher activity	Student activity	Instruction tools
		2.Analysis of each hardware features and price 3.Analysis of the advantages and disadvantages of several software control interface 4.Guide students through group discussion, and let them report on the best software and hardware systems portfolio 5.The proposed justification for STEM vision	2.Understand the software environment and syntax 3.Through group discussions, ask questions to determine the best system solution	5.Visual Studio software
Engineer	1.Construct a prototype 2.Test and evaluate the solution 3.Communication the solution 4.Redesign	1.Guide students on how to purchase materials needed for the system 2.Guide students on the combinations of each component and material, in accordance with the system design, to complete the prototype 3.Guide students on how to write and debug the system program 4.Instruct students how to match up hardware and software, and test and adjust its functions 5.Ask questions and find ways to improve STEM from their point of view 6.Instruct students on how to question, and how to discuss ways to improve the team 7.The system testing: Make improvements and re-test until	1.Guide discussions in each group based on the completion of the assembly materials, program writing and debugging 2.The system has been tested, debugged, optimized, corrected, until the work was completed 3.Nearing completion of the project, update and refresh	1.Course presentation file 2.Projector 3.Class list 4.The quadcopter hardware material 5.Visual Studio software

(*continued*)

Table 1. (*continued*)

6E	Engineering design	Teacher activity	Student activity	Instruction tools
		problems were resolved 8.Guide students on how to optimize the system 9.Make adjustments in accordance with the results of re-organizing the structure of the system		
Enrich	1.Completion	1.The group publishes the results of the competition and allow each group to learn from each other	1.The Groups prepare for an on stage briefing report and summary presentation 2.Each group will make a presentation	1.Course presentation file 2.Projector 3.Class list
Evaluation		1.Prepare and publish the results of the awards competition 2.The discussions of this topic can lead to further exploration in any direction 3.Discussion of the topic areas of application can be extended 4.For information about using STEM instruction method of each team to share experiences and summary reports	1.The Group listens to the teacher evaluation and analysis 2.Each group shares their experiences and summary reports	1.Course presentation file 2.Projector 3.Class list

groups in instructional design, will be in Facebook as a group, the group set up a chat room, a group of teachers each day in a chat room to ask questions, ask students after school to a group chat room discussions and answer questions. After the end of the course, the present study will be to each group chat room to discuss message collected. To use quantitative content analysis and sequential analysis to discussions quality and knowledge links of assess the two groups. Every student need to complete a quadcopter. In addition to teachers were available after school to submit questions via Facebook which allowed students to discuss and share as a community over the internet. These online discussions were after school, in order not to interfere with students' learning in class. Students' slow typing skills, limited time and access may have affected the quality of comments, and discussion.

2.3 Coding Scheme and Analysis

In order to understand whether the students have discussions quality and knowledge links. In this study use 6E as QCA coding scheme of discussions quality and knowledge links were adopted. (shown in Table 2) Four skilled coders were recruited that have education or psychology trained. To ensure the consistency, reliability and validity of the data, the complete discussion messages of one sampled group was first encoded by all four coders to test the data's reliability. Analysis revealed the reliability of the Multi-rater Fleiss Kappa coefficient k to be 0.67, which achieved a high degree of consistency [17]. Because the design of this study was classroom learning and participation in the after school discussion, students will be taught extensively by teachers in the classroom. Design and arrangement of teachers in their activities will affect students' knowledge and understanding. This design of the experimental study hopes to be able to evaluate the quality of the group discussions, and to understand the extent of the students' knowledge and cross concept understanding. Student's discussions will also include off-topic, content hence the addition of the Else Phase (Code: E7), and so a more complete and true of their discussions. Although 6E was a instruction method used in the experimental group, 6E was also often used to normal instruction method, with the only difference being in the amount of different items, and the order used. So the use of 6E coding scheme, for the purposes of the control group was reasonable. The Cohen's Kappa coefficient value was 0.67 which reached the 0.001 level of significance [17].

Table 2. The coding scheme for the content analysis of discussions quality and knowledge links

Code	Phase	Description	Examples
E1	Engage	Identify and define problem	Let me ask you some questions. Let's see if you have any answers
E2	Explore	Research the need or problem Development possible solutions	You can check on Wikipedia You can do a quick Google
E3	Explain	Select the best possible solution	A person was shocked by a current flowing through the body to the ground
E4	Engineer	Construct a Prototype Test and evaluation the solution Communication the solution	Quadcopter of propeller forward and reverse should be so mounted How do you save or upload the code to the IC? Why was my quadcopter unstable during flight?
E5	Enrich	Redesign	The parking apron was complete, so how can we use it for night flight?
E6	Evaluation	Completion	My quadcopter could stable flight
E7	Else	Messages irrelevant to the discussion task	Are you sister picking you up from school today? Today's lunch was pretty bad

3   Results and Discussion

The use of quantitative content analysis tools resulted in the control group 1265 messages, and the experimental group 1564 messages. The control group's largest proportion, as seen in Fig. 1, in which the majority of coded E7 (Else), 624 messages and accounted for 49% of all discussions. That was followed by E4 (Engineer), which 305 messages, and accounted for 24% of all discussions. The experimental group's largest proportion was E4 (Engineer), which 619 messages and accounted for 40% of discussions, was followed by E7 (Else), which 308 messages, and accounted for 20% of all discussions proportion. Notice that within the control group of students who were taught with lecture instruction method, nearly half (49%) of these discussions off-topic, although E4 (Engineer) accounted for 24% of discussions. It was a significant difference. Other lesser proportions reflect less productive after school discussions, which may be due to the limited content and poorly instructional design. In contrast to Fig. 2, using E6 instruction method in the experimental group presented data in which the highest percentage of the E4 (Engineer) was 40%, while the second highest E7 (Else) was 20%. The experimental groups' students in the internet chat rooms discussed topics related to the subject more than they engaged in unrelated social dialogue. The quantity and quality of relevant topic discussions was greater in the experimental group than that for the control group. (experimental group: 1564 messages, control group: 1265 messages) From this data we have collected from the experimental group taught with the 6E instruction method, compared to the control group who were not using 6E instruction method, there was a significant difference in the quality and quantity of its after school discussion online question. The quality and quantity of the experimental group than the control group to discuss the issue of after school on-lines were good.

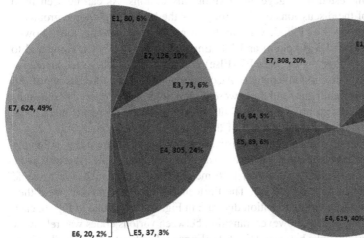

Fig. 1. Distribution of the codes for quantitative content analysis for all the students of control group.

Fig. 2. Distribution of the codes for quantitative content analysis for all the students of experiment group.

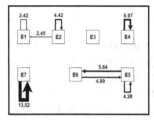 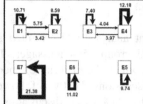 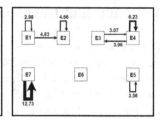

Fig. 3. The behavioral transition diagram of group 1 of control group.

Fig. 4. The behavioral transition diagram of group 2 of control group.

Fig. 5. The behavioral transition diagram of group 3 of control group.

Figure 3, 4 and 5 were behavioral transition diagrams for the discussion of the three groups of students in control groups. The control group 1 as Fig. 3 that E1, E2, E4, E5 and E7 codes was significant that E7 was the most significant of the 5 codes with a z-score = 13.52, accounted for 47.4% of all the group discussions. The behavioral transition between E5 and E6 compared higher than other behavioral transitions, showing that the group was more interested in doing discussions related to Enrich and Evaluation. Also notice this group had no significant E3 (Explain) discussions. There were no other code generated or connections. The results corresponded with the in class behavior of this group of students, with fewer raised hands and fewer interactions with teachers. As can be seen from Fig. 3, the status of the discussions of this group was not ideal. The control group 2 as Fig. 4, shows their group discussions have some of the highest scores in a group, but notice their off-topic E7 discussion's z-score = 21.38 which accounted for 52.8% of the contents of all of their discussions, also the highest in three groups. In addition higher scores of E1 and E2 behavioral transition show that the group was more interested in Engage and Explore discussions. As can be seen from Fig. 4, the status of the discussions of this group was the best of these three groups of data. The control group 3 as Fig. 5, was similar to group 1, except that they showed greater interest between E3 (Explain) and E4 (Engineer) behavior when compared to other behavioral transitions, while their E7 (Else) z-score = 12.73. These accounted for 43.8% of the group discussion content. Also notice this group discussion of E6 (Evaluation) was not significant, and there were no link with other codes. These results was compliance with the group of three students did not complete the quadcopter. From Fig. 5, show the status of the discussions of this group was not ideal.

Data from the three control groups discussions was integrated using computer software to did MEPA sequential analysis. Adjusted residuals table (z-score) were shown in Table 3. A z-score greater than 1.96 means that the sequence of a row and column was significant ($p < 0.05$) [18]. The thirteen significant sequences were then compiled to form the behavioral transition diagram in Fig. 6. Notice that in Fig. 6, each code has reached a significant, however transition between various codes was relatively unchanged. The various links between {E1, E2} (Engage, Explore), {E3, E4} (Explain, Engineer) and {E5, E6} (Enrich, Evaluation) in the control group were not significant in the discussion and students to discuss topics unrelated to content (E7) as much as 49.3%. The control group's highest z-score and frequent discussions were {E3, E4}

Table 3. The results of the sequential analysis of behaviors demonstrated by control group students.

z	E1	E2	E3	E4	E5	E6	E7
E1	9.55*	6.06*	−0.80	0.17	−1.63	−0.25	−5.52
E2	3.61*	10.48*	1.94	0.32	−0.40	−0.78	−6.65
E3	-0.75	−0.07	5.64*	4.99*	1.38	1.85	−5.79
E4	0.28	−0.10	5.46*	15.12*	0.47	0.10	−12.63
E5	1.14	−1.98	−0.10	0.37	11.80*	4.60*	−3.44
E6	0.68	−1.43	−0.15	0.54	3.21*	8.46*	−2.22
E7	−9.80	−10.82	−10.21	−19.73	−6.59	−5.58	28.24*

*$p < 0.05$

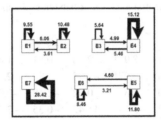

Fig. 6. The behavioral transition diagram of all the students of control group.

(Explain, Engineer) (still behind E7). This behavioral transition between each code, the highest being E1 → E2 with z-score = 6.06 ('→' indicates a unidirectional sequence), means that students showed the strongest knowledge links from Engage to Explore, but not in the return direction. From E3 → E4 the z-score = 4.99 while the E4 → E3 z-score = 5.46. This behavioral transition between the quantity of Explain and Engineer codes was very similar in the control group of students.

Behavioral transition diagrams gathered from the three experimental groups of students (Figs. 7, 8 and 9). The experimental group 1 as Fig. 7. Besides E3, the rest of the codes has been discussed as shown by the number of connecting lines. Code lines connecting the five (E1 → E2, E1 → E3, E3 → E4, E5 → E6 and E6 → E5) were significant, with the sum of z-score = 17.43. Although experimental group 1 of z-scores was not high, the number of discussions was up to 531, wherein the ratio of off-topic accounted for 23.7%, which was significantly higher than the control group. Group 2 and 3 were also better. In addition, the line connecting E1 (Engage) → E3 (Explain) was significant, as it's z-score = 4.56 demonstrates more leaps of knowledge and subject crossover. In Fig. 8, experimental group 2, there were six connecting lines between the code (E1 → E2, E1 → E3, E3 → E1, E2 → E3, E3 → E2 and E5 → E6), and the sum of their z-score = 23.44. With z-score of 9.78 the closed circuit grouping of E1 → E2 → E3 → E1 was significant. The discussion group's use of Engage → Explore → Explain demonstrates good knowledge of connections and crossover topics. Figure 9, experimental group 3, there were five connection lines between the codes in this group (E2 → E1, E3 → E2, E1 → E3, E3 → E1 and E5 → E6). The sum of the

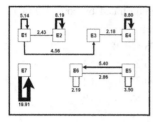 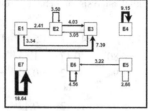 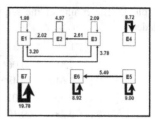

Fig. 7. The behavioral transition diagram of group 1 of experiment group.

Fig. 8. The behavioral transition diagram of group 2 of experiment group.

Fig. 9. The behavioral transition diagram of group 3 of experiment group.

Table 4. The results of the sequential analysis of behaviors demonstrated by experiment group students.

z	E1	E2	E3	E4	E5	E6	E7
E1	3.84*	3.09*	8.95*	−2.70	−0.51	−1.69	−5.97
E2	2.43*	9.56*	2.97*	−1.95	−1.38	−2.90	−5.12
E3	4.30*	3.30*	1.32	0.02	−2.18	−0.02	−5.33
E4	0.07	−3.42	−3.19	15.42*	−0.35	−3.52	−15.59
E5	−3.59	−2.12	−2.12	−0.22	9.86*	8.35*	−3.68
E6	0.11	−1.58	−1.58	−0.90	2.56*	9.27*	−2.97
E7	−6.25	−6.33	−5.35	−11.95	-4.32	−3.54	33.78*

*$p < 0.05$

z-score was 17.10. Similar to Fig. 8, this closed loop grouping of E3 → E2 → E1 → E3 was significant with z-score = 8.41, except that the knowledge path of this group was ordered from Explain → Explore → Engage, because this group of students has a richer knowledge of the group discussions. Excited students often first tell you the results, which then in turn guide the discussion.

In this study MEPA software was used to do comprehensive sequential analysis of the three experimental groups engaged in online discussions. The adjusted residuals table (z-score), as shown in Table 4, with a z-score greater than 1.98 means that the sequence of a row and column was statistically significant ($p < 0.05$) [18]. The fourteen significant sequences were then compiled to form the behavioral transition diagram in Fig. 10. From Fig. 10 it can be found that, like E3, each code shows significance, especially in the E1 → E2 → E3 (z-score the sum of 10.36) and E3 → E2 → E1 (z-score the sum of 14.68). Forming a closed double loop between Engage, Explore and Explain in the experimental group discussions demonstrates a good grasp of concepts, a knowledge of links, and crossover connections to topics and discussions. In addition, E5 → E6 (z-scores of 8.35) and E6 → E5 (z-scores of 2.56) also showed significance, indicating that the experimental group achieved significant linking between the Enrich and Evaluation.

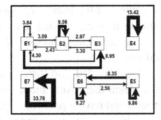

Fig. 10. The behavioral transition diagram of all the students of experiment group.

4   Conclusions and Suggestions

STEM was the integration of science, technology, engineering and mathematics education. STEM aims to link and combine the various disciplines' related courses, so that students take theory and actually implement in a relatable real world way. This STEM approach can improve students' interest in learning and improve their outlook on life challenges.

In this study, students were taught using the STEM instruction architecture and 6E instruction method, through the production of quadcopter. Group chat rooms were created in Facebook for students to use for after school on-line discussions, in order to investigate the effectiveness of STEM instruction and the quality of knowledge and crossover of core topic the students showed in their discussions. The results found that the 6E method used on the experimental group had significant results on the quality of discussion and knowledge links. In addition, the online student discussions were found to be more focused and on-topic than discussions among the control group of students. After the multi leveled 6E instructional the students in the experimental group successfully completed production of a quadcopter. In contrast, 49% of the discussions among a control group (taught with non-6E method) had nothing to do with the subject. The majority of the control group students' chat discussions were limited in scope, including a lower incidence (insignificant amount) of Explaining, Evaluation and other important 6E aspects. In the control group, each phase of knowledge was not as rich as it was in the experimental group. Several students in the control group failed to successfully produce quadcopter.

Based on the findings of this study, were the following suggestions and recommendations for future researchers and teachers interested in the implementation of online reference STEM instruction and discussion.

(1) Present the results of experimental and control groups in an exhibition, so that each group must publish their results or work, and give an onstage presentation. This study was originally designed to have students create a video, then QCA and LSA for analysis, but this was altered due to limited time for students and data for analysis. Recommend increasing the number of students, increase published learning outcomes for all students including questionnaire, so there was more data and the results were more complete.

(2) Regarding online students, when teachers did not participate or guide, it lead to a discussion of poor quality in the control group of students, and discussing up to

52.8% unrelated topics. Recommend the implementation of online discussions, in which teachers or teaching assistants can be added, as the presentation and timing plays an important role for appropriate guidance [19] that the quality of the discussion was helpful and important.

(3) The course included 24 students divided into three groups, but only one teacher, which will lead to problems when there were more students, as teachers will not be able to effectively cope with and have a positive impact on student learning and results. Recommend more assistants (one per group), who, at any time can deal with student's problems, and more researchers in related fields to assist in the lessons. It was found at times that when the group environment became too serious it was quite dull, but with intervention and assistants to help guide, there were better learning outcomes.

(4) To practice the course, it's design must take into account the student's focus in class and during the after school discussion [20, 21]. The teachers should design a variety of educational activities for students to maintain a long focus.

References

1. Han, S.W.: Curriculum standardization, stratification, and students' STEM-related occupational expectations: evidence from PISA 2006. Int. J. Educ. Res. **72**(3), 103–115 (2015)
2. Johnson, J.R.: Technology: Report of the Project 2061 Phase I technology Panel. American Association for the Advancement of Science, Washington, DC (1989)
3. Sadaf, A., Newby, T.J., Ertmer, P.A.: Exploring pre-service teachers' beliefs about using Web 2.0 technologies in K-12 classroom. Comput. Educ. **59**(3), 937–945 (2012)
4. Kim, C.M., Kim, D., Yuan, J., Hill, R.B., Doshi, P., Thai, C.N.: Robotics to promote elementary education pre-service teachers' STEM engagement, learning, and teaching. Comput. Educ. **91**(4), 14–31 (2015)
5. Aladé, F., Lauricella, A.R., Leanne, B.R., Wartella, E.: Measuring with murray: touchscreen technology and preschoolers' stem learning. Comput. Hum. Behav. **62**(3), 433–441 (2016)
6. Pinelli, T.E., Haynie III, W.J.: A Case for the nationwide inclusion of engineering in the k-12 curriculum via technology education. J. Technol. Educ. **21**(2), 52–68 (2010)
7. Sanders, M.: STEM, STEM education, STEM mania. Technol. Teach. **68**(4), 20–26 (2009)
8. Becker, K., Park, K.: Effects of integrative approaches among science, technology, engineering, and mathematics (STEM) subjects on students' learning: a preliminary meta-analysis. J. STEM Educ. **12**(1), 23–36 (2011)
9. Keefe, B.: The perception of STEM: analysis, issues, and future directions. Survey. Entertainment and Media Communication Institute (2010)
10. National Research Council (NRC): Exploring the intersection of science education and 21st century skills: a workshop summary. National Academies Press, Washington, DC (2010)
11. Bybee, R.W.: Advancing STEM education: a 2020 vision. Technol. Eng. Teach. **47**(3), 30–35 (2010)
12. Lindberg, R.E., Pinelli, T.E., Batterson, J.G.: Sense and sensibility: the case for the nationwide inclusion of engineering in the K-12 curriculum. In: American Society for Engineering Education (ASEE), Southeastern Section, April 6–8, 2008, Memphis, TN (2008)

13. Fore, G.A., Feldhaus, C.R., Sorge, B.H., Agarwal, M., Varahramyan, K.: Learning at the nano-level: accounting for complexity in the internalization of secondary STEM teacher professional development. Teach. Teach. Educ. **51**(3), 101–112 (2015)
14. Bybee, R.W., Taylor, J.A., Gardner, A., Van Scotter, P., Carlson Powell, J., Westbrook, A., Landes, N.: The BSCS 5E Instruction Model: Origins, effectiveness and applications. (2006). http://www.bscs.org/bscs-5e-instruction-model
15. Barry, N.: The ITEEA 6E learning byDeSIGN™ Model. In: Technology and Engineering Teacher, 14–19 March 2014 (2014). http://www.oneida-boces.org/cms/lib05/NY01914080/Centricity/Domain/36/6E%20Learning%20by%20Design%20Model.pdf. Accessed 27 Sept 2014
16. Hynes, M., Portsmore, M., Dare, E., Milto, E., Rogers, C., Hammer, D., Carberry, A.: Infusing engineering design into high school STEM courses. National Center for Engineering and Technology Education (2011)
17. Landis, J.R., Koch, G.G.: The measurement of observer agreement for categorical data. Biometrics **33**(1), 159–174 (1977)
18. Bakeman, R., Gottman, J.M.: Observing interaction: An introduction to sequential analysis, 2nd edn. Cambridge University Press, UK (1997)
19. Hou, H.T.: A case study of online instructional collaborative discussion activities for problem solving using situated scenarios: an examination of content and behavior cluster analysis. Comput. Educ. **56**(3), 712–719 (2011)
20. Gilbert, P.K., Dabbagh, N.: How to structure online discussions for meaningful discourse: a case study. Br. J. Educ. Technol. **36**(1), 5–18 (2005)
21. Kanuka, H., Rourke, L., Laflamme, E.: The influence of instructional methods on the quality of online discussion. Br. J. Educ. Technol. **38**(2), 260–271 (2007)

Emerging Technologies Enhanced Language Learning

Improving Students' English Technical Terms Learning and Willingness to Communicate Through Meaning Negotiation

Yaming Tai[1], Yu-Liang Ting[2(⊠)], and Pei-Shan Hsieh[1]

[1] Department of Children English Education,
National Taipei University of Education, Taipei, Taiwan
[2] Department of Technology Application and Human Resource Development,
National Taiwan Normal University, Taipei, Taiwan
yting@ntnu.edu.tw

Abstract. This study attempts to enhance students' willingness to communicate in the field of English technical terms learning. The proposed learning design aims to train students in using various meaning negotiation strategies to discuss and clarify the meaning of given English technical terms and acquire the different aspects of word knowledge of these terms. Twenty-five senior students in a technology institute were provided with interesting corporative films introducing these English technical terms. At the end, participants completed a video-making project demonstrating the target English technical terms. The pre- and post-test of English technical terms and survey of willingness to communicate showed that the proposed learning not only improved students' vocabulary, but also increased significantly their willingness to communicate in English. The results could provide a new way of English technical terms learning.

Keywords: Meaning negotiation · English technical terms · Willingness to communicate

1 Introduction

In English for Special Purpose (ESP) courses, students must be taught to master, in addition to basic or general-purpose vocabulary, a repertoire of professional/technical terms specific to a certain field/discipline related to their studies/career. Even for students in the field of engineering and science, the mastery of English language is of paramount importance in their academic and future professional lives. Engineering students and engineers are engaged in various types of communicative events, including delivering or listening to professional presentations in a meeting, reading professional texts and writing reports [1]. In addition, a critical factor in the success of high-tech organizations is innovation, which requires mutual sharing of new information, knowledge and ideas. For engineers to excel in the workplace and remain competitive, not only should they be able to convey effectively technical information, they also need to have acceptable communication skills [2]. In Asia, despite substantial attention to the teaching of communicative approaches, students are heavily exposed to a grammar-translation method in learning English with an over emphasis on rules,

© Springer International Publishing AG 2017
T.-T. Wu et al. (Eds.): SETE 2016, LNCS 10108, pp. 195–204, 2017.
DOI: 10.1007/978-3-319-52836-6_21

structures and vocabulary [3]. Asian learners are generally regarded as reticent and passive learners, and have appeared to be reluctant to speak up in English class [4].

As engineers are required to interact and communicate with people either in academic or professional activities, ESP for engineering students should focus on equipping them with communicative proficiency. Since language development can occur through communicative interactions, more interactions lead to more language development and learning. Given the potential benefits of participating in communicative interactions, the goal of second language education should include the creation of Willingness to Communicate (WTC) in the language learning process. That is, learners are encouraged to seek out communication opportunities and to use the language for authentic communication [4]. WTC, which has been found to influence the frequency of communication, can contribute to the development of language. Hence, higher WTC among learners translates into increased opportunity for practice in an second language (L2) and authentic L2 usage [4, 5]. WTC should be emphasized in helping students acquire the technical terms of their subject domain [6].

WTC emerges from the joint effect of interacting situational variables such as topic, interlocutors, and conversational context [6]. Because of the changeability of these variables through pedagogical intervention, WTC can be generated by appropriate learning design. This study aims to explore the use of meaning negotiation activities to improve students' vocabulary acquisition performance and enhance their willingness to communicate in English using technical terms learned in the ESP course.

2 The Literatures Review

Willingness to Communicate (WTC). The notion of WTC was originally introduced with reference to communication of first language, and it was considered to be a personality-based, trait-like predisposition [7]. That is, WTC is thought to be fairly stable over time and relatively consistent across situations/contexts and receivers. WTC entails an intention to initiate a communicative behaviour, and this behavioural intention is often predictive of actual behaviour [7, 8]. While personal character has major influence on WTC in first/native-language communication, in the context of L2 communication, individual WTC may differ significantly because of the potentially wide variation in linguistic competence and social relationships in different contexts [9].

Trait WTC and situational WTC are complementary [7]. "Trait WTC prepares individuals for communication by creating a tendency for them to place themselves in situations where communication is expected. Situational WTC, on the other hand, influences the decision to initiate communication in particular situations" [7, p. 469]. WTC of L2 is related to various individual and social variables [7]. In the classroom context, situational WTC was found to be under the influence of situational variables including the class interactional pattern (teacher-fronted situation, small group and dyad), familiarity with interlocutor(s), familiarity with topics under discussion, task type, medium of communication, self-confidence, and topic [4, 8, 10]. These findings contribute to an understanding of the dynamic nature of WTC in second language learning. Prior research has also found a strong correlation between perceived competence and WTC [8, 10]. In particular, WTC in L2 would depend greatly on the communicative competence an individual feels in L2.

Vocabulary (Technical Term) Learning. Vocabulary is the glue that holds stories, ideas and content together, and make knowledge accessible [11]. It is essential not only in learning new concepts but also in conveying thoughts and emotions as well as making ideas comprehensible to others. Deep processing of content has been suggested as a means to facilitate learning; and negotiation of meaning, a process of resolving communication breakdowns, has been considered as an effective approach to vocabulary acquisition [12]. In other words, vocabulary learning should go beyond memorizing definitions; in the case of Taiwan, remembering the Chinese translations. In learning, students should be encouraged to employ their background knowledge and practice proper vocabulary recognition strategies to work out the meaning of new/difficult lexical items [13]. Moreover, students need to be involved in active learning which requires them to make connection between vocabulary acquisition and their experiences. The instructions should help students integrate word meanings into their existing knowledge in order to build conceptual representation of vocabulary in multiple contextual situations.

While the attempt to improve students' general vocabulary is not easy, the teaching of technical lexicon is particularly challenging. Technical vocabulary comprises terms for concepts and phenomena central to a specific discipline [14]. The meaning of these terms is specialized and restricted but may vary across disciplines [10]. Various pedagogical approaches to vocabulary improvement have been proposed for engineering and science students, including the computermediated multimedia presentation [14]. These approaches aim not only to enhance students' vocabulary and attitudes towards L2 learning, they also target at enriching students' language experience and raise their language awareness.

The topic of communication significantly affects the ease of language use [9]. If learners have the topic-related content knowledge and are familiar with a certain register, their linguistic self-confidence could be increased for their communication. Previous studies have also shown that background knowledge of a topic is essential for learners to feel secure and confident enough to talk about the topic [4, 6]. Hence, it is important to select appropriate topics and adequate content in teaching the terms used in a specific subject domain.

Negotiation of Meaning. Activities that involve negotiation of meaning give L2 learners the opportunity to develop communicative competence. Negotiation of meaning entails conversational adjustments characterized by clarification requests, confirmation checks, comprehension checks, as well as self-and other-repetitions (both exact and semantic) [15]. During the interactive negotiation process, learners have the chance to provide comprehensible input and to produce modified output [16]. In their study on the value of meaning negotiation in language classroom, Foster and Ohta [17] found that learners expressed interest and felt encouraged while seeking and providing assistance and initiating self-repair of their own utterances, all in the absence of communication breakdowns. Moreover, words negotiated during communicative activities were more easily acquired and better retained than non-negotiated ones [12].

In designing communicative activities, providing the meaning negotiation context alone is not enough, learners should feel obliged to negotiate. The interaction among learners should be task-based, which involves learners to comprehend, manipulate, produce or interact with each other in the target language [18]. Participants are required to make their content explicit through explanation, modeling, representations, and examples [19]. Such task-based communication is an authentic, pragmatic, contextual and functional use of language.

3 Proposed Learning Design

The proposed learning design is task-based wherein students were given the assignment to learn technical terms. This vocabulary acquisition task involves two processes: the receptive process meaning the reception of comprehensible input on vocabulary definitions, and the productive process referring to the modification of information output by rephrasing the definitions of the vocabulary. After understanding and learning the terms, students were required to prepare a video presentation for explaining the functions and applications of the technical terms acquired. The completion of this learning task would involve learning new technical terms and negotiation of their meanings between learners, not that between teacher and learners, via group discussion and word explanation activities. In sum, the proposed task-based learning design creates a context for students to practice their receptive and productive skills of vocabulary acquisition as well as their communication skills in explaining the words they have acquired.

For constructing a motivating context to engage students into the acquisition and use of technical terms, this study recognizes that mobile communication corporative uses videos to introduce advanced technologies and to promote the related products and services they provide. These videos illustrate versatile mobile technologies used or being used by corporations to provide communication services to their customers. This study values the video content associated with interesting stories on the process of introducing technology without boring the audiences.

The videos are episodic style. The scenarios show how mobile technologies can be used in people's daily life and provide better living in the near future. The videos illustrate the applications of mobile communication technology in human lives, and provide viewers the strong impression that this mobile technology makes human lives more convenient, innovative, and interesting. When the technologies and related terms are introduced on the screen, the videos focus on explaining how the technology is designed to support an application, and what kind of services and benefits the application brings to people. This type of videos is assumed to be interesting because of its story-based scenario and the use of attractive multimedia. In addition, the video's simple explanations and association of rich multimedia are deemed to be comprehensible to the general public, including students.

One additional reason of using the video made by an well-known international corporative is to echo the so-called "image international community" [20]. For students engaged in classroom practices, the realm of their community can be extended to the imagined world outside the classroom – their imagined community. Research has shown that when EFL learners may envision an imagined international community that they can be part of using English, their motivation and L2 WTC could be enhanced [20]. The proposed corporative videos may help students' vividly recognize the vocabulary delivered in classroom is useful and practical in the industry such that they are more willing to use these technical terms outside classroom. Through introducing global study content, it should be possible to link EFL classroom practices to an imagined international community and improve WTC.

Transcripts of verbal explanation of the technical terms in both English and Chinese were also provided to make the videos more comprehensible to students. The use of multimedia presentation in the learning activity not only served to arouse students' interest in the content but also to stimulate them in having conversational negotiation. Learning efficiency seems to be enhanced by multiple, verbal and imagery, representations [21]. Nevertheless, to avoid cognitive overload, the video clips were presented at a pace controlled by the instructor in view of the students' response and the presentation was in form of small segments. The videos shown also served as a reference for students in preparing their own video presentation.

In addition to the issue of selection of curriculum content, the instructional design is based on the framework proposed by Willis [22], task-based learning (TBL) involves two phases, pre-task phase and task-cycle phase. The task-cycle phase is further divided into three stages: task stage, planning stage and report stage. Meaning negotiation can be implemented at different task phases and stages. The detailed design of a 3-hour session for a 7-week course is as follows.

Pre-task phase (Weeks 1–2): Before assigning the vocabulary acquisition and video production tasks, the instructor showed NTT DoCoMo technology films to help students relate to the videos they were to produce. Strategy orientation was implemented in this stage, with instructor teaching students meaning negotiation strategies by demonstrating the communicative skills for comprehension checks, confirmation checks and clarification requests [23]. Suggested strategies were provided during meaning negotiation. Students were given the chance to practice the suggested strategies with the instructor. At the end of this phase, students were asked to form groups and each of them was assigned to look up the meaning of technical terms and explain them to their group members in the next phase.

Task-cycle phase Task stage (Week 3): In this stage, a group discussion activity was implemented, in which students took turns in their group to present the meaning of the technical terms they had looked up. Meaning negotiation strategies were applied in order to reach mutual understanding of those terms.

Planning stage (Week 4): This stage concerned the production of videos for introducing the functions and applications of all the technical terms they had previously discussed. Communicative skills were exercised and meaning negotiation strategies were used for exchange of thoughts and ideas. In the planning process, students go through the provision of comprehensible input to the production of modified output.

Report stage (Weeks 5–7): The groups took turns to present the videos they produced and each student provided verbal explanation for the technical terms they had looked up. Students had to take notes on what was presented and used the suggested strategies for comprehension check, confirmation check and clarification request.

4 Instruments

The vocabulary test evaluated students' knowledge of the 25 technical terms selected. Participants were asked to match the form and meaning, and each correct matching would score four points. As mentioned above, the vocabulary test was given pre-task, post-task, and four weeks after the completion of learning activity.

The WTC questionnaire probed into three dimensions: perceived competence in L2, WTC in group discussion context, and WTC in meeting context. Items in the WTC questionnaire were adapted from McCroskey and Richmond [24] and MacIntyre et al. [5]. The participants were asked to indicate their agreement with the questionnaire items (Table 1) using a 5-point Likert scale, with 1 being strongly disagree and 5 being strongly agree. The questions were translated into Chinese as participants' first language, and were reviewed and revised by two experts in the field of education. The questionnaire was tested in a pilot survey with three students.

Table 1. WTC questionnaire

Perceived competence	Items
	1. I love to learn English
	2. I am afraid of speaking English in front of people
	3. I think English is boring
	4. I feel confident when I give my opinions in English class
	5. It is easy for me to complete the assigned English activities
	6. It is easier to communicate in English if I know the strategies
	7. I am willing to participate in English activities assigned by the teacher
WTC in group discussion context	1. I am willing to share my experience with my classmates in English
	2. During group discussion, I can communicate with classmates in English
	3. During group discussion, it is easy for me to give opinions in English
	4. I am willing to share my opinions with classmates in English
	5. I am willing to share my opinions during group discussion in English
	6. I am willing to have conversation with classmates in English
	7. I am willing to answer classmates' questions in English
WTC in meeting context	1. I will ask the teacher if I cannot solve the problems
	2. I am willing to describe one of my favorite things in English
	3. It is difficult for me to answer teacher's questions in English
	4. It is difficult for me to express my opinions in front of the class in English
	5. I am willing to have conversation with teachers during class in English

Data of the three vocabulary tests were analyzed using SPSS version 16. The paired t-test (two-tailed) was employed to investigate the differences in vocabulary acquisition performance to shed light on the progress in learning English technical terms through negotiation of meaning. Data collected from pre-task and post-task WTC question-naires were analyzed by paired-sample t test to examine the difference in students' WTC before and after the proposed learning activity. Although there were 35 partic-ipants, the validated sample size was 25 because 10 students were absent at least once during the 7-week study.

5 Results and Discussions

Table 2 lists the results of paired-sample t test on scores of pre- and post-task vo-cabulary test. There was significant in pre- and post-task mean scores ($t(24) = 8.20$, $p<$ .001), indicating marked improvement in students' vocabulary.

Table 2. Paired-sample t test on pre- and post-task vocabulary test (*** $P < .001$)

	Mean	SD	N	df	t
Pre-task	29.28	13.15	25	24	8.20***
Post-task	57.73	15.13	25		

Whether such improvement can last over time can be examined by the retention test. Table 3 lists the results of paired-sample t test on scores of post-task- and retention vocabulary test. The retention test scores did not decrease, implying no regression in their performance and the technical terms acquired can be retained by students.

Table 3. Results of paired-sample t test on post-task and retention vocabulary test

	Mean	SD	N	df	t
Post-task	57.73	15.13	25	24	1.18
Retention test	62.48	14.80	25		

Results of vocabulary tests indicated that the proposed learning activity that involves meaning negotiation can lead to enhancement in acquisition and retention of technical vocabulary. The present findings were consistent with the literature. Pica, Young and Doughty [25] showed that the act of negotiation was beneficial for the acquisition of vocabulary items and had a lasting effect. Words that were negotiated during communicative activities were more easily acquired and better retained than non-negotiated ones [12, 26] While previous research involved interaction between native speakers and non-native speakers (NS-NNS), the current investigation focused on NNS-NNS negotiation.

Survey results of participants' WTC are listed in Tables 4 and 5. The reliability (Cronbach's alpha) coefficients of WTC in the three dimensions were 0.75, 0.72, and 0.73, respectively, and the overall alpha was 0.77, which exceeded the minimum of 0.60 generally recommended for internal reliability [27].

As seen in Table 4, there was significant difference in mean pre-task and post-task WTC scores (t(24) = 2.24, p < .05), indicating increase in students' WTC in English

Table 4. Results of Pre- and Post-task WTC (*$p < .05$)

	Mean	SD	N	df	t
Pre-task WTC scores	59.00	11	25	24	2.24*
Post-task WTC scores	62.69	9	25		

Table 5. Results of Paired-sample t Test on Pre- and Post-task WTC Scores (*$p < .05$)

Dimensions		Mean	SD	N	df	t
Perceived competence	pre	21.36	3.45	25	24	2*
	post	22.4	2.25	25		
Group discussion	pre	20.2	5.15	25	24	1.71
	post	21.8	4.86	25		
Meeting context	pre	17.44	3.35	25	24	2.16*
	post	18.68	2.86	25		

after the proposed learning activity. When WTC performance was further analyzed in three dimensions, the results, listed in Table 5, also revealed higher perceived competence and greater WTC in both group discussion and meeting contexts. In other words, the meaning negotiation activities do enhance students' WTC in English (L2).

Scrutinizing further the WTC findings revealed greater increase in WTC in meeting context than in group discussion context. Such difference may be accounted for by two factors. First, in the meeting context, the topic, mobile phone applications, is of interest and relevance to students and the multimedia presentation format is both appealing and entertaining. Thus, they are more motivated to communicate and participate. Second, after going through the proposed learning, the students have gained better understanding of the vocabulary. Hence, their enhanced mastery of the technical terms makes them feel more confident to engage in communication with peers.

The proposed learning design aims to enhance students' perception of the pragmatic utilitarian value of the technical terms and also their motivation to acquire the language in order to facilitate communication with that group on a topic of interest to them. According to MacIntyre *et al.* [5], a person who intends to behave in a particular manner and who holds the belief that positive results will occur has a positive attitude toward that behavior. Hence, enabling the students to perceive the benefits of learning the technical words and the contribution of meaning negotiation to better linguistic performance would in turn improve their vocabulary acquisition performance and WTC with peers.

In the context of L2 communication, a person's WTC may differ significantly because of the potentially wide variation in his competence and social relationships in different contexts [9]. The present findings further show that students' WTC in L2 can be improved by equipping them with meaning negotiation strategies. In addition, previous research also highlighted a situational distinction, referring to the classroom versus "real world" in which WTC arises [5]. In other words, doubt is cast on whether students engaged in immersion classroom L2 learning may also become motivated in L2 communication outside classroom. This study attempts to bridge the gap by adopting videos clips produced by real-world corporations for use in classroom learning. By having students practice in classroom the use of L2 technical terms employed in the business world is to prepare and equip them better for the authentic use of such vocabulary in actual everyday situations. This teaching practice should be desirable and applicable to other subject domains for making up the difference in WTC inside and outside classroom.

6 Conclusions

This study tackles the challenges of ESP in the field of engineering education by proposing a novel approach to vocabulary acquisition. The proposed learning design that involves meaning negotiation was integrated into the learning of English technical terms in classroom. As L2 teachers should promote facilitating factors of WTC as much as possible, this study used out-of-classroom corporative videos and in classroom meaning negotiation activity to construct an authentic L2 learning context. This study should help teachers recognize that there is much more involved in the students' WTC behaviour in class, given the illustrated curriculum and instruction factors that might impact on WTC.

References

1. Kaewpet, C.: Communication needs of Thai civil engineering students. Engl. Specif. Purp. **28**, 266–278 (2009)
2. Kassim, H., Ali, F.: English communicative events and skills needed at the workplace: feedback from the industry. Engl. Specif. Purp. **29**, 168–182 (2010)
3. Kang, D.-M.: The effects of study-abroad experiences on EFL learners' willingness to communicate, speaking abilities, and participation in classroom interaction. System **42**, 319–332 (2014)
4. Cao, Y.-Q., Philp, J.: Interactional context and willingness to communicate: a comparison of behavior in whole class, group and dyadic interaction. System **34**, 480–493 (2006)
5. MacIntyre, P.D., Baker, S., Clément, R., Conrad, S.: Willingness to communicate, social support, and language learning orientations of immersion students. Stud. Second Lang. Acquisition **23**, 369–388 (2001)
6. Kang, S.-J.: Dynamic emergence of situational willingness to communicate in a second language. System **33**, 277–292 (2005)
7. Cao, Y.: Investigating situational willingness to communicate within second language classrooms from an ecological perspective. System **39**, 468–479 (2011)
8. MacIntyre, P.D.: Variables underlying willingness to communicate: a causal analysis. Commun. Res. Rep. **12**, 241–247 (1994)
9. MacIntyre, P.D., Clément, R., Dörnyei, Z., Noels, K.A.: Conceptualizing willingness to communicate in a L2: a situational model of confidence and affiliation. Mod. Lang. J. **82**, 545–562 (1998)
10. Baker, S., MacIntyre, P.: The role of gender and immersion in communication and second language orientations. Lang. Learn. **50**, 311–341 (2000)

11. Rupley, W.H., Logan, J.W., Nichols, W.D.: Vocabulary instruction in a balanced reading program. Reading Teacher **52**, 336–346 (1998)
12. Newton, J.: Task-based interaction and incidental vocabulary learning: A case study. Second Lang. Res. **11**, 159–177 (1995)
13. Pritchard, R.M.O., Nasr, A.: Improving reading performance among Egyptian engineering students: principles and practice. Engl. Specif. Purp. **23**, 425–445 (2004)
14. Rusanganwa, J.: Multimedia as a means to enhance teaching technical vocabulary to phys-cs undergraduates in Rwanda. Engl. Specif. Purp. **32**, 36–44 (2013)
15. Pica, T., Doughty, C.: The role of group work in classroom second language acquisition. Stud. Second Lang. Acquisition **7**, 233–248 (1985)
16. Shehadeh, A.: Task-based language learning and teaching: theories and applications. In: Edwards, C., Willis, J. (eds.) Teachers Exploring Tasks in English Language Teaching, pp. 13–30. Palgrave Macmillan, U.K. (2005)
17. Foster, P., Ohta, A.S.: Negotiation for meaning and peer assistance in second language classrooms. Appl. Linguist. **26**, 402–430 (2005)
18. Nunan, D.: Task-Based Language Teaching. Cambridge University Press, Cambridge (2004)
19. Kearney, E.: A high leverage language teaching practice: Leading an open ended group discussion. Foreign Lang. Ann. **48**(1), 100–123 (2015)
20. Yashima, T., Zenuk-Nishide, L.: The impact of learning contexts on proficiency, attitudes, and L2 communication: creating an imagined international community. System **36**, 566–585 (2008)
21. Mayer, R.E.: Applying the science of learning: eidence-based principles for the design of multimedia instruction. Am. Psychol. **63**, 760–769 (2008)
22. Willis, J.: A framework for task-based learning. Longman, London (1996)
23. Long, M.H.: Inside the 'black box': methodological issues in classroom research on language learning. Lang. Learn. **30**, 1–42 (1980)
24. McCroskey, J.C., Richmond, V.P.: Willingness to communicate. In: McCroskey, J.C., Daly, J.A. (eds.) Personality and Interpersonal Communication, pp. 129–156. Sage, Beverly Hills, CA (1987)
25. Pica, T., Young, R., Doughty, C.: The impact of interaction on comprehension. Tesol Q. **21**, 737–758 (1987)
26. Ellis, R., Tanaka, Y., Yamazaki, A.: Classroom interaction, comprehension, and the acquisition of L2 word meanings. Lang. Learn. **44**, 449–491 (1994)
27. Aron, A., Aron, E.N., Coups, E.J.: Statistics for Psychology, 4th edn. Pearson Education, Upper Saddle River, N.J. (2006)

A Study on the Usability of Multimedia E-Books with Problem-Based Learning (PBL) Model in Junior High School Students' English Classes

Yi-Tung Lin[✉], Yi-Chien Huang, I-Ting Wang,
and Kuei-Chih Chuang

National Yunlin University of Science and Technology, Yunlin, Taiwan
s107@ms26.hinet.net, {dl0443012,chuangkc}@yuntech.
edu.tw, 21stars@yahoo.com.tw

Abstract. The study aimed to explore whether using multimedia e-books with PBL (Problem-Based Learning) teaching approach had impact on junior high school students' personal epistemo-logical beliefs and English academic achievement. In the study, the participants were two classes of 2nd graders of a junior high school in the central Taiwan. One class was the experimental group with 32 students, and the other was the control group with 32 students as well. The two classes were taught by the same teacher with 12 classes. The study adapted English multimedia e-book, English learning achievement tests, and a questionnaire on individual English epistemological beliefs as tools, which was examined by experts to ensure reliability and validity, as the study tool. The study indicated that applying multi-media e-books with PBL teaching approach promoted students English academic achievement. Moreover, it had positive effect on students' tense analysis ability and reading when learning English.

Keywords: Multimedia E-Book · PBL (Problem-Based Learning) · English academic achievement

1 Introduction

Many research reports in Taiwan indicated that, integration of technology with teaching can enhance students' learning motivation (Wang 2001; Wang 2006; Su 2006; Wu 2008). Therefore, the integration of multimedia e-books with PBL teaching can not only improve students' learning interest and effectiveness but also increase teaching quality. During learning process, the influence of epistemological beliefs on learning process cannot be overlooked. Epistemological beliefs are human beings' opinions and beliefs on knowledge perception, namely, how individuals' perception of human beings and how individuals' beliefs affect their perception process (Hofer and Pintrich 1997). The studies on epistemological beliefs should focus on understanding of students' epistemological beliefs, improvement of their critical thinking, and the changes of teachers' and students' epistemological beliefs. This study particularly applied PBL model to teaching. PBL teaching approach (Problem-Based Learning) refers to the use

© Springer International Publishing AG 2017
T.-T. Wu et al. (Eds.): SETE 2016, LNCS 10108, pp. 205–218, 2017.
DOI: 10.1007/978-3-319-52836-6_22

of problems or contexts to induce students' thinking, set up learning objectives, and enable students to engage in self-directed learning to increase new knowledge or correct the old knowledge content. PBL can not only help students to solve problems in the learning process, but also create the opportunities for them to improve knowledge when solving problems. In PBL teaching, students are required to work as a team because working as a team facilitates students' knowledge absorption, teaches students the importance of mutual respect and information sharing, and improves students' communication skills, teamwork attitude, and problem-solving abilities. Therefore, PBL is viewed as a learning method combining knowledge acquisition with cultivation of skills and attitudes. In general, the background for implementation of PBL is that the core courses have been clearly defined and the foundation and subjects have been closely integrated. There are four factors in PBL learning, which are as followed: (1) Progressive and accumulative learning: Learning should be unlimited to time and place. Students can always learn new material any time and any place; (2) Integrated learning: Subjects should be combined in terms of correlation; (3) Attention to learning progress: When students' knowledge advances, the course should also be changed; (4) Consistent learning: As for the spirit of PBL, students should learn consistently and stably. Therefore, this study aims to investigate how the application of multimedia e-books integrated with PBL teaching model influence junior high school students' English learning, and whether it can improve students' academic achievement.

2 Literature Review

2.1 Relevant Theories of Teaching of Multimedia EBooks

1. Dual-coding theory

Dual coding theory explains human behavior and experience in terms of dynamic associative processes that operate on a rich network of modality-specific verbal and nonverbal representations (Clark and Paivio 1991). Dual coding theory assumes that cognition occurs in two independent but connected codes: a verbal code for language and a nonverbal code for mental imagery (Sadoski 2005). Information can be processed through both the verbal and nonverbal channels. This occurs, for example, when a person sees a picture of a dog and also processes the word "dog". Information processes through both channels has an additive effect on recall (Mayer and Anderson 1991; Paivio and Csapo 1973).

Cognitive psychologists investigate the information process of how human brain, the "black box", deals with information through sensory attention, encoding, storage, and retrieval. During the entire learning process, learners' role also has to be changed from passive information receiver to active participant to construct their own learning.

2. Mayer's cognitive theory of multimedia learning

Richard E. Mayer is a well-known cognitive psychologist in the U.S. He used the theory proposed by Paivio as the foundation to further investigate how to simplify information input during the process of multimedia teaching and reduce the interference of irrelevant sounds. Mayer defined computer multimedia learning as the learning using texts and images. Using multimedia in learning can be regarded as a helper for students' acquisition of teaching information or knowledge construction. During such a learning process, multimedia is the tool for transferring teaching information, as well as the means for assisting students' understanding.

2.2   Meaning and Development of Individual Epistemological Beliefs

Perry (1970) suggested that, individuals' opinion on the nature of knowledge and knowing process is "epistemological beliefs". Most of the researchers suggested that, epistemological beliefs are individuals' basic assumptions of the nature of knowledge and the nature of knowing, as well as individuals' beliefs in what knowledge is and how it is acquired. Epistemological beliefs refer to individuals' hypothesis in nature of knowledge and knowing process, which can reflect individuals' psychological state for the knowledge, acquisition approach, and degree of difficulty in knowledge. In this study, epistemological beliefs refer to students' opinion on or beliefs in knowledge and knowing, which covers four dimensions: stability of knowledge, organizational structure of knowledge, control of learning, and speed of learning. The following theories advocated by scholars are related to the development of studies on epistemological beliefs:

1. Piaget's Genetic Epistemology

The integration of philosophy and psychology of developmental psychology is originated from the "genetic epistemology" proposed by Piaget in 1950. Constructivism investigates the origin of knowledge, but actually it emphasizes the interaction between two dimensions – mental structure and knowledge content. Genetic epistemology suggests that the individuals' cognitive development will change stage by stage with individuals' growth. Children's opinion on natural world experiences a series of changing stages, including Sensorimotor stage, Preoperational stage, Concrete operations stage and Formal operations stage. When individuals' cognitive development reaches formal operation stage, they learn by deductive thinking. That is to say, individuals may integrate all of the possible relationships into a closed formal logical structure.

2. Perry's intellectual and ethical development forms

The studies on epistemological beliefs conducted from the perspective of specific psychological orientation started from Perry's *"Forms of Intellectual and Ethical development in the College Years: A Scheme"* published in 1970. Perry used questionnaire surveys and interviews to conduct a 4-year longitudinal study on 110 students studying at Harvard University, hoping to understand how students' nature and knowledge evolve, and how students' understanding as learners changes with time. In the study, Perry discovered that the development of college students' epistemological beliefs can be divided into three forms and nine knowledge positions.

3. King and Kitchener's Reflective Judgment Model

King and Kitchener (1980) enrolled high school students, college students, and PhD students as the research participants. Based on the theoretical foundation of Perry (1970), they analyzed the cognitive development of individuals' epistemology. King and Kitchener suggested that, because individuals have to make explanatory judgments for problems with poor structures, they have to ponder upon the limitations of their knowing, uncertainty, and perception of epistemology. In other words, they emphasized individuals' intellectual development and the ability to deal with poor-organized problems.

4. Baxter Magolda's Reflective Model of Epistemology

In this model, individuals' cognitive development includes 4 orders: (1) absolute knowing – individuals receive knowledge form educators. Only when students don't know the exact answers to the questions does the feeling of uncertainty about knowledge occur; (2) transitional knowing – individuals start to realize that educators may not necessarily know all of the knowledge. They gain some knowledge through inter-personal interactions, and acknowledge the existence of uncertain knowledge; (3) independent knowing – individuals start to question the perspectives of educators, and develop uncertain knowledge through individuals' independent thinking. They expect educators' encouragement on their thinking and expression; (4) contextual knowing – individuals can develop their own perspectives through the interactions with various situations.

5. Kuhn's internal argument

Kuhn was interested in the thinking models in daily life. He proposed a concept about thinking model: people would conceptualize the individuals' internal reasoning and thinking into an internal argument.

6. An embedded systemic model of epistemological beliefs

Schommer (1990) was different from the scholars mentioned above, and suggested that epistemological beliefs are developed in a single dimension, but a multidimensional belief system which is actively constructed by individuals, and includes five dimensions as follows:

(1) Certainty of knowledge: The theory evolves from the perception that knowledge is unchangeable to the perception that knowledge is temporal.
(2) Structure of knowledge: The theory evolves from the perception that the structure of knowledge in independent small units to the perception that the structure of knowledge is highly integrated.
(3) Origin of knowledge: The theory evolves from the perception that knowledge is transferred by authority to the perception that knowledge needs to be observed and reasoned.
(4) Speed of knowledge acquisition: The theory evolves from the perception that the speed of knowledge acquisition is fast and does not need to be understood to the perception that knowledge acquisition is progressive learning.
(5) Control over knowledge acquisition: The theory evolves from the perception that knowledge is inherent to the perception that knowledge grows with time.

3 Methodology

3.1 Participants

The participants were two classes of 2nd graders of a junior high school in the central Taiwan. One class was the experimental group and the other was the control group. The experimental group, including 32 students, learned with multimedia e-books with PBL approach. On the other hand, the control group with as well as 32 students, learned with the conventional teaching approach. The two classes were taught by the same teacher so as to avoid teacher-student interaction-related interference. The number of male students was almost equal to the number of female students, because it reduced the influence of gender difference. The students in both groups were divided into high achievers and low achievers according to the average rank of the previous two English sectional examinations before the experiment. The students whose ranks were top 40% were assigned as high achievers, while those whose ranks were bottom 60% were assigned as low achievers.

3.2 Experimental Procedures

This study used quasi-experimental research method to implement experimental teaching, and enrolled two classes of 2nd graders of a junior high school in the central Taiwan as the participants. The two classes were taught by the same teacher. The teacher implemented teaching at the experimental group and the control group respectively. Before the teaching, the students were asked to take the pre-test. After the two groups of students completed 12 classes' learning, they took the post-test to compare the differences in dependent variables. The design of this study was mainly to implement e-books teaching approach to the experimental group and conventional teaching approach to the control group. This study intended to investigate whether the integration of teaching with e-books could increase students' English learning interest and motivation, and in this way, further improve their learning effectiveness. Based on the research design mentioned above, the teaching procedures in experimental group were divided into the following three steps. The descriptions are given as follows:

Step 1: To trigger students' learning motivation by incentive system.

Before the teaching, the students were divided into groups according to PBL learning model. The multimedia e-books approach was used in the class. Taking advantage of incentive system, the teacher guided students to participate in speaking training in class, enabling them to be confident to speak and glad to answer questions. In this way, their learning motivation was triggered.

Step 2: To integrate the PBL model with brainstorming to stimulate continuous learning.

The students progressively learned the grammar content of present perfect tense. Moreover, the teacher conducted PBL model team competitions for team members to learn collaboratively, and designed some issues for students to brainstorm. Students were encouraged to engage in group discussion so as to cultivate their active learning, critical thinking, and problem-solving abilities.

Step 3: To use summative learning test to test the learning effectiveness.

After finishing learning of step 2, students were required to take English learning achievement test to examine their learning effectiveness and to confirm whether the expected teaching objectives were achieved.

3.3   Tools

1. English multimedia e-book

The content of English multimedia e-book was "Lesson 7: Have You Packed Your Gloves Yet?" and "Lesson 8: Have You Ever Been to England?" of Book 4 of English Textbook for junior high schools published by Kang Hsuan Educational Publishing Group, as shown in Fig. 1:

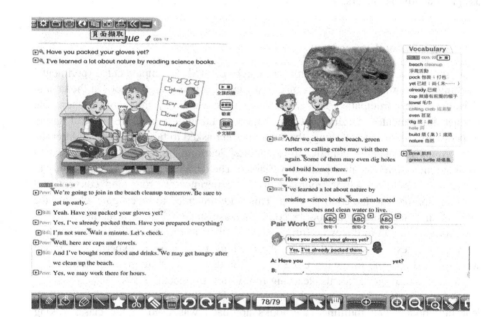

Fig. 1. Example of content of eBook

2. English learning achievement test

According to step 3 of the teaching procedures, this study used learning achievement test to examine students' English academic performance. According to the teaching materials, the teacher designed an English learning achievement test where three dimensions were included: character recognition ability, tense analysis ability, and reading comprehension ability. After 12 classes, students took the test as the post-test.

3. Questionnaire on Individual English epistemological beliefs

In the study, this teacher reviewed the studies of Hofer and Pintrich (1997), Lu (2004), Tsai (2005), Wang (2008), and Chu (2009) and designed a questionnaire on individual English epistemological beliefs, which included three dimensions: authority of knowledge, dialectics of knowledge, and control of knowledge, with a total of 19 questions, to measure the maturity of epistemological beliefs. The content was amended by scholars and experts to ensure the validity.

The answers to each item included strongly agree, agree, uncertain, disagree, and strongly disagree, which was the 5-point Likert scale. The way to score was 5, 4, 3, 2, and 1. The higher score a student got, the more mature his or her epistemological beliefs were. The lower score a student got, the less mature his or her epistemological beliefs were. Time was not limited, and the questionnaire was completed until the all the items were filled out (Table 1).

Table 1. Distribution of various dimensions (Sub-scales) of the questionnaire on Epistemological beliefs

Dimension	Item no. included in each dimension	Total number of items
Authority of knowledge	Questions 1 to 7	7
Dialectics of knowledge	Questions 8 to 13	6
Control of knowledge	Questions 14 to19	6

3.4   Data Collection and Analysis

This study used relevant research tools to implement experimental teaching. The data sources were mainly the quantitative data collected from achievement test and scale on epistemological beliefs. This study used SPSS statistical software to perform data analysis. To-way ANOVA was expected to be performed to investigate the significant differences.

4   Results and Discussion

4.1   Comparison on Differences and Dimensions of Junior High School Students' English Learning Achievement Caused by Different Teaching Methods and Students' Learning Abilities

4.1.1   The Differences of Junior High School Students' English Learning Achievement Caused by Different Teaching Methods and Students' Learning Abilities

Since the experimental group and the control group were implemented multimedia e-books with PBL teaching approach and conventional teaching approach respectively, the study investigated the influence of different teaching methods on English academic performance of junior high school students with different learning abilities. In the study, the teaching methods was independent variable, students' learning ability was dependent variable, and students' pre-test score was the covariance which was used to investigate whether there was any significant relation. According to the results of independent sample two-way ANOVA (see Table 2), the statistical outcome showed that the interaction between teaching method and students' learning ability did not reach significance $(F = 0.367, P = 0.547)$, suggesting that, there was no significant relation between teaching method and students' learning ability in the pre-test. Since there was no major interaction between teaching method and learning ability, this study only focused on the main effect of individual factors. As shown in Table 2, the independent variable, teaching method, reached significance (F = 21.749, P < 0.05), which meant that different teaching methods led to the significant difference in pre-test score. Moreover, the dependent variable, the students' learning ability, also reached significance (F = 5.278, P < 0.05), which suggested that different learning abilities also led to the significant difference in pre-test score.

Table 2. Summary on ANOVA on students' English academic performance with different teaching methods and different learning abilities

Source	Sum of squares of deviation from mean	DOF	Mean of sum of square	F	P
Teaching method	2831.090	1	2831.090	21.749	.000*
Learning ability	687.078	1	687.078	5.278	.025*
Teaching method *learning ability	47.719	1	47.719	.367	.547
Error	7680.031	59	130.17		

* p < .05

Besides, this study compared the adjusted mean score of post-test between the experimental group and control group. As shown in Table 3, the adjusted mean scores of post-test were 85.22 and 71.65 respectively, suggesting that, students who learned with multimedia e-books with PBL approach performed better than those who learned with the conventional teaching approach. Moreover, in terms of division of abilities, the adjusted mean score of low achievers was 74.85, while that of high achievers was 82.02, suggesting that, high achievers' English academic performance was obviously superior to low achievers'.

Table 3. Students' adjusted mean score of post-test of students with different learning abilities and different teaching methods

Learning ability	Experimental group	Control group	Adjusted mean
High achievers	87.92	76.12	82.02
Low achievers	82.52	67.18	74.85
Adjusted mean	85.22	71.65	

4.1.2   The Dimensions of Junior High School Students' English Learning Achievement Caused by Different Teaching Methods and Students' Learning Abilities

In the study, students' English academic achievement was mainly divided into three dimensions: character recognition ability, tense analysis ability, and reaching ability. The comparison of the dimensions was performed as follows, and the results of the statistical tests were summarized in Table 4:

Table 4. Summary on ANOVA on students' post-test score of the influence of different teaching methods and different learning abilities

Learning achievement	Source	Sum of squares of deviation from mean	DOF	Mean of sum of square	F	P
Character recognition ability	Teaching method	90.676	1	90.676	10.584	.002
	High achievers	7.118	1	7.118	.831	.366
	Teaching method	.008	1	.008	.001	.976
	*High achievers and low achievers					
	Error	505.474	59	8.567		
Tense analysis ability	Teaching method	640.865	1	640.865	21.783	.000
	High achievers	301.828	1	301.828	10.259	.002
	Teaching method	60.408	1	60.408	2.053	.157
	*High achievers and low achievers					
	Error	1735.814	59	29.421		
Reaching ability	Teaching method	287.647	1	287.647	7.044	.010
	High achievers	332.841	1	332.841	8.151	.006
	Teaching method	14.733	1	14.733	.361	.550
	*High achievers and low achievers					
	Error	2409.143	59	40.833		

1. Character recognition ability

In terms of the character recognition ability of English academic achievement, there was no significant interaction between teaching method and students' learning ability ($F = 0.001$, $P = 0.976$). However, as for the main effect of individual factors, the teaching method reached significance ($F = 10.584$, $P < 0.05$). However, students' learning ability did not reach significance ($F = 0.831$, $P = 0.366$). According to the statistical results mentioned above, different learning methods affected students' character recognition ability of English academic achievement. However, there was no significant difference between high achievers and low achievers, suggesting that both of them possessed basic character recognition ability.

2. Tense analysis ability

In terms of the tense analysis ability of English academic achievement, there was no significant interaction between teaching method and students' learning ability $(F = 2.053, P = 0.157)$. However, as for the main effect of individual factors, the teaching method reached significance $(F = 21.783, P < 0.05)$. As well, students' learning ability reached significance $(F = 10.259, P < 0.05)$. According to the statistical results mentioned above, the different teaching methods and students' different learning abilities led to a significant difference in performance of tense analysis ability of high achievers and low achievers.

3. Reaching ability

In terms of the reading ability of English academic achievement, there was no significant interaction between teaching method and students' learning ability $(F = 0.361, P = 0.550)$. However, as for the main effect of individual factors, the teaching method reached significance $(F = 7.044, P < 0.05)$. As well, students' learning ability reached significance $(F = 8.151, P < 0.05)$. According to the statistical results mentioned above, different teaching methods and students' different learning abilities led to a significant difference in performance of reading ability of high achievers and low achievers.

This study compared the adjusted mean score of post-test in terms of three dimensions between the experimental group and control group, and the statistical results and findings are as follows. Firstly, as shown in Table 5, the adjusted mean scores of post-test on character recognition ability of experimental group and control group were 85.22 and 71.65, respectively, suggesting that, students who learned with multimedia e-books with PBL approach had better character recognition ability than those who learned with the conventional teaching approach. Besides, in terms of division of abilities, the adjusted mean score of low achievers and of high achievers were equally close to 20, meaning that high achievers' and low achievers' character recognition abilities were almost the same. Secondly, as shown in Table 5, the adjusted mean scores of post-test on tense analysis ability of the experimental group and control group were 29.7845 and 23.289, respectively, suggesting that, students who learned with multimedia e-books with PBL approach performed better on tense analysis. Besides, in terms of division of abilities, the adjusted mean score of low achievers and of high achievers were 24.2585 and 28.8150, respectively; suggesting that, the performance of tense analysis ability of high achievers was significantly superior to that of low achievers. Thirdly, as shown in Table 5, the adjusted mean scores of post-test on reaching ability of the experimental group and control group were 32.7335 and 29.4170 respectively, suggesting that students who learned with multimedia e-books with PBL approach performed better on reading. Moreover, in terms of division of abilities, the adjusted mean score of low achievers and of high achievers were 29.1720 and 33.9785, respectively, suggesting that high achievers' reaching ability was superior.

Table 5. Students' adjusted mean score of posttest in terms of three dimensions of students with different learning abilities and different teaching methods

Sub-dimension	Learning ability	Experimental group	Control group	Adjusted mean
Character recognition ability	High achievers	22.140	19.740	20.9400
	Low achievers	21.475	19.028	20.2515
	Adjusted mean	21.8075	19.384	
Tense analysis ability	High achievers	31.073	26.557	28.8150
	Low achievers	28.496	20.021	24.2585
	Adjusted mean	29.7845	23.289	
Reaching ability	High achievers	35.648	32.309	33.9785
	Low achievers	31.819	26.525	29.1720
	Adjusted mean	32.7335	29.4170	

4.2 Analysis on Students' Individual "Epistemological Beliefs" on the Influence of Different Teaching Methods and Different Learning Abilities

4.2.1 Analysis of Two-Way ANOVA Independent Sample

As for the significance test on the main effect of teaching method shown in Table 6, F value = 5.526, P value = $0.022 < 0.05$, which reached significance, suggesting that teaching method had an impact on students' academic achievement.

Table 6. Summary on ANOVA on posttest on individual Epistemological beliefs with different teaching methods and different learning abilities

Source	Sum of squares of deviation from mean	DOF	Mean of sum of square	F	P
Teaching method	203.372	1	203.372	5.526	0.022
Learning ability	176.758	1	176.758	4.802	0.032
Teaching method *learning ability	4.204	1	4.204	0.114	0.737
Error	2171.550	59	36.806		

Besides, as for the significance test on main effect of students' learning abilities, F value = 4.802, P value = 0.032 < 0.05, which reached a significant difference, also suggesting that students' learning abilities had an impact on students' academic achievement.

4.2.2   Adjusted Mean Score

As shown in Table 7, the adjusted mean score was 74.0650 and 70.4290 respectively, suggesting that students' individual epistemological belief with multimedia e-books teaching approach was more mature. In terms of division abilities, the mean score of low achievers was 70.4300, and that of high achievers was 74.0640. That is, students' individual epistemological belief with high achievers was more mature.

Table 7. Adjusted mean of posttest on individual Epistemological beliefs of different teaching methods in students with different learning abilities

Learning abilities	Experimental group	Control group	Adjusted mean
High achievers	75.619	72.509	74.0640
Low achievers	72.511	68.349	70.4300
Adjusted mean	74.0650	70.4290	

4.3   Analysis on the Mediation Effect on Individual Epistemological Beliefs with Different Teaching Methods and English Learning Effectiveness

This study performed regression analyses on the influence of teaching methods on epistemological beliefs, the influence of teaching methods on students' English academic achievement, and SPSS on the influence of students' English academic achievement with different teaching methods and the epistemological beliefs. The analysis results are summarized in Table 8. As shown in Table 8, the regression coefficient between teaching methods and epistemological beliefs was 0.272^*, which reached significance. The regression coefficient between teaching method and English learning effectiveness was 0.401^{**}, which reached significance as well. Teaching methods and epistemological beliefs were independent variables, and the regression coefficient between them and English learning effectiveness was 0.211^* and 0.7^{**}. Lastly, this study tested the mediation effect. As shown in Table 8, after epistemological beliefs were included, the regression coefficient of teaching methods decreased from 0.401 to 0.211. Therefore, epistemological beliefs had a partial mediation effect on teaching methods and English learning achievement.

Table 8. Regression analysis on the influence of teaching methods and Epistemological beliefs on English learning achievement

Predictor	Epistemological beliefs	English learning achievement	
Teaching methods	0.272*	0.401**	0.211*
Epistemological beliefs			0.7**
R2	0.074	0.161	0.614

* p < .05 ** p < .01

5 Conclusion and Suggestions

The results of this study suggest that, students who received multimedia e-books with PBL teaching approach had better English learning achievement than those who received conventional teaching approach, suggesting that multimedia e-books had a positive influence on English learning. As for the three dimensions of English academic achievement, almost all dimensions of high achievers were superior to those of low achievers except for character recognition ability. Therefore, teachers are encouraged to use multimedia e-books teaching more frequently, which can help improve students' learning effectiveness and is significantly beneficial to tense analysis ability and reading ability when learning English. However, this study only enrolled two classes of 2nd graders of junior high school in the central Taiwan as the subjects, so subsequent research was required for the extension of application to the students in Taiwan. Moreover, the e-books conducted to the experimental group in the study were the teaching materials published by Kang Hsuan Educational Publishing Group. Therefore, the results only represent the positive effect on English multimedia e-books teaching and cannot be extended to other subjects. They can only be provided as reference for teaching in other fields. Last, this study mainly investigated the grammar of "present perfect" in grade 2 of junior high school. Subsequent studies can be performed and developed to understand whether the results can be extended to other grades or other grammar forms.

References

Abdullah, N., Gibb, F.: Students' attitudes towards e-books in a Scottish Higher Education institute: Part 3 — search and browse tasks. Libr. Rev. **58**(1), 17–27 (2009)

Clark, J.M., Paivio, A.: Dual coding theory and education. Educ. Psychol. Rev. **3**(3), 149–210 (1991)

Cobb, T.: Breadth and depth of lexical acquisition with hands-on concordance. Comput. Assist. Lang. Learn. **12**(4), 245–360 (1999)

Chang, Y.F., Peng, H.C.: A case study on the application of computer CD teaching materials to English teaching of Junior High Schools. Educ. Res. Inf. **8**(2), 28–45 (2000)

Chu, Y.S.: Epistemological Beliefs of Gifted Students in Music Class of Elementary Schools and the Its Influence on Objective Orientation. Master's thesis, Department of Elementary Education, National Taipei University of Education (2009)

Huang, S.Y.: A Study on Multimedia Collaborative Learning in English Teaching –Taking Elementary Schools in Remote Coastal Areas of Yunlin County for Example. Unpublished Master's thesis, Graduate Institute of Elementary Education National Chiayi University, Chiayi (2002)

Hofer, B.K., Pintrich, P.: The development of epistemological theories: beliefs about knowledge and knowing and their relation to learning. Rev. Educ. Res. **67**(1), 88–140 (1997)

Johanna, K., Philip, M.: Enhancing English language skills using multimedia: tried and tested. Comput. Assist. Lang. Learn. **12**(4), 281–294 (1999)

Lu, H.L.: A Study on Junior High School Students' Epistemological Beliefs, Parents' Expectations and Learning Achievement. Master's thesis, Graduate Institute of Education, National Changhua Normal University, Unpublished, Changhua City (2004)

Mayer, R.E., Anderson, R.B.: Animations need narrations: an experimental test of a dual-coding hypothesis. J. Educ. Psychol. **83**, 484–490 (1991)

Mayer, R.E., Moreno, R.: Nine ways to reduce cognitive load in multimedia learning. Educ. Psychol. **38**(1), 43–52 (2003)

McLure, M., Hoseth, A.: Patron-driven e-book use and users' e-book perceptions: a snapshot. Collect. Build. **31**(4), 136–147 (2012)

Paivio, A., Csapo, K.: Picture superiority in free recall: imagery or dual coding? Cogn. Psychol. **5**, 176–206 (1973)

Sadoski, M.: A dual coding view of vocabulary learning. Read. Writ. Q. **21**, 221–238 (2005)

Su, P.C.: Influence of Online Game-based Evaluation on Learning Motivation and Learning Achievement of Scientific Leaning of Grade 8 Students. Graduate Institute of Science Education, National Changhua Normal University, Changhua (2006)

Tsai, C.H.: A Study on Epistemological Beliefs, Learning Style and Learning Achievement of Senior High School Students. Master's thesis, Graduate Institute of Education, National Changhua Normal University, Unpublished, Changhua City (2005)

Wang, C.H.: Relationship among Learning Behavior, Learning Satisfaction and Learning Performance of Students Receiving Web-based Instruction. Master's thesis, Department of Information Management, Da-Yeh University, Changhua (2001)

Wang, K.S.: Influence of Multimedia-assisted Teaching on Learning Motivation and Class Atmosphere of Physical Education Class of Elementary School Students. Master's thesis, Graduate School, National Taiwan Sport University, Taoyuan (2006)

Wang, S.C.: A Study on the Relationship among Objective Structure of Mathematics Classroom of Elementary School, Mathematics Epistemological Beliefs, and Patterns of Learning Behaviors. Graduate Institute of Education, Tunghai University (2008)

Wu, C.M.: A Study on the Integration of Information with Satellite Technology Teaching Activities and Its Influence on Learning Effectiveness – Taking Higher Graders of Fu-Sing Elementary School in Taitung County for Example. Master's thesis, Graduate School, Department of Education, National Taitung University (2008)

An Inquiry-Based Digital Storytelling Approach for Increasing Learner Autonomy in English

Ming-Chi Liu and Yueh-Min Huang[✉]

Department of Engineering Science,
National Cheng Kung University, Tainan, Taiwan
{Benliu,huang}@mail.ncku.edu.tw

Abstract. Digital storytelling has been shown by many research studies as an effective learning tool in achieving learner autonomy in language learning. Although the previous studies have worked on the providing students with multimedia authoring tools to unleash their imagination in developing stories, the complexity of the digital story construction still erects challenging barriers to students. Specifically, lacking an appropriate guidance can have a debilitating effect on students' autonomous behavior and learning performance. This study thus introduced the inquiry-based learning strategy to scaffold learners in creating stories. An experiment comprised of 28 Grade 6 elementary students involving in an inquiry-based digital storytelling project, was conducted to examine their learning outcomes. The results revealed that the students improved their learner autonomy.

1 Introduction

Learner autonomy defined as "the ability to take charge of one's own learning." Sanprasert (2010) has been considered to be the most vital ability of language learning in a new media age. Apparently, an autonomous language learner can independently set goals; appropriately search and organize learning resources; continually perform the learning tasks; and critically reflect and evaluate their own progress by chose criteria (Collentine 2011). In other words, they ultimately equipped with a capacity for detachment, critical reflection, decision-making, and independent action. With the situation of globalization in the twenty-first century, teachers are necessary to providing opportunities for self-directed language learning through self-access facilities inside or outside the classroom (Kim 2014).

The popular appeal of computers has resulted in facilitating self-directed language learning through using the technology. In particular, having easy access to digital recording tools can support the unlimited oral practice in language classrooms. As shown by research studies (Hafner and Miller 2011; Kim 2014; Thang et al. 2014), the learning tool such as digital storytelling, which combines the art of storytelling with a variety of digital multimedia contents, has been effective in achieving autonomy in language learning. One reason is that storytelling help learners develop a sensitivity to the way language works (Tsou et al. 2006). The other reason is that these digital tools

T.-T. Wu et al. (Eds.): SETE 2016, LNCS 10108, pp. 219–224, 2017.
DOI: 10.1007/978-3-319-52836-6_23

are able to support language learners in checking performance data to monitor their learning progress (Kim 2014).

However, the construction of a digital story is a complex and challenging task, which involves students combining multiple skills (Liu et al. 2011). As noted by Hafner and Miller (2011), these skills include: research skills (e.g., searching and analyzing information), writing skills (e.g., preparing a script), technology skills (e.g., manipulating digital multimedia), presentation skills (e.g., effectively communicating the information), and evaluation skills (e.g., critiquing their own and others' work). Therefore, the previous studies demonstrated by Hwang et al. (2014); Liu et al. (2011) have worked on the providing students with multimedia authoring tools to unleash their imagination in developing digital stories. However, the previous research lacks to provide students an appropriate guidance to facilitate autonomous learning behavior. Collentine (2011) pointed out that learners lacked a well-defined storytelling task to encourage autonomy. Also, Alshumaimeri and Almasri (2012) argued that using free search environment would put students at risk of accessing inappropriate materials during storytelling tasks. In other words, students need a supportive autonomous learning environment to take an active part in decision-making and problem solving during digital storytelling tasks.

In order to promote high levels of learner autonomy during digital storytelling activity, the inquiry-based learning strategy was introduced to scaffold learners in creating stories. This approach is a research activity that requires the learner "to collect information about a subject using the web" (Laborda 2009). Researchers (Alshumaimeri and Almasri 2012; Hung 2015) found that this approach helps language learners engage with texts related to their discipline and develop critical thinking in the choice of Internet sources promoting. Those benefits are the key to preparing language learners for autonomous learning. Therefore, this study is aimed at an investigation intended to evaluate the effectiveness of the inquiry-based digital storytelling in increase the competence of students' autonomous learning.

2 Methodology

2.1 Participators

A total of 28 Grade 6 elementary students took part in this study. All of them were taking an English course at a public elementary school in southern Taiwan. These students started to take English class in Grade 3, thus, all of them had the basic English language skills necessary to complete the project.

2.2 The Design of the Inquiry-Based Digital Storytelling

The project "I am a weather forecast anchor" contained three topics: weather, activities, and clothes. It was designed on the basis of inquiry-based learning and digital storytelling. Six learning tasks, including "Choosing the city", "Web questing for information", "Composing the weather forecast script", "Shooting a short video clip", "Class presentation," and "Peer-evaluation and feedback" are listed in Table 1.

Table 1. Learning tasks of "I am a weather forecast anchor"

Learning activities	Task missions
1. Choosing the city	1. Watch the weather forecast flip and analyze the elements of the script 2. Choose a city in Taiwan as the topic for weather forecasting
2. Web questing for information	1. Utilize the website "yahoo weather" to gather the information for the weather forecast 2. Use the Google image search engine to collect the pictures of activities and clothes
3. Composing the weather forecast script	1. Combine the information and pictures that collected from the websites to compose the script 2. Revise the script and memorize the lines
4. Shooting a short video clip	1. Use the APP "Noteledge" to make a weather forecast flip
5. Class presentation	1. Present the short video clips
6. Evaluation and feedback	1. Evaluation sheet was used in the process 2. Write down suggestions and feedback in the evaluation sheets

During the learning tasks, the students needed to collect the data from the Internet. There were five websites the students used in the tasks. Figure 1 show how students gathered the weather information and details from the website "yahoo weather" by using the "Noteledge" app. The students gathered the weather information and details. After data collection, the students started to compose their weather forecast script by filling in the worksheet. Following that, the students memorized the script and began to shoot a video clip based on the script they wrote before. The students made their short

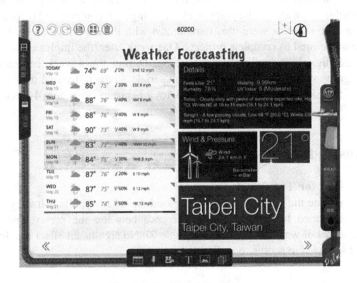

Fig. 1. The "Noteledge" app.

video clips around the classroom. Finally, all short video clips were posted on the teacher's blog for the students to vote and peer-evaluation.

2.3 Instruments

The Knowledge Test About Weather Forecast

The knowledge test was developed by the elementary English teacher, who has taught English for many years. The test was designed to examine students' understanding about word meanings, word choices, and reading comprehension in the situation of the weather forecast. It contained 17 questions with a total score of 17.

The Language Learner Autonomy Questionnaire

The Language Learner Autonomy Questionnaire (LLAQ) developed by Cotterall (1995, 1999) was adapted to measure students' autonomy in language learning. In this study, the test consisted of 12 items using a five-point Likert scale to measure autonomous language learning in the four subscales: four items for learning strategies, two items for motivation, four items for metacognitive awareness, and two items for students' perceived language learning responsibility. The Cronbach's α of this 12-item questionnaire was .881 (Lee 2011; Wang 2013). The Language Learner Autonomy Questionnaire was administered to all the students at the beginning and end of this inquiry-based digital storytelling intervention.

2.4 Procedure

The entire procedure covered seven 45-minute classes over a period of ten weeks. In the first week, the pretests of knowledge, and LLAQ were given to the students during a regular class session. After three weeks, the teacher instructed the students in the use of the Noteledge software for the purpose of searching web contents and recording their presentation. The students were thus familiarized with the experimental environments and the skills required to complete projects. One week later, the implementation of the inquiry-based digital storytelling project began. During the 4-week implementation period, the group was exposed to the course materials. In the last week, the posttests of knowledge, and LLAQ were administered to the group after the 4-week project practice.

3 Results and Discussion

Knowledge Test for Two Work Types

In order to examine the effect of the inquiry-based digital storytelling strategy, a paired t-test was performed to determine the difference between the pretest and posttest knowledge scores of weather forecast (see Table 2). No significant effect was found for the posttest knowledge scores, p = .958.

Table 2. Pre-/post- knowledge test mean scores, standard deviations, and analysis of Paired t-test results

	N	Pretest		Posttest		Paired t-test
		Mean	SD	Mean	SD	T
Knowledge test	28	13.21	3.47	13.18	2.91	0.53

* p < .05

Notes: The maximum score of each test is 17

Autonomous Language Learning Scores for Two Work Types

A paired t-test was also performed to determine how the difference between the pretest and posttest scores of autonomous language learning was influenced (see Table 3). No significant effect was found for the posttest autonomous language learning scores, p = .543. However, the outcomes show that students gain higher posttest autonomous language learning scores than the pretest.

Table 3. Pre-/post- autonomous language learning mean scores, standard deviations, and analysis of the paired t-test results

Work types	N	Pre-autonomy		Post-autonomy		Paired t-test
		Mean	SD	Mean	SD	T
Individual	28	3.09	0.79	3.16	0.55	-6.16

* p < .05

The likely explanation for this finding would be that the project can drive learners to take responsibility for inquiry-based digital storytelling project. For example, the inquiry-based digital storytelling project provided an authentic context for language learning where learners should teach the peers either English or technology skills (Hafner and Miller 2011). In other words, the findings of Table 3 may imply that the better way to achieve autonomy in language learning should be based on authentic learning context.

4 Conclusion

The assumption of this study predicted that the inquiry-based digital storytelling approach would bring two types of benefits to the students: on the one hand, the development of learners' practical language knowledge; on the other, the improvement of their autonomous language learning (Laborda 2009; Snodin 2013). In order to examine these assumptions, an experiment was conducted to investigate that the outcomes of language knowledge, and autonomy in language learning during the proposed inquiry-based digital storytelling project. Overall, the students improved their learner autonomy.

Digital technology alone would not give learners the opportunity to develop language learning autonomy in ways the teachers hoped. These findings imply that the necessity of scaffolding learners in creating stories. Therefore, more work in the future would be needed to further examine the approach of learner autonomy development across different student groups such as learning strategies.

References

Alshumaimeri, Y.A., Almasri, M.M.: The effects of using WebQuests on reading comprehension performance of Saudi EFL students. Turk. Online J. Educ. Technol. **11**(4), 295–306 (2012)

Collentine, K.: Learner autonomy in a task-based 3D world and production. Lang. Learn. Technol. **15**(3), 50–67 (2011)

Cotterall, S.: Readiness for autonomy: investigating learner beliefs. System **23**(2), 195–205 (1995). doi:10.1016/0346-251X(95)00008-8

Cotterall, S.: Key variables in language learning: what do learners believe about them? System **27** (4), 493–513 (1999). doi:10.1016/S0346-251X(99)00047-0

Hafner, C.A., Miller, L.: Fostering learner autonomy in English for science: a collaborative digital video project in a technological learning environment. Lang. Learn. Technol. **15**(3), 68–86 (2011)

Hung, H.T.: Flipping the classroom for English language learners to foster active learning. Comput. Assist. Lang. Learn. **28**(1), 81–96 (2015). doi:10.1080/09588221.2014.967701

Hwang, W.-Y., Shadiev, R., Hsu, J.-L., Huang, Y.-M., Hsu, G.-L., Lin, Y.-C.: Effects of storytelling to facilitate EFL speaking using Web-based multimedia system. Comput. Assist. Lang. Learn., 1–27 (2014). doi:10.1080/09588221.2014.927367

Kim, S.: Developing autonomous learning for oral proficiency using digital storytelling. Lang. Learn. Technol. **18**(2), 20–35 (2014)

Laborda, J.G.: Using WebQuests for oral communication in English as a foreign language for Tourism Studies. Educ. Technol. Soc. **12**(1), 258–270 (2009)

Lee, L.: Blogging: promoting learner autonomy and intercultural competence through study abroad. Lang. Learn. Technol. **15**(3), 87–109 (2011)

Liu, C.C., Chen, H.S.L., Shih, J.L., Huang, G.T., Liu, B.J.: An enhanced concept map approach to improving children's storytelling ability. Comput. Educ. **56**(3), 873–884 (2011). doi:10.1016/j.compedu.2010.10.029

Sanprasert, N.: The application of a course management system to enhance autonomy in learning English as a foreign language. System **38**(1), 109–123 (2010). doi:10.1016/j.system.2009.12.010

Snodin, N.S.: The effects of blended learning with a CMS on the development of autonomous learning: a case study of different degrees of autonomy achieved by individual learners. Comput. Educ. **61**, 209–216 (2013). doi:10.1016/j.compedu.2012.10.004

Thang, S.M., Lin, L.K., Mahmud, N., Ismail, K., Zabidi, N.A.: Technology integration in the form of digital storytelling: mapping the concerns of four Malaysian ESL instructors. Comput. Assist. Lang. Learn. **27**(4), 311–329 (2014). doi:10.1080/09588221.2014.903979

Tsou, W.L., Wang, W.C., Tzeng, Y.J.: Applying a multimedia storytelling website in foreign language learning. Comput. Educ. **47**(1), 17–28 (2006). doi:10.1016/j.compedu.2004.08.013

Wang, Z.: Language learner autonomy: validate its constructs and investigate Taiwanese students' tendency. (Master's thesis), National Changhua University of Education, Changhua, Taiwan (2013)

Investigating Students' Use and Evaluation of Video as a Form of Computer Assisted Language Learning Material

Hsiu-Ting Hung[1], Yu-Fang Lu[1], and Hui-Chin Yeh[2]($\boxtimes$)

[1] National Kaohsiung First University of Science and Technology,
Kaohsiung, Taiwan
hhung@nkfust.edu.tw
[2] National Yunlin University of Science and Technology, Douliu, Taiwan
hyeh@yuntech.edu.tw

Abstract. This study examined a group of English language learners' use and evaluation of digital videos as a form of computer assisted language learning (CALL) material, as they were engaged to complete a video-based vocabulary learning task using a CALL system. The results indicated that the students were able to watch the assigned video clips for task completion with reasonable time and effort, without any major learning difficulties. It was also found that the top three most frequently used functionalities of the CALL system that enabled learner-content interaction were video subtitles, followed by the built-in dictionary, and adjustable playback speed. On the whole, the students considered the way that the video material was integrated in the vocabulary learning task was facilitative and capable of enhancing their English learning experiences, indicating the overall appropriateness of such video use.

Keywords: Computer assisted language learning (CALL) · Vocabulary learning · English as a foreign language (EFL) · Digital video

1 Introduction

The widespread use of computers and technology in the learning and teaching of vocabulary has led to the emergence of Computer Assisted Vocabulary Learning (CAVL) in the broader context of Computer Assisted Language Learning (CALL). Historically, there are three developmental stages of CALL, including behavioristic CALL (with an emphasis on drills and practices from 1970s to 1980s), communicative CALL (with an emphasis on communicative tasks facilitated through CALL materials from 1980s to 1990s), and integrative CALL (with an emphasis on language use in a meaningful and authentic context in the first two decades of the 21st century) [1]. As a subfield of CALL, the development of CAVL has arguably followed a similar path. At present, the development of CALL and CAVL has progressed to the integrative stage. According to a review article on CALL research [2], various forms of CALL tools or activities have now been integrated in the teaching and learning of all four skills (i.e., reading, writing, listening, and speaking) and three language areas (i.e., pronunciation, vocabulary, and grammar). As for CAVL, common tools or activities used to assist

© Springer International Publishing AG 2017
T.-T. Wu et al. (Eds.): SETE 2016, LNCS 10108, pp. 225–239, 2017.
DOI: 10.1007/978-3-319-52836-6_24

students' learning of vocabulary are courseware, electronic dictionaries, corpora and concordances, and computer mediated communication activities.

Although not included in the research synthesis [2], which was conducted nearly a decade ago, many CAVL researchers and practitioners have advocated the use of multimedia-rich resources or materials to enrich and enhance the process of vocabulary learning. Some of these applied animation as a medium [3–6], others used podcasts [7, 8], and still others used video-based materials available on CD-ROMs or in TV programs [9–12] to facilitate vocabulary learning. The findings of these studies have generally supported the idea that multimedia materials can assist language teachers and learners in their teaching and learning of vocabulary.

Currently, the rise of the Internet and web-based learning technologies continue to have a positive impact on student learning, with online or digital video being one of the fastest-growing learning materials [13]. While previous research investigated various forms of multimedia, the use of video as a form of CALL material is gaining popularity in recent years [14]. It follows that learning vocabulary with video appears to be a reasonable research agenda in the literature on CAVL.

2   Theoretical Framework

This study draws upon the cognitive theory of multimedia learning (CTML), proposed by Mayer and his colleagues [15, 16], to highlight the use of multimedia material in the field of CALL. The CTML is probably the most influential theory for learning via multimedia. This theory explains how the presentation of verbal information (e.g., words, narration, or printed text) and visual information (e.g., illustrations, images, animations, or videos) interacts with learners' sensory memory, working memory, and long-term memory in learning. As applied to the learning of vocabulary in a multimedia environment, to achieve effective learning, "the learner must engage in five cognitive processes: (1) selecting relevant words for processing in verbal working memory, (2) selecting relevant images for processing in visual working memory, (3) organizing selected words into a verbal mental model, (4) organizing selected images into a visual mental model, and (5) integrating the verbal and visual representations" ([17], pp. 70–71). Briefly, the CTML argues that learning is more likely to occur when learners can build meaningful connections between the verbal and visual presentations of information [18].

The CTML has been used as a theoretical basis by many studies [5, 6, 9, 19]. Mayer and his colleagues demonstrated in a series of works that the integration of words and pictures can result in better learning [17, 20, 21], and thus it was concluded that "people learn better from words and pictures than from words alone" ([22], p. 548). Video, inherent with these two forms of multimedia, thus appears to be a promising form of multimedia learning material for language learning [18, 23].

3 Method

3.1 Research Questions

To contribute to the CAVL literature in CALL contexts, the present study adopted the theoretical framework of CTML to explore a group of English language learners' use and evaluation of online or digital videos as a form of CALL material, as they were engaged to complete a video-based vocabulary learning task using a CALL system. The following research questions were addressed in this study: (1) To what extent did the students use the video material in the CALL system for the completion of the video-based vocabulary learning task? (2) How did the students evaluate the overall appropriateness of using video to learn English in the CALL system?

3.2 Participants

The present study was conducted at a university in Taiwan. Two intact classes of sophomore students enrolled in an English language course were recruited, and 47 out of the 48 enrolled students agreed to voluntarily take part in this study. There were 12 males and 35 females who participated in the study, and most of them had been learning English as a foreign language (EFL) for more than 10 years before their participation in this study. Nearly half of them had experience of learning English with CALL systems featuring multimedia content, or something similar, although the majority had never done so before.

3.3 The CALL System

This study utilized VoiceTube (http://tw.voicetube.com) as the CALL system through which to deliver digital material in the form of video for English language learning. As a video-based CALL system, VoiceTube provides a huge amount of English subtitled videos (over 30,000 video clips were hosted on its official site as of August 2016), from a wide array of sources, such as TED Talks and CNN Student News, for various purposes of self-study, training, or classroom teaching. The digital videos afforded by the CALL system were thus operationalized as the CALL material in this study.

This particular technology, VoiceTube, was chosen because it is an award-winning video-based CALL system, specifically developed for EFL learners by a group of Taiwanese system designers, and most of its language learning functionalities are freely accessible to subscribers. Specifically, this study focused on how the participating students learned vocabulary intentionally through the use of video or CALL material made available in this system. The major system functionalities involved in this study are briefly described, as follows:

- *Adjustable playback speed:* This makes it possible to slow down or speed up any sentence when the students want to review and watch the videos more clearly.
- *Sentence repetition:* This can be used to replay specific sentences, if needed.

- *Video subtitles:* The students can watch the videos along with synchronized subtitles either in English, Chinese, or both languages in parallel.
- *Synchronized transcripts:* The students can read transcripts of the videos to look up certain vocabulary items. The transcripts can also be synchronized to play along with the related videos.
- *Built-in dictionary:* The built-in dictionary can be used at all times with both the video subtitles and synchronized transcripts. By clicking on any vocabulary item, a pop-up window will then appear and the students can thus see its pronunciation, English definition, example sentence, and synonyms.
- *Word lists:* All the vocabulary items and phrases that the students mark for each video will be added automatically to the students' personal word lists.

3.4   The CALL Task

The students' assignment was to watch two to three weekly assigned videos and generate their own word lists based on these for English vocabulary learning, using the CALL system. This video- based vocabulary learning task (also referred to as the CALL task in this study) was designed to be done outside the classroom with three major steps, as described below.

- *Watching video clips:* Each week the students were assigned two to three short videos for self- study, with each lasting three minutes on average. The course instructor posted details of the assigned videos on the system's bulletin board every week. The students were then given a week to watch these via the CALL system out of class.
- *Organizing target words:* The students were instructed to click on any vocabulary items they were interested in while they were watching the weekly assigned videos in the CALL system, as a way to organize the target words in their own word lists. The resulting word lists from different videos were then merged into a single learner-generated word list for each student.
- *Submitting word lists:* The students needed to submit their own student-generated word lists each week by uploading them to an institution-wide course management system.

Throughout the course of the study, a total of 24 video clips corresponding to ten weekly lesson themes of the curriculum were assigned to the students, for which they needed to generate ten associated weekly word lists to complete the video-based vocabulary learning task.

3.5   Data Sources

The data sources included CALL system logs, student-generated word lists, and individual student interviews. The data obtained from these was then analyzed to answer the two research questions of this study.

CALL System Logs. During the study period, the students had to watch a number of assigned videos using the CALL system. The students' online learning behaviors, such as the time spent on the CALL task and the number of video clips watched, were recorded in the system and retrieved for later analysis.

Student-Generated Word Lists. The CALL system allows the students to add vocabulary items to their own word lists by clicking on any selected words. The students could then review vocabulary items based on the alphabetical order of the words, the date when they were entered into the system, or the number of times they had been viewed, in whatever way best suited their needs.

Individual Student Interviews. To gain more insights into the students' learning experiences in this study, all 47 students were invited to participate in interviews. The interviews were conducted individually in Chinese, the participants' first language, which allowed them to express their ideas fluently. Each interview lasted for an average of 12 min. All the interviews were audio recorded and then transcribed and translated into English for the content analysis. The interview protocol can be broadly divided into two parts, involving seven generic questions with related prompts. The first part of the interview contained six questions developed based on a framework for CALL evaluation [24] to elicit student perspectives. This framework involves a set of six evaluation criteria that can be used to determine the appropriateness of the mediating resources of CALL (e.g., a given CALL task, material, or tool) for supporting second language acquisition from an interactionist perspective. These criteria helped to focus the students' evaluation of English language learning with the use of CALL material as they were engaged in completing the video-based vocabulary learning task. The second part of the interview aimed to find out the students' use of system functionalities for learner-content interaction while learning vocabulary through watching videos. To get more detailed information about the students' learning processes in the CALL system, the interviewees were asked one overarching question (i.e., What is your typical approach to learning vocabulary through video watching?), with some follow-up prompts (e.g., Do you usually watch videos with English or Chinese subtitles on? Do you pause the videos to look up or highlight every word that you don't know? Do you re-watch the videos to gain a fuller understanding or to study the language?).

3.6   Procedure

The procedure used in this study started with the teacher introducing the learning objectives as well as the CALL system to the students, followed by the students being guided to experience a trial lesson and complete a sample task in the first two weeks. Next, the students preceded to self-study the ten weekly lessons using the CALL system out of class, and on completion of the CALL task they were asked to submit their word lists produced on the basis of the weekly lessons to the teacher during this study period. After finishing the CALL task as one of their course requirements, the students took part in individual interviews during the last two weeks of this study.

4 Results

4.1 Students' Use of Video for Task Completion

To better understand the students' use of or interaction with the video material during the completion of the video-based vocabulary learning task, the students' learning records, as kept by the CALL system, were analyzed to reveal information about the time they devoted to completing the task and the number of vocabulary items that they logged in their word lists. In addition, the interview data were analyzed to reveal the students' frequency of using the system functionalities for task completion.

Time Spent on Task. The findings for the time on task indicated that each student spent approximately 198 (SD = 73.79) min creating word lists for the video clips they reviewed over the course of ten weeks. Moreover, the descriptive statistics also revealed that the most time a student spent per week on the task was 48 min, and the least was 13. On average, each student spent around 20 (SD = 7.37) min per week on the task.

As shown in Fig. 1, all of the students spent more than 11 min working on the task weekly, with the largest group spending within the range of 11 to 15 min (N = 17), and this was closely followed by 15 students who spent between 16 and 20 min. As for the students who spent more than 21 min (N = 15), the interview data showed that they viewed the video clips twice, both with and without subtitles, and thus spent much more time on the online learning and completion of the task. In the interviews, the students indicated that the length of the selected video clips (approximately three minutes) was reasonable – long enough to allow them to engage with the material, but not so long that they lost interest.

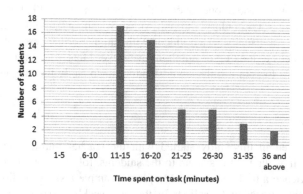

Fig. 1. Distribution of the time that each student spent on the task per week

Number of Vocabulary Items Logged. There were a total of 24 videos assigned to the students for the 10-week online learning. Table 1 shows that the average number of total items that each student collected in the word lists was 126, and that the standard

Table 1. Descriptive statistics for the total vocabulary items logged per student and the number of vocabulary items logged per video

	Minimum	Maximum	Median	Mean	SD
The number of vocabulary items logged for ten weeks	53	216	111	126.34	50.56
The number of vocabulary items logged per video	2	9	5	5.34	2.09

deviation was 50.56. It also shows that the average number of vocabulary items logged per student per video clip was five, with a standard deviation of 2.09.

Figure 2 shows the distribution of the average number of vocabulary items each student logged per video. Among the 47 students, only seven logged between two and three vocabulary items for each video, 27 logged between four and six, and 13 between seven and nine. As seen in Table 1 and Fig. 2, the results indicate that the majority of the students would intentionally study about five vocabulary items from each video clip.

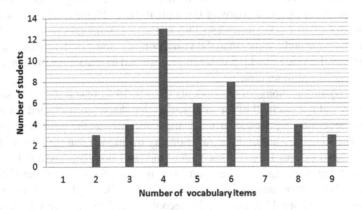

Fig. 2. Distribution of the average number of vocabulary items each student logged per video

Common Functionalities Used for Learner-Content Interaction. The selected video clips were available for use with many embedded functionalities of the CALL system during the intervention. Based on the content analysis of the interview data, the commonly used functionalities for learner- content interaction are summarized in Table 2. The functionalities of video subtitles, built-in dictionary, and adjustable playback speed were favored by most of the students, and thus were used more frequently. In contrast, the functionalities of sentence repetition and others (e.g., self-quiz and recording) were less commonly used.

- *Video subtitles:* This was the most frequent type of learner-content interaction resulting from the use of system functionality. All of the students (N = 47, 100%) used subtitles when viewing the online videos. According to their interview

Table 2. Commonly used system functionalities for learner-content interaction

Functionalities	Frequency	Percentage (%)
Video subtitles	47	100%
Built-in dictionary	40	85%
Adjustable playback speed	28	60%
Sentence repetition	9	19%
Others	8	17%

responses, 26 of the 47 students (55%) used English subtitles to gain better understanding of the video content, while 17 of them (36%) used both English and Chinese subtitles, and only four of them (9%) used Chinese subtitles. In addition, the students agreed that the use of subtitles could lower their anxiety and assist their vocabulary learning.

- *Built-in dictionary:* Most of the students (N = 40, 85%) watched the entire video containing a number of unknown words, and then looked some of these up in the built-in dictionary, which they said could be used to increase their video comprehension and vocabulary acquisition. They were thus more likely to find the correct definition of an unfamiliar word in the dictionary than guessing it from the context.
- *Adjustable playback speed:* Many of the students (N = 28, 60%) used the adjustable playback speed, and in the interviews they stated that sometimes they wanted to rely a bit more on the audio rather than the visual content. Some of the students also said that slowing the video was helpful when they wanted to imitate the pronunciation or to hear a sentence more clearly.
- *Sentence repetition:* Some of the students (N = 9, 19%) repeated certain sentences when they did not catch all of the information that the video contained. In practice, sentence repetition functioned in much the same way as the adjustable playback speed. The students who used this functionality mentioned that they did so in order to focus on sentences they did not understand, and that they preferred to simply listen to it again and again, rather than slowing down the speed of the video.
- *Others:* There were additional functionalities in the CALL system, such as self-quizzing and speaking practice by recording, and these were only used by a small number of students (N = 8, 17%). For example, five students watched the videos and then completed the associated quizzes to see how well they comprehended the video content. Three students stated that the recording functionality aroused their curiosity, and thus they used it to record some utterances and then work to improve their pronunciation.

4.2 Students' Evaluation of Using Video for English Learning

The interview data were analyzed with regard to the second research question, as to how the students evaluated the overall appropriateness of video use in this study. As summarized in Table 3, the students' perceptions of using video as a form of CALL material were categorized and tallied for frequency based on [24] evaluation framework.

Table 3. Major findings regarding the students' perceptions of video use

Criteria	Interview Questions	Major Findings
Language learning potential	Did your English improve from using the video material? Why or why not?	Overall, 85% of students reported that the video material helped them improve their vocabulary knowledge, and 55% stated that their listening comprehension also improved because of their enhanced vocabulary knowledge resulting from studying with the video material
Meaning focus	How much did you understand the content of the video material as you studied on your own?	The majority of students (75%) were able to self-study and comprehend most of the video content and only needed help occasionally, and under such situations they often re-watched the videos with captions on or consulted the pop-up dictionary in the CALL system
Learner fit	How suitable was the content of the video material for you?	Nearly all the students (96%) felt that the content of the video material matched their English proficiency levels
Authenticity	Do you think what you have learned from the video material is useful outside of class? Why or why not?	Almost all the students (96%) thought that what they had learned from the video material was useful and could be transferred across contexts
Positive impact	Would you like to use video to learn English afterwards? Why or why not?	Approximately 91% of students perceived video as a beneficial form of CALL material, and thus would like to continue using it to learn English in the future
Practicality	Do you think video can be used to support English learning? Why or why not?	All the students (100%) were satisfied with the video material and task design of this study, which they thought were well integrated to support their English learning and development

The criterion of language learning potential examined the students' self-perceived improvement in their English proficiency. The students expressed clear agreement that their English skills were enhanced by learning with the video material. In the interviews, 85% reported that they made good progress in vocabulary acquisition. The students stated that they enjoyed learning vocabulary with video because such material was authentic and multimedia-rich, which helped them in applying English knowledge in realistic situations. They also felt that the video material helped them memorize vocabulary and retain it longer. An example comment is presented below to illustrate this point:

"Some video clips contain words which I don't know, thus I can learn many new and useful words and idioms from them. Many such words, for example, "discount" and "on sale," are relevant to our daily life, so that I can remember them easily. I often see them when the department store is having an annual sale, which reinforces my vocabulary knowledge." – *[Student 17]*

Although listening is not the focus of this study, 55% of the students stated that their listening comprehension improved after they studied with the video material, due to their larger vocabularies. Students were allowed to rewind and repeat the video clips as many times as necessary in order to enhance their listening comprehension. One related comment from the students is presented below:

"I continue to increase my vocabulary from the video material, and I feel that my listening comprehension became better after this learning experience. As I study with any video, I try to listen carefully to the clip and repeat it again and again until I can understand it. I think learning English with video is a good way to practice my listening skill." – *[Student 27]*

The criterion of meaning focus looked at whether the students could understand and thus be able to follow the video content. It was found in the interviews that 75% of the students thought that the video material was at a good level of difficulty, and thus neither too easy nor too difficult for self-study, as seen in the following comment.

"I thought I could understand most of the video content, say 70% to 80%, and I often guessed the meaning from the context for the rest. Some video clips were hard to comprehend because of technical terms and idioms, so I always watched English subtitles to learn those unknown words and phrases." – *[Student 38]*

The criterion of learner fit measured whether the difficulty level of the online videos was appropriate. Nearly all the students (96%) felt that the teacher's selection of video clips was set at an appropriate level. They did not feel frustrated when they watched these videos, and they also believed that any difficult vocabulary, idioms, and sentences could motivate their learning. The following comment illustrates this point:

"I am at an intermediate level. I think most of the selected videos are appropriate for me. Some videos contained a few difficult vocabulary items, but I can adjust somehow. I believe that if I work hard, I will reach an advanced level." – *[Student 33]*

This criterion of authenticity explored the usefulness and relevance of the video material to the students' real lives. The students stated that they liked to learn English with online videos, because they could learn both new vocabulary and knowledge from doing so. Almost all the students (96%) felt that they would benefit from the video content, and that it would be helpful outside the classroom for various purposes, such as preparing for a standardized English proficiency test or applying for a job. This can be seen in the following comments:

"I liked to watch video clips about business, and I did learn many words from them. When I took the TOEIC test, I saw some of the words on the test paper. I was glad that I had already learned them in the video clips beforehand. I believe that I really learned many useful words and phrases from the video material, and they helped me get good grades on the TOEIC test." – *[Student 45]*

"I thought learning from video was more practical than from textbooks. I think what I have learned will serve me well in my job after I graduate." – *[Student 34]*

The criterion of positive impact observed the impact of the video use on the students' English learning. The majority of students (91%) perceived digital video as a beneficial form of CALL material and even expressed their desire to continue to learn with it after the course was finished. One typical comment is shown below:

"I would like to continue to improve my English via watching videos, because I am exposed to a variety of authentic contexts by doing so. The use of video makes learning more interesting. I like to spend time on them rather than studying textbooks." – [Student 28]

The criterion of practicality investigated whether the use of video in the adopted CALL system was easy for the students to manipulate, and whether the incorporation of the video material was capable of assisting in their English learning. All of the students (100%) reported that they were satisfied with the video material and task design of the study, stating that the CALL system offered them an user-friendly and easy-to-use interface, with its functionalities for supporting their interaction with the video material. The video material was presented in ways that made the content more understandable, as the following comments made clear:

"I was pleased with the video material. The varied topics illustrated by the vivid images in the clips made English learning more fun and interesting." – [Student 16]

"I was satisfied with the use of video material in two aspects: convenience and system design. In terms of convenience, the video clips were available for us to learn English anytime and anywhere. We can use any mobile devices, such as smartphones and tablets for online learning purposes. As for the system, the interface was very simple and easy for users to manipulate. I was thus able to make good use and interact with the video material effectively and efficiently." – [Student 29]

Taken together, the results regarding how the students evaluated the overall appropriateness of using video to learn English in the CALL system provide ample evidence to suggest that the students considered the way that the video material was integrated in the intentional vocabulary learning task was facilitative and capable of enhancing their English learning experiences.

5 Discussion

This study was an effort to explore how the students used online videos to learn vocabulary in a deliberate manner, and how they perceived the overall value of the video material for vocabulary learning in specific and English learning in general. With regard to the first research question, the analysis of the participants' video use in this investigation revealed that all the students were able to watch the weekly assigned video clips and complete the required video-based vocabulary task with reasonable time and effort, without any major learning difficulties. More specifically, the students' average time spent on task was 20 min per week, which resulted in an average of 13 vocabulary items logged in each student's weekly word list. It was also found that the students exhibited sufficient learner-content interaction with the video material during the 10-week task completion period, and that the top three most frequently used functionalities that enabled such interaction were video subtitles, followed by the built-in dictionary, and adjustable playback speed.

The most commonly used functionality that enabled learner-content interaction in the CALL system was that of video subtitles. All the participants reported using video subtitles either in English, Chinese, or both languages in parallel for repeated viewing as needed. They reasoned that the use of video subtitles provided a more comprehensible and less stressful form of input, helping them to be more confident and thus more likely to engage in language learning. Along the same line, many scholars have cautioned that language learners might experience a variety of difficulties when watching videos without captions, such as rapid speech, unclear accents or utterances, an overload of technical terms or slang, and unfamiliarity with culturally specific knowledge [25]. The use of subtitles could serve to overcome many such problems by reinforcing the connection between the oral and written form of the language. To gain more insights into the potential of video subtitles, one study [26] investigated the effects of L2 audio/video with L1 or L2 subtitles on EFL learners' informal and colloquial language learning. It was found that the participants who watched TV series with English (L2) subtitles outperformed those who watched with Spanish (L1) subtitles. The participants also reported that they tended to use English subtitles for enhanced L2 input, as their main aim was to get an English degree. Likewise, more than half of the participants in the present study preferred to use L2 subtitles to better expose themselves to the target language, while some of them preferred to watch videos with dual subtitles in both L2 and L1, and only a small number of them preferred to use L1 subtitles. The students in the present work thus had different preferences in their choices of L1 and/or L2 subtitles when watching the videos, and this might have an impact on their comprehension and vocabulary learning, although this interesting issue is beyond the scope of this study.

The built-in dictionary, operating in a pop-up form, was the second most frequently used system functionality. The students relied heavily on this to figure out the meanings of words, and then to comprehend the messages embedded in the videos. The built-in dictionary offers information on word usage (e.g., definitions, model sentences, and pronunciations) that can help students better understand the language in the given video context, leading to more successful vocabulary learning. Moreover, using a built-in pop-up dictionary may save both time and mental effort compared to using an external dictionary, because it allows the students to obtain the needed information immediately by clicking on the unknown words in the context [27, 28]. Another study [27] examined students' use of different types of dictionaries (i.e., pop-up, type-in, book dictionaries, and no aid) and their effects on reading comprehension and vocabulary learning. The results indicated that those students who used the pop-up dictionary showed greater improvements in their vocabulary learning compared to those who used the type-in and printed dictionaries, although no significantly different effects were found on the students' reading comprehension.

The third most commonly used functionality in the CALL system was adjustable playback speed. The students often used this to control the speed of the video and hear particular sentences more clearly. A recent study [29] developed an automatic video-text synchronization system for EFL college learners, and found that although synchronized subtitles did help the learners comprehend the videos, the students still needed more functionalities while viewing them. For example, an adjustable playback speed was recommended in order to help the learners gain more access to what they had missed in authentic videos that were somewhat challenging for them to understand. This is in line with the results of the present study, which showed that the students made good use of the adjustable playback speed to review or re-listen to parts of the video content.

The results pertaining to the second research question revealed that the students expressed overwhelmingly favorable perceptions of their learning experience in this investigation in terms of the six CALL evaluation criteria: language learning potential, meaning focus, learner fit, authenticity, positive impact, and practicality. These positive findings reinforce the pedagogical benefits of video identified in recent studies [9, 14, 30]. Researchers have argued that videos can help students understand the meanings of words they hear by providing them with various clues for meaning construction [31], and thus incorporating more types of clues (e.g., verbal, visual, and contextual clues) would help students learn better. The current study confirmed this claim, indicating that the video material was able to provide certain supportive information that enabled the students to better understand the vocabulary and content. Another well recognized pedagogical benefit of video is the authenticity it affords. It is conducive to successful language learning "when linguistic aspects are not singled out and when words and phrases are used and learned in their syntactic, semantic and pragmatic contexts" ([32], p. 315). One would agree that learning with video material creates a fostering environment in a similar vein by exposing learners to the use of authentic language. Likewise, in this study the students' comments also indicated their preferences for and appreciation of learning vocabulary from and with video. In other words, the students found it relatively meaningful to understand and learn vocabulary from authentic contexts, and apply it in authentic situations.

6 Conclusion

Although this study has demonstrated positive findings regarding a group of EFL learners' perceptions on the use of video to assist their vocabulary learning, the results should be interpreted with consideration to the limitations of this work. First of all, given that the current study recruited only a small number of students, the results cannot be generated to all EFL students, and a larger sample is thus needed in future research. Second, this study adopted a one-group design, measuring the students' self-reported perceptions after they had taken part in the instructional intervention with a focus on computer assisted vocabulary learning. The present study thus did not include a control group to compare the students' vocabulary learning performance. In future research, a quasi-experimental research design is recommended, using both experimental and control groups to determine the effects of engaging students to learn vocabulary from digital video in an online learning system. It is also suggested that future studies apply a pretest-posttest design in order to obtain more accurate assessments regarding the effects of video use on students' vocabulary gains and improvement. Based on the results of such a study, it would be possible to be more confident in attributing students' vocabulary development to the use of video. Despite of these limitations, the findings of the current study have two practical implications for EFL teachers and system designers working with the design and implementation of CALL material, particularly in the form of video within a CALL system. It is suggested that EFL teachers incorporate online or digital videos into their classrooms to make vocabulary learning more engaging and enjoyable. Furthermore, system designers are recommended to take into consideration the frequently-used and positively-perceived system functionalities identified in this study when developing EFL systems for vocabulary learning.

References

1. Warschauer, M.: Computer-assisted language learning: An Introduction. In: Fotos, S. (ed.) Multimedia Language Teaching, pp. 3–20. Logos International, Tokyo (1996)
2. Stockwell, G.: A review of technology choice for teaching language skills and areas in the CALL literature. ReCALL 19(2), 105–120 (2007)
3. Kayaoglu, M.N., Dag Akbas, R., Ozturk, Z.: A small scale experimental study: Using animations to learn vocabulary. Turk. Online J. Educ. Technol. 10(2), 24–30 (2011)
4. Lin, C.C.: Learning action verbs with animation. JALT CALL J. 5(3), 23–40 (2009)
5. Lin, C.C., Tseng, Y.F.: Videos and animations for vocabulary learning: A study on difficult words. Turk. Online J. Educ. Technol. 11(4), 346–355 (2012)
6. Samur, Y.: Redundancy effect on retention of vocabulary words using multimedia presentation. Br. J. Educ. Technol. 43(6), 166–170 (2012)
7. Farshi, N., Mohammadi, Z.: Use of podcasts in effective teaching of vocabulary: Learners' attitudes, motivations, and limitations. Theory Pract. Lang. Stud. 3(8), 1381–1386 (2013)
8. Putman, S.M., Kingsley, T.: The atoms family: Using podcasts to enhance the development of science vocabulary. Read. Teach. 63(2), 100–108 (2009)
9. Lin, L.F.: English learners' incidental vocabulary acquisition in the video-based CALL program. Asian EFL J. 12(4), 51–66 (2010)
10. Naraghizadeh, M., Barimani, S.: The effect of CALL on the vocabulary learning of Iranian EFL learners. J. Acad. Appl. Stud. 3(8), 1–12 (2013)
11. Karakaş, A., Sariçoban, A.: The impact of watching subtitled animated cartoons on incidental vocabulary learning of ELT students. Teach. Engl. Technol. 12(4), 3–15 (2012)
12. Yuksel, D., Tanriverdi, B.: Effects of watching captioned movie clip on vocabulary development of EFL learners. Turk. Online J. Educ. Technol. 8(2), 48–54 (2009)
13. Giannakos, M.N.: Exploring the research on video learning: A review of the literature. Br. J. Educ. Technol. 44(6), 191–195 (2013)
14. Goldstein, B., Driver, P.: Language Learning with Digital Video. Cambridge University Press, Cambridge (2014)
15. Mayer, R.E.: Applying the science of learning: Evidence-based principles for the design of multimedia instruction. Am. Psychol. 63(8), 760–769 (2008)
16. Mayer, R.E., Moreno, R.: Nine ways to reduce cognitive load in multimedia learning. Educ. Psychol. 38(1), 43–52 (2003)
17. Mayer, R.E.: Multimedia Learning. Cambridge University Press, New York (2009)
18. Mayer, R.E., Moreno, R.: Aids to computer-based multimedia learning. Learn. Instr. 12(1), 107–119 (2002)
19. Jones, L.C.: Supporting listening comprehension and vocabulary acquisition with multimedia annotations: The students' voice. CALICO J. 21(1), 41–65 (2003)
20. Mayer, R.E., Moreno, R.: Animation as an aid to multimedia learning. Educ. Psychol. Rev. 14(1), 87–99 (2002)

21. Clark, R.C., Mayer, R.E.: E-learning and the Science of Instruction: Proven Guidelines for Consumers and Designers of Multimedia Learning. Pfeiffer, San Francisco (2011)
22. Mayer, R.E.: Applying the science of learning to medical education. Med. Educ. **44**(6), 543–549 (2010)
23. Canning-Wilson, C.: Practical aspects of using video in the foreign language classroom. Internet TESL J. 6(11) (2000). http://iteslj.org/Articles/Canning-Video.html
24. Chapelle, C.A.: Computer Applications in Second Language Acquisition. Cambridge University Press, Cambridge (2001)
25. King, J.: Using DVD feature films in the EFL classroom. Comput. Assist. Lang. Learn. **15**(5), 509–523 (2002)
26. Frumuselu, A.D., De Maeyer, S., Donche, V., del Mar Gutiérrez Colon Plana, M.: Television series inside the EFL classroom: Bridging the gap between teaching and learning informal language through subtitles. Linguist. Educ. **32**, 107–117 (2015)
27. Liu, T.C., Lin, P.H.: What comes with technological convenience? Exploring the behaviors and performances of learning with computer-mediated dictionaries. Comput. Hum. Behav. **27**(1), 373–383 (2011)
28. Levy, M., Steel, C.: Language learner perspectives on the functionality and use of electronic language dictionaries. ReCALL **27**(2), 177–196 (2015)
29. Chen, H.J.H.: Developing and evaluating SynctoLearn, a fully automatic video and transcript synchronization tool for EFL learners. Comput. Assist. Lang. Learn. **24**(2), 117–130 (2011)
30. Huang, P., Hwang, Y.: An exploration of EFL learners' anxiety and E-learning environments. J. Lang. Teach. Res. **4**(1), 27–35 (2013)
31. Jung, R., Lee, C.H.: Using Internet video clips for university students' vocabulary development in blended learning. Multimedia Assist. Lang. Learn. **16**(4), 67–96 (2013)
32. Tschirner, E.: Language acquisition in the classroom: The role of digital video. Comput. Assist. Lang. Learn. **14**(3–4), 305–319 (2001)

The Effects of Peer Interaction-Based Learning Community Through Facebook on Students' English Learning Attitude and Motivation

I-Ting Wang[1(✉)], Yi-Tung Lin[1], I-Ying Tsai[2],
and Kuei-Chih Chuang[1]

[1] National Yunlin University of Science and Technology, Yunlin, Taiwan
21stars@yahoo.com.tw, sl07@ms26.hinet.net,
chuangkc@yuntech.edu.tw
[2] National Kaohsiung University of Hospitality and Tourism,
Kaohsiung, Taiwan
i_ying_tsai@hotmail.com

Abstract. The present study aims to investigate how teaching integrated with Internet multimedia affects college students' English learning attitude and motivation in EFL classrooms. Of particular interest to this study is the use of social network Facebook to engage students in the process of language learning. Peer Interaction-Based Learning Community through Facebook (PIBLCF) was developed in the study to assist learners of English as a foreign language. The usage of PIBLCF provides learners with opportunities to develop a sense of group, and maintain the idea of a community as a unit that can interact and learn collaboratively. The results of this study indicate that PIBLCF can help students improve English learning performance and elevate students' English learning attitude and motivation as well. Students in this study highly valued PIBLCF as a helpful learning method allowing them to have more opportunity and less pressure to interact with peers in group work online.

Keywords: English as a foreign language · Peer interaction-based learning community through Facebook · Learning attitude and motivation

1 Introduction

1.1 Background and Motivation

English has been the main medium of communication and cross-cultural information exchanges with other nations in the world in many different aspects. Taiwan, therefore, has established crucial moves to promote English instruction to increase its global competitive strength. In the past two decades, many researchers have pointed out that quite a few educational problems have existed for many years in the EFL teaching and learning contexts in Taiwan. The traditional teaching method oftentimes is led by a teacher in a classroom and has been the main stream in English classrooms in Taiwan since 1950s. In such environments, students sit row by row facing the blackboard directly in front of them, take notes of teacher's instructions, and listen passively to the

© Springer International Publishing AG 2017
T.-T. Wu et al. (Eds.): SETE 2016, LNCS 10108, pp. 240–256, 2017.
DOI: 10.1007/978-3-319-52836-6_25

teachers' lectures, with little or no opportunity of peer interactions during class sessions.

Recently, abundant studies have documented the benefits of Web 2.0 tools in many areas such as languages, science, math, and social studies; and in various levels from pre-schooling to higher education to colleges. The impact of the Internet on language learning in the context of higher education has been growing exponentially. A number of years ago, early incarnations of the Internet provided students the opportunity to find information online and share their findings with other language learners. For today's generation, Web 2.0 tools, namely "the writable web", (Karpati 2009: 140) allow for the creation of new content; thus previously unexplored communication channels have been opened, providing language learners with new incentives and opportunities to easily interact with people from across the globe. With blogs, wikis, forums and social networking sites (SNSs), the new generation of students can express themselves in various ways that are electronically intertwined. During the last decade, the numbers of students and educators becoming active members of SNSs such as FB surged. As there are 28 million students between the ages of 18-25 using FB and over 500 million users worldwide (Facebook Press Room Statistics), it is not surprising that teachers are finding ways to use social networking in academia.

In educational terms, these social tools redefine learning in different ways. First, time constraints often limit the amount of face-to-face student socialization; however, SNSs offer new opportunities for students to connect easily with their classmates, peer learners and instructors on a new level that is more personal and motivating in many respects. As Mazer et al. (2007) suggest, this type of interaction may have a positive effect on the student-student and student-teacher relationships, and may consequently lead to a more positive learning environment. Second, by using such emerging tools, learners have greater autonomy and are actively involved in knowledge development since they have more control over learn-ing itself. Rather than exclusively delivering information from textbooks, new technologies heighten the engagement of students in finding, recognizing, and analyzing resources on their own. However, although SNSs such as FB are an integral part of the Net Generation students' life (Tapscott 1997, 2009) and can be a viable resource in the context of education, learners do not nec-essarily know how to take advantage of Web 2.0 tools in ways that would benefit them in computer-assisted language learning (CALL). Therefore, they need guidance in selecting the strategies to adopt in order to efficiently take advantage of this dynamic environment as well as to understand the implications of the public nature of Web 2.0 tools.

This study probed into the effects of integration of a social networking community website Facebook in learners' English learning, since familiarity with technology does not necessarily imply that students possess the skills to use it in an educational context (Winke and Goertler 2008). The results of questionnaires and the examination on this social networking community revealed that students view the integration of FB as a positive element at different levels. It appears that today's language learners are receptive to using emerging tools and the use of SNSs has a place in the context of language learning, provided that the language educator is viewed as a facilitator of knowledge, guiding learners through the process of learning (Lantolf and Appel 1994; Vygotsky 1978). In addition, this study attempted to explore workable and efficient models benefitting teachers in their effective guidance of their students' language learning outside language classroom.

1.2 Purposes of the Study

The purpose of this study is to investigate the effects of the social networking community website Facebook on English learning ability of college students in EFL classrooms. The present study identifies students' reading performance in English and online interaction as the keys to representing the effects of Facebook. Because a heterogeneous class has been common in colleges, the study further aims to probe the effects of Peer Interaction-Based Learning Community through Facebook (PIBLCF) on enhancing students' English proficiency and developing their autonomy in learning English.

1.3 Research Questions

The present study aims to probe research questions proposed as follows:

1. Do students prefer Peer Interaction-Based Learning Community through Facebook (PIBLCF) to traditional teaching (TT) in terms of the learning style?
2. Does PIBLCF motivate students to perform better in their language learning as compared with TT?

2 Literature Review

2.1 The Traditional Teaching Approach in EFL

In this section, the discussion is mainly focused on three points. They include features, strengths, and shortcomings of the traditional teaching approach.

1. The Features: The term "Traditional Approach" in this study is used to refer to the Grammar-Translation method, which dominated European and foreign language teaching from 1840s to 1940s (Richards and Rogers 1986). Richards and Rogers (1986) proposed some principal features of the Grammar-Translation Method as follows:

   First, it is a representative of a deductive approach. That is, teachers first offer detailed analysis of grammar rules and linguistic items, followed by the application of this knowledge to the task of translating sentences and texts into and out of the target language. Hence, it views language learning as consisting of memorizing rules and facts in order to understand and manipulate the morphology and syntax of the foreign language. Second, reading and writing are the major focuses; little or no systematic attention is paid to speaking or listening. Third, the grammar rules are presented and illustrated. A list of vocabulary items based only on the reading texts are presented with their translation equivalents. Fourth, the sentence is the basic unit of teaching and language practice. Much of the lesson plan is oriented to translating sentences into and out of the target language. The focus on the sentence is the distinctive characteristic of the method. Fifth, accuracy is emphasized and is a prerequisite for passing the formal written examination. Teachers are the authorities that students get the correct answer from. Sixth, students' native language is maintained as the medium of instruction. It is used to explain new items and to make comparison between the foreign language and students' first language.

2. The Merits and Shortcomings: Grammar-Translation method and its modified form are widely used in some parts of the world today. Brown (1994b) pointed out that the Grammar-Translation method is useless to enhance a student's communicative ability in the language. To thousands of foreign school learners, they experience the method as just boring and endless memorization of lists of unusable grammar rules or new words in an attempt to make the translation of literary propose perfect. Furthermore, no advocates or related literature, such as linguistics, psychology, or educational theory are provided to justify the method and offer the theoretical foundation (Richards and Rogers 1986).

As it is, the Traditional Approach is still used or suggested by many EFL language teachers, such as those in Taiwan due to its advantages in helping teachers with less specialized skills, in preparing for easily constructed tests and in the possible superiority to improve students' accuracy in reading and writing. Nevertheless, the approach shows theoretical inadequacy and is incongruent with the nature of language use. Therefore, it is necessary to explore whether there is another teaching and learning method which may be more beneficial to help students learn language usages in a beneficial way. The Peer Interaction-Based Learning Community through Facebook (PIBLCF) is therefore proposed as a better learning method for assisting students' English learning in the present study.

2.2 Social Networking Facebook as One of Web 2.0 Tools

Computer mediated social networks have been growing at an exponential rate. Recently, Buffardi and Campbell (2008) pointed out that having a web presence and being in touch with a large number of individuals via SNSs has become part of the daily routine of people, many of whom are higher education students. In other words, according to Downes 2006, the emergence of Web 2.0 is not simply a technological revolution, but rather a social transformation that enables and encourages communication as these websites allow members to express themselves and to interact with others (McBride 2009). Multiple SNSs exist, but a particular one – FB – which was initially created by a Harvard student in 2004 for intracampus socializing, now includes more than 500 million active members, one-third of whom are university students (Facebook Press Room Statistics). FB has become the most popular SNS among college students (Cassidy 2006; Downes 2006).

FB offers a wide array of technological affordances supporting a diverse range of interests and practices which integrate several modes of Computer Mediated Communication (CMC) such as self-presentation, and one-to-one or one-to-many written exchanges. Blattner and Fiori (2009) postulate that staying in touch with FB friends has taken on a new dimension, as it is facilitated by a series of notifications that users can receive informing them for instance of friends' status or profile changes, new pictures, and so forth. Therefore, users are able to tailor their privacy settings, which ultimately will impact their online presentations to various friends on FB, as they do offline. Another aspect that is unique to sites like FB is that they enable users to bond with individuals, an event which may otherwise not have taken place without this electronic tool (Schwartz 2009). In fact, nowadays it is common for classmates to become friends on FB, as a way to share personal information with their peers as well as class information, including discussions of personal interests. Schwartz (2009) recently pointed out that for many students FB has become an extension of the classroom where all types of connections take place, some routine and some more substantial. For these various reasons, educators started to view FB as a resourceful tool in language pedagogy and higher education.

2.3 Language Learning Through Facebook

In the context of second language acquisition, the sociocultural approach to language learning views students as active learners who become involved in their own learning process by engaging with others through authentic interaction (Lantolf and Thorne 2006). Given the versatility of the FB site, it is likely that such an online public resource could positively impact the learning experience of many students and be a spring board for real-world activities that are not necessarily associated with the educational environment.

Some studies focused on the teaching and learning implications that SNSs bring to an educational setting. One recent experimental investigation (Mazer et al. 2007) examined the effects of teacher self-disclosure via FB on anticipated college student motivation, affective learning, and classroom climate. The results showed that participants who accessed the FB page of a teacher exhibited high levels of self-disclosure (i.e. showed personal pictures, revealed information about political views, hobbies, etc.) and anticipated higher levels of motivation and affective learning as well as a more positive classroom climate. In a similar vein, Rovai (2002) suggested that online environments such as SNSs provide learners with a new, stronger feeling of community belonging, which ultimately increases the willingness to share information, support each other, and encourage collaborative efforts. These findings are consistent with Kok (2008), who argued that it is important to provide learners with opportunities to develop a sense of group, but also to maintain the idea of a community as a unit that can interact, learn and work collaboratively. He further claimed that virtual communities may enhance the spirit, trust, interaction and the learning experience among students as a whole.

In a more recent investigation, Stevenson and Liu (2010) explored the pedagogical and technical use of foreign language learning websites that use Web 2.0 technologies (i.e.: Palabea, Livemocha, Babbel) in the context of foreign language learning. The results of this exploratory study provided insight into how the goals and designs of such Web 2.0 tools fit with the goals and needs of current and potential language learners. The online survey results showed that the participants were interested in and excited about the possibilities of collaboration on social networking sites in terms of learning directly from other users including native speakers. However, the data also revealed that some sites were considered more user friendly and consequently more appreciated than others.

Furthermore, Mills (2011) conducted a study focusing on the nature of student participation, knowledge acquisition, and relationship development within social networking communities. Students used the FB as a complement to the classroom environment and as an interactive tool where they could share collective reflection and access resources that enhanced the various topics discussed in class. She noticed that students not only made connections to course content, developed identities through the enhancement of interpersonal, presentational, and interpretative modes of communication, which are all typically used on FB, but also engaged in meaningful learning experiences and contextualized interactions within electronic francophone communities. To sum up, many research advocates the positive and beneficial impact of using FB in the context of higher education.

3 Methodology

3.1 Participants

In this study, 80 freshmen in two classes at one college in Kaohsiung city were recruited in this present study. 40 students are male, while the other 40 students are female. The 80 students were divided into two groups: one is Experimental Class; the other is Control Class. The division is based on students' English scores of the Inter-media Level of GEPT.

The English teacher in these two classes is the researcher of this study. The teaching time scheduled for the two classes in this study was finished in one semester, in which two-hour classroom instruction will be implemented each week.

In Experimental Class the English teacher gave students some questions as after-class assignments based on the contents of their textbooks so as to make students do online group discussion through Facebook during this semester. With respect to Control Class, the English teacher instructed students with the contents based on their textbooks without giving students any questions for online group discussion.

3.2 Instruments

The instruments utilized in this study include the examination paper, the questionnaire and SPSS for Windows as the statistical tool for data analysis. The following is the discussion of these instruments.

1. The Examination Paper. The examination paper that was used to test students' learning achievement at the end of the semester are composed of vocabulary test, idiom test, grammar test, conversation test, and sentence pattern test, cloze test and reading comprehension test. All the tests are made in the multiplechoice form.

Those test items were designed, checked and revised by two native speakers teaching at colleges in Kaohsiung.

2. Questionnaire. The questionnaire designed by the researcher includes two sections. The first section consists of 25 questions for students in terms of their opinions about Peer Interaction-Based Learning Community through Facebook (PIBLCF).

3. SPSS for Windows. The statistical models of SPSS for Windows (16.0) used in the present study was T-test models. These models was used to analyze the data collected from students' answers to the questionnaire and examination paper so as to find out whether there was any significant difference between the two group students' opinions of PIBLCF and whether there was any significant difference of academic performance between students in the Experimental Class and those in the Control Class at the end of the semester. The statistical results were the important indicators of teaching method and learning style for language teachers' instruction and students' studying foreign languages respectively.

3.3   Data Collection and Analysis

The data in this study consisted of students' answers to the questionnaire and were collected from the students' performance on their taking the examination at the end of the semester. In addition, the answers to the questionnaire and the scores of examination were analyzed quantitatively.

4   Results and Discussion

4.1   Effects on Students' Preference of the English Learning Style Through *Facebook* and *Traditional Teaching*

Q1.   Do students prefer Peer Interaction-Based Learning Community through Facebook (PIBLCF) to traditional teaching (TT) in terms of the learning style?

According to Table 1, the statistical result of students' English proficiency before the treatment reveals that the difference of pretest scores between the experimental and the control groups does not reach the significance level ($t = -1.035$, $p = .259$). Therefore, it shows that these two groups are homogeneous.

Table 1. Analysis summary of independent samples test on the comparison of the pretest scores of English proficiency between students in the experimental and the control group.

Class	N	M	Sd.	t	p
Experimental group	40	63.055	15.573	−1.035	0.259
Control group	40	67.602	12.132		

$P > .05$

Actually, it could be further inferred that students may not have the preference of one learning style over the other one with respect to PIBLCF and TT before the implementation of the treatment.

However, to find out if students prefer PIBLCF to TBI after the treatment, data collected from the 25 selected-response items (second part) of questionnaire regarding attitudes toward cooperative Facebook learning were analyzed through Independent Samples.

Test between the experimental and the control groups and Paired Samples Test within the experimental group.

In Table 2, data analyzed from the second part of questionnaire after the treatment indicated that there was a significant difference ($t = 4.635$, $p = .000$) in the preference for English learning style between the experimental group ($M = 85.62$, $SD = 11.61$) and the control group ($M = 73.69$, $SD = 9.38$). In other words, it showed that the students in the experimental group had significantly stronger preference for Peer Interaction-Based Learning Community through Facebook (PIBLCF) than their homogeneous counterparts in the control group. This is also true when we especially take students who have finished the treatment (PIBLCF) in the experimental group into consideration.

Table 2. Analysis summary of independent samples test on the comparison of preference for English learning style between students in the experimental and the control groups via questionnaire employed after the treatment.

Class	N	M	Sd.	t	p
Experimental group	40	85.620	11.610	4.635	.000
Control group	40	73.689	9.385		

*$p < .05$

Based on Table 3, data analyzed from the second part of the same questionnaire before and after the experiment indicated that the experimental group's attitudes toward or preference over Peer Interaction-Based Learning Community through Facebook (PIBLCF), as one English learning style, moved forward from the mean of 87.828 and SD of 5.367 before the treatment to the mean of 92.621 and SD of 12.510 after the treatment significantly (t = 2.130, p = .012). Thus, regarding the attitudes toward or preference over PIBLCF as an English learning style in this present study after the treatment, the experimental group showed significant changes in their perspectives. The experimental participants held positive attitudes toward or prefer studying English through PIBLCF. As a matter of fact, such kind of learning style did enhance both their interest and motivation in EFL learning, as can be found in the answers to Research Question 2 in Sect. 4.2.

Table 3. Analysis summary of paired-samples test for the experimental group' attitudes toward peer interaction-based learning community through Facebook before and after treatment (N = 58).

Group		M	Sd.	t	p
Experimental	Before	87.828	5.367	2.130	.012
	After	92.621	12.510		

*p < .05

4.2 Effects of the Peer Interaction-Based Learning Community Through Facebook (PIBLCF) on Students' Motivation Toward Performing Better in Their Language Learning

Q2. Does PIBLCF motivate students to perform better in their language learning as compared with TT?

4.2.1 The Comparison of Students' Learning Motivation Between the Experimental and the Control Group

In Table 4, the results of the comparison between the two groups' pre-motivation in English learning reveal that the scores of students' pre-motivation ($t = .673$, $p = .583 > .05$) does not reach the significance level. Therefore, it indicated that there was no significant difference in English learning motivation between the experimental and the control groups before the treatment (PIBLCF) was implemented in the former group.

Table 4. Analysis summary of independent samples test on the comparison of students' pre-motivation scores in the experimental and the control groups before the treatment.

Class	N	M	Sd.	t	p
Experimental group	40	35.086	3.508	.673	.583
Control group	40	35.733	4.013		

$p > .05$

We could infer that most students in both the experimental and the control groups had similar motivation in learning English before the treatment. However, the comparison of post-motivation between the two groups was shown in Table 5.

Table 5. Analysis summary of independent samples test on the comparison of students' post-motivation scores in the experimental and the control groups after the treatment.

Class	N	M	Sd.	t	p
Experimental group	40	42.672	1.693	5.705	.000
Control group	40	32.544	2.530		

*p > .05

Based on Table 5, the post-motivation mean score of the experimental group is 42.67 with a standard deviation of 1.69, while the post-motivation mean score of the control group is 32.54 with a standard deviation of 2.53. Besides, the statistical results of the comparison of the same questionnaire after the experiment indicated that the difference between the experimental and the control groups in their motivation toward English learning actually reached a significant difference level ($t = 5.705$, $p = .000 < .05$). Obviously, the students in the experimental group had significantly more scores of the first part of the same questionnaire on English learning motivation than those in the control group. Therefore, it proved that the effects of PIBLCF on the students in experimental groups were significantly and positively better than those of TT on the students in the homogeneous control group in terms of their motivation towards learning English in class.

4.2.2 Effects of TBI and PIBLCF on Enhancing Students' Learning Motivation Within the Control Group and the Experimental Group Respectively Before and After the Experiment

In Table 6, the statistical results of the comparison of motivation scores in the control group before and after the experiment showed that students in this group did not get motivated toward learning English. The pre-motivation mean score is 37.133 with a standard deviation of 4.113, while the post-motivation mean score is 35.244 with a standard deviation of 2.529. The difference between the scores of pre-motivation and post-motivation actually reached the significance level ($t = 2.57$, $p = .032 < .05$). Besides, there was significant decrease in the post-motivation scores as compared with the pre-motivation scores. Therefore, it obviously revealed that students in the control group did not obtain any motivation towards learning English under the teacher-based instruction.

Table 6. Analysis summary of paired-samples test for the comparison between student' pre-motivation and post-motivation scores in the control group via questionnaire.

Group		M	$Sd.$	t	p
Control	Before	37.133	4.113	2.571	.032
	After	35.244	2.529		

$*p < .05$

Based on Table 7, the statistical results of the comparison of motivation scores in the experimental group before and after the treatment indicated that students in this group were really motivated toward learning English better. As it is, there was significant increase in the post-motivation scores when it was compared with the pre-motivation scores. That is, the pre-motivation mean score is 37.586 with a standard deviation of 3.507, while the post-motivation mean score is 42.372 with a standard deviation of 1.393. In addition, the difference between the scores of pre-motivation and post-motivation actually reached the significance level ($t = 2.879$, $p = .026 < .05$). Therefore, it proved that PIBLCF had great effects on the students' motivation toward learning English better and that PIBLCF could be better than TT in terms of the enhancement of students' positive learning motivation.

Table 7. Analysis summary of paired-samples test for the comparison between student' pre-motivation and post-motivation scores in the experimental group via questionnaire.

Group		M	Sd.	t	p
Experimental	Before	37.586	3.507	2.879	.026
	After	42.372	1.393		

*p < .05

4.3   Conclusion of Chapter 4

After the treatment, the experimental group's motivation toward English learning changed significantly; in addition, the students' learning motivation in the control group fell considerably. The experimental subjects regarded PIBLCF as a better learning method for them to interact and cooperate with their group members so that they could obtain mutual online assistance and develop individual responsibility after school.

5   Conclusions and Implications

5.1   Summary of the Major Findings and Results

This study aimed to investigate the effects of Peer Interaction-Based Learning Community through Facebook (PIBLCF) on college students in EFL classrooms. The results of this study indicate that PIBLCF can help students improve their English learning performance and elevate students' motivation toward English learning as well. Students in this study highly valued PIBLCF as a helpful and interesting learning method, thus allowing them to have more opportunity and less pressure to interact and cooperate with peers in group work online.

1. The Major Findings. First, most students in the experimental did like PIBLCF a lot after the treatment. This is also true when we especially take students who have finished the treatment (PIBLCF) in the experimental group into consideration. Second, students became more interested in, held positive attitudes toward, and preferred PIBLCF than in the traditional lecture instruction. Third, there was no significant difference in English learning motivation between the experimental and the control groups before the treatment (PIBLCF) was implemented in the former group. Fourth, most students in both the experimental and the control groups had similar motivation in learning English before the treatment. Fifth, the effects of PIBLCF on the students in experimental groups were significantly and positively better than those of TT on the students in the homogeneous control group in terms of their motivation towards learning English in class.
2. Motivation toward English Learning through PIBLCF. After the experiment, the control group students' motivation toward English learning seemed to drop via TBI; instead, the experimental group ones' motivation was enhanced enormously and positively. The afore-mentioned findings revealed that the enthusiasm and motivation toward English learning existed in the experimental group, primarily because PIBLCF activities had made the English learning vivid like a collaborative business

that students could run on their own, instead of just a general school subject. The more motivation the students can obtain, the greater learning achievements they will make. With respect to positive interdependence and the spirit of online cooperative learning (Johnson et al. 1998), each group member in this study marched for the shared goal.

Students realized they could have the priority and responsibility of giving their contributions to the group (Putnam 1997). As a result, the experimental group students' motivation toward English learning became significantly positive because they thought learning English with PIBLCF was for fun and for the sense of achievement based on mutual benefit, not for individual scores and parents as they had done before. In a nutshell, the students under PIBLCF have become autonomous learners with intrinsic motivation.

3. Conclusions. Unlike the traditional learning group, the PIBLCF group benefited tremendously in their academic performance and obtained positive motivation toward EFL learning through student-centered online activities. Thereby, the findings confirmed that PIBLCF can promote college students' academic achievement and learning motivation via harmonious, interactive, and online cooperative environment.

As for teachers, they act no more as the soloists but as facilitators and observers in the process of the PIBLCF. Therefore, teachers can find out students' learning difficulties and give immediate help while monitoring students' online learning through Facebook during the group-work session. As a result, teachers could develop tasks relating to students' personal concern. Due to sufficient time interacting with students, the tacit understanding between teachers and students is generated.

From such PIBLCF environment, students can understand that the mutual interests can be triggered through cooperation not competition, so that they are apt to share resources with others and to accept others' assistance. Besides, students tend to have affirmative emotions due to the harmonious environment. In the long term, the features of tendency to help others online and the efficient communication skills through Facebook could provide critical factors to students' success in their future career.

5.2   Pedagogical Implications

This study aimed to investigate the effectiveness of Peer Interaction-Based Learning Community through Facebook (PIBLCF) on EFL learning in colleges in Taiwan. The findings of this study might provide English teachers in Taiwan with the picture of how learners benefit from and value online cooperative learning, and thus inspiring teachers to incorporate PIBLCF activities in their own teaching. Particularly in most big-sized classes with achievers of various levels, the PIBLCF as a learning strategy will be a useful tool for EFL teachers to meet individuals' needs and improve students' achievements.

In the present study, that the experimental students achieved significantly could awake some of the school administrators, who would be likely to separate high achievers and low achievers into different classes. The above achievement could show those school administrators that students with various levels could cooperate online among themselves to make progress together in the PIBLCF.

5.3 Limitations of the Study

The participants of the present study were freshmen in a college. To maintain the original nature of the class and to avoid affecting their normal school time and teaching environment, a quasi-experimental design was used in the study. The limitation of this study is the limited number of samples of 80 students in two classes from the same grade in the same college. Thus, the results might not prove generalized to that of a larger scale of college students. Also, due to the constraint of time and resource, no proficiency test at the end of the semester was employed to examine whether students' language abilities were enhance through this PIBLCF.

5.4 Suggestions for Future Studies

One limitation in this study was the small sample size of two classes belonging to the same college, limiting the generalization of the results. Thus, future researchers may implement PIBLCF on more classes to become more general. Another limitation concerned was the short experimental period which impeded the exploration of the long-term effectiveness of the PIBLCF on the college students' competence in EFL. Future researchers may be interested in exploring the effectiveness of PIBLCF in EFL classrooms for at least one semester or six months to analyze whether the students' achievement or motivation toward English learning is affected. Another limitation was the fact that no assessment tests were made to find out the effects of PIBLCF on the oral, listening, reading and advanced writing abilities in this study. Thus, the language skills could be included in future PIBLCF studies.

Appendix

Questionnaire of English Learning and Peer Interaction-Based Learning Community through Facebook
Part I. Opinions about English Learning

List	Questions	Strongly agree	Agree	No opinion	Not agree	Strongly not agree
1	English is an important tool for both further study and employment					
2	I have no interest in English learning even there are no tests					
3	I hope I can be capable of having conversation with foreigners in English					
4	I'll correct the mistakes after the tests to improve my English ability					

(continued)

(continued)

List	Questions	Strongly agree	Agree	No opinion	Not agree	Strongly not agree
5	I feel bored at learning English					
6	I hope to master English so as to know the foreign culture and get the chance to study abroad					
7	I have no interest in English, so I don't care about the English assignment					
8	I like learning English and is an active learner					
9	I often doze off in English classes and have a tough time in learning English					
10	I like English whoever the teacher is					
11	I often feel nervous in English classes, so learning English is tough for me					
12	I'm willing to spend time in learning English					

Part II. Opinions about learning English on Facebook

List	Questions	Strongly agree	Agree	No opinion	Not agree	Strongly not agree
1	I like to learn English on Facebook					
2	I'm satisfied with my English performance on Facebook					
3	In learning English on Facebook, the team will get good grade as long as I do my best					
4	In learning English on Facebook, I learn better when the online members help each other					
5	In learning English on Facebook, I often feel frustrated and don't want to learn					

(continued)

(continued)

List	Questions	Strongly agree	Agree	No opinion	Not agree	Strongly not agree
6	Learning on Facebook helps me learn English better					
7	Learning on Facebook motivates me to learn English better					
8	In learning English on Facebook, I'll be more motivated if I perform well or be rewarded					
9	I think learning English on Facebook is interesting, and it makes English classes much more fun					
10	I hope the English classes can be integrated with Facebook					
11	In learning English on Facebook, I have more opportunities to practice					
12	My teammates perform well in learning English on Facebook					
13	In learning English on Facebook, I often disturbed by the noise made by other teams					
14	My thinking perspective broadens through the teammates' collaborative online assist					
15	I learn the skills of communication and collaboration through learning on Facebook					
16	When learning on Facebook, some students seldom participate in group discussion					
17	I study harder for the team honor					
18	Team members can be more responsible and study					

(continued)

(continued)

List	Questions	Strongly agree	Agree	No opinion	Not agree	Strongly not agree
	harder when learning on Facebook					
19	I'm easily distracted in learning English on Facebook					
20	Learning on Facebook is good because teammates can help each other to enhance the English ability					
21	Compared to traditional teaching, I prefer learning on Facebook.					
22	Compared to traditional teaching, I think learning on Facebook less interesting.					
23	When learning on Facebook, we can discuss online easily, which creates better learning atmosphere and makes English learning more interesting.					
24	Because of teammates' help, I understand the material easier than before when learning on Facebook					
25	It is better to help each other in learning on Facebook than compete with each other					

References

Blattner, G., Fiori, M.: Facebook in the language classroom: promises and possibilities. Instr. Technol. Distance Learn. (ITDL) **6**(1), 17–28 (2009). http://www.itdl.org/journal/jan_09/article02.htm

Buffardi, L.E., Campbell, W.K.: Narcissism and social networking web sites. Pers. Soc. Psychol. Bull. **34**(10), 1303–1314 (2008)

Cassidy, J.: Me media–how hanging out on the Internet became big business. The New Yorker (May 15). 50–59 (2006). http://www.newyorker.com/archive/2006/05/15/060515fa_fact_cassidy

Council for Economic Planning and Development: Challenge 2008 National Development Plan. Taiwan Executive Yuan, Taipei (2005)

Downes, S.: E-learning 2.0. National Research Council of Canada e-Learn Magazine. (2006). http://www.elearnmag.org/subpage.cfm?article=29-1&section=articles

Lantolf, J., Thorne, S.L.: Sociocultural Theory and the Genesis of Second Language Development. Oxford University Press, Oxford (2006)

Liao, P.: Teachers' beliefs about teaching English to elementary school children. Engl. Teach. Learn. **31**(1), 43–76 (2007)

Chang, M.M.: Teacher-oriented learning vs. cooperative learning in English reading class. J. Pingtung Polytech. Inst. **4**, 271–277 (1995)

Chen, H.C.: The performance of junior college students studying English through cooperative learning. In: Proceedings of 7th International Symposium on English Teaching, Crane, Taipei, pp. 231–240 (1998)

Johnson, D., Johnson, R., Holubec, E.: Cooperation in the Classroom. Allyn and Bacon, Boston (1998)

Karpati, A.: Web 2 technologies for net native language learners: a 'social CALL'. ReCALL **21** (2), 139–156 (2009)

Kok, A.: Metamorphosis of the mind of online communities via e-learning. Instr. Technol. Distance Learn. **5**(10), 25–32 (2008)

Lantolf, J.P., Appel, G.: Vygotskian Approaches to Second Language Research. Ablex, Norwood (1994)

McBride, K.: Social-networking sites in foreign language classes: opportunities for re-creation. In: Lomicka, L., Lord, G. (eds.) The Nextgeneration: Social Networking and Online Collaboration in Foreign Language Learning. CALICO Monograph Series, vol. 8, pp. 35–58. CALICO, San Marcos (2009)

Mazer, J.P., Murphy, R.E., Simonds, C.J.: I'll see you on 'Facebook': the effect of computer-mediated teacher self-disclosure on student motivation, affective learning and classroom climate. Commun. Educ. **56**(1), 1–17 (2007)

Mills, N.: Situated learning through social networking communities: the development of joint enterprise, mutual engagement, and a shared repertoire. CALICO **28**(2), 345–368 (2011)

Putnam, J.: Cooperative Learning in Diverse Classroom. Merrill, Upper Saddle River (1997)

Rovai, A.P.: Sense of community, perceived cognitive learning, and persistence in asynchronous learning networks. Internet High. Educ. **5**, 319–332 (2002). doi:10.1016/S1096-7516(02) 00130-6

Schwartz, H.L.: Facebook: the new classroom commons? The Chronicle Review. (2009). http://gradstudies.carlow.edu/pdf/schwartz-chronicle_9-28-09.pdf

Solomon, G., Schrum, L.: Web 2.0 New Tools. International Society for Technology in Education, Washington (2007)

Stevenson, M.P., Liu, M.: Learning a language with Web 2.0: exploring the use of social networking features of foreign language learning websites. CALICO J. **27**(1), 233–259 (2010)

Tapscott, D.: Growing Up Digital: The Rise of the Net Generation. McGrawHill, New York (1997)

Tapscott, D.: Growing Up Digital: How the Net Generation is Changing Your World. McGrawHill, New York (2009)

Winke, P., Goertler, S.: Did we forget someone? Students' computer access and literacy for CALL. CALICO J. **25**(3), 482–509 (2008)

Vander Veer, E.A.: Facebook the Missing Manual. Pogue Press O'Reilly, Sebastopol (2008)

Vygotsky, L.: Mind in Society: The Development of Higher Psychological Processes. Harvard University Press, Cambridge (1978)

Emerging Technologies Supported Innovative Learning

A Novel Web Publishing System Architecture for Statistics Data Using Open Source Technology

Md Mostafizur Rahman[✉], Hans Dicken, and Dirk Huke

German Centre for Research on Higher Education and Science Studies (DZHW),
Hannover, Germany
mostafiz.de@gmail.com
https://www.dzhw.eu

Abstract. Web applications have become the primary source of information and transactions over the internet. The number of statistical research organizations, with focused interests in publishing result data on the web, is increasing rapidly in recent years. Statistical report publishing is typically requested to publish reports using different documentation formats. In this research, we examine different web publishing frameworks and effects of saturation trends that appear during implementation. The existing publishing solutions sometimes may or may not cover these requirements. We introduce a simple architectural model that describes the basic steps and overall model to publish statistical reports coming from tabular data sources on the web. Finally, we describe the implementation of such a model and indicate what technologies can be used to enforce it in order to increase productivity and work quality when comparing it with other solutions.

Keywords: Web publishing · Statistics data · XML · Java · Open source technology

1 Introduction

The World Wide Web (WWW) is one of the greatest technologies to have ever come into present existence. In the early 90s, it served as a medium of communication with static content, and later became the medium of rendering web-based software applications as a user requirement.

Publishing refers to the production and distribution of media products. Media content is in the form of images, text, video and audio. A medium is used in storage, transmission or reproduction of this content. Such as, print media (analog) and Internet (digital media). Digital publishing on the Internet has numerous advantages (cost, topicality, availability, added value) [1]. Nowadays, publishing organizations has been dramatically changed in order to digitize the production and distribution of information on the web. In addition, depending on the requirement, information published on the web has different prospective. Contrarily, the question of how multiple uses of content within a publishing framework can be possible is often asked. For these multi-use

© Springer International Publishing AG 2017
T.-T. Wu et al. (Eds.): SETE 2016, LNCS 10108, pp. 259–269, 2017.
DOI: 10.1007/978-3-319-52836-6_26

purposes, a markup language is required, which separates content from a concrete representation, then converts it to any destination document format.

The presentation of content requires the selection of a suitable presentation format. In this regard, there are numerous formats for different media types. HTML is a standardized language of the W3C (World Wide Web Consortium) [2]. The Portable Document Format (PDF) is a data exchange format created by Adobe Systems [AdobJa]. It is suitable for a template-faithful transformation of print files and a distribution of electronic documents on the internet [3]. A Microsoft Excel spreadsheet (XLS) is a proprietary file format that manages data in a tabular form. Furthermore, an XLS document can be handled by many different applications. One example is Open Office, a free Office product, which is available for use on different operating systems. XLSX is another file extension, similar to the XML spreadsheet file format used by Microsoft Excel. Microsoft introduced this XML standard excel file format for Microsoft Office 2007 and upper as an open file format to transfer data between applications and other working areas [4].

This research work is organized as, first, we address the basic functionality at the heart of the publishing system. In the second layer, we study findability via the following question: In a web populated with a number of existing solutions, how can we identify the right one, the framework that provides the right service for our unique publishing system? To answer this question, we address the existing solution limitations, depending upon the general project requirements. In the third layer, we propose a platform architecture that leverages these graphs encapsulated by real life experience. We demonstrate how this helps to publish reports in a straightforward way, by building a user-friendly web-based publishing system. Our primary goal is to propose publishing system architecture for statistical data, using open source technologies that facilitate their integration into composite applications. Finally, to test our architectural model, we apply them to a real life statistical project (FOSTAT) [5]. After implementation, we are able to study the qualitative benefits of applying this proposed model. Then, to better understand how the architecture can facilitate the development of a real-world application, we illustrate its benefits with respect to this prototype.

2 Research Motivation

When developing a publishing system, the most important point needing consideration is the accommodation of collaborative development. A good framework allows collaborative development along with the smooth integration between independent development components. The idea to develop a more robust model for web publishing emerged when I started to work in DZHW (German Centre for Research on Higher Education and Science Studies) on one project (FOSTAT) [5], which leveraged to publish statistical research data on the web. The FOSTAT project is working to publish statistical report data for the Federal Ministry of Education and Research (Germany). One of the main requirements was to develop a web-based publishing system to publish different presentation formats by using the same data, and while following the open source technologies. The idea to bring a new architecture to this manner has hitherto been applied to web-based statistical report publishing.

2.1 Requirement of Publishing System

The functional requirements are derived from the application business process, which consists of several contiguous tasks that are performed by an actor to create a desired result.

Access to the application system: Users access the application system via an internet-connected personal computer and a web browser installed on it.

Selection and display of a table in a defined data format: Users have the option to select a table displaying, the home page of the application forms via the UI.

Import of databases in the system: Administrators can import databases with appropriate functions in the system.

Data format:

- HTML, for presentation in the browser.
- PDF, to view in the Adobe Application Compatible
- XLS, to display the Microsoft Excel application
- XLSX, to display the Open XML spreadsheet file format
- XML, represent the XML format in the browser
- XSL-FO, display the XML Formatting Object format

To resolve this research problem via providing a way to integrate design science and object oriented principles. To address this problem, we consider our research approach as "Design Science" [6]. This approach is widely used in many research disciplines, especially in engineering and computer science, but also in information systems [7, 8]. Java Server Faces (JSF) framework was chosen to solve this research question - which is a Java standard and satisfy the MVC pattern.

3 Related Work

Several papers and news articles relevant to the web publishing framework were studied during the course of development of publishing architecture. There are number of business intelligence (BI) and reporting tools available in the marketplace. The Eclipse Business Intelligence and Reporting Tools (BIRT) and the Jasper soft Community Edition are mostly using open source tools to generate the report in a variety of document formats [9–12]. Well, there is inauspicious news against these tools [13]. Withal, this is out of the scope to consider these reporting tools in this research work because; the dissertation focuses on the publishing.

3.1 Apache Cocoon

The Cocoon is a top-level project of the Apache Software Foundation (ASF) [14]. Apache Cocoon is an XML publishing framework based on the servlet API model. It was built around Separation of Concerns (SoC) and component based development (COP), providing pipeline SAX processing [15, 16].

Apache Cocoon uses an integrated configuration mechanism called the site-map, as a declarative XML document describing a set of pipelines that will be invoked, depending upon a URI (Uniform Resource Indicator) pattern match. An XML document is pushed through a pipeline that exists in several transformation steps. The pipeline consists of three main components, beginning with a generator, zero or more transformers, and a serializer [17, 18].

A sitemap is shown schematically in Fig. 1. Here, a matcher defines each pipeline. Within the illustrated pipeline, data is generated from an XML document using XSLT and an HTML document. The supported output formats include PDF, XML, VRML, etc., which can be controlled by changing transformation rules. The latest stable release of Apache Cocoon is version 2.2.0, released in May of 2008, which is a spring-based framework. Cocoon 1 version 2.2, however, has the advantageous compatibility with Apache Maven 2, which allows for much more efficient building management, as well as perfect integration with the spring framework [19]. Apache Cocoon uses the Apache FOP API to leverage the PDF output format. However, the last stable release of Cocoon framework supports the older version 1.0 of FOP [20], while the recent version of Apache FOP is 1.1. The lack of documented serializer, there is a considerable gap of information explaining the methods for creating Microsoft Excel (.xls) and Open XML spreadsheet (.xlsx) file formats.

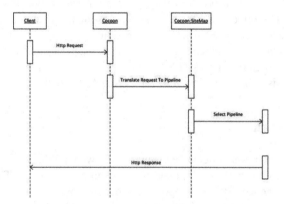

Fig. 1. Cocoon pipeline with Sitemap

3.2   Oracle XSQL Framework

The Oracle XSQL page publishing framework is a publishing platform capable of publishing XML documents in any format using SQL, XML and XSLT. The Java-based XSQL servlet is the controller port that provides a declarative interface to publish web content dynamically with relational data. However, the biggest limitation of this publishing framework, it is a proprietor base initiative, not a completely open source commencement [21]. It has only little available documentation and a bit cumbersome to implement it. In addition, the XSQL servlet can connect to any JDBC-supported database. However, the object-relational functionality only works when using an Oracle database coupled with the Oracle JDBC driver [21].

3.3 Maverick Framework

Maverick is an MVC framework for web publishing using Java technology. This framework focuses solely on MVC logic to allow for generating presentations using a variety of templates and transformation technologies [22]. The most recent update of the Maverick framework was released in 2006. The documentation of this framework is very poor, that makes it difficult to find all the features relative to the frameworks specific requirements.

3.4 Apache AxKit

Another Apache initiative was Apache AxKit, which is also an XML Application Server for data publishing. AxKit provides XML document conversion on-the-fly to any format such as HTML, WAP or text [23]. However, this framework is retired in August 2009.

Most of the framework described in this section has some limitations when considering for statistical report publishing. Despite of these, our initiative is novel that can manage both general and domain-specific statistics report publishing.

4 Technology and Software Selection

To tests our architecture how compatible it is for statistical report publishing, we select different technologies and software to demonstrate the implementation of the prototype. We use XML as middleware a medium-neutral data format that is not tied to a specific purpose or special software due to its separation of content and layout. After generating XML document, it is used as an input for the report publishing. JAXB (Java Architecture for XML Binding) API is used to generate the XML document [24]. JAXB is a Java mapping standard that defines how Java objects are converted from and into XML. For the persistence layer, an Object Relational Mapping (ORM) persistence framework was chosen. To achieve this functionality, we used the Hibernate persistence tool. Hibernate is an open source high performance object relational mapping (ORM) tool and the query service provider. After considering these aspects, the freely available RDBMS PostgreSQL database server version 9.4.4 version chosen for our application prototype. Higher versions are also usable. However, the concept of persistence offers a switch to any other RDBMS with very little effort.

To develop the prototype, we select the Apache Tomcat server, version 7.0,54. Note, however, our prototype application can be run using any of the 7.x subversions of this software. For the middle and front layers of the application, we chose JSF framework version 2.0. JSF is distributed as an open source under the Oracle Standard Web Framework software license.

5 Architecture of the Prototype

To manage the complexity of a software application, the application architecture should be structured with loosely coupled subsystems. This means that each subsystem defines clear responsibilities, minimizing the dependencies between these subsystems. Our architecture is divided into multiple logical layers: a presentation layer, application layer and persistence layer. Figure 2: shows different layer structures and demonstrates the relationships and interactions between applications components contained within those layers. Each individual layer has no knowledge the internal structure of the other layers, but provides services that are used exclusively by the neighboring layers. The use of these services is carried out via a Java class, which is located in the respective underlying layers and provides a narrow interface with fewer methods.

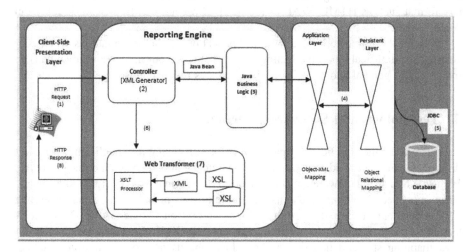

Fig. 2. The application architecture of the prototype

The application architecture of the prototype is presented. As the first step of the process, the Presentation layer asks for a request to the Reporting Engine. Then, within the Reporting Engine, the Controller takes this request and calls upon the respective Java Business Logic. The resulting Java object is annotated as an XML tree structure by JAXB API. Using Hibernate API, the Java object is mapped to the corresponding database table. The database (PostgreSQL) is connected with a JDBC driver. The XML document, or response, goes to the Web Transformer engine. This XML document is used as the input. Afterwards, the XSLT parses this XML document along with the respective XSL style sheet. Finally, the desired output result is displayed to the user.

Figure 5: PDF and XSL-FO Report Publishing Architecture, Apache FOP parser to generate the final PDF document sent to the user. Figure 4: HTML Report Publishing Architecture, the HTML Transformer parser which processes the data and presents it in the final HTML document for user view. Figure 3: Excel (.xls, .xlsx) Report Publishing Architecture, with the help of the Apache POI API, to generate the final Excel

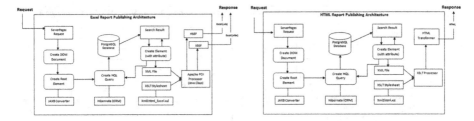

Fig. 3. Excel (.xls, .xlsx) report publishing architecture

Fig. 4. HTML report publishing architecture

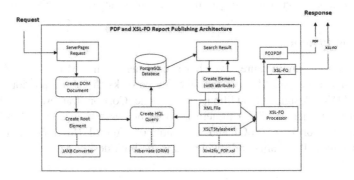

Fig. 5. PDF and XSL-FO report publishing architecture

document. In the Java class, HSSF method is used to generate .xls format and XSSF method is used to generate .xlsx format Excel report. This architecture is designed to publish an Excel format report. The first request to create a DOM document is received via a JAXB converter. The resulting Hibernate query is used to create the XML document, including the element and attribute and their respective values. XSL file is used as the XSL declaration. These two files are then used as input for the Excel parser Java Class with the help of Apache POI API, to generate the final Excel document. In this Java class, HSSF method is used to generate .xls format and XSSF method is used to generate .xlsx format Excel report.

6   Evaluation

The publishing architecture was evaluated, with a reference of standard web application requirements, to test the social acceptability, maintenance, scalability and operational feasibility of the prototype. Measurements were considered based on functional requirements of statistical report publishers. The significant differences in the measurements favoring this architecture will portray the advantages of report publishing.

Comparison between the existing solution and our proposed architecture is based upon the requirements of a report publishing system, as well as the list of parameters necessary to develop a common web-based publishing application. Figure 6 shows the comparison between different system architecture.

No.	Parameter	Specification	Our System	Apache Cocoon	Oracle XSQL	MAVERICK	Apache AxKit
1	Design Pattern	Separation of Concern	YES	YES	YES	Lack of Info	
		Inversion of Control	YES	NO	YES	Lack of Info	
		MVC (Model 2)	YES	YES	YES	Lack of Info	
2	Document Format	HTML	YES	YES	YES	NO	
		PDF	YES	YES	YES	YES	
		MS EXCEL (.xls & .xlsx)	YES	No Block Serializer	YES	NO	
3	Unified API	Apache FOP 1.1 / 2.0	YES	NO (FOP 1.0)	YES	Lack of Info	Retired 2009
4	Form Design	UI Component	JSF (Java Standard)	Cocoon Forms	YES	JSP, Velocity	
5	Database Persistence	ORM Support	YES	YES	Only Oracle	NOT WELL	
6	Data Representation	XML Technologies	YES	YES	YES	YES	
7	Documentation	User Guide	YES	NOT Healthy	YES	NOT WELL	
8	Stable Release	Version	Untill today	2008 Cocoon 2.2.0	2009	2006	
9	Technology	Open Source	YES	YES	NO	YES	

Fig. 6. Functionality comparison between different system architecture

6.1   Design Pattern

In the proposed architecture, we have considered the Model-View-Controller (MVC) design principal. Most of the other frameworks discussed previously follow the same MVC design. In addition, the Apache Cocoon framework follows the Separation Of Concerns (SoC) principal, while our architecture considers both the Separation Of Concerns (SoC) and Inversion of Control (IoC) 6design patterns. Notably, we used JSF framework, which supports both design patterns.

6.2   Document Publishing Format

A statistical report is required to publish in various publication formats, such as PDF, Excel, HTML, and other possible file formats. To publish these formats, the publishing architecture needs to allow the respective parser API. Our publishing architecture applies the separation of the Concern (SoC) principle, where individual format architecture is used to generate an individual document format. The prototype shows the individual format model that gives the flexibility to introduce numerous document formats. Sequentially, Oracle XSQL page publishing architecture also supports different documentation formats, while Apache Cocoon framework does not carry the serializer to support Excel 2007 or Open XML spreadsheet formats, and Maverick framework also has lack of declaration to support the Excel format output.

6.3   API Upgradetion

When designing system architecture, flexibility of API upgradetion is an important concern. Regarding this, the proposed architecture is designed with a sub-function strategy, meaning the individual output format is a sub-function with the respective API. Using this process, it is very easy to upgrade the API version to get the latest API facility. For example, when considering the PDF output format, Apache FOP parse the data with the help of XSL Formatting Object. The Cocoon framework uses Apache FOP version 1.0 while the latest version is FOP 2.0. In our system, the individual sub-function is independent of the others, making it very easy to update the latest version of the API. The Oracle XSQL framework also has this flexibility.

6.4   Form Design

In this architecture, we used JSF to design the form. The JSF UI component provides very simple functionality to design a form while the Apache Cocoon Form design concept is much more difficult. For example, suppose you want to design 10 forms. When using the Cocoon platform, you have to define 10 form definitions, plus 10 JXTemplates with controller logic, as well as the pipeline definitions in the sitemap [.xmap] file. This process raises the productivity scalability issue. On the other hand, when using JSF, the process of form design has been simplified to negate the added step in the process. The Oracle XSQL framework also supports JSF to design user interface.

6.5   Database Persistence

Persistence delivers the ability of an object to remain alive throughout the lifetime of the OS (Operating System) process in which it resides. In our proposed architecture, we considered Hibernate as an object relational mapping (ORM) tool. However, Oracle XSQL only supports the Oracle database system to give the ORM flexibility. This is a big limitation for the Oracle XSQL publishing framework.

6.6   Documentation (User Guide)

A User Guide is an important way to understand all steps of the system. We preferred standard framework and APIs to design the architecture. Our considered framework and APIs are Java and W3S standard, which are well documented within their respected areas. In contrast, Apache Cocoon and Oracle XSQL systems documentation are not healthy enough to understand their functionality easily. The last stable Apache Cocoon release 2.2.0 came out in 2008, whereas the latest version of Oracle XSQL6 was introduced in 2009. Consequently, the Maverick systems documentation is very poor in the sense of availability, especially since the latest release occurred in 2006 and the Apache AxKit was retired in 2009.

6.7   Open Source Technology

Many authors have referred to the advantages of using open source software [25–27]. The first perceived advantage of open source software is a low cost and in gratis availability. With us, all publishing frameworks that we considered are open source initiatives except the Oracle XSQL Publishing framework. It is a collaboration system following the parameters of the Oracle database, therefore preventing the framework from being a truly open-sourced tool.

7 Conclusion

As presented through this work, we studied various demands towards statistical report publishing on the web. We proposed an architectural direction to most efficiently meet these demands. We also built a prototype implementation of a real life project (FOSTAT) in order to report our resulting solutions. The prototype has all the essential characteristics and satisfies demands by the arrangement. The parameters resulted in a reduced learning curve, which were discussed in the evaluation section, proving that this architectural model is most suitable for a developer desiring to implement a web based statistical report publishing system with much flexibility. In addition, when compare to existing solutions, this publishing architecture is a clear winner in all aspects.

Acknowledgements. I gratefully acknowledge the financial support towards my thesis from the German Center for Research on Higher Education and Science Studies (DZHW GmbH) [www. dzhw.eu] under the grant FOSTAT Project, Funded by The Federal Ministry of Education and Research (BMBF), Germany.

References

1. Renear, A.H., Palmer, C.L.: Strategic reading, ontologies, and the future of scientific publishing. Science **325**(5942), 828–832 (2009)
2. Maglott, D., Ostell, J., Pruitt, K.D., Tatusova, T.: Entrez gene: gene-centered information at NCBI. Nucleic Acids Res. **33**(suppl 1), D54–D58 (2005)
3. Massand, D.: System and method for reflowing content in a structured portable document format (pdf) file. US Patent App. 12/413,486, 27 March 2009
4. Neyeloff, J.L., Fuchs, S.C., Moreira, L.B.: Meta-analyses and forest plots using a microsoft excel spreadsheet: step-by-step guide focusing on descriptive data analysis. BMC Res. Notes **5**(1), 52 (2012)
5. Dicken, H.: Data Warehouses für die Forschungsstatistik. In: HIS (2006)
6. Peffers, K., Tuunanen, T., Rothenberger, M.A., Chatterjee, S.: A design science research methodology for information systems research. J. Manag. Inf. Syst. **24**(3), 45–77 (2007)
7. Salminen, A., Jauhiainen, E., Nurmeksela, R.: A life cycle model of XML documents. J. Assoc. Inf. Sci. Technol. **65**(12), 2564–2580 (2014)
8. Zhang, F., Zhang, R.: The research and application of JasperReports in project management system. In: 2009 IEEE International Workshop on Open-Source Software for Scientific Computation (OSSC), pp. 56–59. IEEE (2009)
9. Layka, V., Judd, C.M., Nusairat, J.F., Shingler, J.: Beginning Groovy, Grails and Griffon. Springer, Berlin (2013)
10. Sapre, B.S., Ulhe, P.R., Meshram, B.: Report generation system using JasperReports and SQL stored procedure. Int. J. Eng. Res. Appl. (IJERA) **2**, 984–988
11. Chlouba, T., Kminek, D.: Building open-source based architecture of enterprise applications for business intelligence
12. Innovent Solutions: Open Source Reporting Review-BIRT, Jaspersoft, Pentaho (2015). http://www.innoventsolutions.com/open-source-reporting-review-birt-jasper-pentaho.html. Accessed 20 May 2016

13. Gonzalez, E.J., Hamilton, A., Moreno, L., Mendez, J., Marichal, G., Sigut, J., Sigut, M., Felipe, J., et al.: Intelligent agents and apache cocoon for a CV generation system. In: IEEE/ACS International Conference on Computer Systems and Applications, AICCSA 2007, pp. 9–15. IEEE (2007)
14. Mazzocchi, S.: Adding XML capabilities with Cocoon. In: ApacheCon Europe (2000)
15. Introduction apache Cocoon. https://cocoon.apache.org/2.1/introduction.html. Accessed 20 May 2016
16. Noels, S.: Standards applied: using apache Cocoon and forrest. In: XML Europe (2003)
17. Singh, A.: Web based system architecture
18. Mohammed, S., Orabi, A., Fiaidhi, J., Passi, K.: Developing a Web 2.0 restful Cocoon web services for telemedical education. In: International Symposium on Applications and the Internet, SAINT 2008, pp. 309–312. IEEE (2008)
19. Apache Cocoon 2.2.0 released. http://cocoon.apache.org/1445_1_1.html. Accessed 20 May 2016
20. Eisenblatter, K., Deckarm, H., Scherer, R.: Context-sensitive information spaces for construction site applications. In: eWork and eBusiness in Architecture, Engineering and Construction, ECPPM 2006: European Conference on Product and Process Modelling 2006, Valencia, Spain, 13–15 September 2006, p. 421. CRC Press (2006)
21. XML developers kit programmers guide. http://docs.oracle.com/cd/B19306_01/appdev.102/b14252/adx_j_xsqlpub.htm. Accessed 20 May 2016
22. Melis, E., Siekmann, J.: ActiveMath: an intelligent tutoring system for mathematics. In: Rutkowski, L., Siekmann, J.H., Tadeusiewicz, R., Zadeh, L.A. (eds.) ICAISC 2004. LNCS (LNAI), vol. 3070, pp. 91–101. Springer, Heidelberg (2004). doi:10.1007/978-3-540-24844-6_12
23. Traffic Accounting System Foundation: Apache AxKit. http://www.axkit.org/. Accessed 20 May 2016
24. Acampora, G., Loia, V.: A proposal of ubiquitous fuzzy computing for ambient intelligence. Inf. Sci. 178(3), 631–646 (2008)
25. Lapa, J., Bernardino, J., Figueiredo, A.: A comparative analysis of open source business intelligence platforms. In: Proceedings of International Conference on Information Systems and Design of Communication, pp. 86–92. ACM (2014)
26. Bitzer, J., Schroder, P.J.: The economics of open source software development: an introduction. Econ. Open Source Softw. Dev. 1–13 (2006)
27. Sauer, R.M.: Why develop open-source software? The role of non-pecuniary benefits, monetary rewards, and open-source licence type. Oxford Rev. Econ. Policy 23(4), 605–619 (2007)

Towards Personalization of Peer Review in Learning Programming

Joseph Sunday[✉], Ghislain Maurice Norbert Isabwe,
Muhammad Usman Ali, and Renee Patrizia Schulz

University of Agder, Grimstad, Norway
{joseps14,muhama14}@student.uia.no,
{maurice.isabwe,renee.schulz}@uia.no

Abstract. Peer review is one of the effective processes for sharing knowledge and improving overall learning performance. This became more popular by the use of ICT. However, it is challenging to implement peer review in learning programming languages due to the complexity of the subject matter. A group of peer reviewers may have different overall performance but similar weaknesses on a given aspect of the programming tasks. Hence, they may not be able to help each other to address individual needs. In this paper, we present a personalized approach to peer review with consideration to criteria based assessment and individual performance on specific programming tasks. This is achieved using a novel peer-matching algorithm to create reviewer groups. The algorithm assigns peer-reviewers in such a way that each student gets reviews from at least three peers with different levels of competence (low, medium and high). Peer matching is tailored to individual student needs with respect to specific aspects of learning programming. This work implemented a web based peer review system, and carried out user-based evaluations with computer science students. There are indications that personalized peer matching, based on relevant assessment criteria, can improve individual learning achievement in programming courses.

Keywords: Peer review · Personalized collaborative learning · Programming

1 Introduction

Most courses in higher education still heavily rely on teachers to make students familiar with new real world tasks [1]. However, in programming courses, students should use their own understanding and reasoning to solve given tasks. It's difficult for students to learn solely from teachers [2]. Collaborative learning could help address this challenge, through a peer review process. By reviewing each other's work, students can get more ideas and techniques for solving programming tasks. Peer review is highly recommended because it reduces teachers' workload [3] and increases learning outcome [4].

Since students are neither experts in the subject matter, nor in assessment practice, they need guidance on the assessment process [5]. Students should be given relevant assessment criteria for the learning tasks. The challenge is how to define the assessment criteria and the amount of criteria that can be used in the process. Topping [6] argued that students should be free to use their knowledge and choose the feedback format.

© Springer International Publishing AG 2017
T.-T. Wu et al. (Eds.): SETE 2016, LNCS 10108, pp. 270–277, 2017.
DOI: 10.1007/978-3-319-52836-6_27

2 State – of – the – Art

Peer assessment is an educational arrangement where students judge each other's performance quantitatively and/or qualitatively [7]. Peer assessment stimulates students to reflect, discuss, and collaborate in their learning process [6]. Nowadays, students learn from many different resources, the first resource being the students as a group.

Satu and Kari [2] presented a student self-assessment tool that could be used to motivate learning and track progression in programming courses. Using a revised Bloom's taxonomy scale, it was found that the tool helped students to improve their knowledge. Further on, a study on a system that supports Peer Code Review (PCR) [8] showed that PCR process helped students to achieve the intended learning outcomes. Students improved their abilities for programming, conforming to coding standards, punctuality, making suggestions, accepting criticism, and collaborative learning.

NovoEd[1] is one of the platforms that uses double-blinded peer review. The platform can either assign reviewers randomly, or a student's submission will get more evaluations if s/he has evaluated other submissions. The common challenge is that the assigning of reviewers does not consider individual strengths and weaknesses.

3 Problem Statement and Research Questions

Even though peer review has been generally successful, the selection and allocation of peer reviewers is primarily random. It is possible that a weak student gets several reviews from equally weak students. So far, to the best of our knowledge, peer-matching process has not been sufficiently researched to optimize the peer review process. Programming courses are of particular interest given that students' tasks may include subtasks that require different skills and approaches to problem solving. A student may do well on one sub-task but struggle on a different one, hence affecting the overall performance. There is a need for assessment criteria covering specific sub-tasks, and personalization of the review process to address each sub-task for individual student.

Previous research has explored assessment criteria [9] but more needs to be done to make it more helpful to students, especially in introductory programming courses. This study proposes a personalized peer-matching algorithm to support peer review processes in programming education. This work addresses following questions:

- What is the more optimal approach to match peers in the peer review process?
- What are the assessment criteria for assignments in the "introduction to programming" course?
- How to implement a personalized peer review solution for programming education?

---

[1] Andrew Linford, Manager of Support and Technical Operations; Internal communication, 2016.

4 Methodology

This work adopts methods from educational research and human-centred design, including both qualitative and quantitative user studies. The study participants are computer science teachers (4 men) and 21 first year bachelor students (6 women and 15 men) at University of Agder (Norway). Semi-structured interviews were conducted and recorded to collect data on assessment criteria and peer-matching, from both the teachers and students. User testing and evaluation of the design solution was done through observations as well as online surveys. Students interacted with the designed system while the researchers observed their interactions and looked for usability problems.

The design and development follows the human-centred design process [10]. That addresses a design problem considering the context of use and the people for whom the system is designed for, in order to produce design solutions that meet user requirements.

5 Personalized Peer Review System Concept

The main functional requirement is to enable students learn from their peers how to correct their solutions and reduce teachers' workload. Teachers should be able to see the reviewed assignments and give feedback if required. Students are more likely to be objective if teachers are involved. However, the process should be anonymous (Fig. 1).

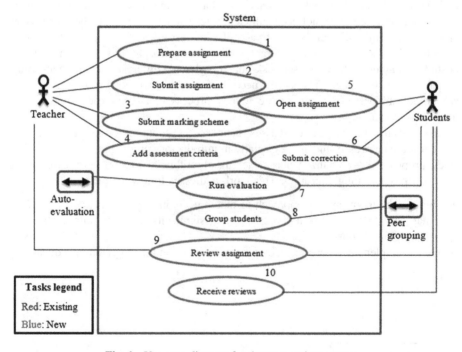

Fig. 1. Use case diagram for the peer review system

Teachers emphasized that students have different capabilities which should be considered for the allocation of reviewers. They suggested that each student should receive 3 to 5 reviews per assignment, in such a way that an assignment is reviewed by at least three students of different performance levels (low [L], medium [M] and high [H]).

Further on, teachers indicated that all the topics covered by an assignment should be reflected in the assessment criteria for peer review. Each criterion gets a certain weight according to its importance in solving the programming problem/task. It's noted that students don't give grades, but performance levels (L,M,H) and comments corresponding with the criteria. More requirements were gathered from teachers and students:

1. Teachers can submit in any of the accepted file formats: pdf, doc/x or txt.
2. A marking scheme is provided as a reference solution (txt, json or java file format)
3. The assignment questions and reference solutions can be resubmitted if necessary
4. Students must be able to submit their answer to the assignment task.
5. All students' performances must be recorded and be retrieved when needed. These performances must be quantifiable for sorting students into levels (L,M,H).
6. Peers (reviewers) must be grouped according to individual performance on the previous assignment.
7. A reviewer must be able to review at least three submissions from other students.
8. A teacher should be able to review any assignment and students' solutions.
9. All students should receive reviews and be able to read them.

Teachers and students also rated the importance of the suggested criteria as shown in Fig. 2. Since it was suggested that every student should get reviews from 3 different performance levels, it is necessary to divide the total number of students (N) into three levels of same size D. D = N/3 if N is divisible by 3, otherwise the high level group will have + or − one student.

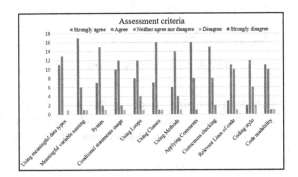

Fig. 2. Users' opinions on rating an assessment criterion as of high importance.

Figure 3, illustrates that each student reviews three other students; one from each level including her/his own level and receives three reviews; one from each level.

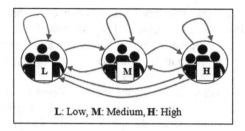

L: Low, M: Medium, H: High

Fig. 3. Students' levels and reviewers' distribution.

In the first round of peer reviews, students are randomly assigned to groups; thereafter, they are assigned based on previous performance as shown in Fig. 4.

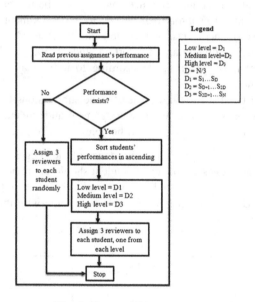

Fig. 4. Peer matching process.

In Fig. 4, D denotes the group size. Assuming that N = 100, D = 100/3 = 33. If sorted in ascending order, the first 33 students belong to L level, named D1; then 34th to 66th student belong to M level (D2). In this example, the H level group D3 has 34 students (67–100).

Students $s_i = \{s_1, s_2 \ldots s_N\}$; $i = \{1, 2 \ldots N\}$, are classified in levels so that reviewers will be distributed from all levels, $D_l, l = \{1, 2, 3\}$. Every student reviews and gets feedback from three other students, one from each level. Every criteria category/aspect has a weight, which is assigned by the teacher as shown in Table 1.

Criterion score C_r is the average of performance scores (Pj) from each reviewer on the criterion r.

Table 1. Assessment criteria with corresponding weights

Criterion no. (r)	Description	Weight (%)
1	How well is the variable declaration made?	20
2	Are the inputs well stated?	20
3	How is the "selection statement" used?	30
4	How well are the comments written?	10
5	Is the overall program working?	20

$$C_r = 1/j \sum\nolimits_{j=1}^{3} \mathbf{p}_j; \ r = \{1,2,3,4,5\}. \tag{1}$$

Each student scores T_i (total score for all criteria) as the overall performance. The total score for the ith student where W_{rq} is the weight "q" for the "r" criterion,

$$T_i = \sum\nolimits_{r=1}^{5} C_r W_{rq}; q = \{0.2; 0.2; 0.3; 0.1; 0.2\}; \ i = \{1, 2, \ldots, N\}. \tag{2}$$

A peer matching algorithm compares each reviewer's performance with the author's both at criterion level and the total performance. The reviewer should not have the same performance score on the same criterion as the author unless all other authors are already assigned to reviewers.

$$T_i \neq T_{i+n}, and \ C_{ri} \neq C_{r(i+n)}; i = \{1, 2, \ldots, N\}; n = (1, 2, \ldots, N-1). \tag{3}$$

This algorithm can help individual students to get reviews from peers with a different score at criterion level, thus allowing them to have personalized reviews that potentially address individual needs.

6 Implementation and Evaluation

A proof of concept system was implemented with MS Visual Studio 2012 (C#); HTML5, CSS3 and MS SQL. User interfaces were developed to support the established requirements for both teachers and students. Several user based evaluations were carried out as part of an iterative design process, to improve usability and user experience.

Twelve (12) first year computer science students took part in user testing. All participants (4 women and 8 men, aged between 18 and 30 years) completed the peer review tasks and received feedback from peers. Five out of twelve students (41.7%) suggested that using this system for peer review was helpful in learning programming whereas the other 7 (58.3%) found that to be very helpful. Additionally, 8 students strongly agreed to have learnt from reviewing their peers 'work, whereas 4 students agreed on the same statement. Generally, students indicated that the peer review system helped them to learn more because they could read the code written by other students. 9 students (75%) strongly agreed that they learnt from the feedback they received.

According to 75% of the respondents, the assessment criteria was not only useful in the review process but also benefitted their learning. Students recommended wide use of such a system, especially in programming courses.

7 Conclusion and Future Work

Research literature suggests that peer review process can help increase learning performance in different disciplines. We argue that students should get personalized peer feedback from peers with different performance at each sub-task level, in order to meet individual needs. We propose a new approach to personalized peer matching for student grouping and allocation of peer-reviewers in programming courses. This considers multiple assessment criteria which contribute to the total performance score, with a different weight for each criterion. Peer matching ensures that the author gets peer-feedback from at least three different performance levels for each programming subtask. That has a potential to increase overall feedback quality since the feedback can include judgment of at least one highly performing student at every criterion. Teachers and students involved in user studies for this work perceive this approach as more useful and helpful to individual student.

In the future, an extended study covering a wide area of programming concepts and a user testing with a larger sample size could help to improve the system and test the pedagogical value of such an intervention.

References

1. Lombardi, M.M.: Authentic learning for the 21st century: an overview. Educ. Learn. Initiat. **1**(2007), 1–12 (2007)
2. Satu, A., Kari, S.: Student self-assessment in a programming course using bloom's revised taxonomy. In: Proceedings of the 15th Annual SIGCSE Conference on Innovation and Technology in Computer Science Education, ITiCSE, Bilkent, Ankara, Turkey (2010)
3. Rochelle, F.R., Traci, T.: Student performance on and attitudes toward peer assessments on advanced pharmacy practice experience assignments. Curr. Pharm. Teach. Learn. **4**(2), 113–121 (2012)
4. Charlotte, M., Christopher, V., Daniel, B.: Turning apathy into activeness in oral communication classes: regular self- and peer-assessment in a TBLT programme. System **40**(3), 407–420 (2012)
5. Mark, L., Phil, W.: Can students assess students effectively? Some insights into peer-assessment. Learn. Teach. Unit **2**(1) (2003). ISSN 1477-1241
6. Keith, T.: Peer assessment between students in colleges and universities. Am. Educ. Res. Assoc. JSTOR **68**(3), 247–276 (1998)
7. Zundert, M.V., Sluijsmans, D., Merriënboer, J.V.: Effective peer assessment processes: research findings and future directions. Learn. Instr. **20**(4), 270–279 (2010)
8. Wang, Y., Li, H., Sun, Y., Jiang, Y., Yu, J.: Learning outcomes of programming language courses based on peer code review model. In: The 6th International Conference on Computer Science and Education (ICCSE 2011), Virgo, Singapore (2011)

9. Jason, C.: IBM DeveloperWorks: 11 proven practices for more effective, efficient peer code review, 25 January 2011. http://www.ibm.com/developerworks/rational/library/11-proven-practices-for-peer-review/. (Accessed 10 Feb 2016)
10. ISO 9241-210: Ergonomics of human-system interaction. International Organization for Standardization, Geneva, Switzerland (2010). http://www.iso.org/iso/iso_catalogue/catalogue_tc/catalogue_detail.htm?csnumber=52075

The Design of TurnTalk for the Scaffolding of Balanced Conversations in Groups of Children

Alessandra Melonio and Mehdi Rizvi[(⊠)]

Free University of Bozen-Bolzano, Piazza Domenicani 3, 39100 Bolzano, Italy
{alessandra.melonio,SRizvi}@unibz.it

Abstract. The proper management of conversation among children is pivotal for any group activity with them. Socio-emotional learning curricula developed experimented activities for teaching children conversation skills, which can be enhanced by tangible interactive playful solutions for conveying conversation rules. This paper moves along such lines and presents the design and current evaluation of a tangible interactive playful object for children: TurnTalk. Enhanced with "calm technology", TurnTalk promotes the scaffolding of a balanced conversation in group, in terms of turns taken in talking. The paper overviews its design rationale, choices and current evaluation results.

Keywords: Playful experience design · Socio-emotional learning · Group dynamics · Children · Deaf

1 Introduction

Technology enhanced learning has focussed on traditional learning domains, such as literacy, and devised adaptive solutions for different children, e.g., [1, 11]. However, nowadays, several schools are increasingly recognising the importance to implement *socio-emotional learning* (SEL) activities for teaching learners how to communicate in a conversation [9]. *Balanced conversations* are at the centre of such activities with children: then each person is actively engaged and takes turns in talking about a topic; each adds to the topic by responding to previous speakers, training a number of communication skills in the process. The positive effects of such activities are many and go beyond improvements in·communication skills; for instance, the meta-analysis reported in [9] found that, compared to controls, SEL participants demonstrated significantly improved social and emotional skills, attitudes, behaviour, and academic performance.

In *human computer interaction* (HCI) and *computer-supported collaborative learning* (CSCL) research, scholars have extensively explored the role of computer or mobile based solutions in mediating and supporting conversation-based activities among humans, in terms of both the outcomes of the activities (e.g., [5]) and the interaction process itself (e.g., [4]). However, a number of SEL activities centre around *synchronous conversations* (briefly, *conversations*, from now onward): face to face, at the same time,

© Springer International Publishing AG 2017
T.-T. Wu et al. (Eds.): SETE 2016, LNCS 10108, pp. 278–287, 2017.
DOI: 10.1007/978-3-319-52836-6_28

in the same place, mainly verbal. Then the mediation of computers or mobile devices is not always feasible or is not perceived natural or effective for SEL, e.g., [21].

SEL activities, centred around conversation, could anyway benefit from HCI and CSCL research—and vice-versa. The survey [24] lists promising directions for such technology-based design solutions. In particular, as envisioned in [8], technology-enhanced embodied interaction and SEL research can profit from each other: tangible interactive objects can represent unobtrusive solutions for SEL. Such objects should be engaging, easy-to-use and easy-to-customise for children.

This paper follows the idea that tangible interactive playful objects, enhanced with technology, can support SEL activities and assist children in becoming aware of their conversation behaviours. Moreover, in line with [6], this paper also sustains that interactive solutions can help stir good practices and avoid systematic flaws in conversation, and hence improve conversation management. Specifically, this paper presents the design of *TurnTalk*: a tangible interactive playful object for 8–10 year old children, enhanced with technology, for scaffolding turn-takings in conversation.

The *turn-taking in talking* is a basic rule for conversation in SEL, and has been assessed as one of the most salient features of conversation by some education experts [26]. It does not often occur automatically and needs scaffolding. Turn-taking starts without the use of words: having a tangible object for turn- taking allows children to practise signalling a turn. TurnTalk can further support the scaffolding of the rule, through unobtrusive or "calm" technology [25] and tangible playful elements: specifically, TurnTalk aims at promoting children's awareness of the rule and reflection on conversation patterns so as to stir a balanced conversation, in which all children are actively engaged.

Besides being rooted in SEL research for building children's conversation skills, the design of TurnTalk is motivated by existing work in the area of tangible interaction design, which is briefly overviewed in Sect. 2. Section 3 outlines the design approach that was followed for incrementally designing TurnTalk prototypes and evaluating them. With the preliminaries out of the way, the paper digs into the design choices of the current TurnTalk prototype. The paper concludes reporting on the available evaluation results and plan for future work.

2 Related Work

The research in this paper is situated in the context of tangible interaction design for communication, with a focus on playful experience design for children.

Related work has been done to cater the need of technology-mediated social interactions, which was mainly assessed with adults in short-term studies. One such examples are wearable *Sociometer* badges, which measure face-to-face social interactions in order to model social dynamics in a group [22]. Such badges were used in *Meeting Mediator*, a real-time portable system which tracks team dynamics and displays them visually, as real-time feedback, on mobile phones, with the aim of promoting positive social behaviours [22]. Similarly, *Second Messenger* used and experimentally evaluated a variety of visualizations to show user participation in order to help users move towards a balanced conversation with equal participation [6].

TurnTalk is also different under several aspects from tabletop solutions such as the *Collaborative Workspace* or *Reflect*, which visualise also complex conversation patterns, and were tested with adults in [3, 19], respectively. For instance, Reflect is a mirroring device: it aims to inform users about their conversation and, to do so, it gives real-time visualisation feedback; then it leaves to the users (adults) to decide if anything needs to be changed in their conversation behaviours. Instead TurnTalk is designed as an active mediator for children's taking turns in talking, besides for enabling children's self-reflection on taking-turn patterns. Moreover, TurnTalk is designed as a portable, tangible, playful solution for children and not as a visualisation tabletop surface, e.g., children have cards to play for regulating and signalling their turn in talking, as well as rewards in the form of coins for the scaffolding of a balanced conversation.

Grouper is another solution for team work but with a different goal than TurnTalk [23]. Developed as a proof-of-concept wireless wearable, it is a group coordinator: through sensory cues, Grouper alerts its users to pay attention to the leader of the group. Users have to wear modules (consisting of a microprocessor, a wireless radio, and various electronics) to provide sensory cues.

TurnTalk aims also at being inclusive and accessible for different users, especially children who are at risk of isolation in social activities at school. The literature of inclusive and accessible design count several interactive solutions, which are often designed according to the specific users' needs. Relevant for this paper is the work reported in [17]: head-mounted displays were used to help deaf users localize sound in order to be effectively part of a group conversation or activity. *SocialMirror* [15] is instead focused on helping individuals with autism by displaying comments and suggestions by family and friends, but the idea can be transferred to team-work settings.

3 Design Process

User eXperience (UX) design, with a lean approach, is the methodology adopted for developing TurnTalk [13]. The design and the evaluation of a series of prototype interactive objects form the significant portion of the research: different prototypes are rapidly delivered and assessed, starting with technology *probes*. Probes, enhanced with technology, evolved from cultural probes and were introduced within an ethnography research project [16].

Probes, enhanced with technology, combine the social science goal of collecting information about the use and the users of the technology in a real-world environment, the user experience goal of field-testing the technology, and the design goal of inspiring users and designers to think of new kinds of technology to support their needs and desires. All prototypes of TurnTalk, realised so far, are Arduino based with a number of sensors and actuators [2].

In line with the UX approach, the design of TurnTalk takes special care of its context of usage. The context of use analysis led to setting requirements for the design of TurnTalk, outlined in Sect. 4, which are then refined in view of evaluation results. In fact, in any lean UX design process, evaluation plays a pivotal role. Also the evaluation of TurnTalk is intertwined with its design.

Evaluation studies are executed with product design experts, interaction design experts as well as with experts of the domain under consideration (SEL and child-development, deafness), e.g., by using inspection methods. Crucially, studies are also conducted with the end users of the objects, that is, children. For instance, the evaluation of an early prototype of TurnTalk, acting as probe, considered unforeseen usages of the object inspired by children; Sect. 5 reports the main evaluation results for the current TurnTalk prototype.

4   Design Choices and Their Rationale

4.1   Design Goal and Primary Users

Two incrementally more refined prototypes of TurnTalk are in Fig. 1. Its primary users are 8–10 children, in groups of 3–5 members: children, older than 8 years, should be able to accurately recognise and manage their emotions and thoughts as well as their influence on behaviour, two abilities that are necessary for the scaffolding of "communication and relationship skills" for group conversation [24]. The main goal of TurnTalk is the scaffolding of taking turns in talking. Specifically it aims at stimulating a balanced conversation in a group: members should take their turn in talking, and encourage fair participation.

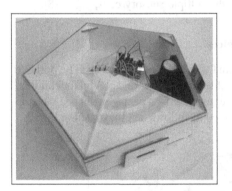 

Fig. 1. Photos of two subsequent TurnTalk prototypes

4.2   Design Requirements

The context of use of TurnTalk was investigated through a literature review and contextual inquiries with four teachers, two experts of SEL, and an expert of cognitive studies. Requirements were formulated in light of the analysis; the main ones are reported informally as follows.

TurnTalk should be used by any teacher in SEL interventions for learning activities, centred around conversation. Thus replicating it should be *economical*.

As it should be used in learning activity centred around conversation, TurnTalk should be an *unobtrusive* portable device that follows the disappearing or calm technology paradigm of ubiquitous computing: paraphrasing Weiser words, technology (instead of "computer") should be "so imbedded, so fitting, so natural, that we use it without even thinking about it" [25].

At the same time, play invites exploration and is a key factor for engaging children in an activity [10]. Therefore TurnTalk should be perceived *playful* by the considered age range of children, and yet it should be unobtrusive in that it does not distract children from the activity they are performing, or even hinder it.

For instance, according to literature of playful interaction design for children, those children enjoy discovering functionalities. They also like being rewarded when they face challenging tasks in an activity [20]. However reward design has to be done with specific care and in line with the balanced conversation goal of TurnTalk, which is cooperative in nature. Therefore rewards of TurnTalk should not foster competition among children. More generally, play social elements, such as rewards and badges, should be cooperative. They should also be contingent to the activity and its tasks, so that children do not feel controlled or manipulated through rewards or badges [14]. Moreover, visual feedback is an important component of any playful interactive object for children. However visual feedback concerning the group conversation should not distract the group from their learning activity but rather support the scaffolding of a balanced conversation during the activity.

Finally, the design of TurnTalk should strive for *affordance* for children. As TurnTalk aims to be *accessible* for children with different conversation needs, multi-modality should be implemented through multiple sensory cues, e.g., [18].

4.3   Physical and Interaction Design Choices

In line with the requirements listed above, TurnTable was designed so as to be portable and not-expensive, as well as affordable, accessible, unobtrusive and playful for children. The main physical components of TurnTalk are: turn-cards; a pentagon-shaped tabletop device; rewards. Each of them is briefly described as follows and illustrated in Fig. 2.

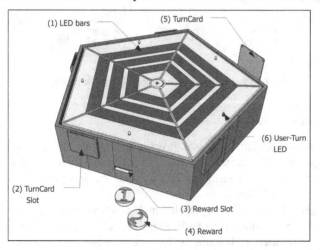

Fig. 2. Physical components of the current TurnTalk prototype (Color figure online)

The turn-card is a 3D printed card, personalised for each group member and identifying him or her ((5), in Fig. 2). Each member plays his or her turn-card to take his or her turn for talking, by placing the card in the pentagon-shaped tabletop device ((2), in Fig. 2).

The pentagon device is the main part of TurnTalk. It is fabricated with a 3D-printer and a laser-cut. Technology takes the form of economical micro-electronics components, hidden in the device: an Arduino UNO micro-controller, sensors and actuators. They enable two things: (1) the interaction with children; (2) the storage and processing of social interaction data, starting with the number of turns taken by each member. The micro-electronics components and their specific interaction design functionalities are described as follows.

Motors are actuators hidden in the tabletop device. These motors trigger the release of rewards in the form of 3D-printed coins, of different value ((4), in Fig. 2). Coins are designed so as to be playful and unobstrusive with respect to the SEL goal of TurnTalk, which is cooperative in nature. Coins act as social rewards for the group, in view of individuals' contributions to the conversation: the more balanced is the number of turns taken in the group, the higher-value coins are released to the group. Moreover, in line with playful design principles, which slot of the pentagon device releases coins varies so as to act as surprise element for children ((3), in Fig. 2). Coins have also a magnet inside, and thus they can be placed on any metallic surface, such as a whiteboard in classroom or a fridge at home. This way coins can serve as badges, as tangible social display of the group's interaction progression.

Finally, the pentagon-shaped tabletop device is divided into five slices; each slice is for a group member. One LED pin ((6), in Fig. 2) is placed at the edge of each slice, so that there is a LED pin for each group member. When a group member takes her or his turn in talking, her or his LED pin flashes green. If, at the same time, another group member tries to take over his or her turn in talking, then the LED pin of this group member flashes red and the overlap in turns is tracked.

Besides LED pins, a series of LED bars are also placed along slices of the tabletop device ((1), in Fig. 2). The LED bars light up in a slice proportionally to the number of

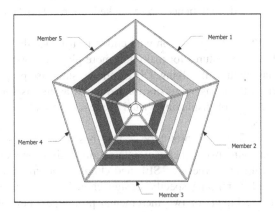

Fig. 3. Visualisation feedback of the current TurnTalk prototype (Color figure online)

turns taken by the member associated to the slice, thereby delivering a visual feedback. Over-participation and under-participation are also tracked, and defined as outliers, computed using upper and lower fences with quartiles, respectively. In line with results of [3, 6], over-participants (albeit adults) tend do moderate their participation in conversation once aware of over- participating. Therefore if a member has been over-participating then his or her LED pin flashes orange to signal it. Under-participation is not highlighted as it may even further inhibit under-participants from more actively engaging in conversation.

The visual feedback is also designed so as to be playful and unobstrusive. Firstly, it can be delivered in different moments, according to the teacher's choice. For instance, depending on the selected scenario, the visual feedback could be given either during a conversation, at specific moments chosen by the teacher, or between two conversation sessions. Figure 3 shows the visual feedback for a conversation session in a group with 5 members. It intuitively shows that Members 3 and 5 were dominating the conversation, and Member 1 was not participating in it at all. This visual feedback can give clear indications about participants who need further scaffolding. Also it may encourage less and more engaged participants to self-reflect on their participation and differently participate in future conversation sessions.

5 Evaluation

TurnTalk is inspired by a gamified probe used in cooperative design activities with 19 9–10 year old children of a primary school, reported in [12], in turn inspired by a non-technology probe, reported in [7]. The probe was meant as an early design non-interactive solution for making tangible the rule of taking turns in speaking in groups of primary-school children. The probe was enhanced with technology, which, however, only logged taking-turn data for statistical purposes (namely, the number of times each group member took a turn in speaking); it was not an interactive object as TurnTalk is, e.g., it had no visualisation feedback nor coins, and hence it was not designed to support children's self-reflection on their conversation patterns. However the probe used and tested cards as physical signals of turns in talking. Cards were mainly used as expected, and hence were picked up by TurnTalk with the same functionality.

Observation results of the evaluation with children sustained the need of enhancing the probe with interaction features for making it more playful as well as for enhancing the scaffolding of taking turns in talking. Observation results also purported the need of avoiding that over-participating members treated cards as means for dominating the conversation. The choice of displaying visual feedback for over-participation is also based on such results.

The design of the TurnTalk prototype is also based on the results of rounds of expert reviews, held with two experts of interaction design, one expert of product design, as well as with two experts of SEL and child development. Results of evaluation sessions helped in refining specific design choices, concerning the product or interaction with it; see Fig. 1 for two incremental prototypes. For instance, the SEL expert highlighted the importance of group rewards (versus individual rewards): the

SEL expert insisted that all group members be rewarded with the same number of coins, according to how balanced the conversation is, so as to reinforce the visual feedback displayed through LED bars. See Fig. 2.

The current TurnTalk prototype will be evaluated through empirical studies as follows. Firstly its visualisation and coin mechanics will undergo small-scale usability studies, and their design will be refined according in 2016. Secondly the usage of TurnTalk in a cooperative learning activity will undergo an empirical study, within an inclusive primary classroom. Its design will be revised and improved in line with the study results. A conclusive empirical study is also planned to compare conversation patterns of groups of children in a cooperative learning activity, with and without TurnTalk.

6 Conclusions

Technology can assist in managing social interactions in activities with children, working in tandem with experimented SEL strategies. Specifically, this paper posits that interaction design of playful objects can enhance SEL strategies and help promote positive social interactions in groups with children.

The paper focused on the design of TurnTalk, a tangible interactive playful object for the scaffolding of turn-taking in talking so as to balance group conversations. The paper overviewed the SEL research on which the design of TurnTalk is based and related work in the area of playful interaction design for communication. Then it focussed on the design goal, requirements and functionalities of the current TurnTalk prototype, after sketching the adopted design approach. The paper ended presenting the current evaluation results, and explaining the next evaluation steps.

References

1. Alrifai, M., Gennari, R., Tifrea, O., Vittorini, P.: The user and domain models of the terence adaptive learning system. In: Vittorini, P., Gennari, R., Marenzi, I., de la Prieta, F., Rodríguez, J. (eds.) International Workshop on Evidence-Based Technology Enhanced Learning. Advances in Intelligent and Soft Computing, vol. 152, pp. 83–90. Springer, Berlin (2012)
2. Arduino: What is Arduino? https://www.arduino.cc/en/Guide/Introduction
3. Bachour, K., Kaplan, F., Dillenbourg, P.: An interactive table for supporting participation balance in face-to-face collaborative learning. IEEE Trans. Learn. Technol. 3(3), 203–213 (2010)
4. Collazos, C.A., Guerrero, L.A., Pino, J.A., Ochoa, S.F.: A method for evaluating computer-supported collaborative learning processes. Int. J. Comput. Appl. Technol. 19 (3/4), 151–161 (2004). http://dx.doi.org/10.1504/IJCAT.2004.004044
5. De Marsico, M., Sterbini, A., Temperini, M.: Assessing group composition in e-learning according to Vygotskij's zone of proximal development. In: Stephanidis, C., Antona, M. (eds.) UAHCI 2014. LNCS, vol. 8514, pp. 277–288. Springer, Heidelberg (2014). doi:10. 1007/978-3-319-07440-5_26

6. DiMicco, J.M., Hollenbach, K.J., Pandolfo, A., Bender, W.: The impact of increased awareness while face-to-face. Hum.-Comput. Interact. **22**(1), 47–96 (2007). http://dl.acm.org/citation.cfm?id=1466595.1466598

7. Dodero, G., Gennari, R., Melonio, A., Torello, S.: Towards tangible gamified codesign at school: two studies in primary schools. In: Proceedings of the First ACM SIGCHI Annual Symposium on Computer-Human Interaction in Play, CHI PLAY 2014. ACM, New York (2014)

8. Dourish, P.: Embodied Interaction: Exploring the Foundations of a New Approach to HCI (1999). http://www.ics.uci.edu/~jpd/publications/misc/embodied.pdf

9. Durlak, J.A., Weissberg, R.P., Dymnicki, A.B., Taylor, R.D., Schellinger, K.B.: The impact of enhancing student's social and emotional learning: a meta-analysis of school-based universal interventions. Child Dev. **82**(1), 405–432 (2011). http://dx.doi.org/10.1111/j.1467-8624.2010.01564.x

10. Ferrara, J.: Playful Design. Rosenfeld Media, Brooklyn (2012)

11. Gennari, R., Mich, O.: Constraint-based temporal reasoning for e-learning with LODE. In: Bessière, C. (ed.) CP 2007. LNCS, vol. 4741, pp. 90–104. Springer, Heidelberg (2007). doi:10.1007/978-3-540-74970-7_9. http://dl.acm.org/citation.cfm?id=1771668.1771679

12. Gennari, R., Melonio, A., Torello, S.: Gamified probes for cooperative learning: a case study. Multimed. Tools Appl. **75**, 1–25 (2016). http://dx.doi.org/10.1007/s11042-016-3543-7

13. Gothelf, J.: Lean UX. O'Reilly Media, Sebastopol (2013)

14. Graves, T.: The Controversy over group rewards in cooperative classrooms. Educ. Leadersh. **48**(7), 77–79 (1991)

15. Hong, H., Kim, J.G., Abowd, G.D., Arriaga, R.I.: Designing a social network to support the independence of young adults with autism. In: Proceedings of the ACM 2012 Conference on Computer Supported Cooperative Work, CSCW 2012, pp. 627–636. ACM, New York (2012). http://doi.acm.org/10.1145/2145204.2145300

16. Hutchinson, H., Mackay, W., Westerlund, B., Bederson, B.B., Druin, A., Plaisant, C., Beaudouin-Lafon, M., Conversy, S., Evans, H., Hansen, H., Roussel, N., Eiderbäck, B.: Technology probes: inspiring design for and with families. In: Proceedings of the SIGCHI Conference on Human Factors in Computing Systems, CHI 2003, pp. 17–24. ACM, New York (2003). http://doi.acm.org/10.1145/642611.642616

17. Jain, D., Findlater, L., Gilkeson, J., Holland, B., Duraiswami, R., Zotkin, D., Vogler, C., Froehlich, J.E.: Head-mounted display visualizations to support sound awareness for the deaf and hard of hearing. In: Proceedings of the 33rd Annual ACM Conference on Human Factors in Computing Systems, CHI 2015, pp. 241–250. ACM, New York (2015). http://doi.acm.org/10.1145/2702123.2702393

18. Knoors, H., Marschark, M.: Teaching Deaf Learners: Psychological and Developmental Foundations. Oxford University, New York (2013)

19. Leonardi, C., Pianesi, F., Tomasini, D., Zancanaro, M.: The collaborative workspace: a co-located tabletop device to support meetings. In: Waible, A., Stiefelhagen, R. (eds.) Computers in the Human Interaction Loop, pp. 187–205. Springer, London (2009). doi:10.1007/978-1-84882-054-8_17

20. Levin Gelman, D.: Design for Kids. Rosenfeld Media, Brooklyn (2014)

21. van der Meijden, H., Veenman, S.: Face-to-face versus computer-mediated communication in a primary school setting. Comput. Hum. Behav. **21**(5), 831–859 (2005). http://www.sciencedirect.com/science/article/pii/S0747563203000761

22. Olguin, D.O., Waber, B.N., Kim, T., Mohan, A., Ara, K., Pentland, A.: Sensible organizations: technology and methodology for automatically measuring organizational behavior. IEEE Trans. Syst. Man Cybern. Part B (Cybern.) **39**(1), 43–55 (2009)

23. Shaw, F.W., Klavins, E.: Grouper: a proof-of-concept wearable wireless group coordinator. In: Proceedings of the 12th ACM International Conference Adjunct Papers on Ubiquitous Computing-Adjunct, pp. 379–380. ACM (2010)

24. Slovák, P., Fitzpatrick, G.: Teaching and developing social and emotional skills with technology. ACM Trans. Comput.-Hum. Interact. 22(4), 19:1–19:34 (2015). http://doi.acm.org/10.1145/2744195

25. Weiser, M.: Creating the invisible interface: (invited talk). In: Proceedings of the 7th Annual ACM Symposium on User Interface Software and Technology, UIST 1994, p. 1. ACM, New York (1994). http://doi.acm.org/10.1145/192426.192428

26. Wiemann, J.M., Knapp, M.L.: Turn-taking in conversations. J. Commun. 25(2), 75–92 (1975). http://dx.doi.org/10.1111/j.1460-2466.1975.tb00582.x

Tangible Design for Inclusive Conversations with Deaf or Hard-of-Hearing Children

Rosella Gennari[1], Francesco Pavani[2,3,4], and Mehdi Rizvi[1(✉)]

[1] Faculty of Computer Science, Free University of Bozen-Bolzano,
Piazza Domenicani 3, 39100 Bolzano, Italy
gennari@inf.unibz.it, SRizvi@unibz.it
[2] Center for Mind/Brain Sciences (CIMeC),
University of Trento, Rovereto, Italy
francesco.pavani@unitn.it
[3] Department of Psychology and Cognitive Science,
University of Trento, Rovereto, Italy
[4] ImpAct Team, Lyon Neuroscience Research Center,
INSERM U1028, CNRS UMR5292, Lyon, France

Abstract. Recent research in the area of deafness stresses that communication difficulties may severely impact the social and emotional development of deaf or hard-of-hearing learners. Education researchers voice the need of an integrated intervention for social and emotional learning at school, which considers deaf or hard-of-hearing learners' communication requirements. In particular supporting conversation with peers can enhance their engagement in school activities, which can positively impact on their academic achievements in turn. This paper presents the design of Compass, a tangible interactive object, enhanced with embedded micro- electronics components, for supporting group conversation in presence of deaf, hard-of-hearing and hearing children. The design choices are motivated in light of the requirement analysis. The paper concludes with an outlook on future work concerning Compass for enhancing conversation among deaf, hard-of-hearing and hearing children.

Keywords: Playful experience design · Socio-emotional learning · Conversation · Children · Deaf · Hard of hearing

1 Introduction

Positive peer interaction is crucial for children's *socio-emotional learning* (SEL) and schools offer plenty of peer interaction opportunities: when children have positive interactions with peers, they tend to show positive self esteem, emotion management, attitudes towards schools, school performances and quality of life in general, whereas negative peer interaction is related to the reverse [1].

Recent evidence-based research in deafness sustains that deaf children encounter specific difficulties in interactions with hearing peers, often in school environments, "due largely to persistent communication difficulties many of them experience at home and, potentially, to neuropsychological or physical difficulties associated with the etiologies of their hearing losses", and yet "precisely because deaf students are at risk

© Springer International Publishing AG 2017
T.-T. Wu et al. (Eds.): SETE 2016, LNCS 10108, pp. 288–297, 2017.
DOI: 10.1007/978-3-319-52836-6_29

for problems in mental health as well as academic achievement, their educational programs need to pay intensive and systematic attention to their social and emotional development" ([2], Chap. 7). A similar concern applies also to children who do not suffer from sever to profound bilateral deafness, but are nonetheless limited in their ability to extract linguistic and social signals through the hearing modality. Note that this includes also deaf children using one or two cochlear implants, who achieve partial recovery of the auditory function through the implanted device. *Deaf or hard-of-hearing children* (DHH) all need support in social interaction with hearing peers.

In the *human computer interaction* (HCI) and *computer-supported collaborative learning* (CSLC) areas, scholars have explored the role of computers or mobile solutions in mediating social activities and supporting positive social interactions. Among social activities, *synchronous conversation in group* of peers (briefly, *group conversation*) plays a crucial role in school contexts: face to face, at the same time, in the same place.

The survey [3] lists promising directions for technology-based interactive solutions for group conversation, at the intersection of CSWC and HCI research. In particular, embodied interaction design, concerning physical objects augmented with technology-enabled interaction, represents a promising approach for supporting group conversation [4]. Such objects should be playful, easy-to-use and easy-to-customise for activities with groups of children. If they aim at supporting group conversation with DHH children, they should primarily consider DHH children's requirements, e.g., [5].

This paper presents the design of *Compass*, a tangible interactive playful object for group conversations with DHH and hearing children. The object should signal who is speaking during a conversation, so as to direct the attention of the DHH child towards the source of conversation, and fix the child's attention on it. The rationale of this facilitation for deaf children is that a reliable and fast signal for directing attention to the speaker in the conversation could have the potentials to help the children to select the relevant speaker with lesser effort and in a timely manner. This rationale also applies to hard-of-hearing children, who typically find it difficult to select the relevant auditory stream during conversations, due to reduced spatial cues to sound location and reduced spectral cues that can help identify voice identity.

The design of Compass is based on related work in the area of interaction design, which is briefly overviewed in Sect. 2. Section 3 outlines the design approach that was followed for designing Compass. Then the paper comes to its main contributions, which is the design of Compass: its goal and primary users; its requirements, especially DHH children's requirements for group conversation; its current design choices and functionalities. The paper concludes reporting on the available evaluation results and plan for future work.

2   Related Work

According to studies reported in Chap. 8 in [2], DHH learners intensively use computers and mobile solutions, which are increasingly adopted in their classes, together with whiteboards. The majority of technology-enhanced solutions designed specifically for DHH learners tackle traditional learning domains, such as mathematics and text comprehension, and not SEL. In spite of that, several existing interactive solutions are potentially beneficial for DHH learners' SEL in general, and their inclusion in group conversation with hearing peers in particular. They are overviewed and compared to Compass as follows.

Wearable. Work has been done in CSLS and HCI to cater the need of tangible social interactions, mainly with adults, through wearable devices. *Grouper* is a wearable solution for group work with an aim similar to that of Compass [6]. Developed as a proof-of-concept wireless wearable, Grouper is a group coordinator: through sensory cues, Grouper alerts its users to pay attention to the leader of the group. To this end, users have to wear modules, each consisting of a microprocessor, a wireless radio, and various electronics.

Relevant for this paper is also the work reported in [7]: head-mounted displays were used to help deaf users localize sound in order to be effectively part of a group conversation. The current version of Compass trades precision in signal recognition for high portability and unobtrusive technology, in line with the calm technology paradigm of [8].

Visual. Different interactive solutions of conversation patterns, albeit mainly for adults, rely on sophisticated visualizations. An example is *Meeting Mediator*, a real-time portable system which tracks team dynamics and displays them visually on mobile phones, with the aim of promoting positive social behaviours [9].

Similarly, *Second Messenger* tracks, with sensors, speaking times in group conversations. The work reported in [10] experimentally evaluated a variety of visualizations of Second Messenger to show group members' participation. Table- top solutions, such as *Reflect* and *Collaborative Workspace*, also aim at visualising complex conversation patterns, and were tested with adults in [11, 12], respectively. *SocialMirror* is instead focused on helping individuals with autism by visually displaying comments and suggestions by family and friends, but the idea can be transferred to group-work settings [13].

Compass is not a visualisation device but a tangible playful portable device for children; it is designed for groups of children, including a DHH child, for stirring the DHH child's attention towards the conversation source.

Playful. Restricting the attention to interactive playful solutions for children, albeit not for group conversations, *Ely the Explorer* focuses on promoting collaborative learning through play with a toy doll, a touch screen display, personal hand held devices as well as RFID cards [14]. Children can take pictures, port them to the system, interact and collaborate with each other in collaborative activities. Playful design is also considered in the ergonomics design of Compass, with a different collaboration goal. Other tangible solutions were proposed for gamified cooperative learning contexts in [15, 16].

3 The Compass Design Process

User eXperience (UX) design is the general approach adopted for designing Compass and the experience of its users with it: design decisions are centred around users and, more generally, their context; design decisions are based on evidence, in the form of qualitative or quantitative data. *Lean UX* is the specific UX design approach chosen for Compass [17].

Therefore the design of Compass starts analysing the context of usage, through literature reviews and inquiries with *domain experts*, that is, of the domains under consideration (SEL and deafness). In line with the lean UX approach, the results of the analyses are stored in brief documents. The design process of Compass proceeds through prototypes that develop a minimal set of top-priority functionalities to evaluate, starting with paper-based prototypes and stepping through technology probes [18].

Evaluation studies are intertwined with the design of Compass prototypes. Evaluations are executed with product design experts, interaction design experts and with domain experts, e.g., by using inspection methods. Crucially, studies are also conducted with the users of Compass, starting with DHH and hearing children, e.g., by considering unforeseen usages inspired by children as well as standard usability metrics, such as success on task [19].

4 Design Choices and Their Rationale

4.1 Design Goals and Users

The *primary* users of Compass are DHH children engaged in group conversations, older than 8 years, an age at which schools tend to implement SEL activities centred around group conversation. Compass should instruct a DHH child to *direct* attention towards the source of conversation in space, *focus* and *maintain* it over time.

The *secondary* users are DHH children's peers and teachers. Other relevant users are speech therapists, who train teachers and family members. Then Compass should make tangible for hearing peers of DHH children, their teachers and family members what DHH children's requirements for conversation are, in particular, DHH children's difficulty of tracking and attending the relevant speaker in a conversational context.

4.2 Design Requirements

The context of use of Compass was investigated through a literature review and contextual inquiries with four teachers, an expert of SEL, an expert of cognitive studies and DHH children, a clinician working with cochlear implanted children, two speech therapists. Requirements were formulated in light of the investigations, and helped in refining the above goals of Compass.

The main requirements are reported below *in italics*. In line with [20], they are divided into requirements concerning: the school environment; users' characteristics, according to whether users are primary (DHH children) or secondary users (hearing peers and teachers); general user experience requirements, which are related to measurable design goals of the product.

School Environment. In the geographic area of Compass, DHH children are in mainstream education; classes tend to be heterogeneous in terms of learning and social skills. Schools do not have a speech therapist per class, who can help DHH children in following conversation in classroom, and hearing children in behaving in conversation with a DHH peer. Psychologists or speech therapists assist teachers when in need of training to the characteristics of DHH children, providing them with behaviour guidelines. Training sessions are usually outside school and conducted with several teachers at the same time. Therefore Compass should be used in any mainstream education class with a DHH child, and potentially in speech therapy sessions with teachers. Therefore Compass should be highly *portable*, *usable* for its different users and *economical* to replicate.

DHH Children. Quality and difficulties of DHH children's relationships with peers, especially in mainstream education, have been recently investigated in the DHH literature. In particular, monitoring conversation in a group with hearing peers and responding appropriately to social cues appear very difficult for DHH children, with or without cochlear implants, even if they function well in one- on-one social interactions [2].

Difficulties of DHH people in group conversation depend on a number of factors [21]. When DHH people look at the current speaker for disambiguating or understanding his or her message, other relevant sources of information have to be *within their line of sight*, or they may miss it. Focussed attention skills are also important for group conversation; monitoring conversation means being able to *focus* and *sustain attention* to a topic or a person as well as the ability to *shift attention* among them during conversation [2]. However, domain experts reported that, if conversation is prolonged or without pauses, fatigue and decrease in attention are easily experienced by DHH children; *breaks* in conversation should instead be solicited.

More generally, DHH learners are at risk of a cognitive overload, particularly DHH children with limited working memory, which hampers their processing of multiple stimuli. In view of that, Knoors and Marschark [2] recommend *multi- media* solutions for DHH people satisfying: *spatial contiguity* of information that pertains together; *no redundant visual* information.

Hearing Peers and Teachers. Hearing peers and teachers encounter their own difficulties in experiencing DHH children's requirements for conversation. For instance, speech therapists reported that DHH children may not react in conversation if teachers or peers forget to explicitly address them or are unaware of the need of doing it, e.g., by calling them by their name or gently tapping on their arms. Similarly, teachers tend to move while talking also outside the line of sight of a DHH child, who thus can miss information, lose concentration and motivation. As speech therapists stressed, even when teachers or peers are caring and aware of DHH children's needs, always behaving accordingly is difficult; then teachers and peers may benefit from interactive objects such as Compass, which may tangibly favour the *contextual recognition* of DHH children's requirements.

User Experience. Compass should be used in school activities requiring group conversation, and hence Compass should be an *unobtrusive* device that follows the calm technology paradigm [8]. Most importantly, DHH children should not perceive Compass as an intrusive object and a source of mockery. At the same time, play invites exploration and is a key factor for engaging children in an activity [22]. Therefore Compass should be perceived *playful* by the considered age range of children, and yet it should be unobtrusive in that it does not distract children from the activity they are performing, or even hinder it.

Compass should be designed in order to help *transfer* training to conversation outside the classroom, e.g., at home or in the playground, by stimulating relevant social support from teachers and family members, besides peers.

Finally, Compass aims at being a *disappearing* interactive *learning* object: over time, with the scaffolding of Compass, DHH children should become able to direct their attention towards relevant social cues, e.g., visual cues, that signal the source of conversation in a group of children [3].

4.3 Design Choices

Compass was designed by considering the aforementioned requirements, given high priority to requirements concerning DHH children, who are its primary users. Figure 1 shows a screenshot of the interior of a prototype component of Compass, which shows some of the Arduino-based electronics hidden inside it [23]. Technology-enabled functionalities of Compass are illustrated in Fig. 2 and explained as follows.

The main component of Compass is a 3D-printed round tabletop device with a red arrow on top. The arrow points towards the current speaker in a group conversation, in which three or four children sit in circle, with the device in the centre; see Fig. 1. The current prototype has an array of eight microphones to detect conversation sources. According to [7], eight is the minimum number of microphones needed to detect conversation sources with sufficient precision in the presence of noise; however the Compass tabletop device has been designed with sufficient empty space to accommodate further microphones and amplification circuitry for enhanced precision. The Arduino board inside the prototype uses the microphones to detect and localize the direction of sound, and triggers a motor that moves the arrow in order to point it towards the conversation source.

A fluctuation or a change in direction of the arrow advise DHH children to turn their face towards the conversation source and assess who the speaker is; no movement of the arrow suggests that DHH children should focus their attention on the current

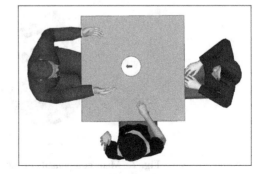

Fig. 1. A screenshot of the interior of a Compass prototype (left) and a sketch of its usage (right)

speaker. As Compass is in the centre with group members around it, any change in the arrow direction can be also easily detected even when the current speaker is outside the DHH children's line of sight.

The arrow-based visual feedback of Compass towards conversation sources can be enhanced with vibrotactile feedback through companion bracelets; see Fig. 3. These are vibrotactile bracelets, two per group member, one for each arm. Bracelets are connected via wireless to the Compass tabletop device, illustrated in Fig. 2. If this detects a sound on the left or right side of a member, the corresponding bracelet mildly and briefly vibrates to indicate the sound direction; in case sound is detected right in front of the member, both bracelets will vibrate.

Finally, given that DHH children seem to require not exceedingly long conversation turns, a design feature under implementation allows teachers or other educators to set a maximum time span for children's interventions. Afterwards Compass will flash a LED light nearby the speaker who exceeds conversation time limits. See the LED pins illustrated in Fig. 2. To this end, Compass will record times for each conversation turn. It will interact via wireless with the educator's mobile or computer through a dedicated interface for setting time limits and eventually displaying relevant speaking time statistics.

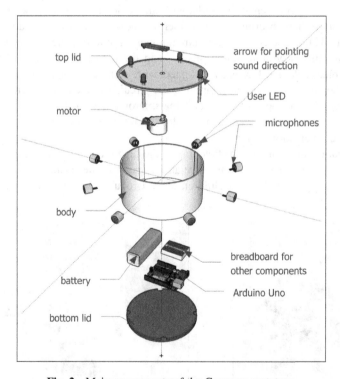

Fig. 2. Main components of the Compass prototype

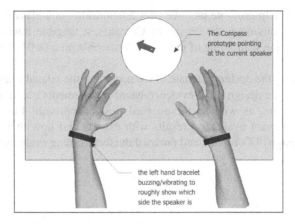

The Compass prototype pointing at the current speaker

the left hand bracelet buzzing/vibrating to roughly show which side the speaker is

Fig. 3. Usage of bracelets for reinforcing the arrow-based feedback of Compass

5 Evaluation Results and Plan

Two main rounds of expert-reviews were conducted with two interaction design experts, a product design expert and a deafness domain expert. Several other smaller evaluation sessions were conducted to refine design decisions taken in light of the two rounds of expert-reviews, reported below.

The first evaluation assessed a cartoon-based prototype of Compass, and a scenario. The evaluation involved all experts and addressed the physical features of the object, such as the size of the arrow as well as of micro-electronics components.

The non-interactive 3D-printed version of Compass was then realised and evaluated first by the interaction experts and then by the domain expert. The prototype functionalities were explained using scenarios, with alternative design choices. Feedback was provided and the suggestion to focus on the arrow-based feedback to test was given high priority.

The current interactive prototype, enhanced with micro-electronics, is going to be evaluated in studies with DHH users in controlled settings and then in the field. Results will be compared and used to guide the final release of Compass.

6 Conclusions

With the aim of balancing the current focus of schools on academic subjects, several education scholars have recently advocated the importance to enhance educational programs with SEL for DHH learners, involving their peers. The impact of such interventions goes well beyond SEL itself and affects academic achievement and quality of life in general [2].

Technology can enhance SEL for DHH children and their peers at school, and also help transfer the benefits of SEL programs outside school, e.g., in the playground or at home. Specifically, this paper posits that interaction design of playful objects can enhance SEL and help promote positive peer relationships in a class with DHH children. The paper focused on the design of Compass, a tangible interactive, playful, portable object for the scaffolding of group conversation with a DHH child and hearing children.

After presenting the design rationale of Compass and the related relevant work, the paper overviewed the design goal, evidence-based requirements and functionalities of the current prototype, as well as the adopted design approach. Finally, the paper overviewed the relevant evaluation results with experts and how they incrementally influenced the design of Compass, and outlined the forthcoming evaluation studies with DHH users.

References

1. Durlak, J.A., Weissberg, R.P., Dymnicki, A.B., Taylor, R.D., Schellinger, K.B.: The impact of enhancing student's social and emotional learning: a meta-analysis of school-based universal interventions. Child Dev. 82(1), 405–432 (2011)
2. Knoors, H., Marschark, M.: Teaching Deaf Learners: Psychological and Developmental Foundations. Oxford University, Oxford (2013)
3. Slovák, P., Fitzpatrick, G.: Teaching and developing social and emotional skills with technology. ACM Trans. Comput.-Hum. Interact. 22(4), 19:1–19:34 (2015)
4. Dourish, P.: Embodied Interaction: Exploring the Foundations of a new Approach to HCI (1999). http://www.ics.uci.edu/~jpd/publications/misc/embodied.pdf
5. Di Mascio, T., Gennari, R., Melonio, A., Vittorini, P.: Designing games for deaf children: first guidelines. Int. J. Technol. Enhanc. Learn. 5(3/4), 223–239 (2013)
6. Shaw, F.W., Klavins, E.: Grouper: a proof-of-concept wearable wireless group coordinator. In: Proceedings of the 12th ACM International Conference Adjunct Papers on Ubiquitous Computing-Adjunct, pp. 379–380. ACM (2010)
7. Jain, D., Findlater, L., Gilkeson, J., Holland, B., Duraiswami, R., Zotkin, D., Vogler, C., Froehlich, J.E.: Head-mounted display visualizations to support sound awareness for the deaf and hard of hearing. In: Proceedings of the 33rd Annual ACM Conference on Human Factors in Computing Systems, CHI 2015, pp. 241–250. ACM, New York (2015)
8. Weiser, M.: Creating the invisible interface: (invited talk). In: Proceedings of the 7th Annual ACM Symposium on User Interface Software and Technology, UIST 1994, p. 1. ACM, New York (1994)
9. Olguin, D.O., Waber, B.N., Kim, T., Mohan, A., Ara, K., Pentland, A.: Sensible organizations: technology and methodology for automatically measuring organizational behavior. IEEE Trans. Syst. Man Cybern. Part B (Cybern.) 9(1), 43–55 (2009)
10. DiMicco, J.M., Hollenbach, K.J., Pandolfo, A., Bender, W.: The impact of increased awareness while face-to-face. Hum.-Comput. Interact. 22(1), 47–96 (2007)
11. Leonardi, C., Pianesi, F., Tomasini, D., Zancanaro, M.: The collaborative workspace: a co-located tabletop device to support meetings. In: Waibel, A., Stiefelhagen, R. (eds.) Computers in the Human Interaction Loop, pp. 187–205. Springer London, London (2009)
12. Bachour, K., Kaplan, F., Dillenbourg, P.: An interactive table for supporting participation balance in face-to-face collaborative learning. IEEE Trans. Learn. Technol. 3(3), 203–213 (2010)

13. Hong, H., Kim, J.G., Abowd, G.D., Arriaga, R.I.: Designing a social network to support the independence of young adults with autism. In: Proceedings of the ACM 2012 Conference on Computer Supported Cooperative Work, CSCW 2012, pp. 627–636. ACM, New York (2012)

14. Africano, D., Berg, S., Lindbergh, K., Lundholm, P., Nilbrink, F., Persson, A.: Designing tangible interfaces for children's collaboration. In: Extended Abstracts on Human Factors in Computing Systems, CHI EA 2004, pp. 853–868. ACM, New York (2004)

15. Dodero, G., Gennari, R., Melonio, A., Torello, S.: Towards tangible gamified co-design at school: two studies in primary schools. In: Proceedings of the First ACM SIGCHI Annual Symposium on Computer-Human Interaction in Play, CHI PLAY 2014. ACM, New York (2014)

16. Gennari, R., Melonio, A., Torello, S.: Gamified probes for cooperative learning: a case study. Multimedia Tools Appl., 1–25 (2016). doi:10.1007/s11042-016-3543-7

17. Gothelf, J.: Lean UX. O'Reilly Media, Sebastopol (2013)

18. Hutchinson, H., Mackay, W., Westerlund, B., Bederson, B.B., Druin, A., Plaisant, C., Beaudouin-Lafon, M., Conversy, S., Evans, H., Hansen, H., Roussel, N., Eiderbäck, B.: Technology probes: inspiring design for and with families. In: Proceedings of the SIGCHI Conference on Human Factors in Computing Systems, CHI 2003, pp. 17–24. ACM, New York (2003)

19. Albert, W., Tullis, T.: Measuring the User Experience. Morgan Kaufmann, Burlington (2013)

20. Preece, J., Rogers, Y., Sharp, H.: Interaction Design: Beyond Human-Computer Interaction. Wiley, Hoboken (2015)

21. Batten, G., Oakes, P., Alexander, T.: Factors associated with social interactions between deaf children and their hearing peers: a systematic literature review. J. Deaf Stud. Deaf Educ. **19** (3), 285–302 (2013)

22. Ferrara, J.: Playful Design. Rosenfeld Media, Brooklyn (2012)

23. Arduino: What is Arduino? https://www.arduino.cc/en/Guide/

Workshop on Active Ageing and Digital Inclusion

Sentiment Analysis for Older People in Cross-Platform Instant Messaging Service

Haoran Xie[1], Tak-Lam Wong[1], Di Zou[2(✉)], Fu Lee Wang[3], and Leung Pun Wong[3]

[1] Department of Mathematics and Information Technology,
The Education University of Hong Kong, Tai Po, Hong Kong
[2] English Language Centre, The Hong Kong Polytechnic University,
Kowloon, Hong Kong
dizoudaisy@gmail.com
[3] Caritas Institute of Higher Education, Tseung Kwan O, Hong Kong

Abstract. The population of older people increases in many developed and developing countries, so that the overall structures of the populations has been changing. However, older people are one of the most disadvantaged and vulnerable groups for digital exclusion in this technocratic society. Therefore, in this article, we aims to predict the sentiments for older people when they use the cross-platform instance messaging service such as WeChat or WhatsApp. Specifically, we adopt semi-annotation approaches to obtaining their sentimental labels from the textual data in the cross-platform instance messaging service. Furthermore, we propose a lexical-based framework for predicting the sentimental labels. The findings give us insight to develop applications for the inclusion of older people in digital world.

Keywords: Sentiment analysis · Text mining · Instance messaging service · Active ageing · Digital inclusion

1 Introduction

Digital devices and applications play key roles in our daily life in a wide range of the society. However, older people are one of the most disadvantaged and vulnerable groups for digital exclusion in this technocratic society. For example, approximately 84% of older adults aged 65 and over are offline in Hong Kong [1]. Enabling older adults to integrate and benefit from the digital technology is a critical issue when we face an inevitable truth of the increasing older populations in many developed and developing countries.

To address this problem, it is important to engage older people to digital devices and mobile applications. The cross-platform instant messaging services such as WeChat[1], Whatsapp[2], or Line[3] are one of most popular mobile applications, which can cater diverse motivations for learning technology by older people. These motivations

---

[1] www.wechat.com.
[2] www.whatsapp.com.
[3] line.me.

© Springer International Publishing AG 2017
T.-T. Wu et al. (Eds.): SETE 2016, LNCS 10108, pp. 301–305, 2017.
DOI: 10.1007/978-3-319-52836-6_30

mainly includes issues as skill, confidence, financial management, healthy lifestyle, management of disabilities and illness, friendships, relationships, passions, hobbies, work, and connection with family and friends [4].

To understand the behaviors and sentiments of older adults who use instant messaging services, we therefore aims to predict the sentiments for older people by analyzing the sentiment polarity in this article. Specifically, we adopt semi-annotation approaches to obtaining their sentimental labels from the textual data in the cross-platform instance messaging service. Furthermore, we propose a lexical-based framework for predicting the sentimental labels. The findings give us insight to develop applications for the inclusion of older people in digital world.

The remaining sections of this article are organized as follows. In Sect. 2, we briefly review the recent research on active ageing and digital inclusion. Section 3 introduces the overall process of data collection and the performance results of the lexical-based framework. In Sect. 4, we draw the conclusion of this research and discuss the future research directions.

2　Related Works

The issue of demographic change has been noted by the research communities for several years. One important issue in active ageing is how to motivate mid age and older adults to learn new skills in order to address the problem of increasing costs of supporting 'non-productive' mid-lifers [6]. The internet can strengthen the older adults' self-worth and improve their quality of life in terms of managing health, nurturing professional interests, maintaining and extending social networks, appreciating the past, and enjoying leisure [8]. Moreover, significant positive relationships were found between Internet/e-mail usage, self-rated health, leisure/recreation participation and leadership, and well-being [9]. Some researchers also found that technology use decreased significantly with greater limitations in physical capacity and greater disability after adjustment for sociodemographic and health characteristics [3]. A more recent study also reveals that there is a positive effect of formal education for ICT adoption by focusing on the impact of older adults [5].

3　Methodology and Experimental Results

In this section, we discuss the overall experimental processes including the participants, experimental settings, data labelling, and results analysis.

Participants. To collect the data from older adults, we have invited 5 participants in our experiments. The participant contains 3 females and 2 males. Their ages are from 52 to 64 years old with the average age of 57.6. They are from China and Hong Kong, and have relatively good education backgrounds (at least hold an associate degree). For the experience of the cross-platform instance messaging service, they have at least 1 year experience of using WeChat to communicate with others frequently.

Experimental Settings. To collect sentimental data from the participants, it is very tedious to annotate the sentimental labels for all their text messages. To reduce the workloads, we encourage participants to use emojis[4] in the messages as the sentimental labels. For those messages without any labels, the human judgement are employed to determine the final labels. Generally, we have three categories of sentiments: positive, neural, and negative. For the experimental period, we select a week without any special holidays [12]. At beginning of the first day, we provides participants the instructions of "adopt as many as possible emojis in your messages" and "use the instance messaging service as usual". In each day, we examine the quality of labels of the messages and remind them to use emojis. After one week, we collect all messages from 5 participants.

Data Labelling. There are totally 1,712 messages collected within a week. By automatically identifying emojis and human annotations, we have obtained sentimental labels attached to all messages. As shown in Table 1, we can find that about a half of the all messages are positive, while there are only less than 20% are negative messages.

Table 1. Total number of message per classes

	Total	%
Positive	831	48.54
Neutral	571	33.35
Negative	310	18.11
Total	1,712	100.00

Lexical-Based Framework. We propose a lexical-based framework to predict the sentiment polarity. As all messages are Chinese, we firstly to adopt a Chinese segmentation technique [11] with accuracy more than 90% to divide sentences to words. Next, we employ Google translator to convert the Chinese to English. Finally, we exploit SentiWordNet 3.0 [2] to obtain the polarity score for each word. The sentiment score of a message is determined by the vote of all words. Formally, the sentiment score of a message is defined as follows.

$$S(m) = \sum_{w \in m} s_w \tag{1}$$

where w is a word in message m, sw is the sentiment score from SentiWordNet 3.0. Note that we actually adopt more complicated formula here as the syntactic structure such as negativity is considered and different weights are assigned according to the position of the words. The prediction results in the form of a confusion matrix are shown in the Table 2. For three classes, the accuracy is 88.32% for positive class,

---

[4] An emoji is an ideogram which is embedded in an electronic message.

Table 2. Confusion matrix for the sentiment prediction

Actual class	Predicted class			
	Positive	Neutral	Negative	Accuracy (%)
Positive	734	41	35	88.32
Neutral	79	435	57	76.18
Negative	35	51	224	72.26

76.18% for neutral class, and 72.26% for negative class. The result verifies the effectiveness of the proposed framework.

4   Conclusion and Future Work

In this article, we have introduced our preliminary research studies on sentiment analysis for older people in cross-platform instant messaging services. We collected a set of labelled data as the ground truth by using emoijs and human annotations. Furthermore, we presented a lexical-based framework for predicting the sentiment of messages. The result has verified the effectiveness of the proposed framework. In the future, we plan to continue our research in the following directions.

- We plan to further develop a supervised machine learning algorithm [10, 13] based on the lexical-based framework. The machine learning algorithm can allow us to apply the framework in a large scale of dataset. In previous study, the machine learning algorithm was normally less accurate than the lexical-based methods [12]. To address this issue, we will adopt deep learning approaches [7] based on the lexical-based framework.
- We also plan to consolidate the individual sentiment information with user profile [18, 19] to facilitate personalized applications. A powerful user profile can improve the accuracy of personalized search and recommendations [14, 16]. The personalized sentiment information can assist users to detect their emotion changes and recommend necessary actions.
- The contextual information in mobile devices can be integrated to the current research and provide us a more complete dataset. By adopting the contextual models [15, 17], the contextual services can be facilitated in cross-platform instant messaging services. For example, with the contextual information such as location, a nearby park can be recommended for a older adult if s/he is not in the positive mood.

Acknowledgement. The work described in this paper was fully supported by a grant from Research Grants Council of Hong Kong Special Administrative Region, China (UGC/FDS11/E06/14), the Internal Research Grant (RG 30/2014-2015) and the Start-Up Research Grant (RG 37/2016-2017R) of The Education University of Hong Kong.

References

1. Census and Statistics Department of Hong Kong. Thematic household survey report C Report No. 52 (2013)
2. Baccianella, S., Esuli, A., Sebastiani, F.: SentiWordNet 3.0: an enhanced lexical resource for sentiment analysis and opinion mining. In: LREC, vol. 10, pp. 2200–2204 (2010)
3. Berkowsky, R.W., Cotton, S.R., Yost, E.A., Winstead, V.P.: Attitudes towards and limitations to ICT use in assisted and independent living communities: findings from a specially-designed technological intervention. Educ. Gerontol. **39**(11), 797–811 (2013)
4. Boulton-Lewis, M.G., Buys, L., Lovie-Kitchin, J., Barnett, K., David, N.L.: Ageing, learning, and computer technology in Australia. Educ. Gerontol. **33**(3), 253–270 (2007)
5. Cattaneo, M., Malighetti, P., Spinelli, D.: The impact of university of the third age courses on ICT adoption. Comput. Hum. Behav. **63**, 613–619 (2016)
6. Davey, J.A.: Active ageing and education in mid and later life. Ageing Soc. **22**(01), 95–113 (2002)
7. Glorot, X., Bordes, A., Bengio, Y.: Domain adaptation for large-scale sentiment classification: a deep learning approach. In: Proceedings of the 28th International Conference on Machine Learning (ICML 2011), pp. 513–520 (2011)
8. Khvorostianov, N., Elias, N., Nimrod, G.: Without it I am nothing: the internet in the lives of older immigrants. New Media Soc. **14**(4), 583–599 (2012)
9. Koopman-Boyden, P.G., Reid, S.L.: Internet/e-mail usage and well-being among 65–84 year olds in New Zealand: policy implications. Educ. Gerontol. **35**(11), 990–1007 (2009)
10. Li, X., Xie, H., Rao, Y., Chen, Y., Liu, X., Huang, H., Wang, F.L.: Weighted multi-label classification model for sentiment analysis of online news. In: 2016 International Conference on Big Data and Smart Computing (BigComp), pp. 215–222. IEEE (2016)
11. Ng, H.T., Low, J.K.: Chinese part-of-speech tagging: one-at-a-time or all-at-once? Word-based or character-based? In: EMNLP, pp. 277–284 (2004)
12. Ortigosa, A., Martín, J.M., Carro, R.M.: Sentiment analysis in Facebook and its application to e-learning. Comput. Hum. Behav. **31**, 527–541 (2014)
13. Rao, Y., Xie, H., Li, J., Jin, F., Wang, L.F., Li, Q.: Social emotion classification of short text via topic-level maximum entropy model. Inf. Manag. **53**(8), 978–986 (2016)
14. Xie, H.-R., Li, Q., Cai, Y.: Community-aware resource profiling for personalized search in folksonomy. J. Comput. Sci. Technol. **27**(3), 599–610 (2012)
15. Xie, H., Li, Q., Mao, X.: Context-aware personalized search based on user and resource profiles in folksonomies. In: Sheng, Q.Z., Wang, G., Jensen, C.S., Xu, G. (eds.) APWeb 2012. LNCS, vol. 7235, pp. 97–108. Springer, Heidelberg (2012). doi:10.1007/978-3-642-29253-8_9
16. Xie, H., Li, Q., Mao, X., Li, X., Cai, Y., Zheng, Q.: Mining latent user community for tag-based and content-based search in social media. Comput. J. **57**(9), 1415–1430 (2014)
17. Xie, H., Li, X., Wang, T., Chen, L., Li, K., Wang, F.L., Cai, Y., Li, Q., Min, H.: Personalized search for social media via dominating verbal context. Neurocomputing **172**, 27–37 (2016)
18. Xie, H., Li, X., Wang, T., Lau, R.Y.K., Wong, T.-L., Chen, L., Wang, F.L., Li, Q.: Incorporating sentiment into tag-based user profiles and resource profiles for personalized search in folksonomy. Inf. Process. Manag. **52**(1), 61–72 (2016)
19. Xie, H., Zou, D., Lau, R.Y.K., Wang, F.L., Wong, T.-L.: Generating incidental word-learning tasks via topic-based and load-based profiles. IEEE Multimedia **23**(1), 60–70 (2016)

English Education for the Elderly in Hong Kong

Di Zou[1], Fu Lee Wang[2], Haoran Xie[3(✉)], and Tak-Lam Wong[3]

[1] English Language Centre, The Hong Kong Polytechnic University,
Kowloon, Hong Kong SAR, China
[2] Caritas Institute of Higher Education, New Territories
Hong Kong SAR, China
[3] Department of Mathematics and Information Technology,
The Education University of Hong Kong, Tai Po, Hong Kong SAR, China
hrxie2@gmail.com

Abstract. Although Hong Kong government has done a great job in various areas for active aging such as social security, residential care services, community care and support systems, the English education for elders is a weak point. This paper analyzes the current situation of English education for elders in Hong Kong from four perspectives: barriers, motivations, styles and methods of English learning for elders. Suggestions, possible solutions and necessary actions are also proposed accordingly.

Keywords: Active aging · English education · Motivation · Learning styles · Elder speak

1 Introduction

To promote active aging, the Hong Kong Government has been offering a wide range of social services and benefits to the elderly, for example, Community Care and Support Services, Residential Care Services and Social Security (The Hong Kong Government, 2016). However, compared to such areas as health, social security and community care, English education for the elderly is an underdeveloped aspect for the Hong Kong government. Few opportunities are available for the elders to develop their English proficiency levels, and the elderly remain a neglected group within the education system. A large number of elders find it difficult to pursue formal or non-formal education.

The elderly learners are very different from learners in other age groups, not only from the aspect of age but also in respects like motivations, expected learning outcomes, learning styles and challenges. It is therefore necessary to differentiate between the English education for the elders and the English education for other age groups. Nevertheless, literature and educational practice often overlook this need for differentiation, and hence probably further limit the engagement of elders in education (Határ and Grofčíková 2016). In the remaining parts of this paper, we analyze the current situation of English education for elders in Hong Kong from four perspectives: barriers,

© Springer International Publishing AG 2017
T.-T. Wu et al. (Eds.): SETE 2016, LNCS 10108, pp. 306–310, 2017.
DOI: 10.1007/978-3-319-52836-6_31

motivations, styles and methods of English learning for elders. Suggestions, possible solutions and necessary actions are also proposed accordingly.

2   Barriers of English Learning for Elders

To better involve elders in English education, it is worth noting some of the factors that might limit elders' participation in learning activities. According to Petřková and Čornaničová (2004), potential barriers for elder people are likely to result from both subjective and objective conditions. Subjective conditions include fear of decreasing sensory and cognitive abilities, anxiety from new situations, low confidence, lack of vitality, etc. Objective conditions include lack of information about educational possibilities and problems with schedule, transport as well as financial support (Petřková and Čornaničová 2004).

Slowey (2008) notes three major barriers for elders: attitudinal, situational and institutional barriers. Elders' attitudes reflect both their and others' perceptions of their decrease of abilities, motivations and interests in learning. Situational barriers (e.g., health, problems with time and money, etc.) relate mainly to personal factors that are beyond the control of learners. From the institutional perspective, educational environments may not be supportive for elders' lifelong learning, and institutions may lack expertise in teaching intergenerational groups (Slowey 2008).

3   Motivations of English Learning for Elders

Motivation for education plays a pivotal role in English learning for elders. Elders' motivations are different from those of other age groups; they focus more on the learning experience and personal interest in the subject (Phillipson and Ogg 2010). Age also to some extent influences elders' attitudes towards and motivations for education (Pollard et al. 2008). Jamieson's (2007) survey also lists personal development and interest in the subject as top motivations for learning.

4   Styles of English Learning for Elders

A significant factor for elders' English learning is health, as many deficits or chronical diseases might place possible influence on elders' learning abilities. Specifically, hearing abilities affect the ability to understand speech; the loss or weakening of viewing abilities and loss of teeth also make language learning challenging for elders. Therefore, educators are advised to take into consideration specific characters of individual learning styles and carry out diagnostic tests through authorized questionnaires, observation and learners' reflective diaries (Határ and Grofčíková 2016).

According to Fleming (2006), there are mainly four learning styles: VARK – visual, aural, read/write, kinaesthetic. Visual type learners organize information by writing it down, and they like making notes to better remember the ideas. Aural type learners learn well when accompanied by others, as they love discussing with others and always seek for opportunities to verbalize ideas. Verbal type learners need chances for communicating what he/she hears and sees. Kinaesthetic type learners learn through experience, and they like feeling and doing things.

In Harmer (1991), four learner categories are noted: converger type, conformist type, concrete type, and communicative type. Converger type prefers individual work; conformist type tends to depend on authorities and enjoy work in non-communicative groups; concrete type is interested in the using of language and enjoys playing and working in a group; and communicative type likes using language for social interactions.

5 Methods of English Learning for Elders

Elderspeak, which is usually characterized by simplified sentence structures, use of simple words, slower talking or exaggerated prosody (Coulmas 2013), is one of the common methods in language education for elders. Many elders are excellent language learners once they overcome such difficulties as affective barriers (mostly fear) and anxiety about new learning environments (Határ and Grofčíková 2016). Effective teaching methods and activities also play important role in strengthening learning effectiveness, styles and strategies of elders.

Many studies on ageing confirm that learning abilities do not decline by age. Schleppegrell (1987) believed that the intellectual abilities of healthy elders do not diminish. Cimermanova (2000) even argued that adults have more advantages in language learning than children after taking psychological knowledge concerning the relation between age and abilities into account. Elders often prefer the grammar - translation methods, and it is indeed a very frequently used method in English education for the elderly (Határ and Grofčíková 2016). As writing exercises are very effective in promoting vocabulary learning, elders may also benefit much from doing sentence-writing and composition-writing exercises (Zou 2016). Moreover, the use of dictionaries in teaching and learning is likely to facilitate elders' English learning (Zou et al. 2015).

However, although vocabulary and grammar structures are normally easy for adults, the sound system and pronunciation are comparatively difficult (Tkacikova 2000). Therefore, to address problems concerning elders' fear and frustration from oral production, methods like drilling pronunciation, intonation and rhythm practices constitute a major part of English education for elders.

The audiolingual method in combination with other procedures also tend to be efficient for elders, as intense practices (e.g., drilling and revision) of listening and pronunciation help elders build up their confidence and become fluent in speaking (Határ and Grofčíková 2016). Cimermanova (2000) also notes that elders have the advantage of being able to repeating and remembering longer sequences of sound, syllables and words.

Additionally, the communicative method and the direct method are suitable for elders with good language skills (Határ and Grofčíková 2016). Others methods like total physical response, natural method and suggestopedia may also work well for elders with different features and needs.

6   Suggestions for English Education for the Elderly

With the fastest-growing number of elders in Hong Kong, one key issue for the Hong Kong government is to construct an effective system to facilitate the elderly to pursue continued learning either in a school setting or through non-formal education.

While analyzing educational needs of elders, it is essential to differentiate "the need to deal with a concrete situation" from "educational need" (Prusakova 2010, p.25). Mitterlechner (2012) also advises educators to take into account the following factors while working with elders: learning takes longer for elders; motivation plays a key role; contents need to be relevant; it is important to emphasize the meaning of education and continue with what was learnt previously.

With the fast development of technologies, English education for elders also need to integrate the use of digital tools or technological platforms, and take into account factors like learners' background knowledge and enjoyment while learning (Zou et al. 2014; Xie et al. 2016).

Acknowledgement. The work described in this paper was fully supported by a grant from the Research Grants Council of the Hong Kong Special Administrative Region, China (UGC/FDS11/E06/14).

References

Cimermanova, I.: Vek, vyber metody a uloha ucitela. In: Pongo, S., Pokrivcak, A. (eds.) Teaching Foreign Langauges to Adults, pp. 24–29. UKF, Nitra (2000)

Coulmas, F.: Sociolinguistics: The Study of Speakers' Choices. Cambridge University Press, Cambridge (2013)

Fleming, N., Baume, D.: Learning styles again: VARKing up the right tree! Educ. Dev. **7**(4), 4 (2006)

Harmer, J.: The Practice of English Language Teaching. London/New York (1991)

Határ, C., Grofčíková, S.: Foreign language education of seniors. J. Lang Cult. Educ. **4**(1), 110–123 (2016)

Jamieson, A.: Higher education in study in later life: what is the point? Ageing. Soc. **27**, 363–384 (2007)

Mitterlechner, Ch.: Staroba neznamena konniec. In: Socioterapia, vol. 2, no. 2, pp. 8–10 (2012). http://www.socioterapia.info/wp-content/uploads/2011/04/Socioterapia_4_2012.pdf

Petŕková, A., Čornaničová, R.: Gerontagogika: Úvod do teorie a praxe edukace seniorů. Univerzita Palackého, Czech Republic (2004)

Phillipson, C., Ogg, J.: Active ageing and universities: engaging older learners (2010)

Pollard, E., Bates, P., Hunt, W., Bellis, A.: University is Not Just for Young People: Working Adults' Perceptions of and Orientation to Higher Education. Department of Innovation, Universities and Skills, London (2008)

Prusakova, V.: Teoreticke vychodiska analyzy vzdelavacich potrieb dospelych. In: Prusakova, V. et al. (ed.), Analyza vzdelavacich potrieb dospelych. Eoreticke vychodiska, pp. 13– 44, Banska Bystrica: UMB

Schleppegrell, M.: The Older Language Learner (1987)

Slowey, M.: Age is just a number? Rethinking learning over the lifecourse. Ageing Horizons **2008**(8), 22–30 (2008)

Tkacikova, M.: Basic principles of teaching foreign language to adults. In: Pongo, S., Pokrivcak, A. (eds.) Teaching Foreign Langauges to Adults, pp. 24–29. UKF, Nitra (2000)

Xie, H., Zou, D., Lau, R.Y., Wang, F.L., Wong, T.L.: Generating incidental word-learning tasks via topic-based and load-based profiles. IEEE Multimedia **23**(1), 60–70 (2016)

Zou, D.: Vocabulary acquisition through cloze exercises, sentence-writing and composition-writing: extending the evaluation component of the involvement load hypothesis. Lang. Teach. Res. (2016). *1362168816652418*

Zou, D., Xie, H., Li, Q., Wang, F.L., Chen, W.: The load-based learner profile for incidental word learning task generation. In: Popescu, E., Lau, Rynson, W.,H., Pata, K., Leung, H., Laanpere, M. (eds.) ICWL 2014. LNCS, vol. 8613, pp. 190–200. Springer, Heidelberg (2014). doi:10.1007/978-3-319-09635-3_21

Zou, D., Xie, H., Wang, F.L., Wong, T.-L., Wu, Q.: Investigating the effectiveness of the uses of electronic and paper-based dictionaries in promoting incidental word learning. In: Cheung, S. K.S., Kwok, L.-f., Yang, H., Fong, J., Kwan, R. (eds.) ICHL 2015. LNCS, vol. 9167, pp. 59–69. Springer, Heidelberg (2015). doi:10.1007/978-3-319-20621-9_5

Photography-Based Intervention:
When the Aged Meets Digital Age

Wai-Yip Chen[(✉)]

School of Social Sciences, Caritas Institute of Higher Education,
Tseung Kwan O, Hong Kong
wychen@cihe.edu.hk

Abstract. The advancement of medical technology has prolonged the life expectancy and improved the quality of life. Ageing becomes a global issue and catches multidisciplinary attention. Contrary to the over-reliance on others and resources consumption by the older people, the concept of active ageing prevails in the past two decades. In this paper, I will discuss, from a social work perspective, the implications of ageing, and suggest the application of photography-based practice model in addressing the issue.

Keywords: Active ageing · Photography-based intervention · Digital inclusion

1 Ageing Population

Ageing is a global phenomenon. In 2015, the number of people aged 60 years or over is 901 million, amounting to 12% of the global population. The figure is projected to be 1.4 billion and 2.1 billion by 2030 and 2050 respectively. In most countries or regions by 2050, about one-quarter or more of the total populations will be aged 60 or over [1]. The population growth is a success in health care. Nevertheless, ageing population drains on the existing scarce resources [2]. This poses political, economic and social implications in which a government has to address to issue likes health, housing, economic and social aspects [3].

2 Active Ageing

In the late 1990s, WHO has adopted the concept of "active ageing" to embody the notion of *"optimizing opportunities for health, participation and security in order to enhance quality of life as people age"* (p.12). It aims at promoting people's holistic well-being, including physical, social and mental aspects. The Active Ageing Model consists of six determinants: (1) health and social services; (2) behavioral; (3) personal; (4) physical environment; (5) social; (6) economic, encompassed in the broader gender and cultural context. Paul, Ribeiro, & Teixeria summarize the key aspects of active ageing as autonomy, independence, quality of life and healthy life expectancy. Further, they state that the focus of interventions lies in the early prevention of health problems since adulthood and the strengthening of psychological resilience, minimizing loneliness or maximizing happiness and subjective well-being [4].

© Springer International Publishing AG 2017
T.-T. Wu et al. (Eds.): SETE 2016, LNCS 10108, pp. 311–314, 2017.
DOI: 10.1007/978-3-319-52836-6_32

3 Photography-Based Intervention

Shortly after its invention in France, Gilman stated that Dr. Hugh Diamond's display of photographs in psychiatry to the London Royal Society of Medicine in 1852 was believed to be the earliest therapeutic use of photography [5]. Early applications of photography remained primarily on institutions like asylum and orphanages [6]. Other applications of photography have been found in the practice of family therapy [7–9], in children and adolescents [10, 11], in ethnics minority and deaf [12]. Apart from using in case counseling, various activities featuring with photography are designed to be used in group work setting [13, 14]. With the development of photovoice, applications on community-based project, aiming at empowerment and community participation, are at the same time phenomenal [15–18]. We can see the therapeutic practices of photography in the helping profession are many and varied, especially entering the digital age. Krauss and Fryrear use the term "Phototherapy" [5] while Weiser with both capitalized letters "PhotoTherapy" [19] to denote both are of equal importance. Wang & Burris, first applying photography in rural Chinese women, apply the term "Photovoice" [20]. With an empowerment perspective, Chen, Lo, Leung, & Wong have adopted the term "photography-based intervention", embedding four aspects of connections: (1) self or individual; (2) interpersonal; (3) community or organization; (4) spirituality which ranges from micro-level to macro-level interventions [21].

4 Application

Photography can be applied in a variety of settings, attributed to its nature and characteristics, including representation, communication, documentation, projection, skills or techniques [5, 18, 19, 22]. Craig pinpointed eight functions that photography plays: (1) promoting communication; (2) aiding memory; (3) promoting feelings of self-esteem; (4) providing cohesion and hence fostering positive relationships; (5) offering a means to communicate what is important; (6) supporting process of change; (7) offering a hobby or interest, and (8) aiding reflection and professional development [13].

In this sense, we can see photography meet the needs of the older people. With the technological advancement, it makes easier for people to operate the once complicated machine to take picture. In line with active ageing, the older people can live a positive life by engaging in photography activities. "Hidden seniors" could voice out their opinions on age-friendly community through a photovoice project [23]. Older people with visual challenges also regained self-esteem and enhanced social and community connections by participating a photography project in a social centre for the Blind [24].

5 Implication

Abreast of the technological conveniences in the digital age, older people can operate camera with much ease. The nature of photography interlocks with the concept of active ageing. Older people can connect with self (self-reflection and self- esteem), with others (sharing and group activities), with the community (community projects and issues) and with spirituality (meaning-searching and integration of life). In this way, there are a lot of possibilities in applying photography-based interventions in working with older people so as to realize active ageing. Apart from a creative blending of the aged and the digital age, evidence-based practice suggests empirical evaluation of this practice approach so that the effectiveness can be measured.

6 Conclusion

The applicability of photography-based intervention covers a variety of service targets. With its empowerment nature, photography-based intervention can integrate with the concept of active ageing so that we can witness the digital inclusion for the older people. I believe the mastery of digital cameras can probably promote an older person's self-esteem. Nevertheless, it is important for practitioners and researchers to conduct relevant and sophisticated researches to validate the effectiveness of this digital intervention model and to formulate the change mechanism of the model in helping the older people.

References

1. United Nations: World Population Prospects: The 2015 Revision, Key Findings and Advance Tables. Working Paper No. ESA/P/WP.241. https://esa.un.org/unpd/wpp/publications/files/key_findings_wpp_2015.pdf
2. World Health Organization. Active Ageing: A Policy Framework. http://www.who.int/ageing/publications/active_ageing/en/
3. United Nations. World Population Ageing 2015. http://www.un.org/en/development/desa/population/publications/pdf/ageing/WPA2015_Report.pdf
4. Paul, C., Ribeiro, O., Teixeira, L.: Active ageing: an empirical approach to the WHO model. Curr. Gerontol. Geriatr. Res. **2012**, 1–10 (2012). doi:10.1155/2012/171857
5. Fryrear, J.L., Krauss, D.A.: Phototherapy introduction and overview. In: Krauss, D.A., Fryrear, J.L. (eds.) Phototherapy in Mental Health, pp. 3–23. Charles C Thomas, Springfield (1983)
6. Stewart, D.: Phototherapy: looking into the history of photography. In: Krauss, D.A., Fryrear, J.L. (eds.) Phototherapy in Mental Health, pp. 25–39. Charles C Thomas, Springfield (1983)
7. Entin, A.D.: The use of photographs and family album in family therapy. In: Gurman, A.S. (ed.) Questions and Answers in the Practice of Family Therapy. Brunner/Mazel Publishers, New York (1981)
8. Entin, A.D.: The family photo album as icon: photographs in family psychotherapy. In: Krauss, D.A., Fryrear, J.L. (eds.) Phototherapy in Mental Health, pp. 117–132. Charles C Thomas, Springfield (1983)
9. Walker, J.: The photograph as a catalyst in psychotherapy. In: Krauss, D.A., Fryrear, J.L. (eds.) Phototherapy in Mental Health, pp. 135–148. Charles C Thomas, Springfield (1983)
10. Wolf, R.I.: Instant phototherapy with children and adolescents. In: Krauss, D.A., Fryrear, J.L. (eds.) Phototherapy in Mental Health, pp. 151–173. Charles C Thomas, Springfield (1983)

11. Ziller, R.C., Rorer, B., Combs, J., Lewis, D.: The psychological niche: the auto-photographic study of self-environment interaction. In: Krauss, D.A., Fryrear, J.L. (eds.) Phototherapy in Mental Health, pp. 95–115. Charles C Thomas, Springfield (1983)
12. Weiser, J.: Using photographs in therapy with people who are "different". In: Krauss, D.A., Fryrear, J.L. (eds.) Phototherapy in Mental Health, pp. 175–199. Charles C Thomas, Springfield (1983)
13. Craig, C.: Exploring the Self Through Photography: Activities for Use in Group Work. Jessica Kingsley Publishers, Philadelphia (2009)
14. Fryrear, J.L.: Photographic self-confrontation as therapy. In: Krauss, D.A., Fryrear, J.L. (eds.) Phototherapy in Mental Health, pp. 71–92. Charles C Thomas, Springfield (1983)
15. Foster-Fishman, P., Nowell, B., Deacon, Z., Nievar, M.A., McCann, P.: Using methods that matter: the impact of reflection, dialogue, and voice. Am. J. Community Psychol. 36, 275–291 (2005)
16. Strack, R.W., Magill, C., McDonagh, K.: Engaging youth through photovoice. Health Promotion Pract. 5(1), 49–58 (2004)
17. Wang, C.C.: Youth participation in photovoice as a strategy for community change. J. Community Pract. 14, 147–161 (2006)
18. Wang, C.C., Redwood-Jones, Y.A.: Photovoice ethics: perspectives from flint photovoice. Health Educ. Behav. 28(5), 560–572 (2001)
19. Weiser, J.: Phototherapy Techniques: Exploring the Secrets of Personal Snapshots and Family Albums. PhotoTherapy Centre Press, Vancouver (1999)
20. Wang, C., Burris, M.: Photovoice: concept, methodology, and use for participatory needs assessment. Health Educ. Behav. 24, 369–387 (1997)
21. Chen, W., Lo, H.Y., Leung, T.Y.K., Wong, K.C. (eds.): Xiang ru fei fei: she ying wei ben huo dong yu she gong jie ru [Touching the extraordinary mind: Photography-based activities and social work intervention]. Riding Publisher, Hong Kong (2015)
22. Loewenthal, D. (ed.): Phototherapy and Therapeutic Photography in a Digital Age. Routledge, New York (2013)
23. Yim, T.W.: Participatory action research by using photovoice with "hidden" senior males. (Unpublished Master Thesis), The Chinese University of Hong Kong, Hong Kong (2014)
24. Chen, W.: A qualitative study of the experiences of people having visual challenges in the use of photography in social work practice. (Unpublished Master Thesis), The Chinese University of Hong Kong, Hong Kong (2012)

A Study of Tag-Based Recipe Recommendations for Users in Different Age Groups

Wei Chen[1,2] and Zhemin Li[1,2(✉)]

[1] Agricultural Information Institute, Chinese Academy of Agricultural Sciences,
Beijing, China
{chenwei,lizhemin}@caas.cn
[2] Key Laboratory of Agri-Information Service Technology,
Ministry of Agriculture, Beijing, China

Abstract. Social tagging becomes prevailing with the emergence of Web 2.0 communities recently. By utilizing this additional valuable information from user-created tags, it is convenient to understand users' interests and behavior so that we can provide good user experience in applications of various domains. Therefore, the definition of profile is crucial for tagging systems. Furthermore, it is important to have recommendations for various groups of users. In recipe recommendations, older people typically have different needs compared with young users. In this paper, we first focus on the definitions of user profile, item feature and how to derive semantics from these sources. Afterwards, we design the framework of the tag-based multimedia recipe recommendation system (MRRS). Finally, we conduct preliminary experimental study of recipe recommendations for different age groups. The result shows that older people concern more about the nutrition aspects of recipes.

Keywords: Social tagging · User profiling · Recipe recommendations · Age groups · User studies

1 Introduction

Coupling with the emergence of Web 2.0 communities in recent years, social annotation (social tagging) becomes prevailing as additional information to describe multimedia objects. Due to diverse modalities and complexity of multimedia object and "semantic gap" problem [1], traditional approaches hit a brick wall in multimedia retrieval.

Taking content-based retrieval (CBR) as an example, it mainly takes low-level features of images such as color, texture and shape to construct feature vectors which is unreliable because of the loss of high-level semantics from multimedia data. In particular, the performance of CBR is even weaker in some specified domains such as e-learning and cooking recipe because the distinction in low-level feature is difficult to figure out [2]. Therefore, some other popular approaches such as semantic-based retrieval (SBR), community profile-based retrieval (CPR) are proposed. However, these approaches have some drawbacks such as semantic derivation and indexing problems in

© Springer International Publishing AG 2017
T.-T. Wu et al. (Eds.): SETE 2016, LNCS 10108, pp. 315–325, 2017.
DOI: 10.1007/978-3-319-52836-6_33

SBR, sparsity and cold start problem in CPR. Different from existing approaches, user-created tags provide additional helpful information which can assist us to understand users' interests and behavior better. Thereby, how to define a profile is crucial for a tagging system.

To address this problem, we exploit user profile, item feature from a 3-dimensional model of user-item-tags. We exploit these sources to obtain semantics which can be incorporated with tag processing mechanisms in our MRRS to enhance expressive capability and handle different kinds of queries. Furthermore, it is important to have recommendations for various groups of users. In recipe recommendations, older people typically have different needs compared with young users. The distinction between different user age groups is to be investigated in this study.

The remaining sections of our paper structures as follows. Section 2 discusses related work, followed by overall architecture of our approach including data organization, definitions of user profile and item features, tag processing mechanisms in MRRS, and neighbor discovery in Sect. 3. In Sect. 4, we conduct preliminary experimental study of recipe recommendations for different age groups and summarize the reasons of the experimental study.

2   Related Work

2.1   Collaborative Tagging Systems

Marking content with descriptive terms, also called tags, for future navigation, filtering or search is becoming popular on the Internet in recent years [3]. Unlike traditional taxonomy-based information indexing approach, which classifies content into predefined categories, collaborative tagging encourages anyone to freely attach user-generated tags to contents. Generally, as summarized in [4], users can create tags from seven aspects, such as identifying what is it about, what is it, who owns it, or even user's emotional feelings/remarks of the content.

The intention of collaborative tagging is to provide users an easy-to-use way for information access [5]. It is considered as an alternative to current effort on semantic web ontology, through its great success in some famous social tagging systems, such as delicious[1], Flickr[2], Last.fm[3], etc. Kerstin et al. [6] have done a survey on the tags distribution in the above three social tagging systems, in order to figure out the problem: can all tags be used for search? They also do experiments to analyze what types of tags users would tend to provide, as well as which tags would be easily remembered and frequently used for search.

---

[1] http://delicious.com/.

[2] http://www.flickr.com/.

[3] http://www.last.fm/.

2.2 Collaborative Filter

Collaborative filtering is a kind of information filtering techniques involving collaboration among multiple agents and viewpoints [7]. Its main idea is to predict a user's affinity for items or information based on the ratings given by his neighborhood who share similar recorded interests. The items with highest predicted ratings among like-minded users will be recommended [8].

Key problems in CF systems include how to define users' personal profiles, how to measure the similarity between users, and how to generate the neighborhood of a particular user [9]. Well-known CF systems in research area include GroupLens [10], a Web news recommender system, and MovieLens[4], a movie recommender website. Both represent a user's personal profile as a vector of his/her ratings on some items, and define the similarity between users using vector distance measures. Notoriously, in commercial area, Amazon is a successful example using CF based techniques [11]. It takes both the contents of items and user profiles [12, 13], which consists of personal information, browsing history and community information to make recommendations, thus to promote its sales.

2.3 Tag-Based Collaborative Filtering

Due to the high popularity of both social tagging and recommender systems, some researchers start to work on the following topic: is there any way to adopt the strengths of both CT and CF to support better recommendation or personal information access? Elke *et al.* [14] point out three ways of learning user profiles from tagging data, which are naive approach, co-occurrence approach and adaptive approach, respectively. Li *et al.* [15] introduce a novel social interest discovery approach based on user-generated tags, by noting that patterns of frequent co-occurred user tags can be used to characterize and capture topics of user interests. The idea of generating user profiles from tagging data has been widely adopted in other domain specific applications [16–18].

3 Overall Architecture

3.1 Data Organization

As mentioned above, tags are popular to be used for describing semantics of multimedia items from the aspect of users' understanding. In typical multimedia resource sharing systems, users can either submit their own items to the system, or select some interested ones from other users' collection lists, with attaching personal tags to them for future navigation, search, etc. The relationship among the users, items and tags is illustrated in Fig. 1. Each user may own an item list in his/her personal account as mentioned above. For each item in a particular user's list, it may have several tags

---

[4] http://www.movielens.org/.

created by the user as content descriptions. Both the items and tag lists may be overlapped between users, because of shared interests and semantic topics.

For example, Item 2 belongs to both User 1 and User 2, and User 1 describes it with Tag 2 and Tag 3, while User 2 tags it with Tag 3 and Tag 4.

In our proposed approach, we organize data and their relationship in a 3-dimensional model as shown in Fig. 2. The U-axis denotes users, the I-axis denotes items and T-axis denotes tags. Points in the model stand for where there are relations among users, items and tags. For example, User 2 has two interested items, I2 and I3, tagged respectively by T3, T4, and T1, T5.

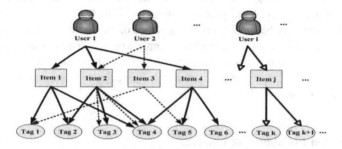

Fig. 1. Relationship among users, items and tags

In Fig. 2, we can derive the user-item and user-tag relationship by projecting the 3-dimesional relationship to the plane UOI and UOT, respectively.

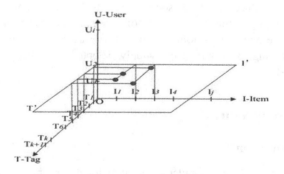

Fig. 2. The 3D model of User-Item-Tag relationship

3.1.1   User-Item Matrix

To derive the user-item matrix, we can project the points in the 3-dimentional model to the plane of UOI. The number of tags attached to an item is not useful to reflect a user's affinity for this item. In other words, it is not meaningful information in our approach. For example, if a user has two interested items, I1 with 3 tags and I2 with 6 tags, it does not always mean that the user has double interest in I2 to I1. As a result, we choose not to record the values, and represent it using binary number (1 and 0) instead, with 1 meaning an owing relationship between a user and an item, and 0 meaning no relation holds.

3.1.2 User-Tag Matrix

The user-tag matrix can be derived by projecting the 3-dimentional model to the plane of UOT. The values in the matrix mean the times that a tag is used by a user. For example, the value of 2 for an entry U1-T2 means user 1 uses tag 2 for two times.

Here we observe that the more a tag is used by a user, the stronger interest the user has in this semantic topic. For example, if a user uses tag T2 for 6 times, and T1 for 3 times, we can assume he/she has double interest in the semantic of T2 than T1.

3.1.3 Item-Tag Matrix

To derive the tag-item relationship, we can project the 3-dimensional model in Fig. 2 to the plane of IOT to get an Item-Tag matrix. The values in the matrix stand for the total count for a tag being attached to an item by all users. For instance, the value of T3-I2 is 2, meaning that Tag 3 is labeled to Item 2 by two users.

3.2 Definitions of User Profile and Item Feature

The definitions of item feature and user profile are the most critical issues in social information filtering problem. Traditional approaches of user profile definition vary from explicitly collecting personal information, or implicitly observing users' behavior in a system, etc. Admittedly, they all achieve some success, but also confront with inevitable difficulties, e.g., few users are willing to provide personal information on the Internet due to privacy risk. Reversely, by witnessing the great success of famous collaborative systems like Delicious, Flickr as mentioned above, we are excited to find that users are active in creating tags for content organization. Moreover, Li *et al.* do experiments with Delicious data in their paper [15] to show that it is feasible and promising to use tags for generating user profile and discovering social interest. Motivated by this, we define both the user profile and item feature in our approach based on user generated tags.

3.2.1 User Profile

As illustrated above, each user in a multimedia system may have relationship with both items and tags, stored in User-Item and User-Tag matrix respectively. In our opinion, both the two kinds of relationships are useful to reflect a user's interest. Specifically, the relationship between user and item tells us what kind of resources a user would like, and his/her tag usage record exhibits his/her preferred semantic topics. The motivation to differentiate these two aspects is that although items shared by like minded users can reflect their common interests to some extent, they are not specific enough, because the reason why users like certain items may be different from person to person. As a result, we define a user's item profile (UIP) and tag profile (UTP) as follows:

Definition 1. A user's item profile consists of a set of items created or collected by him/her:

$$UIP[item_1, item_2, \ldots, item_n]$$

Definition 2. A user's tag profile is a set of tags that the user has used as labels for some items:

$$UTP[tag_1, tag_2, \ldots, tag_n]$$

Definition 3. A user's profile is a two-tuple array, with UIP and UTP as its tuples:

$$UP\{UIP,UTP\}$$

Thus, each user can be described from both item and tag respects. For example, in Fig. 1, the profile of User 1 can be represented as $UP1\{[I1,I2,I4], [T1(1),T2(2), T3(1),\ldots]\}$.

The advantages of defining user profile in this way include the following:

- It has been justified that user-generated tags are effective to summarize the content of resources as well as capturing user interests, for they can reflect human's judgments more concisely and are closer to user understanding [17].
- The profile represents a user's interest in both item level and tag level. We will discuss how to use these two kinds of semantic later.
- Deriving a user profile in this way is easy to implement thanks to the prevailing of the Internet and collaborative tagging techniques.

3.2.2   Item Feature

In our approach, we define item feature (IF) with its semantics derived from user generated tags attached to it.

Definition 4. An item's feature vector consists of all the associated tags to this item and respective tag usage frequencies.

$$IF[tag_1(n_1), tag_2(n_2), \ldots, tag_n(n_n)]$$

For example, in Fig. 1, the feature of Item 2 can be represented as $IF2[T2(1), T3(2), T4(2)]$. Similar to user profile, the derivation of item feature is easy to implement in our approach, and it benefits us to capture the semantic relationship between items in a convenient way.

3.3   Tag Processing Mechanism in MRRS

We implement the user profiles defined above in MRRS to discover the way in obtaining semantics. To concentrate on estimating potentiality of our proposed approach, we construct tag processing mechanisms in MRRS to alleviate impact from

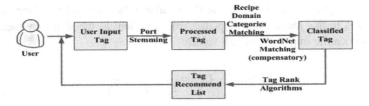

Fig. 3. Tag processing mechanism in MRRS

existing problems such as polysemy, synonymy and basic level variation in the tagging system [4]. The mechanisms in MRRS are illustrated in Fig. 3.

Firstly, a user generates some tags to describe the collective recipes, and we can assist the user in the tagging phase through the tag recommend which has discussed in [12]. By applying Port Stemming[5] to initial user input tag set. For example, the tags "chicken" and "chickens" are standardized. Then, we map processed tags to a predefined taxonomy in the recipe domain (Table 1).

Table 1. Pre-defined categories in MRRS

Category	Example term (Tag)
Taste	Sweet, spicy
Cooking Pattern	Steam, fry
Ingredient	Pork, egg
Cuisines	Cantonese cuisine

3.4 Neighborhood Discovering in MRRS

In the process of recommending multimedia objects, we always encounter the semantic subjectivity problem. For example, movie "Titanic" can be interpreted as "a catastrophic shipwreck event" or "a moving love story", even as "an Oscar-winning film". Users might have different tags to express their subjective semantics.

3.4.1 Similar Users

Different tags of a single item reflect users' different interests to the item, and vice versa. Moreover, overlapped items between two users exhibit their same interest in some particular categories. These two types of user interest can be taken into consideration to measure the similarity between users. We define two kinds of similarities as follows:

Definition 5. Similarity of User's Item Profile. This similarity is in the item level to catch the similarity of specified classes of items, denotes as SimUIP.

---

[5] http://tartarus.org/martin/PorterStemmer/.

We use User-Item matrix to define the similarity between UIPs. Since there are binary values in this matrix, we adopt Jaccard coefficient as the similarity measure in order to reduce the impact from null values.

$$Sim_{UIP}(U_a, U_b) = \frac{I_{11}}{I_{01} + I_{10} + I_{11}} \tag{1}$$

where U_a and U_b denote two users, I_{11} denotes the number of items involved in "1&1" matches in UIP_a and UIP_b in User-Item matrix, and I_{10} and I_{01} are defined similarly.

Definition 6. Similarity of User's Tag Profile. This measure is in the tags level to capture the similarity of users' interested aspects of items, denotes as Sim_{UTP}.

It can be measured by Extended Jaccard coefficient (Tanimoto coefficient) because it relieving the limitation of binary values in Jaccard coefficient [19]. This measure is suitable as there are still many binary values in the User-Tag matrix especially for the newly coming users.

$$Sim_{UTP}(U_a, U_b) = \frac{T_a \cdot T_b}{\|T_a\|^2 + \|T_b\|^2 - T_a \cdot T_b} \tag{2}$$

where $\mathbf{U}_a$ and $\mathbf{U}_b$ denote two users, T_a and T_b denotes the vectors of $\mathbf{UTP}_a$ and $\mathbf{UTP}_b$ in the User-Tag matrix.

To construct community to facilitate the multimedia object retrieval, the most similar users could help the query issuer. Therefore we define the user similarity measure based on the above similarities Sim_{UIP} and Sim_{UTP}.

Definition 7. The similarity between two users is defined as:

$$Sim(U_a, U_b) = \alpha Sim_{UIP}(U_a, U_b) + (1 - \alpha)Sim_{UTP}(U_a, U_b) \tag{3}$$

where U_a and U_b denote two users, α denotes a weighted value. With this measure, we can find top-k nearest neighbors to derive a dynamic community for a particular user. In the next section, we will discuss how to use the community to enhance query in our approach.

3.4.2   Similar Items

Based on the defined item feature vector, the semantic similarity between items can be defined based on row-row correlation in the Item-Tag matrix as follows.

$$Sim(I_a, I_b) = \sqrt{\sum_i (tag_i(n_{a\_i}) - tag_i(n_{b\_i}))^2} \tag{4}$$

where I_a and I_b denote the selected item by the query issuer and any other item.

3.4.3   Tag-Based Recommendation

Tag-based search needs to be triggered by a user provided Boolean tag expression. The concept of Boolean tag expression is similar to the classic Boolean model in information retrieval [20]. Each result of a Boolean tag expression corresponds to an item set including all items in a specified tag column with non-zero values (e.g. the corresponding set of T2 = {I_1, I_2}). For example, a user can issue a query in the form of (Tag 1 ∩ Tag 2) which finds the set of {I_1}. Following is the step illustration of tag-based search:

- The query issuer starts a query by providing his/her interested tags, which will then be transformed into Boolean tag expression automatically, denoted as Q_T;
- Find the top-K nearest neighbors of the query issuer according to user similarity measure defined in (3);
- For all users in the top-K neighbors list, perform Boolean operation based on Q_T on their item-tag matrixes to get a item set that satisfied the conditions;
- Summarize the item sets returning from calculations on all top-K neighbors' Item-Tag matrix, and get the sum-up count as the ranking of items;
- Return items in descending order according to their ranks as the final result.

4 Experimental Study and Summary

In the experiment, we have conducted a preliminary study on two user groups: young users (age from 18 to 30) and older users (age from 50 to 60). Each group has 5 users, and we evaluate the performance by user judgment as well as their feedbacks. More specifically, 25 queries are generated in each group and we ask them to select the best candidate to meet their interests for each query. To compare the performance without taking user profiles into account, we examine the position of the best candidate selected by users in the recommendation lists generated without eliminating user profiles. The results are shown in Fig. 4. We have adopted P@N as the metric to evaluate the accuracy of the result. In other words, if the best candidate is in the top-N, we consider that it is a successful recommendation (denoted as "1"). Otherwise, it is considered as a failed recommendation (denoted as "0"). The overall P@N score is the ratio of successful recommendations in all queries. From the result, we can find that the employment of user profile will increase the precision for both young and older groups. Also, the older group has relative worse performance than young group.

There may be various reasons to explain why the older group has worse performance. From the feedback we have collected, one reason is that the older people have more constraints in food. Some of them are unable to take a specific kind of food due to

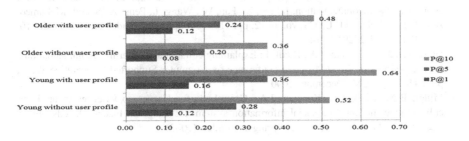

Fig. 4. The performance of the experimental study

certain diseases, while young users do not have such constraints. It is much easier for young users to select the desired recipes. Another reason is that the older people care more about the nutrition aspect of the recipes. They may filter out some recipes without specific nutrition elements.

Acknowledgement. This paper is supported by the MOA International Cooperation Project "The Comparative Study of Agricultural Information between BRICS" funded by Ministry of Agriculture of China, the MOA Innovative Talents Project "Key Techniques of Main Agricultural Products Market Monitoring And Early Warning" funded by Ministry of Agriculture of China, the CAAS Science and Technology Innovation Project "Innovation Team on Agricultural Production Management Digitization Technology" (CAAS-ASTIP-2015-AII-02) funded by Chinese Academy of Agricultural Sciences, and sub-project "Agricultural Data Collection Methods and Technology Analysis" of project of Ministry of Agricultural of China "Monitoring and Statistics Fund for Agriculture and Rural Resources".

References

1. Xie, H., Li, Q., Mao, X., Li, X., Cai, Y., Zheng, Q.: Mining latent user community for tag-based and content-based search in social media. Comput. J. **57**(9), 1415–1430 (2014)
2. Wang, L., Li, Q., Li, N., Dong, G., Yang, Y.: Substructure similarity measurement in Chinese recipes. In: Proceedings of the 17th international conference on World Wide Web, pp. 979–988. ACM, April 2008
3. Xie, H., Li, Q., Mao, X.: Context-aware personalized search based on user and resource profiles in folksonomies. In: Sheng, Q.Z., Wang, G., Jensen, C.S., Xu, G. (eds.) APWeb 2012. LNCS, vol. 7235, pp. 97–108. Springer, Heidelberg (2012). doi:10.1007/978-3-642-29253-8_9
4. Golder, S.A., Huberman, B.A.: Usage patterns of collaborative tagging systems. J. Inf. Sci. **32**(2), 198–208 (2006)
5. Xie, H., Li, Q., Mao, X., Li, X., Cai, Y., Rao, Y.: Community-aware user profile enrichment in folksonomy. Neural Netw. **58**, 111–121 (2014)
6. Bischoff, K., Firan, C.S., Nejdl, W., Paiu, R.: Can all tags be used for search? In: Proceedings of the 17th ACM Conference on Information and Knowledge Management, pp. 193–202. ACM, October 2008
7. Sarwar, B., Karypis, G., Konstan, J., Riedl, J.: Item-based collaborative filtering recommendation algorithms. In: Proceedings of the 10th International Conference on World Wide Web, pp. 285–295. ACM, April 2001
8. Yu, L., Li, Q., Xie, H., Cai, Y.: Exploring folksonomy and cooking procedures to boost cooking recipe recommendation. In: Du, X., Fan, W., Wang, J., Peng, Z., Sharaf, Mohamed, A. (eds.) APWeb 2011. LNCS, vol. 6612, pp. 119–130. Springer, Heidelberg (2011). doi:10.1007/978-3-642-20291-9_14
9. Herlocker, J.L., Konstan, J.A., Riedl, J.: Explaining collaborative filtering recommendations. In: Proceedings of the 2000 ACM conference on Computer Supported Cooperative Work, pp. 241–250. ACM, December 2000
10. Miller, B.N., Ried, J.T., Konstan, J.A.: GroupLens for Usenet: experiences in applying collaborative filtering to a social information system. In: Lueg, C., Fisher, D. (eds.) From Usenet to CoWebs, pp. 206–231. Springer, London (2003)

11. Linden, G., Smith, B., York, J.: Amazon.com recommendations: item-to-item collaborative filtering. IEEE Internet Comput. **7**(1), 76–80 (2003)
12. Xie, H.R., Li, Q., Cai, Y.: Community-aware resource profiling for personalized search in folksonomy. J. Comput. Sci. Technol. **27**(3), 599–610 (2012)
13. Xie, H., Li, X., Wang, T., Lau, R.Y., Wong, T.L., Chen, L., Wang, F.L., Li, Q.: Incorporating sentiment into tag-based user profiles and resource profiles for personalized search in folksonomy. Inf. Process. Manag. **52**(1), 61–72 (2016)
14. Michlmayr, E., Cayzer, S.: Learning user profiles from tagging data and leveraging them for personalized information access (2007)
15. Li, X., Guo, L., Zhao, Y.E.: Tag-based social interest discovery. In: Proceedings of the 17th International Conference on World Wide Web, pp. 675–684. ACM, April 2008
16. Xie, H., Zou, D., Lau, R.Y., Wang, F.L., Wong, T.L.: Generating incidental word-learning tasks via topic-based and load-based profiles. IEEE Multimedia **23**(1), 60–70 (2016)
17. Xie, H., Chen, L., Wang, F.: Collaborative compound critiquing. In: Dimitrova, V., Kuflik, T., Chin, D., Ricci, F., Dolog, P., Houben, G.-J. (eds.) UMAP 2014. LNCS, vol. 8538, pp. 254–265. Springer, Heidelberg (2014). doi:10.1007/978-3-319-08786-3_22
18. Xie, H., Li, X., Wang, T., Chen, L., Li, K., Wang, F.L., Cai, Y., Li, Q., Min, H.: Personalized search for social media via dominating verbal context. Neurocomputing **172**, 27–37 (2016)
19. Wu, L., Hua, X.S., Yu, N., Ma, W.Y., Li, S.: Flickr distance. In: Proceedings of the 16th ACM International Conference on Multimedia, pp. 31–40. ACM, October 2008
20. Baeza-Yates, R., Ribeiro-Neto, B.: Modern Information Retrieval. Addison Wesley, Boston (1999)

Social Support and Sense of Loneliness in Solitary Older Adults

Xue Bai[1(✉)], Shuyan Yang[2], Fu Lee Wang[3], and Martin Knapp[4]

[1] Department of Applied Social Sciences,
The Hong Kong Polytechnic University, Hong Kong, China
xuebai@polyu.edu.hk
[2] Department of Social Work, The Chinese University of Hong Kong,
Hong Kong, China
agenis5027@hotmail.com
[3] Caritas Institute of Higher Education, Hong Kong, China
pwang@cihe.edu.hk
[4] Personal Social Services Research Unit,
London School of Economics and Political Science, London, UK
m.knapp@lse.ac.uk

Abstract. Older people are vulnerable to loneliness and isolation. Solitary seniors are more likely to suffer the feelings of loneliness with inadequate social networks. Based on a face-to-face questionnaire survey with 151 community-dwelling solitary seniors, the present study examined the associations between social support and the sense of loneliness among solitary older adults in Hong Kong. The results showed that poor mental health status, financial inadequacy and weak social support networks were significantly associated with the sense of loneliness of solitary older adults, with social support being the most prominent risk factor. Frequent contacts with siblings, relatives or friends were found to be important sources of social support to combat loneliness. Policy and service implications are discussed.

Keywords: Loneliness · Social support · Hong kong · Solidary older chinese

1 Introduction

Population is aging rapidly in Hong Kong. It is estimated that every three people in Hong Kong will be 65 years or above by the year of 2040. [1] Notably, the percentage of older adults living alone has increased from 11% to 13% in the past decade. [2] A rising trend of living alone among older adults is observed due to late marriage, the declining fertility rate and the lengthening of life expectancy [3, 4].

Loneliness refers to feelings of depression and anxiety about being left alone, [5] which is one of the most common and distressing problems facing older adults. [3] Older people may have a higher chance of inadequate social networking or access to close relationships [6] if they are living alone. Although previous research pointed out that various forms of social support may buffer the negativities of loneliness, [3] little is known about the relationship between social support and loneliness in older people

© Springer International Publishing AG 2017
T.-T. Wu et al. (Eds.): SETE 2016, LNCS 10108, pp. 326–330, 2017.
DOI: 10.1007/978-3-319-52836-6_34

living alone. Therefore, it is the aim of the present study to examine health and social support associated with solitary older adults' sense of loneliness to inform future service and programme development.

2 Method

Ethical approval of the present study was obtained from the first author's affiliated institution. A purposive sampling strategy was used for recruiting eligible participants. Inclusion criteria were: (1) aged 65 years and over, (2) Hong Kong permanent residents, (3) living alone without other persons living under the same roof, and (4) cognitively capable of answering survey questions. A total of 151 participants participated in the study and completed the survey ($N = 151$).

Data was collected between January and March 2015. Five undergraduate students with educational backgrounds in aging studies and good communication skills with older people conducted the interviews. Training and supervision were provided during the course of data collection. Forty-four pilot interviews were conducted to ensure the clarity and relevance of the measures in the questionnaire. Each interview lasted approximately 30 min.

2.1 Measurements

Background information of respondents were collected which included: gender (male or female), age (65 or above), educational attainment (uneducated, primary, secondary, tertiary or university level), place of birth and number of years living in Hong Kong. Their self-rated financial situations were classified as very inadequate, inadequate, merely adequate, adequate and more than adequate.

The Chinese version of the seven-item Lawton Instrumental Activities of Daily Living (IADL) was adopted to measure *functional health* of older adults. [7] Scores range from seven to twenty-eight, with higher scores indicating a greater ability to perform daily activities independently. The Cronbach's alpha coefficient of IADL in the present study was .74, which is satisfactory. Respondents' *mental health status* was measured by the Chinese Mental Health Inventory (MHI-5) which was widely used to measure mental health problems such as anxiety and general distress. [8] Total scores range from five to thirty, with higher scores indicating better mental health. In the present study, the reliability of MHI-5 was satisfactory as indicated by Cronbach's alpha value which equaled to .79.

Social support network was assessed by the Chinese version of 10-item Lubben's Social Network Scale (LSNS) (alpha = .70). This scale has been widely used in examining social networks of older people. [9, 10] A higher rating on this scale represents a stronger social support network. A satisfactory reliability level of Cronbach's alpha in the present study was reported as 0.77.

Respondents' *most frequently contacted person* was included in the analysis since it may represent the main source of informal support for solidary older adults. Respondents were asked to elucidate their most frequently contacted person. It could be their 'offspring', 'sibling or relatives', or 'friend'. These responses were coded as 0 = 'no' and 1 = 'yes'. Respondents' *sense of loneliness* was rated by an 8-item Chinese Version of Loneliness Scale (alpha = .73). [11] A 5-point Likert scale was adopted ranging from '1 = strongly disagree' to '5 = strongly agree'. Total scores range from five to forty, with higher scores indicating greater feelings of loneliness. In the present study, the Cronbach's alpha of the loneliness scale was .88, representing a satisfactory reliability level.

2.2 Data Analysis

SPSS version 21.0 was used in data analysis. Descriptive statistics were first performed to describe the socio-demographic characteristics of this sample. Then, multi-collinearity of included independent variables was checked, with *variance inflation factor* (*VIF*) calculated for independent variables. All the VIF values were below 10, indicating no multicollinearity issue. Finally, a series of hierarchical regression analyses were performed to unearth the relative contribution of demographic characteristics, health status and social support factors to solitary seniors' sense of loneliness.

3 Results

Hierarchical multiple regressions were employed to understand the correlates of loneliness. Social demographic characteristics including age, gender, education level and financial status were entered as Block 1. Self-perceived health, functional health and mental health were entered as Block 2. The strength of social support, dummies of the most frequently contacted persons (children, sibling and friends) were entered as Block 3. The three blocks of variables significantly increased explained variance of loneliness by 16%, 10%, and 17% respectively. Accumulatively, these three blocks of variables accounted for 43% of the variance in the sense of loneliness. It was found that older persons' feeling of loneliness was significantly associated with whether they were born in Hong Kong, length of residence in Hong Kong, mental health, social support networks and most frequent contact with kinships and friends.

The final model showed that reduced loneliness was most strongly associated with social support networks ($\beta = -.39, p < .001$), sibling and other relatives being the most frequently contacted person ($\beta = -.26, p < .05$), children ($\beta = -.24, p < .05$) and friends ($\beta = -.21, p < .05$) after controlling age, gender, educational level, perceived financial adequacy, indigenous or not, length of stay in Hong Kong, mental health and functional health.

4 Discussion

The present study showed that after controlling for socio-demographic factors and health status, the strength of social support networks could predict the sense of loneliness among solitary older Chinese in Hong Kong. Consistent with previous research,

[3, 12, 13] the significant role played by social support in reducing feelings of loneliness was confirmed with a sample of Chinese older people living alone. The findings of present study further revealed that solitary older people with siblings, other relatives and friends as their most frequent contacts were less likely to feel lonely than those whose adult child(ren) were reported to be most frequently contacted person(s). A possible explanation is that peer support from persons who may have similar experiences will enable better exploration of feelings and make people feel genuinely understood, thus combating the feelings of loneliness. Additionally, compared with indigenous Hong Kong people, those solitary older people who were not locally born were found to be more vulnerable to the feelings of loneliness. It is understandable that immigrants are more likely to be separated from relatives, have narrower social networks which are mostly ethnically bounded, and may encounter more barriers in building supportive and emotionally satisfying social networks.

Programmes and social services should be developed to strengthen solitary older adults' social support networks to reduce their feelings of loneliness in later life. Public education should be strengthened to raise awareness about the importance of enhancing social support for solitary older adults. Practitioners and service providers should be trained to be aware of the problems facing solitary older adults, a special group of people who are less likely to establish close, intimate ties with kinships or peers due to their living arrangement. Tailored progammes aimed at enhancing their abilities in using internet or mobile phones to maintain social contacts could be implemented among community dwelling seniors, especially for those who are living alone. Communications with families and friends either face to face or via technology could largely alleviate their feelings of loneliness. [14] Advancements in social media technologies and other digital platforms have huge potential benefits for older adults to build up relationships with peers and keep in touch with the larger society and community [15].

Acknowledgement. The work described in this study was supported by a grant from The Hong Kong Polytechnic University (1-ZVGD) and a grant from Research Grants Council of Hong Kong Special Administrative Region, China (UGC/IDS11/15).

References

1. Census-and-Statistics-Department. Hong Kong Population Projections 2015–2064. Hong Kong Special Administrative Region (2015)
2. Census-and-Statistics-Department. Population Census Thematic Report: Older Persons. In: Department of Census and statistics (ed.) Hong Kong Special Administrative Region (2013)
3. Chen, Y., Hicks, A., While, A.E.: Loneliness and social support of older people in China: a systematic literature review. Health Soc. Care Community 22, 113–123 (2014)
4. Chen, Y., Hicks, A., While, A.E.: Quality of life and related factors: a questionnaire survey of older people living alone in mainland China. Qual. Life Res. 23, 1593–1602 (2014)
5. Netz, Y., Goldsmith, R., Shimony, T., Arnon, M., Zeev, A.: Loneliness is associated with an increased risk of sedentary life in older israelis. Aging Mental Health 17, 40–47 (2013)

6. Adams, K.B., Sanders, S., Auth, E.A.: Loneliness and depression in independent living retirement communities: risk and resilience factors. Aging Mental Health **8**, 475–485 (2004)
7. Lawton, M.P., Brody, E.M.: Assessment of older people: self-maintaining and instrumental activities of daily living. Nurs. Res. **19**, 278 (1970)
8. Veit, C.T., Ware, J.E.: The structure of psychological distress and well-being in general populations. J. Consult. Clin. Psychol. **51**, 730–742 (1983)
9. Chi, I., Yip, P.S.F., Chiu, H.F.K., Chou, K.L., Chan, K.S., Chi, W.K., Conwell, Y., Caine, E.: Prevalence of depression and its correlates in Hong Kong's Chinese older adults. Am. J. Geriatr. Psychiatry **13**, 409–416 (2005)
10. Lubben, J.E.: Assessing social networks among elderly populations. Family Community Health **11**, 42–52 (1988)
11. Shi, Y.Z.: The development of elderly loneliness scale. J. Family Educ. Bimonthy **16**, 74–95 (2008). (in Chinese)
12. De Jong Gierveld, J., Keating, N., Fast, J.E.: Determinants of loneliness among older adults in Canada. Can. J. Aging **34**, 125–136 (2015)
13. Rodrigues, M.M.S., De Jong Gierveld, J., Buz, J.: Loneliness and the exchange of social support among older adults in spain and the Netherlands. Ageing and Soc. **34**, 330–354 (2014)
14. White, H., McConnell, E., Clipp, E., Bynum, L., Teague, C., Navas, L., Craven, S., Halbrecht, H.: Surfing the net in later life: a review of the literature and pilot study of computer use and quality of life. J. Appl. Gerontol. **18**, 358–378 (1999)
15. Bai, X.: Alignment or struggle? Exploring socio-demographic correlates of individual modernity in Chinese older people. Ageing Soc. **36**, 133–159 (2016)

Using iBeacon Technology
for Active Aging Learning

Tak-Lam Wong[1](✉), Haoran Xie[1], Di Zou[2], and Fu Lee Wang[3]

[1] The Education University of Hong Kong, Tai Po, Hong Kong
{tlwong,hxie}@eduhk.hk
[2] The Hong Kong Polytechnic University, Kowloon, Hong Kong
dizoudaisy@gmail.com
[3] Caritas Institute of Higher Education, Tseung Kwan O, Hong Kong
pwang@cihe.edu.hk

Abstract. Participation in educational activities is found to be helpful to lead to successful aging. We have developed a framework for enhancing learning for older learners using iBeacon technology. Personalized and location-aware learning applications can be designed to improve the learning experience of older learners. A learning analytics engine is designed in our framework for better understanding the learners' learning progress and status. Immediate intervention by the instructors can then be conducted based on their learning pace and level of ability. We presented a case of language learning of older learners as a proof of concept.

Keywords: Location-aware · Context-aware · iBeacon · Active aging

1 Introduction

Lifelong learning has becoming a hot topic attracting researchers and policy makers from different regions [8, 9]. The rationale of lifelong learning is that learners cannot rely on the learning from schools, colleges, and universities. People need to enhance their learning skills so that they can continuously acquire new knowledge and skills to tackle any possible challenges in their lifetime. From the social policy perspective, lifelong learning can enhance, enlarge and empower human resources in the society [7]. To achieve this, a number of strategies have been proposed to promote lifelong learning [6, 14, 17]. Recently, different research findings [13, 16] show that the participation of older learners in educational activities can lead to successful aging, which is defined in terms of health, life satisfaction and happiness, and physical and cognitive functioning [12]. On the other hand, the ageing tendency also increases the proportion of people affected by significant disabilities in the society [11]. As a result, different types of activities, especially learning activities, are important for engaging elderly with different needs to achieve healthy and successful lives.

With the growth of digital technology and the Internet, Information and Communication Technology (ICT) plays a crucial role in education and has been adopted to enhance lifelong learning [1]. For example, Sharples proposed a framework of adopting mobile and context-aware technology for lifelong learning [15]. Bong and Chen

T.-T. Wu et al. (Eds.): SETE 2016, LNCS 10108, pp. 331–336, 2017.
DOI: 10.1007/978-3-319-52836-6_35

investigated how Massive Open Online Courses (MOOCs) can help elderly people in learning [3]. The results indicate that older learners are positive to utilize MOOCs to acquire new knowledge online. However, the accessibility of MOOCs and the Web interface are the major obstacle for old learners to achieve efficient and effective learning. This leads to need of an easily accessible learning tool for older learners.

Location technology has been adopted in learning for various types of learners [4, 5]. For example, Brown et al. developed a location-based learning approach for people with intellectual disabilities and additional sensory impairments, so that they can plan and rehearse new learning tasks, and then to carry these tasks out independently in a safe manner [4]. Recently, micro-location based technology, which can detect the in-door location of an object accurately, has been applied to various application [2, 10]. One example is the use of iBeacon that employs Bluetooth Low Energy (BLE). It continuously broadcasts Bluetooth signals, which contain a proximity Universally Unique IDentifier (UUID). A mobile device can accurately detect the fine region that it resides in. One characteristic of iBeacon is that it can "wake-up" and invoke an application that is not running in a mobile device. Personalized and context-aware information or activities can then be actively feed to the users.

In this paper, we aim at presenting our framework for enhancing learning of older learners using iBeacon technology. In our framework, context-aware and location-aware learning activities can be designed to help older learners, who may be affected by different levels of disabilities. One characteristic is that iBeacon can "awake" and invoke a not-running application in a mobile device. This can greatly reduce the accessibility and enhance the learning experience. Learning analytics can also be achieved as the data about the individual older learners can be collected. As a result, the learning deficiency or even disease like Alzheimer's disease of the older learners can also be detected.

2 Our Framework

Figure 1 depicts our overall framework for enhancing learning for aging using iBeacon Technology. The framework consists of several components as follows:

1. iBeacon: It is a small device or sticker which is essentially a sensor emitting signals in Bluetooth Low Energy (BLE) continuously. The signal contains proximity Universally Unique IDentifier (UUID). Mobile devices near the iBeacon can detect their fine location or proximity based on the UUID and the signal strength. Practically, several iBeacons will be installed in different indoor locations, such as rooms, booths or shops. One example is to use iBeacon in personalized and location-aware marketing by installing iBeacons in a shop.
2. Mobile device: Each older learner carries his/her own mobile device running on iOS operating system. The mobile device contains the user's authentication and identity information. One characteristic of iBeacon technology is that the iBeacon signal can invoke and launch an application via the iBeacon signal. This can significantly improve the accessibility and the ease of use of the applications. A learning

application can be installed in the mobile device and invoked when the user is close to a particular iBeacon.

3. Server: The Web server or application server hosts the learning applications or content. The learning applications can be launched either in the mobile device or on a Kiosk. Since the server will receive both the location information and authentication information from the mobile device, personalized, context-aware and location-aware applications can be designed and developed for enhancing learner's experience and learning progress.

4. Kiosk: Besides launching the learning applications in the mobile devices, the kiosk can run the learning applications when the mobile device is detected to be close to the kiosk or the iBeacon. As a result, the personalized and location-aware learning materials can be delivered to the learners via the kiosk, to further improve the accessibility.

5. Learning analytics engine: When the learner interacts with the learning applications, which either run in mobile devices or the kiosks, the learning process data can be collected from the server. Recalled that the identity and the location of the learner can be identified by the iBeacon. These data are very useful to analysis the learners' learning progress and behaviour. In our framework, the learning analytic engine is designed to analysis the interaction data. The engine contains models for determining the learning path or any abnormal status of the learners. For example, when an older learner is found to have sudden memory deficiency and possible Alzheimer's disease, medical examination can be arranged for early intervention.

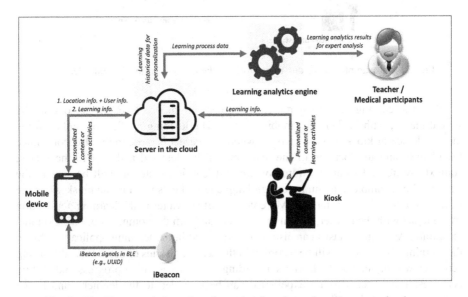

Fig. 1. The Framework for enhancing aging learning using iBeacon technology.

3   An Example of Language Learning for Aging

Learning a new language is no easy task for any learner, especially elderly people. Our framework can facilitate the learning of new language by providing a realistic context and location-aware situation for older learners. Figure 2 shows a sample use of our framework for language learning. In a learning centre, virtual places like restaurant, clinic, supermarket, etc. can be set up in different rooms or booths. Ideally, these virtual places are the places commonly visited by elderly. An iBeacon and an optional kiosk are installed in each of the virtual place. As mentioned in Sect. 2, a context-aware and location-aware learning application, which serves as the client to interact with the server, can be installed in the mobile device and kiosk.

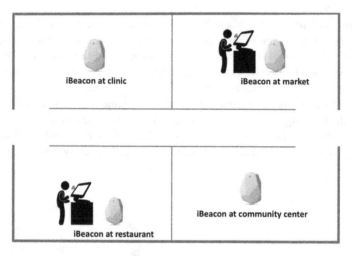

Fig. 2. An example use of our framework for language learning for older learners.

When a learning activity starts, each learner can choose to enter any one of the virtual places, with his/her own mobile device. The learning application, either in the mobile device or kiosk, will be invoked when the learner is close to the iBeacon. Since the identity and the location of the learners will be detected and sent to the server, context- aware and location-aware content and learning materials will be sent to the learners. For example, a menu in foreign language will be shown in the kiosk when the learner is in the virtual restaurant. Moreover, a virtual waiter in the learning application will interact with the learner, so that the learner can learn the common conversation in a restaurant. Assessment tasks can also be incorporated in the learning application. Since the learning process data will be recorded in the server, a series of personalized learning activities will be feed to the learners according to his/her learning progress and ability. As a result, a better learning experience can be provided to the learners, and hence improve their learning efficiency. On the other hand, the learning process information will be recorded in the server. The learning analytics engine can analysis the data individually or collectively. For example, common mistakes can be discovered or learners with similar ability can be identified. Intervention can then be designed by the instructional designers to enhance their learning.

4   Conclusions and Future Work

We designed a framework for enhancing learning for aging using iBeacon technology. Personalized and location-aware learning activities can be designed and carried out. iBeacon technology can improve the accessibility of a learning application and enhance the learning experience of older learners. As the learning data can be continuously recorded, learning analytics can be conducted to achieve better understanding or the learners. A better decision making and assessment can be accomplished.

We intend to extend our framework in several directions. One possible direction is to develop an instructional model for enhancing learning using location and context information. For example, our framework can be integrated into task-based learning, so as to achieve better learning outcome. Another possible direction is to apply our framework in other areas such as provision training or other age group education.

Acknowledgement. The work described in this paper was supported by a grant from the Research Grants Council of the Hong Kong Special Administrative Region, China (Project No. UGC/IDS11/15).

References

1. Arrigo, M., Kukulska-Hulme, A., Arnedillo-Sánchez, I., Kismihok, G.: Meta-analyses from a collaborative project in mobile lifelong learning. Br. Educ. Res. J. **39**(2), 222–247 (2013)
2. Bassbouss, L., Güçlü, G., Steglich, S.: Towards a remote launch mechanism of TV companion applications using iBeacon. In: Proceedings of the IEEE 3rd Global Conference on Consumer Electronics (GCCE), pp. 538–539 (2014)
3. Bong, W.K., Chen, W.: How accessible are MOOCs to the elderly? In: Miesenberger, K., Bühler, C., Penaz, P. (eds.) ICCHP 2016. LNCS, vol. 9758, pp. 437–444. Springer, Heidelberg (2016). doi:10.1007/978-3-319-41264-1_60
4. Brown, D.J., McHugh, D., Standen, P., Evett, L., Shopland, N., Battersby, S.: Designing location-based learning experiences for people with intellectual disabilities and additional sensory impairments. Comput. Educ. **56**(1), 11–20 (2011)
5. Chu, H.C., Hwang, G.J., Tsai, C.C., Tseng, J.C.: A two-tier test approach to developing location-aware mobile learning systems for natural science courses. Comput. Educ. **55**(4), 1618–1627 (2010)
6. Cornford, I.R.: Learning-to-learn strategies as a basis for effective lifelong learning. Int. J. Lifelong Educ. **21**(4), 357–368 (2002)
7. Fernández-Ballesteros, R., Molina, M.Á.: Lifelong Learning. The Encyclopedia of Adult-hood and Aging. Wiley, Hoboken (2016)
8. Jarvis, P.: Adult Education and Lifelong Learning: Theory and Practice. Routledge, Abingdon-on-Thames (2004)
9. Knapper, C., Cropley, A.J.: Lifelong Learning in Higher Education. Psychology Press, Hove (2000)

10. Lin, X.Y., Ho, T.W., Fang, C.C., Yen, Z.S., Yang, B.J., Lai, F.: A mobile indoor positioning system based on iBeacon technology. In: Proceedings of the 37th Annual International Conference of the IEEE Engineering in Medicine and Biology Society (EMBC), pp. 4970–4973 (2015)
11. Marin, B., Prinz, C.: Facts and Figures on Disability Welfare. European Centre for Social Welfare Policy and Research Vienna, Vienna (2003)
12. Menec, V.H.: The relation between everyday activities and successful aging: a 6-year longitudinal study. J. Gerontol. Ser. B: Psychol. Sci. Soc. Sci. **58**(2), S74–S82 (2003)
13. Merriam, S.B., Kee, Y.: Promoting community wellbeing: the case for lifelong learning for older adults. Adult Educ. Q. **64**(2), 128–144 (2014)
14. Müller, R., Remdisch, S., Köhler, K., Marr, L., Repo, S., Yndigegn, C.: Easing access for lifelong learners: a comparison of European models for university lifelong learning. Int. J. Lifelong Educ. **34**(5), 530–550 (2015)
15. Sharples, M.: The design of personal mobile technologies for lifelong learning. Comput. Educ. **34**(3), 177–193 (2000)
16. Sloane-Seale, A., Kops, B.: Older adults in lifelong learning: participation and successful aging. Can. J. Univ. Contin. Educ. **34**(1) (2013)
17. Yang, J., Schneller, C., Roche, S.: The Role of Higher Education in Promoting Lifelong Learning. UIL Publication Series on Lifelong Learning Policies and Strategies: No. 3. UNESCO Institute for Lifelong Learning (2015)

Workshop on Emerging Technologies
for Language Learning

Learner Feature Variation in Measuring the Listenability for Learners of English as a Foreign Language

Katsunori Kotani[1(✉)] and Takehiko Yoshimi[2]

[1] Kansai Gaidai University, Osaka, Japan
kkotani@kansaigaidai.ac.jp
[2] Ryukoku University, Shiga, Japan

Abstract. Previous research on the ease of listening comprehension (henceforth, listenability) has measured listenability on the basis of sentence properties such as the length of words/sentences and speech rate. Recent research has included features of listeners, which are required for the measurement of listenability for English learners because their listening proficiencies vary greatly from the beginner to the advanced level. Given the importance of listening proficiency as a listener feature, this study developed listenability measurement methods based on the costs of compiling listener features: expensive features extracted from test scores and inexpensive features extracted from learners' experiences. The experimental results showed that inexpensive features made substantial contributions to the measurement of middle-range listenability.

Keywords: Listenability · Learner features · English as a foreign language

1 Introduction

Research on the ease of listening comprehension (henceforth, listenability) aims to explain listenability based on the linguistic complexity of sentences/words (henceforth, linguistic features). Listenability has been measured based on linguistic features from the perspectives of vocabulary, sentence/text structure, and phonological representation [1–5]. Listenability has also been measured on the basis of listeners' knowledge/abilities (henceforth, listener features), which are assumed to affect listening comprehension. In addition, listenability has been measured in native English speakers based on the depth of listeners' background knowledge [3].

In measuring listenability for learners of English as a foreign language (EFL), it is necessary to include the features of listeners that explain their listening proficiency (henceforth, learner features), because learners demonstrate different levels of listening proficiency [6]. The issue of learner features has been addressed in previous studies [4, 7]. To explain difficulties regarding the acquisition of vocabulary for learners at the intermediate level, one of those studies [7] used linguistic features as opposed to learner features in the listenability measurement. Therefore, that method [7] was limited to intermediate-level learners. By contrast, the other study [4] included learner features, in this case, listening scores on the Test of English for International Communication

© Springer International Publishing AG 2017
T.-T. Wu et al. (Eds.): SETE 2016, LNCS 10108, pp. 339–348, 2017.
DOI: 10.1007/978-3-319-52836-6_36

Table 1. Linguistic and listener/learner features used in previous studies on listenability

Type	Feature
Lexicon	Word length [4]
	Word difficulty [4, 7]
	Noun collocation [5]
	Type–token ratio [5]
	Frequency of word types [5]
Syntax	Sentence length [1, 3–5]
Discourse	Presence of long sentences [5]
Phonetics	Presence of multiple syllable words [2–4]
	Speech rate [3–5]
	Pause length [3]
	Presence of repairing [3]
	Presence of accent [3]
	Presence of intensity [3]
	Phonological modification patterns [4]
	Silence [5]
	Distance between stressed syllables [5]
	Vowel duration [5]
Listener/Learner	Depth of background knowledge [3]
	TOEIC listening test score [4]

(TOEIC), to explain listening proficiency. Therefore, they expanded the applicability of a listenability measurement method from beginners to advanced-level learners, as test scores cover all of these levels. A summary of the linguistic and listener/learner features used in these previous studies is shown in Table 1.

The TOEIC listening score is a learner feature that can plausibly be used as an evaluation criterion for listening proficiency. However, from the perspective of practical listenability measurement in language classes or computer-assisted language learning systems, the use of test scores is problematic because of the time gap between the time the test was taken and the listenability measurement. Under the listenability measurement method [4], the longest time gap accepted is a year, because learner features consist of test scores up to a year before the listenability measurement. If learners took the TOEIC immediately before the listenability measurement, no gap-related issues would be expected; however, because taking the TOEIC is both time- and cost-consuming, an easier and more appropriate method for evaluating learner features is necessary.

Therefore, this study examined the effectiveness of variety of learner features for listenability measurement with the goal of confirming the applicability of more inexpensive learner features—experimental learner feature: the duration of English-learning experience (henceforth, Learning exp.), the amount of experience in countries/areas where English is a primary language (henceforth, Visiting exp.), and frequency of English listening in daily life (henceforth, Freq.)—as an alternative to their more expensive counterpart—control learner feature: TOEIC listening scores (henceforth, Test scr.). In the present paper, experimental results on listenability measurement using these alternative learner features are reported. The results showed that the alternative and more inexpensive features made substantial contributions to listenability measurement for learners in the middle range of listenability.

2 Learner Listenability

As our listenability measurement methods were developed using regression analysis, it was necessary to collect training/test data composed of both independent and dependent variables. The independent variables consist of linguistic and learner features, which demonstrate the difficulty of listening at lexical/syntactic/discourse/phonological levels and EFL learners' listening proficiency, respectively, whereas the dependent variables demonstrate listenability.

Listenability was collected as scores on a five-point Likert scale (1: easy, 2: somewhat easy, 3: average, 4: somewhat difficult, or 5: difficult). Listenability scores were assigned by 90 EFL learners (48 males, 42 females) who were university students and whose first language was Japanese. Scoring was carried out on a sentence-by-sentence basis where each learner listened to and rated 80 sentences from four news clips taken from the Voice of America website (http://www.voanews.com).

Although for a valid listenability score, the training/test data should have comprised 7,200 instances (90 learners × 80 sentences), only 6,804 were observed; that is, 396 instances were missing. It was assumed that learners did not rate some sentences due to their level of difficulty, so scores for these instances were determined as 5, the lowest listenability score. A distribution of listenability scores can be seen in Fig. 1. Most instances (25.2%) were observed in the middle range of listenability (3), while the fewest (15.8%) were seen in a high range of listenability (2).

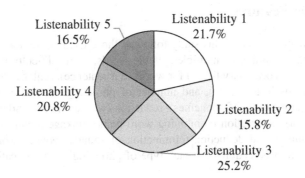

Fig. 1. Distribution of listenability scores

3 Learner Features

Learner features were extracted from corpus data [4]. Listenability measurement was then evaluated through a comparison between the control learner features (TOEIC listening scores) and the following experimental learner features, which were assumed to reflect the growth of learners' proficiency [8–10].

- Learning experience (Learning exp.): how long learners have studied English
- Experience in countries or areas where English is a primary language (Visiting exp.): amount of time learners have spent in such areas
- Frequency (Freq.): frequency of English use (infrequently, somewhat infrequently, moderate, somewhat frequently, and frequently) rated on a five-point Likert scale

Table 2 shows descriptive statistics for the learner features, where "N" refers to the number of instances (learners), "Min" to minimum, "Max" to maximum, "Med" to median, and "SD" to standard deviation.

Table 2. Descriptive statics of learners' features

	Control feature	Experimental feature		
	Test scr. (points)	Learning exp. (months)	Visiting exp. (months)	Freq. (score)
N	90	90	90	90
Min	130	53	0	1
Max	495	243	138	5
Mean	334.8	123.2	11.3	2.1
Med	327.5	108.0	1.0	2.0
SD	97.6	36.6	25.8	1.1

4 Linguistic Features

The linguistic features used in this study followed those used in previous research [4]: mean word length, number of multiple-syllable words, word difficulty (rate of words absent from a basic vocabulary list [7] for words in a sentence), sentence length, speech rate (spoken words in a minute), and number of phonological modifications, which refer to elision (elimination of phonemes), reduction (weakening a sound by changing a vowel to a schwa), contraction (combining word pairs), linkage (connecting final and initial word sounds), and deduction (elimination of sounds between words). Table 3 shows the extraction procedures for each type of phonological modification.

Table 3. Extraction procedures for each type of phonological modification feature

Type	Procedure
Elision	a. Convert to phonetic symbols b. Search conditions for elision [4] c. Calculate the number of condition-matched words per number of words in a sentence
Reduction	a. Parse part of speech [11] b. Search conditions for reduction [4] c. Calculate the number of condition-matched words per number of words in a sentence
Contraction	a. Count the number of apostrophes* b. Calculate the number of apostrophes per number of words in sentence *Contractions using apostrophes in written form, such as "I've".
Linkage	a. Convert to phonetic symbols b. Search conditions for linking [4] c. Calculate the number of condition-matched words per number of words in a sentence
Deduction	a. Convert to phonetic symbols b. Search conditions for deduction [4] c. Calculate the number of condition-matched words per number of words in a sentence

5 Experiment

5.1 Methods

Listenability measurement methods were developed by support vector regression [12], which was performed using an algorithm implemented in mySVM software [13]. The first order polynomial was set as a type of kernel function, and the other settings were retained as defaults. The listenability measurement methods were then examined using five-fold cross validation.

The dependent variable was the listenability score, and the independent variables were the linguistic and learner features. The listenability measurement method used either one of the four types of learner features (Test scr., Learning exp., Visiting exp., or Freq.) or all of the experimental learner features (multiple).

First, the listenability measurement methods were examined in a correlation analysis between listenability scores measured by a method and listenability scores assigned by the learners.

Second, the listenability measurement methods were examined using analysis of variance (ANOVA) for measurement errors. A measurement error was calculated as the absolute value of a difference between a listenability score measured by a method and a listenability score assigned by a learner. When a statistically significant difference was observed, Tukey's post-hoc test was carried out to specify which method(s) using the experimental learner feature(s) differed from those using the control learner features.

Third, listenability measurement errors were further examined using ANOVA for each listenability score. Tukey's post-hoc test was also carried out to specify the experimental learner feature(s) showing lower measurement errors than the control learner features.

5.2   Results

Table 4 summarizes the correlations observed between listenability scores from the learners and those from the measurement methods. The strongest correlation was observed for the method using Test scr. Among the methods using experimental learner features, the strongest correlation was observed for that using all of the experimental learner features (Multiple).

Table 4. Correlation (r) between observed and measured listenability

Method with control feature	Method with experimental feature			
Test scr.	Learning exp.	Visiting exp.	Freq.	Multiple
0.52	0.38	0.35	0.36	0.41

Table 5 shows descriptive statistics of the measurement errors. A one-way ANOVA identified a statistically significant difference in measurement errors ($F(4,35995) = 28.68$, $p < 0.01$). Table 6 shows the results of Tukey's post-hoc test. The measurement errors using the experimental learner feature(s) were significantly higher than those using the control learner features ($p < 0.01$).

Table 5. Descriptive statics of measured errors

	Control feature		Experimental feature		
	Test scr.	Learning exp.	Visiting exp.	Freq.	Multiple
N	7,200	7,200	7,200	7,200	7,200
Min	0.00	0.00	0.00	0.00	0.00
Max	4.45	4.55	4.99	4.74	4.82
Mean	0.95	1.05	1.06	1.05	1.02
Med	0.77	0.96	0.99	0.97	0.91
S.D.	0.74	0.74	0.78	0.76	0.76

Table 6. Results of Tukey's post-hoc test

Tested pair	Significance
Test scr. vs. Learning exp.	p < 0.01
Test scr. vs. Visiting exp.	p < 0.01
Test scr. vs. Freq.	p < 0.01
Test scr. vs. Multiple	p < 0.01

Table 7. Mean absolute measurement errors for the listenability levels

	Control feature	Experimental feature			
	Test scr.	Learning exp.	Visiting exp.	Freq.	Multiple
Score 1 (N = 1563)	1.07	1.45	1.62	1.46	1.33
Score 2 (N = 1135)	0.80	0.87	0.95	0.85	0.84
Score 3 (N = 1813)	0.57	**0.46**	**0.41**	**0.44**	**0.45**
Score 4 (N = 1498)	0.79	0.82	**0.70**	0.82	0.78
Score 5 (N = 1191)	1.68	1.88	1.87	1.94	1.94

Table 7 shows the mean measurement errors for the listenability scores assigned by learners. Values in boldface indicate better performance for the experimental learner feature compared with the control. Table 8 summarizes the results of a one-way ANOVA and Tukey's post-hoc test between the control and experimental learner features. For the scores of 1 and 5, all of the experimental learner features showed worse performance; for the score of 2, performance in terms of Freq. and Multiple (figures in boldface) was similar to that of the control features, that is, the differences were not statistically significant; for the score of 3, all of the experimental learner features showed better performance (boldface); for the score of 4, similar performance was seen for Learning exp., Freq., and Multiple, and better performance was seen for Visiting exp. (boldface).

Table 8. Summary of ANOVA results

ANOVA		Tukey's post hoc test (vs. control)			
		Learning exp.	Visiting exp.	Freq.	Multiple
Score 1	$F(4, 7810) = 164.88$, $p < 0.001$	$p < 0.01$	$p < 0.01$	$p < 0.01$	$p < 0.01$
Score 2	$F(4, 5670) = 13.32$, $p < 0.001$	$p < 0.01$	$p < 0.01$	**$p > 0.10$**	**$p > 0.10$**
Score 3	$F(4, 9060) = 41.13$, $p < 0.001$	**$p < 0.01$**	**$p < 0.01$**	**$p < 0.01$**	**$p < 0.01$**
Score 4	$F(4, 7485) = 11.83$, $p < 0.001$	$p > 0.10$	**$p < 0.01$**	$p > 0.10$	$p > 0.10$
Score 5	$F(4, 5950) = 13.22$, $p < 0.001$	$p < 0.01$	$p < 0.01$	$p < 0.01$	$p < 0.01$

5.3 Discussion

The results demonstrated that the experimental learner features made a lower contribution to listenability measurement than the control learner features. However, the results also suggest that the experimental learner features may be promising if accompanied by fine tuning or supported with other features.

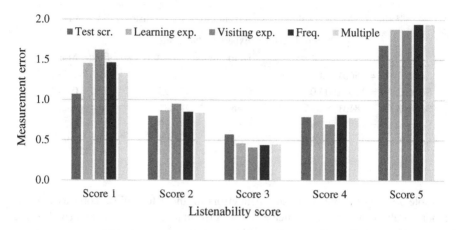

Fig. 2. Distribution of measurement errors (Table 7)

Listenability measurement using the experimental learner features was successful in terms of multiple features (Learning exp., Visiting exp., and Freq.). Each of the experimental learner features contributed to the listenability measurement, so the combination of features should also make a contribution. Hence, this result supports the use of the experimental learner features. Based on a review of the experimental learner features, it was considered that they should include more detailed information. Learning experience should include not only the duration of learning, but time learning began, because the earlier the age at which one begins to study English, the more advantageous it is considered for listening proficiency [14, 15]. In addition, visiting experience should include not only the time span, but also age, because of the similar advantages associated with visiting at an earlier age. Frequency should include not only temporal information, but also information regarding the communication medium, such as in-class/out-of-class communication, radio, TV, or the Internet, because face-to-face communication improves listening proficiency more than non- face-to-face communication [16].

The experimental learner features made a greater contribution to listenability measurement for the score of 3, the middle range of listenability; this result also supports the use of the experimental learner features. The mean absolute measurement errors for the listenability levels tended to be larger for high and low scores, as shown in Fig. 2. The distribution of the experimental learner features followed that of the control learner features, which suggests that errors may be affected by factors other than listening proficiency. One such possibility is the influence of background knowledge, which has been previously reported [3], while another is sentence position in the text, because discourse information depends on sentence position in a news article; for example, the first part of an article typically summarizes an event, while the following part provides more detailed information. The listenability of the former part might be easier than that of the latter due to the lack of detailed information.

6 Conclusion

We examined listenability measurement for EFL learners on the basis of learner features, explaining listening proficiency in terms of duration of English learning, visits to English-speaking areas, and frequency of English use. Although previous research [4] has measured listenability for learners based on TOEIC listening scores, this type of learner feature raises problems in terms of practical listenability measurement because it is both time- and cost-consuming.

The results of our experiment demonstrated that the general measurement performance of these experimental learner features was lower than that of the control learner features. However, the experimental learner features outperformed the control learner features in measuring the middle range of listenability. In addition, the present results suggest that the performance of the experimental learner features may be improved by including more detailed information or by adding other linguistic features such as sentence position in the spoken text.

Acknowledgments. This work was supported by JSPS KAKENHI Grant Numbers, 22300299, 15H02940.

References

1. Chall, J.S., Dial, H.E.: Listener understanding and interest in newscasts. Educ. Res. Bull. **27**(6), 141–153+168 (1948)
2. Fang, I.E.: The easy listening formula. J. Broadcast. Electron. Media **11**(1), 63–68 (1966)
3. Messerklinger, J.: Listenability. Cent. Eng. Lang. Educ. J. **14**, 56–70 (2006)
4. Kotani, K., Ueda, S., Yoshimi, T., Nanjo, H.: A listenability measuring method for an adaptive computer-assisted language learning and teaching system. In: Proceedings of the 28th Pacific Asia Conference on Language, Information, and Computation, pp. 387–394 (2014)
5. Yoon, S.-Y., Cho, Y., Napolitano, D.: Spoken text difficulty estimation using linguistic features. In: Proceedings of the 11th Workshop on Innovative Use of NLP for Building Educational Applications, pp. 267–276 (2016)
6. Saville-Troike, M.: Introducing Second Language Acquisition. Cambridge University Press, Cambridge (2006)
7. Kiyokawa, H.: A formula for predicting listenability: the listenability of English language materials 2. Wayo Women's Univ. Lang. Lit. **24**, 57–74 (1990)
8. Ockey, G.: The use of TOEFL to measure a change in English proficiency. Working Papers on Language Acquisition and Education, vol. 10, pp. 1–12 (1999). http://works.bepress.com/gary-ockey/13/
9. Tanaka, K., Ellis, R.: Study-abroad, language proficiency, and learner beliefs about language learning. JALT J. **25**(1), 63–85 (2003)
10. Brewer, E., Sively, R., Gozik, N., Doyle, D.M., Savicki, V.: Beyond the study abroad industry: perspectives from other disciplines on assessing study abroad learning outcomes. In: Savicki, V., Brewer, E. (eds.) Assessing Study Abroad: Theory, Tools, and Practice. Stylus Publishing, Sterling (2015)

11. Schmid, H.: Probabilistic part-of-speech tagging using decision trees. In: Proceedings of International Conference on New Methods in Language Processing, Manchester, UK, pp. 44–49 (1994)
12. Vapnik, V.: Statistical Learning Theory. Wiley-Interscience, New York (1998)
13. Rüping, S.: MySVM-Manual. University of Dortmund, Lehrstuhl Informatik VIII (2000). http://www-ai.cs.uni-ortmund.de/SOFTWARE/MYSVM/
14. Seright, L.: Age and aural comprehension achievement in francophone adults learning English. TESOL Q. **19**(3), 455–473 (1985)
15. Marinova-Todd, S.H., Marshall, D.B., Snow, C.E.: Three misconceptions about age and L2 learning. TESOL Q. **34**(1), 9–34 (2000)
16. Warscauer, M.: Comparing face-to-face and electronic discussion in the second language classroom. CALICO J. **13**(2), 7–26 (1996)

Corpus-Based Correlational Study of Terms and Quality in Business English Writing

Shili Ge[1,2], Jingchao Zhang[1], and Xiaoxiao Chen[1(✉)]

[1] School of English for International Business,
Guangdong University of Foreign Studies, Guangzhou 510420, China
geshili@gdufs.edu.cn, 774588349@qq.com,
gracekot@qq.com
[2] Guangdong Collaborative Innovation Center for Language Research and
Service, Guangdong University of Foreign Studies, Guangzhou 510420, China

Abstract. One of the most important tasks in automated essay scoring (AES) is feature selection. Terms are indispensable in Business English (BE) writing. In order to analyze the possibility of involving terms in BE writing automated scoring feature set, the strength of correlations between terminological features and writing quality or scores is studied. A Business English term bank (BETB) was built based on a term dictionary. With BETB and a self-coded Python program, business terms and their categories in a BE writing corpus were identified and extracted. The analysis shows that, among ten categories of terms and total term numbers in BE writing, human resource terms and total term numbers have a moderate correlation with writing scores. This result means business terms, especially writing content related terms, should be covered in business AES feature set, which can improve the performance of AES systems and facilitate BE learners' writing proficiency.

Keywords: Automated essay scoring · Business English writing · Terminology · Feature selection

1 Introduction

"Automated essay scoring (AES) has been a real and viable alternative and complement to human scoring for many years" [1]. It has been being adopted in GMAT and TOEFL essay scoring instead of one human rater since the end of last century. Business English (BE), as an area of English for Specific Purposes (ESP), has become the dominant lingua franca in international business world for more than 30 years and also attracted great attention in global education field. Yet, there is no research about automated scoring of BE writing reported. Besides the features of general English, BE "implies … emphasis on particular kinds of communication in a specific context" [2]. As an interdisciplinary discourse, BE includes not only general linguistic features, but also a wealth of business knowledge. Terms are a kind of representation of knowledge. Through this research, moderate correlational relationships between composition scores and human resource term and total term numbers are found, which first indicates that the special lexical features, terms, can be involved in AES studies.

© Springer International Publishing AG 2017
T.-T. Wu et al. (Eds.): SETE 2016, LNCS 10108, pp. 349–358, 2017.
DOI: 10.1007/978-3-319-52836-6_37

2 Related Works

2.1 Automated Essay Scoring

There are already many AES systems in use or under study, such as PEG, IEA, E-Rater and BETSY [3]. The common procedures are usually as following:

(1) Collect a few hundred papers of a certain prompt and get the human score of each paper by writing experts or multi-raters.
(2) Divide the human rated papers into training set and testing set, withdraw values of dozens or even hundreds of textual features from every paper in the training set, fit the values with the score of the same paper mathematically, obtain some features that have more effect on the score and their weight in scoring, and construct a scoring model.
(3) Test the model on the testing set papers and apply it when it meets the requirement of scoring.

AES systems first have to meet the demand of essay scoring in large scale language testing and the requirement of this demand mostly "focuses on the relationship between automated and human scores of the same prompt", which is "typically found that the agreements are very similar" [1]. That means all the systems are applicable in essay scoring. This is firstly due to the adequate study of the field, but on the second thought, it is in fact not a strict requirement because "the simplest form of automated scoring which considers only essay length could yield agreement rates that are almost as good as human rates" [1].

Then, AES systems have to meet the demand of essay scoring in language teaching and this demand mainly needs feedback about writing quality besides a score. In this aspect, feature selection considers not only the relationship between features and the final score but features that should be "intimately related to meaningful dimensions of writing" as well [1]. Huang et al. [4] emphasizes the importance of feature selection in AES study for foreign language writing like HSK, and Ge [5] points out that lexical and phrasal features that can provide meaningful feedback for students are important in English as a foreign language (EFL) AES studies.

Most AES systems or studies adopt lexical features according to Valenti et al. [3]. The earliest system, PEG, takes essay length, i.e., total word number of an essay, number of different types of words, such as prepositions, relative pronouns and other parts of speech, as the main features. The system that claims to assess writing quality based on the essay content, IEA, takes all the words in an essay as its feature set. Two of the eight features in the most famous system e-rater V.2 are lexical features, which are lexical complexity and prompt-specific vocabulary usage [1]. Term usage, as a special type of lexical unit in BE writing, is worth exploring to see if it is effective in AES studies.

2.2   Business English Writing and the Importance of Business Terms

BE writing is a major subject in the syllabus of BE undergraduate program, with purpose of building students' writing ability to produce business discourse appropriately. According to Feng [6], taken as an important course in developing business purpose language ability, BE writing sets its teaching goal as using English effectively in business context so as to complete business communication and fulfill business action. Zhang [7] defines BE writing as a particular type of writing that people create to meet their demands for communications in the domain of international business and international finance. It relates to language use and involves interaction between industry and socio-cultural context. In short, BE writing refers to the creation of written discourse by using English as a lingua franca in business situation. Therefore, it inevitable involves business knowledge.

Business terminology is a salient linguistic feature of business knowledge, thus a good breakthrough point to study the connection between business knowledge and BE writing. Since the standardization of business terminology encounters the same dilemma that other social sciences encounter—the fuzzy boundaries of disciplines make it difficult to construct a clear-cut concept system—no business nomenclature is available now in the term labeling work. In this case, terminology analysis in business context has not been well explored so far. However, in the light of descriptive approach in terminological research, business terminology analysis can be carried out without concept organization, as long as specified corpus or reference materials can be found. Terminology is the language expression of specialized knowledge and the nods in knowledge structure of specific domains. Therefore business terminology can be the quantifiable observation of business knowledge and, consequently become a measurable component of it.

2.3   Corpus and Term Identification

"It is a well-known fact that terminology has attracted the interest of researchers with very different backgrounds and motivations" [8]. Terms are defined as "the words that are assigned to concepts used in the special languages that occur in subject-field or domain-related texts" [9]. This idea is echoed in Business English. "In the late 1960s and early 1970s, specialist vocabulary was seen to be what distinguished Business English from General English, and there was a preoccupation with business-related words and terminology" [2].

Based on Communicative [10] and Cognitive Terminology [11], the new descriptive approach is invented. Unlike the traditional prescriptive approach, the new one cares less about terminology standardization. Terms can be organized and described according to their semantic relations. Specialized corpus as well as other authentic materials are used as reference to analyze the distribution of terms in authentic texts.

"Since terminologies are domain-specific, terminologists will generally need to build a new corpus each time they embark on building a new terminology" [12].

As pointed by Ahmad and Rogers [12], in terminological corpus building, some properties, such as representativeness, text attributes, unbiased sample, corpus size and corpus design have to be taken care of. With a deliberately designed corpus, comparing with a large general language corpus, terms can be identified statistically, e.g., words with significant higher frequency in special corpus than in general corpus are obviously term candidates.

In fact, "identifying and selecting terms is both the first step and an ongoing concern in the creation of terminological resources" [12], which is also the first step in AES with terminological features.

Term identification "methods include statistically based procedures, linguistically-based procedures and hybrid procedures" [12]. But no matter what procedures are adopted, it cannot be 100% accurate because the problems of over-generation and under-generation always exist.

There are many reasons for the problems. For single-word terms, many words do double duty as words in general language and terms in special languages, e.g. platform and bus; for multiword terms or compound terms, term boundaries are difficult to pin down. The solution for the former problem mainly depends on expert knowledge while most researches focus on the latter problem.

In traditional terminology management, researchers mainly rely on linguistically-based methods of extracting compound terms by identifying typical noun phrase structures and morphological patterns (e.g., Picht and Draskau [13] for English, German, and Spanish), which is later applied for purposes of term extraction (e.g., Drouin [14] for French). Linguistic rules may be supplemented by a statistical measure to assess whether the occurrence of such phrases is statistically significant. Statistical method usually starts from a certain kind of statistical analysis before filtering the output using linguistic rules or patterns. The statistical procedure assigns a value for every term candidate based on its frequency, distribution and many other termino-logical properties in the text. With the ranking of the values, terms and non-terms can be separated because effective statistical method assigns a higher value for terms [15].

Certainly, statistical method cannot be 100% accurate in identification of terms, no matter precision or recall. "The output of current systems still requires human filtering by, for example, domain experts, to identify string boundaries and to distinguish valid terms from mere term candidates" [12].

One of the rule-based term extraction methods, dictionary-based method, is the simplest method, which compares the candidate term with the term entries in a term dictionary. If they match, the candidate is a term. Otherwise, it is not [16, 17]. This method is effective and efficient, only that it needs a comprehensive term dictionary.

3 Automated Identification of Business Terms

As mentioned above, three methods are widely adopted in automated term identifi-cation and extraction: linguistically-based, statistically-based and hybrid. Chinese college English learners' business writing, as an interlanguage [18], is quite different from native speakers' language. There may be various textual mistakes or errors that may hinder statistical analysis of terms. In this case, linguistically-based or rule-based method is more appropriate. In order to achieve the detailed analysis of students' use of different types of terms in their business writing, a dictionary-based approach is adopted in this research.

3.1 Term Resources

An authoritative dictionary, An English-Chinese Dictionary of Business Management [19], with more than 20,000 term entries in ten categories is adopted as term resources. Most of entries are noun and noun phrases, and fall into at least one category. Information about the covered disciplines and categories is presented as following with abbreviations in brackets:

Accounting [ACC]: accounting, corporate finance, auditing;

Economics [ECO]: managerial economics, industrial organization, international economics, balance of payments, exchange rate;

Finance [FIN]: banking, insurance, securities, investment, financing, international finance;

Human resources [HR]: human resources, organizational behavior, culture, training and education, leadership;

International business [IB]: international business, international trade, foreign direct investment, multinational corporations, cross-cultural management;

Information technology [IT]: information technology, electronic commerce, artificial intelligence, enterprise resources planning;

Law [LAW]: commercial law, business ethics, environment protection, intellectual property rights, taxation, contract, arbitration;

Management [MAN]: management, strategy, merger and acquisition, change management, innovation, entrepreneurship, corporate governance, business environment, consulting, negotiation;

Marketing [MAR]: marketing, consumer behavior, advertising, retailing, public relations, business communication;

Operating [OPE]: logistics, manufacturing, quality assurance, operations research, statistics, forecasting, decision sciences.

Considering its coverage and the quantity of its entries, there is a reason to believe that this dictionary contains most of business terms that BE undergraduates can apply in writing practice. All term entries and their categories are digitalized manually to build a Business English term bank (BETB).

3.2 Business Writing Corpus Construction

To accomplish this research, Chinese college English learners' compositions have to be collected to build a corpus first. Considering the universal recognition of Business English Certificate (BEC), three writing tasks from the second part of writing module in authentic BEC Higher examination are taken as assignments. Business English majors in sophomore, junior and senior years are invited to join the writing practice. They are required to finish one of the three tasks after class. 122 compositions are collected and among them, 80 are about a same task, which form the research corpus. The brief statistics are presented in Table 1.

Table 1. Brief statistics of students' writing

Grade	Number	Ave. length	SD	ANOVA F	P
2	25	249.68	31.45	0.74	0.48
3	38	251.24	37.70		
4	17	263.06	46.06		
Total	80	253.26	37.72		

From Table 1, we can see that for the same business writing task, sophomore and junior students write roughly the same length and senior students write longer with a large standard deviation, but the ANOVA test shows no significant difference in the length of writing for the three groups ($p = 0.48 > 0.05$).

3.3   Term Identification and Annotation

To identify and annotate terms in students' writing, a maximum matching algorithm is designed and coded in Python. The algorithm is rather simple:

```
Read in all term entries and categories from BETB
for each composition in the corpus:
  for each sentence in a composition:
    Lemmatize all words
    Match the longest term from the first word with the
original word or lemmatized word
    if matched:
      Annotate the first category of the term
      Move on to the next word after the term
    if not matched:
      Move on to the next word
Output the annotated result
```

To illustrate the identification and annotation procedure, an annotated sample is given as following:

Dear Mr. Principal,

I am writing to invite you to cooperate with our company's <internship program> [HR], in which capable students in your business school can attend the three-month work <placement> [HR] program in my company, the ABC Holdings Ltd.

ABC Holdings Ltd. is one of the top company making <fast-moving consumer goods> [MAR] in China. We proudly own <brands> [MAR] like Dello Chocolate, Mrs. Waffle Taffy, and Gunman Chewing Gum.

When striving to make the best <FMCGs> [MAR] in China, we also convince the importance of talented people who are willing to devote themselves to this <industry> [ECO] and own the most sound <employee training> [HR] <system> [OPE] in the world. The <placement> [HR] program is one of our core <training> [HR] programs aiming at cultivating <leaders> [HR] in <marketing> [MAR] and <management> [MAN] and prepare undergraduate students for the future <work-force> [HR].

The work of <placement> [HR] would include developing <marketing strategies> [MAR] for our products, analyzing the products of our major <competitors> [MAN], and processing related <data> [IT] using excel or SPSS.

<Applicants> [HR] are supposed to be able to work 3 days a week lasting 3 months; students major in <strategic management> [MAN] or <marketing> [MAR] or related experience are preferred.

Students can receive professional <marketing> [MAR] <training> [HR] and develop <marketing> [MAR] insight, learn from other senior <employees> [HR] and will have the chance to sign long-term <contract> [LAW] with our company.

If this is of your <interest> [ACC], or if you have any questions, please feel free to <email> [IT] me and I am looking forward to cooperate with your school.

Yours,

Tony Lok

<Senior Manager> [HR] of ABC Holdings Ltd.

There are 29 terms in the 256 words composition, among which 24 are single-word terms and 7 are two or more words. Terms are annotated with angle brackets, <>, and their categories are annotated with square brackets, []. Most terms are matched with their original forms, such as <training>; some are matched with lemmatized form, such as <marketing strategies> with <market strategy>.

There are also some problems in the identification and annotation of terms. Some quasi-terms should be annotated as business terms only when their semantic meanings match the definitions given in the dictionary. For example, the word "interest" should be identified as a term in accounting category [ACC] when it means "a return earned by a creditor" in the context. Otherwise, it should be treated as a common word. Yet, in the above composition, it is labeled as a term though it is in fact only a common word. In present study, we just annotate this kind of words as terms.

Another problem is the multiple category that a term belongs to. In this case, the category label should be annotated according to its context. For example, if the term "placement" means "Find job opportunities for graduates", it should be classified in human resources category, [HR]. And if it means "During an issue's primary market distribution, selling the related securities to investors", it should be put into finance category, [FIN]. The solution of this problem for present study is to annotate the first label.

At last, only matched original or lemmatized words are identified as terms. Some other words, such as "ABC Holdings Ltd.", in fact, is a term in the form of "holding company [LAW]" in BETB, but they are not annotated.

Ten compositions are randomly selected from the annotated corpus to manually check for the three types of annotation errors, and we find that the errors occupy only a minor proportion.

The term distribution in the corpus is presented in Table 2.

Table 2. Term distribution of Chinese college EFL business writing corpus

	ACC	ECO	FIN	HR	IB	IT	LAW	MAN	MAR	OPE	Total
Mean	1.70	0.91	0.10	8.43	0.45	0.44	0.23	1.05	4.89	1.44	19.63
SD	2.28	1.10	0.49	3.80	1.05	0.79	0.64	1.42	4.14	2.29	6.87

From this table, we can see that there are about 20 terms for every composition, which means 7.75 terms for every 100 words, with HR the most and MAR the second. This distribution comes from the writing task of an invitation letter for business school students to the work placement of a company. This is a typical human resource communication.

4   Correlational Analysis of Terms and Scores

The aim of terminological analysis is to find out the relationship between term using and writing quality. In order to accurately and reliably evaluate the writing quality of Business English compositions, the general impression mark scheme for BEC higher writing assessing is adopted as scoring criteria, and two experienced Business English teachers are involved in the scoring process. They are required to assign an integer score from 0 to 10 to every piece of writing independently. When the difference of two scores is no more than 2 points, they are considered as consistent and averaged to get the final score of the writing. Otherwise, two raters have to discuss to reach an agreement on the score. After rating, the Pearson correlations of composition scores and term numbers are calculated. Among them, only total and HR term numbers show significant correlations with writing scores, which are presented in Table 3.

Table 3. Correlations between term numbers and BE writing quality (n = 80)

	Total	HR	Length
Pearson correlations	0.42	0.51	0.57
p		0.00	0.00

For comparison, the correlation between composition lengths and scores is also calculated. Table 3 shows that both HR and total term numbers have a moderate correlation with scores while HR terms have a higher correlation coefficient. The reason is as mentioned in last section that the writing task requires HR terms and the use of this type of terms shows writers' proficiency in their textual communication. While every student writes about their companies, the company type and business are quite different, which leads to many different types of terms in different compositions.

Due to the sparse distribution of various types of terms, on one side, they do not show significant correlation with scores, and therefore, cannot be adopted in AES; on the other side, they interfere with the correlation between total term numbers and scores, which causes a lower coefficient than pure HR term numbers and scores.

This result shows that, for different business writing, there is a possibility that one or more or the total term numbers can have a relatively high correlational relationship with writing quality, which means it or they can be applied in AES process. At last, the relationship between composition length and score is tested, which is high and significant as studied by many researchers. This indicates that confident students usually write long and high quality compositions.

5 Conclusion and Limitation

Though this research shows only a moderate correlation between composition scores and HR and total term numbers, terms, especially writing content related terms, as a key point of teaching in BE writing, should be covered in the AES feature set for automatic evaluation of BE writing. From the correlational study, it is obvious that term using, as an automated scoring feature, can definitely reflect BE writers' confidence and proficiency. At the same time, the involvement of term features will give specific feedback so as to improve Chinese college EFL learners' writing accuracy, and finally improve their writing skills and communicative ability in business context.

The tentative exploration of terms in BE writing and its relationship with writing quality arrives at a positive conclusion but there is still more work to do. First, the result needs to be tested on a larger BE writing corpus of much more compositions in different genres. Then, term identification method should be further probed into to extract terms and their categories more accurately. BETB can be used in combination with large BE corpus so as to construct a context around the term as a classifier to decide if a candidate in a composition is a term or which category it belongs to. BETB should also be modified to accommodate the fuzzy identification of terms in BE writing. At last, with a more accurate extraction and a finer categorization of terms used in BE writing, what type of terms or what structure of terms can reflect writers' proficiency needs more analysis.

Acknowledgements. This work is financially supported by the National Social Science Fund (No. 13BYY097).

References

1. Attali, Y., Burstein, J.: Automated essay scoring with e-rater® V.2. J. Technol. Learn. Assess. **4**, 3–30 (2006)
2. Ellis, M., Johnson, C.: Teaching Business English. Oxford University Press, Oxford (2014)
3. Valenti, S., Neri, F., Cucchiarelli, A.: An overview of current research on automated essay grading. J. Inf. Technol. Educ. **2**, 319–330 (2003)

4. Huang, Z., Xie, J., Xun, E.: Study of feature selection in HSK automated essay scoring. Comput. Eng. Appl. **50**, 118–122 (2014)
5. Ge, S.: A Research on General Computerized Composition Scoring and Feed-Back for College English Teaching in China. Shanghai Foreign Language Education Press, Shanghai (2015)
6. Feng, L.: The Writing of Business. Jiling Publishing Group Co. Ltd., Changchun (2010)
7. Zhang, Z.: Business English students learning to write for international business: what do international business practitioners have to say about their texts? Engl. Specif. Purp. **32**, 144–156 (2013)
8. Bourigault, D., Jacquemin, C., L'Homme, M.: Introduction of Recent Advances in Computational Terminology. John Benjamins Publishing Company, Amsterdam/Philadelphia (2001)
9. Wright, S.E.: Term selection: the initial phase of terminology management. In: Wright, S.E., Budin, G. (eds.) Handbook of Terminology Management, vol. 1, Basic Aspects of Terminology Management, pp. 13–23. John Benjamins Publishing Company, Amsterdam/Philadelphia (1997)
10. Cabré, M.T.: Theories of terminology: their description, prescription and explanation. Terminology **9**, 163–199 (2003)
11. Temmerman, R.: Towards New Ways of Terminology Description: The Sociocognitive-Approach, vol. 3. John Benjamins Publishing, Philadelphia (2000)
12. Ahmad, K., Rogers, M.: Corpus-related applications. In: Wright, S.E., Budin, G (eds.) Handbook of Terminology Management, vol. 2, Application-Oriented Terminology Management, pp. 725–760. John Benjamins Publishing Company, Amsterdam/Philadelphia (2001)
13. Picht, H., Draskau, J.: Terminology: An Introduction. University of Surrey, Guildford (1985)
14. Drouin, P.: Une Methodologie d'identification automatique des syntagmes terminologiques: l'apport de la description du non-terme. META **42**, 45–54 (1997)
15. Pazienza, M.T., Pennacchiotti, M., Zanzotto, F.M.: Terminology extraction: an analysis of linguistics and statistical approaches. In: Sirmakessis, S. (ed.) Knowledge Mining: Proceedings of the NEMIS 2004 Final Conference, vol. 185, pp. 255–279. Springer, Heidelberg (2005)
16. Ananiadou, S., Sullivan, D., Black, W., Levow, G.A., Gillespie, J., Mao, C., Pyysalo, S., Kollu-ru, B., Tsujii, J., Sorbarai, B.: Systematic association of genes to phenotypes by genome and literature mining. PLoS ONE **6**, e14780 (2005)
17. Bunescu, R., Ge, R., Kate, R., Marcotte, E., Mooney, R., Ramani, A., Wong, Y.: Comparative experiments on learning information extractors for proteins and their interactions. Artif. Intell. Med. **33**, 139–155 (2005)
18. Selinker, L.: Interlanguage. Int. Rev. Appl. Linguist. **10**, 209–241 (1972)
19. Wang, J.M., Fang, X.J.: An English-Chinese Dictionary of Business Management. Foreign Language Teaching and Research Press, Beijing (2010)

Speech Verbs' Typology and Their Translation in Chinese

Nana Jin[1]([⊠]) and Zili Chen[2]

[1] School of Foreign Languages, Shenzhen University, Shenzhen, China
nanajin7@163.com
[2] School of Professional Education and Executive Development, CPCE,
The Hong Kong Polytechnic University, Hong Kong, China
spczili@speed-polyu.edu.hk

Abstract. Speech event is not a simple "saying" event, and speech verbs are likely construed and translated differently and evaluatively. This paper argues that English and Chinese have different typologies of "saying" in terms of word forms. English speech verbs are comparatively highly lexicalized (for examples: *declare, announce, scold, praise*), but Chinese speech verbs are more grammaticalized than English, i.e. they are usually formed by a certain pre- adverbial modifier plus a core root "shuo (say)". Because of the complexity of speech verb forms, a software called Words Location is designed to extract all speech verbs in a text and furthermore to group the speech verbs with their articulators, which directly and visually demonstrates their distribution and facilitates the evaluation of the accumulative evaluating effect of speech verbs and/or some hidden meaning and stance held by speakers in a text. The study offers a computer-aided way of analyzing and translating speech verbs from English to Chinese consistently and scientifically.

Keywords: Speech verbs · Typology · Translation

1 Introduction

Every sentence in a text necessarily implies some stance, for language is a powerfully committing medium to work in [1]. It is impossible to write a "statusless" clause, and therefore in this respect it is impossible to write a non-evaluative clause [2]. Speakers and writers code these evaluative signals in their texts, directly or indirectly. How much do listeners and readers decode these signals? In which ways are the evaluation and value coded in speech verbs? How speech verbs are translated in Chinese?

Researchers [3–5] have been aiming at uncovering the mysterious veil of inter-personal meaning, and studying the various forms of the veil. In discourse, many terms have been nominated to define a speaker/writer's ideology, such as connotation, affect, attitude, appraisal, evaluation and modality. As for rhetoricians, they tend to express these similar concepts in terms of "persona". Since people's ideology is multi-layered and multi-angled, the linguists have many terms concerned. Some of them are synonymous, and cover slightly different overlapping areas. These studies set up a broad platform for speech verbs study.

© Springer International Publishing AG 2017
T.-T. Wu et al. (Eds.): SETE 2016, LNCS 10108, pp. 359–369, 2017.
DOI: 10.1007/978-3-319-52836-6_38

Children's literature is chosen for the present study, which has its own general features and forces: a recognition of its proper language matter. The proper language matter of children's literature, apart from informational or didactic works, is children. Children are often "colonized" by adults, because adults speak on behalf of children instead of letting children express themselves. Children's identities are created and not "inherent", and that in the case of an identity such as "childhood" it is created by "adults" in the light of their own perceptions of themselves. The question about how evaluative attitudes are encoded, and in what forms is worth of studying.

This paper focuses on speech verbs in children's literature and evaluative attitudes expressed by speech verbs in context. This paper is specifically working on solving the inconsistency problem of English speech verbs and their Chinese translation in texts. Based on a general observation, English speech verbs have a high lexicalization level, which means the volume, the effect and the mood of saying could all be fused within the speech verbs. Translators who fail to find the matched lexicalized speech verbs in Chinese will resort to a grammaticalization strategy, listing the saying features (in what way, with what affect, and in what mood) in a grammatically right way. Thus these grammaticalized Chinese speech verbs not only share one common character "说" (pinyin: shuo), which means "say" in English, but also have all the saying features placed before the character "说" as pre-modifiers.

2 Speech Verbs and the Typology

English speech verbs have a continuum of saying verbs ranging from general saying meaning to saying in specific manner and with specific preference [6]. A large number of speech verbs, bearing meanings more than "say", provide a potential to express evaluations metaphorically. Usually, attitudes are realized by adjectives, but this is not always true. It means that the tension is resolved through the simultaneous use of overt words that are affectively neutral, and of covert words that have the affective content.

Although there are some studies about word learning tasks [7, 8], they are not tailed for the present study of speech verbs' typology. To observe speech verbs in data more scientifically, a software named Words Location is developed. It is introduced first in this paper for the convenience of discussion.

The software is shown in Fig. 1. The software can extract all instances of given words from a given corpus. This allows us to observe the typical contexts of the given words. In addition, Words Location can also set the given words or phrases in different colors and/or different sizes in the original text, which gives us a quick impression of the given words' mappings in a certain text.

The study on speech verbs and the typology takes two steps. First, apply the software Words Location to locating the given verbs in the text, and to extracting all the instances of the given verbs. Second, compare and analyze the speech verbs in the extracted instances. Figure 1 shows that Words Location is applied to searching for speech verbs claim, ask, and praise in a given text. All the instances are listed, which are not shown fully in Fig. 1 for the reason of space limit. This software can significantly help analyzing speech verbs in long texts or a big corpus.

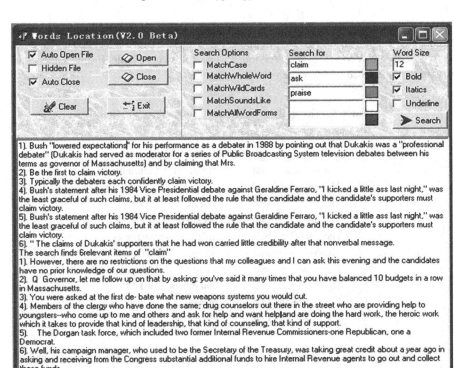

Fig. 1. The software Words Location designed for this present research

To have a pilot study of how speech verbs express attitudes, we will take the following text as an example. It is extracted from The Strange Musician (in Collection of Grimms' Fairy Tales) [9]. There are 10 speech verbs which are underlined in the extract below.

There was once a wonderful musician, who went alone through a forest and thought of all manner of things, and when nothing was left for him to think about, he <u>said</u> to himself: "Time is beginning to pass heavily with me here in the forest, I will find another companion here," and took his fiddle and played in the forest. It was not long before a fox came creeping through the trees towards him. "Ah, there's a fox coming!" <u>said</u> the musician. "I have no desire for him." The fox came up to him and <u>said</u>: "Oh, dear musician, how beautifully you play! I should like to learn that, too." "That is soon learnt," <u>said</u> the musician. "You have only to do everything that I <u>bid</u> you." "Oh, musician," then <u>said</u> the fox, "I will obey you as a scholar obeys his master." "Follow me," <u>said</u> the musician, and when they had walked apart of the way, they came to a footpath, with high bushes on both sides of it. There the musician stood still, and from one side bent a young bush down to the ground, and put his foot on the end of it. Then he bent down a young tree from the other side as well, and <u>said</u>: "Now, little fox, if you will learn something, give me your left front paw." The fox obeyed, and the musician fastened his paw to the left bush. "Little fox," <u>said</u> he, "now reach me your right paw," and he tied it to the right bough. When he had examined whether the knots were firm enough, he let go, and the bushes sprang up again, and jerked up the little fox, so that it hung struggling in the air. "Wait there till I come back again," <u>said</u> the musician, and went his way.

We replaced no other word in the extract but the ten speech verbs and produced another two versions of the extract. Suppose the original extract is Version 1, the other two versions are Version 2 and Version 3. The following Table 1 shows the comparison of the speech verbs among the three versions.

Table 1. The total 30 speech verbs in the three versions

No.	Speaker	Speech verbs		
		Version 1	Version 2	Version 3
1	The musician	said	promised	murmured
2	The musician	said	cried	cried
3	The fox	said	praised	shouted
4	The musician	said	declared	answered
5	The musician	bid	order	suggest
6	The fox	said	begged	claimed
7	The musician	said	shouted	suggested
8	The musician	said	commanded	asked
9	The musician	said	ordered	asked
10	The musician	said	cried	cried

The three versions are the same except for the speech verbs. They were all sent to 30 college students of English majors at Guizhou University for Nationalities, and the students were required to answer the following questions.

1. *Which version do you like most?*
A. *Version 1* B. *Version 2* C. *Version 3* D. *None of them*
2. *Why do you like the version?*
A. *It's plain.* B. *It's vivid.* C. *It sounds natural.*
D. *I like the version because* —————————————————.
3. *Which version would you recommend to children?*
A. *Version 1* B. *Version 2* C. *Version 3* D. *None of them*
4. *If you were the musician in the story, which version you like most?*
A. *Version 1* B. *Version 2* C. *Version 3* D. *None of them*
5. *If you were the fox in the story, which version you like most?*
A. *Version 1* B. *Version 2* C. *Version 3* D. *None of them*

Much more details of the experiment are in [10]. With the analyses of all the answers they gave, there are some significant findings: a. Speech verbs have strong evaluation potential; b. Speech verbs analysis helps reading comprehension; c. The ability of analyzing speech verbs can be transferred in analyzing other verbs or other classes of words, and it helps writing.

3 Speech Verbs' Translation and Cognition

It's important to demonstrate that speech verbs have strong evaluative potential. But the next issues to be explored are whether speech verbs in different languages work the same, and whether the translation of speech verbs also expresses the evaluative meaning. Little Tiny [11] is a worldly famous fairy tale by Anderson, and was translated in many languages. The following Table 2 shows the number of consistent translation and inconsistent translation from English version to Chinese version on each page.

Table 2. Comparison of the speech verbs and their translation in *Little Tiny*

	Consistent translation		Inconsistent translation
English version → Chinese translation	said → 说、道、讲 (Pinyin: shuo, dao, jiang)	said → 说 道 (Pinyin: shuo dao)	exclaimed → 说 (Pinyin: shuo); said → 想到 (Pinyin: xiangdao)
Page 1	5	0	0
Page 2	3	0	0
Page 3	3	0	0
Page 4	1	2	0
Page 5	1	2	1
Page 6	2	1	1
Page 7	2	0	0
Page 8	2	1	0
Page 9	2	0	2
Page 10	1	2	0
Total	22	8	4
Percentage	64%	24%	12%

Generally speaking, most speech verbs in both the English and Chinese versions are "say" and its other forms, with a high percentage of 88% (64% + 24%). They are labeled consistent translation in the table. But there are about 4 pairs of speech verbs whose Chinese translations are inconsistent with the English speech verbs. The 4 inconsistent pairs are as follows:

Page 5 exclaimed → 说 (Pinyin: shuo; Meaning: said)
Page 6 said → 想到 (Pinyin: xiangdao; Meaning: thought about)
Page 9 replied → 说道 (Pinyin: shuodao; Meaning:said)
Page 9 cried → 说 (Pinyin: shuo; Meaning:said)

With the analyses of the 4 inconsistent translations, an important fact is found out, that is, the inconsistency refers that the Chinese translation is generalized or twisted:

Page 5 exclaimed → 说 *(Pinyin: shuo; meaning: said)* shows the meaning is generalized.

Page 6 said → 想到 *(Pinyin: xiangdao; meaning: thought about)* shows the meaning is twisted.

Page 9 replied → 说道 *(Pinyin: shuodao; meaning: said)* shows the meaning is generalized.

Page 9 cried → 说 *(Pinyin: shuo; meaning: said)* shows the meaning is generalized.

Here are the findings from analyzing the speech verbs in English version of Little Tiny and their Chinese translation.

i. Children's literature is not satisfying in terms of choosing speech verbs. (e.g. "say" accounts for 88% in Little tiny)

ii. Translators don't pay enough attention to the meaning of speech verbs. Usually they do an easy job, because most of the speech verbs are forms of "say". But for those "non-say" speech verbs, they generalize the meaning or even twist the meaning. (in Little tiny, there is only one of the five "non-say" speech verb translated well among the total 34 speech verbs, i.e. whispered 悄悄地说, Pinyin: qiaoqiaode shuo, Meaning: speak with a low voice).

iii. English and Chinese have different categorizations of "saying" in terms of word forms. English speech verbs are different words forms, but Chinese speech verbs are usually formed by a common word and some other pre-modifiers, sharing a core root "shuo (say)". For example:

say → 说 *(Pinyin: shuo; Meaning: say, speak)*
shout → 大声说 *(Pinyin: dasheng shuo; Meaning: say loudly)*
stumble → 结结巴巴地说 *(Pinyin: jiejie baba de shuo; Meaning: say with pauses)*
whisper → 小声地说(Pinyin: xiaosheng de shuo; Meaning: say in a low voice)*

It is because of the root "-shuo" in Chinese speech verbs, children can establish their categorization of the experience of saying with a very clear clue. And this clue demands to be an important parameter to evaluate whether a story is written or translated well.

4 A Model of Speech Verbs' Translation in Chinese

Some children's books are sensitive to choosing speech verbs in translating. The Little Cat Rose (Chinese version) [12] is an interesting story which has dialogues and many speech verbs. The speech verbs are vivid and various. The following table lists all the speech verbs in its Chinese form, Pinyin and literal English translation.

Table 3 shows that almost all the Chinese speech verbs share the root "说" (Pinyin: shuo), which means "say" in English. In Chinese, saying in what way, with what affect and in what mood can all be placed before the character "说" (Pinyin: shuo) as pre-modifiers. That is to say, the meanings of Chinese speech verbs are conspicuous and their grammaticalization level is very low. This is quite different from English speech verbs which have a high grammaticalization level, for example declare, announce, scold, praise. It is obvious that speech verbs with low grammaticalization level have stronger relation with the features of saying than those high grammaticalized speech verbs. And thus these low grammaticalized speech verbs have stronger cognitive effects and are easier to be construed by children. Table 3 also shows the literal English translation of the low grammaticalized speech verbs and makes a good example for English speech verbs in children's literature.

Table 3. A list of all of the speech verbs in *The Little Cat Rose*

Speech verbs		
Chinese form	Pinyin	Literal translation
欢天喜地地说	huantian xidi de shuo	said happily
说	shuo	said
结结巴巴地说	jiejie baba de shuo	stumbled
悲伤地说	beishang de shuo	said sadly
交头接耳地说	jiaotou jie'er de shuo	talked to each other
说	shuo	said
说	shuo	said
急切地说	jiqie de shuo	said worriedly
很坚持，说	hen jianchi, shuo	insisted, (and) said
说	shuo	said
说	shuo	said
说	shuo	said
兴奋地说	xingfen de shuo	said excitedly
生气地说	shengqi de shuo	said angrily
问	wen	asked
惊喜地说	jingxi de shuo	said happily surprised
说	shuo	said

In the process of analyzing the speech verbs and their cognitive effect, articulators of the speech verbs will definitely be included. Table 4 adds the articulators of the speech verbs and thus easily shows the speech verbs with their characters in the story.

In Table 4, speech verbs are grouped into several articulators, and it's helpful to analyze the character based on his group of speech verbs. For example, there are 6 speech verbs in Mr. Guan's group, and their literal English translations are said happily, stumbled, said sadly, said angrily, said happily surprised. This group of speech verbs shows that Mr. Guan's saying action changes through a process of happiness, sadness and a final happiness. It's easy to predict that Mr. Guan was so happy at first (said happily), and soon he became very sad (said sadly), and he was at lost (stumbled), and he was angry (said angrily), but finally he was happy again (said happily surprised). Though we haven't read the story, we already know the character Mr. Guan and his stance in the story. With the aid of the plot, we finally know Mr. Guan said happily because his wife

Table 4. Speech verbs and their articulators in *The Little Cat Rose*

Articulators	Speech verb (Chinese)	Speech verb (Pinyin)	Speech verb (English translation)
Mr. Guan	欢天喜地地说	huantian xidi de shuo	said happily
Mrs. Guan	说	shuo	said
Mr. Guan	结结巴巴地说	jiejie baba de shuo	stumbled
Mr. Guan	悲伤地说	beishang de shuo	said sadly
Neighbor cats	交头接耳地说	jiaotou jie'er de shuo	talked to each other
Mrs. Guan	说	shuo	said
Rose	说	shuo	said
Mrs. Guan	急切地说	jiqie de shuo	said worriedly
Rose	很坚持，说	hen jianchi, shuo	insisted, (and) said
Rose's uncle	说	shuo	said
Mrs. Guan	说	shuo	said
Mr. Guan	说	shuo	said
Mrs. Guan	兴奋地说	xingfen de shuo	said excitedly
Mr. Guan	生气地说	shengqi de shuo	said angrily
Rose	问	wen	asked
Mr. Guan	惊喜地说	jingxi de shuo	said happily surprised
Rose	说	shuo	said

gave birth to several new baby kittens; and he said sadly when he knew there was one baby who was not black as the rest of the family but red, he was very sad; then Mr. Guan stumbled because he has never come across such a case, he didn't know what to do; when the red kitten Rose left home and lived her own life, Mr. Guan found his release, on the other hand, he couldn't be happy, the little kitten is his daughter after all, and thus he was neither happy nor sad, and there is no modifier to the speech verb said; Mr. Guan said angrily because he had always thought the red cat was a shame to his family and when he saw Rose singing and dancing on TV, he couldn't control himself and was very angry, finally Mr. Guan said happily surprised because Rose finally came back home visiting them with her four little children, among which there was a very black kitten. Suppose all the vivid speech verbs are replaced by only one speech verb "say", the story will lose its clear and vivid feature which can never be construed by children themselves through reading, for example they couldn't know whether Mr. Guan would be happy or sad about the coming of the little red kitten based on the content of his saying "My god, I have a red baby kitten." With the same clue, we can easily know what characters Mrs. Guan has and Rose has. If the turns of saying and the saying situations are included in the speech verbs anlyzing, more information is accessed.

Table 5 shows the speech verbs in dialogue turns and dialogue situations. Focusing on speech verbs only, we get to know the characters deeper than Table 4. For example, the speech verbs in the second column belonging to Mrs. Guan are "said, said, said worriedly, said, said excitedly", which indicate Mrs. Guan is calm almost in various situations, because three fifths of the speech verbs for her are "said", which does not

Table 5. Illustration of the speech verbs with articulators in dialogue turns in *The Little Cat Rose*

Articulators dialogues	Mr. Guan	Mrs. Guan	Rose	Neighbor cats	Rose's uncle
Dialogue 1	(1) said happily	(2) said	Φ	–	–
Dialogue 2	stumbled	Φ	Φ	–	–
Dialogue 3	said sadly	Φ	Φ	–	–
Dialogue 4	Φ	Φ	Φ	talked to each other	–
Dialogue 5	–	(1) said (3) said worriedly	(2) said (4) insisted, said	–	–
Dialogue 6	(3) said	(2) said	–	–	(1) said
Dialogue 7	(2) said angrily	(1) said excitedly	–	–	–
Dialogue 8	(2) said happily surprised	Φ	(1) asked (3) said	–	–

Note: "–" means "not present in the dialogue"; "Φ" means "present in the dialogue but said nothing"; (1), (2), (3)" refer to the order of saying in a dialogue.

carry any more meaning than she is cool. Furthermore, this table has the advantage of offering more information about the characters of the articulators. Take Mrs. Guan as an example, she appears in the total eight dialogues, but she only articulates in four of them (Dialogue 1, Dialogue 5, Dialogue 6, Dialogue 7). In the rest of the dialogues (Dialogue 2, Dialogue 3, Dialogue 4, Dialogue 8), she didn't say anything no matter his husband was nervous or happy, which also indicates that she is cool and unhurried. In Dialogue 1, when Mr. Guan said happily "Today is one of my happiest days" for their kids were born that day, Mrs. Guan said "I don't think so. There is one more kid behind you". Compared with Mr. Guan, Mrs. Guan is the same as usual in such a situation. When Mr. Guan noticed the red hair kid, Mr. stumbled "How could this be possible?" in Dialogue 2, and said sadly "My God, we have a red hair kid. It's a shame. What will people talk about this?" in Dialogue 3, while Mrs. Guan behaved cool and didn't say anything. In Dialogue 4, when their neighbors talked behind them, both Mr. Guan and Mrs. Guan kept quiet. In Dialogue 5, when Mrs. Guan knew that the red hair kid Rose's abnormal behaviors and making friends with a dog, which can never be allowed in such a noble cat family, she controlled herself well and said: "You made your family ashamed! How dare you make friends with a dog?" After Rose said "Mum, let me go. I want my own life.", Mrs. Guan said worriedly "But Mum loves you, stay at home for good!". This is for the first time that Mrs. Guan got nervous when she knew her unpopular child Rose would like to leave home. This indicates that Mrs. Guan cares her children at heart, especially when Rose said to leave, which also reflects that Mrs. Guan doesn't care there is a red hair one among the new babies, doesn't care that Mr. Guan is so nervous about the unusual case, doesn't care about what neighbors will talk about Rose. In Dialogue 6, Rose left home already, once Rose's uncle brought back some news about Rose, both Mrs. Guan and Mr. Guan took the message calmly and said "it's the old dog who misled Rose", "I had said that Rose were not like us". In Dialogue 7, Mr. Guan and Mrs. Guan happened to watch Rose singing on TV, they acted differently. Mrs. Guan said excitedly "Isn't that our daughter?", but Mr. Guan said angrily "My hair will turn white again". In the light of the speech verbs, it's easy to know that Mrs. Guan and Mr. Guan hold different opinions toward Rose's performance on TV. Finally in Dialogue 8, when Rose took her red hair kids and a black one back to home, Mr. Guan said happily surprised "He is as black as us!". Mrs. Guan was there too. Though she didn't say anything, it's obvious to know that all she cares is that the family is reunited. Based on the speech, it's obvious to get to the conclusion: Mr. Guan gets angry and happy easily and he likes to express his feelings with no concern, while Mrs. Guan is calm in various situations and she cares about the whole family.

5   Conclusion

All in all, speech verb is a form of evaluative resources and it is definitely not a major form. However, speech verbs also help create evaluative functions in a text: (a) expressing a speaker/writer's attitudes, and in doing so to reflect the value system of that person and their community, (b) constructing and maintaining relations between the speaker/writer and the listener/reader, and (c) organizing the discourse.

For language learning, this research provides a critical learning method by analyzing different constructions of speech verbs in English and in Chinese. Language learners may use the software Words Location to locate and extract all speech verbs in the source text to have a clear view of the distribution of speech verbs in text. By grouping all the speech verbs with their articulators, language learners can easily see the differences of one articulator's speech verbs pool from another's, which can also be automatically illustrated. This layer of understanding is above conceptual meaning, and it is called interpersonal meaning in Systemic Functional Linguistics, or illocutionary meaning in pragmatics, and the meaning between the lines, etc. As this layer of understanding is a core meaning which dominates the stance of a text, computer-aided exploration of it may facilitate its learning by machines in future study.

References

1. Fowler, R.: Linguistics and the Novel, p. 76. Methuen, London/New York (1977)
2. Hunston, S.: Evaluation and ideology in scientific writing. In: Ghadessy, M. (ed.) Register Analysis: Theory and Practice, pp. 57–73. Pinter Publishers, London and New York (1993)
3. Stubbs, M.: Text and Corpus Analysis: Computer-Assisted Studies of Language and Culture. Blackwell, Oxford (1996)
4. Martin, J.R.: Beyond exchange: appraisal systems in English. In: Hunston, S., Thompson, G. (eds.) Evaluation in Text: Authorial Stance and the Construction of Discourse, pp. 142–175. Oxford University Press, Oxford (2000)
5. Halliday, M.A.K.: An Introduction to Functional Grammar, 3rd edn. Arnold, London (2004)
6. Thompson, G.: Reporting, pp. 44–52. Foreign Languages Press, Beijing (2000)

7. Xie, H., et al.: Generating incidental word-learning tasks via topic-based and load-based profiles. IEEE Multimedia **23**(1), 60–70 (2016)
8. Zou, D., Xie, H., Li, Q., Wang, F.L., Chen, W.: The load-based learner profile for incidental word learning task generation. In: Popescu, E., Lau, Rynson, W.,H., Pata, K., Leung, H., Laanpere, M. (eds.) ICWL 2014. LNCS, vol. 8613, pp. 190–200. Springer, Heidelberg (2014). doi:10.1007/978-3-319-09635-3_21
9. 13 July 2016. http://www.pitt.edu/~dash/grimm008.html. Accessed
10. Jin, N., Chen, Z.: A study of verb recognitive modes and reading comprehension of college students. J. Guizhou Univ. Ethnic Minorities (Philos. Soc. Sci.) **6**, 171–176 (2007)
11. 13 July 2016. http://ivyjoy.com/fables/thumbelina.html. Accessed
12. 13 July 2016. http://www.abc-school.com.tw/kids/h/story1/0225.htm Accessed

An Empirical Study of Corpora Application in Data-Driven English Lexical Learning

Xiaowen Wang[1] and Tianyong Hao[2(✉)]

[1] School of English and Education,
Guangdong University of Foreign Studies, Guangzhou, China
55736436@qq.com
[2] School of Informatics, Guangdong University of Foreign Studies,
Guangzhou, China
haoty@126.com

Abstract. Though there have been revolutions applying corpora in L2 teaching, empirical studies on the integrated use of corpora in English lexical learning are very limited. The paper takes an empirical study on a DDL approach applying corpora concordance to enhance lexical learning in the teaching of a college English course in mainland China. The corpora resources include a self-built English movie script corpus, a list of publicly available online corpora resources and the WebCorp. After asking students to post their DDL learning results of idiomatic words or expressions in English movies using the three kinds of resources on the course blog for a semester, observation of students' blog posts shows that their use of corpora has achieved promising learning effects for decoding and/or encoding purposes. Questionnaire and interview surveys also indicate that students have not only recognized the advantages and limitations of each corpus, but also found suitable ways to use each kind of resources accordingly in their lexical learning. We conclude that the DDL approach of English lexical learning proposed by this study could be practical and acceptable if carefully planned and conducted.

Keywords: Corpora · Data-driven learning · Lexical learning · Empirical study

1 Introduction

Ever since Johns (1988, 1991) proposed the Data-driven learning (DDL) approach - an advanced learning model based on direct application of corpus and concordancing, there have been increasing studies on how to use corpora in L2 teaching and learning (Flowerdew 1996, 2012; Cheng et al. 2003; O'Sullivan and Chambers 2006; Lee and Swales 2006; Gilmore 2009; Charles 2014). As corpora offer language learners great amount of vivid real-life discourse in the target language (Yoon and Hirvela 2004), the use of corpora has been advocated as one of the significant areas in language pedagogy revolution (Wang et al. 2013). It has been applied directly in writing, grammar and vocabulary teaching in undergraduate and postgraduate education (Römer 2011), but empirical studies on the integrated use of corpora in English lexical learning are very limited.

© Springer International Publishing AG 2017
T.-T. Wu et al. (Eds.): SETE 2016, LNCS 10108, pp. 370–381, 2017.
DOI: 10.1007/978-3-319-52836-6_39

Aiming at addressing the three research questions: (1) How do students use the corpora in the lexical learning assignments? (2) Which kind of corpus do students tend to choose in doing their DDL assignments? (3) How do students perceive the use of corpora in lexical learning?, the present paper describes an empirical data-driven teaching reform in an English course - "Learning English through Movies". The course (hereafter referred as "Movie English" for short) is offered to non-English major sophomore students in a university in mainland China. Its teaching aim is to cultivate the students' comprehensive English skills, especially listening, speaking abilities and cultural awareness through watching movie clips and doing related exercises and activities. This class is featured of students' exposure to rich context of authentic English language resources in movies (Wang et al. 2013), and teachers believe it important for students to explore and summarize the rules and patterns of English words and expressions in movies.

To achieve this goal, dictionaries are relied on for consultation traditionally, but the support provided by this traditional way is far from enough (Frankenberg-Garcia 2012; Lai and Chen 2015). DDL, the "corpus approach to language learning based on the assumption that the use of authentic language together with a concordancer will enable learners to gain insights into the language used in real-life situations" (Li 2015), could just serve the purpose to compensate dictionaries in helping teachers and students to make the largest use of such authentic language in movies in their English learning. Equipped with corpora, students can be provided with instances of word usage in the authentic context, so that they can discover the meaning and recurrent patterns of words and can make comparisons of word usage in different contexts. In empirical teaching experiments of the data-driven teaching, we find it practical to guide the students using several kinds of corpora to achieve the most efficient way of learning in Movie English. Therefore, we carry out qualitative and quantitative studies on students' learning behaviors and responses in the use of corpora to enhance the lexical learning of idiomatic language expressions in the Movie English class.

2 Literature Review

Johns (1988, 1991) is the pioneer for direct application of the corpus, carrying out studies in vocabulary and grammar courses at the University of Birmingham (UK) in the 1980s. After him, many scholars have followed this approach, applying the corpus in various classroom teaching at undergraduate or postgraduate education level, in writing class (O'Sullivan and Chambers 2006; Cresswell 2007; Gilmore 2009), grammar class (Vannestål and Lindquist 2007), ESP class (Lee and Swales 2006; Flowerdew 2012; Charles 2014) and in vocabulary teaching of intensive English class (Cobb 1997), but empirical studies on the integrated use of corpora in English lexical learning are still very limited, and few has focused on corpus application in the lexical teaching of English through movies.

Although there have been great number of publications on how a corpus could be applied in language teaching and learning (Bernardini 2000; Sun 2003; Sun and Wang 2003; Aston, Bernardini and Stewart 2004; Sinclair 2004; Chambers 2005; Braun et al. 2006; Lee and Swales 2006; Hidalgo et al. 2007; Vannestal and Lindquist 2007;

Boulton 2009; Gilmore 2009; Varley 2009; Kennedy and Miceli 2010), "most of them have traditionally focused on learners' opinions and learning outcomes, failing to give an account of students' interaction with the resources" (Pérez-Paredes et al. 2011). Researchers (Hafner and Candlin 2007; Pérez-Paredes et al. 2011) emphasize the importance of providing direct evidence of students' self-directed use of corpus tools, but publications on how learners consult corpus resources, exact queries, search results or even discoveries are still very few in number, no matter asking students to record their activity manually (Chambers and O'Sullivan 2004; Frankenberg-Garcia 2005; Ma 1994; O'Sullivan and Chambers 2006; Varley 2009, cited in Pérez-Paredes et al. 2011), or generating log files automatically by a computer program (Chan and Liou 2005; Cobb 1997; Gaskell and Cobb 2004; Hafner and Candlin 2007; Johns 1997; Yoon 2008; Pérez-Paredes et al. 2011). Yet we find that in those studies, concordance records are mostly kept by the researchers, but students themselves have seldom been reported to share each other's concordance records. In view of this, our study takes a different way to observe students' interaction with the resources, i.e., asking students to post their search results and learning reflections directly on the course blog, which will be openly shared among all the students in the Movie English class taught by the teacher. In this way, not only the teacher researcher, but also the students could benefit from the concordancing records greatly.

3   The Design of the Empirical Study

3.1   Research Design

The present study made both qualitative and quantitative analysis of multiple data resources, including students' blog posts, questionnaire surveys and interviews. It was carried out in the Movie English course delivered to two classes in the computer lab 80 min per week for 18 weeks. 76 Chinese language majors enrolled in the movie English course were invited for this study. Before class, students were registered into the course website on Blackboard system in terms of class group by the teacher. In the first week, the teacher made a course introduction to students, including the course website. The students were instructed how to read notices and posts, how to use blogs, and how to download teaching materials from the website, which paved the way for latter DDL assignments on this website. The notion of DDL was briefly mentioned in the introduction to arouse students' interests. Then after finishing the regular content of Unit 1, the teacher gave a special training of the three kinds of corpus resources for 80 min in Week 4. With the help of a worksheet, the teacher explained the ideas of corpus, concordance, and DDL, showed how to use the three kinds of corpora with examples of lexis from Unit 1, and then asked students to work in groups to finish exercises on the worksheet on their computers.

After the training session, students realized the purpose for using corpora in this course. The teacher created course blogs per unit on the course website, and set the blog section as the designated entrance page. Whenever students opened the website, they could easily target on the unit they needed to work on in the blog section, and their posts on the blog were shared by all registered students as well as the teacher. In Week

5–18, the students were asked to post per unit in this blog section their DDL learning results for at least five idiomatic words or expressions from every key movie they watched (except the last unit due to limit of time). A sample for the assignment was given, containing three parts: way of search, search results, analysis and findings. Students were asked to follow its format, i.e., to firstly state the corpus resource they chose, then post a screenshot of their search results, and sort out from the search results the main meaning/usages of the target lexis. Finally, in the analysis and finding part, they should summarize the meaning and/or usages of the lexis. At the end of semester, a total of 528 blog posts were collected. Course blogs for Unit 1 and Unit 9 were selected as samples for in-depth comparative analysis.

Moreover, the questionnaire survey and semi-structured interviews were conducted to the participants in Week 18. The questionnaire was developed based on Yoon and Hirvela (2004)'s Questionnaire about using the Collins COBUILD Corpus in ESL writing with adaptations to serve specific purposes of the present research. Its reliability examined by means of Cronbach's Alpha with SPSS is .944, showing a high level of reliability. Finally, 10 interviews and 69 valid questionnaires were analyzed to answer the research questions. 7 questionnaires were counted as invalid because of incomplete answer or casual repeated answer. Being sophomores, all students have passed CET-4, an English level test for college students which requires a master of about 4500 English vocabulary, before they started to take this class.

3.2 Corpus Resources

There are three kinds of corpus resources introduced to the students, the first being a self-built corpus specific for the course, the latter two being online resources. They were chosen mostly because they are not only available to the students for free, but also relatively convenient to use.

(1) English Movie Script Corpus (M)

A corpus of movie scripts built by the teacher researcher was introduced to the students. The data were collected from scripts of 21 movies or sitcoms involved in the textbooks of the Movie English course. There were altogether 303770 word tokens (18900 word types) in the basic corpus provided to the students on Blackboard class website. The recommended analytical tool of the corpus was AntConc (Anthony 2008). Basic functions of AntConc, including word search, frequency information and keyword in context were introduced to students at the beginning of the semester.

(2) Seven English corpora on http://corpus.byu.edu/ (B)

Seven corpora offered for free by Mark Davies at Brigham Young University on http://corpus.byu.edu/ were also recommended to students – GloWbE (Mark Davies), COCA (Mark Davies), COHA (Mark Davies), Times Magazine Corpus (Mark Davies), BYU-BNC (Oxford University Press), the Strathy Corpus of Canadian English (Queen's University). (The other latest corpora such as Wikipedia Corpus were not available at the time of the teaching experiment). With very similar interfaces, those large-size free resources are relatively easy to use.

(3) **WebCorp (W)**

WebCorp is a suite of tools which allows access to the World Wide Web as a corpus on http://www.webcorp.org.uk/. The concordance lines are all displayed on a single results page, with links to the websites where they came. Created, operated and maintained by the Research and Development Unit for English Studies (RDUES) in the School of English at Birmingham City University, it can be used on the internet by anyone for free. As indicated in its online guide, it is especially useful for learning language expressions that are too new or too rare to appear in the standard corpora or dictionaries, so we introduced this website to the students as a complement to the above two kinds of resources.

4 Results and Discussion

Results are presented with regard to each research question. Due to limited space, only questionnaire items directly relevant to the above research questions and interview quotes that reflect commonly expressed ideas are discussed.

(1) **How do students use the corpora in the lexical learning assignments?**

To understand how students carried out the use of corpora, a careful examination of their blog posts was conducted. At the end of semester, 59 posts per unit at average were created by the students, indicating that the majority of students completed the assignments as the teacher required. The students' DDL learning results using M, B and W are presented. An example selected from the blog posts is shown as follows.

This is a student's DDL learning post using English Movie Script Corpus (M). The students were asked to search for "*ought*" in M with Antconc. The result, as shown in Fig. 1, was further sorted out as (1) "*We ought to keep an eye on him.*" and (2) "*Indiana Jones – and the other, who seriously ought to have known better*". They further analyze the results as (1) "*You use ought to when saying that you think it is a good idea and important for you or someone else to do a particular thing, especially when giving or asking for advice or opinions*" and (2) "*You use ought to have with a past participle to indicate that something was expected to happen or be the case, but it did not happen or was not the case.*"

In the example, the student made use of M, and completed the task in the format required by the teacher. Concordance results of the word "*ought*" were sorted out and classified into two types. It seemed that he was familiar with the word "*ought*", but was a little vague on the grammatical rules when using this word, so he explained the two main usages he figured out from the concordance results one by one after confirming its meaning and usages in the dictionary. The combined use of the dictionary with M fostered students' learning of English expressions from authentic movies, serving for both decoding and encoding purposes in Humblé (2001) terms.

However, when using B and W, in most cases the students did not sort out the concordance results as what they did while using M. Nevertheless, they could still offer analyses and findings of the meaning or usage of the target word or expression. For example, when using B to learn the word "*scramble*", the student listed point by point

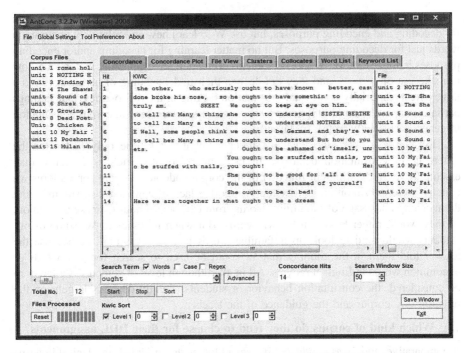

Fig. 1. The screenshot for the concordance results of "*ought*" in English Movie Script Corpus

what he had learnt from the concordance results in corpus COCA and explained as:
(1) "*They tried to scramble up the cliff*", (2) "*scramble to do sth.: to try to do sth.
difficult very quickly. e.g., The liberals had to scramble to get ready to run for elec-
tion.*" and (3) "*The senior officer called for a scramble*". The student had not figured
out all the meaning of "*scramble*" in the context, but could still gain much knowledge
of this word, like the most commonly adopted meaning and the typical collocation of
the word - "*scramble to do sth*". Clearly, the student could make successful learning of
the target lexis for not only decoding but also encoding purposes by using B.

As for the use of W, students seemed to focus on the unfamiliar word(s) for
understanding the meaning. For example, the key word "*tripe*" is not a commonly used
word, ranking 40112 in terms of word frequency in the BNC wordlist. This uncommon
word hardly had more than one hit in M. In fact, the student just copied the explanation
of the word "*tripe*" in English from an online dictionary. In the concordance lines from
W, only examples of "*tripe*" bearing the first meaning in his explanation as a kind of
food were shown. Just as we observed from many other blog posts, students seldom
sorted out the results when they adopted W. In the follow-up interview, they explained
that results in WebCorp were always complicated and the sentences were often repeated, it was hard to sort out learning results from the concordance lines. It seemed that
students used W mostly for decoding purposes, and they did get many authentic
sentences in real context from W to help them understand at least part of the meaning
defined in the dictionary for the target word.

All in all, we discovered that students tended to use M and B to learn known words for decoding and encoding purposes, but use W to learn new and relatively uncommon words just for decoding purposes. But no matter learning for decoding and/or encoding purposes in the use of M, B, and W, students seemed to have generally understood how to make use of corpora, and they did deepen their understanding of target words to a large extent, especially contextual information lacking in the dictionaries. Our findings partially support Yoon (2008) in students' favor of known words in corpus consultation in general, especially in use of M and B.

However, we deem the level of students might not be the only factor for the difference of consultation behavior. In fact, the reason for such a difference may essentially lie in the different function of the corpora adopted. As the corpus tools we adopted were only monolingual, students reported lack of confidence in summarizing the meaning and usage of unfamiliar words from corpora without Chinese translation, so they would rather target on known words. But when it comes to W, some of our students would tend to look up unfamiliar words instead. This may be because the teacher told them in the training that W could be used to search for new words or uncommon words in English movies. All in all, although level of students is a factor to be considered, the consultation behavior of students actually depends largely on the function of a corpus and the guidance of the teacher.

(2) Which kind of corpus do they tend to choose for their DDL assignments?

A comparative study was conducted between blog posts for Unit 1 and Unit 9 in terms of corpus use. As shown in Fig. 2, in both units, M was used most frequently (more than 90 times), B came the second (more than 40 times), and W the last (only 14 times in Unit 1 and 28 times in Unit 9). The interview results could explain why students got to use B more frequently as the time went. A student said: *"When I began to try a corpus on* corpus.byu.edu *such as COCA, I felt it very complicated, so I was reluctant to use that. Movie English Script Corpus seemed easier to operate. However, when I got more and more familiar with the online corpora on that BYU website, I realized that they were very powerful and got to use that more often."*

To deeper understand this, the questionnaire survey also investigated the students' commonly used corpus resource(s) to solve problems in general English learning, 78.26% of the subjects chose M, 72.46% chose B, and only 36.23% chose W, as shown in Table 1. Different from the results of using corpus resources in doing the assignments mentioned above, B was viewed as a much more commonly used resource: the percentage of people in favor of B was just 5.8% smaller than M. Students claimed that M was more suitable to be used in doing assignments in Movie English in comparison to other kinds of English learning, because it was especially designed for this course, and sometimes the number of concordance results turned out to be a little insufficient. B, however, was rather practical in English study in general, including both oral and written English.

(3) How do students perceive the use of corpora in lexical learning?

Table 2 illustrates students' attitudes towards using corpora for lexical learning. For our approach to summarize lexis meaning and usages with combined use of corpora, students' responses were surveyed in the questionnaire. The great majority of respondents

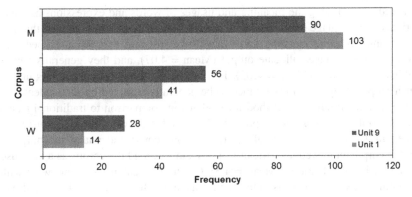

Fig. 2. Frequency of corpus use in blog posts for Unit 1 and Unit 9

Table 1. The statistics of commonly used corpus resources by students

Options	Num.	%	
Movie English Script Corpus	54		78.26%
WebCorp	25		36.23%
corpus.byu.edu	50		72.46%
Total students	**69**		

Table 2. Students' responses to the use of corpora to summarize lexis meaning and usages in Movie English course

Option\Item	Summarizing the meaning and usages of words and expressions is a useful experience for language learning		It is easy to summarize the meaning and usages of words and expressions based on the analysis of concordance/collocate output		I feel confident in summarizing the meaning and usages of words and expressions based on the analysis of concordance/collocate output	
1	0	0%	1	1.45%	1	1.45%
2	0	0%	3	4.35%	3	4.35%
3	3	4.35%	12	17.39%	12	17.39%
4	15	21.74%	28	40.58%	28	40.58%
5	32	46.38%	20	28.99%	20	28.99%
6	19	27.54%	3	4.35%	2	2.90%
N/A	0	0%	2	2.90%	3	4.35%
SD	0.82		0.99		0.97	
Mean	4.97		4.07		4.05	

(Option: 1 = strongly disagree; 2 = disagree; 3 = generally disagree; 4 = generally agree; 5 = agree; 6 = strongly agree; N/A = not sure.)

considered summarizing the meaning and usages of words and expressions as a useful experience for language learning (Mean = 4.97). Students generally agreed that it was easy to summarize the meaning and usages of words and expressions based on the analysis of concordance/collocate output (Mean = 4.07), and they generally felt confident in doing this task (Mean = 4.05). The DDL approach of lexical learning in Movie English proposed by this study seemed to be generally accepted by the students.

DDL is a relatively new method for students in comparison to traditional teaching approach, so it is necessary to be prudent about students' evaluation of corpus use. As revealed in Table 3, over 80% of the respondents could understand the purpose of using the corpus in this course (Mean = 4.24) and regarded the corpus as a very useful resource for English learning (Mean = 4.3). Generally speaking, students were willing to recommend using the corpus in the same course in future (Mean = 4.12), and would like to recommend the corpus to other students (Mean = 4.12). These results seemed to

Table 3. Students' overall evaluations of corpus use

Item\Option	1	2	3	4	5	6	N/A	SD	Mean
I understand the purpose of using the corpus in this course	0 0%	1 1.45%	8 11.59%	35 50.72%	22 31.88%	2 2.9%	1 1.45%	0.755	4.24
Overall, the corpus is a very useful resource for my English learning	1 1.45%	1 1.45%	7 10.14%	36 52.17%	15 21.74%	9 13.04%	0 0%	0.975	4.3
I use the corpus for other English courses too	3 4.35%	6 8.7%	21 30.43%	25 36.23%	12 17.39%	0 0%	2 2.9%	1.034	3.55
As I have learned more about the corpus, I have come to like them more	4 5.8%	3 4.35%	16 23.19%	32 46.38%	11 15.94%	2 2.9%	1 1.45%	1.077	3.72
I will use the corpus for my English learning in the future	4 5.8%	2 2.9%	9 13.04%	38 55.07%	11 15.94%	3 4.35%	2 2.9%	1.066	3.88
I recommend using the corpus in the same course in future	2 2.9%	2 2.9%	6 8.7%	38 55.07%	14 20.29%	5 7.25%	2 2.9%	0.993	4.12
I will recommend the corpus to other students	3 4.35%	1 1.45%	7 10.14%	35 50.72%	16 23.19%	5 7.25%	2 2.9%	1.052	4.12

encourage us to further carry out the DDL approach in the College Movie English course, but we should also pay high attention to those negative answers. The mean scores for students' responses to "*I use the corpus for other English courses too*", "*As I have learned more about the corpus, I have come to like them more*", "*I will use the corpus for my English learning in the future*" were between 3.5 to 4 on the six-point scale. This suggests that the DDL approach could not be simply generalized to all English learning courses. Although the use of corpora has been proved to be generally practical in the lexical learning of the Movie English Course, it is just a small part integrated into the basic teaching plan of that course. Corpus analysis should not be used as the only means of English language teaching, nor could it be regarded as a common practice for L2 teaching.

5 Conclusion

The present paper took an empirical study on a DDL approach to enhance lexical learning in the teaching of a college Movie English course for a semester. Three kinds of corpus resources - Movie English Script Corpus, Davies' list of Seven English corpora, and WebCorp, were recommended to the students. To explore the integrated use of corpora in this approach, participants' DDL behaviors were investigated by looking into their assignments posted on the course blog, and the results showed that the majority of participants were able to complete the DDL assignments, achieving promising learning effects. Drawing on the advantages of multiple corpus resources under the teacher's guidance, this DDL lexical learning approach has been proved to be practical and generally accepted by the students.

Acknowledgements. This paper is supported by the Science and Technology Project of Guangdong Province, China (2016A040403113), Guangdong Provincial Project for Higher Education Teaching Reform (GDJG20142204), Teaching and Research Project for Guangdong University of Foreign Studies (GWJYQN14002), and Innovative School Project in Higher Education of Guangdong, China (GWTP-LH-2015-10 and YQ2015062).

References

Anthony, L.: AntConc [Computer software]. Waseda University, Tokyo (2008). http://www.laurenceanthony.net/

Aston, G., Bernardini, S., Stewart, D.: Corpora and language learners. John Benjamins, Amsterdam (2004)

Bernardini, S.: Competence, Capacity, Corpora: A Study in Corpus-Aided Language Learning. CLUEB, Bologna (2000)

Boulton, A.: Testing the limits of data-driven learning: language proficiency and training. ReCALL **21**, 37–54 (2009)

Braun, S., Kohn, K., Mukherjee, J. (eds.): Corpus Technology and Language Pedagogy. Peter Lang, Frankfurt (2006)

Chambers, A.: Integrating corpus consultation in language studies. Lang. Learn. Technol. **9**(2), 111–125 (2005)

Chambers, A., O'Sullivan, I.: Corpus consultation and advanced learners' writing skills in French. ReCALL **16**, 158–172 (2004)

Chan, T., Liou, H.: Effects of web-based concordancing instruction on EFL students' learning of verb-noun collocations. Comput. Assist. Lang. Learn. **18**, 231–250 (2005)

Charles, M.: Getting the corpus habit: EAP students' long-term use of personal corpora. Engl. Specif. Purp. **35**, 30–40 (2014)

Cheng, W., Warren, M., Xun-feng, X.: The language learner as language researcher: putting corpus linguistics on the timetable. System **31**, 173–186 (2003)

Cobb, T.: Is there any measurable learning from hands-on concordancing? System **25**, 301–315 (1997)

Cresswell, A.: Getting to 'know' connectors? Evaluating data-driven learning in a writing skills course. In: Hidalgo, E., Quereda, L., Santana, J. (eds.) Corpora in the Foreign Language Classroom, pp. 267–287. Rodopi, Amsterdam (2007)

Flowerdew, J.: Concordancing in language learning. In: Pennington, M. (ed.) The power of CALL, pp. 97–113. Athelstan, Houston (1996)

Flowerdew, L.: Exploiting a corpus of business letters from a phraseological, functional perspective. ReCALL **24**(2), 152–168 (2012)

Frankenberg-Garcia, A.: A peek into what today's language learners as researchers actually do. Int. J. Lexicogr. **18**, 335–355 (2005)

Frankenberg-Garcia, A.: Learners' use of corpus examples. Int. J. Lexicogr. **25**(3), 273–296 (2012)

Gaskell, D., Cobb, T.: Can learners use concordance feedback for writing errors? System **32**, 301–319 (2004)

Gilmore, A.: Using online corpora to develop students' writing skills. ELT J. **63**(4), 363–372 (2009)

Hafner, C.A., Candlin, C.N.: Corpus tools as an affordance to learning in professional legal education. J. Engl. Acad. Purp. **6**, 303–318 (2007)

Hidalgo, E., Quereda, L., Santana, J. (eds.): Corpora in the Foreign Language Classroom. Rodopi, Amsterdam (2007)

Humblé, P.: Dictionaries and language learners. Haag & Herchen, Frankfurt (2001)

Johns, T.: Whence and whither classroom concordancing? In: Bongarerts, T., de Haan, P., Lobbe, S., Wekker, H. (eds.) Computer Applications in Language Learning, pp. 9–35. Foris, Dordrecht (1988)

Johns, T.: Should you be persuaded: two samples of data-driven learning materials. Engl. Lang. Res. J. **4**, 1–16 (1991)

Johns, T.: Contexts: the background, development and trialling of a concordance-based CALL program. In: Wichmann, A., et al. (eds.) Teaching and Language Corpora, pp. 110–115. Addison Wesley Longman, Harlow (1997)

Kennedy, C., Miceli, T.: Corpus-assisted creative writing: introducing intermediate Italian learners to a corpus as a reference resource. Lang. Learn. Technol. **14**(1), 28–44 (2010)

Lai, S., Chen, H.H.: Dictionaries vs concordancers: actual practice of the two different tools in EFL writing. Comput. Assist. Lang. Learn. **28**(4), 341–363 (2015)

Lee, D., Swales, J.: A corpus-based EAP course for NNS doctoral students: moving from available specialized corpora to self-compiled corpora. Engl. Specif. Purp. **25**, 56–75 (2006)

Li, L.: An empirical study of English corpus as a reference tool for PhD students. In: Li, L., Mckeown, J., Liu, L. (eds.) Proceedings of the 9th International Conference of Asian Association of Lexicography, pp. 331–343. Hong Kong Polytechnic University, Hong Kong (2015)

Ma, K.C.: Learning strategies in ESP classroom concordancing: an initial investigation into data-driven learning. In: Flowerdew, J., Tong, A. (eds.) Entering Texts, 197-214. The Hong Kong University of Science and Technology, Hong Kong, Language Center (1994)

O'Sullivan, I., Chambers, A.: Learners' writing skills in French: corpus consultation and learner evaluation. J. Second Lang. Writ. **15**, 49–68 (2006)

Pérez-Paredes, P., Sánchez-Tornel, M., Calero, J.M.A., Jiménez, P.A.: Tracking learners' actual uses of corpora: guided vs non-guided corpus consultation. Comput. Assist. Lang. Learn. **24** (3), 233–253 (2011)

Römer, U.: Corpus research applications in second language teaching. Annu. Rev. Appl. Linguist. **31**, 205–225 (2011)

Sinclair, J.: New evidence, new priorities, new attitudes. In: Sinclair, J. (ed.) How to Use Corpora in Language Teaching, pp. 271–299. John Benjamins, Amsterdam (2004)

Sun, Y.: Learning process, strategies and web-based concordancers: a case study. Br. J. Educ. Technol. **34**, 601–613 (2003)

Sun, Y., Wang, L.: Concordances in the EFL classroom: cognitive approaches and collocation difficulty. Comput. Assis. Lang. Learn. **16**, 83–94 (2003)

Varley, S.: I'll just look that up in the concordancer: integrating corpus consultation into the language learning environment. Comput. Assist. Lang. Learn. **22**, 133–152 (2009)

Vannestal, M.E., Lindquist, H.: Learning English grammar with a corpus: experimenting with concordancing in a university grammar course. ReCALL **19**(3), 329–350 (2007)

Wang, X., Ge, S., Wang, Q.: Corpus-based teaching in college "movie English" class in China. In: Lee, G. (ed.) Lecture Notes in Management Science, vol. 18, pp. 120–125. Singapore Management and Sports Science Institute, Singapore (2013)

Yoon, H., Hirvela, A.: ESL student attitudes towards corpus use in L2 writing. J. Second Lang. Writ. **13**, 257–283 (2004)

Yoon, H.: More than a linguistic reference: the influence of corpus technology on L2 academic writing. Lang. Learn. Technol. **12**, 31–49 (2008)

Automatic Essay Scoring Based on Coh-Metrix Feature Selection for Chinese English Learners

Xia Li[1(✉)] and Jianda Liu[2]

[1] Key Laboratory of Language Engineering and Computing, Guangdong University of Foreign Studies, Guangzhou, China
shelly_lx@126.com
[2] National Key Research Center for Linguistics and Applied Linguistics, Guangdong University of Foreign Studies, Guangzhou, China
ahda_liu@aliyun.com

Abstract. Automatic essay scoring can be based on essay's content or form. We believe that both classes of features can reflect some aspects of an essay's quality and they should be combined. In this paper, we use Coh-Metrix and importance measure to extract features that cover a wide range of features relating to the essay's grammatical structure, content, form, cohesion, and so on, and more related to the Chinese English Learners. This is a more complete set of features than those used in the literature and it is expected to better cover an essay's characteristics. SVM and C5.0 classification methods based on these features are used to predict the essay's score. Our experiments show that this set of features can produce good results on Chinese English essays even when we use top 5 and top 15 features with higher importance score.

Keywords: Automatic scoring of English essay · Feature selection · Machine learning

1 Introduction

Writing is an important way to evaluate students' language ability. Each year, a large number of EFL (English as Foreign Language) learners in China participate in various English tests such as college entrance examination, level 4 and level 6 examinations of college English test, college English final examinations, etc. More and more English teachers are needed to correct compositions, which is a big challenge to Universities of Chinese.

Automated Essay Scoring (AES) is use of the computer to evaluate and score the essays automatically. AES has advantages of real-time, objective, and economic. It can also provide diagnostic feedback to candidates or learners. The research of AES for English native speaker began in 1960's [1]. Some systems have been used in some countries, E-Rater is one of writing evaluation system used in the TOEFL [2].

However, there are some differences between Chinese English learners and English native speakers for their different cultures and thinking habits [3, 4]. For example, Chinese students are more prone to use high frequency words, preposition phrases, and easy to make a variety of grammatical errors. They prefer to use discourse function

© Springer International Publishing AG 2017
T.-T. Wu et al. (Eds.): SETE 2016, LNCS 10108, pp. 382–393, 2017.
DOI: 10.1007/978-3-319-52836-6_40

words, such as "well", "now", "anyway", "however", etc. However, English native speakers are more focused on the changes and flexibility of the sentences, such as writing longer sentences, using various clauses. So there should be different features to be used to score the essays written by Chinese English learners and English native speakers.

Automatic essay scoring can be based on essay's content or form. Method based on content mainly relies on semantic information. IntelliMetric [5] is a typical system of this class. She uses LSA to extract a set of semantic features to reflect the essay's content. The methods based on forms usually rely on surface features such as the essay's length, the number of paragraphs, the number of words, the number of prepositions, etc. PEG [6] is a typical system of this class. PEG determines the quality of an essay according to its average sentence length, the total length of the essay, the number of commas, etc. We believe that both classes of features can reflect some aspects of an essay's quality and they should be combined.

In this paper, we use Coh-Metrix to extract features that cover a wide range of features relating to the essay's grammatical structure, content, form, cohesion, and so on. We use Information Gain (IG) to select more relative features to Chinese English learners to evaluate the essays more accurate. SVM, C5.0 classification algorithm based on those features are used to predict the essay's score. Our experiments show that this set of features can produce good results.

2 Related Work

With the development of machine learning research, some automatic essay scoring methods based on machine learning are proposed. In these methods, the problem of essay scoring is treated as a problem of classification or regression. First, we need to extract features from the training essays, and take each essay from the training and test data as a vector. The items of the vector are features pre-extracted from training data. Then, essay scoring model can be trained and constructed with machine learning method in the training data. The score of the new essay can be predicted or regressed by the scoring model. Figure 1 is a classic automatic essay scoring model based on machine learning method.

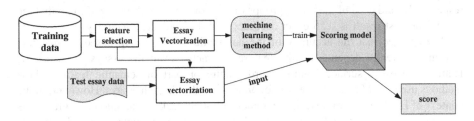

Fig. 1. Automatic essay scoring model based on machine learning method

Previous studies show that classification method like Naive Bayesian, K Nearest Neighbor, Support Vector Machine, etc. are widely use in automatic essay scoring. These methods achieved good results based on different feature selection algorithms.

Larkey [7] compared the differences of scoring results carried by different text classification methods. The experiments show that Naive Bayesian text classification method, K nearest neighbor text classification method, multiple linear regression method all get good results. But Bayesian classification method is relatively consistent with a stable rating. These results tell us that we can use the text classification method to score English essays. Hongbo Chen [8] takes automatic essay scoring as a ranking problem. Learning to rank sorting algorithm is used in the paper to automatically construct sorting model. The numerical score of the new essay is made by the value of mapping from sorting position. In this paper, features of the word, sentence fluency and content quality such as the number of modal verbs, word length, prepositional phrases, grammatical errors, the number of clauses, essay length, the number of conjunctions are used.

Rudner [9] uses unigrams and bigrams of word features to represent and classify essays with Bayesian classifier. The experiments show that using word based features can also achieve accuracy of 0.8 with Bayesian classifier. Zhou [10] construct three neural networks to represent scores of word, syntax and readability respectively by training and learning on essays extracted with word features, syntactic features and readability features. The new essay's score is predicted by the combination of the three scores. Experimental results show that the proposed model has consistency of 0.84 with the manual scoring. Bin [11] uses the combination of Naive Bayesian classification algorithm, K Nearest Neighbor classification algorithm and Support Vector Machine algorithm to score the English composition. In the experiment, stop words are erased from the text of the essay, and the features of content of writing and linguistics are extracted to represent the essay. Experimental test results on the CLEC corpus of grade 4 show that the precision of the algorithm is an average of 0.73.

McNamara [12] proposes a hierarchical classification scoring method. The assumption in the paper is that essay scoring method should be different for long essay and short essay. The method first divide essays into long essay group and short essay group. When the length of the essay is less or equal to 250 and the number of paragraph is 1 or 2, then the essay is divided into short group, the remaining essays are into long group. DFA is used to find the most predictive power variables in these two groups respectively, and each of these two groups of test composition is analyzed to predict the score. The best result is 0.55 exact accuracy and 0.92 adjacent accuracy.

We can see that the accuracy of the automatic essay scoring based on machine learning is greatly depends on the features extracted from the essays. Most of the features are essay surface feature, word feature or part of semantic features. Few methods use Coh-Metrix feature extraction to score the English essays. However, in the context of English writing teaching, another important task of the automatic grading is to give students positive feedback [13, 14]. This paper attempts to use the feature selection based on Coh-Metrix to improve the results of automatic essay scoring system and get more personalized features as feedback to the students.

3   Automatic Essay Scoring Based on Coh-Metrix Feature Selection

3.1   Classic Feature Selection Method

Generally speaking, there are two kinds of feature selection methods. They are the traditional text feature selection method and special feature selection method based on the quality or the level of the composition.

From the perspective of text mining, an essay is regarded as a short text, scoring for the short text is considered as a text classification or regression problem. In this point, we can use classic feature selection method to extract features of the essay text. There are some classic feature selection methods in text mining, such as Information Gain [15], Chi-Square statistic [16], Mutual Information [17], etc. Some AES system use classic feature selection method to extract features of the essay and score the essay with machine learning algorithm. BETSY [9] is typical this kind of class. BESTY extracts classic features of text and classify the essay using Bayesian classification method.

As an example, we extract unigrams, bigrams from Chinese Learner English Corpus (CLEC) [18], and we score and sort these unigrams and bigrams with information gain. Tables 1 and 2 are the top 50 features of bigrams and unigrams extracted from the essays with the theme of "global shortage of fresh water" and the theme of "haste makes waste". From the table, we can find some interesting patterns in the essays written by Chinese English learners. For example, Chinese English learners like use "Chinese way English" such as "very shortage", "people not", "but not", "are also", "we also", "much time", etc.

Table 1. Feature selection with unigrams and bigrams from essays with theme of "global shortage of fresh water"

Top 50 unigrams	Top 50 bigrams
people's// industry,// third,// average// needs.// everyone// out.// recent// actions// already// under// second// future// present,// done// should// percent// on,// also// searching// increase// abundant.// researches// reasonable// earth,// but// mustn't// realized// usually// ever.// granted// amount// please// out// which// cause// obtain// solved// hand// problem,// fresh// those// because// every// abundant// rid// circle// industy// our// millions//	is_important// use_them// under_the// are_also// very_shortage// that_can// the_average// must_be// do_our// the_serious// unfit_for// people's_daily// done_to// should_also// be_done// at_present,// people_to// second_we// in_recent// we_can// global_shortage// all_the// need_of// people_not// but_in// know_the// so_on,// will_not// this_condition,// is_limit// countries_have// nowadays,_many// already_used// for_ever.// we_also// by_controlling// large_of// can_put// are_increasing,// present,_the// water_economically// thing_in// realized_the// what_measures// we_had// for_man// our_needs.// large_of// by_controlling// for_man//

Table 2. Feature selection with unigrams and bigrams from essays with theme of "haste makes waste"

Top 50 unigrams	Top 50 bigrams
waste."// easy// last// going// meaning// they// some// brother// to// sit// classroom,// decided// important,// usually,// understood// failure// chinese// impossible// successfully.// who// finds// later,// aspects.// refused// angry// sentence:// quality// invited.// goods,// cartons// play.in// birthday// intelligence,// kinds,// director// answered,// dollar.// 200// continues// amount.// client.// client// american// payment// invite// guests// accepted// high,// family// deliver//	makes_waste."// for_my// try_to// it_must// therefore,_we// easy_to// much_time.// you_did// say_"haste// the_knowledge// is_easy// makes_us// things_quickly.// everyday_life,// the_classroom,// however, _we// is_that// the_matter// and_then// but_not// that_how// something_done// my_brother// brother_was// failure_if// do_must// it_tells// is_so// we_need// a_hurry,// to_cut// save_time// to_achieve// example,_one// to_work// he_finds// school_in// sometimes_haste// knowledge_of// do_what// usually,_we// speed,_but// refused_to// one_time// nothing. _from// mind_how// he_forgot// i_can// all_kinds,// because_usually,//

For the special feature selection method based on the quality and level of the composition, they are the surface features, language form features, and essay's content features. The surface feature, also called language feature, including the number of sentences, the number of words, the number of paragraphs, the number of verbs, the number of adjectives and so on. Surface feature of Composition can be extracted by natural language processing tools. Essay's content features are that reflect essay's content or semantic characteristic variables. Latent semantic analysis (LSA), LDA technique, WordNet based on semantic analysis technique can be used in extracting the essay's content features. IntelliMetric is a typical system of this class, which uses LSA to extract a set of semantic features to reflect the essay's content.

3.2   Feature Selection Based on Coh-Metrix

Coh-metrix [19] contains features such as word information, word frequency, part of speech, density scores, logical operators, connectives, token ratio, polysemy and hypernym, concept clarity, syntactic complexity, readability, co-reference cohesion, etc. Some details of the Coh-Metrix features are listed in Table 3. From Table 3, we can see that essay's surface features such as sentence count, paragraph count, word count are considered, and essay's content features like LSA overlap, sentence syntax similarity, familiarity for content words, polysemy for content words. Some complexity features like Coh-Metrix L2 Readability are also extracted by Coh-Metrix.

Coh-Metrix measures text complexity, text structure, and cohesion through the integration of lexicons, pattern classifiers, part-of-speech taggers, syntactic parsers, shallow semantic interpreters, and other components that have been developed in the field of computational linguistics. Coh-Metrix reports that hundreds of linguistic

Table 3. Part of Coh-Metrix features

Tag name	Description
DESPC	Paragraph count, number of paragraphs
DESSC	Sentence count, number of sentences
DESWC	Word count, number of words
PCNARz	Text Easability PC Narrativity, z score
PCSYNz	Text Easability PC Syntactic simplicity
PCCNCz	Text Easability PC Word concreteness
PCREFz	Text Easability PC Referential cohesion
PCDC	Text Easability PC Deep cohesion
PCVERB	Text Easability PC Verb cohesion
PCCONN	Text Easability PC Connectivity
PCTEMP	Text Easability PC Temporality
CRFNO1	Noun overlap, adjacent sentences, binary, mean
CRFAO1	Argument overlap, adjacent sentences, binary, mean
CRFSO1	Stem overlap, adjacent sentences, binary, mean
CRFCWO1	Content word overlap, adjacent sentences, proportional, mean
LSASS1	LSA overlap, adjacent sentences, mean
LSAPP1d	LSA overlap, adjacent paragraphs, standard deviation
LDTTRc	Lexical diversity, type-token ratio, content word lemmas
CNCLogic	Logical connectives incidence
SMCAUSv	Causal verb incidence
SYNSTRUTa	Sentence syntax similarity, adjacent sentences, mean
DRVP	Verb phrase density, incidence
WRDFAMc	Familiarity for content words, mean
WRDPOLc	Polysemy for content words, mean
RDL2	Coh-Metrix L2 Readability

variables are primarily related to text difficulty. Coh-Metrix also provides a replication of features reported by Biber (1988) including tense and aspect markers, place and time adverbials, pro-nouns and pro-verbs, questions, nominal forms, passives, subordination features, prepositional phrases, adjectives and adverbs, modals, specialized verb classes, reduced forms, dispreferred structures, and coordinations and negations.

This paper uses Coh-Metrix tool to extract semantic feature, content feature, surface feature and other complex feature to represent essays. The results show that with Coh-Metrix, we can get more than 0.9 adjacent accuracy in our data and get more personalized features as feedback to the students.

3.3 Essay's Representation

In our algorithm, vector space model, which is widely used in information retrieval, is used to represent the essay. Each essay corresponding to one vector, which is in the form of $V(d_j) = (<f_1, w_1>, \ldots, <f_i, w_i>, \ldots, <f_m, w_m>)$ $(i = 1, 2, \ldots, m)$, here

$f_i(i = 1, 2, \ldots, m)$ corresponding to the i-th feature, and $w_i(i = 1, 2, \ldots, m)$ corresponding to the characteristic values.

Table 4 shows that essays with the themes of "health gains in developing countries" represented by the vectors. Rows represent composition vectors, and columns represent corresponding features of each composition vector. For example, The first row vector is like (224, 9, 24.89, 1.402, ...) which represent one essay's vector, here 224 means that there are 224 words in the essay, 9 means that there are 9 sentences in the essay.

Table 4. Essay vector of "Health Gains in Developing Countries"

DESWC	DESPL	DESSL	DESWLsy	DESWLlt	PCNARp	PCSYNp	PCCNCp	PCREFp	PCDCp	PCVERBp
224	9	24.89	1.402	4.161	95.45	9.34	17.11	96.99	52.39	99.38
172	14	12.29	1.628	4.576	93.32	54.78	12.92	99.75	81.06	74.86
122	8	15.25	1.361	4	96.25	25.78	18.41	99.81	74.86	78.81
177	16	11.06	1.39	4.266	86.43	76.11	35.94	76.11	94.06	95.45
201	18	11.17	1.438	4.204	83.65	84.38	4.18	36.69	92.51	86.65
155	9	17.22	1.49	4.406	74.54	59.48	51.2	94.74	75.17	80.23
188	12	15.67	1.457	4.064	88.1	55.17	30.85	99.95	96.56	74.54
188	17	11.06	1.468	4.261	86.43	90.82	9.34	52.39	97.06	41.68
167	10	16.7	1.287	3.808	93.82	58.32	18.41	51.6	95.64	93.82
125	11	11.36	1.296	3.896	86.21	82.12	6.3	82.38	28.1	93.82
128	9	14.22	1.422	4.063	97.19	76.73	72.91	98.08	88.69	9.01
138	9	15.33	1.21	3.674	90.99	47.21	41.29	60.26	92.65	98.57
169	11	15.36	1.391	4.325	85.31	57.14	19.77	82.12	99.18	55.96
122	10	12.2	1.279	3.77	92.07	57.53	53.59	70.54	77.64	64.8
142	10	14.2	1.289	3.965	95.73	31.21	5.48	99.11	95.35	90.99
153	10	15.3	1.438	4.131	86.43	62.55	41.68	47.21	84.61	63.31
169	13	13	1.621	4.497	71.9	63.68	55.17	67	91.31	51.99
118	9	13.11	1.415	4.051	84.38	58.71	0.99	33.72	35.2	95.15
120	5	24	1.408	4.1	90.32	25.46	93.06	99.31	46.02	65.54
169	11	15.36	1.379	3.728	81.59	56.36	19.22	91.77	6.94	95.05
149	14	10.64	1.483	4.081	88.88	84.13	7.64	84.13	94.74	33

3.4   Feature Importance Measure

Information Gain is widely used in machine learning to score features of the text. The information gain can be used to measure the overall class discrimination ability of the feature in the whole training dataset. Generally speaking, the higher the value of the information gain, the more important the feature is. The information gain formula is listed as below. In the formula, $P(c_i)$ represents the probability of each document in the category, $P(t)$ means the probability of containing feature t in the training. $P(c_i|t)$ represents the probability of the feature t which belongs to class c_i. $P(\bar{t})$ means the probability that the training set does not contain the feature t. $P(c_i|\bar{t})$ represents the probability that the training set does not contain the feature but belongs to class c_i.

$$IG(t) = - \sum_{i=1}^{m} P(c_i) \log P(c_i)$$
$$+ P(t) \sum_{i=1}^{m} P(c_i|t) \log P(c_i|t)$$
$$+ P(\bar{t}) \sum_{i=1}^{m} P(c_i|\bar{t}) \log P(c_i|\bar{t})$$

In the problem of automatic essay scoring, essays are regarded as documents and the scores of the essays are the classes of the training set. Classification in automatic essay scoring is to classify each essay into the correct class, and the score of the class is assigned to the test essay.

3.5 Algorithm Description

In order to extract more complex features and the important feature variables related to Chinese English learners, we proposed an automatic essay scoring algorithm based on Coh-Metrix. The algorithm is described as below.

Input: training essays $D_{train} = \{d_1, d_2, \ldots, d_m\}$

test essays $D_{test} = \{e_1, e_2, \ldots, e_n\}$

Output: The scores of the test essays, the accuracy of the scoring algorithm.

(1) Feature Selection according to training essays with Coh-Metrix: $F = \{f_1, f_2, \ldots, f_{106}\}$

(2) Represent training essays with Coh-Metrix features:

$$V(d_i) = (w_1, w_2, \ldots, w_{106}) \quad for \ d_i \in D_{train}$$

(3) Represent test essays with Coh-Metrix features:

$$V(e_i) = (w'_1, w'_2, \ldots, w'_{106}) \quad for \ e_i \in D_{test}$$

(4) Calculate feature score:

$$Score(f_i) = IG(f_i)$$
$$Accumulate \ Score(f_i) = \sum_i Score \ (f_i)$$

(5) Select features whose Accumulate Score is larger or equal to a threshold α

$$F' = \{f'_1, f'_2, \ldots, f'_k\}$$
$$V'(d_i) = (w'_1, w'_2, \ldots, w'_k)$$
$$V'(e_i) = (w'_1, w'_2, \ldots, w'_k)$$

(6) Using Support Vector Machine to classify test essays

(7) Calculate the accuracy of the classifier.

4 Experiment Result and Analysis

4.1 Experiment Data

Our experiment data is named Chinese Learner English corpus (abbreviated as CLEC). The CLEC project was directed by Professor Gui Shichun of Guangdong University of Foreign Studies, and Professor Yang Huizhong of Shanghai Jiaotong University, both from China. CLEC corpus contains 1 million words of English compositions collected from Chinese learners of English with differing levels of proficiency, covering senior secondary school students, English-major, and non-English-major university students in China. The corpus is error tagged according to an error marking scheme of 61 types of error, including various lexical, grammatical, semantic and sentence level errors. Now CLEC corpus has become a public corpus for studying and test automatic essay scoring of EFL.

Taking into account the actual composition, there is no error tagging information. We cleared the error tagging information from the composition. In our experiment, we use 160 number of essays with theme of "health gains in developing countries" to test our scoring algorithm. The detail of the data is described in Table 5.

Table 5. Details about essays with the theme of "Health Gains in Developing Countries"

Score	Number of essays	Average number of word	Average number of sentence	Average length of word	Average number of syllable for word	Average number of letters for word
6	10	144	8.6	17.88	1.47	4.62
7	22	150	8.14	19.44	1.54	4.77
8	34	149	8.88	18.48	1.53	4.71
9	41	151	8.93	18.10	1.52	4.71
10	23	149	9.48	16.40	1.53	4.71
11	14	150	8.29	18.97	1.56	4.84
12	9	163	8.89	19.01	1.51	4.67
13	6	161	10.67	15.14	1.52	4.81

4.2 Evaluation Index

In this paper, the accuracy and the adjacent accuracy are used to evaluate the algorithm. Accuracy is the percentage of the predicted essay which is predicted by the number of correctly predicted. The adjacent accuracy means that if a essay's score is predicted by ±1 score of the correct score, then we take that is correct.

$$accuracy = \frac{\#correct\ essays}{\#all\ test\ essays}$$

4.3   Experiment Results

In the experiment, 106 features are extracted to construct the vectors of the essays. And then, information gain is used to measure the importance of the features. We use Support Vector Machine (SVM) and C5.0 decision tree classifier to score the essay respectively with Coh-Metrix features and top 5, top 15 features with the score of importance. The accuracy of our scoring algorithm in test data is listed in Table 6. The results show that we can get 0.93 adjacent accuracy in training data with 106 features extracted with Coh-Metrix tool in C5.0 classification algorithm. And when we use top 15 features as input, we can get 0.9 adjacent accuracy. This result is useful when we want to give feedback to students about their writing problem and suggestion. That means, we can know which features are important to the students about their essays, and that can help the students to improve their English learning ability. Table 7 is the top 10 features with highest importance measure score in our test data. From the table, we can see that in Chinese English essays, text easability is the most important feature, it's score of importance is 0.18. That means that we can help students to improve their English writing ability with specific items from the important score of the feature.

Table 6. Accuracy of our scoring algorithm

Number of features	SVM	C5.0
Accuracy with 106 features	99.38	93.75
Top 5 features with larger importance measure score	63.12	68.12
Top 15 features with larger importance measure score	74.38	90.62

Table 7. Important features according to Accumulate importance score

Features	Description	Importance score	Accumulate importance score
PCTEMPp	Text easability PC temporality, percentile	18%	18%
SYNSTRUTt	Sentence syntax similarity, all combinations, across paragraphs	11%	29%
SMCAUSr	Ratio of casual particles to causal verbs	9%	38%
SYNMEDpos	Minimal edit distance, part of speech	9%	47%
CRFCWO1	Content word overlap, adjacent sentences, proportional	7%	54%
SMTEMP	Temporal cohesion, tense and aspect repetition	6%	60%
WRDADV	Adverb incidence	5%	65%
DRINF	Infinitive density, incidence	5%	70%
CNCADC	Adversative and contrastive connectives incidence	5%	75%
CNCCaus	Causal connectives incidence	4%	79%

5 Conclusion

As more and more Chinese people learning English, more and more English essays needs to be corrected and give feedback by the teacher. This brings a big challenge to Chinese English teachers and universities and colleges. However, the use of computers to correct and score electronic composition can give good feedback and scores to the students. And automatic correct essays with computer has advantages of economic, real-time, objective and fair.

In this paper, we propose an automatic essay scoring algorithm with Coh-Metrix feature selection. The results show that our algorithm can get more than 0.9 adjacent accuracy in the CLEC dataset, even with top 15 features as data feature input. In the future, we will test our algorithm in more Chinese Essays datasets and we will compare the results on different essays written by Chinese English learners and English native speakers.

Acknowledgment. This work is supported by the National Science Foundation of China (61402119).

References

1. Valenti, S., Neri, F., Cucchiarelli, A.: An overview of current research on automated essay grading. J. Inf. Technol. Educ. **2**, 319–330 (2003)
2. Attali, Y., Burstein, J.: Automated essay scoring with e-rater® V. 2. J. Technol. Learn. Assess. **4**(3), 1–30 (2006)
3. Guang-Hui, M.: A contrastive analysis of the characteristics of Chinese and American college students' English compositions. Foreign Lang. Teach. Learn. **34**(5), 345–380 (2002)
4. Burstein, J., Chodorow, M.: Automated essay scoring for nonnative English speakers. In: Proceedings of a Symposium on Computer Mediated Language Assessment and Evaluation in Natural Language Processing, pp. 68–75. Association for Computational Linguistics (1999)
5. Shermis, M.D., Burstein, J.: Automated essay scoring: cross-disciplinary perspective. Comput. Linguist. **30**(2), 245–246 (2004)
6. Shermis, M., Mzumara, H.R., Olson, J., Harrington, S.: On-line grading of student essays: PEG goes on the world wide web. Assess. Eval. High. Educ. **26**(3), 247–259 (2001)
7. Larkey, L., Croft, W.B.: A text categorization approach to automated essay scoring. In: Shermis, M.D., Burstein, J. (eds.) Automated Essay Scoring: A Cross-Disciplinary Perspective, pp. 55–70. Lawrence Erlbaum Associates, Inc., Hillsdale (2003)
8. Chen, H., He, B., Luo, T., Li, B.: A ranked-based learning approach to automated essay scoring. In: The Second International Conference on Cloud and Green Computing, pp. 448–455 (2012)
9. Rudner, L.M., Liang, T.: Automated essay scoring using Bayes' theorem. J. Technol. Learn. Assess. **1**(2), 3–21 (2002)
10. Zhou, Y., Fan, T., Huang, G.: An Automatic English Composition scoring model based on neural network algorithm. In: 13th International Conference on Computer and Information Science (ICIS), pp. 149–152. IEEE Press (2014)

11. Bin, L., Jian-Min, Y.: Automated essay scoring using multi-classifier fusion. In: Wu, Y. (ed.) ICCIC 2011. CCIS, vol. 233, pp. 151–157. Springer, Heidelberg (2011). doi:10.1007/978-3-642-24010-2_21

12. McNamara, D.S., Crossley, S.A., Roscoe, R.D., Allen, L.K., Dai, J.: A hierarchical classification approach to automated essay scoring. Assessing Writ. **23**, 35–59 (2015)

13. Xie, H., Zou, D., Lau, R.Y., Wang, F.L., Wong, T.L.: Generating incidental word-learning tasks via topic-based and load-based profiles. IEEE Multimedia **23**(1), 60–70 (2016)

14. Zou, D., Xie, H., Li, Q., Wang, F.L., Chen, W.: The load-based learner profile for incidental word learning task generation. In: International Conference on Web-Based Learning, pp. 190–200 (2014)

15. Sebastiani, F.: Machine learning in automated text categorization. ACM Comput. Surv. (CSUR) **34**(1), 1–47 (2002)

16. Yang, Y., Pedersen, J.O.: A comparative study on feature selection in text categorization. ICML **97**, 412–420 (1997)

17. Church, K.W., Hanks, P.: Word association norms, mutual information, and lexicography. Comput. Linguist. **16**(1), 22–29 (1990)

18. Gui, S., Yang, H.: Chinese English Learners Corpus. Shanghai Foreign Language Education Press, Shanghai (2002)

19. Graesser, A.C., McNamara, D.S., Louwerse, M.M., Cai, Z.: Coh-Metrix: analysis of text on cohesion and language. Behav. Res. Methods Instrum. Comput. **36**(2), 193–202 (2004)

Text Analysis of Corpus Linguistics in a Post-concordancer Era

Simon Ho Wang[✉]

Language Center, Hong Kong Baptist University,
Kowloon Tong, Kowloon, Hong Kong
simonwang@hkbu.edu.hk

Abstract. In this methodological paper, I review a number of studies in corpus linguistics that rely heavily on off-the-shelf computer programs known as concordancers. While acknowledging the fruitful research findings generated using concordancers, it is argued that natural language processing (NLP) tools such as Stanford parser and SyntaxNet should be used to automate certain analytical procedures that are often performed manually by corpus linguistics researchers using concordancers. More collaboration efforts between NLP researchers and corpus linguists are called for to help advance the field of corpus linguistics into a post-concordancer era.

1 Introduction

The past two decades have witnessed the emergence of corpus-based approaches to language research and teaching with numerous studies published focusing on data-driven learning, learner corpora, collocation, meta-discourse. At the core of these lines of research studies is a type of computer program known as concordancers, which can automatically process a large amount of textual data and generate concordance lines that contain keywords pre-selected by the researchers. While this computer tool has been very useful for text analysis among corpus linguists and, more recently, been introduced to students to investigate the use of language by themselves, in this short article, I would argue that concordancers are limited in the ways how the texts can be analyzed and this 20th century technology should be phased out among corpus linguists and replaced by more advanced and sophisticated natural language processing (NLP) technologies.

In Sect. 2, I will first review a few studies in corpus linguistics in which corcordancers have been used as a dominant tool. While acknowledging the insights that can be generated through the analysis of corpora using this tool, in Sect. 3, I discuss how the tool is limited for two reasons: first, it ignores the sentence boundaries in texts and, as a result, the researchers miss the opportunities to automatically analyze the texts at sentence level; second, the tool also provides little information about the syntactic functions of the words in the corpora, which can be revealed through more recent tools such as Stanford parsers and SyntaxNet. After exploring how the NLP tools can analyze the corpus more effectively in Sect. 4, a call is made in concluding section (Sect. 5) for more collaboration between computer scientists and applied linguists to make the advanced NLP technologies available to the corpus linguistics and ELT research communities.

© Springer International Publishing AG 2017
T.-T. Wu et al. (Eds.): SETE 2016, LNCS 10108, pp. 394–400, 2017.
DOI: 10.1007/978-3-319-52836-6_41

2 The Dominance of Concordancers in Corpus-Based Studies

Since the advent of inexpensive computing, concordancers have been recognized as a very useful tool in discourse analysis and language teaching. In an article published in 1993, Flowerdew highlighted the utility of concordancers in developing learning materials for language courses based on the word frequency information revealed by using the tool [9]. Following a similar line of research, Thurstun and Candlin also recognized the potential of using concordancers to teach academic vocabulary [19]. More than a decade later, in 2011, Yoon offered an overview of research and issues related to the use of corpus approaches in L2 writing class in which concordancers were still the predominant tool at the center of the discussion [20].

The benefits of taking the corpus-based approach to language teaching using concordancers are well-documented. In a case study of US graduate students developing corpora of published journal articles and their own writing, Lee and Swales demonstrated how the comparison of expert corpora and learner corpora can lead to insights for student writers in terms of specific usage issues [13]. For students who do not have the time to compile their own corpora, Chambers and Yoon reported the usefulness of existing corpora such as British National Corpus (BNC) and the Collins COBUILD Corpus in their 2007 and 2008 studies, respectively [4, 21]. More recently, Davies had led the efforts of creating a large corpus known as Corpus of Contemporary American English (COCA) which provided a free online user interface to generate concordance lines for keywords submitted by users, a feature that can also be available through Google Scholar [6]. English as an additional language (EAL) scholars have been using Google Scholars as a virtual corpus to look up the usage of specific lexical items while revising their manuscripts for international research journals [10].

In addition to being used as a pedagogical tool, concordancers have also been widely used in discourse analysis that inform language teaching. Hyland and Tse, for example, examines the use of evaluative *that* in abstracts of research articles and masters/doctoral dissertations by focusing on concordance lines that contain the keyword *that*. In a study focusing on self-mention and identity construction in graduate student presentations, Zareva used the concordance software MonoConc Pro Version 2.0 to identify all the instances of self-mention (i.e. sentences that contain keywords such as *I*, *me*, and *my*) [23]. In a more recent study, Jiang used the concordance software AntCont and part-of-speech taggers CLAWS to study the use of nominal stance construction in L1 and L2 writing.

3 The Limitations of Concordancers

There are two major problems with the concordancers that have limited the researchers using this tool. First and foremost, concordancers ignore the sentence boundaries when generating concordance lines that contain keywords selected by researchers. When the researchers use concordance software such as AntConc to analyze the texts, sentences are not the default units of analysis. Instead, researchers are provided with concordance lines based on the pre-determined "search window size." Researchers will have to manually extract the texts that have been chopped off by the software in order to obtain the complete sentences that contain the keywords. A second related problem is that, as a result of overlooking sentence boundaries, the concordancers also offer little insights into the syntactic roles played by specific words within the sentences.

The two problems discussed above force the researchers to manually examine the output produced by the concordancers. Hyland and Tse, for example, after using the concordancers to identify the texts that contain the keyword "that", had to examined each concordance line laboriously to identify the sentences "where the subject of the projecting clause referred to a participant, where the lexical verb, noun, or adjective presented the type of projecting, and where the that clause presented the projected idea or speech" but eliminate the cases "where *that* was used to perform other grammatical functions, such as where it acted as a demonstrative or relative pronoun" [11].

There is no doubt that both sentence boundaries and syntactic roles of words within sentences are important issues in corpus linguistics. Researchers in L1 and L2 language teaching have long focused on the syntactic complexity of student writing by examining the frequencies of different grammatical features at sentence levels [14, 15, 17, 18, 22]. In all the studies cited above, researchers used individual sentences as unit of analysis to measure the level of grammar sophistication among student writers. Lu, for example, used Stanford parser to develop an L2 syntactic analyser and the first step of his analysis was to use Stanford parser to segment the texts into individual sentences [14]. In Jiang's study of nominal stance construction, the author used POS tagger CLAWS to investigate the use of specific grammatical structures such as N that clause, to-infinitive, of-prepositional and preposition plus wh-clause. The combined use of concordancers and POS taggers may help reveal more useful information about the corpus than relying on concordancers alone. But the analysis is still inefficient and time-consuming, thereby constraining the corpus size (e.g. in Jiang's study, only 366 essays were analyzed.)

4   The Potential of Stanford Parser and SyntaxNet

Some corpus linguists have overcome the limitations of concordancers by using other tools. In a study of subject it-extraposition, Zhang extracted the sentences with target patterns from academic and popular writing subcorpora in the British component of the International Corpus of English (ICE-GB) by taking advantages of a retrieval program International Corpus of English Corpus Utility Program (ICECUP III) that contain syntactic information of the sentences in the corpus [24]. This approach, while effective for this particular study, cannot be replicated for other corpora that have not been pre-processed for syntactic features. In a more comprehensive study of L2 student writing, Staples and Reppen analyzed a learner corpus using Biber tagger that is not publicly available for the corpus linguistics research community.

For researchers without access to proprietary tools such as Biber tagger or interested in using corpora other than International Corpus of English, there is a need for more sophisticated tools for text analysis that are readily available. Stanford parser, an open-source software package widely used in natural language processing (NLP) research community may address such needs.

Stanford parser is a computer software package that can be used to analyze English texts at sentence level and generate dependencies among the words to describe their syntactic relations. The dependency design of the Stanford parser is based on the framework of Lexical-Functional Grammar [2] and the syntactic relations named by researchers such as Carroll et al. [3], De Marneffe and Manning [7] and King et al. [12]. The set of dependencies are organized in hierarchy to describe different grammatical functions including auxiliary verbs (passive auxiliary and copula), conjunctives, coordination, subject (nominal subject, clausal subject), complement (object, attributive, clausal complement, complementizer) and modifier (adverbial clause modifier, purpose clause modifier, temporal modifier, relative clause modifier, adjectival modifier, infinitival modifier, participial modifier, numeric modifier, appositional modifier, noun compound modifier, adverbial modifier, possession modifier), and other miscellaneous elements.

In addition to Lu's syntactic analyzer mentioned earlier that is based on the Stanford dependency parser, this software package (Stanford parser) has been widely used in other research areas or and projects, such as bioinformatics [5, 8], opinion extraction (e.g. [25], sentiment analysis [16], and building information extraction system TEXTRUNNER [1]. Lu's decision to encapsulate the Stanford parser in his own syntactic analyzer is helpful for the research community of applied linguistics and language education to use the technology for monitoring syntactic complexity development of students without paying attention to the technical details about the parser. Nevertheless, such encapsulation also masks the true potential of the Stanford parser for developing pedagogical applications for language teaching and learning. More recently, a few corpus tools have been available that incorporate Stanford parser, for example, UAM corpus tool. Yet, such tools are still designed following the conventions of concordancers allowing little flexibility for researchers to perform tailor-made analysis, e.g. taking into account the position of sentences in paragraphs or considering words in adjacent sentences.

To use Stanford parser for more tailor-made text analysis, the first step is to segment the texts into individual sentences using the sentence segmentation tool which is part of the software package. Dependencies can then be generated by analyzing the sentences in the corpus to identify the specific grammatical features. To illustrate the functions of this tool, the following sentences are analyzed by Stanford parser via its online interface (http://nlp.stanford.edu:8080/parser/):

The two sentences in Table 1 are used as examples because they contain evaluative *that* and it-subject extraposition that have been the focus of the studies by Hyland and Tse [11] and Zhang [24], respectively. To identify the sentences with evaluative *that*, a tailored-made program may be developed based on Stanford parser to search for dependencies such as ccomp (V1, V2) and mark (V2, that) which indicate that V1 is the verb of the main clause and V2 is that verb of the *that* clause. Similarly, a program based on Stanford parser can be used to identify it-extraposition structures in sentences by searching for dependencies such as nsubj (adj, it) and cop (adj, is) in which adj represents the adjective found in the extraposition structure.

More recently, Google Inc. has released SyntaxNet, which is touted as the most accurate syntactic parser, as an open source software available for the NLP community. Similar to Stanford parser, SyntaxNet can serve as the core technology to generate

Table 1. Dependencies generated by Stanford parser

Sentences	Dependencies generated by Stanford parser
It is important for children to exercise regularly	nsubj(important-3, It-1) cop(important-3, is-2) root(ROOT-0, important-3) case(children-5, for-4) nmod(important-3, children-5) mark(exercise-7, to-6) xcomp(important-3, exercise-7) advmod(exercise-7, regularly-8)
The author argues that corpus linguists should get more help from computer scientists	det(author-2, The-1) nsubj(argues-3, author-2) root(ROOT-0, argues-3) mark(get-8, that-4) compound(linguists-6, corpus-5) nsubj(get-8, linguists-6) aux(get-8, should-7) ccomp(argues-3, get-8) amod(help-10, more-9) dobj(get-8, help-10) case(scientists-13, from-11) compound(scientists-13, computer-12) nmod(get-8, scientists-13)

dependencies among words to help the researchers understand the grammatical structures found the texts. The major advantage of both Stanford parser and SyntaxNet compared to concordancers is that the grammatical relations can be analyzed automatically, making it possible to process a large amount of data for grammatical analysis. While such parsers have yet to achieve 100% accuracy rates and the analysis results require human attention and correction, these NLP tools provide far more information about the corpus than what is available through concordancers. On the other hand, everything that is possible with concordancers can also be done with the NLP tools.

5 Conclusion: The Need of More Collaboration Among Computer Scientists and Applied Linguists

Despite the clear superiority of NLP tools such as Stanford parser and SyntaxNet, a large number of researchers in corpus linguistics still rely on the 20th century technology (concordancers) for their need of text analysis. There might be two reasons why this is the case. First, a large number of corpus linguists and ELT researchers do not have the programming skills necessary to take advantages of NLP tools such as

Stanford parser and SyntaxNet. They feel much more comfortable using concordancers that provide a straight-forward interface for text analysis. The NLP tools, as a result, are outside the radar of many corpus linguists, with notable exceptions such as Lu's L2 syntactic analyzer which only provide quantitative measurements of syntactic complexity. Second, despite the huge potential of NLP tools in advancing corpus linguistics and ELT research, most NLP experts are too busy with even more lucrative projects led by Internet giants such as Google, Facebook, Tencent, Alibaba and Baidu. These companies engaged the best NLP scientists in the world, for whom corpus linguistics and ELT are really not that important.

As a result, despite the giant leaps in NLP and artificial intelligence community in recent years, the corpus linguistics and ELT research community are left behind and still using concordancers, missing the endless opportunities that could have been available with more advanced NLP tools. Therefore, to remedy the situation and advance the fields of corpus linguistics and ELT research into the post-concordance era, corpus linguists and ELT researchers must reach out the NLP researchers for collaboration and technical support. Without realizing the full potential of NLP technologies for corpus linguistics and ELT, the practitioners in both fields may not be able to produce the best research work that is possible in 21st century.

References

1. Banko, M. et al.: Open information extraction from the web. In: Proceedings of the 20th International Joint Conference on Artificial Intelligence (IJCAI 2007) (2007)
2. Bresnan, J.: Lexical-functional syntax. Blackwell, Malden (2001)
3. Carroll, J. et al.: Corpus annotation for parser evaluation. arXiv preprint arXiv:cs/9907013 (1999)
4. Chambers, A.: Integrating corpus consultation in language studies. Lang. Learn. Technol. **9** (2), 111–125 (2005)
5. Clegg, A.B.: Computational-linguistic approaches to biological text mining, University of London (2008)
6. Davies, M.: Google Scholar and COCA-Academic: two very different approaches to examining academic English. J. Engl. Acad. Purp. **12**(3), 155–165 (2013)
7. De Marneffe, M.-C., Manning, C.D.: The Stanford typed dependencies representation. In: Coling 2008: Proceedings of the Workshop on Cross-Framework and Cross-Domain Parser Evaluation, pp. 1–8. Association for Computational Linguistics (2008)
8. Erkan, G. et al.: Semi-supervised classification for extracting protein interaction sentences using dependency parsing. In: Proceedings of the 2007 Joint Conference on Empirical Methods in Natural Language Processing and Computational Natural Language Learning (EMNLP-CoNLL) (2007)
9. Flowerdew, J.: Concordancing as a tool in course design. System **21**(2), 231–244 (1993)
10. Flowerdew, J., Wang, S.H.: Author's editor revisions to manuscripts published in international journals. J. Second Lang. Writ. **32**, 39–52 (2016)
11. Hyland, K., Tse, P.: Hooking the reader: a corpus study of evaluative <i> that </i> in abstracts. Engl. Specif. Purp. **24**(2), 123–139 (2005)
12. King, T.H. et al.: The PARC 700 dependency bank. In: 4th International Workshop on Linguistically Interpreted Corpora (LINC 2003) (2003)

13. Lee, D., Swales, J.: A corpus-based EAP course for NNS doctoral students: moving from available specialized corpora to self-compiled corpora. Engl. Specif. Purp. **25**(1), 56–75 (2006)
14. Lu, X.: Automatic analysis of syntactic complexity in second language writing. Int. J. Corpus Linguist. **15**, 4 (2010)
15. Lu, X., Ai, H.: Syntactic complexity in college-level English writing: differences among writers with diverse L1 backgrounds. J. Second Lang. Writ. **29**, 16–27 (2015)
16. Meena, A., Prabhakar, T.V.: Sentence level sentiment analysis in the presence of conjuncts using linguistic analysis. In: Amati, G., Carpineto, C., Romano, G. (eds.) ECIR 2007. LNCS, vol. 4425, pp. 573–580. Springer, Heidelberg (2007). doi:10.1007/978-3-540-71496-5_53
17. Ortega, L.: Syntactic complexity in L2 writing: progress and expansion. J. Second Lang. Writ. **29**, 82–94 (2015)
18. Ortega, L.: Syntactic complexity measures and their relationship to L2 proficiency: a research synthesis of college-level L2 writing. Appl. Linguist. **24**(4), 492–518 (2003)
19. Thurstun, J., Candlin, C.N.: Concordancing and the teaching of the vocabulary of academic English. Engl. Specif. Purp. **17**(3), 267–280 (1998)
20. Yoon, C.: Concordancing in L2 writing class: an overview of research and issues. J. Engl. Acad. Purp. **10**(3), 130–139 (2011)
21. Yoon, H.: More than a linguistic reference: the influence of corpus technology on L2 academic writing. Lang. Learn. Technol. **12**(2), 31–48 (2008)
22. Youn, S.J.: Measuring syntactic complexity in L2 pragmatic production: investigating relationships among pragmatics, grammar, and proficiency. System **42**, 270–287 (2014)
23. Zareva, A.: Self-mention and the projection of multiple identity roles in TESOL graduate student presentations: the influence of the written academic genres. Engl. Specif. Purp. **32**(2), 72–83 (2013)
24. Zhang, G.: It is suggested that… or it is better to…? Forms and meanings of subject it-extraposition in academic and popular writing. J. Engl. Acad. Purp. **20**, 1–13 (2015)
25. Zhuang, L. et al.: Movie review mining and summarization. In: Presented at the Proceedings of ACM Conference on Information and Knowledge Management (CIKM) (2006)

Comparing the Performance of Latent Semantic Analysis and Probability Latent Semantic Analysis Models on Autoscoring Essay Tasks

Xiaohua Ke and Haijiao Luo[(⊠)]

Cisco School of Informatics, Guangdong University of Foreign Studies,
Guangzhou, People's Republic of China
{carrieke,luohaijiao}@gdufs.edu.cn

Abstract. This paper evaluates the performance variances of Latent Semantic Analysis (LSA) and Probability Latent Semantic Analysis (PLSA) by judging essay text qualities as automated essay (AES) scoring tools. A correlation research design was used to examine the correlation between LSA performance and PLSA performance. We introduced 3 weight methods and performed 6 experiments to produce the scoring performances of both LSA and PLSA from a total of 2444 Chinese essays. The results show that there were strong correlations between the LSA scores and PLSA scores. While the overall performance of PLSA is better than that of LSA, the findings from the current study do not corroborate the previous findings for PLSA methods that claim a significant improvement. The implications of our research for AES reveal that both LSA and PLSA have a limited capability at this point and those more reliable measures for automated essay analyzing and scoring, such as text formats and forms, still need to be a component of text quality analysis.

Keywords: LSA · PLSA · Text analysis · Automated essay scoring

1 Introduction

Latent Semantic Analysis is a statistical latent class model (or aspect model) that has shown encouraging results in scoring content features, such as essays and short-answer responses, and related tasks in the last 20 years (Shermis and Burstein 2013). New methods, such as Probability Latent Semantic Analysis, using probabilistic methods and algebra to search the latent space in the corpus are further applied in document clustering. LSA and PLSA are now in wide use around the world in many applications and in many languages including Internet searches, psychological diagnoses (Gui 2003), signal intelligence (Thomas 2001), educational and occupational assessments, intelligent tutoring systems (Landauer and Dumais 1997) and basic studies of collaborative communication and problem solving (Thomas 2001). The accuracies of the LSA and PLSA representations have been empirically tested in many ways. For example, LSA improves recall in information retrieval, usually achieving 10–30% better performance cetera paribus via standard metrics by matching documents with

© Springer International Publishing AG 2017
T.-T. Wu et al. (Eds.): SETE 2016, LNCS 10108, pp. 401–411, 2017.
DOI: 10.1007/978-3-319-52836-6_42

similar meanings (Landauer et al. 2003). However, little interest or work has been put forth with regards to proposing PLSA as a supporting method for language testing, especially automated essay tasks (Ke et al. 2014). Further insights can be obtained by comparing the variance of using LSA and PLSA, especially the performance of autoscoring human essays when adopting different weight calculation methods, to offer a promising and challenging research arena for the forthcoming years.

The purpose of this study was to explore and evaluate the scoring performance of LSA and PLSA. In Sect. 2, the processes of performing LSA along with 3 different weight methods are introduced. In Sect. 3, PLSA is introduced. In Sect. 4, we illustrate the scoring systems' frameworks and design 6 experiments to examine the variance of LSA performance and PLSA performance. In Sect. 5, the results, discussions and findings from the current study are presented. In the final section, conclusions and implications are provided with suggestions for the various stakeholders and educational software designers.

2 Building an LSA Model

The LSA model was proposed in the 1990s specifically for the area of information retrieval. LSA has been utilized to score essays by many theoretical advances and relevant applications (Shermis and Burstein 2013). LSA derives semantic models of English (or any other language) from an analysis of large volumes of text. For essay scoring applications, we typically use a collection of texts that is equivalent to a reading that a student is likely to encounter when learning this topic. LSA builds a co-occurrence matrix [A] of words as follows

$$
\text{Matrix A} = \begin{bmatrix} A_{11} & A_{12} & \cdots & A_{1n} \\ A_{21} & A_{22} & \cdots & A_{2n} \\ \cdots & \cdots & \cdots & \cdots \\ A_{m1} & A_{m2} & \cdots & A_{mn} \end{bmatrix}. \tag{1}
$$

Matrix A represents the word usage in texts, with each column in [A] representing one essay sample and each row representing a unique word-type that appeared in at least two samples. Aij represents the frequency with which the ith word-type appeared in the jth essay sample. To build the LSA scoring model, 3 weight methods, TF*iDF, Entropy, and Cosine, can be used before the SVD calculation.

2.1 TF*iDF Method

We adopted the TF-iDF method to retrieve a unique measurement of the importance of each word-type in a single essay sample and the total context (Landauer and Dumias 1997),

$$W_{ij} = TF_{ij} * iDF_i = freq_{ij} * \log\left(\frac{n}{n_i}\right), \tag{2}$$

where $TF_{ij} = freq_{ij}$ represents the frequency of a word-type, iDF_i represents how many essay samples contain that word-type, n represents the number of essay samples, n_i indicates the number of essay samples containing the ith word-type, and W_{ij} represents the weight value of the ith word ($word_i$) in the jth document ($document_j$).

2.2 Entropy Method

According to Landauer and Dumias (1997), the Entropy of W_{ij} in [A] can be obtained from the formula

$$W_{ij} = \frac{\log(freq_{i,j} + 1)}{-\sum_{1-j}\left(\left(\frac{freq_{i,j}}{\sum_{1-j}freq_{i,j}}\right) * \log\left(\frac{freq_{i,j}}{\sum_{1-j}freq_{i,j}}\right)\right)}. \tag{3}$$

Note that formula (3)'s $\log(freq_{i,j} + 1)$ becomes 0 when the frequency of a word-type is 0. However, a frequency of 0 means something, while a value of 0 means nothing. It makes sense to keep a rather small value instead of simply putting a 0 in formula (3). Thus, we change $\log(freq_{i,j} + 1)$ into $\log(freq_{i,j} + 1.001)$, and $\log(freq_{i,j} + 1)$ can contain a very small number to keep information in. Therefore, formula (3) is transformed into formula (4):

$$W_{ij} = \frac{100 * \log(freq_{i,j} + 1.001)}{-\sum_{1-j}\left(\left(\frac{freq_{i,j}}{\sum_{1-j}freq_{i,j}} + 0.001\right) * \log\left(\frac{freq_{i,j}}{\sum_{1-j}freq_{i,j}} + 0.001\right)\right)}. \tag{4}$$

Similarly, formula (2) is transformed into formula (5):

$$W_{ij} = (freq_{ij} + 0.001) * \log\left(\frac{n}{n_i} + 0.001\right), \tag{5}$$

where $\mathbf{W}_{ij}$ represents the weight value of the ith word ($\mathbf{word_i}$) in the jth document ($\mathbf{document_j}$).

2.3 Cosine Normalization Method

There exists the possibility that one or two very high frequency word-types could disturb the semantic meaning of matrix [A]. The solution is cosine normalization, by which each weight (W_{ij}) is normalized (Landauer et al. 2003) over the specific essay-samples' Euclidean Lengthvia formula (6):

$$W'_{ij} = \frac{W_{ij}}{\sqrt{\sum_{j=1}^{j=n} W_{ij}^2}}, \tag{6}$$

where W'_{ij} represents the new weight value of the ith word (word$_i$) in the jth document (document$_j$).

2.4   SVD

Noting that using too many factors resulted in a very poor performance (Landauer and Dumais 1997), matrix $[A]$ then underwent a Singular Value Decomposition (SVD) calculation, a technique similar to factor analysis, as shown in formula (7).

$$\text{Matrix } A = A' = \begin{bmatrix} A_{11} & A_{12} & \cdots & A_{1n} \\ A_{21} & A_{22} & \cdots & A_{2n} \\ \cdots & \cdots & \cdots & \cdots \\ A_{m1} & A_{m1} & \cdots & A_{mn} \end{bmatrix} = T \times S \times D'$$

$$= \begin{bmatrix} T_{11} & T_{12} & \cdots & T_{1l} \\ T_{21} & T_{22} & \cdots & T_{2l} \\ \cdots & \cdots & \cdots & \cdots \\ T_{m1} & T_{m2} & \cdots & T_{ml} \end{bmatrix} \times \begin{bmatrix} \sqrt{\lambda_1} & 0 & \cdots & 0 \\ 0 & \sqrt{\lambda_2} & \cdots & 0 \\ \cdots & \cdots & \cdots & \cdots \\ 0 & 0 & \cdots & \sqrt{\lambda_l} \end{bmatrix} \times \begin{bmatrix} D_{11} & AD_{12} & \cdots & D_{1n} \\ D_{21} & D_{22} & \cdots & D_{2n} \\ \cdots & \cdots & \cdots & \cdots \\ D_{l1} & D_{l2} & \cdots & D_{ln} \end{bmatrix}, \tag{7}$$

where the matrix $[S]$ needs a singular key l subject to the reduction of matrix $[A]$. The power of the LSA model comes from dimensionality reduction by using SVD. Hence, the variation of l represents different performances of LSA's autoscoring of essays. To determine the similarity between two essays, a vector space model and the cosine similarity measurement are performed as in Antiqueira (2006).

3   Building a PLSA Model

The PLSA is a generative model that aims to find a latent topic $Z = \{z1, \cdots, zk\}$ from a vocabulary $W = \{W1, \cdots, Wm\}$ given a set of documents $D = \{D1, \cdots, Dn\}$ (Hofmann 1999). Zk indicates a probability relationship between the essay samples, LSA, and word-types. PLSA transforms each cell value in $[A']$ via formula (8):

$$p(w_j|d_i) = \sum_{k=1}^{k} p(w_j|z_k)\, p(z_k|d_i), \tag{8}$$

where the probabilities are estimated using the EM algorithm given in Hofmann (1999); k is defined as a hidden-factor and needs an integer value; $p(w_j|z_k)$ represents the distribution probability of each word-type over all contexts, which is shown in

$$p\left(w_j | z_k\right) = \frac{\sum_{i=1}^{n} a(d_i, w_j)\, p\left(z_k | d_i, w_j\right)}{\sum_{j=1}^{m} \sum_{i=1}^{n} a(d_i, w_j)\, p\left(z_k | d_i, w_j\right)}; \qquad (9)$$

and $p(z_k|d_i)$ represents the distribution probability of the contexts over all essay samples, as shown in formula (10),

$$p(z_k | d_i) = \frac{\sum_{j=1}^{m} a(d_i, w_j)\, p\left(z_k | d_i, w_j\right)}{a(d_i)}. \qquad (10)$$

To obtain a mathematical optimization and the convergence of PLSA, an iterative computation is introduced using formula (11). $p\left(z_k|d_i, w_j\right)$ can be obtained from formula (11):

$$p\left(z_k | d_i, w_j\right) = \frac{p\left(w_j | z_k\right) p\left(z_k | d_i\right)}{\sum_{l=1}^{k} p\left(w_j | z_l\right) p\left(z_l | d_i\right)}, \qquad (11)$$

where l is a predefined threshold (in this paper, we assign an integer in the range of 10 to l); it decreases with an iterative computation until the formula converges. Then, an optimized value of PLSA can be obtained. We will focus on the variation of k considering the scoring performance in this paper.

4 Experiment Setup

To analyze the scoring performance of the LSA and PLSA models, we designed 6 correlating experiments combining different weights methods. They are listed in Table 1. In the standard procedure for calculating the weights, we start with the traditional TF*iDF method as experiment 1 and the Entropy method as experiment 2. Then, both the TF*iDF and Entropy methods are applied in experiment 3. Next, the TF*iDF and Cosine methods are applied in experiment 4, and the Entropy and Cosine methods are applied in the 5th experiment. The last experiment contains all of the methods.

Table 1. The 6 experiments combining different weight methods.

	TF*iDF	Entropy	Cosine	All of above
TF*iDF	Experiment 1	Experiment 3	Experiment 4	Experiment 6
Entropy		Experiment 2	Experiment 5	

Figure 1 shows our proposed autoscoring essay system based on the LSA/PLSA models. We collected over 2444 essay responding to the same prompt. They were written by native speakers who were residents of mainland China. Then, all of the texts were transcribed into text files, with an average article size of 586 words. Each essay was subsequently scored holistically by two human raters on a six-point scale (scores ranging from 1–6), where a score of "6" indicates the *highest* quality essay and a score of "1" indicates the *lowest* quality essay. By having scores from 2 human raters,

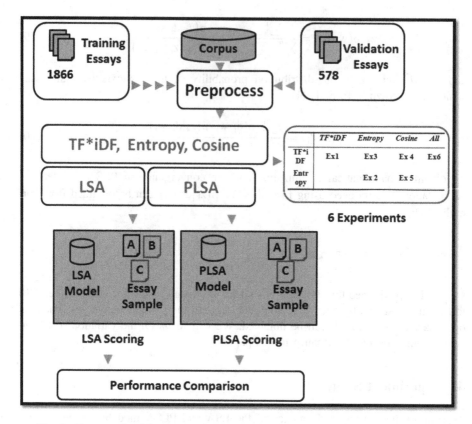

Fig. 1. Framework of the autoscoring essay system based on the LSA/PLSA models

LSA/PLSA model can be trained on essays closer to the true score (e.g., the mean of 2 human raters' scores) rather than the scores from one rater. All scored 2444 essays were separated into a training set (n = 1866) and a validation set (n = 578). A Chinese corpus was used to preprocess all of the texts into word-types. Then, the weights methods were calculated, and the LSA or PLSA models were built for essay scoring.

5   Results and Discussion

To investigate the scoring performance of the LSA and PLSA models, exact agreement and adjacent agreement between human-machine scores were calculated and compared. The scores are designated as *exact* if the LSA/PLSA model and human rater agree with each other. Scores are designated as *adjacent* if the LSA/PLSA model has exact + adjacent[1] agreement with the human score. The results are listed in Table 2.

---

[1] According to Burstein and Chodorow (1999), adjacent is defined as between 1 mark with a full-score of 6.

Table 2. LSA/PLSA performance: exact and adjacent agreement between human-machine scores.

	Description	LSA ec-agm	LSA adj-agm	PLSA ec-agm	PLSAadj-agm
Experiment 1	*TF*iDF*	0.385	0.811	0.398	0.827
Experiment 2	*Entropy*	0.443	0.694	0.402	0.781
Experiment 3	*TF*iDF-Entropy*	0.416	0.764	0.435	0.786
Experiment 4	*TF*iDF-Cosine*	0.437	0.784	0.457	0.811
Experiment 5	*Entropy-Cosine*	0.443	0.822	0.421	0.842
Experiment 6	*TF*iDF-Entropy-Cosine*	0.435	0.821	0.468	0.837

The LSA/PLSA scores on each essay sample were compared to the corresponding human score, and the best performance was listed in Table 2. To investigate the difference between the score performance of the LSA and PLSA methods, we used the two bar charts of Figs. 2 and 3.

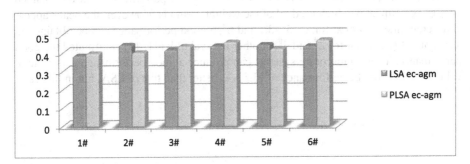

Fig. 2. Difference of exact agreement between human-machine scores via LSA and PLSA

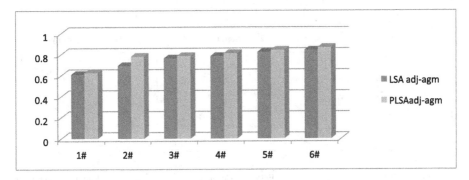

Fig. 3. Difference of adjacent agreement between human-machine scores via LSA and PLSA

The performance of PLSA is clearly better than that of LSA in these two figures. However, there are several variances concerning the comparison of LSA and PLSA, especially for the singular value k, and the chance to obtain the best scoring performance. In the practical LSA and PLSA scoring systems, we illustrated the linear trendlines of LSA's performance and PLSA's performance in each experiment while $k \in (1, 15)$

We attempt to correlate the scoring performance of LSA and PLSA using combinations of 3 weight methods. Because of the large performance dispersion for all k ($k \in (1, n)$), we perform the analysis taking only the first 16 digits ($k \in (1, 15)$), which represents the core idea of SVD and the significant variation. This analysis results in the two sets of trendlines in Figs. 4 and 5. They are organized with the k distributed along the horizontal axes and the agreement between human and machine scores positioned along the vertical axes. The labels $1^\#$, ..., $6^\#$ refer to the 6 experiments in Table 1.

Figure 4 indicates that the exact agreements of LSA and PLSA, with the three weight methods, are very sensitive to the increasing value of k. More significant are the results for the $2^\#$ and the $5^\#$. Similar trendlines can be easily recognized from the result of the $1^\#$ and the $4^\#$, as well as the $3^\#$ and the $6^\#$. While the performances of LSA and PLSA are similar, roughly between 0.39–0.46, the best performance can be obtained only in experiment 6, which used all of the weight methods. However, the peaks appear at different intervals of k: for $1^\#$, $5^\#$, $3^\#$, and $6^\#$, a good performance can be obtained in terms of $k \in (5, 7)$, but for $2^\#$ and $4^\#$, another interval of k (11, 12) contributed the good performance. Thus, autoscoring systems can produce a good performance with a small value of k. In sum, the performance of PLSA is better than that of LSA, but in this case,

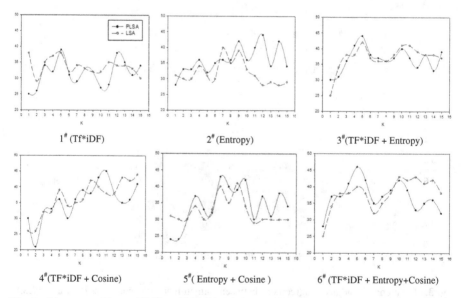

$1^\#$ (Tf*iDF) $2^\#$ (Entropy) $3^\#$ (TF*iDF + Entropy)

$4^\#$ (TF*iDF + Cosine) $5^\#$ (Entropy + Cosine) $6^\#$ (TF*iDF + Entropy+Cosine)

Fig. 4. Linear trendlines of LSA and PLSAs' exact agreement of human-machine scores in 6 experiments where $k \in (1, 15)$

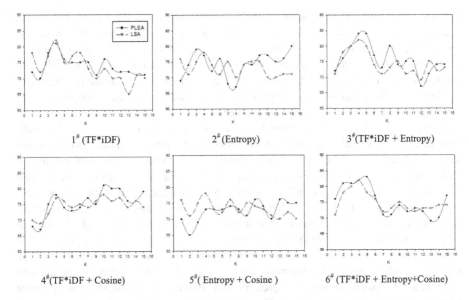

$1^{\#}$ (TF*iDF) $2^{\#}$ (Entropy) $3^{\#}$(TF*iDF + Entropy)

$4^{\#}$(TF*iDF + Cosine) $5^{\#}$(Entropy + Cosine) $6^{\#}$ (TF*iDF + Entropy+Cosine)

Fig. 5. Linear trendlines of LSA and PLSAs' adjacent agreement of human-machine scores in 6 experiments, $k \in (1, 15)$.

it is not as much as we expected or as much as was reported previously (Chen et al. 2012).

Similar conclusions can be drawn from Fig. 5, which shows that the adjacent agreements of LSA and PLSA, with the three weight methods, are sensitive to the increasing value of k, though most of them tend to decrease with the increasing value of k. It appears that the trendlines of the LSA and PLSA models allow one to easily capture the peaks of performance from the interval of k. While the good performances of LSA and PLSA are similar, roughly between 0.78–0.85, again, the best performance can be obtained in experiment 6, which used all of the weight methods. However, the peaks appear at different intervals of k: for $1^{\#}$, $2^{\#}$, $3^{\#}$, $5^{\#}$, and $6^{\#}$, a good performance can be obtained via $k \in (5, 7)$, but not for $4^{\#}$. Additionally, while there is practically no difference in the performances using weight methods, the results for $3^{\#}$ and $6^{\#}$ more significant. From a linguistic point of view, one may infer that using all of the weight methods could effectively retrieve semantic features from the data set, positively promoting the machine scoring approach. It should be mentioned that, again, the performance of PLSA is only slightly better than that of LSA.

6   Conclusion and Perspectives

We have applied the LSA and PLSA models to calculate the scores of essays that were written by university students in the Chinese language and were pre-scored by human raters. A correlation research study was designed to investigate the scoring performances of the LSA/PLSA models considering 3 weight methods, i.e., TF*iDF,

Entropy, and Cosine normalization, in the 6 experiments. From the exact and adjacent agreements of the machine scores and human scores, we found that both the LSA/PLSA models could be applied to essay scoring systems supplementing human judgment. However, when analyzing the specific performance of these 2 models with different weight methods, variation trends in terms of the k value were easily identified. The overall performance of PLSA is generally better than that of LSA, along with all of the weight methods. We interpreted the latter results as being due to the presence of more semantic features, e.g., the word meaning in the context and the word's coefficient in a data set could be retrieved by using more weight methods. However, the scoring performance of PLSA is only slightly better than the scoring performance of LSA, which disagrees with research studies in the information retrieval area (Chen et al. 2012). This discrepancy calls for further, more detailed research into the possible correlation between LSA and PLSA applications. The results here have important implications for computer-based educational measurements as well. While an increasing amount of automated essay scoring systems may be established, their utility is limited to providing scores, and well-documented assessment strategies, such as writing portfolios, writing conferences, and the process writing approach, should still be included in computer-assisted teaching and learning programs. Moreover, more reliable measures for assessment, such as text formats and forms, still need to be a part of the text quality analysis in our future research.

Acknowledgements. The authors are very grateful to the anonymous referees for their very detailed referencing and helpful suggestions to improve this paper. Also, the author would like to express their sincere acknowledgements to the Guangdong Province Natural Science Fund Project (2015A030313575), the Innovative School Project in Higher Education of Guangdong (GWTP-LH-2015-06), and the University innovation projects of Guangdong province (2014).

References

Antiqueira, L., Costa, L.F.: Using complex networks for language processing: the case of summary evaluation. In: Communications, Circuits and Systems Proceedings 2006, pp. 2678–2682 (2006)

Ke, X., Zeng, Y., Ma, Q., Zhu, L.: Complex dynamics of text analysis. Phys. A. **415**, 307–314 (2014). http://dx.doi.org/10.1016/j.physa.2014.08.022

Burstein, J., Chodorow, M.: Automated essay scoring for nonnative English speakers. In: Proceedings of the ACL99 Workshop on Computer-Mediated Language Assessment and Evaluation of Natural Language Processing (1999)

Chen, Y., et al.: A topic detection method based on semantic dependency distance and PLSA. In: The Proceedings of Computer Supported Cooperative Work in Design (CSCWD), vol. 5, pp. 703–708 (2012)

Gui, S.: The theory of latent semantic analysis and its application. Liguist. Appl. Linguist. **1**, 76–85 (2003)

Hofmann, T.: Probabilistic latent semantic indexing. In: Proceedings of SIGIR 1999 (1999)

Landauer, T.K., Dumais, S.T.: A solution to Plato's problem: the latent semantic analysis theory of acquisition, induction, and representation of knowledge. Psychol. Rev. **104**(2), 211–240 (1997)

Landauer, T., Laham, D., Foltz, P.: Automatic essay assessment. Assess. Educ. Princ. Policy Pract. **3**, 295–309 (2003)

Shermis, M.D., Burstein, J.: Handbook of Automated Essay Evaluation: Current Applications and New Directions. Routledge, New York (2013)

Thomas, H.: Unsupervised learning by probabilistic latent semantic analysis. Mach. Learn. **2**, 177–196 (2001)

Workshop on Online Adaptive Learning Techniques and Applications

Look Taiwan Education Big Data Research and Development

Yu-Sheng Su[1,2(✉)], Chester S.J. Huang[2], Sheng-Yi Wu[3],
and Chiu-Nan Su[4]

[1] Research Center for Advanced Science and Technology,
National Central University, Taoyuan, Taiwan
addison@csie.ncu.edu.tw
[2] Department of Computer Science and Information Engineering,
National Central University, Taoyuan, Taiwan
shinjia.huang@gmail.com
[3] Department of Science Communication, National Pingtung University,
Pingtung, Taiwan
digschool@gmail.com
[4] Department of Information Management, Nan-Jeon University of Science
and Technology, Tainan, Taiwan
cnsu@mail.njtc.edu.tw

Abstract. With the coming of 4G era, the popularity of various kinds of online equipment, the maturity of Web 2.0 skills, and the effects of increased ability of internet of students and teachers, Taiwan Education Cloud has been progressively emerging with the characteristics of large volume, velocity, and variety of education big data. This has made the currently familiarized techniques of statistical learning and data mining of all departments of MOE (Ministry of Education), such as news briefing, artificial retrieving and synthesizing information, and personnel experience judgment, unable to efficaciously analyze education big data that rapidly accumulate. We develop a new analytical steps and logical thinking so that, while facing such digital information accumulation trend, composedly extract information of valuable teachers and students feedback from such education big data mighty torrent. The paper is to aim for "Look Taiwan Education Big Data Research and Development", and we use the currently big data techniques to analyze the learning background of individual learners in Taiwan Education Big Market. Through the collection, conduction, and analysis of the past using experience, it was further predicted, suggested, and giving feedback on the need of Taiwan Education Big Market for teachers and students.

Keywords: Big data techniques · Taiwan education cloud · Taiwan education big market

© Springer International Publishing AG 2017
T.-T. Wu et al. (Eds.): SETE 2016, LNCS 10108, pp. 415–421, 2017.
DOI: 10.1007/978-3-319-52836-6_43

1 Introduction

In 2012, the Ministry of Education (MOE) implemented "Application of Education Cloud and Interface Service Promoting Plan," and established infrastructure of education cloud environment [1]. The goal of MOE integrated on cloud learning resource and service, and they aimed at the following four perspectives: (1) to integrate the various existing cloud learning materials and service of MOE, universities, and industries, to induce the categories according to the areas and phases, etc., and to help learners search and access easily, which will accomplish a "learner-centered" resource requirement; (2) under the learner-centered concept, to provide learners with autonomous learning service, which will make each learner refer to the learning advice and guidance, based on his/her own learning phase, and to arrange personal learning progress for autonomous learning ability; (3) to integrate various learning resources and learning services through education cloud, which will avoid the waste of learning resources from repeated development and static investment; (4) to expect that teachers and students can "Bring Your Own Device, (BYOD)" at school, as a world-wide trend. Many schools have implemented mobile learning, and the MOE has supplied tens of tablets at school to enhance e-learning environment.

Taiwan education cloud [1] makes relevant websites of teaching resources (learning station, exchange platform, learning resource, interscholastic resource share, and creative commons), through common regulations of the platforms, back-end data standardized learning materials, and cross-platform search engine, etc., integrate as a convenient and functional "MOE Digital Learning Resource Entrance," providing with single portal sites for teachers and learners to easily grab digital teaching resources. Hence, it can make more interactive applications for teachers' communities. Taiwan education cloud, for the instantaneity of the future and characteristic of mobile digital learning, integrates the education resources from direct-controlled municipalities, city and county governments, organizations affiliated to the Ministry of Education, and some folk units through "Taiwan Education Big Market [2]." Figure 1 shows, based on the statistics by May 23rd 2014, the Web education resources, educational e-books, and education APPs. There are approximately 150,000 Web education resources of education ISP website, 900 market teaching APPs of nationwide education, 5,000 city and county education resources, and 14,000 resources from the affiliated units.

With the coming of 4G era internet, high speed network will enhance the digital data traffic of the internet, and it also boost the need of e-traffic. The need of applying education cloud big data will be increasing in the coming 3 years [5]. In a published and authorized document from the US Department of Education [6], it emphasized the importance between data exploration and learning analysis on education. In this paper, we use the existing Taiwan Education Big Market Data to execute basic exploration as well as analysis on the practical education application of the future. Therefore, we want to look Taiwan education big data to analyze the applied information accumulated from Taiwan education big market, and further figured out the value of the date and extracted usable information.

Fig. 1. Taiwan education big market shows the statistics of the Web education resources, educational e-books, and education APPs.

2 Literature Review

Based on the prosperity of world-wide web and cloud technology, the operation history of users is totally recorded. The foci of the communities are not only the analyzing skills and the development of the tools but also the abundant information extracted and decoded from the great number of data. Furthermore, the feedback of people on various cases is elicited to predict the trends of the future. To use the huge data to analyze, evaluate, improve, and predict like this is the application [1, 4] on Taiwan education big data. The trend of using Taiwan education data has gradually influenced education. The recently grown up Massive Open Online Course (MOOC), Online Tutoring, Learning Management System (LMS), integration of technology into teaching, and so on [8–10]. Students' learning progress will thus be recorded, and the records provide teachers with tips to improve teaching and carry out adaptive teaching as well. Therefore, some researchers [3] remained reserved. They worried too much dependence on the technology-oriented data will narrow and limit the development of education and influence students' privacy. No matter how we concern about the application on Taiwan education data, this issue has been a trend of analysis. The educators must remain concerned about this issue and make discussion on the relative applications as well as limitations.

Some high education studies [7–9] indicated that the concept and analysis of big data can be used on various educational administrations and teaching applications, taking examples of manpower hiring and management, financial planning, donation following, or monitoring students' performance. Generally, the exploration and analysis of data can offer instant feedback or prediction. On students' learning, we can predict their learning behaviors through digital data, like if they will drop out the school, need helps or be able to face more difficult challenge, and so on. This seems to help us to discern which pedagogy will be effective to some students, which corresponds adaptive teaching [5, 6].

Besides this, the application of big data can also develop core architecture and technique instrument [10] to evaluate the performance of students or teachers. Therefore, the model of education treatment on these choices will base on existing recommendation systems. From this, it can be seen that the development and application of big data on education will be necessary and promotable. Using big data [7, 9] to estimate and predict the development of education and so on seems a good way to progress. However, to use these data remains risky and needs awareness. According to the findings from two researchers [5, 7], it was necessary to have data provided by professional analysts to ensure the accuracy of the research. Therefore, the practicality of big data may limit the research questions because we would not have the data of all kinds of cases. The data would confine our study. Hence, it would be more important to sort and analyze the available data in the paper. Privacy would be the most vital but perhaps the most neglected case. To analyze, users' digital data need to be collected. That is why we need to be aware of their privacy to protect the rights and interests.

3   Methodology

Figure 2 depicts the framework diagram, and it shows the application and research of Taiwan education big market in Taiwan education cloud. Through big data technique, we can have deeply analyze contents and records of education application in Taiwan education big market. We hope to improve the procedures of adaptive education and boost educators' teaching efficiency. Moreover, we also hope to, through big data analysis, expand the high quality and multielement teaching contents, and then to enhance learners' learning attitude and immersive effect.

In the framework diagram in Fig. 2, we designed the integration of big data core architecture, big data analysis, and instrument techniques. From the right to the left, we can see (A) taking Taiwan education big market data, (B) big data core architecture, and (C) big data tools. Aiming at the big digital data base of Taiwan education big market, we used big data core architecture and technique instrument to analyze the learning history of teachers and learners, and through various statistics learning and data exploration, to understand the learners' learning condition.

(A)   Taking Taiwan Education Big Market Data

First, we needed to understand the needs of Minister of Education and data characteristics of Taiwan education big market, shown in Fig. 1. Second, the accessibility of data should be confirmed and thus categorized to confirm the field, which provide the back-end data analyzing system with assess to application and ensure the research directions of Taiwan education cloud. Hence, limits of authority should be also confirmed to protect privacy and copyright.

(B) **Big Data Core Architecture**

We provide a core architecture conducting education big data analysis, and develop the technique based on this framework. The smart resource managing mechanism can effectively control the computing learning resources, and let multimedia learning data analyzing applications work rapidly under the limited resources. Therefore, the global big data analyzing tasks will work directly on these physical machines, to avoid efficacy losses during data transit and duplication.

(C) **Big Data Tools**

We overcame the challenge of big data management, and to fill the need of the organization, we carried on big data handling analysis mechanism on Taiwan education cloud condition through collecting, integrating, and analyzing the mass user history on Taiwan education big market. From the past using experience data, including words, emotional contents, interpersonal network, relative communication, as well as message flows, we presented quantitative statistical data and saved them on big data database. At last, the users can present quantitative statistics through visualizing user interface and understand efficiently student's learning condition. Thus, they can predict, suggest, and give feedback to students, which boosts the efficiency of work.

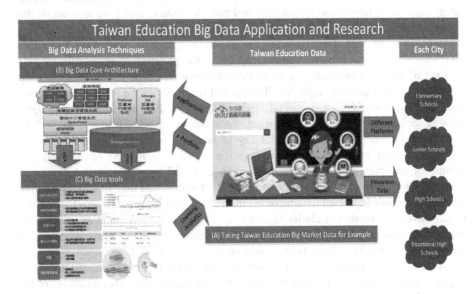

Fig. 2. The framework diagram of Taiwan education big data application and research.

4 Conclusion and Further Work

We focus on the communication and consultation with professionals of every field, in order to confirm the execution of every task. In view of this, we establish consulting group and invite, on or off scheduled, group members to attend the meetings about the need analysis of Taiwan education big market application, category platform data record, resource field confirmation, judging mechanism of digital resources, and authority limits of resource confirmation, etc.

The preparation of a lesson by a teacher is like that of a delicious dish, which needs a lot of ingredients. Beside textbooks, teacher's manuals, and some basic materials, in order to enhance students' interest and learning effect, we would collect more extracurricular materials about the lessons, including Web learning resources, education e-books and teaching Apps, etc. Taiwan education big market provides these resources, but the included ones are so many and complicated that they need to induce the way to categorize its recourses. Therefore, we will make thorough inspection and categorization on the mass included resources and users' behavior records in Taiwan education big market to sum up the practicability of the characteristics and application of the resources. For example, how will the teaching resources in various educational systems (elementary school, junior and senior high school and vocational high school, etc.) influence the users' browsing behaviors? Thus, we will carry on the users' resource recommendation based on this concept.

The resource exchange and sharing mechanism of Taiwan education big market is therefore understood, and we will verify the possible data field in education analysis. When more and more future users entering the terrace collect or share learning resources, there will be increasing system logs. Hence, how we extract the meaningful categorized items from these system logs and conduct relative data field analysis on the operation behaviors for the sake of the future studies seems significant. In this paper, we will provide metadata recording explanation Standard Operation Procedure (SOP) for the users to browse, consult, and orient the planning of application.

One of the most concerned issue of the retrieving and applying of education big data is the privacy and copyright, etc. The present study clarify the related issue on two aspects: first, copyright, and second, right of privacy. For the sake of copyright, through the assistance of law professional, the authority range of resource use will be acquainted in order to insure the usability of teaching resources. According to the filling-in of metadata, ways of sharing resource authority, uploading of data and presenting of complete data structure, the usable data will be retrieved and computed analysis. On the aspect of right of privacy, we shall understand the "limit" of objective data. In other words, not all data recorded in the back-end terrace can be retrieved and used. Therefore, we should clarify the relative using range information as anonymous processing. However, whether these processing will influence the application of Taiwan education big data needs further estimation.

At last, we had negotiation and cooperation with professionals of related areas and acquired usable Taiwan education big data. Then, we analyzed the characteristics of the data, clarified relative data field and authority limit in order to provide practicability of resource application and further establish the applicable environment of the future. Hence, it provided with back-end big data analyzing system for applying to ensure the direction of applied study of Taiwan education cloud. For basic estimation and comprehension of the possible influence of the future in the present study to accomplish the planning of the complete Taiwan education big data research, we need to invite professionals, scholars, teachers, students, and so on to carry on discussion of the issue and give suggestion of the planning, in order to ensure the correctness of the research direction and avoid negative impacts.

Acknowledgements. This study is supported in part by Research Center for Advanced Science and Technology and Ministry of Science and Technology, Republic of China, Taiwan under contract numbers MOST 105-2914-I-008-025-A1.

References

1. Taiwan Education Cloud. http://cloud.edu.tw/
2. Taiwan Education Big Market. https://market.cloud.edu.tw/
3. Chen, D.-Y., Hu, L.-T., Tseng, K.-C.: Engaging citizens through E-government 2.0: hopes and problems as evident in the case of Taiwan. In: Shark, A.R., Toporkoff, S. (eds.) Beyond eGovernment - Measuring Performance: A Global Perspective, pp. 99–108 (2010)
4. Eynon, R.: The rise of big data: what does it mean for education, technology, and media research? Learn. Media Technol. **38**(3), 237–240 (2013)
5. West, D.M.: Big Data for Education: Data Mining, Data Analytics, and Web Dashboards. Governance Studies. Reuters, Brookings (2012)
6. Picciano, A.G.: The evolution of big data and learning analytics in American higher education. J. Asynchronous Learn. Netw. **16**(3), 9–20 (2012)
7. Siemens, G.: What are learning analytics? (2013)
8. Tabaa, Y.: LASyM: a learning analytics system for MOOCs. IJACSA Int. J. Adv. Comput. Sci. Appl. **4**(5), 113–119 (2013)
9. Chen, H., Chiang, R.H.L., Storey, V.C.: Business intelligence and analytics: from big data to big impact. MIS Q. **36**(4), 1–24 (2013)
10. Eaton, C., Deroos, D., Deutsch, T., Lapis, G., Zikopoulos, P.: Understanding Big Data: Analytics for Enterprise Class Hadoop and Streaming Data. McGraw Hill Companies, New York (2012)

VisCa: A Dashboard System to Visualize Learning Activities from E-learning Platforms

Chan-Hsien Lin[(⊠)], Shih-Shin Hu, Horng-Yih Lai,
Chieh-Feng Chiang, Hsiao-Chien Tseng, and Yuan-Che Cheng

Institute for Information Industry, Digital Education Institute, Taipei, Taiwan
chanhsienlin@iii.org.tw

Abstract. With the advance of ICT technology, the e-learning platform from higher education to K12 becomes increasingly prevalent in recent years. Furthermore, as the emerging trend of data science, several educational platforms have introduced learning analytics and data-driven learning in their system, leading to more adaptive and personalized learning services. Therefore, it is crucial time to develop a mechanism to manage and visualize the data of learning experience. To achieve this goal, we created a web-based dashboard system called VisCa to track, store, and show learning experience from e-learning platforms. The data model is based on the standard of Experience API (xAPI) to communicate with third-party platforms. The whole system brings a general framework for the data flow of learning experience, as well as supports the students and teachers to understand their leaning status. The development of this study will provide an infrastructure to collect the data of learning activities, which can be used for further learning analytics or data-driven learning in the future.

Keywords: Data visualization · Learning analytics · Learning record store · Experience API

1 Introduction

The advance of cloud computing provides a convenient environment to share all kinds of information on network, and leads to various innovations and online applications in recent years. It has also given rise to the development of many e-learning platforms, which aimed at self-learning students and open access through the network. The appearance of these platforms not only has the effect of amplifying the conventional and social use of network environments, but also contributes the use of educational technology in all possible contexts. Many platforms provide a large number of open courses to all students, and serve interactive user forums or communities between students and professor 1. Some adaptive or personalized learning platforms, such as Knewton or Smart Sparrow, can based on student's proficiency in the platform to provide directions about learning pathway, or to give suggestions of learning materials 2. With the pervasiveness of e-learning environment, we have more opportunities to analyze the learning behavior or pattern from learners. When a user regularly accesses learning services on an e-learning platform, data of activities on the platform can be

© Springer International Publishing AG 2017
T.-T. Wu et al. (Eds.): SETE 2016, LNCS 10108, pp. 422–427, 2017.
DOI: 10.1007/978-3-319-52836-6_44

quickly accumulated, and these data can promote the research of learning analytics or educational data mining 3. Learning analytics is a new research area that has rapidly gained attention in recent years. The purpose of learning analytics is to understand and optimize the learning environment for a learner, and it includes the study of measurement, collection, analysis and reporting of learning data 45. There are several research teams focusing on the learning data extracted from e-learning platforms 67. For example, a large-scale study of video engagement on edX platform indicates that the characteristics of videos are related to students' engagement 8. Another research teams on Coursera also explored the video lecture interaction to see the relation between watching sessions and students' engagement 9. Moreover, the low-level data in the form of user events are transformed as high-level parameters to evaluate the engagement and learning process on the platform of Khan Academy 10. Therefore, considering the above research cases on MOOCs, the long-term user events stored on the e-learning platform provide a good data resource for the presentation of students' learning status, and for the large-scale researches on learning behaviors.

However, there is no generally standard data model for user records, and this fact reduces the interoperability of learning events in different platform. Hence, a standard specification, called as Experience API (xAPI), was currently developed by Advanced Distributed Learning (ADL) to solve the problem 11. The purpose of this standard is to store and access the learning experiences by a unified format. It describes an interface and the retrieval rules that can record the detail events of learners' actions, including watching a video, taking an assessment, or reading an e-book. After tracking on learning experiences from users through the xAPI, the experience data will be delivered to and stored in a database called learning record store (LRS), which can be subsequently used as the data source of learning analytics and visualization. In our work, we created a dashboard system called VisCa to catch all kinds of learning experience from e-learning platform, and visualized these data by several dashboards on the web. VisCa can help students and teachers leverage the latest learning experiences by xAPI standard, and solve data silos problems and support innovative learning designs and technologies without limit. Because of the structure and semantic interoperability of xAPI, VisCa can integrate and visualized data from different systems or applications. The statistical result of experience data shown in dashboards can represent the learning status, behavior, or pattern across diversity platforms. The real-time data feedback loops aim to benefit instructors, learners, administrators and product developers, and will be used to support data-driven learning.

2   Overview of System

2.1   The Standard of Experience API

To enable tracking on learning experiences, the xAPI is designed to allow the statements of experience to be delivered to and stored in an LRS. The format of these statements is based on activity stream to syndicate activities across social web applications and services. A statement is composed of three principal fields including actor, verb, and object. The actor is the agent which the statement is about, such as a learner, teacher, or

Table 1. Properties of xAPI statement

Properties	Description
Actor	Indicate an agent or group object
Verb	Represent the action between Actor and Object
Object	Indicate the target what the Actor interacted with
Result	Show a measured outcome related to the statement
Context	Provide a place to add contextual information to a statement
Timestamp	Record the time at which the learning experience occurred
Stored	Record the time at which a statement is stored into LRS
Authority	Provide information about whom or what asserted that this statement is true
Version	xAPI specification version
Attachments	A digital artifact providing evidence of a learning experience

group. The object represents what the actor interacted with, and can be any learning material such as videos, tests, or books. The verb is the interaction between the actor and the object, so that it depends on the type of objects. In addition to three basic fields, there are some extra properties to supplement an xAPI statement as shown in Table 1.

For each property in a statement, there are still sub-properties to describe the details of the property, and that means the structure of a complete statement is hierarchical. Therefore, as shown in the Fig. 1, an xAPI statement is stored in JSON format, which is an open standard format that can represent hierarchical data object with the form of attribute-value pairs. Based on the xAPI standard, we designed several data recipes to communicate with the third-party e-learning platforms.

```
"id": "2a1cf4dc-364b-463f-975f-d4dfd9548cb9",
"actor": {
    "objectType": "Agent",
    "mbox": "mailto:tyler@example.com"
},
"verb": {
    "id": "http://example.com/verbs/highlighted",
    "display": {
        "en-US": "highlighted"
    }
},
"object": {
    "objectType": "Activity",
    "id": "http://example.com/activities/paragraph%207"
},
"result": {
    "response": "insightful"
},
"context": {
    "contextActivities": {
        "parent": [
            {
                "objectType": "Activity",
                "id": "http://example.com/activities/page%209",
                "definition": {
                    "name": {
                        "en-US": "page 9"
                    },
                    "description": {}
                }
            }
```

Fig. 1. The format of an xAPI statement

2.2   System Architecture

We used the MongoDB, which supports JSON-like documents, as our LRS to store all xAPI-based learning records. The learning experience from the users in third-party platform will be transferred into our LRS via xAPI statements. The low-level user events will be tracked as learning behaviors when students watch an online video and e-book, or take an assessment in an e-learning platform. We also created a wrapper module which can be quickly used or embedded for any e-learning platform to generate standard learning records. After processing and analyzing the raw data of learning experiences data in LRS, some visualized dashboards via a web server are provided for students and teachers to see their learning pattern. We show the flowchart of the system architecture in Fig. 2, as well as the web page of dashboard system in Fig. 3.

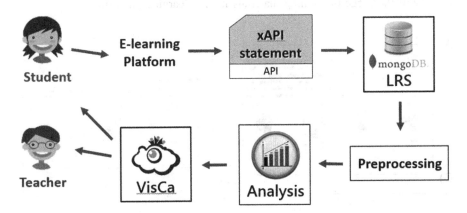

Fig. 2. The flowchart of system architecture

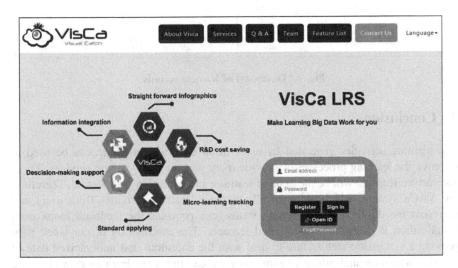

Fig. 3. The web page of VisCa

2.3   Dashboard of Learning Experiences

As concern as the friendly representation of learning records in LRS, a dashboard which can show the statistics of learning behaviors is needed. A student can see the learning pattern or style in the learning platform, while a teacher can check the usage of learning materials and improve them. Four kinds of dashboard showing the statistics of learning records were depicted in Fig. 4. The overview of collected learning records in recent days is shown in Fig. 4A. The level of engagement of different kinds of materials including video, e-book, practice, or assessment, is illustrated in Fig. 4B. The watching pattern for a video and the assessment result in a class are shown in Fig. 4C and D, respectively. These dashboards enable students, teachers, web administrators, and researchers to view the statistics of their learning records in a favorable way, and these visualization can be used as a report of learning status of each student, or as a summary of the usage of learning materials in an e-learning platform.

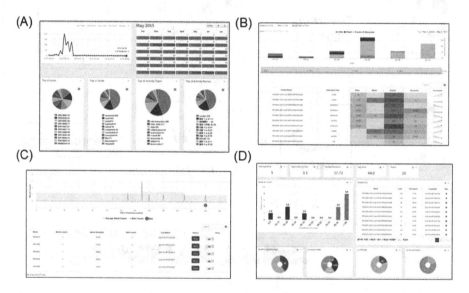

Fig. 4. Dashboard of learning records

3   Conclusion

The learning activities generated by users in an e-learning platform can be used to improve the learning processes or provide more personalized learning services. These data-driven learning will be the trend of learning and education in the future. Therefore, the VisCa system, which automatically retrieve learning activities from users and represent the dashboards of learning status, can provides the feedback loops from visualization to benefit instructors and learners. The contribution of our work is to provide a systematic architecture to deal with the enormous and unorganized data of learning activities, and primarily show how we can use these learning data via some dashboards of visualization. The goal behind the work in this study is to build a standard model to process and represent the learning data, and it will benefit to further learning analytics or data-driven learning in the future.

Acknowledgements. This study is conducted under the "III Innovative and Prospective Technologies Project" of the Institute for Information Industry which is subsidized by the Ministry of Economy Affairs of the Republic of China.

References

1. Johnson, L., Adams Becker, S., Estrada, V., Freeman, A.: NMC Horizon Report: 2015 Higher Education Edition. The New Media Consortium, Austin (2015)
2. Johnson, L., Adams Becker, S., Estrada, V., Freeman, A.: NMC Horizon Report: 2015 K-12 Edition. The New Media Consortium, Austin (2015)
3. Masud, M.A.H., Huang, X.: An e-learning system architecture based on cloud computing. System **10**(11) (2012)
4. Picciano, A.G.: The evolution of big data and learning analytics in American higher education. J. Asynchronous Learn. Netw. **16**(3), 9–20 (2012)
5. Siemens, G., Long, P.: Penetrating the fog: analytics in learning and education. Educause Rev. **46**(5), 30 (2011)
6. Siemens, G.: Learning analytics: envisioning a research discipline and a domain of practice. In: Proceedings of the 2nd International Conference on Learning Analytics and Knowledge, New York, pp. 4–8 (2012)
7. Greller, W., Drachsler, H.: Translating learning into numbers: a generic framework for learning analytics. J. Educ. Technol. Soc. **15**(3), 42–57 (2012)
8. Guo, P.J., Kim, J., Rubin, R.: How video production affects student engagement: an empirical study of MOOC videos. In: Proceedings of the First ACM Conference on Learning@ Scale Conference, New York, pp. 41–50 (2014)
9. Sinha, T., Jermann, P., Li, N., Dillenbourg, P.: Your click decides your fate: inferring information processing and attrition behavior from MOOC video clickstream interactions. Presented at the 2014 Empirical Methods in Natural Language Processing Workshop on Modeling Large Scale Social Interaction in Massively Open Online Courses (2014)
10. Muñoz-Merino, P.J., Valiente, J.A.R., Kloos, C.D.: Inferring higher level learning information from low level data for the Khan Academy platform. In: Proceedings of the Third International Conference on Learning Analytics and Knowledge, New York, pp. 112–116 (2013)
11. ADL-Co-Laboratories: Experience API Version 1.0.0 (2013)

Building an Online Adaptive Learning
and Recommendation Platform

Hsiao-Chien Tseng[1](✉), Chieh-Feng Chiang[1], Jun-Ming Su[2],
Jui-Long Hung[3], and Brett E. Shelton[3]

[1] Digital Education Institute, Institute for Information Industry, Taipei, Taiwan
tseng.tsc@gmail.com
[2] Department of Information and Learning Technology,
National University of Tainan, Tainan, Taiwan
[3] Department of Educational Technology, Boise State University, Boise, USA

Abstract. In the traditional e-learning environment lack of immediate learning assistance. This online adaptive learning and recommendation platform (ALR) provide tracking tool for instructors to "observe" or "monitor" individual students' learning activities. Students can learn through the ALR platform using the learning path to get the immediate assistance. Individual students' learning strengths and weaknesses can be revealed via analyzing learning activities, learning process, and learning performance. Related analysis results can be utilized to develop corresponding automatic interventions in order to achieve goals of adaptive learning. Therefore, the purpose of this study aims to construct the concept map for adaptive learning, provide educational recommender for individual students. On the top of these prior projects, this project will develop the following intelligent components: (1) personalized dynamic concept maps for adaptive learning; (2) personalized learning path recommendation; and (3) context-based recommendation for meeting personal learning needs. Each of components will be strictly validated to ensure its practicability. This study introduce the ALR platform.

Keywords: Concept mapping · Adaptive learning · Educational recommender

1 Introduction

Online learning has become popular in recent years, especially the online self-regulated learning platforms (such as Coursera, edX, and Udacity). For example, the self-regulated learning platform (www.junyiacademy.org) provides over 7,600 free learning videos for junior and senior high school students in Taiwan (Junyi Academy 2016). However, how to select suitable (meeting with personal learning needs and capability) learning materials from a huge amount of learning resources becomes a challenge for students. In addition, these platforms heavily replies on learner's autonomy. A standardized package cannot meet learning needs from individual students. Therefore, it is crucial to provide "customized" learning materials or paths in order to cultivate successful students.

© Springer International Publishing AG 2017
T.-T. Wu et al. (Eds.): SETE 2016, LNCS 10108, pp. 428–432, 2017.
DOI: 10.1007/978-3-319-52836-6_45

However, in the self-regulated learning platforms, students encounter two major learning barrier—metacognition and information overload (Riverin and Stacey 2008). Learners are usually designed to accept a huge amount of learning resources, including videos, written lectures, and online discussions. However, learners might not have sufficient knowledge and ability to diagnose personal learning needs or learning weakness and then locate suitable correct learning resources.

In order to overcome above challenges, adaptive learning has attracted attentions by scholars and educators (Brusilovsky 2003). Adaptive online learning environments emphasizes the following advantages to attract learners:

1. Instant feedback: studies have shown that the immediacy and frequency of feedback significantly influences learning performance. Adaptive online learning platforms usually embed mechanisms aiming to provide instant feedback (Šimko et al. 2010).
2. Personalized learning: theoretically, more than one learning paths can achieve the same learning goals. An adaptive (smart) learning system can diagnose student's learning preferences and current status in order to recommend personalized learning path (Chen 2008).
3. Self-paced learning: on the adaptive learning platforms, students will not be blamed by failing in basic questions. On the other hand, students can skip units which have been mastered and focus on their own learning weaknesses. Quick or slow learners can take their own pace without considering others (Chan et al. 2001).

With the support of Taiwan's Ministry of Economic Affairs, this project aims to develop online adaptive learning and recommendation platform (ALR). The purpose of this study is to introduce the framework of the project and the adaptive learning and recommendation platform.

2 Literature Review

The major components of the adaptive learning systems contain two parts: the component of dynamic concept map and the component of context-based recommender. The framework will be presented in a latter section, here will discuss prior work in concept map and education recommender systems.

2.1 Concept Map

Concept maps are graphical tools for organizing and representing knowledge. They include concepts, usually enclosed in circles or boxes of some type, and relationships between concepts indicated by a connecting line linking two concepts. Concept maps were developed in 1972 in the course of Novak's research program at Cornell University where he sought to follow and understand changes in children's knowledge of science (Novak and Musonda 1991). Concept map presents concept structures via nodes and connections. Nodes represent concepts and connections between two nodes represents relationships. The relationships can be non-, singular-, or bi-directional. In a concept map, the entire "map" is shown as a hierarchical structure. Generic concepts are located at the upper levels and concrete, specific concepts are located at the lower levels. The sequence of learning order (i.e. learning path) becomes more organized and systematic via concept map.

2.2 Education Recommender Systems

Burke (2002) defined recommender systems as any systems which can generate personalized recommendation in order to provide guidance among choices. The recommendations usually contain interesting or useful options. In today's online learning, learners are exposed to a huge amount of learning resources. Therefore, learners need an effective mechanism which can recommend suitable resources. Educational Recommender systems also attracted lots of research efforts in recent years (such as Park et al. 2012; Santos 2011). Buder and Christina (2012) suggested educational recommender systems should focus on the non-technical factors, instead of the algorithms. The algorithms used in the e-commerce might not be suitable for educational environments. The systems should combine with education related theories, especially when the system applies to non-traditional learning environments. Vasilecas (2007) also suggested to combine multiple algorithms in order to avoid the issues of cold start and data sparsity. In addition, in order to achieve the goal of personalized learning, learning recommendations should take individual learners' situation into consideration in order to provide the most appropriate recommendations.

3 The Framework of the Adaptive Learning Platform

Figure 1 shows the framework of the whole project. The platform contains the following major components:

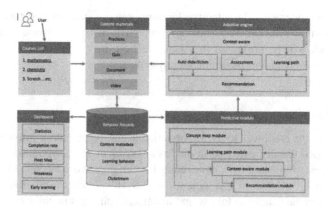

Fig. 1. Framework of the adaptive learning platform

- **Course list:** a database table which stores courses offered on the platform;
- **Content materials:** a cloud-based database which stores course materials. The major formats of course materials include instructional videos, written course materials, and assessment;
- **Behavior records:** in order to track student's learning behaviors performed on the platform, this project adopts xAPI standards (reference here) to store content metadata, learner metadata, learning behaviors, and clickstreams;
- **Adaptive engine:** the engine is used to generate real-time recommendations based on learner's learning contexts. Recommendations will be triggered by personalized learning path (context 1), by learner's self-learning behaviors (context 2), or by learner's assessment results (context 3). The sequence of personalized learning path is based on dynamic concept map; (e) Predictive module: the module implements computations of dynamic concept map and context-based recommendation and stores results in the database;
- **Dashboard:** the dashboard module visualizes real-time results for instructors and students to support educational decisions.

4   Discussion

Table 1 compares adaptive learning platforms on the market. Most platforms provide modules of concept map and learning path. However, learning path and concept map are fixed, not personalized. In addition, only Renaissance learning and this project offers recommendation on the platform. The comparison indicates current adaptive learning platforms mainly focus on the content development. The smart "adaptive" components are still not the major functions of the platform.

Table 1. Comparisons of adaptive learning platforms

Adaptive learning platforms	Concept map	Learning path	Recommendation
Renaissance learning			✓
Knewton	✓	✓	
RealizeIt		✓	
ALEKS	✓	✓	
Smart Sparrow	✓		
This project	✓	✓	✓

Although the platform can construct personal concept map from the results of pre-test, the system should have another mechanism to compare the student's concept map structure with the expert's. If the structures have huge differences, which mean the student's concept map might contains significant false concepts or misunderstanding. Then using expert's concept map structure to guide the student's learning can obtain better learning outcomes.

Acknowledgements. This study is conducted under the "III Innovative and Prospective Technologies Project" of the Institute for Information Industry which is subsidized by the Ministry of Economy Affairs of the Republic of China and sponsored by the Ministry of Science and Technology MOST, under Grant No. MOST 105-2511-S-024-009 and MOST 104-2511-S-468-002-MY2.

References

Brusilovsky, P.: Adaptive and intelligent web-based educational systems. Int. J. Artif. Intell. Educ. **13**(2–4), 159–172 (2003)

Burke, R.: Hybrid recommender systems: survey and experiments. User Model. User-Adap. Inter. **12**(4), 331–370 (2002)

Chan, A.T., Chan, S.Y., Cao, J. (2001). SAC: a self-paced and adaptive courseware system. In: Proceedings IEEE International Conference on Advanced Learning Technologies, 2001. pp. 78–81. IEEE (2001)

Chen, C.M.: Intelligent web-based learning system with personalized learning path guidance. Comput. Educ. **51**(2), 787–814 (2008)

Junyi Academy (2016). http://www.junyiacademy.org/

Novak, J.D.: Learning, Creating, and Using Knowledge: Concept Maps as Facilitative Tools in Schools and Corporations. Lawrence Erlbaum and Associates, New Jersey (1998)

Park, D.H., Kim, H.K., Choi, I.Y., Kim, J.K.: A literature review and classification of recommender systems research. Expert Syst. Appl. **39**(11), 10059–10072 (2012)

Riverin, S., Stacey, E.: Sustaining an online community of practice: a case study. Int. J. E-Learning Distance Educ. **22**(2), 43–58 (2008)

Santos, O.C.: Educational Recommender Systems and Technologies: Practices and Challenges. IGI Global, Hershey (2011)

Šimko, M., Barla, M., Bieliková, M.: ALEF: A Framework for Adaptive Web-Based Learning 2.0. In: Reynolds, N., Turcsányi-Szabó, M. (eds.) KCKS 2010. IAICT, vol. 324, pp. 367–378. Springer, Heidelberg (2010). doi:10.1007/978-3-642-15378-5_36

Adaptation of Personalized Education in E-learning Environment

Kateřina Kostolányová[(✉)]

Faculty of Education, University of Ostrava,
Fr. Sramka 3, 708 00 Ostrava, Czech Republic
katerina.kostolanyova@osu.cz

Abstract. We know from the classic instruction that some students might be hindered and bored by collective teaching. Others, on the other hand, might find it too fast, as a result of which they are not able to understand everything. Other students are satisfied with the pace of instruction but may not be satisfied with the teaching style of a particular teacher. Consequently, such students dislike some teachers and courses and their study results become worse. Those reasons lead to the idea of the optimization of the learning process through the individualization of instruction. [1, 2] The individualization of instruction mirrors each student's learning style, skills and the already acquired knowledge. Such a method cannot be applied in typical face-to-face classes where the students cannot be treated individually. In the time of the informatization of society, the Internet, and suitable SW and HW instruments, the computer-based (specifically e-learning and web technologies) instruction can easily be realized. [3] The paper describes the proposition and solution of adaptive instruction through e- learning aimed at the personalization of instruction according to each student's learning style and current knowledge.

Keywords: Individualization of instruction · Personalization · Adaptive e-learning · Evaluation · Study material · Adaptive instruction model

1 Introduction

Lifelong learning in all areas of the productive and post-productive life is one of the cornerstones of the progress and development of today's society.

Instruction supported by web technologies and all kinds of tools has become a topic of current interest. The same can be said about individualization, personalization and adaptation of the education process, all of which is related to the electronic-based instruction. The term personalization covers the adaptation of solution of various problems, situations and environments to specific conditions and requirements of individuals [4, 5].

E-learning is one of the modern and popular forms of education. However, due to technical limitations, most of them remained in the theoretical realm as they have not been practically realized.

© Springer International Publishing AG 2017
T.-T. Wu et al. (Eds.): SETE 2016, LNCS 10108, pp. 433–442, 2017.
DOI: 10.1007/978-3-319-52836-6_46

2 Approaches to Personalization of Education

There have been efforts to individualize education since the 1990s. Similar adaptation methods have appeared in a number of adaptive systems:

- Conditional layer technique (a layer containing particular content is displayed when a predefined condition is fulfilled) [8].
- Change of a frame variant – a variant suitable for a particular student is selected. In order to do so, however, a number of instruction variants need to exist. As this method is time consuming, it is rarely used [6, 7].
- Adaptation of navigation (the way of displaying the course content, i.e. the sequence of chapters and frames, is modified in a number of ways) [8, 13].

Sometimes, instruction modes modifying the entire adaptation process are being considered [6, 21]. For instance, in addition to the common instruction mode, there may also be a testing mode in which only testing questions are displayed and the explanation is displayed only after an incorrect answer [8–10].

These techniques have been used in a number of adaptive systems, from which we have selected the following two: ELM-ART and AHA! ELM-ART–advanced adaptive systems aimed at the instruction of programming in Lisp. The systems use a special type of adaptation based on a detailed analysis of the student's example solutions in Lisp, which enables it to predict how they will approach other problems and select following examples accordingly. The AHA! (Adaptive Hypermedia for All) system monitors and models the student's knowledge. The system allows the author of the study material to add conditional references and layers which are displayed only if a particular condition is met. In this system, the authors of courses create HTML sites enhanced with special tags containing evaluation conditions. The conditions should help the authors create content and propose the method of adaptation [11, 12].

3 Adaptive Education Theory–Pedagogical Solutions

Basic didactic principles concerning individual approach must be reflected in the education of students. The principles are rooted in personality psychology. They presuppose that each student is an individual and should be approached as such [16]. When assessing the student's characteristics, it is important to consider the optimal mediation of the curriculum in order to provide as comprehensive knowledge and skills as possible. This can be achieved through personalized instruction adapted to a specific person – the student. Adaptation of instruction can be characterized as a change in the way of teaching the same curriculum; always in a different way that is most suitable for the needs of specific students. This is not achievable in classic classroom instruction, but possible in computer-based and managed instruction [17].

The most important aspect of our approach to personalization is the definition of the term learning style. It is this type of characteristics of an individual that will serve as the basis for the adaptation and personalization of instruction. The research of a number of authors focuses on the classification of learning styles. The most often quoted definition of the term learning style is the one from the pedagogical dictionary [13]:

"A learning style is learning techniques an individual uses in pedagogy-related situations during a particular period of life. They are, to a certain degree, independent of the content of learning. They are innate (cognitive style) and can be developed through the interaction of internal and external influences".

Snider [14] argues that learning styles are a typical example of the interaction of human propensities and the way in which they are approached, while Sternberg [20] argues that they are "propensities rather than skills". Kolb [15] defines a learning style as preferring one learning method to another, not rejecting the other method completely – in a different situation, the other method may be preferred. Coffield et al. [16], on the other hand, describes it as a set of cognitive, affective and psychomotor factors which is a relatively stable indicator of the student's perception and reactions in the educational environment. Keefe [20] defines learning styles as cognitive, affective and physio-logical manifestations typical of an individual which are a relatively stable indicator of the student's perception, interactions and reactions in the educational environment. Kolb defines a learning style as follows (a citation): *"Learning styles can be considered to be general differences in learning orientation based on a relative level of emphasis which people put on the four learning methods, i.e. methods that can be measured through a "self-report" questionnaire called Learning Style Inventory"* [15, 19]. For our purposes, a learning style is a set of the student's characteristics that can be taken into account in e-learning and define each individual's learning style [20].

4 Design of Adaptive Education Model

Taking into consideration the theoretical foundations of personalization in general, the system of adaptive education is divided into three parts – the area for which personal ization is prepared, the area in which personalization is created and the mechanism used for its practical realization.

The theoretical model of adaptive e-learning can be seen in Fig. 1. The system consists of 3 parts – the student module, the author module and the Virtual Teacher module [20].

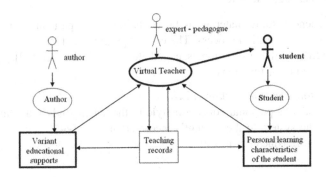

Fig. 1. Basic model of adaptive E-learning education management

4.1   Student Module

After the completion of the extensive background research and the analysis of available publications on the issues of learning styles [9], characteristics that define the student's learning style and that can be affected in the e-learning instruction (e.g. *sensory perception, social aspects, affective aspects, learning tactics, etc.*) have been selected. Since the existing questionnaires determining those characteristics did not meet our requirements, a new questionnaire was created. The questionnaire determines the values of the characteristics considered to be essential for the instruction in the e-learning environment [21]. The content of the created questionnaire was verified and pilot tested on a sample of five hundred students.

4.2   Author Module

The author module is used for preparing, storing and maintaining adaptive study materials. Considering the possibilities of adaptability, we further divided the curriculum into the so-called frames – they represent the smallest unit of information. Furthermore, we know that teaching methods consist of the sequence of elementary learning steps – the beginning of instruction, explanation, exercise, examination and conclusion. To be able to use the principle in the field of adaptable education, we will divide the instruction process according to R. Gagné [22]. The methodology for the creation of adaptable study materials was based on this approach. A frame is a section of the studied curriculum and is further divided into sub-sections, e.g. layers. There are three types of layers – instructional, testing and other. Other layers include the motivational layer, the navigational layer and the layer with additional resources. The created parts of the study material come in four sensory variants (verbal, visual, auditive and kinaesthetic) and in three depths of the detail of the curriculum (average, more comprehensive – slower, and more comprehensive instruction – enhanced by additional information and interesting facts) [20].

4.3   Virtual Teacher Module

A suitably sequenced study material (as far as its individual parts are concerned) is a suitable form of the education process. The control program that structures and verifies the understanding of the instruction is called the Virtual Teacher [22]. This expert system has a number of functions:

- find the personal education style (PES)
- apply the student's personal education style to the actual study material
- reaction of the system to the student's incorrect answers [24]
- record the entire education process.

5 Formal Structure of Adaptive Rules and Its Verification

To determine the theoretically optimal personal education style of a specific student means to choose the most suitable sensory variant and add the optimal sequence of layer types and depths for each frame (theoretically complete; with all types of layers) [20].

The student's personal sensory variant is defined by the most prolific type of their sensory perception, i.e. the form with the highest value of verbal, visual, auditive or kinesthetic perception. As far as the remaining characteristics are concerned, general elementary rules are formulated:

If the student has qualities V1 = a and V2 = b, then use layer sequence and depth X, Y, Z, ...

where X, Y, Z ... individual layers (theoretic, ...), V1, V2 ... learning style characteristics (motivation, self-regulation, ...), a, b, ... values of the particular characteristics.

The rules assigning the sequence and depth of layers when displaying the frame are based on the student's static (those acquired at the beginning of the studies) and dynamic qualities (those determined regularly, e.g. continuous testing). These are expert rules created by an expert – a pedagogue. There are a number of such "elementary" rules – for each value of each quality, or even some of their combinations. The creation of the rules requires close cooperation of a pedagogue, psychologist and informatician.

The first step to testing the designed rules is to verify their correct functioning by modeling the education process. To completely debug the functions of the Virtual Teacher, all basic types of virtual students and all variants and layers of the study material need to be defined.

Learning characteristics are assigned to virtual students. By combining their values (2–4 values for each characteristic), we arrive at 2,000 possible types of students. Instruction is simulated for these individual types or groups with one or more identical values of each characteristic. The virtual study material is modeled using only their metadata.

After completing the research and analysis of the modeling tools, we decided to create our own modeling tool that would best suit our needs. The tool uses the already mentioned expert rules and algorithms to determine the personal education style and actual education style. It can visualize a way through the study material for different types of students, thus enabling the inspection of their education styles. Moreover, it provides data for the analysis of the frequency of a way through the individual parts of the study material. A special method of the visualization of the PES and AES results displays a pattern of all theoretical variants of one frame (sensory perception and depth of instruction) with all possible layers. Into this pattern it can draw the progress of instruction recommended by the Virtual Teacher (in the form of polygonal line connecting individual layers in the recommended sequence and depth). This diagram will be called a trace of the adaptive education process, the education trace in short. Each trace corresponds with one education style for one type of student [22, 23].

6   Adaptive Education Process Modeling

As far as the pilot modeling of the education process is concerned, the elementary rules are tested first; for this reason the individual characteristics are added to modeling gradually, not all at once. A complete study material (represented by metadata) with no variants or layers missing will be used to model the functionality and correctness of all elementary rules. The procedure of modeling individual elementary rules:

- simulation of teaching a student "average" in all characteristics;
- simulation of teaching with the value of the tested characteristic changed to high and low; verification of the functionality and correctness of the proposed expert rules.

If the resulting diagram does not correspond with the expert's notion of PES, an error is generated- an incorrectly formulated expert rule or an incorrect function of the PEStyl algorithm.

Using the same modeling tool, it is verified if the rules are correctly designed for the case when it is necessary to combine several rules corresponding to different student characteristics [23].

In the second phase of modeling, the functionality and correctness of the AEStyl algorithm was tested. In real-life education, the VT does not have an ideal study material containing all the layers in every variant of instruction. And because the theoretically complete study material is not always available, we focused on the use of suitable substitute variants and layers of the study material - substitute the missing layer with a "closest related" one (if such exists), or omit it completely (if it is not available in any other version).

During the simulation of the education process, some mistakes in the formulation of adaptive rules have been discovered (see more in [20, 23]) and corrected. The described form of adaptive instruction is based on a quality study material and the formulation of rules for the adaptation of a study material to the student's needs.

Some of the elementary rules can be formulated as follows:

- If a student has a quality Understanding = 1, then for the instructional and testing layers use first Depth 2 and then Depth 1.
- If a student has a quality Motivation = 75 (highly motivated), use a motivation layer from Depth 3; if it is missing, leave it out completely.
- If a student has a quality Self-regulation = −50 (highly dependent), use a navigation layer from Depth 3 (detailed pedagogical instructions to study).

7   Ways of Adaptive Education Evaluation

A high quality study material verified through evaluation is an integral part of high quality instruction. Evaluation of textbooks includes all methods which can contribute to the evaluation of the success of instruction:

- Professional or pedagogical reviews.
- Evaluation questionnaires.
- Protocol about the student's behavior during logging into the course [27].

We will introduce two original methods of the adaptive instruction theory, which automate evaluation – first before the instruction (by analyzing the textbook) and then again after the instruction (by analyzing the education process protocol, thus objectively evaluating students' behavior in the on-line instruction).

The first method [29] uses a semantic network of terms which occur in the study material. Due to the detailed structuralization of the study material, the definitions of terms are stored in the theoretical layers of each frame. As a result, the terms can be automatically distinguished, filed and managed.

First of all, a semantic network is designed. The semantic network is a graph of the nodes-edges type where the node represents the term and the edge in between the nodes represents the relations between the terms. The following types of relations and meta-relations are defined: relations – the predecessor, the successor and the synonym; meta-relations – occurrence_before and occurrence_after the definition. Such a network makes it possible to monitor whether the main pedagogical principles have been met. If some of those principles have not been met, the system generates an error report for the author of the study material. An example may be using terms before they are defined, introducing terms which are not explained, used or tested later, etc.

The second method [28] analyzes the instruction that has already taken place and the students' behavior during the course of it. It uses mathematical statistics and data mining.

Through simple statistics, we can acquire the following information about the online instruction of a subject:

- The number of students, the number of sessions (logging into the system), the number of sessions per student (min, max, median); time of studying (date, day of the week, exact hour)
- The number of teaching and testing layers; the time students spent on them (seconds).

The new analyses aim to answer 3 main questions, which can be achieved through the method of finding associations or the construction of the decision tree [28]. Those can find all the combinations of attributes – potential causes, which result in different values of attributes, i.e. consequences. The 3 main questions are:

- Under what circumstances (i.e. values of attributes which may be the cause) do students achieve different levels of knowledge?
- Under what circumstances do students spend a different amount of time on indi-vidual parts of the study material?
- Under what circumstances do students find the offered instruction insufficient and search for other variants?

8 Partial Research Results

The defined theory is experimentally verified and extended by the results of a number of partial researches.

The verification of the effectiveness of the sensory variants in the teaching of a foreign language was a part of Ph.D. students' dissertations. As far as a foreign language is concerned, it is vital that the student learns to use all of the senses (auditive – listening, verbal – reading and writing, etc.). Two original realizations of adaptive instruction of a foreign language have already been created, verified and described [25, 26, 28, 29].

The first experiment [25] proved that using the individual sequence of sensory variants is effective. Before the start of instruction, the student is tested and the values of the individual sensory perception types are determined. As a result, the sensory variants used in the instruction reflect the sequence of the determined values, beginning with the most prominent sense. The aim of this method was maximum effectiveness with minimum effort on the student's part: the first variant reflects their most prominent sense, which means the student can solve it with minimum effort; every other variant adds a small part of the curriculum so the use of a less preferred sense does not involve a lot of effort.

The second research and experiment [26] used a completely different approach. It examined the relation between the student's current English skills (listening, reading, writing) and their sensory preferences. The results of the pedagogical experiment showed that the most effective way of teaching the above skills is through a corresponding sensory variant, regardless of the student's sensory preference.

The theory of adaptive testing was a natural extension of the theory of adaptive education [19, 20]. The basic education mode contains test layers of three types: theoretical questions, application tasks and practical tasks. They are used as immediate feedback and help the student determine whether or not they have mastered particular parts of the studied curriculum. The results of the partial researches have been acquired through the real implementation of the adaptive Barborka LMS into university instruction. Nearly 1,000 students participated in the instruction.

9 Conclusion

Today, e-learning in its classic form is almost obsolete. Personalization, individualization and instruction tailored to students' needs have caught the attention of a number of experts. The theory of personalized education as introduced above is based on the use of the student's personal characteristics for the adaptation of a special study material to their individual needs. The adaptation is carried out through the elementary formulated expert rules. The proposed solution is original in its new structure of a study material which, however, is based on the verified pedagogical rules. Further research in this field will be aimed at the issue of consistency between a learning style and real instruction with regard to elimination of the student's inappropriate learning habits (surface learning, not realizing the links between sub-units, etc.) [18]. As far as the creation of the adaptive study material (mainly the parts of the curriculum that are difficult to understand) is concerned, the research will be aimed at the use of the so called scaffolding.

References

1. Felder, R. M.: Are Learning Styles Invalid? (Hint: No!) (2010). http://www4.ncsu.edu/unity/lockers/users/f/felder/public/Papers/LS_Validity(OnCourse).pdf
2. Gregorc, A.F.: Learning/teaching styles: potent forces behind them. Educ. Leadersh. **36**(1), 234–238 (1979)
3. Zou, D., Xie, H., Li, Q., Wang, F.L., Chen, W.: The load-based learner profile for incidental word learning task generation. In: Popescu, E., Lau, R.W.H., Pata, K., Leung, H., Laanpere, M. (eds.) ICWL 2014. LNCS, vol. 8613, pp. 190–200. Springer, Heidelberg (2014). doi:10.1007/978-3-319-09635-3_21
4. Chen, Ch., Lee, H., Chen, Y.: Personalized e-learning system using item response theory. Comput. Educ. **44**(3), 237–255 (2005)
5. Özpolat, E., Akar, G.B.: Automatic detection of learning styles for learning systems. Comput. Educ. **53**, 355–367 (2009)
6. Beaumont, I.: User modelling in the interactive anatomy tutoring system ANATOM TUTOR. User Model. User-Adap. Inter. **4**(1), 21–45 (1994)
7. Gilbert, J.E., Han, C.Y.: ARTHUR: an adaptive instruction system based on learning styles. In: Proceedings of International Conference on Mathematics/Science Education and Technology, Association for the Advancement of Computing in Education (AACE) (1999)
8. Debra, P., et al.: Aha! the Adaptive Hypermedia Architecture. In: Proceedings of the ACM Conference on Hypertext. ACM (2003)
9. Weber, G., Brusilovsky, P.: ELM-ART: an adaptive versatile system for webbased instruction. Int. J. Artif. Intell. Educ. **12**, 351–384 (2001)
10. Wu., H., Houben, G.J., Debra, P.: AHAM: a reference model to support adaptive hypermedia authoring. In: Zesde Interdisciplinaire Conferentie Informatiewetenschap, Ant werp: AACE (1998)
11. Smits, D., Debra, P.: GALE: a highly extensible adaptive hypermedia engine. In: Proceedings of the 22nd ACM Conference on Hypertext and Hypermedia (HT 2011). ACM, New York (2011)
12. Brusilovsky, P.: Adaptive navigation support. In: Brusilovsky, P., Kobsa, A., Nejdl, W. (eds.) The Adaptive Web. LNCS, vol. 4321, pp. 263–290. Springer, Heidelberg (2007). doi:10.1007/978-3-540-72079-9_8
13. Průcha, J., Walterová, E., Mareš, J.: Pedagogický slovník [Pedagogical dictionary]. Portál, Praha (2009). ISBN 978-80-7367-647-6
14. Snider, V.E.: What we know about learning styles from research in special education (1990). Educational Leadership. http://www.ascd.org/ASCD/pdf/journals/ed_lead/el_199010_snider.pdf
15. Kolb, A.Y., Kolb, D.A.: Learning styles and learning spaces: Enhancing experiential learning in higher education [Electronic version]. Acad. Manage. Learn. Educ. **4**(2), 193–212 (2005). http://search.ebscohost.com/login.aspx?direct=true&db=bth&AN=17268566&site=ehostlive
16. Coffield, F., et al.: Learning styles and pedagogy in post-16 learning. In: A Systematic and Critical Review. Learning and Skills Research Centre, London (2004)
17. Paramythis, A., Loidl-Reisinger, S.: Adaptive learning environments and e-Learning standards., In: ECEL. Academic Conferences and Publishing International, Linz (2003)
18. Simonova, I., Poulova, P.: Learning and assessment preferences in the ICT-enhanced process of instruction. In: Hybrid Learning. Theory and Practice, Proceedings of the 7th International Conference (ICHL 2014), pp. 281–288. Springer (2014)

19. Sak, P.: Man and education in the information society: education and life in the computerized world (2007)
20. Kostolányová, K.: The theory of adaptive e-learning. University of Ostrava, Ostrava (2012). ISBN 978-80-7464-014/8
21. Novotný, S.: Individualization of teaching through e-learning. development of students-learning profile questionnaire. In: Theoretical and Practical Aspects of Distance Learning, pp. 105–116. Studio NOA, Katowice (2010)
22. Kostolányová, K., Šarmanová, J.: Methodology for creating adaptive study material. In: Proceedings of the 12th European Conference on e-Learning, Sophia, pp. 218–223. Academic Conferences and Publishing International Limited, Antipolis (2013)
23. Kostolányová, K: Simulating personalized learning in electronic environment. In: Proceedings of the 10th International Scientific Conference on Distance Learning in Applied Informatics. Wolters Kluwer, Praha, pp. 105–115 (2014)
24. Prextová, T.: Increasing the level of student's knowledge via adaptive testing. Dissertation. University of Ostrava, Ostrava (2014)
25. Horký, E.: Autonomous learning of foreign languages in e-learning. Dissertation. University of Ostrava, Pedagogical Faculty, Department of Information and Communication Technologies (2014)
26. Nedbalová, Š.: Application of Sensory Characteristics in Adaptive Language Learning. Dissertation. University of Ostrava, Ostrava (2016)
27. C Attwell, G.: Evaluating e-learning: a guide to the evaluation of E-learning, 46 s. Creative Commons, California, USA (2006). http://www.pontydysgu.org/wpcontent/uploads/2007/11/eva_europe_vol2_prefinal.pdf
28. Dvořáčková, M.: Auto-evaluation algorithms of e-learning courses. Dissertation. University of Ostrava, Ostrava (2015)
29. Šeptaková, E.: The semantic network of concepts in adaptive e-learning. Dissertation. University of Ostrava, Ostrava (2015)

Closing the Reading Gap with Virtual Maze Environments

Lisa Gabel[1], Evelyn Johnson[2], Brett E. Shelton[2(✉)],
and Jui-Long Hung[2]

[1] Lafayette College, Easton, USA
gabell@lafayette.edu
[2] Boise State University, Boise, USA
{evelynjohnson,brettshelton,andyhung}@boisestate.edu

Abstract. The purpose of the proposed project is to develop and validate a virtual Hebb-Williams (vHW) maze task for use as a low-cost, time-efficient, and easy-to-use assessment for the early detection of children at risk for reading impairment. The vHW maze offers the potential to serve as a reliable, non-language based predictor of reading difficulty, which can improve early identification and intervention efforts. Unlike current screening measures of reading impairment, the vHW maze could be administered in the classroom, with a fully integrated analytical system. With the successful attainment of this project, the vHW maze task will fill important gaps in early identification screeners by examining a broader range of cognitive processes associated with reading and enhancing our understanding of factors underlying reading impairment. This paper comprises the proposed work and significance while highlighting previous findings related to reading impairments and virtual maze environments.

Keywords: Reading impairment · Special education · Educational technology · Virtual environments

1 Introduction

The purpose of the proposed project is to develop and validate a virtual Hebb-Williams (vHW) maze task for use as a low-cost, time-efficient, and easy-to-use assessment for the early detection of children at risk for reading impairment. A recent report from the National Assessment of Educational Progress (NAEP) noted that 31% of fourth graders scored at Below Basic levels, and 33% scored at the Basic level (USDE, 2015). These data suggest that a significant number of US students struggle with reading, and many more experience significant difficulty learning to read. Throughout early education (i.e. K-3) to middle school, children should be learning to read and reading to learn through a simultaneous and continuous process. Poor reading achievement can have a serious negative impact throughout a person's life, including increased risk for dropping out of school, higher rates of unemployment and other negative social outcomes. Ferrer and colleagues (2015) recently reported findings from a longitudinal study demonstrating significant achievement gaps for poor readers as early as first grade that persist

© Springer International Publishing AG 2017
T.-T. Wu et al. (Eds.): SETE 2016, LNCS 10108, pp. 443–454, 2017.
DOI: 10.1007/978-3-319-52836-6_47

throughout school. When interventions are delayed until after first grade, they are substantially less effective in closing the reading achievement gap (Torgesen 2004). Therefore, early detection efforts are critical.

A major challenge with early detection is the complexity of the reading process; difficulties with reading may arise from deficits in one or more cognitive processes. Research criteria often refer to a score below the 30th percentile in a basic reading skill as an impairment. These skills may include trouble with accurate and fluent word recognition due to phonological processing deficits, poor word recognition speed and automatic recall without phonological deficits, or poor comprehension with typical word decoding skills. Subtypes of reading difficulties have been categorized in many ways. For example, Catts et al. (2006) developed a classification model aligned to the simple view of reading (Gough and Tunmer 1986) that results in four types of readers as shown in Table 1 below. A recent analysis of large data sets across elementary school grades provided support for the validity of these classifications, and indicated that the majority of students experience difficulties with both decoding and comprehension, with smaller percentages of students experiencing specific impairments restricted to a single domain (Spencer et al. 2014).

Table 1. Classification of types of readers (adapted from Catts et al. 2006)

	Good decoding	Poor decoding
Good comprehension	Adequate reader	Specific reading impairment
Poor comprehension	Specific comprehension disorder	Poor reader (poor decoder and comprehender)

Under this classification model, reading difficulties may be experienced at the word level (e.g. dyslexia or specific reading impairment), as a difficulty with comprehension, or as a combination of both, in which poor word level reading skills lead to poor comprehension ability. Different predictors are needed to identify these specific subtypes. For example, Adlof et al. (2010) found that different combinations of predictor variables in kindergarten were required to optimally predict reading impairments in second grade versus those in eighth grade. Phonological measures were more predictive of second grade reading impairments, whereas language measures were more predictive of reading impairments encountered in later grades (Adlof et al. 2010).

Findings from similar studies suggest the need for multiple predictors to more accurately identify children at risk for poor reading outcomes. For example, in a study designed to identify students with reading disability (RD), Pennington et al. (2012) created single and multiple deficit models that included measures of phonological awareness, language skill, processing speed and naming speed. They found that multiple deficit models of RD more accurately identified cases at the individual level than single deficit models (Pennington et al. 2012). However, even the best fitting model in their study, which allowed for both single and multiple-predictor models, only accurately identified 46% of their sample of students with RD. These findings suggest that there may be other important predictors of RD, and that a *multiple-risk* framework of identification that includes measures beyond those which are phonological may lead to more accurate identification of the heterogeneous manifestations of RD (Pennington et al. 2012).

Measures of EF, attention, working memory and visual processing may have predictive value above and beyond phonological skills in the identification of reading difficulties (Frijters et al. 2011). Including measures of EF, attention, working memory and visual processing may enhance the practitioner's ability to accurately identify children at risk for poor reading outcomes. In turn, early identification of the specific deficit associated with poor reading ability could inform individualized intervention planning. For practitioners however, administering a full battery of tests that include all of the specific cognitive processes related to reading would not be practical or feasible. Screening methods need to be brief, accurate, and easy to implement to make them feasible to administer in schools (Jenkins et al. 2007). However, a number of studies have indicated that current screening tools are inadequate. Current assessments do not screen for the range of processes and skills that are highly associated with reading difficulty. This is problematic, because intervention research consistently shows a persistent group of nonresponders to evidence-based reading interventions (Compton et al. 2014). A stronger understanding of an individual student's specific challenges may allow for interventions tailored to meet a student's unique learning needs. Currently however, there are a lack of instruments that *efficiently* measure processes such as executive function, attentional control, spatial processing and working memory.

Therefore, the goal of the proposed project is to develop and validate a virtual Hebb Williams (vHW) maze task for use in the early detection of reading difficulties. The vHW maze is a virtual maze environment patterned after the physical Hebb-Williams, a closed-field maze typically used for mice (Hebb and Williams 1946). The task consists of 12 distinct maze configurations, with three measured levels of difficulty (Hebb and Williams 1946; Meunier et al. 1986; Robinovitch and Rosvold 1951). We successfully created a virtual environment for the Hebb Williams mazes that mimicked the physical version of the maze used in our laboratory to examine visuo-spatial abilities in animal models of reading disabilities (see Fig. 1). We used this virtual environment to compare human performance to mouse performance on a physical version of the maze (Gabel et al. 2016). A cross-species (i.e. mouse – human) comparison demonstrated similar performance efficiencies on this task. In addition, we demonstrated that both 5–6 year old, and 8–13 year old children with reading difficulties exhibited a similar impairment to animal models of the disorder [i.e. mice which were genetically altered to create a microdeletion in a candidate dyslexia susceptibility gene (CDSG)] (Gabel et al. 2016).

Our data thus far suggest that regardless of the nature of a child's reading impairment (e.g. specific reading impairment, reading comprehension, reading fluency), there are significant differences in their overall performance on the vHW maze task compared to typical readers (Gabel et al. 2016). We theorize that the vHW maze task employs a number of underlying processes associated with reading, such as executive function, working memory, attentional control and visual processing skills, and that developing a more thorough understanding of how the vHW maze taps these constructs will provide valuable insight into its use as an early screening for reading

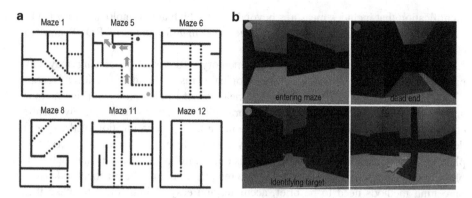

Fig. 1. (a) Schematic of HW mazes 1, 5, 6, 8, 11, and 12. Colored dots indicate location of first person when traveling through maze 5 as pictured in b. (b) Scenes from virtual HW maze 5: entering the maze, reaching a dead end, and identifying the goal box. If the participant did not locate the target in 120 s, yellow arrows appeared to guide the participant from the start box to the goal box. Data were no longer collected after 120 s had elapsed from the time the participant entered the maze

difficulties. To achieve the overall goal of this proposal, we will accomplish the following research aims.

2   Research Aims

Aim 1. Develop a more complete understanding of how performance on the vHW maze task is associated with reading, and what cognitive processes are engaged in navigating the task. To accomplish this aim, we will examine the performance efficiency on the maze task (both overall performance, and through a finer grained path analysis), and an assessment of the participant's problem solving strategy using eye tracking measurements. Briefly, performance efficiency is measured based on standardized scores for the errors made during the completion of the maze, and the total time it takes to reach the goal. The average scores for these measures provide an overall performance efficiency across mazes and trials completed (Shore et al. 2001). This provides a composite measure where large positive numbers reflect a relatively poor performance. Heat maps are created by taking composite standard scores for the distance traveled and the time spent in each of the 6 × 6 cells that make up the interior of the maze. This analysis provides us with an examination of the specific path the individual took with additional measures of time spent and distance traveled within each region of the maze. Lastly, eye-tracking data will provide us with information toward understanding the strategies employed by the participant to solve the maze. In studies of both pre-readers (5 & 6 year olds, unpublished observations) and upper elementary age readers (8–13 year old), our findings indicate significant differences in performance on the vHW task for students identified as reading impaired, regardless of the type of reading difficulty they experience (Gabel et al. 2016). In this aim, we seek to better understand the processes involved in completing the vHW maze task, and determine its relationship with other cognitive processing instruments. To accomplish this aim, in Years 1–2 we will explore the construct validity of the vHW maze with other diagnostic measures of cognitive processes and reading, and determine differences in problem solving abilities and strategies using path analysis and eye tracking.

Aim 2. Determine the vHW maze task's utility as a non-language based task that informs the identification of students who are at risk for reading difficulties. Early detection of reading difficulties is important because early intervention has been found to be more effective in addressing students' learning needs. To accomplish this aim, we will conduct concurrent and predictive validity studies. Concurrent studies will examine the validity of the vHW with measures of executive function, working memory, attentional control and visual processing skills, as well as with measures of reading ability. Predictive studies will examine the extent to which performance on vHW is associated with performance on reading measures. Once important predictors have been identified, the predictive model can be used to assist with diagnostic functions for reading disability.

Aim 3. Develop a web-based version of the vHW maze task that can be easily administered and automatically scored, with output that will indicate the level of risk by age level for reading impairment. Using the data that we collect to address the other research aims, we will develop a web-based version of the vHW maze to visualize maze results and prepare for larger scale implementation. There are 4 main developmental *parts* of this portion of the research program:

A. Provide the design, development and implementation of a revised and more robust vHW maze for data collection.
B. Provide more evidence as to the key indicators of vHW maze that can predict reading impairment through navigation of a vHW.
C. Use the most innovative methods and varieties of statistical models to ensure the highest accuracy in building a predictive model for identifying students at risk for reading impairment.
D. Integrate the statistically derived model into a diagnostic tool, delivered through web browsers, which can test children independently for reading impairment. Ensure the tool provides the parents/teachers of the child with appropriate feedback and instruction for next steps, whatever the results of the test.

3 Data Analysis

Data Collection. A total of 150 participants, ages 5 & 6, from the Northeast and Mountain West regions will be included in the sample. This sample will include the following demographics: 51% female, 50% White, non-Hispanic, 16% Black, 25% Hispanic, 5% Asian or Pacific Islander, 1% American Indian, 3% Two or more races. Additionally, we will ensure that we obtain unique student identification numbers in addition to demographic information to facilitate follow-up during years 3 & 4, when participants will be 7–8 years old. We will oversample students at high risk for reading impairment.

Students will be categorized as either 'typical readers' or 'reading impaired'. Students whose performance is 1 standard deviation (SD) below the mean on one aspect of reading (e.g. phonological awareness, vocabulary, comprehension) will be categorized as reading impaired. Then, a 2 (typical vs. reading impaired) × 4 (mazes 6, 8, 11, 12) × 6 (trials 1–6) mixed factorial ANCOVA will be performed with maze and trial as the within-subject factors. For univariate measures of within-subject effects, Mauchly's test of sphericity will be performed. If the sphericity assumption is not met, a Huynh-Feldt correction will be applied. Performance efficiency on the vHW maze will be calculated based on a composite z score for both error and latency measures. The slope will be calculated from performance efficiency T scores across the six trials. Heat maps will be created by taking composite standard scores for the distance traveled and time spent in each of the 6 × 6 cells that make up the interior of the maze. The composite score will be calculated in a similar way as the performance efficiency score; however, the distance traveled and the time spent in each cell will be converted into a z score, and then the two z scores will be weighted equally providing a Pesky efficiency score (PES).

To determine the concurrent validity of the vHW maze with measures of cognitive processing, we will conduct similar analyses except we will classify students as either typical or impaired on the various cognitive measures and repeat the analyses described above. Participants will be identified as either typically developing or as impaired (scores of 1 SD < mean) on the relevant cognitive process, and the same analysis as described f above will be conducted. The results will provide evidence of the vHW maze task's concurrent validity with these various cognitive processes. A power analysis using G*Power indicates that setting power at .80 and an effect size of 0.2, to detect a significant moderate difference between groups a sample size of approximately 124 students are needed. Our projected sample is sufficient to address this research aim, allowing for 17% attrition.

vHW Computational Model. Building a computational model of vHW participants will determine which variables are significant in navigating the maze. Theoretically significant variables are included in the model (e.g. demographic data), and data mining techniques are used to derive models that target the research aims. The term "data mining" refers to the process of applying specific algorithms for extracting patterns (models) from data. It is a particular step in Knowledge Discovery in Databases (KDD) (Fayyad et al. 1996). Therefore, researchers usually follow the KDD process when conducting data mining studies. The KDD process includes the following major steps (Fayyad et al. 1996): (a) identifying the goal and creating a target dataset, (b) data preprocessing, (c) data transformation, (d) data mining, and (e) interpretation and evaluation.

Figure 2 represents the derivation of the computational model proposed for the vHW. The model was derved from the KDD model, educational data mining literature reviews, and results from previous model-building efforts.

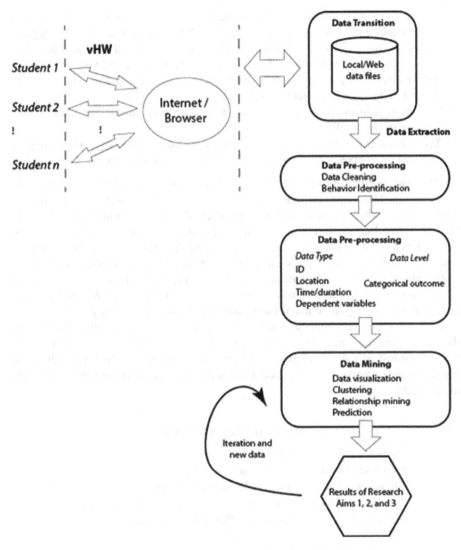

Fig. 2. Process of computational model building for the vHW maze task

Data Source and Data Extraction

Based on Romero and Ventura (2010), Baker and Yacef (2009), data derived for the model will be collected from the following sources:

1. vHM activity logs—Existing data from pilot sources, as well as newly acquired data from the improved vHM is stored locally and/or through a shared, protected database. Dynamic data consists of every action performed on the platform with their associated timestamps. The aggregated frequencies will be used as potential predictor variables, as well as the sequence of the duration between actions. The behavioral tracking tool records mouse clicks from users and the eye-tracking data

records attenuations during the vHW navigation. A tool such as *Pygaze* will be used to code and analyzed eye-tracking data (http://www.pygaze.org/2015/06/pygaze-analyser/). All sequential codes will be combined into textual strings, then a tool such as *Word2Vec,* software useful for textual data analysis, will be used to group students based on pattern similarity. The output of the activity logs will be part of derived variables for predictive modeling.

2. Student/participant data—Specific student data gathered during controlled administration of the vHW.
3. Technology Data—Other types of data with regard to versions of vHW may be gathered for purposes of monitoring bias and technology validation.

The data pre-processing stage includes two steps: data cleaning and behavior identification. These steps remove all superfluous, irregular, or missing records, impute data (possibly, when necessary and meaningful), and will assist in identifying learning behaviors from location and time data. The goal of the behavior identification step is to define useful learning behaviors from the collected data and associate them with the rest of the variables, such as identifiers and demographic data. In the data transformation stage, variables are aggregated for analysis. Types of variables—IDs (e.g. user ID or country ID), learning behaviors (e.g. location and time of vHW activity), category (e.g. type of cognitive impairment), and dependent variables (e.g. variable associated with maze performance)—are suggested for levels of accumulation. Other theoretical variables are expected to emerge and may be included for mining. To address our research aims, techniques of pattern discovery and predictive modeling are applied to data analyses. Table 2 recommends data mining techniques and data levels at this stage.

Table 2. The data mining stage

Method	Example
Data visualization	2D or 3D data visualization
Clustering	K-mean or Hierarchical clustering
Relationship mining	Association; Sequential association; Path analysis
Prediction	Decision tree; Regression; neural network

The computational model building techniques proposed by gathering location and time-based inputs into the model we propose include a method of clustering time-elements into categories that can possibly provide more robustness in prediction accuracy. Developing such algorithms as applied to learning tasks is noted in recent research (Shelton et al. in review; Shelton et al. 2015).

For example, a variety of computational models can be tested through training (60% of data, including static and dynamic inputs) and validation (remaining 40% of data) using a variety of time-series clusters as well as aggregate (traditional) groupings. Most recent results show that validation through low misclassification rankings of clustering have better accuracy rates for many time-based tasks. We commonly use six models for the nominal dependent variable: decision tree, boosting, logistic regression (forward, backward and stepwise), and rule induction. For this project, we will consider additional analytic methods which include outlier supervised and semi-supervised outlier detection methods in machine learning, including K-nearest neighbor (Knorr et al. 2000), score normalization (Kriegel et al. 2011), neural network (Hawkins et al. 2002), ensemble model (Nguyen et al. 2010), support vector machines (SVM) (Schölkopf et al. 2001), random forest (Ho 1998), and feature bagging (Lazarevic and Kumar 2005). The best model will be selected based on the lowest validation mean of squared errors or the lowest validation classification rate. We validate the predictive models concurrently with the process of predictive modeling. Regardless of which models prove to emerge as best-fit, using maze locations and timeliness of completion values will offer a computational model of students' actions, which can then be applied to new vHW tasks. The results can be integrated into the test for real-time feedback of the performance in the form of at-risk percentages for reading impairment (Fig. 3).

Model Name	Validation: Misclassification	Training: Misclassification
TS_Decision Tree	0.101942	0.092409
TS_Gradient Boosting	0.106796	0.09571
TS_Rule Induction	0.11165	0.082508
TS_R_Stepwise	0.135922	0.108911
TS_R_Forward	0.135922	0.108911
R_Foward	0.150485	0.138614
R_Stepwise	0.150485	0.138614
Decision Tree	0.150485	0.138614
Gradient Boosting	0.150485	0.138614
TS_R_Backward	0.160194	0.092409
R_Backward	0.174757	0.132013
Rule Induction	0.203883	0.151815

Fig. 3. Sample model comparison results for training and validation of computational models.

Finally, valuable rules and patterns are discovered through data interpretation and evaluation. Through data triangulation, domain experts evaluate and identify interesting rules and patterns for decision-making. If the results are not deemed valuable, stages of data mining and data interpretation and evaluation are repeated. Note that there are two types of data being used in the computational modeling process: one is static data (such as students' profiles) and the other is dynamic data (such as students' behaviors). We can construct multiple models for different purposes to address separate research aims. For example, one model with static and dynamic data can derive results for real-time diagnosis. Having multiple years to implement the diagnosis system with effects of interventions, the system can do diagnosis resulting in recommendations for personalized interventions.

4 Summary

Contributions of the proposed research. The vHW maze offers the potential to serve as a reliable, non-language based predictor of reading impairment which can improve our early identification and intervention efforts for young children. Unlike current measures of cognitive processing areas, the vHW maze could be administered in the classroom, providing valuable information about a child's learning processes that will inform instructional practice. With the successful attainment of these research aims, the vHW can fill important gaps in the extant range of early identification screeners, and further our understanding of the cognitive processes associated with reading.

Need for the vHW maze task and limitations of current reading screeners. Given the complexity of reading, some researchers question whether early identification of reading impairment is practicable. For example, reading impairment at the word level is most often conceptualized as a weakness in phonology (Ferrer et al. 2010), and screening tools that assess phonological abilities have been shown to be useful in identifying children at risk for word-level reading impairments. Phonological skills such as segmenting and blending are particularly useful predictors, as are skills related to rapid automatic naming (RAN) (Frijters et al. 2011). There are a number of assessments that reliably measure phonological and early reading constructs and are in wide-use in schools. Examples include the Comprehensive Test of Phonological Processing (CTOPP-2), the Test of Word Reading Efficiency (TOWRE-2), the Texas Primary Reading Inventory (TPRI), and numerous others, including a variety of curriculum-based measures of reading. These measures assess phonological processes, word level reading abilities and fluency. There are fewer measures available that screen for early language impairments, which have been associated with reading comprehension. Although group level differences on measures that are consistently reported in the research, they have been found to be less accurate when used to make diagnostic decisions at the individual level (Adlof et al. 2010; Pennington et al. 2012).

In our previous work, we have found that there are significant differences in performance on the vHW maze between children who are good readers and those who are reading impaired. In our studies, we defined reading impairment as performance on a cluster score of the Woodcock Reading Mastery Test (WRMT-3) or the Woodcock Johnson Reading Tests of Achievement (WJ-IV) was more than 1 SD below the mean. We used the cluster scores for Basic Reading Skill, Reading Comprehension and Reading Fluency. Our results indicated that performance on the vHW maze task was impaired for students with one or more reading scores at this level, regardless of the area of reading impairment (e.g. poor decoding, poor comprehension or both). This suggests that the vHW may be a useful early predictor of reading difficulties, especially if we can further investigate performance on the vHW task through additional means such as path analysis.

References

Adlof, S.M., Catts, H.W., Lee, J.: Kindergarten predictors of second versus eighth grade reading comprehension impairments. J. Learn. Disabil. **43**, 332–345 (2010)

Baker, R., Yacef, K.: The state of educational data mining in 2009: a review and future visions. J. Educ. Data Min. **1**(1), 3–17 (2009). http://www.educationaldatamining.org/JEDM/images/articles/vol1/issue1/JEDMVol1Issue1_BakerYacef.pdf

Catts, H.W., Adlof, S.M., Weismer, S.: Language deficits in poor comprehenders: a case for the simple view of reading. J. Speech Lang. Hearing Res. **49**(2), 278–293 (2006)

Compton, D.L., Miller, A.C., Elleman, A.M., Steacy, L.M.: Have we forsaken reading theory in the name of quick fix interventions for children with reading disability? Sci. Stud. Reading **18**(1), 55–73 (2014). doi:10.1080/10888438.2013.836200

Fayyad, U.M., Piatetsky-Shapiro, G., Smyth, P.: The KDD process for extracting useful knowledge from volumes of data. Commun. ACM **39**(11), 27–34 (1996)

Ferrer, E., Shaywitz, B.A., Holahan, J.M., Marchione, K., Shaywitz, S.E.: Uncoupling of reading and IQ over time: empirical evidence for a definition of dyslexia. Psychol. Sci. **21**(1), 93–101 (2015). doi:10.1177/0956797609354084

Frijters, J.C., Lovett, M.W., Steinbach, K.A., Wolf, M., Sevcik, R.A., Morris, R.D.: Neurocognitive predictors of reading outcomes for children with reading disabilities. J. Learn. Disabil. **44**(2), 150–166 (2011). doi:10.1177/0022219410391185

Gabel, L.A., Manglani, M., Escalona, N., Cysner, J., Hamilton, R., Pfaffmann, J., Johnson, E.: Translating dyslexia across species. Annals of Dyslexia (2016)

Gough, P., Tunmer, W.: Decoding, reading, and reading disability. Remedial Special Educ. **7**, 6–10 (1986)

Hawkins, S., He, H., Williams, G., Baxter, R.: Outlier detection using replicator neural networks. In: Kambayashi, Y., Winiwarter, W., Arikawa, M. (eds.) DaWaK 2002. LNCS, vol. 2454, pp. 170–180. Springer, Heidelberg (2002). doi:10.1007/3-540-46145-0_17

Hebb, D.O., Williams, K.: A method of rating animal intelligence. J. Gen. Psychol. **34**, 59–65 (1946)

Ho, T.K.: The random subspace method for constructing decision forests. IEEE Trans. Pattern Anal. Mach. Intell. **20**(8), 832–844 (1998)

Jenkins, J., Hudson, R.F., Johnson, E.S.: Screening for service delivery in an RTI framework: candidate measures. School Psychol. Rev. **36**(4), 582–601 (2007)

Knorr, E.M., Ng, R.T., Tucakov, V.: Distance-based outliers: algorithms and applications. VLDB J. Int. J. Very Large Data Bases **8**(3–4), 237–253 (2000). doi:10.1007/s007780050006

Kriegel, H.P., Kröger, P., Schubert, E., Zimek, A.: Interpreting and unifying outlier scores. In: Proceedings of the 2011 SIAM International Conference on Data Mining, pp. 13–24, Mesa, AZ, April 2011

Lazarevic, A., Kumar, V.: Feature bagging for outlier detection. In: Proceedings of 11th ACM SIGKDD International Conference on Knowledge Discovery in Data Mining, pp. 157–166, August 2005

Meunier, M., Saint-Marc, M., Destrade, C.: The Hebb-Williams test to assess recovery of learning after limbic lesions in mice. Physiol. Behav. **37**(6), 909–913 (1986)

Nguyen, H.V., Ang, H.H., Gopalkrishnan, V.: Mining outliers with ensemble of heterogeneous detectors on random subspaces. In: Kitagawa, H., Ishikawa, Y., Li, Q., Watanabe, C. (eds.) DASFAA 2010. LNCS, vol. 5981, pp. 368–383. Springer, Heidelberg (2010). doi:10.1007/978-3-642-12026-8_29

Pennington, B.F., Santerre-Lemmon, L., Rosenberg, J., MacDonald, B., Boada, R., Friend, A., et al.: Individual prediction of dyslexia by single vs. multiple deficit models. J. Abnorm. Psychol. **121**(1), 212–224 (2012)

Rabinovitch, M.S., Rosvold, H.E.: A closed-field intelligence test for rats. Can. J. Psychol. **5**(3), 122–128 (1951)

Romero, C., Ventura, S.: Educational data mining: A review of the state of the art. IEEE Trans. Syst. Man Cybern. Part C Appl. Rev. **40**(6), 601–618 (2010)

Schölkopf, B., Platt, J.C., Shawe-Taylor, J., Smola, A.J., Williamson, R.C.: Estimating the support of a high-dimensional distribution. Neural Comput. **13**(7), 1443–1471 (2001)

Shelton, B.E., Hung, J., Lowenthal, P.: Predicting student success by modeling student interaction in asynchronous online courses. IEEE Trans. Learn. Technol., 8 pages (under review)

Shelton, B.E., Hung, J., Baughman, S.: Online graduate teacher education: establishing an EKG for student success intervention. Technol. Knowl. Learn. **21**(1), 21–32 (2015). doi:10.1007/s10758-015-9254-8

Shore, D.I., Stanford, L., MacInnes, W.J., Klein, R.M., Brown, R.E.: Of mice and men: virtual Hebb-Williams mazes permit comparison of spatial learning across species. Cogn. Affect Behav. Neurosci. **1**(1), 83–89 (2001)

Spencer, M., Quinn, J.M., Wagner, R.K.: Specific reading comprehension disability: major problem, myth, or misnomer? Learn. Disabil. Res. Pract. **29**(1), 3–9 (2014)

Torgesen, J.K.: Avoiding the devastating downward spiral: the evidence that early intervention prevents reading failure. Am. Educ. **28**, 6–19 (2004). Reprinted in the 56th Annual Commemorative Booklet of the International Dyslexia Association, November 2005

U.S. Department of Education, Institute of Education Sciences, National Center for Education Statistics, National Assessment of Educational Progress (NAEP), 2015 English Language Arts Assessment

A Comparison of Adaptive Learning Within the SOI Model Using Paper and Computer Presentation

Huei-Ping Chen[1(✉)], Wen-Yi Lin[2], and Fang-Ming Hwang[2]

[1] Taipei College of Maritime Technology, Taipei, Taiwan
febychen@mail.tcmt.edu.tw
[2] National Chiayi University, Chiayi, Taiwan
afrapupu@gmail.com

Abstract. The main purpose of this paper is to analyses adaptive learning of elementary students' reading comprehension within multi-strategy using different tools. By applying the SOI model (Mayer 1996), three knowledge constructions of cognitive process, the reading comprehension for guiding three cognitive processes is developed in our design website tool named Multiple Online Reading Strategies System. The three multifunctional strategies in online reading strategies system, Selecting relevant information, Organizing incoming information, and Integrating incoming information with exist knowledge, could be applied to highlighting important information, concept mapping, and summarizing to determine topic sentences or important sentences in an article. Data are collected from elementary school in Taiwan and 245 questionnaires are collected in our study. These data are analyzed by the SPSS-for-windows software with statistical methods, descriptive statistics, t-test, one-way analysis of variance (ANOVA). The results of the empirical study suggest that adopting the highlighting method for students to understand articles and employing concept mapping and summarizing strategies to improve students' comparative analysis capabilities are conducive to establishing compact reading strategies for them whether students use online or on paper.

Keywords: SOI model · Multiple online reading strategies system · Reading comprehension · One-way analysis of variance (ANOVA)

1 Introduction

Based on the SOI model by Mayer (1996) as framework, this study designed a multiple online reading strategies system by simulating guided reading of printed expositive texts. The multiple online reading strategies system was from knowledge construction by learning would follow three step of cognitive process. The three multifunctional strategies in online reading strategies system, Selecting relevant information, Organizing incoming information, and Integrating incoming information with exist knowledge, could be applied to highlighting important information, concept mapping, and summarizing to determine topic sentences or important sentences in an article. The three multifunctional strategies in online reading strategies system of highlighting important

© Springer International Publishing AG 2017
T.-T. Wu et al. (Eds.): SETE 2016, LNCS 10108, pp. 455–460, 2017.
DOI: 10.1007/978-3-319-52836-6_48

information, concept mapping, and summarizing to determine topic sentences or important sentences in an article would be applied to comprehending facts explicitly stated in the text, comparing/analyzing the facts stated in the text, and deriving main idea from the text - between reading expositive text in this study. The purpose of this study is to investigate whether differences exist in students' reading comprehension abilities - comprehending facts explicitly stated in the text, comparing/analyzing the facts stated in the text, and deriving main idea from the text - between reading expositive text using the multiple-strategy reading comprehension system and using printed paper.

2   Literature Review

In the competitive 21st century, knowledge quality and creativity play a vital role to the country. It is also the era with rapid development of information technology. Reading is considered as basic learning and acquiring new knowledge skills. Mayer and Wittrock (1996) indicate three processes of cognitive include selecting relevant information from what is happened, organizing selected information into a coherent representation, and integrating submitted information with existing knowledge. The graphic organizer process is helpful for continuous processing of the concepts and the interrelations among them (Armbruster and Anderson 1984). The teaching of learning strategies has a growing consensus and legitimate place in the curriculum (Weinstein and Mayer 1986). Chang et al. (2002) test 126 fifth graders in primary school indicated that the map-correction method and the scaffold-fading method enhanced text comprehension, summarization abilities and summarization ability. Although scholars affirm the important of graphic organizers and knowledge maps when learning process, some important issues from previous studies have yet to be considered such as new technology applied in learning process.

3   Methodology

This study used unequal-group quasi-experimental design to conduct experimental teaching to investigate whether differences exist in students' reading comprehension ability between reading expositive text using the multiple online reading strategies system and using printed paper. The convenience sampling method was used, and two classes from the fifth and two classes from sixth grades, respectively, were selected for the online test. Another two classes from the fifth and two classes from sixth grades, respectively, were selected for the printed test. In total, there are four experimental groups (two classes from the fifth and two classes from sixth grades respectively for the online test) and four control groups (two classes from the fifth and sixth grades respectively for the printed test). The experimental group used the multiple online reading strategies system, while the control group used traditional printed reading material and written test.

3.1   Participants

Participants of this study included fifth-grade and sixth-grade students from two public elementary schools in central Taiwan, who were distributed to classes using normal class grouping. Therefore, the prior knowledge and learning abilities of the students were in normal distribution. One class from the fifth and sixth grades in both schools, respectively, were randomly selected for the reading comprehension tests using online multi-strategy reading comprehension system and printed paper. One of the classes was randomly assigned the online reading and reading comprehension test, while the other class participated in reading and reading comprehension test using printed paper.

3.2   Samples

Two fifth-grade classes and two sixth-grade classes were assigned online reading and reading comprehension test; another two fifth-grade classes and two sixth-grade classes were assigned reading and reading comprehension test using printed material. The tests returned 245 valid questionnaires in total.

3.3   Reading Comprehension Tasks

Chinese Reading Comprehension Test preparation by Lin and Chi (2000) was used as the material for reading and testing. Articles number 7, 9, 10, and 12 were used for both online and printed tests, which consisted of comprehending facts explicitly stated in the text, comparing/analyzing the facts stated in the text, and deriving main idea from the text.

3.4   Multiple Online Reading Strategies System Design

The three multifunctional strategies in online reading strategies system, we designed highlighting important information, concept mapping, and summarizing to determine topic sentences or important sentences in an article to stand for selecting relevant information, organizing incoming information, and integrating incoming information with exist knowledge. The multiple online reading strategies system was designed by 3 parts as Fig. 1.

4   Results

Based on the multiple online reading strategies system (F value = 52.986; p value = 0.000 < 0.001), the means for comprehending facts explicitly stated in the text, comparing/analyzing the facts stated in the text, and deriving main idea from the text were 0.6034, 0.2102, and 0.2932, respectively. Table 1 shows the results of post hoc comparison. For the multiple online reading strategies system test, comprehending facts explicitly stated in the text scored higher than both comparing/analyzing the facts stated

Fig. 1. The multiple online reading strategies system

Table 1. The results of multiple online reading strategies system

Abilities in online reading	Mean	Standard deviation	F value	Post hoc tests
Comprehending facts explicitly stated in the text	0.6034	0.6482	52.986***	Comprehending facts explicitly stated in the text
Deriving main idea from the text	0.2102	0.2450		Deriving main idea from the text
Comparing/analyzing the facts stated in the text	0.2932	0.3398		Comparing/analyzing the facts stated in the text

***p < 0.001

in the text and deriving main idea from the text. From these results, we can infer that in multiple online reading strategies system, the selecting process (strategy of underlining key points) scored higher than the organizing (strategy of filling in concept maps) and integrating (strategy of deriving summaries) processes.

Based on multiple reading strategies system test using paper (F value = 54.365; p value = 0.000 < 0.001), the means for comprehending facts explicitly stated in the text, comparing/analyzing the facts stated in the text, and deriving main idea from the text were 0.5333, 0.1667, and 0.2680, respectively. Table 2 shows the results of post hoc comparison. For the printed-material reading comprehension test, comprehending facts explicitly stated in the text scored higher than both comparing/analyzing the facts stated in the text and deriving main idea from the text. From these results, we can infer that in multi-strategy reading comprehension, the selecting process (strategy of underlining key points) scored higher than the organizing (strategy of filling in concept maps) and integrating (strategy of deriving summaries) processes.

Table 2. The results of multiple reading strategies system using paper

Abilities in printed reading	Mean	Standard deviation	F value	Post hoc tests
Comprehending facts explicitly stated in the text	0.5333	0.5891	54.365***	Comprehending facts explicitly stated in the text
Deriving main idea from the text	0.1667	0.2176		Comparing/analyzing the facts stated in the text
Comparing/analyzing the facts stated in the text	0.2680	0.3003		Deriving main idea from the text

***p < 0.001

5   Conclusion

From the study, it is indicated that the purpose of the multiple online reading strategies system was to investigate whether differences exist in students' reading comprehension abilities - comprehending facts explicitly stated in the text, comparing/analyzing the facts stated in the text, and deriving main idea from the text - between reading expositive text using the multiple online reading strategies system and using printed paper. The multiple online reading strategies system was used to measure students' performance in comprehending facts explicitly stated in the text, comparing/analyzing the facts stated in the text, and deriving main idea from the text. The results showed that in both online and printed reading comprehension, the selecting process (strategy of underlining key points) scored higher than the organizing (strategy of filling in concept maps) and integrating (strategy of deriving summaries) processes.

References

Armbruster, B.B., Anderson, T.H.: Mapping: representing informative text diagrammatically. In: Holley, C.D., Dansereau, D.F. (eds.) Spatial Learning Strategies: Techniques, Applications, and Related Issues. Academic Press, New York (1984)

Chang, K.E., Sung, Y.T., Chen, G.A.: The effect of concept mapping to enhance text comprehension and summarization. J. Exp. Educ. **71**(1), 5–23 (2002)

Lin, B.G., Chi, P.H.: The development of test of reading comprehension. Bull. Spec. Educ. **2000**(19), 79–104 (2000)

Mayer, R.E.: Learning strategies for making sense out of expository text: the SOI model for guiding three cognitive processes in knowledge construction. Educ. Psychol. Rev. **8**(4), 357–371 (1996)

Mayer, R.E., Wittrock, M.C.: Problem solving transfer. In: Befliner, D., Calfee, R. (eds.) Handbook of Educational Psychology, pp. 47–62. Macmillan, New York (1996)

Weinstein, C.E., Mayer, R.E.: The teaching of learning strategies. In: Wittrock, M.C. (ed.) Handbook of Research on Teaching, 3rd edn, pp. 315–327. Macmillan, New York (1986)

Workshop on Social and Personal Computing for Web-Supported Learning Communities

Wikis as a Mediation Platform
for Developing Learning Communities:
The WEKI Framework

George Palaigeorgiou[1(✉)] and Ioannis Kazanidis[2]

[1] University of Western Macedonia, Florina, Greece
gpalegeo@uowm.gr
[2] Eastern Macedonia and Thrace Institute of Technology, Kavala, Greece
kazanidis@teiemt.gr

Abstract. Wikis provide unique affordances for collaboration and delivering public products and have been explored extensively as learning spaces. Most studies have underlined that triggering productive collaborative learning in wikis may be challenging and that an effective learning design is an important prerequisite for their successful exploitation. Several related design guidelines have been proposed such as setting group goals, design a rich context and problem, motivating progress monitoring, establishing structured collaboration processes etc. By following these guidelines and taking advantage of community of learners principles, we have designed the instructional approach WEKI which aims to help students to familiarize with a new learning domain by co-developing an open educational book about the domain. Twenty-four 4th-year undergraduate students of an Electrical and Computer Engineering Department applied the WEKI approach and formed a learning community for 15 weeks. The undergraduates successfully managed to design and develop an e-book and relevant learning resources about Microsoft Kodu in the context of a Teaching IT course. Interviews about students' perceptions of WEKI were conducted with all of the students before and after the project. In the beginning, students considered the proposed framework as a complicated and challenging process but in the end, the vast majority of students stated that their experience and the final products exceeded their best expectations. Our results indicate that well-structured instructional approaches focusing on communities of learners' principles, may realize the potential of wikis.

Keywords: Wikis · Blended learning · Collaborative learning

1 Introduction

Wikis are easy to use, lightweight services which allow participants to create collective documents by editing, revising, discussing, and sharing information. Wikis are of special interest in education due to their ability to create a virtual innovative space of coordination and collaborative writing, to produce and share public products or resources and to allow participation from a high number of students.

© Springer International Publishing AG 2017
T.-T. Wu et al. (Eds.): SETE 2016, LNCS 10108, pp. 463–472, 2017.
DOI: 10.1007/978-3-319-52836-6_49

Several studies from early on tried to validate the promises of wikis. Yan [1] supported that collaborative work through a wiki motivates students' active participation while other researchers claimed that collaborative learning is facilitated when wikis are integrated as an instructional strategy in tertiary education courses [2]. Wikis seem to facilitate peer review [3], to encourage students to reflect on the potential audience of their writing [4, 5], to develop more powerful connections between students and the learning task [5], to endorse casual and flexible discussion [6], to enhance peer interaction and sharing of knowledge in groups projects [7] etc.

Nevertheless, the list of problems related with the educational exploitation of wikis is equally impressive. For example, studies have shown that tertiary level students have a reluctance or "discomfort" to edit one another's contributions [8], tend to read only those pages to which they had contributed [5], even feel offended if their own work has been edited by peers [9], are reluctant to be the first to post and lack confidence in sharing their writing on a wiki [10], appear to favor individual work over collaboration using wikis [11], prefer face-to-face discussion during collaborative writing [12], experience feelings of isolation and disconnection [13], confront difficulties in managing the group dynamics within the developing community [14] and do not perceive their wiki tasks as authentic activities that require authentic audiences [15]. Kummer in his meta-analysis of 73 articles on wikis [16] have extracted three barriers in achieving optimal collaboration: lack of ownership, fear of publicity and poor group climate. Some researchers consider that there is relatively little research on successful implementations of wikis that support collaborative writing [17].

Therefore, one of the major encounters in applying wikis in an educational setting seems to be how to trigger and maintain students' coordination, collaboration, and production activities. Instructional guidance and a sound pedagogical model seems to be needed. Several design guidelines have been proposed such as to create positive interdependence, to promote interaction and individual accountability, to trigger group processing [18], to be clear on expectations for editing, to model expected behaviors, to provide timely feedback, to offer rewards for contributions, to establish clear timelines, create a sense of ownership, to provide a structured model by setting "rules of engagement," and proposing "navigation paths" [19], to incorporate social rewarding mechanisms [20], to help and engage students in monitoring their group progress and evaluating group accomplishments [21], to establish a purpose for the wiki project, to design a rich context and problem that support the achievement of the purpose [22], to give students authority to choose topics based on their interests [23], to offer face-to-face meeting opportunities in early collaboration to build empathy and trust [24] and a lot more. Although the list of design guidelines is big, there are a few instructional frameworks right now which try to address all the previous issues holistically and managed to offer real learning value.

2 Weki Framework

In this paper, we present the WEKI instructional framework which aims at exploiting wikis as a mediation platform for developing and sustaining communities of learners (CoL) [25]. WEKI tries to foster a culture of learning based on wiki's affordances where both individuals and the community as a whole are learning how to learn with the aim of producing and delivering an authentic product.

With WEKI, an academic course is transformed into a project where undergraduates are asked to create collaboratively an educational book about the course subject matter. For example, in a ICT Teaching course, students may be asked to address the lack of material for a kids programming tool such as Microsoft Kodu, or Scratch. In that case, the end product is enormously useful for its final recipients (i.e. primary school students) and that becomes a significant motivation for undergraduates.

The WEKI framework consists of two phases. In the first and shorter phase, three face to face meetings are conducted where:

- the instructor informs the students about the procedure to be followed and publishes the rules of the CoL and the project timetable on the wiki.
- students are organized in teams; the instructor meets with each team separately, explains its role and defines together with the team the objectives and the plan for its deliverables.
- students take the responsibility and decide about the domain and the audience that they will address (i.e. in a ICT Teaching course, whether to deal with Microsoft Kodu, Scratch, Python, etc.).
- each team proposes its own outline for the book and in the third and final meeting, the different content proposals are synthesized into a common outline.
- the instructor presents and shares in the wiki related educational resources in order to get the undergraduates acquainted with the course subject.

In the second phase, the teams start working collaboratively towards their goals and three or more milestones for uploading the work in progress are specified. These time points are crucial for assessing the evolution of the project and reflecting on its sustainability.

Each student must participate in two teams, one "vertical" and one "horizontal". Vertical teams are the ones focusing on the writing of a book chapter. Horizontal teams may either support the coordination processes or produce supplementary material for the book. Exemplary horizontal teams for the project coordination:

- *Contents team*: supervises and coordinates the content of the chapters, assesses publicly their progress in the specific milestones, provides feedback on the writing norms and the common mistakes.
- *Typography team*: creates specifications for the layout of the chapters and the book in general and composes all the deliverables into one single book.
- *Experience assessment team*: collects information about participants' experience of the project by conducting interviews, monitors and publishes cooperation and coordination problems on the wiki and, prepares a video documentary for the project.
- *Experts team*: provide answers to questions regarding the course subject. It is composed of students with the best knowledge of the subject domain.

Exemplary horizontal teams which concern the enrichment of the book with supplementary learning material include:

- *Links team*: selects and shares relevant links and information sources for each chapter. At the end of the project, the team also creates a list of the best external resources that will be included in the book
- *Comics team*: creates comics that will be included in the beginning or at the end of each chapter.
- *Presentation team*: creates presentations for each chapter i.e. in Prezi.
- *Screencasts team*: create video tutorials for all related computer tools.

The first group of horizontal teams, pursue their goals from the very beginning of the project while the second group of horizontal teams starts working after the first drafts of the book.

The wiki enables the accurate reflection of the CoL organization into three group of pages which function as discussion hubs:

- *Instructor pages*: the instructor shares material with the students i.e. the community norms and rules, the description of the project and the course-related educational material.
- *Chapter pages*: the second group of pages corresponds exactly to the number of the book chapters. Each vertical group is responsible for one chapter and one corresponding wiki page. The discussion forum in all these pages, is placed on the top of the page layout in order to encourage discussions between and within vertical teams.
- *Horizontal teams pages*: The third group of wiki pages relates to the horizontal teams. Each horizontal team is responsible for its own page and there, it uploads deliverables, provokes discussions about their form and content, organize votes, etc.

An important community rule is that all horizontal teams have to propose different drafts of their deliverables and invite the CoL to discuss, evaluate and select the preferred ones. The communication of the learners is being done mainly through the discussion forums of the wiki pages and the messages mechanism of the wiki platform.

3 Learners Experience

The WEKI framework transfers the responsibility of studying, cooperating, coordinating, writing, executing and ensuring the quality of the products to the undergraduates. The instructor helps the Contents team to specify the quality criteria and to assess the intermediate deliverables of each team, while he meets with the other teams whenever they ask for it. After each milestone, face to face meetings are taking place with all of the community of learners. In that way, all problems and questions are resolved quickly and the book contents are homogenized.

The WEKI framework was designed with the aim of provoking a daily intense engagement within the community. The initiative in the community constantly changes hands, different teams ask their colleagues to create things, evaluate deliverables or express their opinion and vice versa. That creates an interesting symmetry of triggering the participation by diverse teams throughout the project.

Although, each member manages two wiki pages, one for his chapter and one for his horizontal team, in reality the students have to participate in all other wiki pages, for example in order to vote for the screencast style in the related horizontal team page or to answer a question in another chapter's discussion forum that concerns his writings. The members have a strong interconnection between them i.e. several horizontal teams wait for the first deliverables of the ebook chapters, each chapter depends on its related chapters etc. The special characteristics of the wikis (revisions history, notifications, forums for each page etc.) are not just "nice to have" affordances but tools without which the learners are unable to do their job in this complex interaction context.

If we try to identify the experience of a participant in WEKI, we will see that the participant has

- to participate in discussions for the contents of the book while looking at the "related" chapters for overlaps and their progress.
- to visit the proposed links from the Links team for writing his chapter.
- to develop and write together with his teammates the chapter and share drafts to of his work at regular intervals which will be studied by the other teams.
- to monitor his chapter assessment from the Contents team and adapt his writings.
- to study the previous chapters systematically in order to understand the learning domain and the reader knowledge when the last reaches his chapter.
- to be responsible for a horizontal team, to prepare and upload the related material in the wiki page of the team, to discuss with his teammates in the corresponding page discussion forum, to organize polls and discussions over the deliverables of his team.
- to offer a video interview to the Experience Evaluation Team in which he reflects on the product and the project in an informal and personal way.
- to study, vote and discuss the form and the content of the deliverables of the other horizontal teams (i.e. layout alternatives from the Typography team, screencasts forms from the Screencast team, Comics form and content from the Comics team, etc.).

As it is evident, the students in WEKI have to participate in the project with a plurality of ways and their involvement in all aspects of the products development is deep and democratic.

4   Methodology

Twenty-four 4th-year undergraduate students of a Greek Electrical and Computer Engineering Department exploited WEKI and formed a learning community for 15 weeks in a "Teaching IT" course. The students selected to design and develop a book about learning programming with Microsoft Kodu. No lectures were conducted and the whole course was focused on establishing the community of learners and delivering a useful and ready to use book for primary school students. The wiki platform used was wikispaces.com. In order to study the students' perceptions about the WEKI frame-work, two interviews were conducted with each student. The first one took place exactly after the first phase of the project and the second one was conducted at the end of the project. The initial semi-structured interviews tried to identify students' views on the project goals, on the community organization, on their expectations for the final product and it consisted of 10 questions. The final semi-structured interviews included 20 questions and focused on students' views on the final products, the knowledge acquired and the effectiveness of the WEKI organization. All audio-recorded interviews were transcribed and then encoded and compared within and between cases using the ATLAS.ti software and the constant comparative method. A concise view of the most significant conclusions will be presented in the following section.

5 Results

5.1 Students Deliverables

The students succeeded in delivering a book for children about how to program with Microsoft Kodu. The book consisted of 12 chapters, 252 pages and 64290 words. The book was shared in a separate site together with educational screencasts while it was promoted through social media and was accepted with great enthusiasm from the teachers' community.

5.2 Wiki Statistics

The wiki statistics indicated that the effort invested was significant and the involvement of the students was intensive. In order to create the book and all the complementary learning material, students edited 2074 times the various pages, exchanged 273 messages in the discussions of the wiki pages, while they viewed the pages for 43077 times. The wiki was visited every day all of those weeks by at least 20 visitors each day (although this statistic offered by wikispaces isn't accurate enough). In any case, these numbers show that the WEKI framework managed to engage students in a daily basis.

5.3 Students Negation at the Start of the Project

Although the majority of the undergraduates claimed that the ultimate goal of the community, the creation of a useful product beyond the borders of their class, intrigued them, at the same time they expressed a number of reservations about this new adventure. Their greatest concern was focused on whether 24 people can cooperate and work together towards a common goal. They did not have similar experiences in the past, while, as they claimed, previous team projects were usually decomposed into individual tasks without the need for extensive communication.

- *Always problems arise when you participate in a team, even if just 3 people cooperate, they have trouble, what will happen now that we are 24 people.*
- *Cooperation problems appear when we are two people, and sometimes do not understand each other as we should...it seems difficult to reach agreement between 24 people.*

Students expressed similar concerns in regards to the book co-writing. They had difficulties imagining how the interdependence of the different chapters will work out.

– *The main difficulty that we will have to deal with, is in the vertical teams, where we have to cooperate with the chapters (teams) that are connected to our content.*
– *I am not sure whether the chapters will be consistent enough because they are written from different teams and I believe that we will have a problem in that respect.*

Few students pointed out that they did not have the skills to write a book, and considered the task at hand as bizarre. This is usually referred as anxiety about writing.

– *It will be difficult, we are not writers, we do not know where to start and where to end, what this book should contain.*
– *Personally, I cannot write something that will address children, in general I am not the "writing" guy, I do not have creativity, imagination, I cannot find easily examples, I believe that I will have a problem.*

Some students were also negative towards the team assignments since they projected that some teams had easier workload than others or that groups formation was unfair. These students were in general not positive to the diversity of roles and deliverables for each team.

From the initial interviews was clear enough that the WEKI framework does not seem as a straightforward project, and its complexity provokes feelings of anxiety and negativity.

5.4 Students Surprised by Their Own Results

Students views on WEKI and their products changed dramatically when the project was completed, the book and the supporting learning material were developed. The vast majority of students was impressed by their deliverables and noted that their products surpass their best expectations.

– *I believed that the results wouldn't be something good enough, now that I am seeing the book, it is too big, well organized and I can say that I was impressed and felt pleasure with the final result...my initial predictions were wrong, the result is very very good.*
– *I thought that it would be very difficult, but finally was easier than I expected. The communication between the teams was easy. I believe that it was a really good experience. The book is much better than expected.*

The students evaluated the WEKI organization as effective, efficient and enjoying while they also characterized it as "common-sense" and "sound". Hence, despite their initial reservations, the cooperation-coordination processes were organically integrated in their daily activities with the help of the wiki.

– *The coordination was very good and through twitter and the wiki we could communicate comfortably and questions were solved immediately, there was no delay.*

- *I really liked the separation in vertical and horizontal teams. 2 or 3 students is a good number for developing a chapter. If we were more, we would have trouble in our collaboration. In the horizontal action, I liked our role which influenced all other teams (Typography team) and we had to be responsible, to respond quickly and to give credits to the best deliverables. And I also liked that some other teams checked our own text and provided us with interesting comments on how to improve it.*
- *Amazing coordination. We managed to deliver a very good result. We were well organized and at the end we managed to have something in our hands.*
- *If there wasn't such a coordination plan and division of labor, I do not believe that we would reach this final result.*
- *Great collaboration, it was reasonable to distribute the workload in such a manner, it was a nice idea.*

Students supported that they learnt a lot from a practical view point about the course contents (Teaching ICT) while they also exercise collaboration and coordination skills.

- *Amazing how many side effects the whole thing had, I have really appreciated how important is to have solid cooperation and communication foundations, how we communicated, how we collaborated and that when there is a central guidance, the result will almost definitely be satisfying. It's an exceptional way of learning, we didn't learn only about how to teach children ICT but also how to prepare and follow a big project, we didn't have the chance until now to live something similar, I liked it a lot, I wish more courses to be done in the same way in our department.*

6 Discussion

Some students claimed that their WEKI experience "will be remembered in the future" and that "more courses should be done in the same way". Our data in this concise presentation showed that the combination of wiki features together with community of learners' principles managed to engage and motivate students to cooperate, collaborate, study and create. Students exploited almost all wiki features, participated successfully with multiple ways in the community, developed diverse expertise, monitored their progress and knowledge, and went beyond the bounds by creating something useful while respecting, cooperating, negotiating and sharing with their co-fellows. Exactly these elements constitute the core of communities of learners [25]. It is interesting that students seemed ready for bigger, more complex projects with the aim of producing authentic and useful results. This gives more meaning to the learning processes and wikis can become an excellent mediation tool for such open coordination and development efforts.

The instructor was not uninvolved, the opposite, he was strongly engaged with each team by offering his feedback continuously. Students asked for his guidance especially in the initial phase where they had to set their goals and the timetable. Afterwards, his help was more focused on the quality and the content of the deliverables and less on the coordination of the teams. The lectures in the course were few but the meetings were a lot and the opportunities for the instructor to work on the course objectives were probably more authentic and effective.

Nevertheless, more applications of the WEKI framework are needed in order to identify its learning value and optimize better its structural elements. More studies should focus also on the details of the interactions between and within teams and on the factors affecting the feasibility of the WEKI framework for different contexts (e.g. group sizes, course domains etc.).

References

1. Yan, J.: Social technology as a new medium in the classroom. New Engl. J. High. Educ. **22** (4), 27–30 (2008)
2. Biasutti, M., EL-Deghaidy, H.: Using wiki in teacher education: impact on knowledge management processes and student satisfaction. Comput. Educ. **59**(3), 861–872 (2012)
3. Xiao, Y., Lucking, R.: The impact of two types of peer assessment on students' performance and satisfaction within a Wiki environment. Internet High. Educ. **11**(3–4), 186–193 (2008)
4. Hemmi, A., Bayne, S., Land, R.: The appropriation and repurposing of social technologies in higher education. J. Comput. Assist. Learn. **25**(1), 19–30 (2009)
5. Wheeler, S., Yeomans, P., Wheeler, D.: The Good, the Bad and the Wiki: evaluating student-generated content for collaborative learning. Brit. J. Educ. Technol. **39**(6), 987–995 (2008)
6. Read, B.: Romantic poetry meets 21st-Century technology. Chronicle High. Educ. **51**, 35–36 (2005)
7. Augar, N., Raitman, R., Zhou, W.: Wikis: collaborative virtual learning environments. In: Weiss, J., Nolan, J., Hunsinger, J., Trifonas, P. (eds.) The International Handbook of Virtual Learning Environments, pp. 1251–1269. Springer, Netherlands (2006)
8. Kale, U.: Can they plan to teach withWeb 2.0? future teachers' potential use of the emerging web. Technol. Pedagogy Educ. **23**(4), 471–489 (2013)
9. Alyousef, H.S., Picard, M.Y.: Cooperative or collaborative literacy practices: mapping metadiscourse in a business students' wiki group project. Australas. J. Educ. Technol. **27**, 468–480 (2011)
10. Cole, M.: Using wiki technology to support student engagement: lessons from the trenches. Comput. Educ. **52**, 141–146 (2009)
11. Hadjerrouit, S.: A co-writing development approach to wikis: pedagogical issues and implications. World Acad. Sci. Eng. Technol. **57**, 579–586 (2011)
12. Yusoff, Z.S., Nik Alwi, N.A., Ibrahim, A.H.: Investigating students' perception of using wikis in academic writing. 3L: Lang. Ling. Lit. **18**(3), 91–102 (2012)
13. Boling, E.C., Hough, M., Krinsky, H., Saleem, H., Stevens, M.: Cutting the distance in distance education: Perspectives on what promotes positive, online learning experiences. Internet High. Educ. **15**(2), 118–126 (2012)
14. Vratulis, V., Dobson, T.M.: Social negotiations in a wiki environment: A case study with pre-service teachers. Educ. Media Int. **45**(4), 285–294 (2008)
15. Grant, L.: 'I don't' care do our own page!' A case study of using wikis for collaborative work in a UK secondary school. Learn. Media Technol. **34**(2), 105–117 (2009)

16. Kummer, C. (2013). Factors influencing wiki collaboration in higher education. doi:10.2139/ssrn.2208522. Retrieved from Social Science Research Network at http://papers.ssrn.com/sol3/papers.cfm?abstract_id=2208522

17. Pifarré, M., Fisher, R.: Breaking up the writing process: How wikis can support understanding the composition and revision strategies of young writers. Lang. Educ. **25** (5), 451–466 (2011)

18. Falcó, J.M., Huertas, J.L.: Use of wiki as a postgraduate education learning tool: A case study. Int. J. Eng. Educ. **28**, 1334–1340 (2012)

19. Zitzelsberger, H., Campbell, K. A., Service, D. & Sanchez, O: Using wikis to stimulate collaborative learning in two online health sciences courses. J. Nurs. Educ. **54**, 352–355 (2015)

20. Hoisl, B., Aigner, W., Miksch, S.: Social rewarding in Wiki systems – motivating the community. In: Schuler, D. (ed.) OCSC 2007. LNCS, vol. 4564, pp. 362–371. Springer, Heidelberg (2007). doi:10.1007/978-3-540-73257-0_40

21. Järvelä, S., Kirschner, P.A., Panadero, E., Malmberg, J., Phielix, C., Jaspers, J., Järve-noja, H.: Enhancing socially shared regulation in collaborative learning groups: designing for CSCL regulation tools. Educ. Technol. Res. Devel. **63**, 125–142 (2015)

22. West, J.A., West, M.L.: Using wikis for on-line collaboration: the power of the read-write web. Jossey-Bass, San Fransisco (2009)

23. Zheng, B., Niiya, M., Warschauer, M.: Wikis and collaborative learning in higher education. Technol. Pedagogy Educ. **24**(3), 357–374 (2015)

24. Garrison, D.R., Vaughan, N.D.: Blended Learning in Higher Education: Frame-Work, Principles and Guidelines. Jossey-Bass, San Francisco (2008)

25. Bielaczyc, K., Collins, A.: Learning communities in classrooms: a reconceptualization of educational practice. In: Reigeluth, C.M. (ed.) Instructional design theories and models, vol. II, pp. 269–291. Lawrence Erlbaum Associates, Mahwah (1999)

Obtaining Assessment Tests After Double Filtration

Doru Popescu Anastasiu[1](⊠), Nicolae Bold[2],
and Ion Alexandru Popescu[3]

[1] Faculty of Mathematics and Computer Science,
University of Pitesti, Pitesti, Romania
dopopan@gmail.com
[2] Faculty of Management Economic Engineering in Agriculture and Rural
Development, University of Agronomic Sciences and Veterinary Medicine,
Slatina Branch, Bucharest, Romania
bold_nicolae@yahoo.com
[3] National College "Radu Greceanu", Slatina, Romania
alexionpopescu@gmail.com

Abstract. Tests are widely used in assessment. Regardless their forms or types, the tests that are formed of a fixed number of questions are the most efficient in the case of checking the proportion of understood information. Usually, tests are formed from a number of question set by the assessor, but the database that contains the number of questions (the pool of questions) can contain as many as thousands of questions. From this pool, the assessor wants to select only the ones which correspond to certain needs. This paper presents a modality of filtering the questions, firstly by their subject and, secondly, by their solving time. Practically, the assessor will obtain tests formed from sequences of questions which match best with the subjects defined by the user and the total solving time of the test is in the range of a time defined by the assessor. This implies notions related to optimization and fitness, alongside reliability, favorability, correctness, efficiency and other useful and needful characteristics of an intelligent tutoring system.

Keywords: Question · Test · Solving time · Keywords · Filter

1 Introduction

Questions are the basic element of assessment. Due to their variety and modality of construction, the questions that form a test require special characteristics (close to adaptability - [4]) within the test. Usually, questions have the same subjects and must form a structure that shows in the most accurate way the gained knowledge by the learners.

That is, the assessor must select the most appropriate questions from a large database of questions of different subjects and characteristics (forming a type of open learning environment - [6]). Usually, the number of the entries in the database is a very large one, which makes the task of filtering the question time-consuming and inefficient.

© Springer International Publishing AG 2017
T.-T. Wu et al. (Eds.): SETE 2016, LNCS 10108, pp. 473–479, 2017.
DOI: 10.1007/978-3-319-52836-6_50

We used genetic algorithms mainly because their characteristic of output existence in cases of large input data. Even if the solutions are approximate, they are close to the optimum. This algorithm includes data related to combinatorics [1]. A part of other types of filters is presented in previous papers of the authors – degree of difficulty, questions not wanted in the test etc. [5, 7] or [8]).

In this domain of education, genetic-based algorithms were also used (as in paper [2, 3]). As we can see, in the literature, several types of systems that are useful in the assessment process are presented. However, giving an additional filter to a primary filtration increases the fidelity of the results and the efficiency of assessment.

2   Method Description and Filters

As we stated in the introduction, the questions that form entries in a database (which can be populated during a period of time with various questions) are numerous and diverse. Thus, the process consumes time and resources.

The database of question is built overtime, the assessors filling it with questions from various disciplines. The questions may be multiple-choice or plain questions, but their solving time must not exceed 10 min, thus they have an order number, a statement and choices (in cases of multiple-choice).

Shortly, our model consists in a method which filters some questions labeled with certain keywords that characterize best their subject and with a given solving time. The assessor wishes to select questions to form a test using two filters: the first one is based on the matching between the user-given keywords and the keywords of a question, using a genetic-based algorithm to generate sequences of questions (namely, tests) that meet this requirement and the second consist in finding the sequences which fit in a total solving time given by the assessor. But, firstly, we will present data related to our method.

Definition 1. A filter (F_j) is considered a user requirement met by a question Q_i, $1 \leq i \leq N$ (number of questions), $1 \leq j \leq NF$ (number of filters).

This paper will present a method which will use two filters (NF = 2).

Observation 1. K is considered the number of questions within a test and Tt represents the limit of solving time set by the user. The questions will be denoted by numbers from 1 to N. The number of keywords set by the user are denoted by $no\_kws = \{kws_1, kws_2, \ldots, kws_{no\_kws}\}$.

Observation 2. Given N questions in a database, a question Q_i (i = 1, N) is considered to be characterized by no_kw_i keywords $\left(kw_i = \{kw_{i,1}, kw_{i,2}, \ldots, kw_{i,no\_kwi}\}\right)$ and a solving time denoted by $time_i$, expressed in minutes ($1 \leq time_i \leq 10$).

Observation 3. Let Q_i be a question from the database (i = 1, N). The number of keywords that characterize $Q_i(kw_i)$ which are common with the kws is considered the intersection of the two sets of keywords:

$$kw'_i = \{kw_1, kw_2, \ldots, kw_{no\_kw_i}\} \cap \{kws_1, kws_2, \ldots, kws_{no\_kws}\}$$

Observation 4. A sequence of k questions $sQ_i = (sQ_1, sQ_2, \ldots, sQ_K)$, also called a test, is defined by kw' keywords that match with the no_kws keywords and a solving time denoted by T_i (which, intuitively, represents the solving time for the test). ($1 \leq i \leq$ NS - number of obtained sequences).

Definition 2 *(filter F_1).* Given a sequence of questions sQ_i, (i = 1, NS), if

$$\sum_{l=1}^{K} kw'_{sQ_{i,l}} > \sum_{l=1}^{K} kw'_{sQ_{j,l}}, any\, j = \overline{1, NS}$$

than the sequence sQ_i has the maximal number of keywords that matches with the keywords set by the user. The number of these sequences will be denoted by NSM.

Definition 3 *(filter F_2).* Given a sequence of questions sQ_i, (i = 1, NSM), which met the filter F_j, if $T_i \leq$ Tt, than the sequence meets the filter F_2.

Note

Obviously, there can be situations in which none sequence meets the two filters. In this case, the sequence which is closest to the filter requirement is output. Thereby, we can identify two cases (with a statistic made out from 105 algorithm runs):

- case 1: after filtering, several sequences are found (48.57%);
- case 2: no sequence is found; here, we can identify two subcases:
  - case 2a: F1 is false and F2 is true, meaning that no sequence with maximum number of common keywords are found, but the solving time is respected $\rightarrow$ the sequence that respect the time with the closest number of maximum is output (35.24%);
  - case 2b: F1 is true and F2 is false, meaning that no sequence has the solving time less than Tt $\rightarrow$ the sequence with the maximum number of common keywords that has the closest time to Tt is output (16.19%).

In Sect. 3 we will present the description of the algorithm used for the method of double filtering.

3 Algorithm Description

The method presented in Sect. 2 is using as solving method a genetic-based algorithm for the first filter and the selection of the resulted sequences by their solving time T_i for the second filter.

The representation of a gene will be an integer number from 1 to N, also the questions being codified with numbers. For example, a question will be denoted by x, $x \in \{1, \ldots, N\}$, and its representation within the chromosome will be marked by x.

Thus, in order to generate and obtain sequences of questions, we will make the next considerations: a question will be symbolized by a gene, a sequence of questions (a test) will be a chromosome and the fitness function, will consist in the number of keywords of the algorithms that match with those given by the user. Methodically, these steps and these data are presented in the next rows.

Step 1. The input data is read. The input data consist in the number of question in the database (N), the number of questions within a test (K), number of generations (NG), total solving time for a test (Tt), the number of keywords set by the user (no_kws), the set of these keywords (kws) and, for each question, the number of keywords that characterize the question (no_kw), the set of these keywords (kw) and the time for each test (T_i).

Step 2. In order to ease the process, the intersection of the keywords is stored as binaries in a bi-dimensional array (TT).

Step 3. The initial population is randomly generated gene by gene. Then, the chromosomes are sorted descending by their fitness value. The next two steps are iterated for NG times.

Step 4. The mutation operation is applied. Mutation consists in the generation of a random gene M and the swap of the gene found at the random position P with this gene. Then, the chromosomes are sorted.

Step 5. The crossover operation is applied. Crossover means replacing the second part of the chromosome M with the second part of the chromosome N and the first part of the chromosome N with the first part of the chromosome M, these parts being delimited at a random position P. Then, the chromosomes are sorted.

Step 6. The chromosomes are then filtered using the second filter.

Step 7. The output data is print. This means the first sequences (chromosomes) are output.

4   Implementation and Results

The algorithm is important due to two main aspects: the results close to reality/the performance of the algorithm and the runtime. The tests were made on a system with the next parameters: a Windows 8 operating system, a i3-3217U 1.80 GHz microprocessor and 4 GB of RAM. Firstly, we will study the first-mentioned aspect. For 1000 questions, 10 questions within a test, 100 generations, 50 min (Tt) and 10 keywords set by the user, we obtained the results from Table 1.

The runtime for the example presented above was 1.51 s. Regarding the runtime for different values of the parameters, we will take examples of databases with 1000, 2000, 3000, 4000 and 5000 questions. Table 2 presents the evolution of runtime for different values of N, K and NG and for Tt = 120 min.

Regarding the runtime, we can observe that the runtime slightly depends on N, the things changing in the case of the variation of K, when the increase is more noticeable. The bigger increase of runtime can be observed for the variation of NG, because the finer the results will be, the higher the runtime will increase.

Table 1. The first five results for the example

Sequence (test)	Sequence solving time	Number of common keywords
628 103 653 542 4 1 520 9 732 400	46 min	22
628 103 653 542 6 9 520 252 732 400	48 min	22
628 2 653 6 7 1 520 252 732 400	50 min	22
628 2 653 4 373 1 520 252 732 400	48 min	22
628 2 653 542 373 1 4 252 732 400	48 min	22

Table 2. Runtimes for different values of N, K and NG

N	K	NG	Runtime (seconds)	Runtime for a previous algorithm
1000	20	500	6.655	8.099
2000			6.682	8.347
3000			6.870	8.200
4000			6.568	8.857
5000			6.760	9.293
2000	30	500	7.125	10.177
	50		7.312	9.690
	70		7.739	12.886
	90		8.296	12.904
	100		8.627	12.423
2000	20	600	8.003	10.171
		800	10.636	13.426
		1000	13.095	16.932
		1200	15.763	19.770
		1400	18.809	23.091

In order to show the usefulness of the double filtration, especially from the structure of questions, we will compare the results from this paper (double filtration) with a previous generation of tests, with a simple filtration related to the number of common keywords. For the same input data applied to the algorithm presented in paper [9], we obtained the results presented in Table 3. For $N = 1000$, $K = 10$ and $NG = 100$, the runtime was 1.80 s.

We can see that the questions obtained in Table 3 are more various in terms of questions. This result is obtained due to the fact that a second filter is applied, which modifies the structure of the test. A more various structure of a test can be obtained by increasing the number of generations or variation of solving time.

In order to show the relatedness of the algorithm to the keywords given by the user, we must observe the evolution of the number of common keywords. We must take into account that the second filter has the trend to lower the number of common keywords.

Table 3. First five values obtained for the compared algorithm

Sequence (test)	Number of common keywords
751 89 33 484 885 227 400 868 672 613	23
544 474 116 608 377 770 254 614 335 375	23
430 316 942 667 36 230 798 251 10 674	23
879 79 854 754 863 145 42 506 850 43	23
700 576 669 384 821 249 363 469 402 277	23

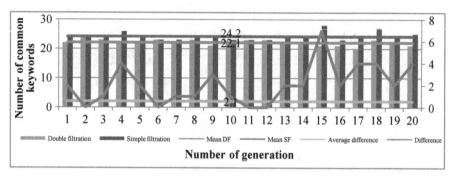

Fig. 1. Comparison between the number of the common keywords in case of simple and double filtration

A situation of obtained number of keywords for the compared algorithms is presented in Fig. 1.

This thing is somehow normal, taking into account that the results of the double filtration are stricter and more close to what the user wants in order to accomplish its requirements.

5 Conclusions

The double filtering is a useful tool in selecting questions for a test. It must be mentioned that the filters can be interchanged or even other types of filters can be used (e.g., the degree of difficulty of the questions, which is strongly related to the solving time, being inversely with the degree of difficulty). Thus, a third filter can be added (e.g. in paper [9]), that is the filtering can be made using the time requested for a test, the number of keywords and the order of questions within a test depending on the degree of difficulty. Another future work would consist in adding a feature to the keywords filter, that is, giving weights to filters, a thing that would increase the accuracy of the results.

References

1. Balcau, C.: Combinatorică şi Teoria Grafurilor. Publishing of Univ. of Pitesti (2007)
2. Hwang, G.-J., Lin, B.M.T., Tseng, H.-H., Lin, T.-L.: On the development of a computer-assisted testing system with genetic test-sheet generating approach. IEEE Trans. Syst. Man Cybern. **35**(4), 590–594 (2005)
3. Wang, F.-R., Wang, W.-H., Yang, H.-Q., Pan, Q.-K.: A novel discrete differential evolution algorithm for computer-aided test-sheet composition problems. In: Information Engineering and Computer Science (ICIECS 2009), Wuhan, pp. 1–4 (2009)
4. Popescu, E.: Adaptation provisioning with respect to learning styles in a web-based educational system: an experimental study. J. Comput. Assist. Learn. **26**(4), 243–257 (2010)
5. Popescu, D.A., Bold, N., Nijloveanu, D.: A method based on genetic algorithms for generating assessment tests used for learning. In: 17th International Conference on Intelligent Text Processing and Computational Linguistics (2016)
6. Holotescu, C.: A conceptual model for open learning environments. In: International Conference on Virtual Learning (ICVL), pp. 54– 61 (2015)
7. Nijloveanu, D., Bold,N., PopescuI, A.: Model of evaluation using questions with specified solving time. In: The 12th International Scientific Conference eLearning and Software for Education, Bucharest (2016)
8. Domşa, O., Bold, N.: Generator of variants of tests using the same questions. In: The 12th International Scientific Conference eLearning and Software for Education, Bucharest (2016)
9. Popescu, D.A., Bold, N., PopescuI, A.: The generation of tests of knowledge check using genetic algorithms. In: 7th International Workshop on Soft Computing Applications, 7th IEEE SOFA, LNCS Proceedings, Arad, Romania (2016)

Automatic Inspection of E-Portfolios for Improving Formative and Summative Assessment

Wolfgang Müller[1(✉)], Sandra Rebholz[1], and Paul Libbrecht[2]

[1] Media Education and Visualisation, University of Education Weingarten,
Weingarten, Germany
{mueller, rebholz}@md-phw.de
[2] Information Center for Education, German Institute for International
Educational Research, Frankfurt am Main, Germany
paul.libbrecht@dipf.de

Abstract. The concept of e-portfolio is finding an ever-growing uptake in secondary and post-secondary education as a tool to measure holistically the effects of learning. Learners document their development process in form of a collection of documents. In this research, we propose an automated method to support teachers in their assessment of e-portfolios by evaluating e-portfolios using automated analysis tools, which operate descriptively and semantically. A first formative evaluation of the system has been performed, to assess how much the quality portfolios are detected by descriptive indicators, which have proven to be already partially expressive. Delivered insights on e-portfolios were considered valuable by lecturers.

Keywords: E-portfolios · Formative assessment · Summative assessment · Learning analytics · Teaching analytics

1 Introduction

E-Portfolios as a modern method to support self-regulated learning and competence-oriented learning find increased recognition and application, especially in higher education. They allow for individual learning paths and provide learners with increased freedom, the possibility to follow own learning objectives, to emphasize self-chosen topics of a learning domain, to present the results of individually performed activities and projects in the context of modules or single classes in learning activities, and to reflect on their learning processes. Compared to paper-based portfolios, they provide students with means to document their experiences and achievements within the world and with the means of their preferred media domain, contributing to the development of desired media competences at the same time.

E-portfolios may be applied as a basis for summative assessment in examinations, introducing a new flexibility compared to classical oral or written examinations by allowing for individual learning paths and focusing on competences.

© Springer International Publishing AG 2017
T.-T. Wu et al. (Eds.): SETE 2016, LNCS 10108, pp. 480–489, 2017.
DOI: 10.1007/978-3-319-52836-6_51

A holistic assessment and evaluation of portfolios requires teachers to get an indepth impression of student portfolios. Important aspects are the comprehensiveness with respect to the covered subjects of the learning domain, a distinct and reflective treatment of individual topics, but also formal aspects such as a sufficiently clear structure of the portfolio, an appropriate connection to and reference of existing work as well as corresponding citations as an approach to prevent plagiarism. Such an indepth analysis of student portfolios requires substantial effort and resources from a teacher, and, as a consequence, is difficult to achieve in practice.

In this paper we describe an experiment and its results to support teachers in the evaluation of e-portfolios by the means of analytical methods, partially based on semantic technologies. This experiment is based on specific procedures applied in the study program on Media Education and Management at the Univ. of Education Weingarten. However, we think that results may be generalized to other domains and other types of applications of assessments based on e-portfolios. We explore in how far typical criteria for the assessment of e-portfolios may be assessed automatically by means of appropriate analytical methods, and in how far corresponding results may provide support to teachers in their assessment. In specific, we analyze which types of analytics are applicable and may provide valuable results, considering both, statistical approaches and approaches based on semantic text analysis.

As a contribution of this paper we present an innovative approach for the support of teachers in the assessment of students' learning portfolios based on analytical methods, which is based on a toolset to access and analyze student portfolios, a set of analytical methods, and a dashboard utilizing various forms of visualization to provide an overview on the set of portfolios under assessment, a specific view on the various aspects of an individual portfolio, as well as means to analyze such individual portfolios in detail, thus allowing teachers to provide valuable feedback more efficiently in reduced time and to get an objective and criteria-driven overview on portfolios supporting a better summative assessment. We describe a concept and corresponding technologies developed to implement this approach, as well as the results of a first evaluation of a practical application.

2 State-of-the-Art

Portfolios can be considered both, an instrument for documentation and assessment of learners' efforts, progress and achievement, as well as a concrete artifact in terms of a collection of representative individual work and products, which may provide evidence on a learner's skills and competences [6]. E-portfolios represent the electronic equivalent to these, often implemented in terms of individual learner's weblogs or Wiki pages. E-portfolio systems such as Mahara (mahara.org) und Elgg (elgg.org) extend corresponding functionalities with social media functionalities, allowing for feedback from tutors and peers, and fostering collaboration.

E-portfolios are attributed with a number of potentials and benefits, such as fostering the development of learner skills and competences, especially in the areas of media literacy, problem solving, and communication; enhanced documentation of learning; more possibilities for individual feedback; motivation to reflect on individual learning processes; support self-directed learning with the possibility to focus on topics on an individual basis (see for instance [10]). Their application as a basis for (summative) assessment is often motivated with an intended shift to more competency-based education and training [3]. Here, the typical approach is an assessment center or face-to-face consultation, where it is being used as a basis for discussion and reflection of learning processes. However, cyclic approaches are recommended, with formative assessments preceding the final summative evaluation, involving the suggestion of improvements and changes, and fostering reflection [2]. However, especially in case of large-scale assessments with large numbers of students the requirement for several assessment cycles can often not be met, and, in practice, teachers may provide only limited formative feedback to individual portfolios.

Portfolio development may be supported by rubrics, which may clearly state the specific requirements for portfolios for learners, make the criteria for assessment transparent in advance, and provide teachers with guidelines for their assessment. While the provision of such rubrics may provide a means to standardization especially in such cases when several tutors and teachers are involved in the assessment, the inspection of portfolios according to rubric's criteria will still prove time-consuming and cumbersome. Clearly, approaches and tools are required to support teachers in the inspection of e-portfolios.

The here presented approach can be related to the fields of Learning Analytics (LA) and Teaching Analytics (TA) in specific. LA denotes the "... measurement, collection, analysis and reporting of data about learners and their contexts, for purposes of understanding and optimizing learning and the environments in which it occurs" [8]. Teaching analytics (TA) can be considered a sub-field of LA, focusing on "... teachers' professional practices with visual analytics methods and tools ... "aiming at"... innovative solutions to assist and augment teachers' dynamic diagnostic decision making in the classrooms of the 21st century" [9]. In general, most approaches in both fields are based on data collected within learning management systems (LMS). While such LMS access data is typically too coarse-grained, and it seems difficult to rely instructional decisions on such data, learning objects delivering fine-grained information on learning processes are largely lacking.

In the context of e-portfolios, examples for the introduction of methods from LA and TA are rare. Aguiar et al. [1] apply analytical methods to learner history and specific data on the usage of an e-portfolio system (e.g., number of logins, number of articles added to the portfolio, number of hits of these articles for searches of other students) to assess engagement and predict performance. Aspects of portfolio contents are not being considered, though.

Approaches on text processing and semantic analysis in the context of e-portfolios are also rare. CONSPECT presents an approach to analyze the network based on LSA generating concept maps automatically from RSS feeds, blogs or portfolios [11]. An overview on approaches for text analysis in the context of learning analytics is presented in [12].

Computer-based tests, especially in terms of "Short-answer free-text", have been the object of several research initiatives, such as [6]. Here, the objective is however on the automatic assessment of features, and the general approach cannot necessarily be considered as broad as LA.

A broad spectrum of text-processing tools exists to analyze e-portfolios, being (rich and interactive) text documents. However, we have been able to observe very few applications of these tools to e-portfolios environments. In this section we describe several applicable text-analysis strategies.

The first family of processing tools are the descriptive statistical tools. Typical measures such as the lexical density, the text length (words, characters), the number of links or the count of pictures all are analysis dimensions that allow the comparison of e-portfolios. Further, configured analysis dimensions can be introduced: measures such as the thematic fields (as measured in the frequency of chosen words in the text), the expected length of sections or the appearance of typical concepts that describe the process and are described as expected in portfolio methodologies. All these measures allow to compare the portfolios and to evaluate how careful the realization of a portfolio is. Visualization of highest word frequencies, for example, can be created automatically; for example, tag-clouds (e.g., [4]).

Finally, an even larger class of text processing tools can be found in the machine learning world, which use the sophisticated tools of natural language processing. They base on the practice of creating a model by selecting samples and their expected labels. These models and labels are specific to the applications and require teachers to *input* these samples and label. While this input can be a considerable task, the analysis possibilities are very broad. Among the classical such approaches, the *Essay Grading* experiment [5] shows that it is possible to get close to the expectations of a teacher using latent semantic analysis (LSA), a process which creates a triple of matrices based on word-frequencies in each document of the training set which then allows to compute a distance between documents or between terms: these matrices can then be used with any other portfolio expected to contain similar words; this document can then be analyzed for its closeness to other model portfolios. Clearly, these indications are insufficient to assess the deep quality of a portfolio, since much freedom is left.

Other approaches based on machine learning include the automatic tag generation using naive Bayes' classifiers. These tags can denote a family of topics, but they can also denote other instructional aspects of the portfolios: dimensions such as the amount of reports of difficulty or progress, the use of scientific jargon, or the quantity of style annotations can indicate important development aspects.

3   Methodology and Conceptual Design

Portfolio assessment typically follows guidelines and observes well-defined criteria, often defined in terms of a rubric. For our purposes, we followed the criteria defined in the guidelines of our study program and defined the levels of achievement in terms of four levels: level 0 - not satisfactory; level 1 - basic; level 2 - advanced; level 3 - excellent. Hence, the main goal of the automatic portfolio analyzer system was to support the teacher in assessing the students' e-portfolios according to this rubric. For a detailed requirements analysis, we used a scenario-based design methodology. Based on concrete usage scenarios, the relevant requirements were derived and a design for the automatic analysis system was developed. A first prototype of the system was used and evaluated in the summer term 2016. In the evaluation, various automatically calculated statistics were compared with the human assessment results. In particular, we investigated whether the statistics can provide additional insight into the portfolios' structure, and thus can be used to enhance the overall assessment process.

Using a scenario-based design approach, we illustrate the requirements for an automatic portfolio analyzer software by describing a typical scenario of how the software can be used. The actor of the scenario is Peter Taylor, a fictional professor, who is using the analyzer software as a supporting tool for assessing e-portfolios (Fig. 1).

Scenario: Summative assessment of e-portfolios

Peter Taylor is a professor at the University of Education in Freiburg and is currently preparing the oral exams for this year's Information Technology module. The exams will be based on the e-portfolios developed and published by the students. As a preparation, Peter has to go through every single e-portfolio and assess it based on a set of predefined criteria. First, Peter logs into the portfolio analyzer software and gets a list of all available e-portfolios. Only e-portfolios that are explicitly shared with him by their owners are displayed in the list. Peter selects the first e-portfolio and is presented with the automatic analysis results from the software. In order to get a rough overview over the e-portfolio's structure, Peter scans the automatically generated table of contents containing headers and word counts for each section. Based on this information, he can find out quickly which sections are well elaborated and which are not, or whether there are topics that are missing completely. Additionally, he checks the number and type of external resources that are used in the e-portfolio, the number and type of integrated media content, as well as links between the individual sections. In the external references list, most of the stated resources have been used in the lectures already. Only a few resources have been investigated and added by the student herself. However, in the miniature view of embedded media artefacts, Peter discovers a lot of interesting material for the focus topic chosen by the student. He finds many graphics and videos related to state-of-the-art research and development, as well as a YouTube video produced by the student herself. Based on this preliminary evaluation, Peter fills out part of the rubric for the student and then links directly from the analysis view to the e-portfolio in order to scan the portfolio contents and complete the assessment.

Fig. 1. Scenario "Performing summative assessment for an e-portfolio"

From the scenario the following claims for a portfolio analyzing system can be derived:

- The main structural characteristics of the e-portfolio have to be easily accessible, e.g., being displayed in a dashboard, presenting information such as an index of contents, the portfolio size, word count per section, thumbnails of all contained images, and a list of references.
- The dashboard view should support focus-and-context analysis, i.e., by supporting zoom-in/zoom-out between summary views and detail views.
- Links have to be provided between analysis views and the corresponding e-portfolio content to provide detail views.
- Adaptable interactive visualizations, e.g., hide or display elements according to the users' needs, should be provided.
- Semantic analysis results indicate the completeness of the portfolio and the level of detail of individual topics should be included.

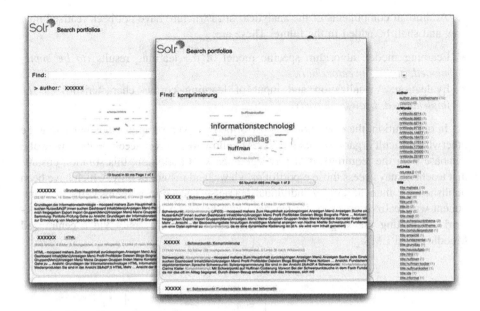

Fig. 2. Student and topic search dashboard

- Only teachers who are granted access to the portfolios should have access to the results of the analyzer software.

4 Technical Solution and Architecture

Based on the sketched requirements we conceptualized and implemented a prototypical solution to support lecturers in the assessment of students' e-portfolios. The solution considers specifics of the institution's e-learning software infrastructure. Figure 2 shows an example of a dashboard providing a summary of a student portfolio to teachers. Figure 3 depicts the architecture of the solution we developed for the analysis of students' e-portfolios. It contains the following central components, complementing the existing e-portfolio infrastructure:

- LMS: Central access point for students and portfolio extractor (*Moodle*),
- e-Portfolio system: Editing and display server for portfolios (*Mahara*),
- Extractor: component for the extraction of relevant information from learners' portfolios (*Ruby-based*),
- Statistical analysis: fundamental analysis based on descriptive features and statistical measures (*Ruby-based*),
- Semantic analysis: analytics of semantic characteristics of individual portfolios and their relations to others (*to be implemented, e.g. semantic-vectors*),
- Index: the storage of portfolios for searching, querying, and displaying values (*Solr-based*),
- Dashboard: Visualization of analytical results and visual analytics (*browser-based*),

Additional components of the analytical infrastructure have not been realized upto now and shall be added in the future. These are:

- Learning model: algorithm specific model of the learning results (*to be implemented, e.g. termvectors.bin*),
- Evaluation: Visualization and input of learning corpus characteristics (*to be implemented, browser-based*)

In our solution, the extraction was performed via web-scraping, thus bypassing the otherwise difficult organisational processes to allow for a direct access to the e-portfolio database with the requirement of privileged access. In addition, this solution ensures that teachers may access those e-portfolios, views, and resources only, which have been published for their access by individual learners. The corresponding extractor component was realized as a tool for teacher usage based on the Ruby mechanize framework, exploiting the single-sign-on mechanism of our university via a centralized Moodle-based LMS.

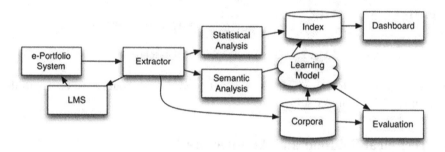

Fig. 3. Architecture of the developed e-portfolio analysis solution

The extraction process triggers a storage of e-portfolio contents in a local database, and a descriptive/statistical as well as a semantic analysis, containing general indicators, such as the total and relative number of hyperlinks and images, as well as the total and relative length (number of words and characters) of the complete portfolio and individual views. In addition, we support the definition of special indicators, such as the frequency of images from dedicated sources (such as Flickr or Instagram) and links to dedicated domains (such as Wikipedia or WordNet).

Semantic analysis, the persistent storage of analytical results, and dashboard functionalities are implemented by the means of data models and views provided based on an Apache Solr server (lucene.apache.org/solr/). The Solr infrastructure takes over the indexing of e-portfolios and the classification of contents. In addition, required functionalities for the navigation between individual portfolios, the search of specific learner portfolios, and the drill-down of portfolio details are realized based on the Apache Solr storage and retrieval functionalities (search, facet and filtering).

5   Application and First Results

In the summer term 2016, a first prototype of the portfolio analyzer software was used for the assessment of the e-portfolios in the module "Information Technology" in the degree program Media Education and Management at the University of Education in Weingarten. The main objective of the evaluation was to identify those assessment criteria that can be backed by automatically calculated statistical parameters such as total word count and the number of uploaded images. The applied rubric contains criteria in 3 categories: Contents, e.g., completeness of depiction, contribution, difficulty of own tasks, professional level; formals aspects, e.g., design, language, media usage, references; process, e.g., depiction of work process, curiosity, cooperation, reflection. Based on the criteria's definition in the rubric, the following assignment of parameters seemed to be useful:

- Work intensity and level of detail (*word count, number of uploaded images*)
- Adequate usage of multi-media (*number of uploaded images*)

For a first formative evaluation of the chosen approach, the manual assessments of 12 e-portfolios were analyzed and compared to the automatically retrieved statistical parameters. Three teachers took part in the evaluation and provided their assessments of the rubric criteria according to the four levels of achievement. As an outcome of the manual assessment phase, the average assessment results for each criterion were calculated and used for further evaluation. In the automatic assessment, the statistical parameters were calculated for a total of 78 e-portfolios. For the selected e-portfolios, the statistical parameters were compared to the minimum, first quartile, median, third quartile and maximum of these data sets, and corresponding assignments to the four levels of achievement were made. Figure 4 depicts the comparison of manual and automatic inspection results.

When considering the results of the evaluation, one can observe differences of up to one level between the manual and automatic assessments. As expected, the manual assessment of a complex documentation of learning experiences and outcomes such as an e-portfolio takes much more aspects into account, as can be achieved by statistical analysis. However, the calculated correlation factor (see last column in Fig. 4) between the manual assessments and the automatic assessments reveals a medium to high correlation between the obtained results. While not providing statistical significant results, this indicates that even simple statistical parameters like the word count or the number of uploaded images can serve as useful information for the human assessor. In addition, all reviewers/lecturers involved in the assessment used the results of the statistical analysis in their assessment and grading of the students' e-portfolios. All reviewers/lecturers reported the toolset to be very helpful in their assessment, and referred to the extracted information during their assessment frequently.

In order to support the evaluation of additional assessment criteria, one estimates that more parameters should be used and that existing parameters should be further differentiated, so as to become even more expressive indicators of e-portfolios. A need for analyzing the diversity of external links or of different types of media appears. Aside of the analysis measures, the portfolio analysis system should also be extended

	p1	p2	p3	p4	p5	p6	p7	p8	p9	p10	p11	p12	Correlation
Work intensity and level of detail													
Manual Assessment (Average)	1,8	1,3	1,7	2,2	0,8	1,5	1,8	1,8	1,5	0,8	2,3	1,5	
Word count (Statistics)	2	2	1	2	1	2	3	3	3	0	2	0	
Uploaded images (Statistics)	2	1	1	2	0	2	3	1	3	1	3	2	
Statistical Parameters (Average)	2	2	1	2	1	2	3	2	3	1	3	1	0,67
Adequate usage of multimedia													
Manual Assessment (Average)	2,0	1,3	1,5	2,2	0,8	2,0	2,0	1,5		1,0	1,8	1,5	
Uploaded images (Statistics)	2	1	1	2	1	2	3	1	3	1	3	2	
Statistical Parameters	2	1	1	2	1	2	3	1	3	1	3	2	0,69

Fig. 4. Comparing manual and automatic assessment results (red: unsatisfactory, yellow: basic, green: advanced, blue: excellent) (Color figure online)

with visualizations which give an overview of the content and of the structure of portfolios so as to support the teacher by the manual evaluation.

It is also interesting to note that some parameters are precious also because they deliver information which is otherwise extremely difficult to detect by a manual evaluation.

6   Summary and Conclusions

In this paper we presented an approach for an automatic inspection of e-portfolios to support teachers in their assessment. Following a scenario-based design approach, the developed prototype provides functionalities to aid teachers in their analysis and contains components, both, for a descriptive/structural and a semantic analysis of e-portfolios.

The prototype has been applied to two examination series and evaluations of the portfolios by experts have been made. Correlations to the statistical indicator values have been studied: for the considered dimensions, medium to high correlations have been found (e.g. the number of words and uploaded images is correlated to 67% to the completeness of an e-portfolio). Nevertheless, deviations of up to one level of achievement were detected between the manual and automatic evaluation of the e-portfolios.

This confirms the role of such analytics devices as a preparatory and hinting instrument before assessing the portfolios as opposed to an assessment instrument. We suspect that several of the dimensions may be specific to the topics studied.

We plan to further strengthen the components for a semantic analysis of e-portfolios, and to provide further support for interactive analysis of the portfolios of a cohort based on visual analytics techniques. A clear objective is to extend the application of our tool to allow for an enhanced formative assessment, preceding a summative assessment, and, as such, fostering valuable instructional feedback and letting students benefit in the sense of student-centered learning analytics [7].

References

1. Aguiar, E., Chawla, N.V., Brockman, J., Ambrose, G. A., Goodrich, V.: Engagement vs performance: using electronic portfolios to predict first semester engineering student retention. In: Proceedings LAK 2014, pp. 103–112 (2014)
2. Buzzetto-More, N.A., Alade, A.J.: Best practices in e-assessment. J. Inf. Technol. Educ. 5(1), 251–269 (2006)
3. Cooper, T.: Portfolio Assessment: A Guide for Lecturers, Teachers, and Course Designers. Praxis Education, Perth (1999)
4. Feinberg, J.: Wordle. http://www.wordle.net. Accessed 28 Aug 2016
5. Foltz, P.W., Laham, D., Landauer, T.K.: Automated Essay Scoring: Applications to Educational Technology. In: Proceedings of EdMedia 1999 (1999)
6. Jordan, S., Mitchell, T.: E-assessment for learning? The potential of short-answer free-text questions with tailored feedback. Br. J. Educ. Technol. 40(2), 371–385 (2009)
7. Kruse, A., Pongsajapan, R.: Student-centered learning analytics. In: CNDLS Thought Papers, pp. 1–9 (2012)
8. 1st International Conference on Learning Analytics and Knowledge (LAK 2011), Call for Papers (2011). https://tekri.athabascau.ca/analytics/. Accessed 11 Aug 2016
9. Mason, R., Rennie, F.: E-Learning and Social Networking Handbook: Resources for Higher Education. Chapman & Hall, Routledge (2008)
10. 2nd International Workshop on Teaching Analytics (IWTA-2013). http://next-tell.eu/iwta-2013/. Accessed 11 Aug 2016
11. Wild, F., Haley, D., Bülow, K.: CONSPECT: monitoring conceptual development. In: Luo, X., Spaniol, M., Wang, L., Li, Q., Nejdl, W., Zhang, W. (eds.) ICWL 2010. LNCS, vol. 6483, pp. 299–308. Springer, Heidelberg (2010). doi:10.1007/978-3-642-17407-0_31
12. Wild, F.: Learning Analytics in R with SNA, LSA, and MPIA. Springer, Heidelberg (2016)

Social Network Sites and Their Use in Education

Blanka Klimova$^{(\boxtimes)}$ and Petra Maresova

University of Hradec Kralove, Rokitanskeho 62,
50003 Hradec Kralove, Czech Republic
{blanka.klimova,petra.maresova}@uhk.cz

Abstract. At present social networks are becoming important in all areas of human activities. The future potential of social networks is high as it can be seen from their statistics on a daily, monthly or yearly increase in the number of their users. Therefore the purposes of this study is to discuss the current concept of social network sites and their classification. In addition, the authors of this study explore their use in education. This is done on the basis of literature review of available sources exploring the issue of social networks sites with respect to their role in education was used. A search was performed in the acknowledged databases Web of Science, Scopus, Springer and ScienceDirect. The findings indicate that SNSs have a big potential for educational purposes despite some limitations such as a lack of legal measures or a possibility of errors when sharing and exchanging information.

Keywords: Social network sites · Classification · Education · Strengths · Weaknesses

1 Introduction

Social network sites (SNSs) have become an important phenomenon nowadays since they can affect an enormous number of people through social networking. Since 2003 a number of SNSs have occurred such as MySpace, YouTube and, of course, Facebook [1], which is the most popular social network site. According to Boyd and Ellison [2], SNSs can be perceived as web-based services that allow individuals to construct a public or semi-public profile within a bounded system; articulate a list of other users with whom they share a connection; and view and traverse their list of connections and those by other within the system. Many research studies now demonstrate that SNSs can be very effective learning tools that contribute to students' engagement and learning experience, stimulating them to take an active part in the learning process and thus, foster big quality exchange of ideas and knowledge among participants (cf. [3–5]).

Therefore the purposes of this study is to discuss the current concept of social network sites and their classification. In addition, the authors of this study explore their use in education on the basis of the findings from the research studies described in Table 1 below.

© Springer International Publishing AG 2017
T.-T. Wu et al. (Eds.): SETE 2016, LNCS 10108, pp. 490–495, 2017.
DOI: 10.1007/978-3-319-52836-6_52

2 Methods

Firstly, a method of literature review of available sources exploring the issue of social networks sites with respect to their role in education was used. A search was performed in the databases Web of Science, Scopus, Springer and ScienceDirect. Secondly, on the basis of evaluation of these literature sources, the researched issue was explored. The research studies were classified according to their relevancy. The keywords searched in the Web of Science were as follows:

- social network sites AND education (number of results 897);
- social network sites AND their role in education (number of results 81).

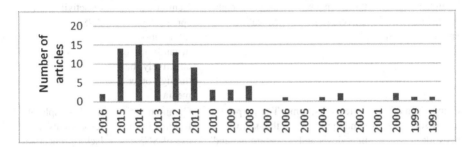

Fig. 1. Number of articles found on the role of SNSs in education in Web of Science from 1991 to 2016 (authors' own processing)

As it can be seen from the number of articles found in the Web of Science and Fig. 1, the issue of SNSs and their role in education has not been much researched yet although the number of research studies on this topic has recently risen.

3 Findings and Their Discussion

Altogether seven research studies exploring the role of SNSs in education were identified and their findings are presented in Table 1 below.

Although there are not many research studies on the use of SNSs and their role in education, the findings in Table 1 indicate that SNSs are predominantly positively perceived in educational processes where they can play an important role in the stimulation and engagement of students into their learning activities. As Helleve, Alams and Bjorkelo [11] report, it is quite common now that both teachers and their students have a profile on some SNS. In fact, 90% of them use Facebook on a daily basis in order to maintain relationships and contacts. Munoz and Towner [12] confirm that students prefer Facebook more than any other official online course for communication since they consider Facebook less formal than the official online course. Therefore Mazer et al. [13] claim that SNSs are suitable for pedagogical work because students are motivated when they connect with teachers who present information about themselves. Students' motivation for the use of SNSs is their desire to integrate into a new school environment,

Table 1. Overview of the research studies on the role of SNSs in education and their findings (authors' own processing)

Study	Methods	The aim	Results/benefits	Limitations
Learning "beyond the classroom" within an enterprise social network system [6]	107 students; In 2012 students participated in an educational course aimed at the use of SNSs	To explore how educational SNSs within a doctoral-level course foster learning	Study showed that SNSs could support learning even in informal learning spaces	Data limitations - the data are from one graduate program, the majority of students are females
Study of social networking usage in higher education environment [3]	300 students; online survey in three private universities	To examine benefits of SNSs usage in higher education	By using SNSs connection, the lecturer can spread the information instantly more effectively than through other media	Analysis of the limited number of activities on SNSs
Comparison of the use of social network in education between North and South Cyprus [7]	35 teachers; semi structured interviews and observations	The purpose of this study is to determine and compare the use of SNSs in education of two schools	Common features in the use of SNSs; there is no school policy for using SNSs in education; teachers have a negative attitude	Small sample of respondents; a lack of objective generalizations of the results
Transformative higher education teaching and learning: using social media in a team-based learning environment [4]	122 students; a quantitative survey; students learning experience and motivation was assessed through the content analysis	This study aims to assess the effectiveness of social media to enhance teaching and learning in a team-based learning	The results clearly showed the positive impact that team-based strategy had on the students' learning experience and motivation	Small sample of respondents; the questionnaire developed for this study has room for further improvement
E-learning in the evaluation of students and teachers: LMS or social networks? [8]	48 teachers, 224 students; survey; statistical data processing and the comparative analysis of result	To examine distinctions in the relation of students and teachers to two various e-learning tools and their preferences in	Results of the research confirm the necessity of an integrated approach to the application of LMS and SNSs in learning	For further development survey from other Russian and foreign universities is needed

(continued)

Table 1. (*continued*)

Study	Methods	The aim	Results/benefits	Limitations
		them: Learning Management System (LMS) and social network sites	process, supplement of classroom lessons with individual work in LMS and collaborative work in SNSs	
Guiding in tertiary education: a case study on social networking and e-learning platforms [9]	150 students; quantitative research - questionnaire with open questions; interviews with students	To measure students' motivation, guidance and language improvement through using blogging in a learning process	The study confirms a positive attitude of the students towards the use of blogging	The use of blogging cannot be generalize for the whole concept of SNSs
Designing a social network to support e-learning activities at the Department of Communications, University of Zilina [10]	238 students; a questionnaire surveye	The aim of this study is to research possibilities of using social network sites at the University of Zilina	The findings of the study show that more than one half of the respondents would like to have their own social network at the University of Zilina	A further analysis is needed since the newly created university social network

communication with their peers, planning events, comment or express their opinions. For example, a student who is quite shy and hardly ever participates in class may get actively engaged in co-constructing his learning experience with his teachers, collaborating with his fellow colleagues, and may feel more comfortable to express himself and to share his resources and ideas on Facebook, Twitter, or YouTube [14].

Thus, SNSs can be a kind of the bridge between informal and formal education because they can support not only the interaction among the students but also enable to share knowledge, information or experience.

However, there are also negative opinions on the use of SNSs in education. For instance, Selwyn [15] or Kirschener and Karpinski [16] claim that students use SNSs mainly for identity building rather than for educational purposes. Helleve, Alams, and Bjorkelo [11] point out that SNS activities for students are to a large extent a combination of school activities and homework and they are initiated by students, not by the teachers who are not participants in this private sphere (Table 2).

Table 2. Strengths and weaknesses of SNSs and their role in education (authors' own processing, based on [17])

Strengths	Weaknesses
Overcoming isolation and shyness; Sharing materials from lectures, exchanging information, helping with assignments; Use of different types study materials such as online videos, which can affect more senses; Access to a much bigger bulk of information at any time and from anywhere; Higher students' involvement, motivation; Students' cooperation and collaboration; Personalization of learning; Development of students' specific skills required for their future industrial occupations; Development of special studying skills such as scanning and skimming skills; Possibility to compare teaching methods and approaches; Teachers can use a variety of teaching methods (e.g. they can share links to foreign sources or lectures online); Preparation for future employment	A lack of legal measures, problem of data security; A possibility of errors when sharing and exchanging information; Necessity of continuous teacher" check and corrections; Reduced reasoning and critical thinking skills; Distraction from studying; Misuse of SNSs, e.g., in form of cyber bullying; A lack of well elaborated pedagogical methodology for the use of SNSs in engineering education; A lack of long-term memory

Although there are opposite views on the use of SNSs in education due to a lack of legal measures, there are evident benefits for learning as the findings of this study have confirmed. In addition, when exploiting SNSs in education, teachers should pay attention to the background and behaviour of user; the university policy on the Internet access; the behaviour of university communication; role and rule of social network in daily communication; and the attitude of user [3].

Acknowledgments. This review study is supported by SPEV project 2017 run at the Faculty of Informatics and Management, University of Hradec Kralove, Czech Republic.

References

1. Pavlicek, A.: Nova media a socialni site [New media and social networks]. Oeconomica, Praha (2010)
2. Boyd, D.M., Ellison, N.B.: Social network sites: definition, history and scholarship. J. Comput. Mediated Commun. **13**(1), 210–230 (2008)
3. Falahah, Rosmala, D.: Study of social networking usage in higher education environment. Procedia Soc. Behav. Sci. **67**(1), 156–166 (2012)
4. Ratnesward, R., Rasiah, V.: Transformative higher education teaching and learning: using social media in a team-based learning environment. Procedia Soc. Behav. Sci. **123**(1), 369–379 (2014)

5. Selwyn, N.: Faceworking: exploring students' education-related use of Facebook. Learn. Media Technol. **34**(2), 157–174 (2009)
6. Scott, K.S., Sorokti, K.H., Merrell, J.D.: Learning "beyond the classroom" within an enterprise social network systém. Internet High. Educ. **29**, 75–90 (2016)
7. Isik, F.: Comparison of the use of social network in education between North and South Cyprus. Procedia Soc. Behav. Sci. **103**, 210–219 (2013)
8. Mozhaeva, G., Feshchenko, A., Kulikov, I.: E-learning in the evaluation of students and teachers LMS or social networks. Procedia Soc. Behav. Sci. **152**, 127–130 (2014)
9. Montero-Fleta, B., Perez-Sabater, C.: Guiding in tertiary education: a case study on social networking and e-learning platforms. Procedia Soc. Behav. Sci. **159**, 410–414 (2014)
10. Madlenak, R., Madlenakova, L., Kianiþkova, E.: Designing a social network to support e-learning activities at the Department of Communications, University of Zilina. Procedia Soc. Behav. Sci. **176**, 103–110 (2015)
11. Helleve, I., Almas, A.G., Bjonkelo, B.: Social networking sites in education – governmental recommendations and accrual use. Nordic J. Digital Litracy **8**(4), 191–207 (2013)
12. Munoz, C.L., Towner, T.: Back to the "wall": how to use Facebook in the college class-room. First Monday (2011). http://journals.uic.edu/ojs/index.php/fm/article/view/3513/3116
13. Mazer, J.P., Murphy, R.E., Simonds, C.J.: I'll see you on "Facebook": the effects of computer-mediated teacher self-disclosure on student motivation, affective learning, and classroom climate. Commun. Educ. **56**(1), 1–17 (2007)
14. McLoughlin, C., Lee, M.J.W.: Social software and participatory learning: extending pedagogical choices with technology affordances in the Web 2.0 era. In: ICT: Proceedings of the 24th ASCILITE Conference on Providing Choices for Learners and Learning, Singapore, pp. 664–675 (2007)
15. Selwyn, N.: Schools and Schooling in the Digital Age: A Critical Perspective. Routledge, New York (2010)
16. Kirschener, P.A., Karpinski, A.C.: Facebook and academic performance. Comput. Hum. Behav. **26**, 1237–1245 (2010)
17. Klimova, B.: Benefits and limitations of social network sites for engineering education – a review study. In: Proceedings of the IEEE Global Engineering Education Conference (EDUCON) (2016)

Automatic Student Group Generation for Collaborative Activities Based on the Zone of Proximal Development

Maria De Marsico[1]([⊠]), Emanuele Giarlini[1], Andrea Sterbini[1], and Marco Temperini[2]

[1] Department of Computer Science, Sapienza University, Rome, Italy
demarsico@di.uniroma1.it
[2] Department of Computer Control and Management Engineering, Sapienza University, Rome, Italy

Abstract. The Zone of Proximal Development (ZPD) theorized by Lev Vygotskij can be considered as one of the most interesting insights on the value of collaborative learning: it specifies the cognitive distance reachable by a student in learning activities, given that some support by teachers, and peers, is available. Group handling is certainly one of the main aspects to be reproduced in an online learning system. This paper aims to offer a twofold contribution. First, with a proposal for the evaluation of the "pedagogical quality" of the partition of a class in groups, over a specific activity, in terms of internal homogeneity, and external balance of expected effort. Second, with policies to automatically, or semi-automatically, make groups according to the cognitive characteristics of single students. An evaluation of group composition is also provided according to a computation of the group ZPD, which is estimated basing on a notion of *Daring Threshold*, shaping the *maximum viable effort*.

Keywords: Zone of proximal development · Group ZPD · Group composition

1 Introduction

Lev Vygotskij can be considered one of the main scientists in social constructivism. His research identifies different dynamic *cognitive zones* that characterize the learning process of a student [1]. The Autonomous Problem Solving (APS) zone includes concepts, knowledge and skills that the learner has firmly achieved, so to be able to autonomously tackle problems therein. The learner is too weakly, or not at all, acquainted with concepts, knowledge and skills falling within the Unreachable Problem Solving (UPS): tackling related problems would only frustrate the student, notwithstanding the possible help by teachers and peers. In the middle, the most pedagogically significant zone: the Zone of Proximal Development (ZPD). Concepts, skills and knowledge falling there are not firmly possessed, maybe even ignored, yet the student can safely tackle related learning activities, especially if supported by group collaboration. Experienced teachers can satisfactorily handle collaboration in face-to-face teaching, by spurring group activities and by guiding group composition:

© Springer International Publishing AG 2017
T.-T. Wu et al. (Eds.): SETE 2016, LNCS 10108, pp. 496–506, 2017.
DOI: 10.1007/978-3-319-52836-6_53

these abilities are conditioned by the actual teacher's experience, yet they are also among the aspects that a distance learning system usually lacks to reproduce.

We have developed a proposal for the evaluation of "quality" of the partition of a class in groups for a specific activity. The evaluation is based on the difficulty each group will meet along the learning path related to the activity at hand. The assessment can be carried out over teacher-created groups, or even over groups created by the system by specific algorithms we propose. This proposal can support both distance activities, and "traditional" face-to-face ones, when relying on a software system that maintains a record of students achievements.

Group creation is usually left to teacher's responsibility and experience. We propose a framework were student achievements, assessed during the educational process, are summarized by the *Student Model (SM)* [2]. This is used to guide the group creation through some policies. In addition, each learning activity (*la*) is specified through an appropriate *Activity Model*. The evaluation of a kind of "group pedagogical quality" relies on both internal homogeneity, and external balance of expected effort. Moreover it can be related to the concept of individual as well as group ZPD.

2   Related Work

Immersing the student in a realistic, "ecologically" meaningful (consistent with real-life context), and comprehensive framework fostering social learning activities, can support better retention and deepening of knowledge over time [3]. In [4], a group composition based on individual knowledge and interests is argued as spurring better discussions/interactions during learning. The work in [5] investigates how collaborative activities better prepare for real-life team-based working. Recent proposals aim at helping teachers in handling huge classes by automatic group composition [6]. Some of them use sophisticated mathematical tools. In [7] Particle Swarm Optimization is adopted. The authors start from individual students' understanding level on course topics and build on it to create groups. Scores can also be used to compute a group aggregate level of understanding, and can be possibly weighted according to teacher's evaluation of topic relevance to tackle a certain activity. The system also stores, for each student, a learning experience (interest) vector with one entry and an experience level per topic. The procedure computes the difference between maximum and minimum understanding level within each group, and aims at minimizing the average of such difference over groups. Furthermore, it minimizes the maximal difference of understanding strength for each topic between any two groups, and maximizes the average number of topics in which members of the same group are interested (interest is inferred from experience). A different approach is proposed in [8], that specifically addressed ubiquitous learning. Here, the student's profile (portfolio) contains essential learner profiles, including the proposed location profile (with student's movements recorded by RFID during learning activities), and the behavior profile (a behavior is in one of eight classes). From individual portfolios a portfolio grid is derived, collecting individual students trait and opposite attributes. The grid is used with a weighting procedure for similarity comparison and heterogeneous grouping: a teacher could use either heterogeneous grouping with a given difference threshold T, or clustering on a fixed number of groups, still using functions in heterogeneous grouping.

3 The Basics of the Proposed Framework

It is worth summarizing the fundamentals of the proposed framework. More details can be found in [9]. The Student Model for a *Learner* l is $SM(l)$. It stores information about l's learning style - $LS(l)$ - and state of knowledge $SK(l)$. Here, we consider only $SK(l)$. It is continuously updated after learning activities, and records the current state of skills for l. A skill represents an ability/knowledge related to a learning domain. A learning activity (*la*) may require a set of prerequisite skills, and may support the acquisition of others. A skill can be defined as a predicate S() whose arguments include a main concept (a conventional name). $SK(l)$ is a set of pairs, each representing an acquired skill and the level of the confidence of its possession (*certainty*):

$$SK(l) = \{ <s_1, c_1>, \ldots, <s_{nl}, c_{nl}> \}$$

The certainty c_i for a skill s_i is a number $c \in [0\ldots1]$ which is computed/updated following the assessment activities related to the course. The first time a learner l acquires a skill, the couple $<s, C_{ENTRY}>$ is added to $SK(l)$, where C_{ENTRY} is a default starting confidence. The certainty is either increased after each further successful assessment for s, or decreased after each unsuccessful one. When the certainty for s decreases below a level C_{DEMOTE} the couple $<s,c>$ is deleted from $SK(l)$: further activities will be required to acquire it back; on the contrary, when in $<s,c>$ the value of c exceeds a conventional value $CPROMOTE$, the s is given as firmly acquired, and no further specific assessment is required for it.

A *learning activity* is designed to be carried out either individually, or with a group. The components of a learning activity *la* are: a collection of learning material (*la.Content*); a set of skills the student is expected to acquire into $SK(l)$ with certainty C_{ENTRY} after tackling it (*la.A*), or for which the corresponding assessment will cause an increase (or decrease) of certainty; a set of skills that are a prerequisite to fruitfully tackle it (*la.P*); and an estimate of the cognitive load/effort implied by it (*la.Effort*).

A repository R of learning activities is a set of *las*, available for building courses related to a specific Knowledge Domain, that in turn is handled as a set skills. The notion of *ZPD* that we adopt is related to the concept of *learning path*. A *learning path* is defined as a set $LP = \{la_i\}_{i \in \{1 \ldots n\}}$, for which it is possible to identify the overall acquirements *LP.A*, the overall requirements *LP.P*, and the overall expected effort as:

$$LP.A = \cup_{i \in \{1 \ldots n\}} la_i.A, LP.P = \cup_{i \in \{1 \ldots n\}} la_i.P \backslash LP.A, LP.Effort = \sum_{i \in \{1 \ldots n\}} la_i.effort$$

The *s-projection* of $SK(l) = \{<s_1, c_1>, \ldots, <s_{nl}, c_{nl}>\}$ is the set of included skills:

$$s - proj(SK(l)) = \{s_i, with <s_i, c_i> \in SK(l)\}$$

The definition of learning activity implicitly enforces a *relation of derivation*: given $<la', la''>$, if $la'.A \cap la''.P \neq \emptyset$, some skills needed to tackle la'' are acquired through la' and la' precedes la''. The induced *relation of partial order* in R allows depicting it as a graph. In this context, the choice of the next learning activity should be limited only by the current possibility to tackle it, determined by the current state of $SK(l)$. Vygotskij's theory underlies a truly social-collaborative approach to taking learning paths. Given a learner l, working on a course LP in a Knowledge Domain $KD(LP)$, significant cognitive areas, related to the learning state of l, can be defined according to Vygotskij's theory as follows.

Autonomous Problem Solving (APS) is the area of firm course knowledge:

$$APS(l) = \{s \in KD(LP)| <s, C_{PROMOTE}> \in SK(l)\}$$

In order for l to profitably tackle a $la \in LP$, all skills in $la.A$ should be in the individual student ZPD. $ZPD(l) = s\text{-}proj(SK(l)) \backslash APS(l)$ wouldn't be challenging enough. This is where the learner is expected to go, with the help of teacher and peers, not only by strengthening skills already owned, yet also acquiring new ones. Beyond ZPD is the area of *Unreachable Problem Solving* (UPS), i.e. the subset of course activities, that are not pedagogically sound for the learner (the complement of the other two).

4   The Definition of Individual and Group ZPD

In order to proceed along a gradual line, we first addressed the "extended" concept (w.r.t. Vygotskij's theory) of individual ZPD [10] of a student, to be expanded when the student enters a group according to the original definition by Vygotskij [11]. With respect to [7, 8] we adopt a finer granularity, since our basic elements are skills instead of topics: their relevance is implicit in the number of activities for which they appear among prerequisites. Groups will be created according to learners' skills, instead of considering overall competence on topics. The proposed approach relies on the student's estimated individual effort in tackling single activities, based on the cognitive state regarding prerequisite skills and skills to be acquired/enforced.

The basic element of the proposed implementation of ZPD is the distance of a skill outside $SK(l)$ from $SK(l)$. Skills within a certain threshold, computed accordingly, will be considered as part of the ZPD of student l, denoted as $ZPD(l)$.

Given a learner l and a skill s still outside $SK(l)$, it is possible to use the above mentioned relation of partial order among learning activities to identify a set of possible (sub)learning paths G, contained in a course LP (a learning path in itself), that take to possibly acquire s, and that are traversable from the current state of skills:

$$Reach\,(s, SK(l), LP) = \{G = \{la_i\}_{i \in \{1...nG\}} \subseteq LP | s \in la_{nG}.A \wedge la_1.P \subseteq s\text{-}proj(SK(l))$$
$$\wedge\ G.P \subseteq s\text{-}proj(SK(l)) \cup G.A\}$$

where $G.P$, $G.A$, and $G.Effort$ are defined as in Sect. 3 (where a generic LP is considered). The first condition indicates that skill s is acquired by the last activity in the path. The second one means that the skills required to tackle the first activity in the path must be already possessed. The last condition, relating G.P to G.A, is the possibility that the prerequisites of some $la_i \in G$ might be acquired through a preceding $la_j \in G$. The distance of s from the present $SK(l)$ is defined as

$$D(s, s - proj(SK(l)), LP) = \min_{G \in Re\ ach(s, SK(l), LP)} G.Effort$$

The subset of skills, already in $SK(l)$, that are necessary to reach s along the minimal-effort path G^* in LP is defined as the *support* set to reach s and denoted as

$$Support(s, SK(l), LP) = G^*.P \cap s - proj(SK(l)).$$

The problem to solve is how to determine G^*. This means finding a minimal cost path in a graph. This point is out of the scope of this paper (see [9]), and we will assume to have computed G^*. Having identified G^* and its distance from $SK(l)$, we have to decide if it is contained in $ZPD(l)$ or not. To do this, we rely on the definition of a highly dynamic and personalized distance threshold that depends on the student (namely, on the current $SK(l)$), on the skill s, and on the identified learning path G^*. We define the two following measures:

$$A1 = AvgEffort(G^*, Support(s, SK(l), LP))$$

as an estimate of the "average" effort required by each activity in G^*, and

$$A2 = AvgCertainty(Support(s, SK(l), LP))$$

as an estimate of the "average" certainty of the skills in the support set for G^*. Of course, we might simply compute such measures as the true average of efforts defined for the *la*s along G^*, and as the true average of certainties of skills in the support set *Support*(s, SK(l), LP). Actually, we take into account the certainty associated to each skill already in $SK(l)$ (weak prerequisites increase the effort) and the possible presence of some acquired skill in $SK(l)$ (that decrease the effort). About this point, not crucial here, the interested reader can refer to [10]. Whichever is the strategy to estimate *A1* and *A2*, we use them to define a suitable *daring threshold,* i.e., the maximum distance from a specific learner's state of knowledge $SK(l)$ of a certain skill s, below which it is acceptable to include s in ZPD(l); this threshold can reasonably be computed as:

$$DTreshold(s, SK(l)) = (A2/A1) \cdot EFF(R) \cdot dF.$$

The ratio represents in some sense the amount of certainty per unit of effort, *EFF(R)* relates the threshold with an estimation of the average effort in the repository, and *dF* is the *daring factor,* an integer regulating how "far" from the present skills/state of knowledge the teacher estimates it is pedagogically acceptable/sustainable to go and place the ZPD boundaries. When *A1* has a value similar to *EFF(R)*, A2 (average certainty) becomes a multiplier for the *daring factor.* When *A1* is very close to *A2*, *dF* determines a linear increase of the threshold according to *EFF(R)*. These considerations are a guide to set a suitable value for dF. Finally, we can then define the ZPD as the set of skills whose distance from $SK(l)$ is within the above stated threshold

$$ZPD(l) = \{s \in KD(LP) \backslash APS(l) | D(s, s - proj(SK(l), LP) \leq DTreshold(s, SK(l))\}$$

We start from a group to determine feasible activities. Next, we will tackle the task of determining the optimal groups in a class given a specific activity. Group activities require to determine the group state of skills (Group Knowledge GK), and ZPD, starting from individual ones. We expect that activities that could not be tackled by single students can become accessible to the group. The group ZPD should maximize members' gain from the collaboration. It could include activities outside of some member ZPD, provided they are not too far away. This is crucial to avoid leaving members behind. A related discussion is in [11]. Being ST a group of students, and LP a learning path, we first define the group APS. It is trivial to assume it as the intersection of individual ones (skills that are firmly possessed by all members). However, this would ignore the reciprocal support. We rather consider a "pseudo-intersection": skills that are not firmly possessed by *all* members yet are in $APS(l)$ for *some* $l \in ST$, and in $SK(l')$ for all the other members $l' \in ST$, with a certainty at least $\tau_C = C_{PROMOTE} - CENTRY/2$. Since the l students will support the l' ones, there must be at least one such leader for every g members, with g chosen by the teacher according to the activity:

$APS(ST) = \{s \in \cup_{l \in ST} APS(l)|$
$\forall l \in ST(<s,c> \in SK(l) \wedge c \geq \tau_C) \wedge Card(\{l\} \in ST|<s,c> \in SK(l') \wedge c = C_{PROMOTE}\}) \geq Card(ST)/g$

The GK is defined basing on the members SKs as an expansion of $APS(ST)$

$$GK(ST) = \{<s,c> /\forall l \in ST(<s,c_l> \in SK(l) \wedge c$$
$$= ((\sum\nolimits_{l \in ST, <s,c_l> \in SK(l)} c_l)/Card(ST))\}$$

We use $GK(ST)$ and $APS(ST)$ to compute $ZPD(ST)$. Again, instead of direct construction a reverse strategy defines the group ZPD, through criteria of *admissibility*.

A first condition requires: (1) *the group members must share a common portion of APS, and (2) each activity prerequisites are firmly possessed by at least one member*:

$$\bigcap\nolimits_{l \in ST} APS(l) \neq \emptyset \wedge LP.P \subseteq \bigcup\nolimits_{l \in ST} APS(l)$$

A second condition states that students in a group ST must share some common proximal development, and that an activity $la \in LP$ is admissible for ST if and only if, though being possibly off the ZPDs of some members, it is *not too distant*, and it is comprised in the ZPD of at least a number of members sufficient to support the others - τ is a threshold to establish admissibility, for learner l, of an la not in $ZPD(l)$:

$$\cap_{l \in ST} ZPD(l) \neq \emptyset \wedge \forall la \in LP \forall s \in la.A \forall l \in ST \, D(s, ZPD(l), LP) < \tau$$
$$\wedge \forall la \in LP \, Card(\{l \in ST | la.A \subseteq ZPD(l)\}) \geq Card(ST/g)$$

where $\tau = \min_{l \in ST} DTreshold(s, SK(l))$ and g is as above. If we used *APS* in place of *ZPD*, in the second condition, we would have some of the brighter members of the group left without anything new to learn, which is pedagogically deplorable.

5   Group Quality Evaluation and Automatic Group Creation

Before the proposed group composition procedures, it is worth presenting our proposal for group quality assessment, that will be useful to discuss those procedures. The main parameter underpinning the assessment of the class partition in groups is the *TargetWorkload (l, la)*, a value representing the workload required from each student *l* in a group *ST* to deal with a learning activity *la*. The *TargetWorkload (l, la)* can be calculated by adding the *AvgEffort ()* (met above) for each skill *s* included in *la.A*.

It is possible now to consider the following four parameters:

- *IntraGroupTotEff (ST)* – sum of *TargetWorkload (l, la)* over all members of *ST*.
- *IntraGroupAvgEff (ST)* – mean *TargetWorkload (l, la)* over all members of ST
- *IntraGroupVarEff (ST)* – variance of *TargetWorkload (l, la)* over ST.
- *InterGroupAvgEff (D)* – mean *IntraGroupAvgEff (ST)* over groups in class *D*.
- *InterGroupVarEff (D)* – variance of *IntraGroupAvgEff (ST)* over groups in *D*.

Evaluation of the groups generated in a class is twofold: inner-balance, and balance across groups are considered. As of the former, inner-balancing can be achieved by monitoring the values of the parameters *IntraGroupAvgEff (G)* and *IntraGroupVarEff (G)*. Notice that the first one controls that the mean effort is not too high over students. However, even a single very proficient student may keep this value low, so that the internal homogeneity is guaranteed by the second parameter. A comprehensive assessment on the class can be carried out using the following two parameters.

Three proposed policies for the automatic creation of groups try to meet the described quality criteria. Through them the system can generate a set of groups according to the number of students and their *Target Workload* (as introduced, it is the sum of the distances between a student and all skills acquired following the completion of a task). Optimal group composition may change according to different activities.

The first group creation policy is totally based on the concept of *Target Workload*. The students are ranked according to this parameter, and selected to create the various groups. This policy creates groups composed mainly by three students. The algorithm first composes a set of pairs $<Student_i, TW_i>$ representing the student and the respective estimated Target Workload. An array stores this set of pairs, and is sorted by increasing TW. Groups of three students are created by iterating the cycle of picking the first array element, the last, and the (approximately) median, and deleting them from the array. The final step might generate a group with either two or four students instead of three. This method, albeit simple from the implementation point of view, does not produce good groups with respect to the internal variance. This especially holds for the first created groups, while this problem tends to fade as the array size decreases and created groups contain students concentrated in its center.

The second policy for the creation of groups incorporates some elements of the first but aims at solving the problems arising from internal variance. After the initial array ordering, the students are divided into three (ordered) subarrays based on TW. The class division will be based on these subarrays. At every group creation, for each subarray the element will be picked that has the TW closest to the subarray mean value. It is easy to consider that this algorithm can be extended to create groups with a different number of students, by simply changing the number of initial subarrays.

The third policy is the one that most reflects the above considerations about group collaboration, since it takes into account the concept of "mentor", and starts from including one or more students with such role in each group. A mentor can be, e.g., a student with higher proficiency, with wider ZPD, or with lower TW. The teacher can decide the maximum number of students that will be supported by each mentor, and a preferred number of students per group. As in the previous cases an array is generated as a ranking of students, from the stronger (closest to the skills to reach) to the weaker (the farthest from the skills). In this case, the parameter used to sort students is given by the product between individual TW and the variance of the distances of each student from skills to acquire. This further enhancement was introduced because the single value TW of a student only describes the total effort required, but it is also interesting to understand how evenly it is distributed. In the present proposal, the lower the variance the better (students with low TW and low variance are the best candidates to be mentors). In a future investigation it might be worth considering cases when the teacher deems some skills to be more relevant to reach the target, and therefore a lower distance from these might rather identify a possible mentor. Once created this array, the system inserts the first array students as initial components of the groups, according to the proportion of mentors decided by the teacher. The remaining part of the array is orderly scanned, and every time a student is picked up, the best group where he/she can be inserted is estimated. This is determined as the one for which the insertion of that student would minimize the derived product of *IntraGroupVarEff* and *Inter-GroupVarEff* (such product can be denoted as *TotVariance*). Generating all possible class subdivisions and choosing the best would guarantee an optimum distribution, but would be too expensive.

6 Experimental Results

This Section presents the results of some "in vitro" hand-configured experiments. We assume an activity *la* with *la.A* = *{s1, s2, s3}*. Each such acquired skill requires an *AvgEffort* from each student, which is assumed to be computed as in Sect. 4. Table 1 shows the way the proposed parameters support group assessment. The results accurately reflect the created groups' composition. The first two groups in table are the most balanced, as confirmed by their internal variance, which is much smaller than it is for the other groups. The last groups both contain "outlier" students: Student9 has Target Workload highest than the others in the group; (s)he can be supported by mates. The second is a "positive" outlier, Student10, whose Target Workload is much lower than the others: (s)he may possibly guide the others. In any case, the last pair of parameters indicates a quite good overall balance.

Table 1. An example of the use of group assessment parameters

Student	Group	s1	s2	s3	TW	Intra-Group TotEff	Intra-Group AvgEff	Intra-Group VarEff	Inter-Group AvgEff	Inter-Group V arEff
Student1	G1	1	3	5	9	33	11	2	12.5	3.64
Student2	G1	7	2	3	12					
Student3	G1	9	1	2	12					
Student4	G2	3	4	1	8	31	10.3	2.89		
Student5	G2	6	3	2	11					
Student6	G2	2	4	6	12					
Student7	G3	8	2	3	13	41	13.6	10.89		
Student8	G3	7	2	1	10					
Student9	G3	8	6	4	18					
Student10	G4	5	3	3	11	45	15	9.6		
Student11	G4	7	1	9	17					
Student12	G4	7	3	8	18					

Two examples of hand-composed classes are used to compare the three policies: one is composed that is quite well balanced, the other is not. Groups include three students, when feasible. Table 2 shows class compositions.

Table 2. Example 1: balanced class. Example 2: class with differences among students

Example 1					Example 2				
Student	s1	s2	s3	TW	Student	s1	s2	s3	TW
Student1	2	3	7	12	Student1	7	5	4	116
Student2	3	3	4	10	Student2	2	2	3	7
Student3	5	3	3	11	Student3	2	5	3	10
Student4	3	4	3	10	Student4	3	3	3	9
Student5	3	5	3	11	Student5	7	4	4	15
Student6	5	1	6	12	Student6	4	4	1	9
Student7	4	3	4	11	Student7	4	4	1	9
Student8	3	4	3	10	Student8	1	1	4	6
Student9	2	4	6	12	Student9	2	5	3	10
Student10	2	3	6	11	Student10	3	2	3	8

For the first example, the groups produced by the three policies are as follows:

- first policy: $G1 = \{S2, S5, S9\}$; $G2 = \{S4, S6, S7\}$; $G3 = \{S1, S3, S8, S10\}$.
- second policy: $G1 = \{S1, S2, S3\}$, $G2 = \{S4, S5, S6\}$, $G3 = \{S7, S8, S9, S10\}$
- third policy (one mentor per group): $G1 = \{S2, S3, S10\}$, $G2 = \{S5, S8, S7\}$, $G3 = \{S1, S4, S6, S9\}$

Table 3 shows that with a balanced class all policies produce similar performance.

Table 3. Results with the three group creation policies on the class of Example 1 in Table 2. Abbreviations: *IntragroupAvgEff = IgAE, IntraGroupVarEff = IgVE*

First policy		Second policy		Third policy	
IgAE	*IgVE*	*IgAE*	*IgVE*	*IgAE*	*IgVE*
G1 = 11,00	G1 = 0,67	G1 = 11,00	G1 = 0,67	G1 = 10,67	G1 = 0,22
G2 = 11,00	G2 = 0,67	G2 = 11,00	G2 = 0,67	G2 = 10,67	G2 = 0,22
G3 = 11,00	G3 = 0,50	G3 = 11,00	G3 = 0,50	G3 = 11,50	G3 = 0,75
InterGroupAE	*IntergroupVE*	*InterGroupAE*	*IntergroupVE*	*InterGroupAE*	*IntergroupVE*
D = 11,00	D = 0,00	D = 11,00	D = 0,00	D = 10,94	D = 0,15

On the second class, the different policies produce the following groups:

- First policy: $G1 = \{S1, S8, S6\}$, $G2 = \{S2, S4, S5\}$, $G3 = \{S3, S7, S9, S10\}$
- Second policy: $G1 = \{S2, S5, S6\}$, $G2 = \{S1, S7, S10\}$, $G3 = \{S3, S4, S8, S9\}$
- Third policy: $G1 = \{S3, S9, S7\}$, $G2 = \{S2, S8, S1\}$, $G3 = \{S10, S4, S5, S6\}$

Table 4 shows that this time the difference is significant. In the case of an heterogeneous class, the first policy behaves as one can expect. The first generated groups present values of internal average effort and variance much higher than the last. This happens because of the way selection works: once the array is shortened, the generated groups are increasingly balanced. Results from the second policy are similar.

Table 4. Results with the three group creation policies on the class of Example 2 in Table 2. Abbreviations: *IntragroupAvgEff = IgAE, IntraGroupVarEff = IgVE*

First policy		Second policy		Third policy	
IgAE	*IgVE*	*IgAE*	*IgVE*	*IgAE*	*IgVE*
G1 = 10,33	G1 = 17,56	G1 = 10,33	G1 = 11,56	G1 = 8,00	G1 = 2,00
G2 = 10,33	G2 = 11,56	G2 = 11,00	G2 = 12,67	G2 = 8,67	G2 = 1,56
G3 = 9,25	G3 = 0,68	G3 = 8,75	G3 = 2,68	G3 = 12,25	G3 = 11,18
InterGroupAE	*IntergroupVE*	*InterGroupAE*	*IntergroupVE*	*InterGroupAE*	*IntergroupVE*
D = 9,97	D = 0,26	D = 10,02	D = 0,89	D = 9,63	D = 3,48

The third policy seems to provide the best results under some points of view. The third group experiments more effort, but this is balanced by more members. The internal variances tend to increase, probably due to the presence of "strong" mentors as opposed to "weak" peers, that on their side can however benefit from this. The *InterGroupAvgEff* is the lowest for this class (the workload is globally balanced among the groups). Overall, the third policy produces lower average effort within groups.

7 Conclusions

Creating groups for collaborative activities is a task which is often neglected in existing distance learning platforms. Also in face-to-face education, it is often left to random strategies, or to the pedagogical experience of single teachers. We propose here an attempt for a computer-supported method. Automatic creation of student groups relieves the teacher from most of the burden, especially in large classrooms, but can be refined by if necessary, according to personal experience and personal knowledge of students characteristics. Much work has still to be done, especially when working, as we propose, at the level of single student skills instead of considering the larger granularity of topics. The results seem to encourage continuing the investigation of this fascinating topic, which is especially relevant to achieve a good yet homogeneous group performance. Preliminary tests, not reported for sake of space, confirmed that group ZPD is wider than individual ones, and both single components and overall groups take advantage from the inclusion of more proficient peers.

References

1. Vygotskij, L.S.: The development of higher forms of attention in childhood. In: Wertsch, J. V. (ed.) The Concept of Activity in Soviet Psychology. Sharpe, Armonk (1981)
2. De Marsico, M., Sterbini, A., Temperini, M.: The definition of a tunneling strategy between adaptive learning and reputation-based group activities. In: Proceeding of 11th IEEE International Conference on Advanced Learning Technologies (ICALT 2011), pp. 498–500, July 2011
3. Kreijns, K., Kirschner, P.A., Jochems, W.: Identifying the pitfalls for social interaction in computer supported collaborative learning environments: a review of the research. Comput. Hum. Behav. **19**, 335–353 (2003)
4. Yang, S.J.H.: Context aware ubiquitous learning environments for peer-to-peer collaborative learning. J. Educ. Technol. Soc. **9**(1), 188–201 (2006)
5. Cheng, Y., Ku, H.: An investigation of the effects of reciprocal peer tutoring. Comput. Hum. Behav. **25**(1), 40–49 (2009)
6. Christodoulopoulos, C., Papanikolaou, K.: Group formation tool in a E-learning context. In: IEEE International Conference on Tools with Artificial Intelligence (ICTAI), 29–31 October, Patras, Greece (2007)
7. Lin, Y.T., Huang, Y.M., Cheng, S.C.: An automatic group composition system for composing collaborative learning groups using enhanced particle swarm optimization. Comput. Educ. **55**(4), 1483–1493 (2010)
8. Huang, Y.M., Wu, T.T.: A systematic approach for learner group composition utilizing U-learning Portfolio. Educ. Technol. Soc. **14**(3), 102–117 (2011)
9. De Marsico, M., Sterbini, A., Temperini, M.: A strategy to join adaptive and reputation-based social-collaborative e-learning, through the zone of proximal development. Int. J. Distance Educ. Technol. (IJDET) **11**(3), 12–31 (2013)
10. De Marsico, M., Temperini, M.: Average effort and average mastery in the identification of the Zone of Proximal Development. In: SPeL 2013 Sinaia, Romania 11–13 October 2013
11. De Marsico, M., Sterbini, A., Temperini, M.: Assessing group composition in e-learning according to Vygotskij's zone of proximal development. In: Stephanidis, C., Antona, M. (eds.) UAHCI 2014. LNCS, vol. 8514, pp. 277–288. Springer, Heidelberg (2014). doi:10. 1007/978-3-319-07440-5_26

sMOOC and Gamification – A Proposed Ubiquitous Learning

Javier Gil-Quintana, Lucía Camarero-Cano, Carmen Cantillo-Valero,
and Sara Osuna-Acedo[(⊠)]

Spanish National Distance Education University, Madrid, Spain
{jgilquintana,lcamarero,
carmen.cantillo}@invi.uned.es, sosuna@edu.uned.es

Abstract. The sMOOCs (Social Massive Open Online Course) respond to a more social type of education, which boosts a greater role for users who come to this training model, thanks both to the communicative model developed and to the interactive and participatory teaching practices. One of these innovative proposals in this type of courses is the immersion of gamification practices in the same digital training environment. Therefore, the communication model is enriched through participants who motivate the rest of peers through their own interaction. Gamification arises through game simulators within the communication tools such as forums and social networks, rewarding the knowledge that has been shared with the aim of promoting collective intelligence.

Keywords: MOOC · High education · Gamification · E-learning

1 Introduction

The fears and insecurities to incorporate gamification in the ubiquitous learning continue to prevail in digital training scenarios; thus, we are moving away from a reality that responds to the development of a more active and participatory learning within a scenario, which poses different challenges in a playful way. This difficulty can be tackled, if it is contemplated as an active methodology, which uses different "hooks" [1] within the educational action. This makes possible to connect empathically [8] with students immersed in a creative virtual reality, responding to their need to encourage all their multiple intelligences within the same learning proposal.

The accessibility to a new way of learning connecting ubiquitously through gamification has been a challenge proposed by the ECO European Project (Elearning, Communication and Open-data: Massive Mobile, Ubiquitous and Open Learning), led by the Spanish National Distance Education University (UNED); an offer of massive, open, and online courses, which "are increasingly taking prominence in the field of training, as well as they are being considered as a resource available to an infinite number of people" [9]. ECO stands up as a pioneering project in incorporating gamification into the MOOC training model, but it should provide greater openness in these processes.

ECO sMOOCs promote a horizontal and bidirectional communication model [10]. In this type of courses the entire virtual learning community is able to interfere with the

© Springer International Publishing AG 2017
T.-T. Wu et al. (Eds.): SETE 2016, LNCS 10108, pp. 507–513, 2017.
DOI: 10.1007/978-3-319-52836-6_54

development of the contents proposed and with the design, planning and structure, as if it were a challenge. The goal to achieve by all media is to spread the social interaction; not only by the interaction among the participants in the learning virtual community, but also outside the "connectivism ecosystems", where it is posed "a pedagogy in which knowledge arises from relationships and debates established among the members of these communities; therefore, learning is conceived as an ongoing and permanent activity" [5]. ECO platform offers new mean of communication among the MOOC participants through the use of new social features such as karma, reputation and badges. A training proposal in a gamification space which objective is the possibility of learning through play, is possible thanks to the karma established in participants, medals assignment, points or levels by people who are part of the learning community, etc. As a result, the participants' motivation in these courses promotes interactivity and participation, which they get strongly consolidated in the sMOOCs, while they collaborate in the construction of the collective knowledge from the universities. As [4] states, "the barrier of individualization in the traditional education gets overcome by applying educational proposals, where interaction and participation are enhanced with the technologies that the sMOOCs put at our disposal".

2 Method

The study focuses on the sMOOCs offered within the platform of the ECO European Project, which started in 2014. Data generated from the participants enrolled in the third iteration of these courses is analyzed using quantitative methodology. Objectivity is key when sampling methods are used. These techniques clearly respond to the hypotheses and intend to be concise in the results in order to facilitate accuracy in the realization of the conclusions formulated, avoiding the possible researchers' interference. The instrument chosen in this study among all the quantitative techniques for data collection is the survey. Its purpose is to collect information of participants in the virtual learning community, which respond to the objectives and hypotheses made. This survey was disseminated to students from the courses offered by ECO platform, getting the answers of the nine hundred twenty-nine participants who were enrolled in different sMOOCs. In consequence, these are the objectives formulated in the study:

- To analyze the impact of recognition systems (badges, karma, databases, challenges, etc.) on the participants' motivation in sMOOC.
- To analyze the effects of gamification in the acquisition of collaborative learning skills.
- To measure the degree of participation and extrinsic motivation of students, using the gamification possibilities within the communication and playful tools offered by ECO platform.

Once the important parts of this study in relation to the specific topic and their justification and delimitation in a real approach have been set up, these are the hypotheses taken into account: (a) the use of gamification tools in sMOOCs improves the collective construction of knowledge, whiles develop the empowerment of students in their own process of teaching and learning; (b) motivational accreditation systems based on granting digital distinctive promote active participation, while they are a mean to recognize the online social reputation; (c) perception of students about the gamification tools within the sMOOC has been positive.

3 Findings

Regarding the objectives and hypotheses proposed, the analysis of the results shows the data considered in this study and for which conclusions have been drawn [2]. Firstly, the communicative and pedagogical model which has strengthened an ubiquitous learning in the playful digital space was analyzed, as well as participants in this training model validated it satisfactorily; secondly, the assessment of subjects who have completed a sMOOC was studied [7], taking into consideration what has been the impact of their contributions and the reaction of peers; finally, the participants' degree of satisfaction with the different gamification tools offered by ECO was observed. These tools contribute to the construction of a more valuable learning. For this purpose, the following codes were formulated by categories to be evaluated in this study, in order to categorize and reflect on the answers given by the sample: interaction and participation of students in sMOOC, impact and reaction to the contributions made in sMOOC, achieving badges and gamification statistics in sMOOC and relevance tools in sMOOC. The potential for social interaction and communication is a powerful incentive by itself: the feeling of belonging to a learning virtual community, connectivity, participation and interaction increase. Thus, students are more motivated to keep themselves moving towards the community of practice [6]. From this perspective, it was possible to confirm according to the data shown in Fig. 1, the satisfaction degree of students about interaction and participation in ECO project sMOOCs is high, offering a positive assessment on this aspect, represented by 20% of students who are completely satisfied and 41% which is largely satisfied.

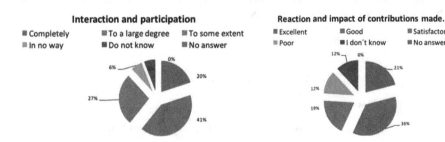

Fig. 1. Interactive and participatory communication development among students of the course.

Fig. 2. Reaction assessment and contributions impact made by students of the course.

Participants analyzed the scores referred to post comments, projects and documents shared by other students in order to measure the impact and the reactions of contributions made in sMOOC. The results were very good. In this regard, as shown in

Fig. 2, participants rated these courses 21% as excellent, 36% good and 19% satis-factory their experience as for the follow-up that their contributions have had and their impact in the learning virtual community.

The challenges and achievements system, which should not be mandatory for course completion, is analyzed. However, participants should be proposed to enable themselves to improve and be more involved in the interaction opportunities and course progress. The implementation of "shadow" is secret and course designers could value it as a way to implement partial reinforcement strategies. These gamification tools are increased by the use of points and levels. This is a gamification karma style where users should be able to earn points in a collaborative and not competitive way, in order to either progress through the content and course activities or to interact with one another in a meaningful way. Nevertheless, as it is possible to see in Fig. 3, although the increase or the decrease of karma is a gamification strategy with great potential in sMOOCs, it still has not been strengthened enough in the students' context. That is why, the project must reflect about the reasons, which have conditioned its majority use. By contrast, it was possible to observe how the use of medals has been further enhanced starting from a total of 1242 medals distributed to 444 students, who have won these awards. Although none of the students used the module type, 74 participants achieved the "activity performed" medal, while 444 participants achieved the "single unit" medal. In this regard, it was not strengthening enough (Fig. 3), highlighting the fact that 1118 participants have had only fifty or so followers. Therefore, it is stated that this aspect of interactivity related to social software has not been developed in the digital environment, becoming an aspect to improve in subsequent iterations. This shows that the challenge of the current online education involves promoting collabo-rative learning experiences, which overcome the traditional procedures of preset knowledge systematization. Additionally, creativity, experimentation and interaction in education have to be stimulated (Fig. 4). This intercreativity [11] environment engages all members in the community and the whole society. New spaces of deconstruction and reconstruction of knowledge in different languages and gamification strategies, which encourage critical thinking, are needed.

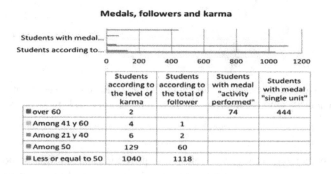

Medals, followers and karma

	Students according to the level of karma	Students according to the total of follower	Students with medal "activity performed"	Students with medal "single unit"
■ over 60	2		74	444
▦ Among 41 y 60	4	1		
▦ Among 21 y 40	6	2		
▦ Among 50	129	60		
▦ Less or equal to 50	1040	1118		

Fig. 3. Medals for students, karma impact and number of followers as gamification tool used by the students of the course.

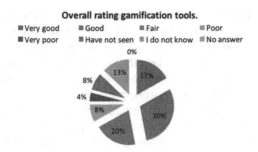

Fig. 4. Overall rating of the different gamification tools used by students of the course.

In the case of gamification, the reward system influences student motivation, since the ratings are replaced by the levels system used in videogames. The fact of using levels and a leader board of the traditional game (where users can see the peers who have acquired the greatest amount of points) could encourage friendly competition and commitment. In this respect, the progress bar also appears among the gamification tools where the course designers can assign completion rates for each unit and activity. Therefore, users can monitor their progress, becoming a way of intrinsic motivation, which it can be used to encourage active participation. Regarding this type of gamification tools offered in ECO sMOOCs, the Fig. 3 shows the positive assessment made by the students. Thus, 17% states it as very good, 30% as good and 20% as fair for this training model.

4 Conclusions

As shown in the study, it is clear that the most important challenges universities face in order to expand sMOOC training spaces are the innovations within the ubiquitous learning environment and their gamification techniques, which grant leadership to students. These challenges change the roles and generate a new "logic of action" in students, as well as in the traditional education system, which considers the teacher as the beginning and end of the learning process. Content and tasks are shown as adventures that may appear in the progress of a particular mission, which the requirement to solve it and move forward is the students' interactivity. That way, the student role goes beyond the traditional methods between teaching and learning functions. These students are immersed in "techno-social communities" [3] typical of the network society, and become mediators for their own learning and their peers who act as contents curators within the sMOOC. Also, advisors and moderators actively engaged in certain actions participate in the process of teaching and learning. From this standpoint, it is necessary to consolidate an alternative communication model, which is based on horizontal and bidirectional structures in order to foster co-authored learning. New lines of research in the field of sMOOCs are added to this challenge, such as the study and development of training platforms with the greater potential in gamification tools. These ones help to convert digital scenarios in playful and participatory spaces, while the citizens' empowerment, their training and, therefore, the improvement of the rest of society, become a reality. Students value very positively the patchwork of contents, learning ecosystems and gamification context as well as the processes of socialization and subjectivation made in sMOOCs. Participants become generators and co-creators of knowledge in a social environment, where the validity of the content is usually fleeting, and therefore, it is likely to search for new and immediately verifiable reconstructions. In addition, "the way in which people's work and functions change when new tools are used" [12]. This facilitates the students' empowerment in the teaching and learning process and the closeness of the academic demands in personal life.

Gamification has yet to gain a foothold in the field of sMOOCs, consolidating additional gamification strategies that engage students with an active motivation. This brings the development getting away from the proposal of the traditional courses. There are many possibilities in the new learning techniques based on gamification, such as avatars in the new roles and playful narrative adventures in the learning experience, which are reflected in social networks thanks to microblogging or co-created stories on blogs. Accordingly, the positive assessment of gamification tools used in ECO sMOOCs confirms the hypotheses. Thus, they contribute to foster creativity and develop competencies and skills as learning objectives, which have been established in this type of educational activities. The challenges of educational practices have an immediate effect on the way they relate to emerging technologies and how they are implemented in the educational world. In this regard, gamification tools are revolutionizing current learning systems, adding new mechanisms of motivation to online learning.

References

1. Burgess, D.: Teach Like a Pirate: Increase Student Engagement, Boost Your Creativity, and Transform Your Life as an Educator. Theoklesia, EEUU (2012)
2. Callejo, J., Viedma, A.: Proyectos y estrategias de Investigación Social: la perspectiva de la intervención. McGrawHill, Madrid (2009)
3. Camarero-Cano, L.: Comunidades tecnosociales. Evolución de la comunicación analógica hacia la interacción analógico-digital. Revista Mediterránea de Comunicación 6(1), 187–195 (2015). http://rua.ua.es/dspace/handle/10045/44257
4. Camarero-Cano, L., Cantillo, C.: La evaluación de los aprendizajes en los sMOOC. Estudio de caso en el Proyecto Europeo ECO. Revista Mediterránea de Comunicación (2016). http://rua.ua.es/dspace/handle/10045/56388
5. Cantillo, C.: Nuevas dinámicas de aprendizaje en entornos virtuales. En Osuna, S. (coord.): Escenarios virtuales educomunicativos. Icaria, Barcelona (2014)
6. Fidalgo Blanco, A., Sein-Echaluce, M.L., García-Peñalvo,F.J.: Desde el acceso masivoa la cooperación: lecciones aprendidas y aprobados resultados de un enfoque pedagógico xMOOC híbrido/cMOOC a MOOCs. Revista Internacional de Tecnología Educativa en la Educación Superior (2016)
7. Fueyo, A., et al.: ECO_D4.5 Report on users satisfaction (2016). http://project.ecolearning.eu/about-eco/results
8. García-Pérez, R., Santos-Delgado, J.M., Buzón-García, O.: Virtual empathy as digital competence in education 3.0. International Journal of Educational Technology in Higher Education (2016)

9. Gómez-Hernández, P., García-Barrera, A., Monge-López, C.: La cultura de los MOOCS. Editorial Síntesis, Madrid (2016)
10. Gil-Quintana, J.: MOOC "Innovación Educativa y desarrollo profesional. Posibilidades y límites de las TIC". Una experiencia desde la educomunicación en el Proyecto Europeo ECO. Qual. Res. Educ. **4**(3), 299–328 (2015)
11. Osuna, S., y Camarero-Cano, L.: The ECO european project: a new MOOC dimension based on an intercreativity environment. TOJET: Turk. Online J. Educ. Technol. **15**(1), 117–125 (2016). http://www.tojet.net/volumes/v15i1.pdf
12. Siemens, G.: Conectivismo: Una teoría de aprendizaje para la era digital (2004). http://www.fce.ues.edu.sv/uploads/pdf/siemens-2004-conectivismo.pdf

Second Screen User Profiling
and Multi-level Smart Recommendations
in the Context of Social TVs

Angelos Valsamis[✉], Alexandros Psychas, Fotis Aisopos,
Andreas Menychtas, and Theodora Varvarigou

Distributed, Knowledge and Media Systems Group,
National Technical University of Athens, Athens, Greece
angval@central.ntua.gr,
{alps,fotais,ameny}@mail.ntua.gr,
dora@telecom.ntua.gr

Abstract. In the context of Social TV, the increasing popularity of first and second screen users, interacting and posting content online, illustrates new business opportunities and related technical challenges, in order to enrich user experience on such environments. SAM (Socializing Around Media) project uses Social Media-connected infrastructure to deal with the aforementioned challenges, providing intelligent user context management models and mechanisms capturing social patterns, to apply collaborative filtering techniques and personalized recommendations towards this direction. This paper presents the Context Management mechanism of SAM, running in a Social TV environment to provide smart recommendations for first and second screen content. Work presented is evaluated using real movie rating dataset found online, to validate the SAM's approach in terms of effectiveness as well as efficiency.

Keywords: Second screen · Social TV · Context management · Recommendations

1 Introduction

The usage of mobile devices has become one of the leading daily activities. This phenomenon extends to the usage of those devices in parallel with other devices also. SAM project [1] aims at exploiting, researching and creating the appropriate technologies that revolve around the usage of mobile devices simultaneously with TV, the so called 2nd screen phenomenon[1]. The software created for the purposes of SAM revolves around the creation of a complete experience for the user delivered in to his mobile device during a TV program. In a very simple way users get multimedia content (in the form of widgets) about the TV program they are watching in to their mobile devices. This Content varies from simple information about the characters of the TV program to social media content about the program.

---

[1] Second Screen Society: http://www.2ndscreensociety.com/.

© Springer International Publishing AG 2017
T.-T. Wu et al. (Eds.): SETE 2016, LNCS 10108, pp. 514–525, 2017.
DOI: 10.1007/978-3-319-52836-6_55

Initially, SAM is planned to use a set of educative-oriented videos, which are created by SAM's Media Providers and selected by didactic teams of schools for educational purposes. Contents linked to such videos will be editorially curated, and its didactic value reviewed by the didactic team of each school. The most common learning scenarios, for example, include short documentaries or nutrition-related video reports, where users (students in this case) will use their mobile devices and computers to have an interactive social experience.

However, delivering multimedia content to user mobile devices poses a variety of challenges and requirements. The creation of a mechanism that delivers personalized content as well as the contextualization of this content are the requirements that drove the research and developments of this paper. The work is summarized into two main objectives:

- Creating sophisticated contextualization of the information and content
- Create recommendation system for personalized content delivery to enrich user experience

There is a vast variety of recommendation algorithms to implement in a system. In this paper the research focus not on creating new algorithms but creating sophisticated data to use as input in these algorithms. More specifically representing relations between users and multimedia content in a more refined way and further more adapt this data to be used as input to the well-established and tested algorithms for recommendation.

The rest of the document is organized as follows: The current section introduces the Social TV Context Management concept. Section 2 presents the related work regarding 2nd screen Context Management and graph Recommendations, while Sect. 3 analyzes the SAM model and approach. In Sect. 4, experiments' configuration as well as their results is provided and finally Sect. 5 concludes the current paper and discusses the work to be done in the future.

2 Related Work

Context management. Social TV and 2nd screen are now some of the most emerging technologies, used for eLearning, Political Surveys or just Social Networking purposes. Cezar et al. [2] analyzed the usages of the 2nd screen in an Interactive Television Environment, to control, enrich, share, and transfer TV content. This work provided an initial market assessment in the areas of media creation and distribution and subjected its prototype implementation to test by a dozen groups of users in a social setting. Giglietto and Selva [3] applied a content analysis to a big dataset of 2nd screen tweets during an entire TV season, in order to clarify the relationship between TV political talk shows and related comments on social media. This study points out the effects of celebritization of politics and confirms the coexistence of different and interlinked forms of participation (with political prevailing on audience participation). Elaborating on personalized experiences, Geerts et al. [4] investigated a 2nd screen application, stimulating social interaction in the living room, offering more insight into how viewers experience second such applications, and contrasted this with the perspective of producers and actual usage data.

Graph analysis and recommendations. Although much work has been carried out concerning movie/TV programs, Second screen and Social TV recommendations are quite immature. Context-based recommendations using graphs are evidently the more efficient, as SQL databases are now obsolete for big data analytics. Demovic et al. [5] presented a suchlike approach, saving movie data in a graph and using Graph Traversal Algorithms to efficiently address user preferences. This work uses explicit user "likes" for movies or genres, but does not collect any contextual or social data. When it comes to Social TV Platforms, authors in [6, 7] highlight the concept of context management and analysis in the frame of social enabled content delivery to 2nd screen devices. These papers present a novel solution for media context management in a Neo4j graph database, and provide the baseline context of the current work.

k-NN and Collaborative Filtering. Collaborative filtering techniques are commonly used for TV program recommendations. Authors in [8] use collaborative filtering for such recommendations, enhanced with singular value decomposition resulting into a low-dimension item-based filtering with promising accuracy. Andrade and Almeida [9] adopt the k Nearest Neighbors (k-NN) algorithm to implement a hybrid strategy that combines collaborative filtering with a content-based method for delivering TV recommendations to individual users. K-NN is also employed in [10, 11] to implement personalized popular program recommendation systems for digital TV data clustered by k-means. Both works generate datasets of user profiles, to examine resulting recommendations in terms of accuracy as well as computation time.

3   SAM Context Management and Recommendations

3.1   Context Management Database

The Context Manager is connected with various key components of the SAM system. In order to contextualize process and create the recommendations, Context Controller needs to be connected with data listeners to gather data from SAM 1st and 2nd screen. After processing the collected data, Context Controller stores the data to the SAM Cloud storage. SAM "Syndicator" component, which is responsible for orchestrating the 2nd screen experience, as well as the 2nd screen component itself are also connected with the Context Manager to retrieve the information needed in order to deliver the recommendations. In the following paragraphs a more in depth analysis of the storage and the recommendation techniques used will be presented.

As mentioned, graph databases are the leading solution for the data analysis and recommendation systems. All data created or imported in SAM are stored in a Neo4j Graph database in order to be further analyzed and used for recommendation purposes.

The structure of the graph database is a very important factor for the optimization of the recommendation algorithms. Graph databases contain two types of data in general, the nodes and the edges. Nodes represent entities such as persons and multimedia

Assets, edges represent relationships between the entities (nodes). In SAM there are three types of nodes:

- **Assets:** which represent any type of multimedia content
- **Persons:** which represent every user that interacts with the Assets
- **Keywords:** which represent words that describe Assets

There are several types of edges that describe the relationships between nodes:

- Has-keyword is the relationship that connects the Assets with the Keywords that most appropriately describes them.
- Consume, like, dislike, comment, full-screen, dismiss and show-more are relationships that describe interactions between a user (Person) and an Asset.
- Is-root-of describes the relationship between a root asset and the assets (widgets) that are appear in the second screen when it is being consumed.

The following paragraphs explain how entities and interactions are used to estimate relevance with an asset and produce recommendations.

3.2   User Interactions and Analysis

SAM first and second screen listeners collect various user actions and store them in order to be able to later recommend videos and/or widgets. In particular, actions concerning videos include:

1. Comment a movie: a comment in Twitter/Facebook/SAM Dynamic Communities that is being processed by SAM's sentiment analysis service.
2. Consume a movie: action of selecting a movie and start watching.
3. Initiate Full screen: action of pressing the enlargement button in order to see the movie in full screen mode.
4. Like/Dislike a movie: action of pressing the like/dislike button under a movie.

Actions concerning widgets appearing in 2nd screen while watching a video are:

1. Like/Dislike a widget: The actions of pressing the like/dislike button under each widget.
2. Dismiss a widget: The action of pressing the dismiss button in order to hide a widget.
3. Show more: The action of pressing the show-more button, located under each widget that enlarge the widget's size and adds more info.

SAM's sentiment analysis service [12, 13], which is used to identify sentiment on widget and movie comments, is also able to perceive the sentiment polarity of a comment in regards to the movie's keywords. For example, if the user commented "That movie was awesome. Jennifer Lawrence's acting was spot on!" the sentiment analysis service will generate a positive number for the comment in regard to the movie, and also a positive number for the movie's keyword "Lawrence". Thus, we also identify an (indirect) action: *"Comment on keyword"*.

A basic part of the analysis of the graph is to apply some kind of "weights" (i.e. relevance scores) to the lines connecting users and assets. Setting +1 and −1 as absolute values of relevancy and irrelevancy respectively, we apply those values to user-asset relations that explicitly show such a rating ("like" weights for +1, "dislike" weights for −1). On the other hand, comments on assets are saved along with their sentiment polarity and intensity (percentage of positivity or negativity), thus we apply for positive comments a decimal weight, ranging from (0, +1] and for negative comments from [−1, 0). Zero value obviously expresses neutrality.

However, consuming or pressing 'Full Screen' on a video also indicates interest by the user. The same applies for pressing 'show more' on a specific widget in 2nd screen, while dismissing it before it automatically closes indicates lack of interest. To capture those implicit patterns, we need to make sure that they will not totally overlap the explicit ones already mentioned. For example, if a user has "liked" an asset, but on the other hand dismissed it early on, this implies a weaker "like" or "interest" relation. The approach that we follow to make sure the overall relevance score (sum of weights) is mainly defined by "likes"/"dislikes" and only partly affected by other interactions is to apply to the latest a weight of

$$w_i = \frac{p_i}{t+1}$$

where p = polarity indication (+1, −1) and t = number of implicit interactions existing for asset type (movie or widget). Following this approach, if an explicit interaction weight we contradicts to all implicit weights wi, the overall weight

$$W = w_e + \sum w_i$$

will still bare the (now normalized) "polarity" of w_e.

Given the aforementioned list of interactions that we collect from SAM Dashboard, the weights of different asset interactions are summarized in Table 1:

Table 1. Polarity contribution of the various user interactions.

Interactions	Movie	Widget	Keyword
Explicit weights w_e			
Comment	(−1, 1)		(−1, 1)
Like	+1	+1	
Dislike	−1	−1	
Implicit weights w_i			
Full screen	+1/3		
Consume	+1/3		
Dismiss		−1/3	
Show More		+1/3	
#Implicit_interations t	2	2	

Taking into account the above, the overall direct weight of a user and an asset is:

$$W_d = \sum w_e + \sum w_i$$

In the example given above, where a user "liked" an asset but dismissed it early on, the overall weight is now: W = +1 −1/3 = +2/3, which is still a positive score.

3.3 Analysis of Indirect Relations

When analyzing interactions, to estimate assets' relevance we identify two cases:

1. An interaction of a user with a widget/keyword of a movie (Fig. 1).

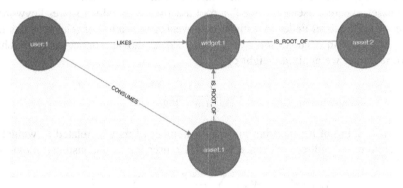

Fig. 1. User interacts with widget.

2. An interaction of a user with a movie, with common widgets to another (Fig. 2).

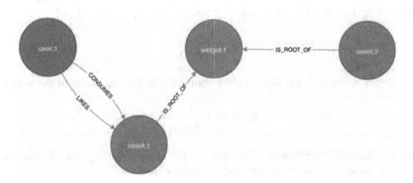

Fig. 2. User interacts with movie.

To estimate user relevance to a movie, we can also use interactions with widgets and keywords related to it and other movies already consumed. Also, we can use interactions with movies that share widgets and keywords with this movie.

For example, if a user has "liked" or commented positively for all widgets or keywords of a root asset (case 1), a strong indication of relevance to this root asset also exists. Similarly to the previous logic, we need to make sure that indirect relations to assets will not overlap a direct weight to it. Thus, for every rating to a connected widget/keyword we apply a weight of

$$W_w = \frac{r_w}{a+k+1}$$

where r_w = rating of neighboring node, a = number of neighboring assets and k = number of keywords connected to the "under investigation" asset.

In cases, where a user has "liked" a root asset (case 2), which shares keywords or widgets with the asset under investigation, a weaker indication of relevance has to be taken into account. Thus, for every rating to a movie connected with shared keyword/widget we apply a weight of

$$W_m = \frac{r_m}{(m+1)2}$$

where r_m = rating of neighboring node, m = number of movies related to widget.

Therefore, the indirect relevance weight of a user for an unconsumed movie is:

$$W_{ind} = W_w + W_m = \sum \frac{r_x}{a+k+1} + \sum \frac{r_m}{(m+1)2}$$

When it comes to widgets of a movie, we use interactions with other widgets/keywords belonging to that movie (case 1) and interactions with movies that share the widget in question (case 2). Similarly to the previous logic, for every rating to a root asset connected to the under investigation widget, we apply a weight of

$$W_r = \frac{r_r}{m+1}$$

and for every rating to a keyword/widget connected to the root asset of the widget:

$$W_k = \frac{r_k}{(a+k+1)2}$$

where r_k = rating of neighboring node, a = number of neighboring to the widget assets and k = number of keywords connected to the root asset.

Therefore, the overall relevance weight of a person for a widget of an unconsumed asset becomes:

$$W_{ind} = W_r + W_k = \sum \frac{r_r}{m+1} + \sum \frac{r_k}{(a+k+1)2}$$

As a result of the analysis above, the overall relevance estimation of an asset is:

$$W = W_d + W_{ind} = \begin{cases} \sum w_e + \sum \frac{p_i}{t+1} + \sum \frac{r_w}{a+k+1} + \sum \frac{r_m}{(m+1)2}, & \text{for movies} \\ \sum w_e + \sum \frac{p_i}{t+1} + \sum \frac{r_r}{m+1} + \sum \frac{r_k}{(a+k+1)2}, & \text{for widgets} \end{cases}$$

3.4   Collaborative Filtering Analysis

The technique described cannot provide rich results for assets that the user has not interacted with or with their neighbours ("isolated" assets). Thus, as a supporting solution, collaborative filtering is applied among users, to estimate their relevance with such assets, based on correlation with other users. A common approach for collaborative filtering on a dataset of simple numeric ratings [14], as in our dataset, is using the Pearson Correlation Coefficient. Its equation is the following:

$$c_{au} = \frac{\sum_{i=1}^{h} (r_{ai} - \bar{r}_a) \times (r_{ui} - \bar{r}_u)}{\sqrt{\sum_{i=1}^{h} (r_{ai} - \bar{r}_a)^2 \times \sum_{i=1}^{h} (r_{ui} - \bar{r}_u)^2}}$$

for users a and u, where in our case $h = |I_{au}|$ is the amount of assets rated by both users, r_{ai} is user a's weight for asset i and $\bar{r}_a = average\ (r_{a1}, r_{a2}, K, \ldots r_{ah})$.

After calculating the correlation coefficients of a user with other users, Pearson collaborative filtering can provide a prediction, estimating her relevance with an asset j, based on other users' relevance for the specific asset and their correlation:

$$p_{aj} = \bar{r}_a + \frac{\sum_{u=1}^{g} (r_{uj} - \bar{r}_u) \times c_{au}}{\sum_{u=1}^{g} |c_{au}|}$$

where g is the number of users that consumed j and p_{ai} is the predicted rating of relevance for user a.

3.5   Asset Recommendations

The analysis of the graph, together with the Collaborative Filtering method described above, provide relevance estimation for every user and asset. Relevance scores per asset allow for the implementation of the following recommendations:

- Recommendation of a ranked list of root assets, based on their relevance to users.
- Recommendation of a ranked list of widgets, while users watch their root videos.

These recommendation methods are used for the personalization of the 1st and 2nd screen environment, based on each user context. Using those, SAM is able to recommend relevant videos in 1st screen, as well as prioritize widgets when watching a video, hiding the irrelevant ones or highlighting the most interesting.

4 Experiments

4.1 Dataset and Configuration

Finding a dataset that contains user interactions, and in general two-level (implicit and explicit) data, proved challenging. For the evaluation of the current solution, we used a well known movie rating dataset found online [15], comprising a huge database of movies and user ratings, as well as keywords linked with those movies.

The dataset imported was interpreted into the SAM logic, generating SAM users, assets and keywords. We analyzed the rating values in order to simulate like/dislike actions based on those values (explicit information), and we were also able to use the implicit information of connected movies to the same keywords, thus having the two-level information that is necessary for our algorithm to display its full potential.

To limit our scale and make a meaningful analysis, we selected a random sample of available movies along with all the associated ratings and keywords. The overall numbers and statistics of the dataset imported can be found in Table 2.

Table 2. Sample retrieved from MovieLens dataset clusters correlation coefficient

	Users	Movies	Ratings	Keywords
Overall metrics	656	1032	9902	495
	Mean Rating	Mean Rating per Movie	#Keywords per movie	#Movies rated by a user
Average metrics	3.48	9.6	0.64	15.09

The dataset was split in a 70/30 ratio into training and a testing set respectively. Note that for k-NN, Pearson as well as SAM algorithm, no training step is really required, although the training set is used in the preparatory step of calculating coefficients (in standalone Pearson's filtering) and clusters (in k-NN algorithm). In case of SAM, training set is used as prior knowledge since interactions of users have to be saved in the graph in order to analyze and recommend new assets/widgets.

Experiments were performed on a desktop machine with an Intel Core TM i5-3400 Processor, 2.80 GHz, 12 GB of RAM memory, running 64-bit Windows 10 Pro N.

4.2 Experiment Results

The graph analysis, supported by the Pearson Collaborative filtering, presented above, was applied and compared with the stand-alone implementation of Pearson Collaborative filtering as well as an implementation of k-NN algorithm run over Neo4j. K-NN is one of the most popular clustering approaches for recommendations using graphs. In our case, we followed the user-based algorithm approach with adjusted cosine similarity function[2]. As evaluation metric we used the variation between the ground truth rating and the relevance computed by the different algorithms. In Table 3 we present the errors of each method using root mean squared error (RMSE), mean absolute error (MAE) and mean percentage error (MPE).

Table 3. Results of different algorithms run over Neo4j database.

Algorithm	Mean absolute error	Root mean squared error	Mean percentage error	Average Response time (ms)
K-NN algorithm	0.3415	0.4242	17.08%	6910
Stand-alone Pearson Collaborative filtering	0.2809	0.3190	14.04%	5882
SAM algorithm sup. by Pearson Collaborative filtering	0.2584	0.2878	12.92%	5529

Based on measured errors, it is evident that the graph analysis is superior to the collaborative filtering approach when there are adequate user interactions. In case where there are not enough user interactions we fall back to Pearson's filtering. In addition, as can be observed, the SAM algorithm outperforms K-NN accuracy-wise, one of the most popular clustering approaches for recommendations using graphs.

Apart from the accuracy experiments, we also measured the response time of the three different algorithms (SAM, Collaborative filtering, K-NN) exposed by SAM's Context Management component as web services. Last column of Table 3 presents the average response time in ms for each algorithm after 1000 requests on each. SAM algorithm's locality search seems to outperform other approaches.

5   Conclusions and Future Work

This work has been focused on an efficient Context Management and Personalized Recommendation system for Social TV First and 2nd screen. 2nd screen Content Listening and related Recommendations is a new promising area that has yet to be explored by the research community. To this end, the authors have proposed an innovative and adaptive model, using social media and user context information, and applied over SAM's Content Syndication and Social learning environment. This model was supported by a collaborative filtering mechanism and evaluated over real-world dataset found online.

---

[2] https://neo4j.com/graphgist/8173017/.

In the future, SAM will be piloted to elementary schools as well as high schools as an eLearning and Media Delivery application, in order to test its functionalities and acquire real datasets of user interactions. Those interactions will constitute a more concrete dataset, to be used in order to evaluate the current representation model and the resulting recommendation system's effectiveness.

Acknowledgment. This work has been supported by the SAM project and funded from the European Union's 7th Framework Programme for research, technological development and demonstration under grant agreement no 611312.

References

1. Socialising Around Media (SAM) Project: Dynamic Social and Media Content Syndication for 2nd Screen. http://samproject.net/
2. Cesar, P., Bulterman, D.C.A., Jansen, A.,J.: Usages of the secondary screen in an interactive television environment: control, enrich, share, and transfer television content. In: Tscheligi, M., Obrist, M., Lugmayr, A. (eds.) EuroITV 2008. LNCS, vol. 5066, pp. 168–177. Springer, Heidelberg (2008). doi:10.1007/978-3-540-69478-6_22
3. Giglietto, F., Selva, D.: Second screen and participation: a content analysis on a full season dataset of tweets. J. Commun. **64**(2), 260–277 (2014)
4. Geerts, D., et al.: In front of and behind the second screen: viewer and producer perspectives on a companion app. In: Proceedings of the 2014 ACM International Conference on Interactive Experiences for TV and Online Video. ACM (2014)
5. Demovic, L., et al.: Movie recommendation based on graph traversal algorithms. In: 2013 24th International Workshop on Database and Expert Systems Applications (DEXA). IEEE (2013)
6. Menychtas, A., Tomás, D., Tiemann, M., Santzaridou, C., Psychas, A., Kyriazis, D., Vidagany, J.V., Campbell, S.: Dynamic social and media content syndication for second screen. Int. J. Vir. Communities Soc. Networking (IJVCSN) **7**(2), 50–69 (2015)
7. Santzaridou, C., Menychtas, A., Psychas, A., Varvarigou, T.: Context management and analysis for social TV platforms. eChallenges e-2015 (2015)
8. Barragáns-Martínez, A.B., et al.: A hybrid content-based and item-based collaborative filtering approach to recommend TV programs enhanced with singular value decomposition. Inform. Sci. **180**(22), 4290–4311 (2010)
9. Andrade, M.T., Almeida, F.: Novel hybrid approach to content recommendation based on predicted profiles. In: Ubiquitous Intelligence and Computing, 2013 IEEE 10th International Conference on and 10th International Conference on Autonomic and Trusted Computing (UIC/ATC). IEEE (2013)
10. Lai, C.-F., et al.: CPRS: a cloud-based program recommendation system for digital TV platforms. Future Gener. Comput. Syst. **27**(6), 823–835 (2011)
11. Chang, J.-H., et al.: 3PRS: a personalized popular program recommendation system for digital TV for P2P social networks. Multimedia Tools Appl. **47**(1), 31–48 (2010)
12. Sánchez-Mirabal, P.A., Torres, Y.R., Alvarado, S.H., Gutiérrez, Y., Montoyo, A., Muñoz, R.: UMCC_DLSI: sentiment analysis in twitter using polarity Lexicons and tweet similarity. In: Proceedings of the 8th International Workshop on Semantic Evaluation (SemEval 2014), Dublin, Ireland, pp. 727–731

13. Gutierrez, Y., Tomas, D., Fernandez, J.: Benefits of using ranking skip-gram techniques for opinion mining approaches. In: eChallenges e-2015 Conference. IEEE (2015)
14. Tserpes, K., Aisopos, F., Kyriazis, D., Varvarigou, T.: Service selection decision support in the internet of services. In: Altmann, J., Rana, O.F. (eds.) GECON 2010. LNCS, vol. 6296, pp. 16–33. Springer, Heidelberg (2010). doi:10.1007/978-3-642-15681-6_2
15. Harper, F.M., Konstan, J.A.: The MovieLens datasets: history and context. ACM Trans. Interact. Intell. Syst. (TiiS) 5(4), 19 (2015). Article 19

Keyword-Based Similarity Using Automatically Generated Semantic Graph in an Online Community of Practice

Oumayma Chergui[1(✉)], Ahlame Begdouri[1],
and Dominique Groux-Leclet[2]

[1] SIA Laboratory, Faculty of Science and Technology,
University of Sidi Mohammed Ben Abdellah, Fez, Morocco
{oumayma.chergui,ahlame.begdouri}@usmba.ac.ma
[2] MIS Laboratory, University of Picardie Jules-Verne, Amiens, France
dominique.groux@u-picardie.fr

Abstract. Communities of Practice (CoPs) allow enhancing members learning and maintaining knowledge in a community memory as they evolve. Pertinent reuse of this knowledge could facilitate learning among the CoP members, increase their productivity and also improve the quality of their artefacts. In our online CoP environment, we include knowledge reuse based on the Case Based Reasoning (CBR) approach as one of the main functions, aiming at capitalizing the community knowledge. In fact, when a CoP member encounters a new problem, the first phase of the CBR cycle consists of retrieving previously experienced cases that are similar to the new problem.

In this paper, we propose a keywords-based similarity using a semantic network that contains all potential keywords of the CoP's domain of interest, organized semantically. We also present our approach for automatically generating this semantic graph based on content extracted from an external source: the Wikipedia knowledge base.

Keywords: Community of Practice · Semantic graph · Keywords similarity · Case based reasoning · Higher education

1 Introduction

The concept of Communities of Practice (CoPs) is based on the idea of interacting to improve a shared practice between the community members. We chose to make use of CoPs in a context of higher education [1], since they allow developing various skills and academic practices along with the shared domain of interest [7], and they can facilitate blending formal and informal learning. Our research revolves around the design and implementation of an online CoP supporting environment, comprising three main functionalities: community interactions knowledge reuse and teacher's assistance.

The knowledge reuse allows creating the community memory based on the community interactions. To achieve this, we use the Case-Based reasoning (CBR), a concept used in maintaining and adapting shared knowledge [2]. The case elaboration consists in a CoP member asking a question (a text description), choosing the question category and

© Springer International Publishing AG 2017
T.-T. Wu et al. (Eds.): SETE 2016, LNCS 10108, pp. 526–532, 2017.
DOI: 10.1007/978-3-319-52836-6_56

its keywords. Then, the first phase of the CBR cycle is the retrieval of similar cases which requires indexing the cases. We use keywords for the case indexing.

In order to improve the effectiveness of this information retrieval scenario, accurate knowledge representation should be adopted to model the keywords. Both the choice of the data structure and the semantic information that resides in them should be taken into account, allowing knowledge to be well organized based on meaning and therefore facilitate the similarity measure.

In this paper, we start by giving an overview about our online environment and the CBR cycle used for knowledge reuse. Then we introduce the keywords-based similarity measure and detail our approach for automatic extraction of a semantic graph of keywords from the Wikipedia knowledge base. We finally conclude by presenting some preliminary results.

2 Research Context

2.1 Our CoP's Supporting Environment

The CoP revolves around students providing mutual help to each other. Whether by directly asking colleagues for help, or based on the community's history of previous questions and answers validated by the teacher. We define three main functionalities of the community's supporting tool: **(i) Community interactions:** using Facebook as the main communication medium for the community members, **(ii) Knowledge reuse:** creating the community memory based on the community interactions, and **(iii) Teacher's assistance:** functionalities allowing him to motivate students, to supervise them, and to evaluate their performance as community members.

Figure 1 presents a summary of the environment we propose as a community supporting tool. In this paper we are focusing on "the community memory" module.

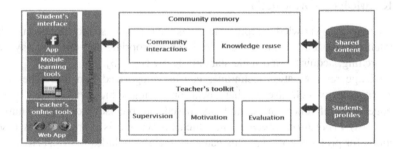

Fig. 1. General architecture of our online CoP supporting environment [1]

2.2   Knowledge Reuse Based on the CBR Approach

One of the most used methodologies in maintaining and adapting shared knowledge for future usage is the Case Based reasoning (CBR), using old experiences to understand and solve new problems [2].

In the CBR approach, a case is defined by two parts: a problem, and a solution for this problem. In our context, CBR is used in an interactive question/answer environment, a student's question can be a difficulty in executing a learning task, a need for clarification, etc. Therefore, our case is represented as: (Question, Answer). *The Question part* includes a *Question description, Keywords,* and a *Question category*. *The Answer part* is composed of a set of Answer steps, at least one, based on members discussions that lead to the solution. It might include an additional indication related to a specific context (represented by a set of keywords). By dividing the answer into steps with an intermediate question for each, we are able to minimize duplications. An answer step could be reused as a part of answering several different questions (Fig. 2).

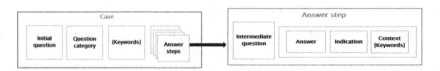

Fig. 2. The "Case" structure

The CBR cycle consists in: (1) *Retrieving* one or more previously experienced cases, (2) *Reusing* the information and knowledge in that case to solve the problem, (3) *Revising* the proposed solution, and (4) *Retaining* it by adding it into the existing knowledge-base (Case-Base).

2.3   Knowledge Representation

For reuse purposes, knowledge representation is the method used to encode knowledge in an intelligent system's knowledge base, in an appropriate and optimal way, facilitating searching, acquiring and understanding knowledge [3].

Knowledge representation techniques can be categorized into four types [4]: **(i)** *Logical schemes* which use mathematical or orthographic symbols to represent knowledge and inference rules, and are based on precisely defined syntax and semantics. **(ii)** *Procedural schemes*, in which knowledge is represented as a set of instructions for problem-solving. This category mainly includes the IF..THEN.. rules, used to formulate the conditional statements that comprise fuzzy logic [5]. *B.* **(iii)** *Networked schemes* use a graph to represent knowledge. Nodes of a graph display objects, and arcs define relationships between objects. This category includes semantic networks, which have no formal semantics and don't allow expressing property characteristics [6]. And **iv)** *Structured schemes* which extend networked representation by displaying each node as a complex data structure. This category includes ontologies, formal explicit descriptions of concepts in a specific domain [6].

The choice of the adequate knowledge representation method differs depending on the knowledge domain, the problem to be solved, the representation purpose and each method's characteristics. An important aspect to consider is "semantics". The power of any data structure lies not only in their structure but also in the semantic information that resides in them, which allows knowledge to be organized based on meaning.

3 Keywords Modeling in a Semantic Graph

3.1 Keywords-Based Similarity for Case Retrieval in the CBR

In the retrieval phase of the CBR cycle, we need to retrieve the similar cases from the case-base. This requires assigning indices to cases to facilitate their retrieval. In our context we chose the question's keywords to be the indexing terms of the cases, since they hold the essence of the text and verbalize the described problem.

When a new case arrives, it will be "classified" according to its keywords to get the most similar cases. This requires an adequate representation for keywords related to the CoP's domain of interest, since all students questions will revolve around it.

We find semantic networks especially adapted to our needs. Other than their semantic nature, networks as a data structure make a better representation than trees, since they include more relations between nodes, which provides more information. In addition, semantic networks are less complex than other representation forms (e.g. ontologies), which is enough for our needs. Therefore, we chose using a semantic graph to model the keywords, in such a way that the main concept represents the graph center, and more the nodes are close to it, more semantically related they are. Each node contains a keyword, and the arcs are automatically weighted in order to provide more information about the semantic closeness of the nodes.

As for the similarity measure, once we have the keywords of the new case, we search for each of the keywords in the graph. If a corresponding node is found, the retrieved questions are the ones related to the found node and also the nodes directly related to it, since they would be semantically the closest questions.

3.2 Our Proposed Method for Automatic Creation of a Semantic Graph

Having a main concept, we need a corresponding semantic graph of keywords related to this concept. Since the teacher is the expert of the community, (s)he is responsible of making this graph and deciding what are the most significant keywords. However, one of our environment's functions is teacher's assistance, therefore, we want to make the creation of the graph of keywords an automatic process, which only requires from the teacher to provide the main concept and to validate the resulting keywords graph.

For the automatic graph creation, we need an external source of information, which could be a knowledge base (e.g. DBPedia), a lexical database (e.g. WordNet), a glossary or encyclopedia (e.g. Wikipedia). In our work, we chose Wikipedia, because of its rich and valid content. Wikipedia is one of the most popular online encyclopedias, it contains millions of articles (over 5.2 million English articles) that are densely structured through inter-wiki links connecting the pages and providing a quick way of accessing additional information.

In our proposed method, the extracted keywords will be "Article titles" from Wikipedia. In fact, according to Wikipedia Manual of Style, "*A title should be a recognizable name or description of the topic that is sufficiently precise, concise, and consistent with the titles of related articles*". Which means that titles make appropriate keywords. We also use Wikilinks, hyperlinks linking to other Wikipedia articles.

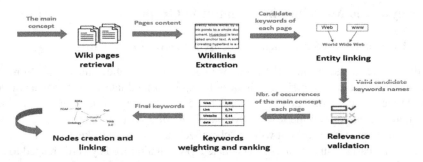

Fig. 3. Our proposed method for extracting a semantic graph of keywords from Wikipedia

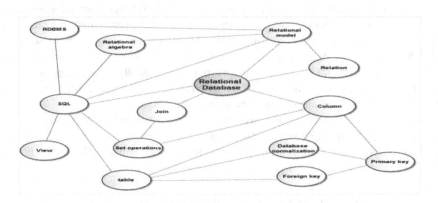

Fig. 4. The generated keywords graph for the concept "Relational Database"

The process in Fig. 3 starts with a query containing a main concept X, the steps we propose to create a semantic network of related keywords are as follows:

Wiki pages retrieval. Consists of searching for the wiki articles which contain the main concept in their titles, and retrieving their full content. (For example, we consider the concept "Relational database").

Wikilinks extraction. Extracting all hyperlinks from the retrieved pages, since they link to other wiki pages, they are meaningful, and the keywords we want to extract are most likely to be among them. So they form an initial list of candidate keywords.

Entity linking. As mentioned above, the final keywords will be Article titles. Usually, a Wikilink refers to the linked article by its exact name, however, sometimes different words are used to refer to the same article. Therefore, in this step we use Entity linking to change the candidate keywords into the corresponding article titles.

Relevance validation. In order to validate the candidate keywords relevance to the main concept (that we call X), the system extracts the content of the corresponding article for each candidate keyword, then calculates the number of occurrences of the main concept $NbOcc(X)$. If the main concept isn't mentioned at all, i.e. $NbOcc(X) = 0$, the candidate keyword will be considered irrelevant and eliminated.

Keywords weighting and ranking. Next, and in order to characterize the closeness of the found keywords to the main concept, the weight of each keyword K is calculated using the following equation: $W(K)=TF(K)*NbOcc(X)$

$TF(K)$: is the Term Frequency of K. $TF(K) = \frac{number\ of\ occurences\ of\ K}{total\ of\ all\ candidate\ keywords\ occurences}$

$NbOcc(X)$ was calculated during the relevance validation.

At this point, we obtain a list of ranked keywords according to the calculated weight.

Nodes creation and linking. Now that we have the keywords which will make the nodes of our semantic graph. We want to connect them with weighted arcs, which will represent the semantic relations between the keywords.

First, we clearly noticed based on the tests that the best ranked keywords are the most relevant to the main concept, especially the top 20% keywords, so we chose to make them the nodes directly related to the central node (main concept). (e.g. for "Relational Database", the top 20% are: Relation model, SQL, Relation, Column and Join).

Next, for each keyword Ki, we want to determine the top related keywords among the less ranked keywords. If they haven't been added in the first phase, they are added and linked directly to Ki. Otherwise, if they are already in the graph, we add new links (arcs) between them and the keyword Ki. To do this, for each keyword we follow the same extraction method used for the main concept, but at the end we only keep the keywords we already have (extracted based on the main concept), no new keywords are added. This process is repeated for each of the keywords until they are all added to the graph, or eliminated. An example of the generated graph is given in Fig. 4.

The resulting keywords graph will be validated by the teacher, who could add or remove some of the graph nodes, based on the specific content of the taught domain.

4   Conclusion and Perspectives

In this paper, we presented our approach for automatically generating a semantic graph of keywords related to a specific concept based on content extracted from an external source, the Wikipedia knowledge base. This keywords modeling is meant to be used in a keywords-based similarity in the context of knowledge reuse in the CBR cycle.

Currently, we are working on the cases' clustering around the most appropriate nodes in the generated keywords graph, which aims at obtaining pertinent results from the similarity measure and therefore having an optimal knowledge reuse. The system's performance will be evaluated based on the accuracy of the retrieved cases.

References

1. Chergui, O., Begdouri, A., Groux-Leclet, D.: CBR approach for knowledge reuse in a Community of Practice for university students. In: the 4th International Colloqium on Information Science and Technology, Tangier, Morocco October 24–26 (2016)
2. Kolodner, J.L.: An introduction to case-based reasoning. Artif. Intell. Rev. **6**, 3–34 (1992)
3. Davis, R., Shrobe, H., Szolovits, P.: What is a knowledge representation? AI Mag. **14**(1), 17–33 (1993)
4. Grundspenkis, J., Anohina-Naumeca, A.: Knowledge representation and networked schemes. http://stpk.cs.rtu.lv/sites/all/files/stpk/lecture_7.pdf
5. Fuzzy logic toolbox. http://www-rohan.sdsu.edu/doc/matlab/toolbox/fuzzy/fuzzytu5.html
6. Salem, A.M., Alfonse, M.: Ontology versus semantic networks for medical knowledge representation. In: 12th WSEAS International Conference on COMPUTERS, Heraklion, Greece, July 23–25 (2008)
7. deChambeau, A.L.: Supported Student Success: Communities of Practice in Higher Education (2014)

Adaptive Video Techniques for Informal Learning Support in Workplace Environments

Miloš Kravčík$^{(\boxtimes)}$, Petru Nicolaescu, Aarij Siddiqui,
and Ralf Klamma

Advanced Community Information Systems (ACIS),
Informatik 5, RWTH Aachen University, Aachen, Germany
{kravcik, nicolaescu, siddiqui,
klamma}@dbis.rwth-aachen.de

Abstract. Learning at the workplace is largely informal and there is a high potential to make it more effective and efficient by means of technology, especially by using the power of multimedia. The main challenge is to find relevant information segments in a vast amount of multimedia resources for a particular objective, context and user. In this paper, we aim to bridge this gap using a personalized and adaptive video consumption strategy for professional communities. Our solution highlights relevant concepts within segments of video resources by means of collaborative semantic annotations, analyzes them based on the user's learning objectives and recomposes them anew in a personalized way. As the preferred adaptation may be context dependent, the user has the opportunity to select a predefined adaptation strategy or to specify a new one easily. The approach uses a Web-based system that outputs a relevant mix of information from multiple videos, based on the user preferences and existing video annotations. The system is open source and uses an extendable approach based on micro-services. The performed evaluation investigated the usability and usefulness of the approach. It showed that effectiveness and especially efficiency of such informal learning could be indeed better with adaptive video techniques applied. On the other hand, collected ideas on how to improve the usability of the system show opportunities for its further improvements. These results suggest that personalization and adaptive techniques applied on video data are a good direction to proceed in facilitating informal learning in workplace environments.

Keywords: Informal learning at the workplace · Adaptive video

1 Introduction

Informal learning is defined as a byproduct of various activities, such as task accomplishment, interpersonal interaction, sensing the organizational culture, trial-and- error experimentation or even formal learning [1]. An example of informal learning is a workplace environment, where learning is achieved through performing tasks and one way to evaluate an individual is based on the completion of these tasks [2]. However, it can be challenging to accomplish informal learning in a workplace environment when there is a large number of individuals eager to learn, but there is a limited number of

© Springer International Publishing AG 2017
T.-T. Wu et al. (Eds.): SETE 2016, LNCS 10108, pp. 533–543, 2017.
DOI: 10.1007/978-3-319-52836-6_57

experts available to guide them. The Learning Layers project (http://learning-layers.eu/) is a European initiative to advance the informal learning at workplace by developing various social, multimedia, and collaborative tools for professional learning communities. Our research [3] highlighted the importance of videos in this context. Here, videos are regarded as a demonstrative, engaging, authentic, and intuitive way of sharing experiences. An adaptive video, in general, is a processed video that is adjusted according to a certain set of requirements. These can be based on the network, domain model, or user model parameters. In this paper, the adaptive video is composed by extracting relevant segments of multiple videos and presenting to the user a personalized and context-specific mix of these video segments, instead of the time consuming traditional approach of watching whole videos in a sequence or searching for relevant content in a video collection.

Our solution should work along with expert guidance and is not intended to replace it completely. We focus on the enhancement of informal learning at the workplace via adaptive video. The aim is to develop a system where the experts no longer have to guide every batch of new recruits. Instead, the learning and guidance is based on videos, which were recorded once, shared within a learning community, and annotated collaboratively in order to be watched in an effective manner. The proposed system, named Vaptor (acronym for Video Adaptor), implements such a scenario: a keyword-based search will return a video with relevant video segments, considering user preferences. Each video segment is specified by its start time, end time, duration and annotation. These segments are extracted collaboratively during a video annotation phase. The annotations are created with SeViAnno [4], a tool for semantic annotation, and an app named "Ach so!" (http://achso.aalto.fi). These were developed to scaffold informal learning using video annotations for the construction industry. They allow simple text annotation of videos by means of Web or mobile devices.

Using this video composition and its corresponding metadata, the learners can clarify the relevant concept, without a direct help of an expert and without the need of an extensive search. The relevance of the video segment is measured by the corresponding annotations and metadata (e.g. title, topic, description, keywords). The adaptation and personalization is based on the user model, which contains user preferences that include time, location, duration of the video segments, and other metadata, such as topics of interest. Finally, Vaptor also provides video recommendations to a user, computed from similar searches done by other peers.

In the following, we first introduce related work. Then we explain our concept and outline the basic features of our system. Implementation details are described next. Finally, we present the results of our evaluation, and conclude the paper with a summary and future work.

2   Related Work

The term "adaptive video" has been used often in the context of network and hardware specifications, e.g. bandwidth or memory [5–7]. The DANAE algorithm [8] works on the dynamic and distributed adaptation of scalable multimedia content in a context-aware environment. The algorithm targets context-aware, dynamic and flexible media adaptation, delivery, consumption and provision of quality multimedia services at a minimal cost for the end-user.

Various algorithms have been proposed to identify important activities in videos [9]. This is often materialized using summaries of videos, like storyboards [10, 11], layered timelines [12], and video skims [13]. Salim [14] attempts to decompose the video content and achieve a personalized recomposition. In a review of multimodal feature extraction to create a video summary [15] the authors have considered all three modalities (audio, visual, and linguistic) to generate summaries. Another approach [16] achieves the recomposition by splitting the video into smaller segments based on PowerPoint slides, combining ontologies and video systems.

Our approach was inspired by the FOSP method [17], which proposed a mechanism for specifying reusable adaptation strategies in educational hypermedia applications. The designer should have an opportunity to create a specific strategy for a particular purpose, considering the learning objective, learner preferences, current context, and available metadata in the domain model. This method was implemented in a system realizing personalized adaptation on the base of emotional intelligence [18].

We build on our previous work with semantic video annotations, which led to SeViAnno 2.0 [4]. This (c.f. Figure 1) is a widget-based application, which focuses on the collaborative annotation of videos for professional communities. It features multimodal annotation options on transcoded videos, using predefined annotation types (e.g. Place, Object, Agent, Event). The annotations can be added from a map or via dedicated forms in a Web widget. It enables informal learning by collaborative video browsing using annotations. After a video has been annotated, users can navigate through it using the available semantic annotations or the video timeline. Once a video is playing, the annotations corresponding to certain video segments are highlighted. Users can jump to specific video segments by using the annotations.

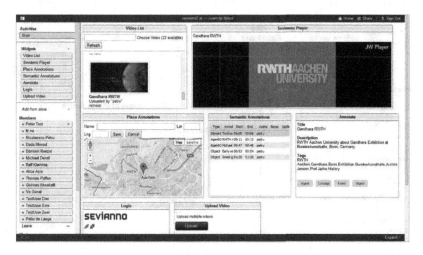

Fig. 1. SeViAnno 2.0 Interface [4]

Using SeViAnno 2.0, it is possible to only work on one video at a time – by visualizing the annotations linked to the specific video. However, it is not possible to compose and visualize the extracted content (segments) from multiple videos, which are linked by certain metadata. This feature is enabled by Vaptor through adaptation and personalization, as presented in the next sections.

3   Concept

Figure 2 outlines a scenario and system functions illustrating the process used by Vaptor to support informal learning at the workplace. The users, who are members of a professional community, can have various *roles* in different times. They can act as video uploaders (possible being also their producers), video annotators or video con-sumers. The aim is to share the knowledge and experience in the community, especially from its experienced members. The annotation process is collaborative, in order to gather and share the non-obvious and domain specific information of the community members.

In the targeted scenario, we distinguish between two *phases* – the preparation phase (using video uploading and annotation tools, e.g. SeViAnno 2.0) and the adaptation (and personalization) phase, processing the available user and video metadata. Thus, in the *preparation phase* Video Uploaders upload the video into Video Repository, available to all community members. Each video is transcoded by Transcoding Service,

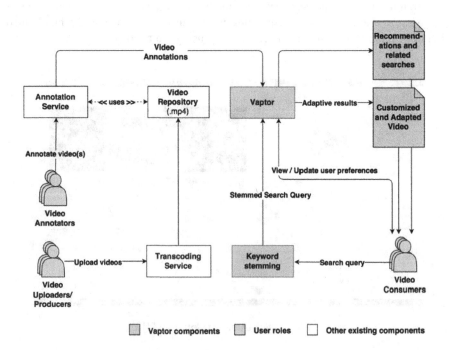

Fig. 2. Vaptor system scenario (simplified)

in order to produce a common, well-defined format for the multimedia objects used by the community. These videos can be annotated collaboratively with textual information (e.g. keywords) or predefined annotation types (e.g. Place, Object and Event as presented in [4]) by Video Annotators using Annotation Service. They are saved in Metadata Repository (can be considered as an extension of Video Repository), which is accessible through Annotation Service.

With the existing pool of annotated videos, the *adaptation phase* can start (as highlighted on the right side of Fig. 2). The personalized and adapted video consumption is supported by the Vaptor service, which based on Video Consumer's profile and Search query delivers Adapted Video data and Recommendations on similar searchers and video compilations to the particular user.

When a Video Consumer enters a Search query, this is first transformed by Keyword Stemming component, which removes all the stop words from the query and forwards it to Adaptation Component (in Vaptor). This in turn sends the query to Annotation Service, from which it receives all the related annotations. Similarly, it receives the preferences of the current user from Preference Service (in Vaptor). The component will also query Segment Analytics Service (in Vaptor) to obtain segment specific data domain, weight) for each annotation. With these two sets of data, Adaptation Service will process the result received from Annotation Service. The outcomes are sent to the user for direct playback and to Compilation Service, which compiles the segments into a new full video and stores it into the repository. Keyword Stemming component also stores the stemmed query and requests for related searches. Here, if they exist, related queries (which were used by other community members) are found and sent to Adaptation Service, and cumulative results are sent back to the user. The result saved in the database is used by Recommendation Service, which obtains user preferences from Preference Service (in Vaptor) and based on those, recommends the adaptive videos to the user. Users can update their user preferences by accessing the Preference Component (in Vaptor). They can also define the adaptive strategies, which can be chosen while entering the search query. Furthermore, users can rate video segments through the Segment Analytics component (in Vaptor), which gets the user's preferences from Preference Service (in Vaptor) and based on those, assigns and updates the weights to the video segments.

The user profile should cover all the relevant aspects of the user, which might influence the adaptation. Our user profile attributes include language, location, preferred duration, domain of interest, and level of expertise (affecting ratings and recommendations). The *user model* of Vaptor consists of the following attributes:

- Search refinement parameters: language and location of the video
- Duration of the resulting video: limit in seconds
- Semantic preferences: domain of interest (community-defined topic) and user's level of expertise (for the respective topic)
- Relevance hierarchy: calculated based on the similarity between search query and metadata (like tags, description, title) of the annotation

The adaptation in Vaptor is based on a sequence of pipes and filters. In computer science literature, this design pattern specifies the scenario of a one-directional flow and sequential processing of data by applying different filters as it passes through specified pipelines. Users have the liberty to design their own, personalized adaptive strategy, choosing various filters and applying them in their desired sequence. An example of a possible sequence of application is illustrated in Fig. 3. Here, after the search is performed and results are obtained from the annotation service, the annotations are first ordered based on the relevance of the query (and the metadata of the annotation). The annotations are then filtered based on language. The results are taken as an input by duration trimming, which ensures the duration of the resulting playlist is approximately the size of user's preferred duration. Then annotations get ordered either by location or segment weight.

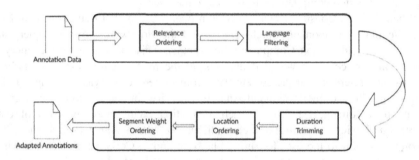

Fig. 3. Adaptive pipeline and alternative strategies

An adaptive strategy is mainly built up from the filters that are applied on the data and the order in which those are applied. Once defined, strategies can be used by other community users directly while performing the search. This feature provides users with a greater control over the obtained results. The following video adaptation filters have been predefined, in accordance to the user preferences presented above:

- Relevance Ordering: calculated based on the text similarity between search query and metadata of the annotation (e.g., tags, description, title)
- Language Filtering: the preferred language of the user is compared with language of the video, in order to filter out non-matching objects
- Duration Trimming: the playlist is composed taking user's preferred duration into consideration for the final result
- Location Ordering: video segments are shown based on the user's location
- Segment Weight Ordering: the playlist is ordered based on weight of the video segment, which depends on its rating

4   Implementation

Vaptor is implemented as a Web application, which is available on the Web as well as on smartphones through the browser by using a responsive Web interface. The main language of development is Java for the server side, and Javascript, HTML, and CSS for the frontend. The architecture of Vaptor is built from multiple components, some of which were previously implemented and used within the Learning Layers project. These components involve Cloud Video Transcoder (ClViTra) and Semantic Video Annotation (SeViAnno 2.0) [4]. Communication with SeViAnno and ClViTra is done using their respective RESTful APIs.

More specifically, Vaptor is based on a set of micro-services, according to a widgetizing methodology specified in [19]. Micro-services are small and independent services, which compose various functionalities of the application. These are designed to perform dedicated tasks and support the modular Vaptor architecture approach. The aim is to enable an agile community-oriented development, deployment, update, and replacement of services. The Vaptor services are the following ones: Adapter Service, Video Compiler Service, User Preference Service, Recommendation Service, Orchestration Service, and Segment Analytics Service.

The user interface of Vaptor (Fig. 4) is based on twelve ROLE SDK [19] widgets. They communicate with various micro-services and with each other. Widgets under Vaptor are placed in three different areas, called activities: Video activity, User preference activity and Alternative adaptation activity.

Fig. 4. User interface of Vaptor (Video activity)

5 Evaluation

In order to validate the user experience with Vaptor and its relevance for informal learning, we have performed user evaluation in a simulated community environment. The evaluation scenario was divided into three tasks. The first two tasks assessed the contribution of Vaptor to informal learning, whereas the last task evaluated its usability and individual features. In the first two tasks users were asked to search for certain terms in a predefined collection of videos, in an effort to learn certain notions on a given task. In order to assess the difference compared with existing non-adaptive applications, one task was performed with Vaptor, using the adapted videos, and another using the SeViAnno 2.0 tool (explained in Sect. 2). After they have viewed the video results, users were asked a set of questions, evaluating their learning process. In the third task, users were formally introduced to Vaptor and given a set of keywords, they were allowed to freely search and explore through the application and understand its features. After this session, users were requested to fill out a questionnaire, comprising of questions about the application, its features, and their usefulness.

Altogether we had 20 participants that used Vaptor in individual sessions. 14 participants belonged to the field of Computer Science, whereas 6 were from other study areas. 75% of the participants had learning experience using videos, but only 15% of them have used a video adaptation tool before.

The first two tasks contained videos with information about microchips and videos from the healthcare domain (cardiopulmonary resuscitation – CPR). Before each of the first two tasks, the users were asked about their knowledge of the topics. Afterwards, they were asked questions about certain domain details and asked to search for videos containing the right answer. It is worth mentioning here that users were not knowledgeable in the given topics, therefore simulating a novice community user. For learning of the microchip construction, the average percentage of correct answers when participants used Vaptor was 60%, whereas while using SeViAnno it was 43%. Making the same comparison for the second task, where user learned about the procedure of giving a CPR, they scored on average 88% using Vaptor, whereas using SeViAnno the average score was 80%. These scores are based on the number of correct answers given to the questions for each topic. Even though the number of participants was rather limited, the findings suggest that Vaptor keeps the user focused on a specific topic, which can represent an indicator towards informal learning.

In the same set of tasks users were also analyzed for the time they spent in learning about the two topics. When the users learned about the microchip using Vaptor, they spent, on average, 05:03 min, whereas when using SeViAnno they spent 08:33 min. In their next task when they learned about giving a CPR, they spent on average 04:32 min using Vaptor, and 07:12 min using SeViAnno. Before reaching any conclusions on this result, it is important to know the factors on which this data is dependent. Each system used the same video and annotation repository for their tasks, however since Vaptor shows the user only relevant data, the playlist created from each system was slightly different for the same topic. The playlist was adapted to the user's given profile and search query in Vaptor. This comparison indicates that Vaptor does assist a user in learning more efficiently by reducing the time required and still getting better results in comparison.

During the third task users were encouraged to explore through the system, and understand all the individual features of Vaptor. By analyzing various sections of the survey it was found out that language was the most liked filter in Vaptor. It was favored by a majority of 15 out of 20 participants, rating it as extremely useful. On the other hand, location based ordering received some questionable ratings regarding its usefulness. Several participants were not very thrilled to have this feature in the system – some showed concerns in giving away their current location, while others were just interested to see more open results.

We also evaluated the component where the user can define and use adaptive strategies. The usage of various adaptive strategies was favored without a doubt by around 60% of the participants, whereas the specification (design) of adaptive strategies was favored by around 50%.

At the beginning of the evaluation session the participants were given a chance to use the systems without any briefing. Once the goal of Vaptor was explained along with the idea of video segments concatenated together for easy viewing, the participants were appreciative of the idea and considering it novel and efficient. For this particular reason many of them rated Vaptor to be more productive than currently available commercial tools like YouTube and Vimeo for the purpose of learning.

6 Conclusion

In this paper, a Web based video adaptation tool is presented, which exploits user preferences and video annotations as primary means of adaptation. An innovative feature is an easy specification of alternative adaptation strategies by the user and their selection based on the user needs and learning context. The aim was to facilitate the informal learning by automating the process, which traditionally consumes significant amount of time and effort.

Our findings from the evaluation phase indicated that majority of the users have not experienced video based online learning in such a scenario before. They strongly believed the idea of basing the whole learning process on video segments, instead of the whole video was unique. According to them, it helps the user get exposed to only a tailored set of information, which is adapted to their own preferences, saving them significant amount of time and effort. Conclusively it can be said, that our evaluation suggests that Vaptor possesses the capability to support and contribute to online learning in its own different perspective. Of course, we are aware of the limitations, including the number of participants involved in our experiments.

During the evaluation, it was found that there were some new features that users recommended, believing that they would add value to the system. It was recommended that video segments (annotations) can be ordered based on their date, and also an option to bookmark them would improve the usability. Users were interested in seeing comments to a video segment (annotation). There were also other comments and suggestions related to new features, improvements in the current ones, and recommendations regarding the user interface.

Our workplace learning research continues in the projects WEKIT (http://www.wekit.eu/), and VIRTUS (http://www.virtus-project.eu). They deal with wearable experiences for knowledge intensive training and development of a virtual VET Centre, respectively.

Acknowledgments. The presented research work was partially funded by the 7th Framework Programme large-scale integrated project Learning Layers (grant no: 318209), the H2020 project WEKIT (grant no: 687669), and the Erasmus + project VIRTUS (grant no: 562222-EPP-1-2015-1-EL-EPPKA3-PI-FORWARD).

References

1. Marsick, V., Watkins, K.: Informal and incidental learning. New Dir. Adult Continuing Educ. **2001**(89), 25–34 (2001)
2. Eraut, M.: Informal learning in the workplace. Stud. Continuing Educ. **26**(2), 247–273 (2010)
3. Kravcik, M., Nicolaescu, P., Klamma, R.: Informal learning at the workplace via adaptive video. In: Proceedings of the UMAP 2014, ProS: Workshop on UMAP Projects Synergy, 1181, pp. 35–38 (2014)
4. Nicolaescu, P., Klamma, R.: SeViAnno 2.0: web-enabled collaborative semantic video annotation beyond the obvious. In: Proceedings of the 12th International Workshop on Content-Based Multimedia Indexing (CBMI), (Klagenfurt, Austria, June 18–20, 2014), pp. 1–6. IEEE (2014)
5. Aharoni, A., Khirman, S., Taits, E., Ariel, O.: System for Adaptive Video/Audio Transport Over a Network. Patent (2000)
6. Miller, K., Quacchio, E., Gennari, G., Wolisz, A.: Adaptation algorithm for adaptive streaming over HTTP. In: Proceedings of the 19th International Packet Video Workshop (PV), pp. 173–178 (2012)
7. Liu, C., Bouazizi, I., Gabbouj, M.: Rate adaptation for adaptive HTTP streaming. In: Proceedings of the Second Annual ACM Conference on Multimedia Systems, pp. 169–174 (2011)
8. Wien, M., Cazoulat, R., Graffunder, A., Hutter, A., Amon, P.: Real-time system for adaptive video streaming based on SVC. IEEE Trans. Circ. Syst. Video Technol. **17**(9), 1227–1237 (2007)
9. Kankanhalli, M., Rui, Y.: Application potential of multimedia information retrieval. IEEE **96**(4), 712–720 (2008)
10. Boreczky, J., Girgensohn, A., Golovchinsky, G., Uchihashi, S.: An interactive comic book presentation for exploring video. In: Proceedings of the SIGCHI Conference on Human Factors in Computing Systems, pp. 185–192 (2000)
11. Uchihashi, S., Foote, J., Girgensohn, A., Boreczky, J.: Video manga: generating semantically meaningful video summaries. In: Proceedings of the 7th ACM International Conference on Multimedia (Part 1), pp. 383–392 (1999)
12. Haubold, A., Kender, J.: Vast mm: multimedia browser for presentation video. In: Proceedings of the 6th ACM International Conference on Image and Video Retrieval, pp. 41–48 (2007)
13. Christel, M., Smith, M., Taylor, C., Winkler, D.: Evolving video skims into useful multimedia abstractions. In: Proceedings of the SIGCHI Conference on Human Factors in Computing Systems, pp. 171–178 (1998)
14. Salim, F.A.: From artifact to content source: using multimodality in video to support personalized recomposition. In: Ricci, F., Bontcheva, K., Conlan, O., Lawless, S. (eds.) UMAP 2015. LNCS, vol. 9146, pp. 391–396. Springer, Heidelberg (2015). doi:10.1007/978-3-319-20267-9_36
15. Evangelopoulos, G., Zlatintsi, A., Potamianos, A., Maragos, P., Rapantzikos, K., Skoumas, G., Avrithis, G.: Multimodal saliency and Fusion for movie summarization based on aural, visual, and textual attention. IEEE Trans. Multimedia **15**(7), 1553–1568 (2013)
16. Dong, A., Li, H.: Ontology-driven annotation and access of presentation video data. J. Theor. Appl. Inf. Technol. **4**(9), 840–860 (2008)
17. Kravcik, M.: The Speciffcation of adaptation strategy by FOSP method. In: Proceedings of AH2004 Conference, pp. 429–435 (2004)

18. Damjanovic, V., Kravcik, M.: Using emotional intelligence in personalized adaptation. In Sugumaran, V. (ed.), Intelligent Information Technologies: Concepts, Methodologies, Tools, and Applications, pp. 1716–1742. IGI Publishing (2007)
19. Nicolaescu, P., Klamma, R.: A methodology and tool support for widget-based web application development. In: Cimiano, P., Frasincar, F., Houben, G.-J., Schwabe, D. (eds.) ICWE 2015. LNCS, vol. 9114, pp. 515–532. Springer, Heidelberg (2015). doi:10.1007/978-3-319-19890-3_33

Workshop on User Modeling for Web-Based Learning

Towards a Characterization of Educational Material: An Analysis of Coursera Resources

Carlo De Medio[1](✉), Fabio Gasparetti[1], Carla Limongelli[1],
Matteo Lombardi[3], Alessandro Marani[3], Filippo Sciarrone[1],
and Marco Temperini[2]

[1] Engineering Department, Roma Tre University,
Via Della Vasca Navale 79, 00146 Roma, Italy
`carlo.demedio@uniroma3.it,`
`{gaspare,limongel,sciarro}@ing.uniroma3.it`
[2] Department of Computer, Control and Management Engineering,
Sapienza University, Via Ariosto 25, 00184 Roma, Italy
`marte@dis.uniroma1.it`
[3] School of Information and Communication Technology, Griffith University,
170 Kessels Road, Nathan, QLD 4111, Australia
`{matteo.lombardi,alessandro.marani}@griffithuni.edu.au`

Abstract. When teachers are surfing the Web to search suitable learning material for their courses it would be very important that web resources were characterized to restrict the scope of the search. Hence, it arises the need of finding characterizing properties for learning materials. This paper proposes an initial reflection on this issue. We exploit the huge potential of the MOOC, in particular Coursera, to discover new educational information that might characterize material of MOOCs. This goal is achieved by means of data mining techniques. Two types of features about resources have been discovered: teaching context and resource attributes. The resulting knowledge can be very helpful for a more accurate recommendation of resources to the particular teaching context of an instructor, as well as improving the creation and arrangement of learning activities.

Keywords: Data mining · MOOC · Learning resources features

1 Introduction

The search and reuse of Web educational material is a difficult and time-consuming activity for teachers. Many elements play an important role in this search, such as the resource content, the learning objective, the style of presentation, the target audience, and so on. A teacher might need to be guided in this search.

A recent trend in web-based learning is the delivery of Massive Open Online Courses (MOOC). These courses are offered worldwide with many instructors and students involved in the process of teaching and learning respectively. MOOCs are collected on platforms like Coursera[1], where hundreds of instructors deliver thousands

---

[1] https://www.coursera.org/.

© Springer International Publishing AG 2017
T.-T. Wu et al. (Eds.): SETE 2016, LNCS 10108, pp. 547–557, 2017.
DOI: 10.1007/978-3-319-52836-6_58

of courses to thousands of students. Therefore, MOOCs represent a very rich mine of resources, teaching and learning data [7].

This contribution aims to analyze typical educational materials taken from MOOCs, Coursera in particular, with the aim of finding some characteristics that can contribute to guide teachers during the search of the educational material.

The analysis is performed on Coursera data that are hosted in the dataset DAJEE [4]. Such dataset is a collection of educational data extracted from Coursera at the end of 2015. Now that Cousera no longer offers previews of their courses and resources, DAJEE remains, to the best of our knowledge, the only publicly available source of structured educational information about this MOOC repository.

The first information comes from the structure of the resources. In this scope, we propose a novel attribute called *specificity* of a resource. The other information is about the teaching context where a resource has been delivered in by instructors. We propose to analyse this aspect exploiting the hierarchical structure of DAJEE. In this way, a resource is described also by data about its instructor. This information seems to provide a better characterization of resources on MOOCs. We expect to provide benefits to many studies focused on recommending teaching resources [3, 10, 11] and evaluating diverse recommendation strategies [12]. In addition, also other MOOC platforms like edX[2] and Udacity[3] present a structure of their courses similar to Coursera, so the same approach can be applied to other popular systems as well.

In the next section we present the dataset DAJEE and introduce the *specificity*. In Sect. 3, we demonstrate that *specificity* is suitable for characterizing educational resources. Section 4 is about the discovery of teaching information able to characterize the context where MOOCs instructors deliver their resources. In Sect. 5, we show how the new data about resources structure and teaching context can be exploited for a comprehensive contextualization of educational resources. Finally, Sect. 6 presents our conclusions and possible future works.

2   The Dataset DAJEE

Coursera is one of the largest platforms which hosts MOOCs, and DAJEE [4] is a MySql DataBase[4] built from the crawling of MOOCs hosted on Coursera that stores structured information on the usage of more than 20,000 resources in 407 courses by 484 instructors.

In particular, it stores two types if information: those that can be directly derived from Coursera, such as university, instructor, course name, lesson name, concept name, resources (videos) associated to that concept and their duration (in sec). There are other information non directly provided from Coursera, such as the concept map associated to a course and its related sequencing. This entity connects one course with its concepts.

---

[2] https://www.edx.org/.

[3] https://www.udacity.com/.

[4] DAJEE can be accessed publicly for research purposes only, following the authors' approval. Apply for it by filling in the form at http://144.6.235.142/dajee.

We apply text-mining tools to the transcripts of resources for discovering further knowledge about instructors and courses, so as to support course and teaching planning and delivering.

2.1   Information About Resources in MOOCs

Popular MOOC platforms such as Coursera, edX and Udacity offer just basic details about their educational material. In general, the data about educational resources hosted on MOOCs are limited to *title*, *type* (e.g., a video) and *duration* (e.g., length of a video or number of questions in a quiz). This is a limitation in reusing resources from MOOCs with other systems. As an example, smart systems in Technology Enhanced Learning cannot provide an effective recommendation of resources coming from MOOCs because there are no educational data.

In order to fulfil such gap, this contribution aims to extract additional data from the content of the resources on Coursera, enriching the description of resources from MOOCs stored in the DAJEE dataset. The methodology here proposed does not depend on the specific platform, because all the different MOOC providers offer the aforementioned basic details about their material. In particular, we propose to extract a set of keywords from the content of the resources (or transcripts in case of videos). Such keywords are then exploited for computing a novel characteristic of a resource, called *specificity*.

2.2   Specificity of a Resource

In this work we propose a novel descriptive information about educational resources in MOOCs, namely the *specificity* of a resource. Such value is computed exploiting the keywords contained in the resource content. The set of keywords consists of the most frequent terms in the transcript of a resource, after removing the stop words and stemming the terms with the Porter stemming algorithm [14]. We propose the following formula for computing the specificity of a resource r:

$$Specificity(r) = \frac{\sum_{t \in keywords} TermFrequency(t)}{\text{\# of words in the resource content}}$$

where t is a term from the resource content and *keywords* is the set of keywords. In practice, the specificity is the ratio of the frequencies of the keywords contained in the resource over the total number of words of the resource. The rationale behind our proposal is that very focused resources present a high frequency of the keywords in their content, leading to a high specificity (close to 1). Otherwise, more general or conversational resources have a high frequency of terms which are not keywords, presenting a low specificity value (close to 0).

The *specificity* of a resource is also a characteristic suitable for describing the instructor that uses such resource during her teaching. In particular, the style of an instructor in delivering an educational material is reflected in the specificity of the resources selected for that task. Our rationale is that straight-to-the-point instructors tend to use very specific resources, while others who adopt a more conversational approach are likely to prefer resources with low specificity. Such consideration is exploited in Sect. 4 of this paper as a feature for clustering instructors with similar characteristics.

3   Deducing Educational Traits of Resources in Coursera

As said in the previous section, only few characteristics of educational resources are offered by Coursera. In essence, only the *length* can be used as a descriptive feature. For this reason, we propose to compute also the *specificity* of each resource (see Sect. 2.2). To understand if those two features can well describe the educational traits of resources in Coursera, and in general on MOOCs, we used the popular machine learning software WEKA [6] for clustering the resources using (i) only the *length*, and (ii) both *length* and *specificity* of the resources. Evaluation of the 1D clustering on *length* is performed in order to demonstrate that the addition of the *specificity* to the feature set improves the clustering, hence *specificity* is a valid descriptive feature. Two different clustering algorithms, K-Means and Expectation-Maximization (EM) are performed. In particular for K-Means, all the values in the range from 2 to around 3000 (a quarter of the total number of resources involved) have been used as k. Once the algorithms terminate, the clustering configurations are evaluated using the Calinski-Harabasz (CH) validity index [2]. The higher the CH index value, the better the clustering. The instances to be clustered are 11,853 which is the amount of resources with transcripts in English.

Validity indices are usually affected by the dataset as well as the clustering algorithm [13, 15]. Hence, it is not possible to compare the CH index values of different feature sets. However, the results are still comparable in terms of the number of clusters generated by the best configuration indicated by the index, called k^* in this study. The CH index formula says thata lower number of clusters gives a better value for the index, i.e. the compactness of the clusters is improved when k^* decreases [13, 15].

Table 1 shows a remarkable drop of k^* introducing the *specificity* feature, from 63 to only 16 clusters in the best configuration of K-Means. The overall trend of the CH index for different values of k is shown in Fig. 1. About EM, it is possible to notice that including the *specificity* in the feature set, the number of clusters is nearly the same, 12 instead of the 10 clusters recognized considering only the *length*. At the end of this evaluation, we can state that the proposed *specificity* significantly improves the clustering of resources using K-Means, hence it can be used for characterizing the resources on MOOCs.

Nevertheless, educational resources should be also described by information about the teaching traits. Some of them are related to the teaching context, expressing in which teaching situation a resource is more appropriate. This contexts can additionally distinguish the resources according to their teaching properties by analysing how they

Table 1. Evaluation of clustering produced by K-Means and EM with *length* only and with *length* and *specificity*. For K-Means, only the best results are reported.

Features	Algorithm	Clusters	CH index
Length	K-Means	63	$1.64x10^8$
Length	EM	10	28254
Length and Specificity	K-Means	16	3766
Length and Specificity	EM	12	5201

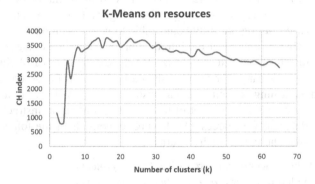

Fig. 1. The overall trend of the CH index according to different values of k for K-Means performed on *length* and *specificity* of the resources. CH presents the highest value when k is set to 16 clusters.

have been delivered by instructors. In this way, a recommender system can suggest to the instructor a resource with a certain structure (e.g., *length* and *specificity*), and also used in specific teaching contexts. Thus, in the following section the teaching data stored in DAJEE are analysed for contextualizing the educational resources on MOOCs with the aim of deducing their teaching properties.

4 Discovering Teaching Contexts in Coursera

The previous section has shown that resources coming from Coursera, and more in general from MOOC platforms, can be characterized by their *length* and a novel feature called *specificity*. More in depth, the length of a resource is provided by the platform which hosts the resource, while the specificity is computed out of the frequency of the keywords appearing in the content of the resource.

Following the principle that an instructor is influenced by the teaching context when choosing which resource to deliver, in this contribution we are exploring the possibility of contextualizing the resources with such information. In a previous work, hierarchical clustering has been applied to instructors, courses and lessons extracted from Coursera and stored in DAJEE [9]. In that study, an instructor has a profile made of three features, namely average duration of resources (*avg_length_resources*), the average number of resources per concept (*avg_number_resources*) and the average duration of concepts (*avg_length_concepts*) according to her teaching experience. In DAJEE, a lesson is made of one or more concepts, and each concept can be taught using one or more educational resources. Hence, the duration of a concept is the sum of the duration of all the associated resources.

After proving the validity of the *specificity* in characterizing resources (see Sect. 3), we add the average specificity of the resources delivered by an instructor to the set of features of the instructor profile. This average value is called *avg_specificity_resources*. The same evaluation presented in [9] has been set up, namely a clustering of instructors using K-Means with K from 2 to 242 (which is the half of the number of instructors in DAJEE) and then selecting the clustering with the highest CH index value. In this way, the results of our clustering are fully comparable to previous findings.

Results in Table 2 shows that the introduction of the attribute *avg_specificity_resources* to the features proposed in [9] does not change the number of clusters, which remains This suggests that other features should be involved for describing the characteristics of the teaching context where an instructor has selected a resource. For that reason, we propose an alternative set of features for profiling an instructor aiming to contextualize educational resources. Our feature set consists of the following average values (in brackets, the corresponding variable):

- Duration of the concepts delivered (*avg_length_concepts*)
- Number of video resources (*avg_number_resources_video*)
- Specificity of the resources (*avg_specificity_resources*)
- Semantic density of the lessons taught (*avg_semantic_density_lessons*)
- Number of concepts in the lessons (*avg_concepts_in_lessons*)
- Duration of the lessons (*avg_length_lessons*)
- Duration of the courses delivered (*avg_length_courses*)
- Duration of video resources (*avg_length_resources_video*)

The clustering of instructors in DAJEE is executed again for testing whether or not there is an improvement using the new feature set. As done previously, such test is performed using K-Means with K in the range from 2 to the half of the instructor instances in DAJEE and selecting the best *k* value according to the CH index.

Table 2. Evaluation of clustering of instructors in DAJEE adding *average specificity of the resources* to the set of features coming from [9], namely *average duration of resources*, *average number of resources per concept* and *average duration of concepts*. Only the results of the best configurations of K-Means are reported.

Features	Algorithm	Clusters	CH index
Same of [9]	**K-Means**	2	827
Same of [9] and *avg_specificity_resources*	**K-Means**	2	801
avg_length_concepts, *avg_number_resources_video*, *avg_specificity_resources*, *avg_semantic_density_lessons*, *avg_concepts_in_lessons*, *avg_length_lessons*, *avg_length_courses*, *avg_length_resources_video*	**K-Means**	7	99.221

Table 2 presents the results of the three different feature sets exploited in this contribution. The best clustering algorithm for instructors is K-Means with the proposed eight features and $k = 7$, as indicated by the CH index shown in Fig. 2, and the centroids of these 7 clusters are reported in Table 3. Therefore, the contextual information in our feature set is able to detect 7 classes of instructors. From a recommender system perspective, it is preferred to have more than only 2 classes of users for enhancing the precision of the recommendation process.

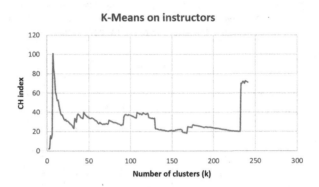

Fig. 2. The CH index for different execution of K-Means on instructors profiled by the proposed eight features, using k from 2 to 242. The best value of CH is obtained when k is set to 7 clusters.

In order to understand the relevance and the possible redundancy of all the eight proposed variables, we set up a feature selection process using the statistical software R. The 7 clusters are used as classes of instructors in DAJEE. Such classes are exploited for training the prototype-based supervised classification algorithm Learning Vector Quantization (LVQ) [8]. LVQ is used with a repeated 10 fold cross-validation for computing the importance of each variable. Then, the Recursive Feature Elimination (RFE) algorithm [5] is executed for selecting the predictors, namely the minimum sub-set of features able to represent all the data with high accuracy. The selection function for RFE is Random Forest with non-repeated 10 fold cross validation. The output of the feature selection process is reported in Fig. 3, where the chart on the left indicates that RFE selected five variables out of eight, while on the right hand side the variables are reported in descendent order of importance as computed by LVQ. The five most important variables form the set of features able to characterize the instructors in DAJEE, namely *avg_length_concepts*, *avg_number_resources_video*, *avg_specificity_resources*, *avg_semantic_density_lessons* and *avg_concepts_in_lessons*.

In conclusion, we demonstrated that the proposed set of features improves the clustering of instructors, with five of the initial 8 features suitable for characterizing 7 different teaching profiles.

Table 3. Centroids of the seven clusters of instructors considering the eigth features extracted from the data in DAJEE. The five features that are selected after the feature selection are reported in bold.

Feature	Cluster 1	Cluster 2	Cluster 3	Cluster 4	Cluster 5	Cluster 6	Cluster 7
avg_length_concepts	**82.6344**	**13.2174**	**17.1858**	**30.8591**	**9.6296**	**23.5608**	**31.1683**
avg_number_resources_video	**5.6433**	**1.2476**	**1.8241**	**1.8045**	**1.6538**	**2.2115**	**2.3411**
avg_specificty_resources	**0.1939**	**0.2572**	**0.2985**	**0.2015**	**0.0127**	**0.2314**	**0**
avg_semantic_density_lessons	**0.0181**	**0.0848**	**0.0972**	**0.0453**	**0.2593**	**0.0708**	**0.0564**
avg_concepts_in_lessons	**1.2124**	**8.9185**	**4.5733**	**4.3256**	**1.7176**	**2.3744**	**3.658**
avg_length_resources_video	11.0922	9.2335	6.9887	15.4728	4.371	8.3982	9.2029
avg_length_courses	803.4796	1799.4367	525.6792	914.9061	220.125	458.3026	596.1678
avg_length_lessons	100.8826	114.3046	75.6398	130.221	16.8607	53.7307	99.1148

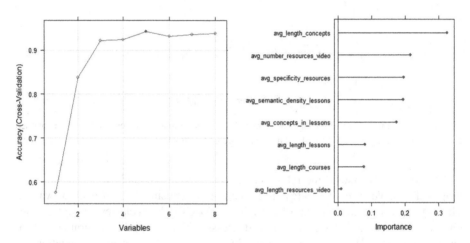

Fig. 3. The details about the feature selection process. On the left the results of RFE algorithm, on the right the LVQ output.

5   Characterization of Resources Using Teaching Data

From the previous section, 7 different teaching contexts have been discovered and characterized with five variables coming from a feature selection process. These variables can then be used for characterizing resources according to their teaching properties as described by the teaching context. However, not all of them are useful for describing the resources; here some considerations about two redundant variables for this scope. The variable *average specificity of resources* is already expressed by the resource attributes. Also the *avg_number_concepts_in_lessons* information is already included in the semantic density of lessons, which is the ratio of the number of concepts over the duration of a lesson. Hence, the semantic density is preferred expressing a more interesting aspect of a lesson.

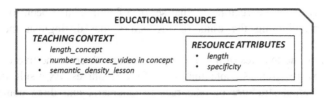

Fig. 4. The characterization of Coursera resources as available in the dataset DAJEE, formed by resources attributes (internal layer) and teaching context (external layer).

Hence, data of concepts and lessons contextualizes the resources defining where they have been delivered in. This additional contextual information is demonstrated to represent diverse teaching contexts, and so those resources that are more appropriate for a particular context. A personalised recommendation of resources that complies with a teaching context would benefit from our comprehensive characterization, as supported by the findings of the previous section. In fact, when it is not possible to deduce further information, contextual information may still help in implicitly define the characteristics of objects, teaching resources in our case [1].

To sum up, the resources in DAJEE are characterized by two types of data: *resource attributes* and *teaching context*, as Fig. 4 summarises. The external layer characterizes the resources focusing on their teaching properties, while the internal layer describes their own structure. Both set of variables have been proved to characterize teaching resources and teaching contexts respectively.

6 Conclusions and Future Work

During this study, we have presented the teaching data that are in Coursera and available in the dataset DAJEE. The dataset itself contains very little information about resources delivered in Coursera, because of the structure of MOOCs. However, this study proposes the *specificity*, a new attribute for describing the conciseness of a material about its keywords, in combination with some teaching properties.

The *specificity* feature can be automatically extracted by a text-analysis of the content of a resource. The clustering of resources has shown an improvement using this feature against not using it. This result remarks the enhanced characterization of resources with their *specificity*. K-Means (with k from 2 to half of the number of resources) and EM clustering algorithms have been used and evaluated with the CH cluster-validity index. CH points to K-Means with $k = 16$ as the best clustering result, so 16 clusters of resources are in Coursera when considering also the *specificity*. Instead, without *specificity*, 63 clusters are identified.

Also the teaching properties of resources can be deduced analysing the teaching data. Eight elements that describe the profile of teaching of instructors on Coursera have been detected. With these features, the same clustering algorithms used previously have been run, producing the best clustering with K-Means when $k = 7$, according to the CH index as shown in Fig. 2. The 7 centroids of instructors are reported in Table 3. Starting from these 8 features, a feature selection phase has been conducted using the clusters as *class* of the instructors. A final set of 5 features have been found relevant (see Fig. 3), highlighting the traits of instructors that distinguish their teaching contexts.

In addition to the features of the resources structure, three of the five variables of a teaching context are used as contextual data of the resources. As result, two features describe the internal structure of resources in Coursera, and three contextual data present their teaching properties. These two layers of characterization of resources can be extracted from other MOOCs similarly to Coursera. Interestingly, the contextual data allow the future application of context-aware recommendation of resources with a very little information. As also proved in this study, with the identification of such features, data mining techniques can now be applied to resources and instructors for extraction of further knowledge.

We also suggest the inclusion of such features in DAJEE, so that they are ready-to-use by other researchers in the field.

References

1. Adomavicius, G., Tuzhilin, A.: Context-aware recommender systems. In: Ricci, F., Rokach, L., Shapira, B., Kantor, P.B. (eds.) Recommender Systems Handbook, pp. 217–253. Springer, New York (2011)
2. Calinski, T., Harabasz, J.: A dendrite method for cluster analysis. Commun. Stat. Theory Methods **3**(1), 1–27 (1974)
3. Drachsler, H., Verbert, K., Santos, O., Manouselis, N.: Panorama of recommender systems to support learning. In: Ricci, F., Rokach, L., Shapira, B. (eds.) 2nd Handbook on Recommender Systems, pp. 421–451. Springer, New York (2015)
4. Estivill-Castro, V., Limongelli, C., Lombardi, M., Marani, A.: Dajee: a dataset of joint educational entities for information retrieval in technology enhanced learning. In: Proceedings of the 39th International ACM SIGIR Conference on Research and Development in Information Retrieval, pp. 681–684. ACM (2016)
5. Granitto, P.M., Furlanello, C., Biasioli, F., Gasperi, F.: Recursive feature elimination with random forest for ptr-ms analysis of agroindustrial products. Chemometr. Intell. Lab. Syst. **83**(2), 83–90 (2006)
6. Hall, M., Frank, E., Holmes, G., Pfahringer, B., Reutemann, P., Witten, I.H.: The weka data mining software: an update. SIGKDD Explor. Newsl. **11**(1), 10–18 (2009)
7. Kay, J., Reimann, P., Diebold, E., Kummerfeld, B.: Moocs: so many learners, so much potential. Technology **52**(1), 49–67 (2013)
8. Kohonen, T.: Learning vector quantization. In: Self-Organizing Maps, pp. 175–189. Springer, Heidelberg (1995)
9. Limongelli, C., Lombardi, M., Marani, A.: Towards the recommendation of resources in coursera. In: Micarelli, A., et al. (eds.) ITS 2016. LNCS, vol. 9684, p. 461. Springer, Heidelberg (2016)
10. Limongelli, C., Lombardi, M., Marani, A., Sciarrone, F.: A teaching-style based social network for didactic building and sharing. In: Lane, H.,Chad, Yacef, K., Mostow, J., Pavlik, P. (eds.) AIED 2013. LNCS, vol. 7926, pp. 774–777. Springer, Heidelberg (2013). doi:10.1007/978-3-642-39112-5_110

11. Limongelli, C., Lombardi, M., Marani, A., Sciarrone, F., Temperini, M.: A recommendation module to help teachers build courses through the moodle learning management system. In: New Review of Hypermedia and Multimedia, pp. 1–25 (2015)
12. Lombardi, M., Marani, A.: A comparative framework to evaluate recommender systems in technology enhanced learning: a case study. In: Lagunas, O.P., Alcántara, O.H., Figueroa, G. A. (eds.) MICAI 2015. LNCS, vol. 9414, pp. 155–170. Springer, Heidelberg (2015). doi:10. 1007/978-3-319-27101-9_11
13. Maulik, U., Bandyopadhyay, S.: Performance evaluation of some clustering algorithms and validity indices. IEEE Trans. Pattern Anal. Mach. Intell. 24(12), 1650–1654 (2002)
14. Porter, M.F.: An algorithm for suffix stripping. Program 14(3), 130–137 (1980)
15. Xu, R., Wunsch, D., et al.: Survey of clustering algorithms. IEEE Trans. Neural Netw. 16(3), 645–678 (2005)

Agent-Based Simulation for Agricultural Learning Resource Recommendation Based on Geographical Similarities

Wei Chen[1,2] and Zhemin Li[1,2(✉)]

[1] Agricultural Information Institute,
Chinese Academy of Agricultural Sciences, Beijing, China
{chenwei,lizhemin}@caas.cn
[2] Key Laboratory of Agri-Information Service Technology,
Ministry of Agriculture, Beijing, China

Abstract. As the development of information technology and intelligent tutoring, web-based learning has been widely used nowadays to help people acquire knowledge in a flexible way. Especially, web-based learning services can greatly facilitate farmers to gain knowledge on farming. It is observed that learning goals and preferences tend to be localized for farming knowledge due to similar climate and soil conditions in an area. Therefore, geographical information can be utilized to recommend agricultural learning resources. In this paper, an agricultural learning resource recommendation approach is proposed using agent-based simulation that takes geographical information into account. The agent simulation environment is introduced. A distance-aware agent reputation model is presented. A multi-agent collaborative recommendation approach is proposed. Simulation experiments are conducted for the evaluation of the proposed approach. The results show good performance of it.

Keywords: Agent-based simulation · Agricultural learning · Recommender system

1 Introduction

In recent years, as the development of information technology and intelligent tutoring techniques, web-based learning has been widely applied in our daily lives. Learning resources are generated in a collaborative manner. Finding appropriate data that are suitable for a learner to learn becomes an important issue. On the other hand, the way that learners acquire knowledge changes in web-based learning systems so that it becomes more learner centric compared with conventional learning style which is teacher centric [3]. In order to enhance learner centric learning, it is important to acquire the goals and preferences of learners in a specific learning scenario [7]. Therefore, user modeling techniques in web-based learning have attracted researchers' attentions.

With the rapid development of modern precision agriculture technology and agricultural information technology, farmers increasingly require ubiquitous assistance with their farming work. Personalized web-based learning services can greatly facilitate

© Springer International Publishing AG 2017
T.-T. Wu et al. (Eds.): SETE 2016, LNCS 10108, pp. 558–563, 2017.
DOI: 10.1007/978-3-319-52836-6_59

farmers to gain knowledge on their farming. It is observed that learning goals and preferences tend to be localized for farming knowledge due to similar climate and soil conditions in an area. Therefore, geographical information can be utilized to recommend agricultural learning resources.

One of the issues for learning resource selection is the information overload problem. As more and more resources are generated, it is hard for a learner to determine his/her suitable resources by directly inspecting them. However, experiences from similar learners can provide a backdrop for him/her to find the resources that match his/her requirement. Agent-based systems can be used in user modeling as well as collaborative resource selection [4]. Software agents interact with each other in a computer simulation environment, in which each agent represents a user in the real world. Each agent has its internal properties according to the preference of the user that it represents. The preferences can be learnt by other agents during the interactions and then be utilized for resource selection. In this way, user modeling can be achieved in a distributed manner and does not require a consistent ontology on the global scale.

In this paper, an agricultural learning resource recommendation approach is proposed using agent-based simulation that takes geographical information into account. The agent simulation environment is first introduced. A distance-aware agent reputation model is presented that takes two sources into account to establish trust between agents. A multi-agent collaborative recommendation approach is proposed. Agent simulation experiments are conducted for the evaluation of the proposed approach.

The rest of the paper is organized as follows. The agricultural learning resource recommendation approach is proposed in Sect. 2. Agent simulation experiments and the results are presented in Sect. 3. We conclude our work in Sect. 4.

2 Agricultural Learning Resource Recommendation

2.1 Agent Simulation Environment

An agent-based simulation approach is utilized in this paper to facilitate collaborative recommendation of agricultural learning resources. Agents interact with each other to share information in an unstructured peer-to-peer network, each of them represents a learner in the system. In an unstructured overlay network, agents are not specifically organized. They can join or leave the network freely at any time. Due to the ad hoc nature of the network structure, information cannot be directly located. Instead, queries are propagated in the network. The receiving parties then execute the queries and forward them to their neighbors. The results of the queries are then sent back to their issuers.

The structure of the agent network is defined as a directed graph $G = (P, E)$, where $P = \{p_1, p_2, \ldots, p_n\}$ is a set of nodes, each of which represents an agent, and $E \subseteq P \times P$ is a set of edges, each of which represents a link from one agent to another.

Each agent $p \in P$ has an agricultural learning resource database in which resources are collected according to p' owner's interest or preference. Agent p also maintains a list of links $E_p \subset E$, each of which is a direct link $p \rightarrow q$, where $q \in P$ is another agent that p has direct access to.

2.2 Distance-Aware Agent Reputation

In a web-based learning system, each learner has different learning goal and preference. Therefore, the learning resources collected by his/her agent can be different in the agent simulation network. Finding agents that have similar preferences can greatly improve the information sharing effectiveness. Conventional approaches utilize agent content summaries to distinguish different agent preferences. However, those approaches suffer from biased content summaries as well as non-cooperative agents.

In our previous work, an agent reputation model was proposed for distributed information retrieval networks [1]. Reputations are handled in three levels, i.e., *individual level*, *social level*, and *community level* [6]. In this section, the concepts of *individual level* and *social level* reputations are adopted to handle trust between agents.

Direct Reputation. The most reliable source of trust between agents is direct interaction. An agent can determine another one's quality of service by evaluating the quality its shared information.

From agent v's point of view, the influence of all the interactions $v \rightarrow b$ occurring between time t_i and t_{i+1} on the reputation of agent b is defined in (1).

$$\Delta R_{v \xrightarrow{D} b}(t_{i+1}) = \sum_r r_{v \rightarrow b} \tag{1}$$

where $r_{v \rightarrow b}$ is defined as the relevancy judgment made by agent v about the results of data returned from b in reply to v's queries.

Witness Reputation. An agent v has to seek for reputation witness in the case that there is a lack of direct interactions to agent b [5]. However, a reputation witness should not be fully trusted since its effectiveness is limited by the information evaluation performance of the third parties. Furthermore, v does not necessarily have the same preference as the witness.

In web-based agricultural learning, it is observed that learning goals and preferences tend to be localized. Learners with small geographic distances tend to seek for farming knowledge for similar plants. Their focuses and learning preferences are also similar in a certain period of time. This phenomenon is caused by the fact that the climate and soil conditions in an area is similar. Farmers in an area usually work on similar tasks in a certain period. Disasters, plant diseases and pests often influence most farmers simultaneously in a region. Therefore, geographical information can be utilized to recommend agricultural learning resources. We argue that agent reputation witnesses provided by nearby agents can be considered more reliable compared with others.

From agent v's point of view, the influence of a reputation witness from agent x on the reputation of a target agent b at time t_{i+1} is defined in (2).

$$R_{v \xrightarrow{W} b}^{x}(t_{i+1}) = \frac{R_{x \rightarrow b}(t_i)}{\left(1 + e^{-(R_{v \rightarrow x}(t_i) - R_0)}\right)\left(1 + e^{-(dist(v,x) - dist_0)}\right)} \tag{2}$$

where $R_{v \rightarrow x}(t_i)$ is the reputation of x at time t_i from v's point of view, R_0 is a parameter adjusted to identify the reputations of average agents, $dist(v, x)$ is the geographic distance between agent v and b, and $dist_0$ is the estimated average distance in which farming condition is considered to be similar.

The witness reputation of agent b from agent v's point of view is the aggregation of all the reputation witness acquired, defined in (3).

$$R_{v \xrightarrow{w} b} = \sum_x R^x_{v \xrightarrow{w} b} \qquad (3)$$

2.3 Collaborative Recommendation with Agent-Based Simulation

An agent-based simulation approach is proposed for collaborative recommendation of agricultural learning resources. Agents in the multi-agent network act as sources of information. Recommendations are propagated in the network through direct links between agents. The method proposed by King et al. [2] is adopted to establish links in the system.

Each agent maintains two kinds of links. *Attractive links* are established according to distance-aware agent reputation model presented in Sect. 2.2. An agent periodically sends a message requesting agent reputation witnesses to its neighbor. Collected data are used to evaluate other agents and those with highest scores are accepted as direct links of the agent. On the contrary, *random links* are picked randomly in order to enhance the connectivity of the network.

Agents with similar learning goals and preferences tend to gather together as the evolvement of the network structure. Agricultural learning resources are shared in the neighborhood of agents to improve accuracy. Recommendations can then be selected from the shared resources.

3 Simulation Experiments

3.1 Experiment Setting

Preliminary simulation experiments are conducted for the evaluation of the proposed method. PeerSim is used as the multi-agent simulation platform.

The number of agents in the simulation varies from 200 to 1000. Agricultural learning resources are divided into 10 topics, each of which represents knowledge of a kind of plant. Each agent has a learning resource database that contains 20 to 40 learning resources. Most learning resources are from a single topic, while others are randomly picked in the dataset. The agents are placed on a two-dimensional space, which is randomly divided into five regions. A random centroid is assigned for each region. Agents in a region are placed randomly around its centroid. Each agent has five links in its direct link set. Three of them are attractive links and the other two are random ones. The links are randomly assigned initially when the simulation starts.

The average precision $\overline{P}$ metric is used for the evaluation of the proposed method. We do not distinguish the overall precision and precision in the top-N list since the proposed method focuses on resource selection, and result ranking is not included in the experiment.

Three methods are compared in the experiments for comparison. M_1 is *recommendation with breath-first search*. The direct links of agents are randomly selected. M_2 is *recommendation with agent reputation model*. The direct links are selected according to the reputation model and $dist(v, x) = dist_0$ in (2). M_3 is *recommendation with distance-aware agent reputation model*. The direct links are selected according to the distance-aware reputation model.

3.2   Experiment Results

The learning resource recommendation precision with different numbers of agents in the network is shown in Fig. 1(a). The query scope, i.e., the percentage of agents visited for a query, is fixed to 10%. From the figure we can see that the average precision $\overline{P}$ declines as the number of agents increases. Method M_3 achieves the best results among the three.

Figure 1(b) shows the learning resource recommendation precision with different query scopes. From the figure we can see that the average precision $\overline{P}$ declines as the number of agents visited increases. This is because that more irrelevant agents are introduced with larger query scope. Again, method M_3 achieves the best results.

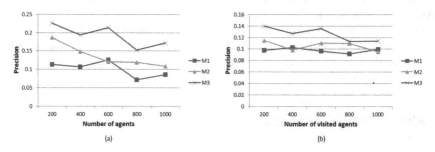

Fig. 1. Recommendation precision with (a) different numbers of agents in the network, and (b) different query scopes

4   Conclusion

In this paper, an agricultural learning resource recommendation approach is proposed using agent-based simulation that takes geographical information into account. The agent simulation environment is first introduced. A distance-aware agent reputation model is presented that takes two sources into account to establish trust between agents. A multi-agent collaborative recommendation approach is proposed. Agent simulation experiments are conducted for the evaluation of the proposed approach. Results show good performance of it.

Acknowledgment. This paper is supported by the monitoring statistics Project on Agricultural and rural resources "Agricultural Monitoring, Early Warning and Informatization" funded by Ministry of Agriculture of China, the Innovative Talents Project "Key Techniques of Main Agricultural Products Market Monitoring And Early Warning" funded by Ministry of Agriculture of China, the Science and Technology Innovation Project "Innovation Team on Agricultural Production Management Digitization Technology" (CAAS-ASTIP-2015-AII-02) funded by Chinese Academy of Agricultural Sciences, and sub-project "Agricultural Data Collection Methods and Technology Analysis" of project of Ministry of Agricultural of China "Monitoring and Statistics Fund for Agriculture and Rural Resources".

References

1. Chen, W., Zeng, Q., Wenyin, L., Hao, T.: A user reputation model for a user-interactive question answering system. Concurrency Comput. Prac. Exp. **19**(15), 2091–2103 (2007). http://dx.doi.org/10.1002/cpe.1142
2. King, I., Ng, C.H., Sia, K.C.: Distributed content-based visual information retrieval system on peer-to-peer networks. ACM Trans. Inf. Syst. **22**(3), 477–501 (2004). http://doi.acm.org/10.1145/1010614.1010619
3. Mandula, K., Meday, S.R., Muralidharan, V., Parupalli, R.: A student centric approach for mobile learning video content development and instruction design. In: 2013 15th International Conference on Advanced Communication Technology (ICACT), pp. 386–390. IEEE (2013)
4. Niinivaara, O.: Agent-based recommender systems. Department of Computer Science, University of Helsinki, pp. 1–48 (2004)
5. Qureshi, B., Min, G., Kouvatsos, D.: A distributed reputation and trust management scheme for mobile peer-to-peer networks. Comput. Commun. **35**(5), 608–618 (2012)
6. Sabater, J., Sierra, C.: Reputation and social network analysis in multi-agent systems. In: The First International Joint Conference on Autonomous Agents & Multiagent Systems, AAMAS 2002, Proceedings, Bologna, Italy, 15–19 July 2002, pp. 475–482. ACM (2002). http://doi.acm.org/10.1145/544741.544854
7. Zou, D., Xie, H., Wong, T.-L., Rao, Y., Wang, F.L., Wu, Q.: Predicting pre-knowledge on vocabulary from e-learning assignments for language learners. In: Gong, Z., Chiu, Dickson, K.,W., Zou, D. (eds.) ICWL 2015. LNCS, vol. 9584, pp. 111–117. Springer, Heidelberg (2016). doi:10.1007/978-3-319-32865-2_12

Topic-Level Clustering on Web Resources

Shiyu Zhao[1], Fu Lee Wang[2(✉)], and Leung Pun Wong[2]

[1] School of Data and Computer Science,
Sun Yat-sen University, Guangzhou, China
zhaoshiyu92@sina.cn
[2] Caritas Institute of Higher Education, Tseung Kwan O, Hong Kong
{pwang,lpwong}@cihe.edu.hk

Abstract. The rapid development of Internet, social media, and news portals has provided a large amount of information in various aspects. Confronting such plenty of resources, it is valuable to develop effective clustering approaches. However, performance of traditional clustering models on web resources is not good enough due to the high dimension. In this paper, we propose a clustering model based on topic model and density peaks. Our model combines biterm topic model and clustering by fast search of density peaks, which firstly extract a set of features with the co-occurrence of two words from the original documents, followed by clustering analysis via topical features. Web resources are translated from raw data into clusters, and evaluation on clustering results of center part verifies the effectiveness of the proposed method.

Keywords: Document clustering · Topic model · Biterm · Density peaks

1 Introduction

With the rapid development of social media services, people collect more and more data from various web resources. Thus, it is important to cluster/group web resources to provide users with more suitable recommendations. The existing clustering algorithms can be divided into partitioning method, hierarchical method and density-based clustering algorithm. Partitioning method such as K-means tends to find clusters of comparable spatial extent [13], making it difficult to handle cluster with different shapes [20]. In general, the complexity of hierarchical clustering is $O(n^2log(n))$, which makes them too slow for large data sets. As for density-based algorithms such as DBSCAN [4], it is difficult to choose a distance threshold if the data and scale are not well understood.

In this article, we present a document clustering topic model called Clustering by Density Peaks based on Biterm Topic Model (CDPBTM), in order to overcome the drawbacks of the previous approaches. We discuss the advantages and disadvantages of each method in relation to better understanding of each clustering method in this context.

The rest of this paper is organized as follows. The related work is given in Sect. 2. The proposed CDPBTM is presented in Sect. 3. The dataset, experimental results and discussions are illustrated in Sect. 4. Finally, we draw conclusions in Sect. 5.

T.-T. Wu et al. (Eds.): SETE 2016, LNCS 10108, pp. 564–573, 2017.
DOI: 10.1007/978-3-319-52836-6_60

2 Related Work

In this section, we briefly summarize the related work from the following three perspectives: topic models, clustering algorithms, and web learning applications.

2.1 Topic Models

Topic models have been proposed to uncover the latent semantic structure from corpora. Research into mining the semantic structure of a textual collection began with latent semantic analysis (LSA) [3], which utilized the singular value decomposition of the document-term matrix to reveal the major associative words pattern. Probabilistic latent semantic analysis (PLSA) [8] improved LSA with a solid probabilistic model based on a mixture decomposition derived from a latent class model. In PLSA, a document is presented as a mixture of topics, while a topic is a probability distribution over words. Extending PLSA, latent Dirichlet allocation (LDA) [2] adds Dirichlet priors on topic distributions, resulting in a more complete generative model. Due to its good generalization ability and extensibility, LDA achieves huge success in text mining domain.

In the last decade, topic models have been extensively studied. Many more complicated variants and extensions of LDA and PLSA have been proposed, such as the author-topic model [17], Bayesian nonparametric topic model [18] and biterm topic model [25]. Different from those methods based on authors' perspective, some frameworks with the idea of user modeling have been proposed, such as the hybrid recommendation system with multicriteria user modeling [11], and the collaborative recommender consist of user modeling and clustering algorithms [14]. Among them, two works close to us are the recently proposed regularized topic model and the biterm topic model, which also employ word co-occurrence statistics to enhance topic learning.

2.2 Clustering Algorithms

Clustering algorithms attempt to classify elements into categories, or clusters, on the basis of their similarity. Several different clustering strategies have been proposed [24], but no consensus has been reached even on the definition of a cluster. In K-means and K-medoids [9] methods, clusters are groups of data characterized by a small distance to the cluster center. An objective function, typically the sum of the distance to a set of putative cluster centers, is optimized until the best cluster center candidates are found. However, these approaches are not able to detect nonspherical clusters. In distribution-based algorithms, one attempts to reproduce the observed realization of data points as a mix of predefined probability distribution functions [15]. The accuracy of such methods depends on the capability of the trial probability to represent the data.

Clusters with an arbitrary shape are easily detected by approaches based on the local density of data points. In density-based spatial clustering of applications with noise, one choose a density threshold, discards as noise the points in regions with densities lower than this threshold, and assigns to different clusters disconnected regions of high density. However, choosing an appropriate threshold can be nontrivial, a drawback not present in the mean-shift clustering method [6]. There, a cluster is defined as a set of points that converge to the same local maximum of the density distribution function. This method allows the finding of nonspherical clusters but works only for data defined by a set of coordinates and is computationally costly.

2.3   Web Learning Applications

The web provides an extremely large and dynamic learning resources. Thus, it is increasingly popular to provide personalized service in learning resource recommendation. In a web-based learning system, topic models can generate a better vector model than traditional methods (e.g., vector space model) for course documents [10]. Specially, after building up a topic model for a course, we can get a low-dimension vector to represent each document in this course, in addition to identify some ambiguity words that have different meanings in different environments.

In recent years, clustering algorithms have been extended and applied to group web learning resources [21], and to discover communities [22, 23]. But most of these studies are based on the classic vector space model, in which, keywords in a document are assigned weights and a high-dimension vector is constructed to represent the instance. Thus, such a kind of method has disadvantage in both effectiveness and scalability. We develop a clustering algorithm by density peaks based on topic models, and it can be well applied to web learning applications.

3   Clustering by Density Peaks Based on Biterm Topic Model

In this section, we propose the clustering by density peaks based on biterm topic model (CDPBTM), a multi-labeled topical clustering model for web resources. The problem is first defined, including the relevant general terms and notations, and then our model is presented in detail. Finally, we describe the estimation and prediction of parameters.

3.1   Problem Definition

For the sake of convenience, we define terms and notations as follows:

An online news collection consists of D documents $\{d_1, d_2, ..., d_D\}$ with word tokens and category labels. In particular, a document d consists of a sequence of N_d word tokens denoted by $w_d = \{w_1, w_2, ..., w_{Nd}\}$, and category labels over $|C|$ categories represented by $C_d = \{C_{d,1}, C_{d,2}, ..., C_{d,|C|}\}$.

We denote the number of latent topics as T, the topic distribution of document d as θ, and the word distribution of topic z as φ_z. The key task of document clustering is to find the similarity and differences between documents through their word tokens and latent topics, in addition to predict the category labels of unlabeled documents.

3.2   Biterm Topic Model

In this part, we first briefly introduce the Biterm Topic Model (BTM) which is the first step of clustering by fast search and find of density peaks [16]. BTM is a topic model based on the co-occurrence of a pair of words. Unlike the traditional Latent Dirichlet Allocation (LDA) and other topic models, BTM uses a distribution θ for the whole corpus.

As a partial generative model, CDPBTM allows us to associate each topic with word tokens jointly, and to infer the probabilities of categories conditioned to unlabeled documents that only contain word tokens.

The graphical model of BTM is shown in Fig. 1, where shaded nodes are observed data, blank ones are latent (i.e., not observed), and arrows indicate dependence. The parameterization of the CDPBTM is as follows:

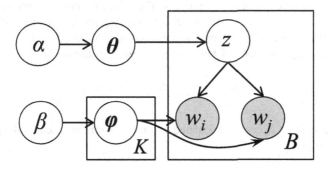

Fig. 1. Graphical model of BTM

$\theta \mid \alpha \sim Dirichlet(\alpha)$
$\varphi z \mid \beta \sim Dirichlet(\beta)$
$zdn \mid \theta \sim Multinomial(\theta)$
$wdn \mid \varphi dn \sim Multinomial(\varphi zdn)$

In the above, α and β are hyperparameters. The hyperparameter α can be interpreted as the prior observation count for the number of times a topic was sampled from a document before any word token is observed [12]. The hyperparameter β can be interpreted as the prior observation count for the number of times a word token was sampled from a topic before having observed an actual word. Similar to the existing models [1, 7], we use fixed symmetric Dirichlet distributions ($\alpha = 50/T$ and $\beta = 0.1$).

Following the above procedure, we can estimate the probability of biterm b_i conditioned to the model parameters θ and φ, as follows:

$$P(b_i \mid \theta, \phi) = \sum_{k=1}^{K} \theta_k \phi_{k,w_i,1} \phi_{k,w_i,2}$$

The likelihood of the whole corpus is:

$$P(B) = \prod_{i,j} \sum_{k=1}^{K} \theta_k \phi_{k,w_i,1} \phi_{k,w_i,2}$$

It can be observed that we directly model the word co-occurrence pattern, rather than a single word, as a unit conveying semantics of topics. This is because the co-occurrence of a pair of words can better reveal the topics than the occurrence of a single word, and then enhance the learning of topics. Moreover, all biterms from the whole corpus, rather than from a single document, are aggregated together for the topic learning. Therefore, we can fully leverage the rich global word co-occurrence patterns to better reveal the latent topics.

A major difference between BTM and conventional topic models is that BTM does not model the document generation process. Therefore, we cannot directly obtain the topic proportions of documents during the topic learning process. To infer the topics in a document, we assume that the topic proportions of a document equal to the expectation of the topic proportions of biterms generated from the document:

$$P(z|d) = \sum_{b} P(z|b)P(b|d)$$

In the above, $P(z|b)$ can be calculated via Bayes' formula based on the parameters estimated by BTM:

$$P(z|b) = \frac{P(z)P(w_i|z)P(w_j|z)}{\sum_z P(z)P(w_i|z)P(w_j|z)}$$

where $P(z) = \theta_z$ and $P(w_i|z) = \varphi_{i,z}$ as for the value of $P(b|d)$, we simply take the empirical distribution of biterms in the document for estimation:

$$P(b|d) = \frac{n_d(b)}{\sum_b n_d(b)}$$

where $n_d(b)$ is the frequency of biterm b in document d.

3.3 Clustering by Fast Search and Find Density Peaks

In this part, we first introduce the Clustering by fast search and find of Density Peaks (CDP) briefly, and then present how our CDP do clustering on the intermediate results of BTM. CDP is a method of hierarchical clustering, however, unlike the traditional BIRCH [26], CDP gathers points based on not only distances, but also densities of points.

The algorithm has its basis in the assumption that cluster centers are surrounded by neighbors with lower local density, and that they are at a relatively large distance from any points with a higher local density. For each data point i, we compute two quantities: its local density ρ_i and its distance δ_i from points of higher density. Both quantities depend only on the distances d_{ij} between data points, which are assumed to satisfy the triangular inequality. The local density ρ_i of data point i is defined as:

$$\rho_i = \sum_i \exp(-(\frac{d_{ij}}{d_c})^2)\chi(d_{ij} - d_c)$$

The above equation is a density function with gaussian kernel, where $\chi(x) = 1$ if $x < 0$ and $\chi(x) = 0$ otherwise, and d_c is a cutoff distance. Basically, ρ_i is related to the number of points that are closer than d_c to point i. The algorithm is sensitive only to the relative magnitude of ρ_i in different points, implying that, for large data sets, the results of the analysis are robust with respect to the choice of d_c.

For the point with highest density, we conventionally take:

$$\delta_i = \min_{j:\rho_j > \rho_i} (d_{ij})$$

Note that δ_i is much larger than the typical nearest neighbor distance only for points that are local or global maxima in the density. Thus, cluster centers are supposed with large ρ and anomalously large δ.

After the cluster centers have been found, each remaining point is assigned to the same cluster as its nearest neighbor of higher density. The cluster assignment is performed in a single step, in contrast with other clustering algorithms where an objective function is optimized iteratively.

3.4   Our Model

The clustering by fast search and find of density peaks based on biterm topic model (CDPBTM) proposed in this paper is an extension of BTM, using CDP to cluster the intermediate probability distribution generated by BTM.

The CDPBTM is proposed to conduct clustering over unlabeled documents. For each document d, the word tokens are generated as follows:

1. Draw $\theta \sim Dirichlet(\alpha)$
2. For each topic $k \in [1, K]$
   (a) draw $\varphi_k \sim Dirichlet(\beta)$
3. For each biterm $b_i \in B$
   (a) draw $z_i \sim M ultinomial(\theta)$
   (b) draw $w_{i,1}, w_{i,2} \sim M ultinomial(\varphi_{zi})$
4. For each document calculate the probability distribution $P (z \mid d)$
   (a) calculate ρ_i
   (b) calculate δ_i
5. Find the cluster centers through ρ and δ
6. For all the remaining points, assign them to the same cluster as its nearest neighbor of higher density.

Here, we assume that the biterms are generated independently for simplicity.

4 Experiments

In this section, we evaluate the performance of the proposed model for document clustering. We design the experiments to achieve the following goals: (i) to analyze the influence of number of topics on the task of clustering accuracy, (ii) to compare the performance between cutoff kernel and gaussian kernel, and (iii) to find the optimal parameter t in CDP.

4.1 Experiment Design

To test the effectiveness of our CDPBTM model, we have collected 9950 news articles from the SogouT corpus which is consist of a large scale of news articles from various kinds of aspects.

As a preprocessing step, Jieba is used to perform the Chinese POS tagging and word segmentation. Jieba is a Chinese word segmentation method based on multilayer HMM and Viterbi algorithm. It takes words' frequency and position into consideration, statistic with the BMES model. Note that Chinese word segmentation are implemented based on phrases, rather than individual Chinese characters.

To estimate the performance of the model we proposed, the existing BTM [25] and LDA model were implemented for comparison. All hyperparameters were set at default.

4.2 Influence of the Size of Window

The size of window indicates how many biterms can be generated and the correlation of words in a biterm which may have an effect on the performance of BTM, which is an important part of our model. To evaluate the influence of this factor, we varied the size of window from 2 to 6 (the amount of different size of window tested was 5 in total).

With respect to those parameters, the accuracy of different models is presented in Table 1. Compared to the traditional BTM, the performance of CDPBTM improved 36.03%, 28.20%, 28.78%, 26.82%, 29.78%, for different size of window respectively. It can be seen that when the size is equal to 2 or 3, the size is too small to find enough correlation. Besides, when the size is 6 or even larger, words in a biterm are probably belongs to different topics actually. While bigger window size consequent on more time complexity, so that the optimal size of window is 4. As LDA is not related to window, their performance is independent of the size of window.

Table 1. The mean of accuracies for different models

Size of Window	2	3	4	5	6
CDPBTM	70.54%	76.79%	82.41%	78.67%	76.60%
BTM	51.86%	59.90%	63.99%	62.03%	59.02%
LDA	64.86%				

4.3   Influence of the Parameter of Radius

For each data point i, we compute two quantities: its local density ρ_i and its distance δ_i from points of higher density. Both these quantities depend only on the distances d_{ij} between data points and radius d_c. In the first step, we have transform each document to a probability distribution of topics through BTM. Thus in the second step, we considered using Kullback-Leibler divergence rather than Euclidean metric to measure the distance between points due to Kullback-Leibler divergence indicates the correlation between data points better [19].

In this way, the only parameter that have to be estimated is the radius d_c. The radius d_c is determined by a parameter t which is set by us. As a rule of thumb, one can choose d_c so that the average number of neighbors is around 1% to 2% of the total number of points in the data set. Thus we can get the radius with the parameter t and the sorted d_{ij}. To evaluate the influence of parameter t, we varied the value of t from 0.001 to 0.2 (the amount of different t is 9 in total). The accuracy of different radius is shown in Table 2.

Table 2. The mean of accuracies for different radius

Radius parameter (t)	mean of accuracies
0.001	79.94%
0.002	80.79%
0.005	81.08%
0.01	81.34%
0.02	81.63%
0.05	81.57%
0.1	81.62%
0.15	81.22%
0.2	72.35%

Obviously, the method is robust with respect to changes in the metric that do not significantly affect the distances below radius parameter t. However, it is not expected to get an ideal result when the radius is smaller than 0.01 or bigger than 0.1. With the window size equals to 4 and radius parameter t equals to 0.02, our model's performance improved 18.72% compared with LDA.

5   Conclusions

Document clustering is an increasingly important task due to the prevalence of news portals. Compared with normal datasets, document clustering brings severe sparsity problems to conventional clustering models. In this paper, a clustering algorithm was proposed based on BTM and CDP. This algorithm do clustering based on the topic probability distribution generated by BTM while Jensen-Shannon divergence is used to estimate the distance between data points. Experiments were conducted to evaluate the effectiveness of the proposed model. The main contributions are summarized as follows:

1. The performance of the proposed CDPBTM is much better than the baseline BTM when the size of window used was varied.
2. The performance of CDPBTM is much better than the baseline BTM and LDA when the value of radius parameter t within certain limits.

As for future works, we plan to build a recommendation system for user's comments based on our model and the frame of user modeling. A good recommendation system should modeling by the conceptual understanding of users, in other words, it needs to "say the right thing at the right time in the right way" [5]. Thus, it is important to develop a clustering system with the unique feature of each user.

Acknowledgements. The research work described in this article was supported by a grant from the Research Grants Council of the Hong Kong Special Administrative Region, China (UGC/FDS11/E06/14).

References

1. Bao, S., Xu, S., Zhang, L., Yan, R., Su, Z., Han, D., Yu, Y.: Joint emotion-topic modeling for social affective text mining. In: Proceedings of the 9th IEEE International Conference on Data Mining (ICDM), pp. 699–704 (2009)
2. Blei, D.M., Ng, A.Y., Jordan, M.I.: Latent dirichlet allocation. J. Mach. Learn. Res. **3**, 993–1022 (2003)
3. Deerwester, S., Dumais, S.T., Furnas, G.W., Landauer, T.K., Harshman, R.: Indexing by latent semantic analysis. J. Am. Soc. Inform. Sci. **41**(6), 391 (1990)
4. Ester, M., Kriegel, H.-P., Sander, J., Xu, X.: A density-based algorithm for discovering clusters in large spatial databases with noise. In: Proceedings of the 2nd International Conference on Knowledge Discovery and Data Mining (KDD), pp. 226–231 (1996)
5. Fischer, G.: User modeling in humancomputer interaction. User Model. User-Adap. Inter. **11**(1–2), 65–86 (2001)
6. Fukunaga, K., Hostetler, L.: The estimation of the gradient of a density function, with applications in pattern recognition. IEEE Trans. Inf. Theory **21**(1), 32–40 (1975)
7. Griffiths, T.L., Steyvers, M.: Finding scientific topics. Proc. Natl. Acad. Sci. **101**(suppl. 1), 5228–5235 (2004)
8. Hofmann, T.: Probabilistic latent semantic indexing. In: Proceedings of the 22nd Annual International ACM SIGIR Conference on Research and Development in Information Retrieval (SIGIR), pp. 50–57 (1999)
9. Kaufman, L., Rousseeuw, P.J.: Finding Groups in Data: an Introduction to Cluster Analysis. Wiley, New York (2009)
10. Kuang, W., Luo, N., Sun, Z.: Resource recommendation based on topic model for educational system. In: Proceedings of the 6th IEEE Joint International Information Technology and Artificial Intelligence Conference (ITAIC), pp. 370–374 (2011)
11. Lakiotaki, K., Matsatsinis, N.F., Tsoukiàs, A.: Multicriteria user modeling in recommender systems. IEEE Intell. Syst. **26**(2), 64–76 (2011)
12. Lin, C., He, Y.: Joint sentiment/topic model for sentiment analysis. In: Proceedings of the 18th ACM Conference on Information and Knowledge Management (CIKM), pp. 375–384 (2009)

13. MacQueen, J.: Some methods for classification and analysis of multivariate observations. In: Proceedings of the 5th Berkeley Symposium on Mathematical Statistics and Probability: Statistics, vol. 1, pp. 281–297. University of California Press (1967)
14. Martın-Guerrero, J.D., Palomares, A., Balaguer-Ballester, E., Soria-Olivas, E., Gómez-Sanchis, J., Soriano-Asensi, A.: Studying the feasibility of a recommender in a citizen web portal based on user modeling and clustering algorithms. Expert Syst. Appl. 30(2), 299–312 (2006)
15. McLachlan, G., Krishnan, T.: The EM algorithm and extensions. Wiley, New York (2007)
16. Rodriguez, A., Laio, A.: Clustering by fast search and find of density peaks. Science **344** (6191), 1492–1496 (2014)
17. Rosen-Zvi, M., Griffiths, T., Steyvers, M., Smyth, P.: The author-topic model for authors and documents. In: Proceedings of the 20th Conference on Uncertainty in Artificial Intelligence (UAI), pp. 487–494 (2004)
18. Teh, Y.W., Jordan, M.I., Beal, M.J., Blei, D.M.: Hierarchical dirichlet processes. J. Am. Stat. Assoc. (2012)
19. Thollard, F., Dupont, P., Higuera, C.D.L.: Probabilistic dfa inference using kullback-leibler divergence and minimality. In: Proceedings of the 17th International Conference on Machine Learning (ICML), pp. 975–982 (2000)
20. Trier, Ø.D., Jain, A.K., Taxt, T.: Feature extraction methods for character recognition-a survey. Pattern Recogn. **29**(4), 641–662 (1996)
21. Wang, S., Tang, Z., Rao, Y., Xie, H., Wang, F.L.: A clustering algorithm based on minimum spanning tree with e-learning applications. In: Gong, Z., Chiu, D.K.W., Zou, D. (eds.) ICWL 2015. LNCS, vol. 9584, pp. 3–12. Springer, Heidelberg (2016). doi:10.1007/978-3-319-32865-2_1
22. Xie, H., Li, Q., Cai, Y.: Community-aware resource profiling for personalized search in folksonomy. J. Comput. Sci. Technol. **27**(3), 599–610 (2012)
23. Xie, H., Li, Q., Mao, X., Li, X., Cai, Y., Rao, Y.: Community-aware user profile enrichment in folksonomy. Neural Netw. **58**, 111–121 (2014)
24. Xu, R., Wunsch, D.: Survey of clustering algorithms. IEEE Trans. Neural Netw. **16**(3), 645–678 (2005)
25. Yan, X., Guo, J., Lan, Y., Cheng, X.: A biterm topic model for short texts. In: Proceedings of the 22nd International Conference on World Wide Web (WWW), pp. 1445–1456 (2013)
26. Zhang, T., Ramakrishnan, R., Livny, M.: Birch: an efficient data clustering method for very large databases. ACM Sigmod. Rec. **25**(2), 103–114 (1996)

When Innovation Meets Evolution: An Extensive Study of Emerging e-Learning Technologies for Higher Education in Hong Kong

Yunhui Zhuang[1,2(✉)], He Ma[3], Haoran Xie[4], Alvin Chung Man Leung[1], Gerhard P. Hancke[2], and Fu Lee Wang[5]

[1] Department of Information Systems, City University of Hong Kong, Kowloon Tong, Hong Kong
yhzhuang2-c@my.cityu.edu.hk
[2] Department of Computer Science, City University of Hong Kong, Kowloon Tong, Hong Kong
[3] School of Creative Media, City University of Hong Kong, Kowloon Tong, Hong Kong
[4] Department of Mathematics and Information Technology, The Education University of Hong Kong, Tai Po, Hong Kong
[5] Caritas Institute for Higher Education, Tseung Kwan O, Hong Kong

Abstract. With the rapid development of sophisticated technologies, many innovative e-Learning tools or applications with increased inter-activities and improved features have been adopted in tertiary institutions. This paper serves as a platform for industry and academia to exchange higher education practices in innovative course and programme design. We investigate current practices in tertiary institutions with e-Learning technologies and applications to enhance academics' teaching excellences and research capabilities in order to achieve social, cultural, environmental, or economic impacts. In particular, we investigate all public universities and one private college in Hong Kong in terms of various e-Learning technologies. The results demonstrate that all these e-Learning technologies for being used in higher education help to enhance teaching and learning experiences, and make it more efficient and effective. Students can also benefit from these e-Learning technologies to become life-long learners. Moreover, by taking a closer look at current e-Learning technology trends, we list some possible e-Learning applications and tools that are expected to surge in the coming years.

Keywords: Higher education · Innovation · e-Learning technology

1 Introduction

In the late 90s, a computer-based training system (or CBT system) named PLATO came around in university campus as a programmed instruction teaching machine that allows a student to work through the materials at any time based on individualized instruction [1]. However, most universities, including

© Springer International Publishing AG 2017
T.-T. Wu et al. (Eds.): SETE 2016, LNCS 10108, pp. 574–584, 2017.
DOI: 10.1007/978-3-319-52836-6_61

Hong Kong, were still using paper-based textbooks and materials as the primary form for teaching purpose.

At the beginning of 21st century, internet-based learning tools expanded, which made it easier and more flexible for students to learn various subjects and develop certain skill sets. In search of an appropriate description for such learning method such as "online learning" or "distance learning", internet-based learning environments began to truly thrive, with students gaining access to plenty of online information and learning opportunities [1].

In the context of the higher education community, the use of advanced technologies have broad connotations that embrace a wealth range of practices. In addition to focusing on online contexts, it also includes the full range of internet-based learning platforms and formats, genres, and delivery methods such as easy-to-learn educational programming, multimedia, simulations, gamification, and the use of emerging new media on mobile devices (e.g., smartphone or pads) across all discipline areas. As rapid evolution of the innovative learning tools and techniques and its associated fields, it is important to understand how the learning environment is used, and the various influences of such tools and techniques that distinguish the differences in learning outcomes.

In this paper, we investigate eight public universities and one private college in Hong Kong in terms of various e-Learning technologies, which can be classified into three categories, including presentation recordings, learning management system, and online course. The results show that all these e-Learning technologies for being used in Hong Kong's higher education help to enhance teaching and learning experiences, and to broaden students' learning horizons. Moreover, with the help of such technologies, instructors are empowered with handful resources so that they can further enrich students' learning experiences through interactive classroom teaching.

The rest of the article is structured as follows: Sect. 2 will introduce a number of emerging e-Learning technologies currently being used in Hong Kong. Section 3 presents a comprehensive study which highlights unique merits and weaknesses for each of three popular learning management systems in Hong Kong, such as Canvas, Blackboard, and Moodle; all of which provide fundamentally different teaching and learning experiences for both instructors and students. Section 4 list some possible e-Learning applications and tools that are expected to surge in the coming years. Section 5 concludes the paper.

2   Innovative and Emerging e-Learning Technologies

This section summarizes the most popular e-Learning technologies being used in eight public universities and one private college in Hong Kong as shown in Table 1, along with easy-to-understand introduction and notable benefits and advantages.

2.1   Echo360

Echo360 is a digital educational environment provided by the Echo360 company. By integrating presentations and course resources altogether, it aims at transforming digital devices into helpful educational tools. Currently CityU is mainly utilizing Echo360's presentation recording function, which records video of the presenter's speech and the presentation notes displayed on computer screens at the same time. Its benefits and advantages include:

- Allow content of presentations to be preserved to a much larger extent.
- Essential to the launch of MOOC program and production of online open courses' material.
- Provides educators a new method to have wider and deeper understanding of students' presentation skills so as to make evaluations more critically.

2.2   Panopto

Panopto is a highly flexible presentation capture platform that lets users easily to create, edit, and search any combination of digital, video and audio elements which preserve critical knowledge. The obvious benefits and advantages can be summarized as follows:

- Videos with rich contents can be created by Panapto.
- Editing, sharing and archiving presentation videos made easy.
- Enable publishers to learn about audiences better.

2.3   Blackboard, Moodle, and Canvas

Blackboard, Moodle, and Canvas are three major Learning Management Systems (LMS) of choice for higher education in Hong Kong. Canvas didn't come to Hong Kong until 2014, when CityU replaced Blackboard to this new LMS in order to meet teaching and learning needs. One year later, HKUST joined CityU to become Canvas's second major customer in Hong Kong after replacing its own developed LMS system. On the other hand, Moodle also offers handful tools that can make course delivery more effective and efficient. It works in a similar way of Blackboard and Canvas to provide one-stop teaching and learning experiences. We will present a detailed case study against three major LMS of their merits and weaknesses in Sect. 3.

2.4   MOOC

A Massive Open Online Course (MOOC) is a web-based course tool that enables students to participate in various courses for free. Different from traditional course arrangements for textbooks, assignments, and even videos, MOOC offers more advanced interactive forums for instructors and students to build an online community. MOOC is also a recent development in distance education. A relatively recent MOOC adopts closed licenses for the course materials (i.e., the

Table 1. e-Learning technologies in Hong Kong

e-Learning Technologies Universities	Presentation Recordings		Learning Management System			Online Course
	Echo360	Panopto	Canvas	Blackboard	Moodle	MOOC
CityU	✓	–	✓	–	–	✓
HKBU	–	✓	–	✓	✓	✓
CUHK	✓	–	–	✓	–	✓
PolyU	–	–	–	✓	–	✓
HKU	–	✓	✓	–	✓	✓
HKUST	✓	–	✓	–	–	✓
EdUHK	–	–	–	–	✓	–
LU	–	–	–	–	✓	–
HSMC	–	–	–	–	✓	✓

CityU: City University of Hong Kong
HKBU: Hong Kong Baptist University
CUHK: The Chinese University of Hong Kong
PolyU: The Hong Kong Polytechnic University
HKU: The University of Hong Kong
HKUST: The Hong Kong University of Science and Technology
EdUHK: The Education University of Hong Kong
LU: Lingnan University
HSMC: Hang Seng Management College

learning resources only available for students). In early stages, MOOC employs open licensing for all users for sharing and promotions.

Tertiary institutions gradually begin to use MOOC since 2016 and currently only offer a limited number of online courses. For example, PolyU offers five verified online courses published through the edX platform, while three courses offered by CityU have been confirmed to be made into MOOC.

2.5   Others

Qualtrics. As one of the powerful and user-friendly online survey tools, Qualtrics can be used by instructors and students for diversed purpose. Its benefits include:

– Easy-to-use and equipped with a powerful set of tools, options and integrations.
– Offer instructors a better insight of students' understanding so as to improve the way of teaching
– Able to handle a big variety of educational and research projects.

iQlickers. It is a multi-functional tool for in-class teaching, feedback collection, idea generation, survey, polling, and assessment. There are a lot of benefits and advantages for institutions to use iQuickers:

– Location Independent: iQlickers can be used inside or outside the classroom via SMS or Internet
– Low cost and no additional software installation is required.
– Support various types of questions and anonymous polling.

KEEP. It is a another one-stop e-Learning platform specifically designed for CUHK instructors and students. KEEP provides a handful set of tools such as KEEP Moodle, KEEP Open edX, KEEPoll, and KEEPAttendance, to facilitate both in-class and off-class teaching and learning. One notable merit is that it aggregates various e-Learning technologies and integrates them into one platform for education. KEEP also encourages students to use their mobile devices for in-class teaching and learning.

CantoSound. It is an innovated gamification e-Learning platform for foreign students in HKU to learn Cantonese [2]. Through the demonstration videos, students can learn the grammars and tones of Cantonese. They can also choose to listen to individual words, or "play" a quiz through various games to test their understanding. Students can gain game points through above actions. The more points they earned, the higher levels they will be promoted. The CantoSound is an innovative and easy-to-use platform to popularize Cantonese. It is also an augmentation of learning, where from the in-class traditional learning experiences to the interest-driven and self-motivated encouraging process of gaining.

Fig. 1. Web services

QR Code. The Quick Response System is composed with a QR Code to foster meaningful engagement among students in the classroom. The system can maintain students' attention to the class engagement, and assist instructors in assessing students' understanding, as well as developing in-class activities. Students can scan the QR Code via the mobile devices (e.g., smartphones, pads, etc.) and answer the questions instantly. This way instructors can get an instant feedback from students on whether they have understood the concepts. Polling and quizzes are two common functions.

Other Web Services. During our survey (as shown in Sect. 3.2) and continuous talking with students, we also identified a handful of web services that could be very supportive to students' learning experiences. Figure 1 shows the web services other than aforementioned e-Learning tools.

3   Case Study: Blackboard, Moodle, and Canvas

Current practices on e-Learning technologies in tertiary institutions for the purpose of learning management not only focus on the self-developed LMS, but also consist of using Canvas, Blackboard, and Moodle. In January 2015, CityU replaced Blackboard to Canvas as their LMS, and HKUST joined CityU to adopted Canvas as their LMS instead of Blackboard one year later. HKUST became the second Canvas user in Hong Kong. Nevertheless, most tertiary institutions are still using Blackboard or Moodle.

3.1   Blackboard and Moodle

Blackboard was launched in 1998. Although it was not recognized as the first modern Learning Management System (LMS), its nature and functions made it widely welcomed by tertiary institutions during the initial launch campaign. However, there are serious weaknesses that have forced Blackboard into becoming less market relevant. Firstly, the cost of using is considerable, such as purchasing and maintenance, which can be a heavy burden to many institutions.

Secondly, the system is neither robust nor stable enough to evolve with new technologies or to enrich useful functions [3]. For example, Blackboard was not providing any cloud service until late 2014 [4]. In addition, the update for user interface was lagging. Despite these problems, Blackboard has introduced their mobile apps for Android and iOS users. Students can access contents posted on their institutional Blackboard through mobile apps, while instructors are offered more apps to handle different tasks.

Moodle is another LMS and was launched in 2002. Different from Blackboard, Moodle is a fully open-source system, which made Moodle a good substitution of Blackboard when considering the cost. Moodle is open to all kinds of plug-ins, add-ons and additional modules. This enables Moodle users to customize the system as they wish. On the other hand, the open-source and easy-to-customize are in fact a double-edged sword. This is because Moodle's built-in functions are too basic and a task can be done with multiple different methods; however, it often requires huge time investments for development of integration with other software and additional functionalities may be massive.

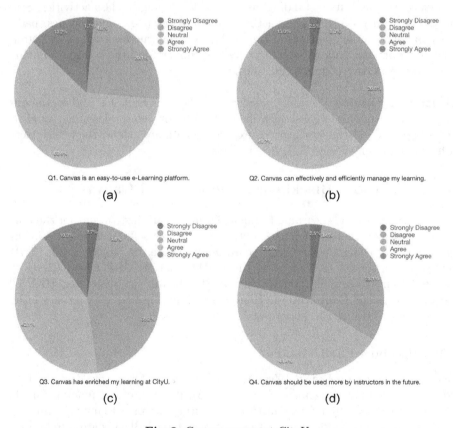

Fig. 2. Canvas survey at CityU

3.2   Canvas

Canvas is an open-source learning application launched in 2012. The service form of Canvas is SaaS (Software As a Service), which means no local installation is required and expedite setup process. Although Canvas is free, paid services ensure that institutions can have more safe and stable use, as well as year round technical support. The user experiences and function flows of Canvas are consistent even accessed from mobile devices. Also, Canvas has built an resource center to provide all kinds of LTI (Learning Tools Interoperability) technologies for users to use. Canvas users can also enjoy the system's extensibility while being able to lower the cost. Moreover, Canvas is also mobile friendly for both Android and iOS users.

Since Canvas has been launched in CityU for over one year, CityU has conducted a survey to see how Canvas changes the way of learning for students in CityU. By doing so, four specifically designed questions try to best describe the overall usage of Canvas, as shown in Fig. 2. The survey received a total of 528 responses and there are five students were never using Canvas as their LMS. Thus, five responses are excluded in the final survey statistics. The survey results show that the overall satisfaction for the initial launch of Canvas is successful.

3.3   The Tradeoff

Choosing LMS for an institution is bound to experience certain kinds of trade-off, such as financial cost, quality of the product, flexibility, maintenance, and service support [5–8]. In this section, we will focus on some important merits and weaknesses of these three LMS.

Being popular over a decade, Blackboard has proved itself to be the leader in the higher education LMS market. From the institutional perspective, considerable user base is one of the merits to become a Blackboard user. Joining the Blackboard user group means large amount of existing resources would turn useful, including training materials, solutions, extensions, and experiences. Another merit is that the system can be run on various OS using several different type of database management methods. Also, Blackboard has been practicing the Building Blocks (B2s) method, which means additional functions, extensions and integrations can be added modularly like piling bricks. In terms of user experience and function usefulness, Blackboard can generally satisfy the needs from both students and instructors. However, the weaknesses of Blackboard are obvious. First, the cost of use is considerable. Second, maintenance work is time-consuming because blocks are less compatible against others, and it takes effort to accurately locate the faulty Block.

Moodle has been some institutions' choice of LMS and its ultimate merit is that it's free. Basic user experience and general operations are ensured to be complete, and if users, especially institutional administrators and instructors, are willing to pay more effort, they can get to interact with the system much deeply and sophisticatedly. Hence, Moodle may be a good choice for institutions having special needs that common LMS cannot accommodate.

One of Moodle's weaknesses is that creating a full adapted Moodle that suits the institution well would be of huge amount of work. Moreover, Moodle is community-supported, which makes Moodle lack of a complete and clear systematic structure and a set of well kept documentations. The Moodle application consists of hundreds of thousands lines of codes, but they are less optimized and refactored. Moodle's legacy interface design and layout are another two problems. Due to the complexity of the system, even upgrading the interface would become a rather tough task, which makes migration from other LMS to Moodle a hard decision to make.

4 Future Development

With the rapid development of sophisticated technology, we can get a glimpse at what will lead the future of e-Learning development in Hong Kong. In particular, Gamification, Wearable Technology, Automated Course Authoring, and Cloud-based Learning Systems, are taking shape in the future development of e-Learning.

Gamification. Integrate gamification into in-class teaching has become increasingly popular in recent years [9–12]. It is expected that gamification will become an integral part of e-Learning in the near future. Games often involve points, badges, or leaderboards that could boost engagement and encourage students to do their best. The games can also be designed in a way that different levels are required for students to complete, with each level focusing on a key topic or concept. What's more, the games do not require prior gaming experience, with the philosophy that everyone could learn through playing games.

Wearable Technology. Apple Watch and Google Glass are two popular wearable gadgets coming to our daily life by storm. These wearable devices give students a golden opportunity to interact with the instructor in a more dynamic way that learning is more accessible and engageable, even those who are too busy to have the time to receive formal training. It is possible that students may have the chance to "walk in" a virtual learning environment and immerse themselves into various teaching and learning activities, e.g., tutorials, e-Learning games, etc. The power of augmented virtual reality has dramatically changed the way of teaching and learning, as well as the nature of online training. In the future, there are even 3D simulations or scenario tools could be applied to make the e-Learning design process easier and more cost efficient.

Automated Course Authoring. Automation in e-Learning is a relatively new concept in the sense that it may extremely reduce the cost and design efficiency of the e-Learning course. Although some existing e-Learning tools do provide course templates for instructors to set up the entire course, the future of automated course authoring is able to interact with the students by customizing individual e-Learning process and automatically detecting their preferences in order to customize every aspect of their e-Learning experience.

Cloud-based Learning Systems. Cloud is everywhere, includes education, which is why so many LMS and authoring tools are now begin to support cloud-based platforms due to steadily growing in popularity over the past years. The cloud approach can not only reduce the cost of learning but also improve the safety of sensitive data being stored on the cloud through multi-level encryption. The learning on the cloud can be scalable very easily.

5 Conclusion

In this paper, we investigated current practices in local higher education institutions with e-Learning technologies and applications on how to enhance teaching and research in order to achieve social, cultural, environmental, or economic impacts. In particular, we investigated all public universities and one private college in Hong Kong in terms of various e-Learning technologies. We have demonstrated that all these e-Learning technologies help to enhance teaching and learning experiences, and make it more efficient and effective. Students can also benefit from these initiatives to become life-long learners.

Acknowledgment. The work described in this paper was fully supported by the Start-Up Research Grant (RG 37/2016-2017R) of The Education University of Hong Kong and a grant from the Research Grants Council of the Hong Kong Special Administrative Region, China (UGC/FDS11/E06/14).

References

1. Nicholson, P.: A history of e-Learning. In: Computers, Education: E-Learning, From Theory to Practice, pp. 1–11. Springer. ISBN: 978-1-4020-4914-9(2007)
2. Lau, C.M.: The Power of Games: Gamifying Cantonese Learning for Exchange Students, 10. http://tl.hku.hk/2016/08/the-power-of-games-gamifying-cantonese-learning-for-exchange-students/. Accessed 15 August 2016
3. Incident Report. http://www.cityu.edu.hk/elearn/incident_report.xml. Accessed 15 August 2016
4. Blackboard Introduces Cloud Version of Flagship LMS. http://www.blackboard.com/news-and-events/press-releases/2014/blackboard-introduces-cloud-version-of-flagship-lms.aspx. Accessed 15 August 2016
5. Moodle vs BlackBoard? That is the Question (2015). http://www.ispringsolutions.com/blog/moodle-vs-blackboard/. Accessed 15 August 2016
6. Coopman, S.J.: A critical examination of Blackboard's e-learning environment. First Monday, [S.l.], ISSN 13960466. http://firstmonday.org/ojs/index.php/fm/article/view/2434/2202. Accessed 15 August 2016
7. Ryan, F.N., et al.: Learning management system migration: An analysis of stakeholder perspectives. Int. Rev. Res. Open Distrib. Learn. 13(1), 220–237 (2012). http://www.irrodl.org/index.php/irrodl/article/view/1126/2078, ISSN 1492–3831. Accessed 15
8. Difference Between Blackboard and Canvas (2015). http://www.alamo.edu/mainwide.aspx?id=22961. Accessed 15 August 2016

9. Strmeki, D., Bernik, A., Radoevi, D.: Gamification in e-Learning: introducing gamified design elements into e-learning systems. J. Comput. Sci. **11**(12), 1108–1117 (2015)
10. Alevriadou, A., Urh, M., Vukovic, G., Jereb, E., Pintar, R.: The model for introduction of gamification into e-Learning in higher education. In: 7th World Conference on Educational Sciences, vol. 197, pp. 388–397 (2015)
11. Bedrule-Grigoruta, M.V., Rusua, M.L.: Considerations about e-Learning tools for adult education. Proc. Soc. Behav. Sci. **142**, 749–754 (2014)
12. Dominguez, A., Saenz-De-Navarrete, J., De-Marcos, L., Fernández-Sanz, L., Pages, C., Martinez-Herráiz, J.J.: Gamifying learning experiences: practical implications and outcomes. Comput. Educ. **63**, 380–392 (2013)

Diachronic Analysis on the Change of Citation Behaviour Based on the Core Medical Journals in Guangdong Province

Shuo Wang[1], Changchen Zhan[1], Yangling Chen[1], Qingyuan Wu[1],
Xinjie Yuan[1(✉)], and Lingnan He[2]

[1] School of Management, Beijing Normal University, Zhuhai Campus, China
233137494@qq.com
[2] The School of Communication and Design, Sun Yat-Sen University,
Guangzhou, China

Abstract. The information embedded in core academic journals is useful to learn effectively, recommend prestigious learning resources, and reflect the academic level of subjects in some areas. This article involves 11 Guangdong medical academic journals published from 1989 to 2015, which are collected from the Chinese Science Citation Database. We divide these journals into 4 small subjects and analyze them from both the time and subject dimensions. From the time dimension, the total cited curve presents an exponential trend. The annual averaged cited quantities are larger than those in the past. The earlier papers are published, the longer the interval between the published year and the year that reaches the cited peak. From the subject dimension, the cited curve of traditional Chinese medicine is apparently different from the other 3 subjects. These journals overall appear relatively consistent cited characteristics. The citation theory of periodical data can help us understand the citation rule of online learning data and use them more efficiently.

Keywords: Citation analysis · Diachronic perspective · Cited characteristic · Medical Journal

1 Introduction

Core academic journals consist of information on one or more certain fields, authoritative journals, the law-fully established periodical publishing units which published academic papers, research reports and comments [3]. These journals reflect the academic level of subjects in some areas. Citation analysis on core academic journals is benefit to scholars in terms of academic exchanging and resource sharing, opening circulation, fusion and development of knowledge in academia, as well as enhancing the public utilization degree of scientific researches and promoting the progress of certain subjects.

This article mines core medical journals from the diachronic perspective, and cites the concept of the journal's lifecycle to focus on differences and the trend. The main contributions of this paper are as follows: First, we study the change of Guangdong province medical core academic journal citation behaviour, and summarize the

© Springer International Publishing AG 2017
T.-T. Wu et al. (Eds.): SETE 2016, LNCS 10108, pp. 585–590, 2017.
DOI: 10.1007/978-3-319-52836-6_62

difference between subdivided medical subjects. Second, we alleviate the limitations of the synchronic analysis in previous studies. The rest of this paper is organized as follows. We describe related work in Sect. 2. The proposed method is presented in Sect. 3. The dataset, results and discussions are illustrated in Sect. 4. Finally, we draw conclusions in Sect. 5.

2 Related Work

Diachronic analysis has been widely applied to scientometrics, online learning, and distance education.

First, it is valuable to conduct citation analysis on academic journals, because they can imply the knowledge communication characteristics of Countries and other entities. For example, Bouabid and Larivière [1] used the model of Diachronic analysis to study the change of literature cited period, and found that developed Countries' literature cited period is shorter than developing Countries. Finardi [2] showed that the trend of the averaged paper cited amount changed over time, and the significant difference existed among different subjects. Larivi`ere et al. [4] concluded that citation dispersion increased significantly and cited papers became comprehensive and diverse. Yang et al. [7] conducted the research on citation behavior in China and got the same conclusion.

Second, a lot of researches presented that the distribution of cited papers had some regularity over time. Generally, as the time goes by, the number of cited papers presents an increasing trend, i.e., the more literature of cited papers. Besides, at different times and different academic conditions, the peak citations of interdisciplinary literature is different. For instance, Weaver and Barnard [6] showed that numbers of sources, use of instructor sources, and use of library's "Subject Guide" sources were positively related to each other. This research expands the literature by examining two successive assignments from a large sample of Online Distance Learning (ODL) students. Nicol et al. [5] explored the social dimensions of online learning, in which learners interacted and communicated with other learners and tutors used electronic communication networks. The longer the online communication is, the larger academic effect it has.

3 Proposed Method

The cited quantities of 11 core academic journals, i.e., Chines Journal of Nephrology, Chinese Journal of Microsurgery, Chinese Journal of Nervous and Mental Disease, Chinese Journal of Pathophysiology, Carcinogenesis: Teratogenesis & Mutagenesis, Chinese Journal of Cancer, Guangdong Medical Journal, Traditional Chinese Drug Research & Clinical Pharmacology, Journal of Chinese Medicinal Materials, Journal of Southern Medical University, and Chinese Journal of Orthopaedic Trauma are collected from 1989 to 2015. We here propose several equations to analyze these core academic journals in terms of cited quantities, the annual average cited quantities, and the average cited quantities.

There are four variables in our method. The first one i denotes the published year. The second one j represents the cited year. We have $1989 \leq i$ and $j \leq 2015$. The third one P_i denotes quantities of published articles in year i. The fourth one C_j denotes quantities of articles cited in year j and published in year i.

The averaged cited number changes after certain published year. After the year of publishing articles (x year), we have

$$MEAN_k = \frac{C_j}{P_i} \qquad (1)$$

where $MEAN_k$ is the averaged cited number after j years since the articles published in year i, and $x = j - i + 1$ includes the publishing year.

In this sample, x could be $1 - 27$, which is called $MEAN_k$ number. The values of $MEAN_k$ are estimated as follows:

$$MEAN_1 = \frac{C_{1991}}{P_{1989}}, MEAN_2 = \frac{C_{1992}}{P_{1990}}, \ldots, MEAN_N = \frac{C_{2015}}{P_{2013}} \qquad (2)$$

In the above, k could be 1 to N, and $N = 2015 - 1989 - x + 2$. Finally,

$$AMEAN_x = \frac{\sum_{k=1}^{N} MEAN_k}{N}, CAC_x = \frac{\sum_{j=1}^{i+x-1} C_j}{x \times P_i} \qquad (3)$$

where $AMEAN_x$ means the averaged cited value after articles published for a certain period of time. Using this formula could avoid the uncertainty caused by a single publishing year. The final result could be expressed by $AMEAN_x$ v.s. x. We use CAC_x to represent the cited-accumulative-average value after a certain year (x year) with publishing articles in a different time. Such as $i = 2010$, $x = 3$, the article is published in 2010, then using cited number of 2010, 2011, 2012, the annual average cited number could be calculated. In the same situation, $MEAN_k$, CAC_x also need the individual subject method to be estimated.

4 Result Analysis

In this section, we describe the citation changing of 11 core academic journals based on our aforementioned mathematical methods.

4.1 Diachronic Analysis of Papers Published in a Particular Year

After calculating cite numbers of papers each year, we observed that different representative subjects published in a particular year changed consistently, that is, they reached the peak of the discipline after being published 2 to 3 years, and then began to decline year by year. We also found that the earlier papers published, the later they reached the cited peak. Conversely, the peak arrived earlier. This phenomenon may be trigged by the development of science and the speed of information dissemination.

The overall trend was similar to the above observations, i.e., the cited amount of papers reached the peak in two years after being published, and then decreased year by year. But there is one exception, the trend of Chinese medicine journals is significantly different from other subjects, that is, the earlier papers published, the slower of aging. For them, the peaks of cited appeared in five years after being published. This phenomenon may be caused by the special nature of medical science.

The overall trend can be concluded as published papers cited increased year by year. At the same time, the Journal of clinical medicine, basic medicine, and the comprehensive discipline of Medicine published in the early years (2000 years ago), after 5 years and 6 years, it has a higher amount of cited quantity. But for papers published in recent years (after 2001), it is the highest value after being published from 2 to 3 years, it also reflects that the paper cited and life cycle of this paper is getting shorter and shorter. In the early published papers, the overall averaged cited amount of the medical comprehensive subjects was significantly lower than that in the recently published papers, also reflects the timeliness of the paper cited. However, the subject of Traditional Chinese Medicine and Pharmacy medicine still reflects the obvious difference between other disciplines, published in early or recent papers were cited for no significant change in trend, the change tends to be stable year after year.

4.2   Diachronic Analysis of Papers Published in a Time Period

In this part, we conduct Diachronic analysis on papers published in a time period.

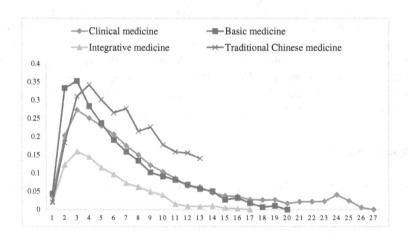

Fig. 1. The annual average cited quantity (y) v.s. time window (x) - $AMEAN_x$

As shown in Fig. 1, the peak of traditional Chinese medicine and pharmacy medicine is in the fourth years after the publication. Compared to other subjects that reach the peak, it declines slowly. The largest average cited of the other three subjects (clinical medicine, basic medicine, and comprehensive discipline of medicine) appeared in the third year after publication, and then began to decline. There is no peak

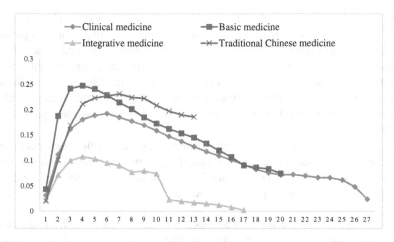

Fig. 2. The annual average cited quantity (y) v.s. time window (x) - CAC_x

appears again, and it shows that the three subjects are more like to quote some new articles, update faster, resulting in the short life cycle of the literature.

The curve of Fig. 2 shows the cumulative average of the cited quantity. Because the cumulative effect decline, the curve is smoother, the corresponding peak was delayed by some extent. Coupled with the cumulative effect, more obvious differences in the curve of the four disciplines, including traditional Chinese medicine and pharmacy medicine curve in papers published to reach peak after five years, has been maintained in higher cited values, and then have a slow decline. This may be related to the nature of the discipline of traditional Chinese medicine and pharmacy medicine, because the subject has a long history, the change is relatively slow, the knowledge system has been more mature and comprehensive, and so the literature has a long half-life and slower aging rate.

5   Conclusions

This paper shows the changes and differences in the process of mining Guangdong Province medical core journals citation behaviour. The following two points can be concluded: worthy of publication and other scholars' attention, and excessive posting may dilute the academic impact of core journals. Guangdong Medical Journal was established in 1963 which reflects the Guangdong medical and health research level, consisting of Guangdong Province clinical medical research results and practical experience of the representative journal reports. The method also played a good role in promoting the development of medical science and research. But Guangdong Medical Journal become a semi-monthly, which has a serious impact on the averaged volume of papers published in the journal and the averaged value of each year. Semi-monthly influences Guangdong medical journal articles in terms of cited number and the citation amount of averaged value, which is easier to ignore the dilution effect of core journals academic influence caused by the slightly lower evaluation. Due to the rapid development of science and technology in the present society, more and more scholars focus on innovation, new technology or concept learning, resulting in articles published in recent years. The averaged citation quantities and cited the averaged values at a high level. But it can not be ignored that a lot of early theories have a certain influence and rationality nowadays. For example, this paper published in different years. The cited amount of the paper shows that the peak will reach in 2–3 years after being published. Therefore, it is suggested that researchers should not ignore the early papers in the innovation.

This paper systematically analyzed the similarities and differences between the changes of the citation behaviour in Guangdong Province, and draws a series of conclusions. But citation behaviour has its complexity, uncertainty and individual differences, there are some content that need our further analysis.

Acknowledgements. The research work described in this article was fully supported by a grant from Innovation and entrepreneurship training program for 2015 Provincial College Students (Grant No. 201513177006), and a grant from the Soft Science Research Project of Guangdong Province (Grant No. 2014A030304013).

References

1. Bouabid, H., Larivière, V.: The lengthening of papers' life expectancy: a di- achronous analysis. Scientometrics **97**(3), 695–717 (2013)
2. Finardi, U.: On the time evolution of received citations, in different scientific fields: an empirical study. J. Informetrics **8**(1), 13–24 (2014)
3. Gui, Q., Zan, Z.: The research on development and the current situation in the medical core journals of china. Med. Philos. (A) **10**, 15–17 (1994)
4. Larivière, V., Gingras, Y., Archambault, E.: The decline in the concentration of citations, 19002007. J. Am. Soc. Inf. Sci. Technol. **60**(4), 858–862 (2009)
5. Nicol, D., Minty, I., Sinclair, C.: The social dimensions of online learning. Innovations Educ. Teach. Int. **40**(3), 270–280 (2003)
6. Weaver, N.E., Barnard, E.: A citation analysis of psychology students' use of sources in online distance learning. J. Libr. Inf. Serv. Distance Learn. **9**(4), 312–329 (2015)
7. Yang, S., Ma, F., Song, Y., Qiu, J.: A longitudinal analysis of citation distribution breadth for chinese scholars. Scientometrics **85**(3), 755–765 (2010)

On Security and Privacy of Quick Response System in Classroom Teaching

Ying Chen[1], Yunhui Zhuang[2,3(✉)], Haoran Xie[4], and Fu Lee Wang[5]

[1] Department of Foreign Language, Minjiang University, Fuzhou, China
[2] Department of Information Systems, City University of Hong Kong,
Kowloon Tong, Hong Kong
yhzhuang2-c@my.cityu.edu.hk
[3] Department of Computer Science, City University of Hong Kong,
Kowloon Tong, Hong Kong
[4] The Education University of Hong Kong, Tai Po, Hong Kong
[5] Caritas Institute for Higher Education, Tseung Kwan O, Hong Kong

Abstract. The Quick Response System (QRS) consists of a 2-D machine-readable QR Codes and a mobile-friendly user interface. The QR Codes can be encoded to different types of information. Because of QR code's high information density and robustness, it has gained popularity in many applications across various industries. Recently, some universities and colleges have adopted QR Code into classroom teaching, by taking advantage of its instant feedback from students, instructors may have immediate understanding of whether students have understood a concept. The QR code can be used for polling, tutorials, and quizzes. However, it is crucial to protect against personal data from disclosure and to prove student identity, especially in the event of an in-class QR Code-based quiz. In this paper, we explore some potential security breaches and privacy concerns for QR codes in classroom teaching, and propose some design requirements with respect to the QR code itself. We also suggest to apply a grouping-proof protocol to authenticate all students identity before starting a quiz. This paper sheds some lights on future research directions in QR code design and processing.

Keywords: QR code · Security and privacy · Classroom teaching

1 Introduction

QRS is very popular in our daily life with a broad range of advantages for various applications, ranging from the venue booking, classroom teaching, polling, to mobile payment system. QR Code was initially launched for supply chain purpose with main focus on tracking automotive parts during the production process in 1994 by Denso Wave in Japan. Nowadays, we can see QR Codes everywhere. The production and deployment of a QR Code are very cheap and easy. As a result, many organizations use QR Codes as their medium of choice in billboard advertising to attract potential customers. Among variety of use cases, URL encoding is the most commonly used one to instantly publish available information.

© Springer International Publishing AG 2017
T.-T. Wu et al. (Eds.): SETE 2016, LNCS 10108, pp. 591–597, 2017.
DOI: 10.1007/978-3-319-52836-6_63

Recently, QR Code has been used in mobile payment in Singapore [3]. PayPal launched first QR Code payment in Singapore subway. Later Alipay wallet, the largest third party mobile payment provider in China, has initialed mobile QR Code payment by encoding simple-to-read data (e.g. a link to an 18-digit one- time pad) that can be read and displayed by a smartphone. There exist some mobile payment applications other than PayPal and Alipay are also using QR codes, such as PayCash[1], LevelUp[2], and GO4Q[3], which all apply the QR code in traditional commercial settings. However, Chinese central bank suspended any mobile payments imposed by QR codes amid security and privacy concerns during the transactions. This was only a tip of the iceberg. QR codes have been misused as phishing attacks as attackers encode malicious links into the code to redirect to phishing sites or to execute fraudulent code [1, 2].

In Hong Kong, QR Code has been adopted in classroom teaching, where instructors can get an instant feedback from students on whether students have understood a concept. This QRS works as follows: (i) the instructor prepares for a set of questions and generates respective QR Code for each of those questions for students to respond, (ii) students scan the QR Code during a class via the mobile devices, (iii) the instructor releases the results to the class after collecting all responses. The responses could be anonymous or recorded. The system can be used for classroom polling, tutorials, and quiz. However, when students scan the unauthenticated data from billboards, posters, screens, or even stickers, QRS provides a phishing attack for attackers, who then lure students to scan the malicious codes and subsequently visit phishing websites. Furthermore, students need to provide proof of presence in the classroom in order to answer the questions via the link imposed by QR Code. This requires proximity authentication from students and their mobile devices to ensure they are in the classroom.

In this paper, we explore QR Code-based phishing attacks and try to identify some ways of improving the security of QR Code interaction. In addition, we suggest some solutions with respect to the proof of presence for QR Code initiated questions or quizzes in the classroom teaching. Finally, we propose a set of design requirements for QR code itself. This paper sheds some lights on future research directions in QR code design and processing.

2   Security of QR Code

In this section, we explore different attack scenarios imposed by QR Code. The most common attack for QR Code is phishing, where the attacker encodes a malicious QR Code to entice users to fraudulent websites and steal sensitive personal information, such as password or credit card information. Kieseberg et al. [5] proposed two commonly used attack vectors to exploit QR Code:

---

[1] http://www.paycash.eu/, accessed at: 08/15/2016.

[2] https://www.thelevelup.com/, accessed at: 08/15/2016.

[3] http://go4q.mobi/, accessed at: 08/15/2016.

1. **QR Code replacement.** This attack is intuitive because an attacker just creates a new QR Code with a malicious link encoded and replace it with the real one. This attack usually happens on billboard advertisement.
2. **QR Code individual module modification.** Since the encoded information in a QR Code is machine readable only, a human cannot distinguish a valid one against a maliciously encoded QR Code. Kieseberg et al. [5] proposed some possible modifications to different parts of QR Codes via ECC (Error Correction Codes) or masking, as shown in Fig. 1. This modification enables an attacker to either modify or inject information into the existing QR Codes. Figure 1b shows a modified QR Code to a malicious City University of Hong Kong website.

(a) www.cityu.edu.hk   (b) www.c1tyu.edu.hk

Fig. 1. QR code modification (Phishing) attack

In light of aforementioned two attack vectors, a series incidents against malicious QR Codes occurred [6, 7, 8]. Later two important papers talking about human computer interaction with respect to QR Code security has been acknowledged to Vidas et al. [1] and Seeburger et al. [9], who found out that the curiosity is the main motivation for mobile device users to scan a QR Code, and quite a number of users refused to continue to visit the encoded URL due to phishing attack concerns. With curiosity being the #1 cause for people to interact with unknown sources, many of them are unconsciously ignoring the security threats imposed by malicious QR codes. Their findings shed some lights on some important research challenges for the security of QR Codes.

1. **Security Awareness.** People from different cultures may have different understanding in terms of security and privacy concerns. As pointed out by Vidas et al. [1] and Seeburger et al. [9], a detailed understanding across cultures would significantly contribute to enhance security awareness.
2. **Design Requirements.** From cryptographic perspective, signing a digital signature would be a more secure way to verify the validity of the QR Code and therefore to check whether the code has been maliciously modified. An alternative solution would be to append a (keyed) Message Authentication Code (MAC). While the latter is faster and cheaper to implement, the former is proven to be more secure from lots of existing applications.

3. **Anti-Phishing Detection.** The scanning app should be able to detect the trust-worthiness of a URL by checking on the phishing blacklists or whitelists, or simply by metrics as proposed by Choi et al. [10].

3 Proof of Presence

If an instructor wants to conduct an in-class quiz in the form of QR Codes, he needs to be sure that every student sitting in the classroom belongs to his class. A proof of presence or proof of proximity for each student needs to provide to the instructor [4, 11]. By doing so, a grouping-proof protocol would suffice. This kind of authentication protocol is often used to prove the presence of a group of Provers to the Verifier at the same time. Therefore, the scanning app that every student has should be incorporated with a grouping-proof protocol to prove each student's physical presence in the classroom to the instructor. After scanning the first QR Code provided by the instructor, this app should launch a grouping-proof protocol and transmit its partial proof to the instructor. By linking all the partial proof together, the instructor is able to generate a group proof to ensure every student belong to this course is physically presented in the classroom. The protocol presented by Zhuang et al. [4] demonstrates such proof with some additional features, such as mutual authentication and privacy preserving. We take advantage of the core design from [4] and make some slight modifications to fit the classroom teaching scenario. The protocol is presented in Fig. 2. The notations are summarized in Table 1.

Table 1. Notations

X_j:	Student j's secret key stored in her mobile device
X_{j1} / X_{j2}:	Student j's two secret keys stored on instructor's server
$F(\cdot)$ / $G(\cdot)$:	Pseudo-random function (PRF)
ID_j:	Student j's identity number
N_T:	The counter, $N_T \to 0$
r_1 / r_2:	A random nounce with length l generated by two parties, respectively
$MAC(\cdot)$:	A keyed message authentication code with student j's secret key X_j
b_{j-1} / b_j:	Student j's partial proof or random nounce for Student l
$P_{1,...,m}$:	Grouping-proof for all students in the classroom

There are some minor differences in the protocol in terms of first student and the remaining students. When an instructor requests all students to authenticate themselves, the first student with the smallest student ID proceeds as follows:

1. Server sends a random challenge message b_{j-1} with length l to student l.
2. After receiving this challenge from instructor, student l immediately updates her counter as $N_T = N_T + 1$, together with her identity ID_1, the challenge b_{j-1} from instructor, her current secret key X_1, as the input to compute an l bit "dynamic pseudonym" $r_1 = F(X_1, ID_1, N_T, b_{j-1})^l$, which is then sent back to the server along with N_T.

3. Upon receiving $\{r_1, N_T\}$ from student 1, instructor picks another l-bit random challenge message r_2 and tries to search for student 1's identity.

4. The server searches the database for the tuple (x_{11}, ID_1) such that $F(X_{11}, ID_1, N_T, b_{j-1})^l == r_1$ holds. If such a tuple exists, it computes $V = G(X_{11}, r_1, r_2)^l$, then sends $\{r_2, V\}$ to student 1. If not, the server searches for the tuple (x_{12}, ID_1) such that $F(X_{12}, ID_1, N_T, b_{j-1})^l == r_1$ holds. If such a tuple exists, it computes $V = G(X_{12}, r_1, r_2)^l$. In the meantime, the server updates two keys as follows: $X_{11} = X_{12}$, $X_{12} = G(X_{12}, r_1, r_2, V)^l$. After that the server sends $\{r_2, V\}$ to student 1. Otherwise, the server responds with $V \in_R \{0, 1\}^l$, r_2, rejects student 1, and terminates the proof session.

5. After receiving $\{r_2, V\}$, student 1 computes the values of V and checks whether $G(X_1, r_1, r_2)^l == V$ holds. If yes, student 1 updates her secret key $X_1 = G(X_1, r_1, r_2, V)^l$ and generates her partial proof by applying a MAC: $b_1 = MAC(X_1, ID_1, b_{j-1})^l$, and sends b_1 to instructor's server. Otherwise, student 1 rejects instructor's response and terminates the proof session.

6. The server keeps $\{ID_1, b_1\}$ for the next protocol execution and verification.

The main difference between the remaining students and student 1 is that: instead of a random challenge message, the server sends previous student's partial proof b_{j-1} as "a challenge message" to student j, where $j = 2, ..., m$. This makes all remaining students' partial proof linked together in order to prevent man-in-the-middle and replay attacks. After receiving b_{j-1}, student j will perform the same task as that of student 1. In the meantime, the server is going to verify student j's identity the same way when verifying student 1 via several if-else decision makings. Finally, student j generates her partial

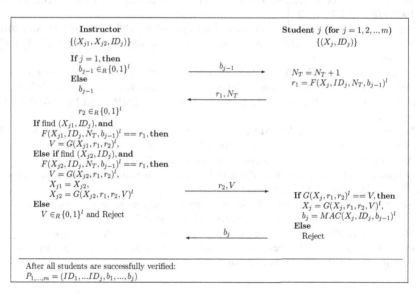

Fig. 2. A grouping-proof protocol for classroom teaching

proof by applying a MAC: $b_j = MAC(X_j, ID_j, b_{j-1})^l$, where one of the inputs is previous student's partial proof b_{j-1}, and then sends b_j to the server.

4   Concluding Remarks

Due to rapid development of e-Learning technologies, many universities start to adopt QR Codes in classroom teaching. Such practices include polling, tutorials, and quizzes. However, it is crucial to protect against personal data from disclosure and to prove a student's identity, especially in the event of an in-class QR Code-based quiz. In this paper, we first explored some potential security breaches and privacy concerns for QR codes in classroom teaching, then proposed some solutions with respect to the design and process of QR code itself. We also suggest to use a grouping-proof protocol to authenticate all students' identities before starting a quiz.

Acknowledgements. The work described in this paper was fully supported by the Start-Up Research Grant (RG 37/2016-2017R) of The Education University of Hong Kong and a grant from the Research Grants Council of the Hong Kong Special Administrative- Region, China (UGC/FDS11/E06/14).

References

1. Vidas, T., Owusu, E., Wang, S., Zeng, C., Cranor, L.F., Christin, N.: QRishing: the susceptibility of smartphone users to QR code phishing attacks. In: Adams, A.A., Brenner, M., Smith, M. (eds.) FC 2013. LNCS, vol. 7862, pp. 52–69. Springer, Heidelberg (2013). doi:10. 1007/978-3-642-41320-9_4
2. Security attacks via malicious QR codes. https://goo.gl/WYO9lr. Accessed 15 Aug 2016
3. Moth, D.: PayPal trials QR code shop in Singapore subway (2012). http://goo.gl/qjalQQ. Accessed 15 Aug 2016
4. Zhuang, Y., Hancke, G.P., Wong, D.S.: How to demonstrate our presence without disclosing identity? evidence from a grouping-proof protocol. In: Kim, H., Choi, D. (eds.) WISA 2015. LNCS, vol. 9503, pp. 423–435. Springer, Heidelberg (2016). doi:10.1007/978-3-319-31875-2_35
5. Kieseberg, P., Leithner, M., Mulazzani, M., Munroe, L., Schrittwieser, S., Sinha, M., Weippl, E.: QR Code Security. In: Proceedings of the 8th International Conference on Advances in Mobile Computing and Multimedia, pp. 430–435 (2010)
6. Borgaonkar, M.: Dirty use of USSD codes in cellular network. http://www.youtube.com/watch?v=Q2–0B04HPhs. Accessed 15 Aug 2016
7. Wagenseil, P.: Anti-Anonymous hacker threatens to expose them. http://www.nbcnews.com/id/46716942/ns/technologyandscience-security/. Accessed 15 Aug 2016
8. Moore, T., Edelman, B.: Measuring the perpetrators and funders of typosquatting. In: Proceedings of the 14th International Conference on Financial Cryptography and Data Security, FC 2010, pp. 175–191 (2010)

9. Seeburger, J.: No cure for curiosity: linking physical and digital urban layers. In: Proceedings of the 7th Nordic Conference on Human-Computer Interaction: making sense through design, pp. 247–256. ACM (2012)

10. Choi, H., Zhu, B.B., Lee, H.: Detecting malicious web links and identifying their attack types. In: Proceedings of the 2nd USENIX Conference on Web Application Development, p. 11 (2011)

11. Zhuang, Y., Yang, A., Wong, D.S., Yang, G., Xie, Q.: A highly efficient RFID distance bounding protocol without real-time PRF evaluation. In: Lopez, J., Huang, X., Sandhu, R. (eds.) NSS 2013. LNCS, vol. 7873, pp. 451–464. Springer, Heidelberg (2013). doi:10.1007/978-3-642-38631-2_33

Workshop on Peer Review, Peer Assessment, and Self-assessment in Education

Improving Peer Assessment Modeling
of Teacher's Grades, The Case of OpenAnswer

Maria De Marsico[1], Andrea Sterbini[1(✉)], and Marco Temperini[2]

[1] Computer Science Department, Sapienza University, Rome, Italy
{demarsico,sterbini}@di.uniroma1.it
[2] Computer, Control, and Management Eng. Department,
Sapienza University, Rome, Italy
marte@dis.uniroma1.it

Abstract. Questions with answers are rarely used as e-learning assessment tools because of the resulting high workload for the teacher/tutor that should grade them, which can be mitigated by doing peer-assessment. In OpenAnswer we modeled peer-assessment as a Bayesian network connecting the sub-networks representing any participating student to the corresponding answers of her graded peers. The model has shown good ability to predict (without further info from the teacher) the exact teacher's grade (ground truth) from the peer grades only, and a very good ability to predict it within 1 mark from the right one. In this paper we explore changes to the OpenAnswer model to improve its predictions. The experimental results, obtained by simulating teacher's grading on real datasets, show the improved predictions.

Keywords: Automatic correction of OpenAnswers · Peer assessment modeling · Bayesian networks

1 Introduction

Student's learning activity is primarily deemed to let the person acquire knowledge, and be able to use it. However, the ability to "evaluate" is crucial for a reasonable use of one's knowledge. *Evaluating* is indeed considered as a high level skill, higher than the well-known *remember*, or *understand* cognitive levels in the Bloom's Taxonomy [1, 2]. As a metacognitive skill, evaluation abilities bridge knowledge/proficiency, on a topic, with activities associated to learning and to the use of what was learnt, namely activities such as: checking on one's own and others' comprehension of a topic, monitoring the proceeding of a task, planning schedules and strategies, and putting actually on trial and to use newly acquired concepts and rules.

In the OpenAnswer system [14–16] (OA), peer-assessment brings in its widely renowned effects on developing better understanding, and learning, of topics, and on achieving higher *metacognitive* abilities by the part of the learners. OA allows for (semi-)automated grading of answers to open ended questions, basing on both peer assessment and teacher's grading. Dealing with open ended questions provides the possibility to have a much more reliable evaluation of students' proficiency (with respect to, e.g., multiple-choice tests) [11]; however this practice is more demanding

© Springer International Publishing AG 2017
T.-T. Wu et al. (Eds.): SETE 2016, LNCS 10108, pp. 601–613, 2017.
DOI: 10.1007/978-3-319-52836-6_64

for both the student and the teacher; in particular, for the teacher, it requires a longer revision activity. So it is important to point out, here, that a significant (expected) effect of using peer-assessment in OA is in that the teacher can be relieved from part of the burden of grading the complete set of answers: basing on peers' and teacher's (partial) assessment, the system can infer the remaining grades. In OA, during an assessment session on a specific question, after submitting her answer each student is requested to grade some (e.g., 3) of her peers' answers to the same question. Then a subset of the answers (selected through the application of certain criteria, that we call "strategies") is directly graded by the teacher. Peers' and teacher's assessments are used as evidence, which is propagated within a Bayesian Network (BN) conceived here. In such network the students are modeled by their *Knowledge* level on the topic (K), and by the ability to evaluate peers' answers, denoted as *Judgment* (J). Moreover each answer has a current estimated *Correctness* (C). K, J, C are discrete variables that can be influenced by evidence propagation throughout the network; they are expressed as probability distributions (how probable each allowed – possible – value is). As a student marks a peer's answer, a corresponding discrete variable *Grade* (G) is added to the network, and propagated as well. Variables C and J are assumed to be conditioned by K ($C|K$ and $J|K$), therefore for each of them we have a Conditional Probability Table (CPT). The usefulness of this process and of peer-evaluation [13], depends on the reliability of the grades inferred by the system for the ungraded answers, so in this paper we evaluate how the reliability of the OA predictions improve when the model is modified as described later.

In particular, we present an analysis of a large series of simulations of the system's behaviors, conducted on datasets composed by peers' assessment and teacher's grading taken from several exercises done in the field. The simulations test the use of the system in different scenarios: a starting case is based on the use of the datasets limited to the peer-assessment data only; then simulations are conducted by using both peers' and teachers' grading from the datasets. When a teacher is involved, the simulations test different combinations of (1) strategies to select the next answer to be graded by the teacher, (2) termination conditions for the grading process, and (3) a variety of constituents of the system: Conditional Probability Tables and Probability Distributions, regarding the Bayesian Network variables, and mapping functions by which the system infers a final grade basing on its current probability distribution. In the next subsection we describe our research questions, anticipating some technical aspects of the system where needed. Then in Sect. 2 some research work on the topics of this paper is recalled. Section 3 will describe the system. In Sects. 4 and 5 we introduce and discuss the experimental work done. Some conclusions are finally drawn in Sect. 6.

1.1 Research Questions

We have anticipated already that our model of peer assessment is based on discrete variables (K, J, C, G) in a BN: at any time, their values are probability distributions, and their dependences are expressed through CPTs. Additionally the K variable needs an initial Probability Distribution (PD) over the class of students where we use OpenAnswer. Moreover, we stress that the final grade for an answer, if not provided by the teacher, is computed "mapping" the current value of the corresponding C (i.e. its probability distribution) over, for instance, the scale A...F. Besides the strategies and termination conditions, that we will describe in Sect. 3, the adoption of different CPTs, PD, and MAPPING methods (cfr. above), may bring different system's performances. With respect to previous work, we designed a new strategy for the selection of the next best answer to be graded by the teacher: we call it a two-phases strategy ([2PHASES]) and describe it later. Moreover, we have devised a different method (based on median computation) for the mapping operation, and introduced a CPT for the variable G, *CPTG*, modeled by Gaussian distributions. So, in our evaluation we considered a general research question, from which three sub-questions stem, regarding the new factors mentioned above:

RQ: Is OpenAnswer improving respect to a simple "pure" peer-evaluation approach? and, in relation to the possible advantages using OpenAnswer,

- [CPTG] *is the system improving by using the Gaussian CPTG?*
- [MAPPING] *is there evidence of a better behavior using the mapping method "Median" instead of the previous "WeightedSum"?*
- [2PHASES] *is the sequencing of two different strategies, each one with its own termination condition, making the final grade inference better?*

2   Related Work

Open ended questions can be a powerful tool in education. In [12] the application of data mining and natural language processing techniques to education is reported. In [3] (semi-)automatic assessment of open-answers relies on methods of the semantic web. An ontology models the knowledge domain and its use supports the educational process. The teacher plays a crucial role in the definition of course ontology and questions' semantic annotations, while such role is less necessary later. Open answers are analyzed also in [7], where they are representing formal transformations used to solve problems in algebra. The analysis of an answer (that are basically made of plain alge expressions) aims to spot misconceptions to be dealt with in the lines of an Intelligent Tutoring System (ITS). The automatic analysis of open answers is applied also in other fields than education, such as in the context of marketing applications, where techniques as those mentioned above are used to extract customer opinions and to define "reputation of product" [17]. In [8] concept mapping and *coding schemes* are used with the same goals. Regarding peer-assessment, a wide study, performed in a prototype educational application is in [5], while [9] states that a relationships does exist between the quality of the peers feedback, on a learner's job, and the quality of the final project submitted by the learner.

The OA system presented here relies on the evaluation of answers coming from peer-assessment, and on the student modeling organized through the use of BNs. There are other approaches based on BN; for instance [6] applies such techniques to support learner's modeling in the framework of an ITS. Examples of modeled activities are knowledge assessment, plan recognition and prediction, the last two deemed to see what intentions are behind a learner's choice, and what following choices might be, during the phase of problem solving. The proper definition of "scoring criteria", and their detailed ratio, is considered an important factor: absence thereof, or lack of specificity might be conducive to bad peers behaviors, such as not all the mark scale being used (and typically only the higher part) [10]. OA is based only on the grades given by peers and teacher, abstracting from the exact definition of how to grade, which is left to the teacher that explains to the students the assessing criteria to be used as marking reference. In our experience too many criteria might result cumbersome for the peers.

An aspect of research in peer-assessment regards the number of peer-evaluations each job should undergo during peer-evaluation. In OA this is a configurable value, three by default. In literature it has been found that more feedbacks on the same job make the peers suitable to perform more complex revisions on their products, ending up with a better assessment result [4].

3   The OpenAnswer Model

OA models peer-assessment as a Bayesian network (BN) made of interconnected sub-networks, each one representing one of the participating students. The student model sub-network is made of three discrete variables, representing respectively:

- K: her **knowledge** about the topic
- C: the **correctness** of her answer
- J: her ability to **judge**/assess the answer of a peer

The student models are interconnected by adding a variable G for each **grade** given to a peer, connected to the peer's C variable. All such Bayesian variables range over the 6-valued discrete domain A (best) … F (fail). Figure 1 shows an example of student sub-network, with the probability computed for each domain value of C, K and J, given the grades G chosen for her three peers.

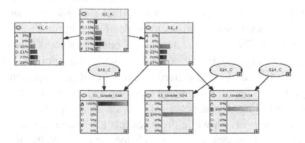

Fig. 1. Bayesian model of student S1, who is grading the answers of students S46, S24 and S14 with grades A, C, B, respectively.

We assume that both C and J probabilistically depend on K because:

1. C: writing an essay cannot easily be solved by guessing, as in multiple-choice quizzes (and we do not model cheating yet);

2. *J*: inspired by Bloom's taxonomy of cognitive levels [3], we assume that judging a peer's answer should be a more difficult task than answering the question.
3. *G*: the grade *G* given to a peer's answer probabilistically depends from both the answer's Correctness and the student's Judgment ability.

Once the Bayesian network is complete we use it to infer what would be the K, J and C of each student, by adding as evidence all the G peer assessment grades and by propagating the values in the BN. Our aim is to analyze the assessment and possibly get a clear picture of the class modeled. Moreover, with a partial grading from the teacher, we refine the network prediction of the student's C by entering as evidence the actual Correctness of the subset of corrected answers, i.e. the teacher's grade. In earlier work we analyzed several parameters affecting the network by simulating teacher's grading, and noticed that the CPTs, defining the probabilistic dependencies (J and C from K, and G from J and C) influence the quality of grade prediction.

To find the model's prediction ability we simulate the teacher correction by selecting the next answer to grade (depending on a specific selection *strategy*) and we stop when a given *termination* criterion is met. The initial probability distribution (PD for short) *P(K)* can be initialized in different ways: **flat** (no information prior of grading), **TgradeDist** (the same distribution of the teacher grades this mimics the situation when the teacher knows the distribution of good, average and bad students in the class), or **synthetic** (hand-made distribution centered on the 'C' grade). When a grade must be inferred from the BN, the current PD of C is mapped to a grade by summing the possible grades, each weighted by the corresponding probability.

According to the research question mentioned in Sect. 1, here we try to improve the predictions by proposing three changes:

1. The introduction of a CPTG modeled as a set of Gaussian functions. We noticed that the Grade CPT was not particularly selective, i.e., the probability distribution *P (G|J, C)* was "flat". For the student model this implied that grades are similarly weighted (as opposed to being more probable when close to the correct mark).
2. Replacing *weightedSum* method of mapping a PD to a grade by the *median* value.
3. The introduction of a new two-phase selection strategy, *maxWrongThenMaxEntropy*. We start using the *maxWrong* selection strategy, and then try to improve its results applying a *maxEntropy* phase. Definitions are in Sect. 4.

4 Methodology

To analyze how much OA improves its predictions we have run simulations of the teacher grading job. A simulation mimics the teacher's grading, which at each step is suggested by OA what answer to correct next (depending on the correction strategy), until a termination criterion is met. Each new grade is inserted in the Bayesian network as evidence of the Correctness (value) of the corresponding answer. Before the next answer is suggested this new evidence is propagated and the termination criterion is tested. As soon as the criterion is met, the remaining grades are predicted and compared with the remaining teacher's grades (ground truth).

More in detail, the *strategies* considered to suggest the next answer to grade are:

- *maxEntropy*: choose the answer OA knows less about (max C information entropy),
- *maxTotalEntropy*: choose the student OA knows less about (max sum of the information entropy of C, J, K),
- *maxInfoGain*: takes an answer ensuring max increase of information (i.e. max decrease of total information entropy over the network) no matter how it's graded,
- *maxStrangeness*: choose the student farthest from the OA model (with J and C most different, i.e. with good judgment of her peers but poor answer, or vice versa, with poor judgment but very good answer),
- *maxWrong*: choose the most wrong answer (as no student would accept an "automatically assigned fail" all wrong answers should be manually graded anyway),
- *random*: choose at random,
- *maxWrongThenMaxEntropy*: a new two-phases strategy, which first applies *maxWrong*, then *maxEntropy*.

The available *termination* criteria are:

- *noFlip(N)*: the inferred grades are stable in the last $N + 1$ corrections,
- *noWrong*: no inferred grade is F(ail),
- *noWrong2*: there is no remaining answer with $P(C = F) > 1/2$,
- *noWrong3*: there is no remaining answer with $P(C = F) > 1/3$,
- *noWrong(X)ThenNoFlip(N)*: (two-phases strategy). When *noWrong(X)* is satisfied the first phase is completed and the second starts with termination *noFlip(N)*.

In general, *maxWrong* is best associated with *noWrong* <p> and *maxEntropy* with *noFlip(N)*, while *random* can be associated with both the termination criteria types.

The *CPTC* describing $P(C|K)$ is chosen among 4 different hand-crafted CPT (Fig. 2):

P(C|K)	A	B	C	D	E	F
A	20%	9%	1%	1%	1%	1%
B	40%	20%	9%	7%	6%	1%
C	20%	40%	20%	12%	10%	1%
D	12%	20%	40%	20%	18%	7%
E	7%	9%	20%	40%	25%	20%
F	1%	2%	10%	20%	40%	70%

P(C|K)	A	B	C	D	E	F
A	40%	5%	5%	5%	5%	2%
B	30%	40%	5%	5%	5%	3%
C	15%	25%	45%	15%	10%	10%
D	10%	15%	20%	45%	15%	15%
E	4%	10%	15%	15%	45%	25%
F	1%	5%	10%	15%	20%	45%

P(C|K)	A	B	C	D	E	F
A	50%	20%	7%	3%	2%	1%
B	30%	50%	13%	7%	4%	3%
C	10%	12%	50%	10%	6%	6%
D	6%	9%	15%	50%	8%	10%
E	3%	6%	10%	20%	50%	30%
F	1%	3%	5%	10%	30%	50%

P(C|K)	A	B	C	D	E	F
A	70%	20%	7%	3%	2%	1%
B	10%	50%	13%	7%	4%	3%
C	8%	12%	50%	10%	6%	4%
D	6%	9%	15%	50%	8%	5%
E	4%	6%	10%	20%	50%	7%
F	2%	3%	5%	10%	30%	80%

Fig. 2. CPT **A** (top left): for each value of K, $P(C|K)$ has its maximum on $K-1$. CPT **M0** (top right): for each value of K, $P(C|K)$ has its maximum on k. CPT **M1** (bottom left): half probability is concentrated on $C = K$. CPT **M4** (bottom right): same as **M1**, except for first and last columns.

- **A**: with max of $P(C|K)$ over one grade less than K.
- **M0, M1, M4**: variations of CPTs with max of $P(C|K)$ over K. The three CPTs differ in how high is the maximum and how much the distribution is spread.

The *CPTG* describing $P(G|J,C)$ instead can be chosen among:

- **A**: a truncated flat distribution (normalized to 1 for any J,C choice):

— $P(G|J,C) = 0$ if $|G−C| >= J$ (with A = 0...F = 5)
— $P(G|J,C) = 1$ otherwise

(a flat distribution falling to 0 when G is more than J grades from the correct C).

- **Gauss** (the new proposal): $P(G|J,C) = Gaussian(mu(J,C), sigma(J,C))$ where

— $mu(J, C) = C$ (with A = 0...F = 5)
— $sigma(J, C) = 0.5 * J + 0.5$ (with A = 0...F = 5)

(here the max is on the correct grade C; the stdev of choosing a wrong grade is linearly related to the Judgment ability (best if J = A, worst if J = F)).

5 Experimental Results

The simulations have been run on datasets representing various peer-assessments, conducted by authors and colleagues mainly at university-level in engineering, or highschool level in physics or information representation (see Table 1).

Table 1. The dataset composition.

Dataset	Level	Topic	Groups	Students
A-6-1	Univ.	6 exercises on multi-level cache systems	2	7 to 15
M-6-1	Univ.	3 exercises on C programming	2	9 to 13
I-6-1	H.School	1 physics exercise	2	14 and 12
A2-5-4	Univ.	1 essay on social tools	5	12 (60 assessments)
F-6-1	H.School	1 number representation exercise	2	12

Overall, our dataset is made of: 14 different questions, which have generated 23 peer assessment (some question was given to 2 groups), the students involved where 240, giving a total of 285 answers (some student participated to more assessments), which have collected 465 teacher grades (some answer has been graded by more teachers) and 1875 peer grades (some answer had more than 3 peer grades).

We first report the performance of pure peer assessment over the whole datasets, i.e., the accuracy of average peer grades compared with the ground truth of teachers' grades. The percentage of average peer grades which are correct (OK/TOTAL) is 47%, while if we admit a difference of ±1 grade (IN1/TOTAL) the average peers get 87%.

In order to deal with RQ, we started comparing the above rates with those obtained by "OA without the teacher", i.e. by just letting the peer grades propagate across the BN. The termination condition in this case is called **none** (no teacher's grading). The results we present show the behavior of the same "percentages of success" mentioned above (OK/TOTAL and IN1/TOTAL) with respect to different simulated combinations of the CPTs, P(K) distributions and mappings described earlier; cfr. Table 2: the choice of *CPTG = Gauss* improves the results (respect to the earlier CPTG = A), especially when *CPTC = M4*, obtaining 50% OK/TOTAL and 88% IN1/TOTAL. As of the way a PD is mapped to a value, the *median* mapping seems to be almost as effective as the old *weightedSum*. Finally, both the *TgradeDist* and the *flat* way to initialize *P(K)* produced good results (with *flat* slightly better), while the *synthetic* is definitely worse (column STAT).

Table 2. Predictions of teacher grades with no teacher correction (termination = none).

CPTC	CPTG								
	A		M0		M1		M4		
PROB2VAL	median	w. Sum	median	w. Sum	median	w. Sum	median	w. Sum	STAT
OK/TOTAL	43%	44%	45%	47%	45%	46%	46%	47%	TgradeDist
	41%	46%	43%	46%	43%	47%	43%	47%	flat
	41%	45%	42%	45%	44%	45%	44%	45%	synthetic
IN1/TOTAL	87%	86%	86%	85%	87%	86%	**88%**	88%	TgradeDist
	86%	85%	86%	85%	86%	86%	86%	85%	flat
	86%	86%	86%	85%	85%	84%	85%	85%	synthetic
CPTG = Gauss									
OK/TOTAL	43%	45%	47%	48%	47%	48%	49%	49%	TgradeDist
	45%	47%	46%	47%	47%	49%	47%	**50%**	flat
	43%	45%	46%	48%	47%	48%	48%	48%	synthetic
IN1/TOTAL	86%	86%	86%	86%	87%	86%	87%	86%	TgradeDist
	86%	86%	85%	87%	87%	86%	86%	86%	flat
	85%	84%	85%	85%	85%	85%	85%	85%	synthetic

Tables 3 and 4 present the results that we obtained for the best candidates identified from Table 2 (*CPTC = M4, weightedSum, CPTG = Gauss, P(K) = flat*). They show the performance results associated to different combinations of *strategies* and *termination conditions*. First (Table 3) we analyze the prediction ability of the OA model, by showing *OK/INFERRED*, the percentage of exact inferred grades and *IN1/INFERRED*, the percentage of grades inferred within 1 mark from the ground truth, for the P(K) initialization *flat* (similar results are obtained for *TgradeDist*). The inference quality, with a partial grading, is well above (56% OK and 92% IN1) both the BN ability alone (termination *none*, 50% OK and 86% IN1), and the raw peer assessment (46% OK and 87% IN1), with a maximum increase of 10% (from 46% to 56%) and of 5% (from 87% to 92%) for both the *OK* and *IN1* ratios. The best strategy seems to be *maxEntropy* (termination *noWrong3*). The new two-phase *maxWrongThenMaxEntropy* (rightmost column) seems to be less effective, when only the prediction precision is considered.

Table 3. Prediction performances in the case CPTG = Gauss, P(K) = flat, CPTC = M4

		CPTG Gauss							MaxWrong then MaxEntropy		
		CPTC M4									
		PROB2VAL WeightedSum									
STAT	STRATEGY (TERMINATION)	noFlip1	noFlip2	noFlip3	noWrong	noWrong2	noWrong3	none		Termination1	Termination2
OK/INFERRED (correctly inferred) flat	maxEntropy	48%	47%	46%	56%	54%	**56%**	50%	46%	**noWrong2**	**NoFlip1**
	maxInfoGain	46%	45%	44%	52%	50%	52%	49%	45%	**noWrong2**	**NoFlip2**
	maxStrangeness	49%	46%	42%	47%	46%	45%	50%	48%	**noWrong3**	**NoFlip1**
	maxTotalEntropy	47%	48%	44%	51%	49%	49%	50%	46%	**noWrong3**	**NoFlip2**
	maxWrong	49%	44%	44%	49%	47%	48%	50%	49%	**noWrong**	**NoFlip1**
	random	47%	47%	47%	47%	48%	49%	50%	48%	**noWrong**	**NoFlip2**
IN1/INFERRED (inferred within 1 mark) flat	maxEntropy	88%	88%	88%	91%	90%	**92%**	86%	90%	**noWrong2**	**NoFlip1**
	maxInfoGain	87%	89%	87%	90%	89%	91%	86%	89%	**noWrong2**	**NoFlip2**
	maxStrangeness	85%	85%	84%	84%	86%	85%	86%	88%	**noWrong3**	**NoFlip1**
	maxTotalEntropy	87%	87%	89%	87%	84%	85%	86%	90%	**noWrong3**	**NoFlip2**
	maxWrong	88%	89%	85%	87%	87%	88%	86%	88%	**noWrong**	**NoFlip1**
	random	85%	85%	85%	89%	86%	90%	86%	89%	**noWrong**	**NoFlip2**

Table 4. Correction length and other results vs. Strategy and Termination.

			CPTG							MaxWrong then MaxEntropy		
			CPTC									
			PROB2VAL									
			Gauss									
			Marco4									
			WeightedSum									
	STAT	STRATEGY	noFlip1	noFlip2	noFlip3	noWrong	noWrong2	noWrong3	none		Termination1	Termination2
L/TOTAL(correction length)	flat	maxEntropy	11%	26%	41%	34%	33%	34%	0%	34%	noWrong2	NoFlip1
		maxInfoGain	11%	26%	43%	31%	30%	32%	0%	31%	noWrong2	NoFlip2
		maxStrangeness	15%	34%	51%	20%	18%	21%	0%	20%	noWrong3	NoFlip1
		maxTotalEntropy	11%	26%	45%	33%	32%	33%	0%	34%	noWrong3	NoFlip2
		maxWrong	11%	27%	46%	10%	8%	10%	0%	21%	noWrong	NoFlip1
		random	15%	35%	52%	28%	22%	28%	0%	19%	noWrong	NoFlip2
OK/TOTAL(precision)	flat	maxEntropy	42%	35%	27%	35%	**35%**	35%	50%	32%	noWrong2	NoFlip1
		maxInfoGain	41%	34%	25%	36%	36%	36%	49%	32%	noWrong2	NoFlip2
		maxStrangeness	41%	31%	23%	40%	40%	40%	50%	39%	noWrong3	NoFlip1
		maxTotalEntropy	42%	36%	26%	35%	35%	35%	50%	32%	noWrong3	NoFlip2
		maxWrong	44%	34%	25%	44%	44%	44%	50%	39%	noWrong	NoFlip1
		random	40%	31%	23%	37%	39%	37%	50%	39%	noWrong	NoFlip2
(OK + L)/TOTAL(exact delivered)	flat	maxEntropy	54%	61%	68%	69%	68%	**69%**	50%	66%	noWrong2	NoFlip1
		maxInfoGain	53%	60%	68%	67%	66%	67%	49%	63%	noWrong2	NoFlip2
		maxStrangeness	56%	65%	74%	60%	58%	61%	50%	60%	noWrong3	NoFlip1
		maxTotalEntropy	54%	61%	71%	68%	68%	68%	50%	**65%**	noWrong3	NoFlip2
		maxWrong	55%	61%	71%	55%	52%	54%	50%	61%	noWrong	NoFlip1
		random	55%	66%	76%	64%	61%	65%	50%	58%	noWrong	NoFlip2
(OK + L)/L(exact per work unit)	flat	maxEntropy	4,7	2,3	1,7	2,0	2,1	**2,0**		1,9	noWrong2	NoFlip1
		maxInfoGain	4,6	2,3	1,6	2,2	2,2	2,1		2,0	noWrong2	NoFlip2
		maxStrangeness	3,7	1,9	1,4	3,0	3,2	2,9		2,9	noWrong3	NoFlip1
		maxTotalEntropy	4,7	2,4	1,6	2,1	2,1	2,1		1,9	noWrong3	NoFlip2
		maxWrong	5,1	2,2	1,5	5,3	6,5	5,5		**2,8**	noWrong	NoFlip1
		random	3,8	1,9	1,4	2,3	2,7	2,3		3,1	noWrong	NoFlip2
IN1/TOTAL(precision within 1 mark)	flat	maxEntropy	78%	65%	52%	60%	60%	**60%**	86%	59%	noWrong2	NoFlip1

(continued)

Table 4. (continued)

	CPTG	Gauss									
	CPTC	Marco4									
	PROB2VAL	WeightedSum							MaxWrong then MaxEntropy		
STAT	TERMINATION	noFlip1	noFlip2	noFlip3	noWrong	noWrong2	noWrong3	none		Termination1	Termination2
	STRATEGY										
(IN1 + L)/TOTAL(delivered within 1 mark) flat	maxInfoGain	77%	66%	51%	62%	63%	62%	86%	62%	noWrong2	NoFlip2
	maxStrangeness	71%	56%	41%	71%	72%	70%	86%	71%	noWrong3	NoFlip1
	maxTotalEntropy	77%	65%	49%	60%	60%	61%	86%	60%	noWrong3	NoFlip2
	maxWrong	79%	65%	49%	79%	80%	80%	86%	70%	noWrong	NoFlip1
	random	73%	55%	41%	65%	68%	65%	86%	73%	noWrong	NoFlip2
flat	maxEntropy	89%	91%	93%	94%	93%	**94%**	86%	94%	noWrong2	NoFlip1
	maxInfoGain	89%	92%	94%	93%	93%	94%	86%	93%	noWrong2	NoFlip2
	maxStrangeness	87%	90%	92%	91%	90%	91%	86%	92%	noWrong3	NoFlip1
	maxTotalEntropy	89%	91%	94%	93%	93%	93%	86%	94%	noWrong3	NoFlip2
	maxWrong	89%	92%	94%	89%	88%	89%	86%	92%	noWrong	NoFlip1
	random	87%	91%	94%	92%	91%	93%	86%	91%	noWrong	NoFlip2
(IN1 + L)/L(within 1 mark per work unit) flat	maxEntropy	688%	246%	129%	178%	184%	**177%**		173%	noWrong2	NoFlip1
	maxInfoGain	678%	253%	120%	199%	206%	194%		197%	noWrong2	NoFlip2
	maxStrangeness	470%	164%	81%	351%	402%	332%		348%	noWrong3	NoFlip1
	maxTotalEntropy	676%	254%	109%	186%	186%	185%		179%	noWrong3	NoFlip2
	maxWrong	737%	239%	107%	766%	989%	814%		330%	noWrong	NoFlip1
	random	496%	156%	78%	234%	310%	230%		389%	noWrong	NoFlip2

Showing how much work the teacher does, w.r.t. strategy and termination, might give a better picture of the results. In Table 4 we show the average correction length *L/TOTAL*, the total amount of exact grades delivered *(OK + L)/TOTAL* and the amount of exact grades obtained for unit of work *(OK + L)/L* (and similarly for *IN1* in place of *OK*). Two competing goals (1) shorter correction, (2) higher percentage of exact grades find a good compromise in the case of *maxEntropy/noFlip3*, where a 34% long correction delivers 69% correct grades to the student (and 94% grades within 1 mark); with an efficiency of 1 exact grade inferred per answer graded. Finally, the two-phase strategy gives similar results, and slightly shorter length, improving work-efficiency.

The results confirm that OA can predict rather well the exact teacher grades even with a relatively short partial teacher correction, with an evident increase in quality when *CPTG = Gauss* and *CPTC = M4*. More investigation is due on the CPTs used, possibly by finding ways to parametrize the CPTs and learn them from the available data.

6 Conclusions and Future Work

In this paper we studied the impact of several parameters on the quality of teacher grade predictions made by the OpenAnswer model. From the simulations we see that the biggest impact respect to raw peer assessment (10% better, i.e. a relative improvement of circa 20%) is obtained by improving both CPTG and CPTC. Moreover, we see that using the PD mapping *median* shows similar (just slightly lower) results respect to *weightedSum*. Finally, the 2-phase strategy *maxWrongThenMaxEntropy* has similar performance than the simpler *maxEntropy*, with a slightly lower workload and a slightly lower precision.

The above mentioned results due to CPT improvements suggest to give further attention to the definition of the CPTs, possibly by learning their parameters from data.

The results shown are aggregated (averaged) over our datasets. It would be interesting to analyze the OA behavior in the single cases. In particular, we think the model would show better prediction results when applied to better classes (as the higher information content of the peer-assessment would allow the BN to deduce more), than when applied to worse classes (as the model would get less information from student with low J). This suggests to investigate a possible correlation between the model output quality and the quality of the class (e.g. their average grade and stdev).

Finally, it is worth to study the sensibility of OA respect to collusion, even if it is discouraged both by anonymizing the peer-graded answers, and by the fact that misjudgment reflects on poor J, K and C, i.e. a worse model for the misbehaving student.

References

1. Anderson, L.W., Krathwohl, D.R.(eds.): A Taxonomy for Learning, Teaching, and Assessing: A Revision Of Bloom's Taxonomy of Educational Objectives. Allyn and Bacon (2000)

2. Bloom, B.S., Engelhart, M.D., Furst,. E.J., Hill, W.H., Krathwohl, D.R.: Taxonomy of educational objectives: The classification of educational goals. Handbook I: Cognitive domain. David McKay, New York (1956)
3. Castellanos-Nieves, D., Fernández-Breis, J., Valencia-García, R., Martínez-Béjar, R., Iniesta-Moreno, M.: Semantic Web Technologies for supporting learning assessment. Inf. Sci. **181**, 9 (2011)
4. Cho, K., MacArthur, C.: Student revision with peer and expert reviewing. Learn. Instr. **20**(4), 328–338 (2010)
5. Chung, H., Graf, S., Robert Lai, K.: Kinshuk: Enrichment of peer assessment with agent negotiation. IEEE Trans. Learn. Technol. **4**(1), 35–46 (2011)
6. Conati, C., Gartner, A., Vanlehn, K.: Using Bayesian networks to manage uncertainty in student modeling. User Model. User-Adap. Inter. **12**, 371–417 (2002)
7. El-Kechaï, N., Delozanne, É., Prévit, D., Grugeon, B., Chenevotot, F.: Evaluating the performance of a diagnosis system in school algebra. In: Leung, H., Popescu, E., Cao, Y., Lau, R.W.H., Nejdl, W. (eds.) ICWL 2011. LNCS, vol. 7048, pp. 263–272. Springer, Heidelberg (2011). doi:10.1007/978-3-642-25813-8_28
8. Jackson, K., Trochim, W.: Concept mapping as an alternative approach for the analysis of open-ended survey responses. Organizational Research Methods, vol. 5. Sage (2002)
9. Li, L.X., Liu, X., Steckelberg, A.L.: Assessor or assessee: how student learning improves by giving and receiving peer feedback. Br. J. Ed. Tech. **41**(3), 525–536 (2010)
10. Miller, P.: The Effect of Scoring Criteria Specificity on Peer and Self-assessment. Assessment & Evaluation in Higher Education, 28/4 (2003)
11. Palmer, K., Richardson, P.: On-line assessment and free-response input-a pedagogic and technical model for squaring the circle. In Proceeding 7th Computer Assisted Assessment Conference, pp. 289–300 (2003)
12. Romero, C., Ventura, S.: Educational data mining: a review of the state of the art. IEEE Trans. SMC Part C **40**(6), 601–618 (2010)
13. Sadler, P.M., Good, E.: The impact of self and peer-grading on student learning. Educ. Assess. **11**(1), 1–31 (2006)
14. Sterbini, A., Temperini, M.: Dealing with open-answer questions in a peer-assessment environment. In: Popescu, E., Li, Q., Klamma, R., Leung, H., Specht, M. (eds.) ICWL 2012. LNCS, vol. 7558, pp. 240–248. Springer, Heidelberg (2012). doi:10.1007/978-3-642-33642-3_26
15. Sterbini, A., Temperini, M.: Analysis of OpenAnswers via mediated peer-assessment. In: Proceeding International Conference on System Theory, Control and Computing, Workshop SPEL (2013)
16. Sterbini, A., Temperini, M.: OpenAnswer, a framework to support teacher's management of open answers through peer assessment. In: Proceeding Frontiers in Education, pp. 164–170 (2013)
17. Yamanishi, K., Li, H.: Mining open answers in questionnaire data. IEEE Intell. Syst. **2002**, 58–63 (2002)

Embedding Interuniversity Peer Review in Virtual Learning Groups

A Research-Based Learning Scenario

Michael A. Herzog[1]([⊠]), Elisabeth Katzlinger[2], and Martin Stabauer[2]

[1] Magdeburg-Stendal University, Magdeburg, Germany
michael.herzog@hs-magdeburg.de
[2] Johannes Kepler University, Linz, Austria
{elisabeth.katzlinger-felhofer,
martin.stabauer}@jku.at

Abstract. Interdisciplinary cooperation in virtual groups has become a reality and challenge for businesses and institutions in the globalised world and thus a main learning objective for business students. This paper reports an inter-university cooperation between a German University of Applied Sciences and an Austrian University, in which students of both institutions work together in virtual learning groups. They collectively develop a research project concerning "ethical issues of digital communication". The students pass the different stages of a typical research process starting with a relevant research question towards the presentation of the findings at a conference. For this research-based learning scenario a process model is developed based on established theory and including a Peer Review process for students from three courses of both universities. An accompanying study collects qualitative and quantitative data on Peer Review as a learning method in an inter-university context and the role of media for virtual cooperation.

Keywords: Interdisciplinary collaboration · Inter-University learning groups · Learning through research · Integrated peer review process · Inquiry based learning · Virtual learning group

1 Introduction

Interdisciplinary collaboration in virtual teams is both challenge and reality for institutions and companies in the globalised world especially when digital business models are involved. This increases the need for virtual communication. This leads to media literacy for virtual learning and collaboration becoming an important learning objective in business education.

In traditional courses, both on-campus and in blended learning style, there is no essential need for the learners to use different media for collaboration in their learning group. That is, because the students can communicate face-to-face in a simple way. This situation changes for non-traditional students in higher education who are working during their studies. For this group of students, virtual collaboration is essential.

© Springer International Publishing AG 2017
T.-T. Wu et al. (Eds.): SETE 2016, LNCS 10108, pp. 614–623, 2017.
DOI: 10.1007/978-3-319-52836-6_65

Because of their diverse professional experience, they are not a homogenous group of learners. Thus, interdisciplinary and intercultural aspects gain importance in virtual teams.

Based on this assumption, an inquiry-based learning scenario was developed, in which three universities in Austria and Germany cooperated. In virtual learning groups with members from both Austria and Germany, the students created and worked on a joint research project and presented the selected papers at an scientific conference. In a double-blind peer reviewing process the students gave feedback to their colleagues and the best rated papers were selected for the conference.

The students organised their virtual learning group autonomously and selected the used tools and media in self-responsibility. The development of media skills and abilities for virtual teams was an intended learning objective of the learning scenario.

2   Learning Through Research

Inquiry-based learning is grounded on the philosophy of John Dewey [1], who believed that education starts with the inquisitiveness of the learner, and that learning and researching are corresponding activities. Both activities are focused on cognitive processes. Since the 1970ies, inquiry-based learning and assessment is a main didactical principle of teaching in higher education and documented in a number of papers [2–4].

Inquiry-based learning is a student-centered active learning approach, where the students are part of the whole research process. Learners complete different phases of the research process [5]. Inquiry-based learning activities start with the development of a research question followed by finding adequate research methods and investigating different solutions. On basis of the gathered information, students create new knowledge. The discussion of discoveries and experiences is an essential part of the learning process. At the end of the process, the findings are comprehensibly documented and presented for third parties. Inquiry-based learning encourages a hands-on approach where students practice scientific methods. The documentation and reflection on the personal learning pathway is part of the learning process.

Figure 1 shows Kolb's experiential learning cycle synchronised with a typical research cycle that is basis for the inquiry-based learning model. It regards learning as an interaction of several different activities on the part of the learners, such as dealing with an authentic learning item in a concrete and direct way, reflection, the development of a personal net of knowledge by means of abstract conceptualization and the use of this theoretical knowledge for planning further learning activities. Kolb's [6] model of an experience based learning model is built upon the idea that learning preferences can be described along two continuums: active experimentation vs. reflective observation and abstract conceptualization vs. concrete experience. These four elements are at the centre of an idealised learning cycle or spiral where learners touch all the bases. This starts with any one of the four elements, but typically begins with a concrete experience. The four stages in this experiential learning cycle include concrete experience being involved in a new experience, reflective observation watching others or developing observations about one's own experience, abstract conceptualization

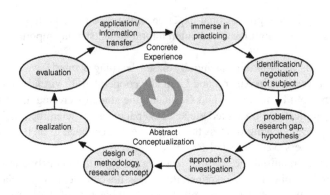

Fig. 1. Kolb's Learning Cycle synchronised with Wildt's Research Cycle [7]

creating theories to explain observations, and active experimentation using theories to solve problems, make decisions.

As it is shown in Fig. 1, Wildt synchronised the research process with the learning cycle. The research process needs to be specified for each discipline, e.g., engineering education differs from social sciences or economic [8]. The research and the learning process starts with observation of problems in the real world and the concrete experience, the students are irritated by a situation or an experience. The defining of questions or problems is part two of the cycle (reflective observation) and ends with the formulation of research questions or hypothesis. The abstract conceptualisation is used to develop a research concept and design. The developed concepts will be verified during active experimentation, and new knowledge will be created. From this findings new learning and research cycles start.

The steps in the research process are connected with the learning steps in the learning process to acquire research competencies and professional expertise. This is the basic principle for developing a learning scenario that connects the two processes.

3 Research Questions and Design Method

For an implementation of inquiry-based learning we evaluated, how far an interuniversity and interdisciplinary scenario, connected to an intercourse approach, could be conducted in a higher education environment (research question 1). Investigation in added values was planned compared to other learning scenarios using Peer Review (2). The intensity and quality of media usage that allows virtual learning in groups was another focus of the study (3). For our design of this learning setting a design-based research approach was employed. Design-based research has demonstrated its potential as a methodology suitable to both research and design of learning environments [9]. Application on inquiry-based learning goes back to problem solving in education practice wherein a "close connection between forming theory and optimizing process development" is allowed ([4] p. 62).

"Design experiments are extended (iterative), interventionist (innovative and designbased), and theory-oriented enterprises whose 'theories' do real work in practical educational contexts" ([10], p 13).

With this focus, a theory driven learning process model was developed and specified that orients on systematics of Wildt using Kolb as evolved in [6, 7] (Chap. 4.2). The resulting process model was first used, evaluated, and refined in three single courses, each in another semester with a homogeneous group of students from only one discipline. It formed a basis to extend and explore the setting internationally over three universities with three different courses, in two different study programs.

As proving evaluation in the design-based research methodology (Chap. 5), a qualitative survey about learning process and learning outcomes was conducted at the end of the course. It is based on 23 protocols and reflections by students and is abstracted on level of 12 learning groups as at least one document per group was submitted.

To collect more data and correlate it to other media based learning scenarios, an online survey about media use and teaching methods was conducted. This quantitative investigation is part of our "CrossTeaching" study, that started in winter term 2010 and includes answers of 770 students of several courses in two German speaking universities. This comparative data from other interregional learning scenarios, such as an interregional case study work, allows to discover specifics and differences regarding the inquiry-based setting.

4 Learning Scenario and Role of Peer Review

4.1 Setting

The conducted learning scenario is based on an intensive cooperation of three different courses embedded in Master programmes of three different educational institutions. This learning scenario is driven by research and utilises Peer Review as one part of its iterative and self-regulated learning process.

The Master programmes involved are "Digital Business Management" (DBM) on one hand, which is run by Johannes Kepler University Linz (JKU) together with University of Applied Sciences (FH) Upper Austria on its Campus Steyr, and "Cross Media" (CM) run by Magdeburg-Stendal University of Applied Sciences on the other hand. Both programmes are characterised by extensive interinstitutional, intercultural and interdisciplinary collaboration. DBM is the first ever Master programme in Austria that is conducted by an University of Applied Sciences together with a research-based University. The curriculum is built by one half of its courses run at JKU in Linz and one half at the FH in Steyr. Students are enrolled in both institutions and utilise the respective learning platforms.

The list of the bespoke courses that are run in a collaborative way and are interlocked in the research process reads as follows: Foundations of Scientific Research (JKU, 3 ECTS); IT-Ethics and Selected Aspects of Gender Studies (JKU, 3 ECTS); Reflexion and Communication (Magdeburg, 5 ECTS).

This makes it clear, that Austrian students need to complete 6 ECTS in their third semester for these two courses, while German students only need to complete 5 ECTS.

This was discussed by students (see Chap. 5), but the fact that in DBM both courses contain contents and works in addition to the cooperation makes up for the difference in credits. 24 students of DBM participated in the courses (12 male, 12 female) and 10 students of CM (4 male, 6 female). Both Master programmes are designed for professionals, which has implications on periods of face-to-face training and on availability for group meetings. Another similarity of both programmes' students is that they share a highly developed media competency and technical affinity. This has significant influence on choice and usage of technology and media for communication.

To increase motivation, a special incentive was provided: If their contributions achieved a certain degree of quality, the students were entitled to participate in the Cross Media conference "Think Cross Change Media" (#TCCM), to present their work at a dedicated track and get their paper published in the conference proceedings [11].

4.2   Process Model

Following Bloom's taxonomy of learning goals [12] inquiry-based learning aims to "higher" dimensions of cognitive processes, which intends a "higher value" of learning progress and knowledge production with students. These higher transfer dimensions *Analyse*, *Evaluate*, and *Create* are mainly addressed by the following process model (Fig. 2).

Students teamed in inter-university learning groups involving one person from master program "Cross Media" and two from master program "Digital Business Management". The exposed task for each learning group was to form a research project and to write an academic article in the broad field of "Ethical Questions of Digital Communication". Principally, groups were responsible for their own organization of

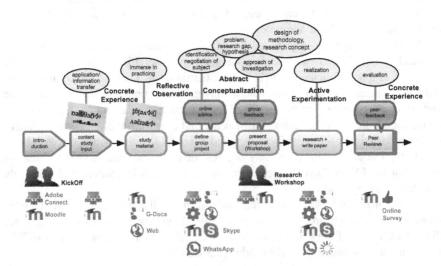

Fig. 2. Research process in first part of the Learning Cycle

group work, choice of tools and communication media, forming research questions, creating their appropriate methodology. This resulted in a broad variety of research methods and approaches. Nevertheless, teachers support like in a seminar about research methods, a research workshop with discussions of all research proposals, or online consulting was highly used.

4.3   Embedded Peer Reviewing Process

As central part of the underlying process a double-blind peer reviewing was conducted, which had high impact on personal motivation, turned out to deliver constructive feedback and acted as a personal learning experience. The students had to hand in a draft of their paper about six weeks before the conference and were then assigned three papers to review from three different groups. The allocation was done manually by the teachers, as the used Moodle Workshop module v2.2 didn't allow for automatic allocation with consideration of working groups. The students received comprehensive oral and written instructions including information on anonymity, feedback and grading as well as detailed evaluation criteria (e.g., quality of content, relevance for theory and practice, originality, formal quality), scales and weights. These instructions have been developed and refined over the last years.[1]

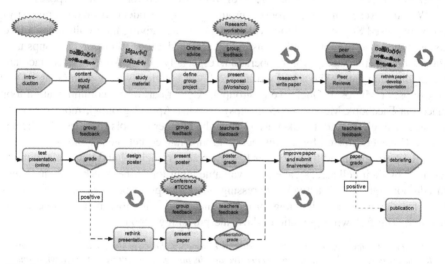

Fig. 3. Full inquiry based learning process model with 4 cycles inspired by Wildt (Fig. 1)

The students had two weeks to hand in the review and then had the possibility to incorporate the received feedback into their own papers (Fig. 3 shows the whole process). This phase of revision was very much appreciated by the students and turned out to improve quality of the papers considerably. A number of papers that were seen

---

[1] Readers can find the bespoken peer reviewing instructions in German language at http://download. idv.edu/crossteaching/PR_Anleitung.pdf.

as average or even below average by the reviewers and the teachers, benefited enormously and at the end of semester met the criteria to be published in the conference proceedings. Not least because of students' wishes, only the final papers were marked by the teachers and the first drafts were not considered.

5 Evaluation and Findings

5.1 Students' Survey

In this section we want to discuss some findings of the qualitative evaluation we have conducted with the students of the winter term 2015/16. The survey consisted of free text questions regarding the process of group work, communication media, situations of conflict and their solutions, scientific paper as learning method, evaluation of Peer Review and collaboration amongst others.

The students were given a free choice of tools and technologies that they could use to communicate with their respective group members. The learning management system 'Moodle' was compulsory for students and was utilised during consolidation of groups and research topics and Q&A regarding issues of general interest. The video conferencing tool 'Adobe Connect' was used for getting in touch with the lecturers. Apart from these two, a diverse variety of tools was used for various purposes.

With the exception of one group (a group of just two students from one university), everybody used Skype; mostly for video telephony and giving their colleagues a face, some groups also used it for file transfer and screen sharing. 10 out of 12 groups used classic e-mail messaging for cooperation, especially for making first contact and finding meeting dates. The actual writing work was commonly done with Google Docs (7 groups) or Microsoft OneDrive (2 groups). A great part of the communication took place via Facebook Messenger (5 groups) or WhatsApp (3 groups), more rarely via Trello or Google Hangout. Taken as a whole the number of tools (besides Moodle and Adobe Connect) utilised by the respective groups ranged between 2 and 6.

All 12 groups stated that the Peer Review was very helpful and that the comments received by their colleagues gave them valuable input for further work on their papers. In addition, the task of actively addressing other groups' papers was seen positively both for the individual learning progress and further improvement of one's own research. The following quotations show the prevailing mood:

> "The Peer Review process was a very special experience, because the feedback of our colleagues was extremely honest, comprehensive and inspiring."; "Drafting a Peer Review and the associated intensive work with another groups' paper was very interesting and rewarding."

Quite diverse approaches, perspectives and strategies of the working groups' members turned out to be both challenging and beneficial for the writing process. It seems logical that a collaboration of highly divergent personalities cannot always be without any frictions. However, there were only two groups facing serious problems. Interestingly enough, the end results of these two groups emerged above-average.

> "Various approaches and educational background of group members were absolutely beneficial. That way, we had a great mix of ideas, methods and strengths, that we could co-ordinate

and distribute the diverse tasks accordingly. "; "Just like in professional life, you can't always choose with whom you want to work together and you might come across difficult characters or people you can't get along very well."

The applied teaching method was seen as positive or very positive by all 12 groups, they all recommend to continue the collaboration. Some groups found the amount of work involved in the process rather high, but the incentive of being able to publish a scientific article during the Master study made it worth the effort.

"The conference provided a worthy setting to our paper and gave it and our efforts a deeper sense. "; "I would prefer this learning method to other methods like exams or tests any time, because the knowledge acquired will last longer and seems more meaningful".

5.2   Lining up with Previous Semesters

The present study is part of an ongoing interuniversity teaching and research project that started in fall 2010 [13]. More than 770 students participated in an online survey, 325 of them collaborated in virtual teams which were part of an interuniversity learning scenario; most of them worked on a case study in interuniversity learning groups. 34 students took part in the inquiry-based interuniversity learning scenario, the response rate of the online survey was 47% (N = 16). The students rated the usefulness of communication media which they used for the virtual learning group (Fig. 4). Over the time face-to-face is the preferred media, chat and forum become less important, social media and video conference gain more importance. For the paper collaboration the students preferred shared spaces like Google Docs or Dropbox (3.9 of 4).

In our survey the students ranked different aspects of Peer Review as a learning method on a scale from poor to excellent (see Fig. 5). The highest rank has Peer Review for improving assessment skills. They agreed to Peer Review in general and as learning method (3.4 of 4). Regarding to the learning scenario the personal learning

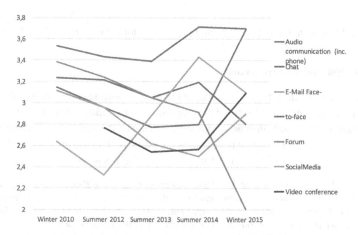

Fig. 4. Rating of media for collaboration [1] not useful, [4] very useful

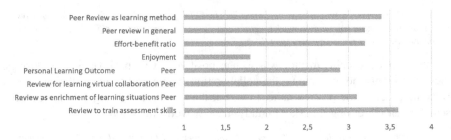

Fig. 5. Student rating of Peer Review as a learning method [1] poor, [4] excellent

outcome, the effort-benefit ratio and the enrichment of learning situations is rated high by the students. The enjoyment was rated lower.

In our model of inquiry based learning the feedback loops are an important part of the learning process. In the survey we asked the students which role the feedback had for their learning process. Figure 6 shows the rating of the students separated by gender, female student rated mostly higher. They see their given feedback as positive and constructive as well as helpful for their colleagues and it encourages their own learning process. The received feedback was positive and constructive as well as helpful. The feedback as contribution to the learning process is not that important. Furthermore, the received feedback didn't change the focus of the paper or brought new ideas.

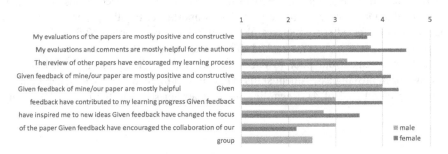

Fig. 6. Student rating of Peer Review feedback [1] totally disagree, [5] totally agree

5.3   Findings and Future Work

In addition to the evaluation results discussed in the previous sections, one of this work's main findings is the tested and refined process model for conducting an interdisciplinary, inter-university collaboration-based course that makes extensive use of research-based learning and embeds an elaborate peer reviewing process. The learning method was very well received by the students, as the following quotation shows:

"Even though the development of this paper was more demanding than any other during my studies, I would recommend the cooperation with the university in Magdeburg for the coming years. Not only have we gained another experience, it was very interesting to see that in some cases students of another university have completely different approaches. The chance to present our paper at the Cross Media conference was great and will not repeat itself too

quickly. The work in virtual teams was rewarding, even though not always simple, and might turn out helpful in modern professional environments."

The learning scenario turned out to be quite demanding for both students and teachers and calls for intense support and coordination. However, the outcome with 6 out of 12 papers being published in the conference proceedings shows that the efforts invested are worthwhile. The discussed process model will therefore be employed again in the next academic year and be evaluated comparatively.

References

1. Dewey, J.: Experience and education. In: The Educational Forum. Taylor & Francis Group, pp. 241–252 (1986)
2. Fichten, W.: Über die Umsetzung und Gestaltung Forschenden Lernens im Lehramtsstudium. Verschriftlichung eines Vortrags auf der Veranstaltung "Modelle Forschenden Lernens" in der Bielefeld School of Education 2012, Schriftenreihe Lehrerbildung in Wissenschaft, Ausbildung und Praxis (2013). https://www.uni-oldenburg.de/fileadmin/user_upload/diz/download/Publikationen/Lehrerbildung_Online/Fichten_01_2013_Forschendes_Lernen.pdf
3. Kergel, D., Heidkamp, B.: Forschendes Lernen mit digitalen Medien. Ein Lehrbuch:# theorie# praxis# evaluation, Waxmann Verlag, Münster (2015)
4. Reinmann, G.: Forschendes Lernen und wissenschaftliches Prüfen: die potentielle und faktische Rolle der digitalen Medien. In: Meyer, T., Tan, W.-H., Schwalbe, C., Appelt, R. (eds.) Medien & Bildung: Institutionelle Kontexte und kultureller Wandel. VS Verlag für Sozialwissenschaften, Wiesbaden (2011)
5. Wolf, D.K.: Forschendes Lehren mit digitalen Medien: wie forschendes Lernen durch Teilhabe und mediale Unterstützung gelingen kann. In: Kergel, D., Heidkamp, B. (eds) Forschendes Lernen 2.0: Partizipatives Lernen zwischen Globalisierung und medialem Wandel. Springer Fachmedien, Wiesbaden (2016)
6. Kolb, D.A., Oslond, J., Rubin, I.: Organizational Behavior. An Experimental Approach. Prentice Hall, Englewood Cliffs (1995)
7. Wildt, J.: Forschendes Lernen: Lernen im "Format" der Forschung. J. hochschuldidaktik **20** (2), 4–7 (2009)
8. Ossenberg, P., Jungmann, T.: Experimentation in a research workshop: a peer-learning approach as a first step to scientific competence. Int. J. Eng. Pedagogy (iJEP) **3**(S3), 27 (2013). doi:10.3991/ijep.v3iS3.2748
9. Wang, F., Hannafin, M.J.: Design-based research and technology-enhanced learning environments. Educ. Technol. Res. Dev. **53**(4), 5–23 (2005)
10. Cobb, P., Confrey, J., Lehrer, R., Schauble, L.: Design experiments in educational research. Educ. Res. **32**(1), 9–13 (2003)
11. Falk-Bartz, S., Stockleben, B. (eds): Think Cross Change Media 2016: Mobil. Ethisch. Kollaborativ, Books on Demand, Norderstedt (2016)
12. Krathwohl, D.R.: A revision of Bloom's taxonomy: an overview. Theor. Pract. **4**, 212–218 (2002)
13. Katzlinger, E., Herzog, M.A.: Intercultural collaborative learning scenarios in E-business education: media competencies for virtual workplaces. In: Issa, T., Isaias, P., Kommers, P. (eds.) Multicultural Awareness and Technology in Higher Education: Global Perspectives, pp. 24–46. IGI Global, Hershey (2014)

Peer Reviews in a Web Design Course:
Now Students like Them Too

Zuzana Kubincová$^{(\boxtimes)}$, Martin Homola, and Veronika Dropčová

Faculty of Mathematics, Physics and Informatics,
Comenius University in Bratislava, Mlynská dolina, 84248 Bratislava, Slovakia
{kubincova, homola, dropcova}@fmph.uniba.sk

Abstract. For several years we have used peer reviews in a web design course. The students published web content, originally in form of blog articles, and they received feedback in form of peer reviews from their colleagues. In the previous run of the course, this method helped us to improve the learning outcomes, however the students did not perceive the publishing/reviewing activity very well; they felt it is too much work and they are forced to do it. In the last two runs of the course we tried to cope with this problem by replacing blog development by more free web design-related assignments the topic of which the students were allowed to choose. They could come up with their own project. The students worked in teams, and peer reviews did not focus entirely on web content, but also on more technical aspects of the task like layout design, and on the team work inside the teams. The learning outcomes were approximately the same, however the students' perception of the usefulness of the publishing/reviewing activities was much improved, as much as their overall satisfaction with the course.

Keywords: Peer review · Team work · Motivation · Acceptance · Web design

1 Introduction

Gaining sufficient insight into front-end web development is not possible without practicing on real web content and understanding also the basics of web publishing. Over the years of existence of our web design course, we faced the problem that the students were reluctant to understand this fact. Their attention centered mainly on programming and technology, and their acceptance of web publishing related activities was low. This was particularly a problem in the practical assignment, where the students did the programming work, but they turned in the content largely underdeveloped which missed many of our didactic goals and diminished the learning outcomes.

Since several years we coupled the web publishing part of the assignment, which was implemented as blogging, with peer reviews, a methodology that was shown to enhance the learning outcomes in different scenarios [4, 8, 9, 13, 15] including that of web design courses [1, 11, 12].

While we achieved encouraging results, especially improved learning outcomes, students' acceptance of blogging and peer review was not completely satisfactory. Some of them were not able to perceive this as beneficial and complained that they were forced to write, which they were not willing to do.

T.-T. Wu et al. (Eds.): SETE 2016, LNCS 10108, pp. 624–634, 2017.
DOI: 10.1007/978-3-319-52836-6_66

We chose to address this problem by implementing changes in the project assignment during the next two runs: we allowed students more freedom in the choice of their development technology and in the second year we relaxed from blogging entirely and allowed them to work on any project of their own. This allowed students to work on an actual content that they considered real: we expected that they would rate the web publishing activity more meaningful. We also restructured the project into three rounds (specification and prototype, application, content) and pegged peer reviews with each round, so that students now reviewed each aspect of their project work, not only the content. We expected that students would perceive the usefulness of such reviews more easily. Finally, to relax a bit from the workload, in the second year we also introduced teamwork, and teamwork reviews which was shown useful by previous research [6, 7, 10, 14].

As we report below after a detailed description of our methodology (Sect. 2), these changes were successful, because while the learning outcomes stayed approximately the same (Sect. 3.1), students' overall satisfaction with the peer review activities as well as with the course significantly increased during the last two years (Sects. 3.2 and 3.3). We summarize our conclusions in Sect. 4.

2 Course Overview

Our web design course is part of the Master's curriculum of Applied Informatics. In the past the course was compulsory, but this has changed in the last year when it has become optional. It is also popular with Bachelor students who can take it optionally too. The course concentrates mainly on front-end web design issues, with emphasis on usability and user experience. We will concentrate on the last three runs of the course. The number of enrolled students was 69 in 2013, 75 in 2014, and 42 in 2015.

The course relies heavily on an all-semester practical assignment, hereafter referred to as *the project*. By development of the project the students exercise (a) technological skills required to put together a web application, especially its front end; and (b) web publishing skills by providing meaningful content for their web application. Depending on how the web publishing part is implemented, this may include further didactic goals such as (c) technical writing skills – e.g., when the assignment is blog based; and (d) extending the knowledge related to the course – when students are required to write on course topics (See [12] for deeper discussion on didactic motivations behind this).

The evaluation of the students work splits between the project, written examination (midterm and final written test), and oral examination. Partial evaluations are summed and the resulting sum is graded on a six-point grading scale from A (excellent) to Fx (failed). The numerical representation of the scale A–Fx is 1–6 (in the charts below).

2.1 2013 Course Run

In our initial setting, the project amounted to 42.5% of the evaluation (split between 25% for the technological part and 17.5% for the web publishing part). The assignment was blog-based; students developed their own blog, and published several articles on the topic of the course. Thus the web publishing part was entirely translated into blog publishing. Using these settings we followed didactic goals (a–d). The publishing was done in multiple rounds, and peer reviews were used to encourage students to read also the articles written by the others and provide feedback.

As we already mentioned, while this setting was undoubtedly useful for the students, some of them were not able to perceive this and complained that they were forced to write, which they did not like to do. The methodology and results were published [1].

2.2   2014 Course Run

In the following run, we largely redesigned the project assignment. It now amounted to 45% of the evaluation (30% for the technological, and 15% for the web publishing part). The project was still blog-based, but we allowed students to freely choose the programming platform they want to use to develop their blog, which was not previously the case. We collected the blogs by web-crawling.

In the web-publishing part we relaxed from the didactic goals (c–d). While students still published blog articles, we focused more on the web formatting issues, and less on technical writing. The topic was no longer necessarily related to the course.

We largely redesigned the peer review activities. Most importantly, the students now reviewed all aspects of the project, including the technological part. The project was submitted in three rounds (back-end and basic desktop front-end; full front-end including mobile; and content) and each part was peer-reviewed. Each submitted project was assigned three peer reviewers; the reviews were blind. The review forms rated different aspects related to development and design quality issues (rounds 1–2) and to content quality and web formatting issues (round 3). Reviewers answered the questions on a scale 1–5 (weak–excellent) and had to provide also verbal justification. Students were given an option to improve their submissions after peer reviews before they were evaluated by the lecturers. This workflow was supported by a dedicated tool [5] that the students used for submission and review of the projects.

As we report below, these changes brought an interesting improvement in students' acceptance of the course activities, however, we were not entirely satisfied. A number of students still expressed their discontent with blogging, in particular.

2.3   2015 Course Run

In the most recent run, the project amounted again to 45% of the evaluation (30% for the technological, and 15% for the web publishing part). We took further steps to improve our course, as described below.

We allowed students not only to choose the programming platform, but we also relaxed from the requirement to develop a blog, and allowed them to choose the topic freely. We especially encouraged them to use any real project they have already been working on. This made the projects harder to evaluate, however, we conjectured that drawing students' attention on the content that they themselves consider real would help to improve their motivation.

Instead of individual assignment, the students now worked in 3–4 person teams. By this decision we wanted to decrease the workload on individual students, and allow them to choose their task within the team by themselves. The project was again split into three rounds, however we updated the split of tasks: specification and prototype were submitted in round 1; the application with full front-end interface design (desktop and mobile) in round 2; and content in round 3.

We relied on the same peer review methodology as in the previous run however, the reviews were part of the team work, so the team could do them together, or delegate them on a selected team member. The review forms were adjusted to reflect the work submitted in the respective rounds.

After each round was completed, students filled in a newly introduced blind review form evaluating the team work. The aim was to assure no students abuse the team assignment by avoiding to contribute; to provide the teams with mutual feedback; and the lecturers with insight about the individual contributions. Regarding the methodology for team peer review, the Fink method [7] was chosen: Each student divided 100 percent points between the remaining team members. Thus a team of n members divides $n \times 100\%$ between themselves. The points received by each team member were summed up and presented to everyone. The students also evaluated each team member by answering three open questions to justify the points division, related to (a) overall contribution, (b) most valued contribution, and (c) possible improvement.

Importantly, the evaluation points the team received from lecturers in rounds 2–3 were split respectively to the team review rating of each student. Round 1 was demonstrative in this respect, the points were split evenly, but the students saw how the points would be split based on the ratings.

We employed the same tool [5] as in the previous year to manage the whole process, which we extended to handle team submissions and team review.

In the next sections we look at the results that we achieved by these changes in our methodology. We first look at the learning outcomes, and then on the students' acceptance of these activities and their opinion about the whole course.

3   Results

As mentioned before, due to the changes in curriculum in 2015, our course was not compulsory any more. As a consequence, the number of students attending the course lowered compared to the previous course runs. There were 42 students enrolled altogether, however, four of them dropped out the course over the semester.

Coupling course activities with peer review brought higher students' engagement and also improved learning outcomes already in previous years. On the other hand, not all students were able to perceive peer-review activities as beneficial [1]. The new settings helped us to reach 100% engagement. In this section we will see that learning outcomes were not affected by these changes. We will then have a look on students' acceptance of the peer review activities, and their overall opinion on the course.

3.1   Learning Outcomes

We found out that the students' learning outcomes did not differ significantly from those achieved in the three previous years. The average grade slightly dropped down (Fig. 1(a)), however, this decrease is too weak to be significant (compared to the years ibution of grades is shown in Fig. 1(b) failed the course (grade Fx) decreased the semester, thus no student who grade Fx (nobody failed the exam).

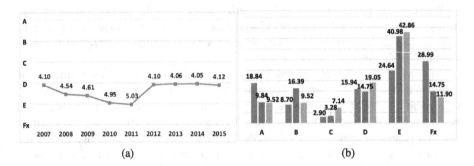

(a)   (b)

Fig. 1. (a) Average grades in years 2007–2015. (b) Distribution of particular grades in years 2013–2015 (in %). ■ 2013; ■ 2014; ■ 2015

Figure 2 provides a better insight into the average evaluation of exams and projects since 2007. The exam results continued in the growing trend of the last few years. More interestingly, the project results improved and thus reversed the falling trend from the last two years. In our opinion, these improved results can be attributed to the introduction of team work, and to more proper alignment of the project with peer review activities.

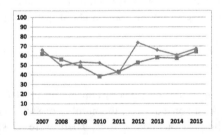

Fig. 2. Percentage in ■ projects and ■ exams in 2007–2015.

3.2   Students' Satisfaction with Peer-Review Activities

As explained in previous sections, the new course settings were intended to solve students' prevailing discontent with the course and course activities. Therefore students' attitudes towards peer review activities and towards the course were explored.

At the end of the semester students completed a questionnaire on their acceptance of peer review. The results were encouraging since students appreciated the possibility to be peer-reviewed (mainly due to the chance to correct or improve their project according to the peer feedback) as well as the experience gained through peer reviewing the projects of the others (see Fig. 3). More detailed findings from this research are published in our other paper [3].

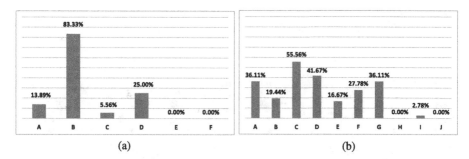

(a)   (b)

Fig. 3. Questionnaire results: (a) How do you think the peer reviews received by your team were useful for you? A: To better understand the project assignment. B: To correct problems we over- looked. C: To correct problems we were not able to solve. D: To improve in my reviewing. E: It was not useful. F: Other. (b) Do you think that it was useful to review others' work? A: I learned how to test web projects. B: I learned how the project assignment was understood by other teams. C: I realized how many different types of problems can appear on websites. D: While reviewing others' projects I realized shortcomings of our own project. E: I trained my language/verbal skills. F: I improved in constructive criticism. G: I could gain more points. H: It was not useful. I: I did not review. J: Other.

3.3   Students' Satisfaction with the Course

To measure the students' attitude towards the course we used the official anonymous education evaluation questionnaire annually conducted by our institution. As a lower number of students participates in the official questionnaire, since 2014 we anony- mously administrated the same questions to a greater sample of students (adding them to the survey related to peer reviews).

The outcomes of both questionnaires differed rather significantly. Both years the outcomes from our questionnaire reflected higher students satisfaction with the course than those from the official one. In our opinion, this could be caused by different sample sizes and different timing of the respective surveys. We refer the reader to a separate study [2] where we analyzed this issue. In this section, the outcomes of both questionnaires are presented side by side.

Course Quality. The overall rating of the course. Answers are on the scale 1–5 stars, where 5 is the best. From both charts plotted in Fig. 4 it is apparent that the overall rating of the course quality improved in 2015. The results from our questionnaire show more significant improvement, since 75% of all students (nearly 34% more than in the previous year) rated the course at least four stars. In our opinion, this improvement can be attributed to the overall adjustment of the course rules enabling students to work on more practical assignments and in the settings closer to the real IT industry environment (teamwork). The official student evaluation of the course improved as well, however, there is still higher percentage of students unsatisfied with the course quality (values 1 and 2). The possible reasons of this difference were mentioned above.

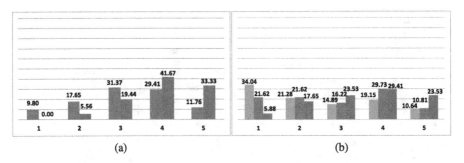

(a)   (b)

Fig. 4. Overall rating of the course quality. Results are in %. (a) Our questionnaire. (b) Official student evaluation of education. ■ 2013 ■ 2014 ■ 2015

Course Difficulty. Students rate how difficult it is to comprehend the course subject matter (*Incomprehensible, Too difficult, Just right, Too easy, Trivial*). This was the only question with comparable and very similar answers in both questionnaires (Fig. 5). In our questionnaire, the students presented almost the same opinions in both years, only minor differences appeared. The percentages of particular answers correspond to the normal distribution which is a positive finding. Moreover, the most desirable option *Just right* was indeed the most frequently chosen and reached almost 70% of all responses.

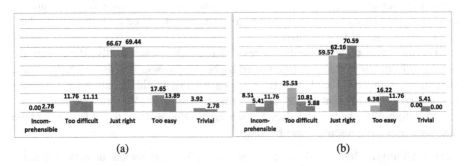

(a)   (b)

Fig. 5. How difficult was the course? Results are in %. (a) Our questionnaire. (b) Official student evaluation of education. ■ 2013 ■ 2014 ■ 2015

Course Interestingness. Responses to this question (values from the scale 1–5) were more positive in the last course run than those collected in the previous year in both surveys (Fig. 6). In our questionnaire, the percentage of students who chose lower values (1 and 2) in 2015 was 7 times lower than in 2014. Regarding the highest value chosen, in our questionnaire this ratio was more than 2.3 times higher in 2015 than in 2014. Surprisingly, in the student evaluation of education it was even 2.5 times higher. These results are likely due to various changes in the course settings especially in the last run: the free choice of the project topic, the course optionality, but the introduction of teamwork as well.

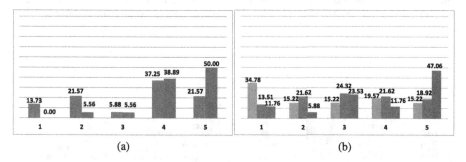

(a)   (b)

Fig. 6. Was the course interesting to you? Results are in %. (a) Our questionnaire. (b) Official student evaluation of education. ▮ 2013 ▮ 2014 ▮ 2015

Amount of Work. To which extent is the amount of work required by the course appropriate to the number of credits acquired (*Absolute killer, Too much, Just right, Too little, What work?*). A significant improvement showed up in our survey (Fig. 7), in 2015 – only about 20% of students considered the amount of course work to be *Too much* (compared to 50% in 2014) and all the other students (nearly 80%) rated it *Just right*. We believe that particularly the introduction of teamwork may have helped here, as students' could split up the task according to their preferences. A moderate improvement occurred in the official evaluation of the course in 2015 as well, however, the percentage of students who rated the amount of course work *Too much* was excessively high (comparable to the option *Just right*).

Recommendation to Other Students. Asked if they would recommend the course to others, the students could choose from four possible answers: *Definitely yes, Yes, No, Definitely no*. Since this question is obviously related to the previous questions that showed an improvement, also here a significant increase in the ratio of positive answers can be seen (Fig. 8). In our survey more than 85% of students would recommend the course which is nearly 30% more than in the previous year. In the official evaluation the number of positive votes increased even more (nearly 33%). This result can be interpreted as a success and large accomplishment of our goals.

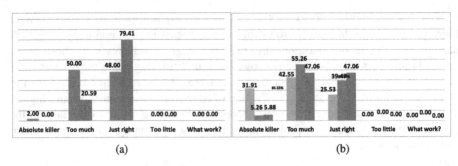

(a)   (b)

Fig. 7. Was the amount of work appropriate considering the number of credits? Results are in %. (a) Our questionnaire. (b) Official student evaluation of education. ■ 2013 ■ 2014 ■ 2015

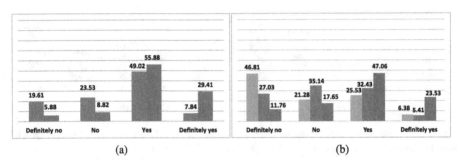

(a)   (b)

Fig. 8. Would you recommend this course to other students? Results are in %. (a) Our questionnaire. (b) Official student evaluation of education. ■ 2013 ■ 2014 ■ 2015

4   Conclusions

We have described our experience with students' acceptance of content-based web publishing assignments within a university course. While we originally thought that blogging is a suitable exercise of this type, we explained how we diverted from it because the students perceived this task as unrelated to the applied informatics curriculum. While the supplementary peer-review activity was undoubtedly useful as it helped to improve the students' engagement in the course activities as well as the learning outcomes; when it was paired with blogging only, students perceived it mostly as additional extra work.

Students' acceptance was significantly improved after we restructured the practical assignment in the last two course runs. Specifically, we believe that this was especially due to: (a) decreased workload on individual students who now worked in teams; (b) the students could also choose the role in the team by themselves depending on their personal interests; (c) they could select the technology but also the topic for the project freely which allowed them to work with content which they themselves considered meaningful; (d) restructuring the overall assignment and pairing peer reviews with all parts thereof, including the team work.

Higher students' acceptance of this course and peer review activities was reflected not only in our survey but also in the official student evaluation of the course which, after years, finally improved.

Acknowledgment. This work was supported from the Slovak national VEGA project no. 1/0948/13.

References

1. Bejdová, V., Homola, M., Kubincová, Z.: Blogging in obligatory course: a bitter victory. In: Popescu, E., Lau, R.W.H., Pata, K., Leung, H., Laanpere, M. (eds.) ICWL 2014. LNCS, vol. 8613, pp. 1–10. Springer, Heidelberg (2014). doi:10.1007/978-3-319-09635-3_1
2. Dropcova, V., Kubincova, Z.: Student questionnaire – can we trust it? In: 2015 International Conference on Interactive Collaborative Learning (ICL), pp. 602–607. IEEE (2015)
3. Dropcova, V., Kubincova, Z.: Team-based projects and peer review. IT works! In: 2016 International Conference on Interactive Collaborative Learning (ICL) (to appear)
4. Gehringer, E.F.: Strategies and mechanisms for electronic peer review. In: 30th Annual Frontiers in Education Conference (FIE 2000), vol. 1, p. F1B/2. IEEE (2000)
5. Homola, M., Kubincová, Z., Čulík, J., Trungel, T.: Peer review support in a virtual learning environment. In: Li, Y., Chang, M., Kravcik, M., Popescu, E., Huang, R., Kinshuk, Chen, N.-S. (eds.) State-of-the-Art and Future Directions of Smart Learning. LNET, pp. 351–355. Springer, Heidelberg (2016)
6. Kennedy, G.J.: Peer-assessment in group projects: is it worth it? In: Proceedings of the 7th Australasian Conference on Computing Education, vol. 42, pp. 59–65. Australian Computer Society Inc. (2005)
7. Levine, R.E.: Peer evaluation in team-based learning. In: Team-Based Learning for Health Professions Education: A Guide to Using Small Groups to Improve Learning, pp. 103–116. Stylus Publishing, Sterling (2008)
8. Lin, S.S., Liu, E.Z.F., Yuan, S.M.: Web-based peer assessment: feedback for students with various thinking-styles. J. Comput. Assist. Learn. **17**(4), 420–432 (2001)
9. Liu, E.F., Lin, S.S., Chiu, C.H., Yuan, S.M.: Web-based peer review: the learner as both adapter and reviewer. IEEE Transactions on Education **44**(3), 246–251 (2001)
10. Michaelsen, L.K., Fink, L.D.: Calculating peer evaluation scores. Team-Based Learning: A Transformative Use of Small Groups in College Teaching, pp. 241–248. Sterling, Stylus Publishing (2004)
11. Popescu, E.: Providing collaborative learning support with social media in an integrated environment. World Wide Web **17**(2), 199–212 (2014)
12. Popescu, E., Kubincová, Z., Homola, M.: Blogging activities in higher education: comparing learning scenarios in multiple course experiences. In: Li, F.W.B., Klamma, R., Laanpere, M., Zhang, J., Manjón, B.F., Lau, R.W.H. (eds.) ICWL 2015. LNCS, vol. 9412, pp. 197–207. Springer, Heidelberg (2015). doi:10.1007/978-3-319-25515-6_18
13. Popescu, E., Manafu, L.: Repurposing a wiki for collaborative learning-pedagogical and technical view. In: 2011 15th International Conference on System Theory, Control, and Computing (ICSTCC), pp. 1–6. IEEE (2011)

14. Reily, K., Finnerty, P.L., Terveen, L.: Two peers are better than one: aggregating peer reviews for computing assignments is surprisingly accurate. In: Proceedings of the ACM 2009 International Conference on Supporting Group Work, pp. 115–124. ACM (2009)
15. Sterbini, A., Temperini, M.: Dealing with open-answer questions in a peer-assessment environment. In: Popescu, E., Li, Q., Klamma, R., Leung, H., Specht, M. (eds.) ICWL 2012. LNCS, vol. 7558, pp. 240–248. Springer, Heidelberg (2012). doi:10.1007/978-3-642-33642-3_26

Exploring the Role of Online Peer-Assessment as a Tool of Early Intervention

Michael Mogessie Ashenafi$^{(\boxtimes)}$, Marco Ronchetti, and Giuseppe Riccardi

Department of Information Engineering and Computer Science,
University of Trento, Trento, Italy
{michael.mogessie,marco.ronchetti,
giuseppe.riccardi}@unitn.it

Abstract. Peer-assessment in education has a long history. Although the adoption of technological tools is not a recent phenomenon, many peer-assessment studies are conducted in manual environments. Automating peer-assessment tasks improves the efficiency of the practice and provides opportunities for taking advantage of large amounts of student-generated data, which will readily be available in electronic format. Data from three undergraduate-level courses, which utilised an electronic peer-assessment tool were explored in this study in order to investigate the relationship between participation in online peer-assessment tasks and successful course completion. It was found that students with little or no participation in optional peer-assessment activities had very low course completion rates as opposed to those with high participation. In light of this finding, it is argued that electronic peer-assessment can serve as a tool of early intervention. Further advantages of automated peer-assessment are discussed and foreseen extensions of this work are outlined.

Keywords: Electronic peer-assessment · Early intervention · At-risk students

1 Introduction

Peer-assessment in education is an assessment method in which students assess the performance of their peers. Topping [1] defines peer-assessment more formally as "... an arrangement in which individuals consider the amount, level, value, worth, quality, or success of the products or outcomes of learning of peers of similar status."

A wide variety of peer-assessment settings exist in which the nature of the work being assessed varies with the discipline and course. Essays, answers to open questions, and oral presentations are examples of work that is assessed in peer-assessment classes.

Reliability, validity, and practicality of peer-assessment as well as its impact on students' learning have been studied for decades. Nonetheless, there is no strong consensus among practitioners on whether peer-assessment is guaranteed to deliver its

© Springer International Publishing AG 2017
T.-T. Wu et al. (Eds.): SETE 2016, LNCS 10108, pp. 635–644, 2017.
DOI: 10.1007/978-3-319-52836-6_67

desired effects. Most recent research seeking to establish whether peer-assessment can be used as alternative assessment method has come in the form of one-off experiments conducted in small classes.[1]

The wide range of scenarios in which peer-assessment is implemented has also made it particularly difficult to reach solid conclusions about its effectiveness as the number and impact of variables being studied varies from one scenario to another. Some variables are however common to all peer-assessment settings. Examples include the number of students involved per assessment task and the total number of participants. Recent studies in peer-assessment have focused on a number of themes including peer-feedback, design strategies, students' perceptions, social and psychological factors, and validity and reliability of the practice.

Large-scale introduction of peer-assessment in educational institutions is very rare for a number of reasons. Given the issues of reliability and validity of student ratings, in particular, integrating peer-assessment into a course's curriculum implies risks both on parts of the institution and students, which stakeholders may not be willing to assume.

Moreover, the manual nature of most peer-assessment practices prevents researchers from carrying out large-scale experiments that would help investigate the impact of variables on the effectiveness of the practice.

Automation of peer-assessment tasks could greatly improve efficiency and enable conducting large-scale, iterative experiments. In addition to the foreseen improvement in efficiency, the move towards automated peer-assessment could reduce, if not eliminate, issues of non-confidentiality, the potential for academic dishonesty, and increase in the workload of instructors.

Automated peer-assessment implies more than simple automation of task assignment and submission. Depending on the nature of the work being assessed, many other features of peer-assessment can also be automated, at least to a certain degree.

Other opportunities that arise from the automation of peer-assessment tasks include mathematical modelling of students and construction of student profiles, ubiquitous peer-assessment practices that go beyond the confines of the traditional classroom, and creation of platforms that allow easy replication and extension of previous studies.

Another prospect worth examining is the potential of online peer-assessment systems to serve as tools of monitoring and supervision of students. Used this way, an online peer-assessment system may provide timely information about students who may be at risk of falling behind or even failing a course.

Two previous studies demonstrated how models of student progress and early intervention could be built on top of an online peer-assessment platform to monitor students who often participate in peer-assessment activities [4, 5]. This study is a follow-up, which sought to determine whether analysis of the digital traces of students who had little participation in peer-assessment activities could lead to a firm conclusion about their success rate of completing their courses.

---

[1] See [2] for a meta-analytic review of peer-assessment studies conducted in the previous century and [3] for a comprehensive review of those peer-assessment studies conducted since 2000.

The findings of three courses involving over 600 students, in which the online peer-assessment system was applied, showed that students who had a participation rate of less than 33% in online peer-assessment activities were significantly more at risk of not completing the courses as those who had over 33% participation rates.

Section 2 provides a brief review of the state-of-the-art in automated peer-assessment, with focus a number of popular tools for peer-assessment and recent topics addressed by the automated peer-assessment community. Section 3 introduces the reader to the peer-assessment system that was used to conducted this study. Section 4 presents analyses and findings across three computer science courses that were taught between mid-2013 and mid-2014. Section 5 provides a discussion of the role automated peer-assessment may play in identifying at-risk students and concludes with a number of final remarks.

2 Previous Work in Automated Peer-Assessment

Peer-assessment has been in use at all levels of education for over half a century. There is a significant amount of literature that documents this use across several course subjects. Writing courses, especially those that focus on improving students written English, constitute the largest share [2, 3]. Adoption of information technology infrastructures geared towards education by many institutions has led to the introduction of electronic peer-assessment systems with a varying designs and levels of sophistication. Educators in computer science have especially benefited from this transformation by introducing such tools in their courses.

There is an extensive number of tools that support automated peer-assessment. For reasons of brevity, four tools that are similar to the peer-assessment system used in this study are presented here.[2]

2.1 PRAISE (Peer Review Assignments Increase Student Experience)

de Raadt et al. [7] presented a generic peer-assessment tool that was used in the fields of computer science, accounting and nursing. The instructor could specify criteria before distributing assignments, which students would use to rate their peers' assignments. The system could compare reviews and also suggest a mark. Disagreements among reviewers would lead the system to submit the solution to the instructor for moderation. The instructor would then decide the final mark.

2.2 PeerWise

Denny et al. [8] presented PeerWise, a peer-assessment tool, which students used to create multiple-choice questions and answer those created by their peers.

---

[2] See [6] for a comprehensive review of tools that support peer-assessment.

When answering a question, students would also be required to rate the quality of the question. They could also comment on the question, in which case the author of the question could reply to the comment.

2.3 PeerScholar

Paré and Joordens [9] presented another peer-assessment tool, which was initially designed with the aim of improving writing and critical thinking skills of psychology students. First, students would submit essays. Next, they would be asked to anonymously assess the works of their peers, assign marks between 1 and 10, and comment on their assessments. An additional feature of PeerScholar is that students could also rate the reviews the received.

2.4 Peer Instruction

Peer Instruction is not a software artifact but a practice that is applied in a classroom setting where instructors provide students with in-lecture multiple choice questions. Students would then vote for the correct answer using Electronic Voting Systems (EVS), also known as clickers [10, 11]. A study by Kennedy and Cutts [12] showed that communication systems such as EVS may serve as indicators of expected student performance. This is an example of assessment that aids in early discovery of challenges students may face in grasping concepts so that appropriate supervision is provided in a timely manner.

Despite its widespread use, peer-assessment had not gained enough of the spotlight to warrant the creation of conferences or workshops dedicated solely to the topic. Now, there are at least two annual workshops that aim to bring together scholars from many disciplines in order to foster the advancement of the practice. The Computer Supported Peer Review in Education (**CSPRED**) and Peer Review, Peer Assessment, and Self Assessment in Education (**PRASAE**) workshops address several issues in electronic peer-assessment such as improving the impact of reviews [13, 14], training reviewers to improve the peer-review process [15, 16] and also aim to provide the current state-of-the-art in electronic peer-review and peer-assessment [17, 18].

3 The Online Peer-Assessment System

A web-based peer-assessment platform was developed and used in three computer science courses between 2012 and 2016. Participation in peer-assessment tasks was optional. However, all students who completed at least a third of the tasks were awarded a bonus worth 3.3% of the final mark. An additional 3.3% bonus was awarded to the top-third students, based on the number of peer-awarded points. For all three courses, it was observed that active participation in peer-assessment activities waned towards the end of the course. Regardless. A total of 83% of students for the three courses completed at least a third of the tasks.

In the latest version of the platform, students completed a weekly peer-assessment cycle composed of three tasks. First, students submitted questions relating to a list of previously discussed topics provided by the teacher. Then, the teacher examined the questions and selected a subset of questions, which were randomly assigned to students in the second task. The assignment procedure ensured that each question was assigned to at least four students. Machine learning techniques were applied to group similar questions in an effort to facilitate the question selection process.

After answers were submitted, question-answer sets were randomly distributed to students to rate each answer. In order to encourage careful assessment of each answer, students were provided with a certain amount of points, referred to as coins, to distribute over the answers.

After the completion of each cycle, questions and answers, together with coins earned, were made available to all students. Students could also monitor their progress by accessing visual and statistical information available in their profile page. In previous studies, how to predict expected performance in final exams was explored using student activity data from the peer-assessment system [4, 5]. The prediction models in those studies, however, considered only those students who had completed over a third of all peer-assessment tasks. The main reason behind this was that the performance of the linear regression models was significantly reduced with the introduction of data of students with little or no participation at all. Because the number of students who did not participate enough in online peer-assessment tasks was considerably low, the attempt to build prediction models only for those students did not produce encouraging results. Therefore, the analyses presented here used less sophisticated statistics to perform comparisons between the two student groups.

4 Analyses and Results

Three undergraduate-level computer science courses, labelled **IG1, LP,** and **PR2**, utilised the peer-assessment system between the early 2013 and mid 2016. The courses were administered at the University of Trento in Italy.

The Italian grading system uses a scale that ranges between 0 and 30, with 30L or 30 Excellent the highest possible mark. In order to pass a course, students have to obtain at least a score of 18. For the purpose of this analysis, the range of scores was categorised into four groups and labels were assigned to each group. Table 1 presents this partitioning of scores. The Italian higher education system permits students to sit for the same exam at most five times within an academic year. Students therefore have an opportunity to improve their grades by making several attempts. The analysis considers the data of those students who both subscribed for peer-assessment tasks and attempted an exam at least once.

For each course, students with less than 33% participation (who completed less than a third of peer-assessment tasks), referred to as *low-participation groups*, and those with over 33% participation, referred to as *high-participation groups*, were assigned to performance groups according to the final scores they obtained for the courses. Table 2 shows the categorisation of students in the low-participation group

Table 1. Mapping of scores to performance groups

Score	Verdict
Below 18	Insufficient
Between 18 and 22	Low performer
Between 23 and 26	Medium performer
27 or above	High performer

into the performance groups and Table 3 does the same for those in the high-participation group. The observation that a large majority of low-participation students did not manage to obtain passing marks was consistent across all three courses, albeit with varying degrees. In the case of PR2, low-participation students were more than twice as likely to score below the passing mark as those with high participation. LP and IG1 low-participation groups were 1.66 and 1.87 times as likely as their high-participation counterparts to score below the passing mark, respectively.

Table 2. Distribution of scores for students in the low-participation group

Course	Number of students	<18	[18.23)	[23, 26]	>=27
IG1	35	25	4	3	3
PR2	42	18	7	11	6
LP	30	22	1	5	2

Table 3. Distribution of scores for students in the high-participation group

Course	Number of students	<18	[18.23)	[23, 26]	>=27
IG1	182	69	46	36	31
PR2	141	23	33	49	36
LP	189	84	40	37	28

Further analysis of the data showed that low-participation students usually stopped participating between the third and fourth weeks of the courses, which spanned at least nine weeks. For this reason, much of the data for students in this group showed little change between the midpoint and end of the courses.

Another observation was the large difference in the percentage of students with insufficient performance between the low-participation and high-participation groups. This difference ranged between 27% and 33% for the three courses.

Therefore, the argument that the peer-assessment system could identify the large majority of students who may be at-risk of failing in a timely manner is supported by these observations. The charts presented in Figures 1, 2, and 3 demonstrate the differences in performance levels between low-participation and high-participation groups for the three courses.

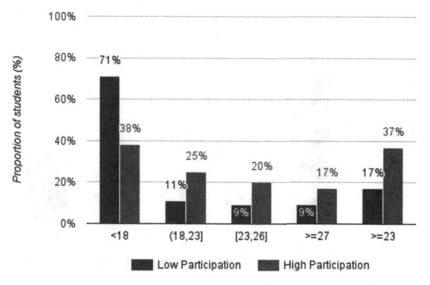

Fig. 1. Participation in peer-assessment tasks and exam scores for course IG1

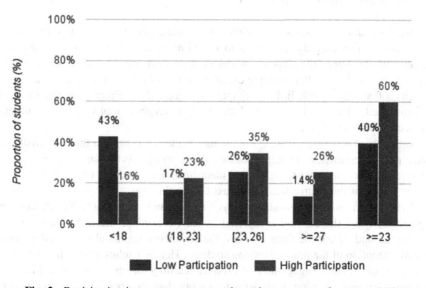

Fig. 2. Participation in peer-assessment tasks and exam scores for course PR2

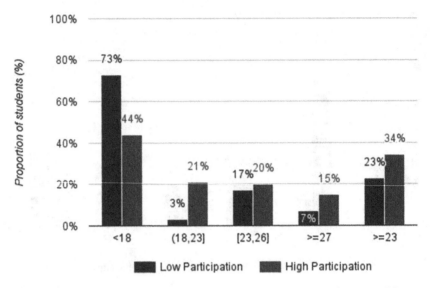

Fig. 3. Participation in peer-assessment tasks and exam scores for course LP

5   Discussion and Conclusion

In order to examine if lack of participation in online peer-assessment activities for a course could fairly identify students who would not successfully complete the course, the data of the over 600 students in enrolled in three courses were analysed. The analyses revealed that, after multiple exam sessions, all of which a student can sit, the majority of students with little participation struggled to either pass the exams or perform well. The findings contribute to yet another motivation to automate peer-assessment activities.

Although, at this stage, there is not enough evidence to suggest that participation in online peer-assessment tasks improves overall student performance, the argument that these activities could provide well-timed identification of students who may fall behind at later stages of the course was supported by the findings.

Participation in peer-assessment activities was not mandatory. Nonetheless, the large majority of student had completed at least a third of the tasks, which ranged between 22 and 27 for the three courses. Earlier survey results also showed generally positive reception of the practice among students. Hence, studies of whether the system could promote student engagement or produce learning effects are in order. Moreover, categorisation and mapping of students into more than two performance groups could provide better insights with respect to identifying students that may not be at risk but may still need closer supervision. These two possible extensions of this work will be explored in an upcoming study.

The case for introducing electronic peer-assessment environments into the class-room is supported by the foreseen significant improvements in efficiency and effec-tiveness of the activities involved. It is hoped that the prospects explored in this study contribute to the case for transitioning into cost-effective, ubiquitous, and highly interactive electronic peer-assessment solutions.

In particular, the transition to a ubiquitous system can be made with little difficulty by taking advantage of the fact that virtually all students own smartphones or tablets. Developing a mobile peer-assessment solution has the potential to increase student productivity given that peer-assessment tasks are designed to be simple, mobile-friendly and with special attention to privacy and other social aspects. Hence, development of a mobile version of the peer-assessment system will be addressed in the near future.

Calibrating peer-assigned marks as well as training students how to grade their peers' answers have been shown to improve the effectiveness of peer-assessment, with what regards its validity and reliability. Hence, future work will also look to improve the quality of peer-assigned marks by applying these techniques.

References

1. Topping, K.: Peer assessment between students in colleges and universities. Rev. Educ. Res. **68**(3), 249–276 (1998). doi:10.3102/00346543068003249, URL: http://rer.sagepub.com/content/68/3/249.abstract, http://rer.sagepub.com/content/68/3/249.full.pdf+html
2. Falchikov N, Goldfinch J (2000) Student peer assessment in higher education: A meta-analysis comparing peer and teacher marks. Review of Educational Research 70 (3):287–322, doi:10.3102/00346543070003287, URL http://rer.sagepub.com/content/70/3/287.abstract, http://rer.sagepub.com/content/70/3/287.full.pdf+html
3. Ashenafi, M.M.: Peer-assessment in higher education twenty-first century practices, challenges and the way forward. Assess. Eval. High. Educ. 1–26 (2015). doi:10.1080/02602938.2015.1100711, URL: http://dx.doi.org/10.1080/02602938.2015.1100711
4. Ashenafi, M.M., Riccardi, G., Ronchetti, M.: Predicting students' final exam scores from their course activities. In: Frontiers in Education Conference (FIE), pp. 1–9, 32614 2015. IEEE. doi:10.1109/FIE.2015.7344081
5. Ashenafi, M.M., Ronchetti, M., Riccardi, G.: Predicting student progress us- ing peer-assessment data. In: 9th International Conference on Educational Data Mining (EDM) (2016)
6. Luxton-Reilly, A.: A systematic review of tools that support peer assessment. Comput. Sci. Educ. **19**(4), 209–232 (2009). doi:10.1080/08993400903384844, URL: http://dx.doi.org/10.1080/08993400903384844, http://dx.doi.org/10.1080/08993400903384844
7. de Raadt, M., Lai, D., Watson, R.: An evaluation of electronic individual peer assessment in an introductory programming course. In: Proceedings of the Seventh Baltic Sea Conference on Computing Education Research (Koli Calling 2007), vol. 88, pp. 53–64. Australian Computer Society, Inc., Darlinghurst, Australia (2007). URL: http://dl.acm.org/citation.cfm?id=2449323.2449330
8. Denny, P., Hamer, J., Luxton-Reilly, A., Purchase, H.: Peerwise: Students sharing their multiple choice questions. In: Proceedings of the Fourth International Work- shop on Computing Education Research (ICER 2008), pp. 51–58. ACM, New York (2008). doi:10.1145/1404520.1404526, URL: http://doi.acm.org/10.1145/1404520.1404526

9. Paré, D., Joordens, S.: Peering into large lectures: examining peer and expert mark agreement using peerscholar, an online peer assessment tool. J. Comput. Assist. Learn. **24**(6), 526–540 (2008). doi:10.1111/j.1365-2729.2008.00290.x, URL: http://dx.doi.org/10. 1111/j.1365-2729.2008.00290.x

10. Fagen, A.P., Crouch, C.H., Mazur, E.: Peer instruction: results from a range of classrooms. Phys. Teach. **40**(4), 206–209 (2002). doi:http://dx.doi.org/10.1119/1.1474140, URL: http:// scitation.aip.org/content/aapt/journal/tpt/40/4/10.1119/1.1474140

11. Simon, B., Kohanfars, M., Lee, J., Tamayo, K., Cutts, Q.: Experience report: peer instruction in introductory computing. In: Proceedings of the 41st ACM Technical Symposium on Computer Science Education (SIGCSE 2010), pp. 341–345. ACM, New York (2010). doi:10.1145/1734263.1734381, URL: http://doi.acm.org/10.1145/1734263.1734381

12. Kennedy, G.E., Cutts, Q.: The association between students' use of an electronic voting system and their learning outcomes. J. Comput. Assist. Learn. **21**(4), 260–268 (2005). doi:10.1111/j.1365-2729.2005.00133.x, URL: http://dx.doi.org/10.1111/j.1365-2729.2005. 00133.x

13. Yadav, R.K., Gehringer, E.F.: Automated met reviewing: a classifier approach to assess the quality of reviews. In: Computer-Supported Peer Review in Education (CSPRED-2016) (2016)

14. Wang, Y., Wang, H., Schunn, C., Baehr, E.: Choosing a better moment to assign reviewers in peer assessment: the earlier the better, or the later the better? In: Computer-Supported Peer Review in Education (CSPRED-2016) (2016)

15. Morris, J., Kidd, J.: Teaching students to give and to receive: improving interdisciplinary writing through peer review. In: Computer-Supported Peer Review in Education (CSPRED-2016) (2016)

16. Song, Y., Gehringer, E.F., Morris, J., Kid, J., Ringleb, S.: Toward better training in peer assessment: does calibration help? In: Computer-Supported Peer Review in Education (CSPRED-2016) (2016)

17. Gehringer, E.F.: A survey of methods for improving review quality. In: Cao, Y., Väljataga, T., Tang, Jeff, K.,T., Leung, H., Laanpere, M. (eds.) ICWL 2014. LNCS, vol. 8699, pp. 92–97. Springer, Heidelberg (2014). doi:10.1007/978-3-319-13296-9_10

18. Babik, D., Gehringer, E.F., Kidd, J., Pramudianto, F., Tinapple, D.: Probing the landscape: Toward a systematic taxonomy of online peer assessment systems in education. In: Computer-Supported Peer Review in Education (CSPRED-2016) (2016)

Workshop on Technology Enhanced Language Learning

An Investigation of Students' Perception on Willingness to Communicate Behavior and Synchronous Communication

Mei-Jen Audrey Shih[(✉)] and Jie Chi Yang

Graduate Institute of Network Learning Technology,
National Central University, Taoyuan City, Taiwan
{audreyshih32,yang}@cl.ncu.edu.tw

Abstract. In English as a target language (TL) learning environment, it always takes effort to encourage learners to open and engage in a conversation for English communication practice. Moreover, the shorts of communication practice might be influencing their perceptions which are corresponding to a variety of willingness to communicate (WTC) behaviors. On the other hand, a mode of engaging synchronous communication (SC) to facilitate English as a TL communication has been positively addressed. As a result, the current study attempts to investigate what features of WTC behaviors would influence English learners' WTC, and whether an engagement of SC would influence to their WTC respectively. The participants were the first year non-English majored college students. Questionnaires with open-ended questions were applied to gather the data. The results showed learners' perceptions on several WTC behaviors were ranked much higher than those were lower. The modes of SCs positively associated with learner's WTC accordingly.

Keywords: English as a target language · Synchronous communication · Willingness to communicate behaviors

1 Introduction

To communicate in English as a target language (TL) has been considered as a difficult but crucial skill in the second language learning. Also, in order to sharpen the skill, it takes time and efforts to engage in the communication context, which may not be emphasized primarily in English as TL setting. So, the communication skill tends to be ignorance to practice in the TL learning comparing to other skills [1, 2]. Gradually, learners encounter some weaknesses and difficulties to practice communication skill, such as reluctance to speak out in TL, speaking anxiety, lacks of speaking confidence and unwilling to communicate [3, 4]. Apart from these mentioned influences, more conditions affect their WTC behaviors to communicate in the classroom should be concerned [5].

Relating to the technology advancement, prior research has noted the means of synchronous communication (SC) was applied as a supplement to benefit several TL learning setting. In·other words, it is seen as an alternative of assisting the communicative practice [6]. In the current study, the SC would be implemented as a text or

© Springer International Publishing AG 2017
T.-T. Wu et al. (Eds.): SETE 2016, LNCS 10108, pp. 647–653, 2017.
DOI: 10.1007/978-3-319-52836-6_68

audio mode to support an instant communication and interaction in the TL classroom communication practice for learners. Therefore, there are two research questions noted in the current study. Research question one: Do the features of WTC behaviors influence learners' WTC in English respectively? Research question two: Do the different modes of synchronous communication (SC) influence learners' WTC in English respectively?

2 Literature Review

2.1 WTC Behavior

With regard to the practice of communication skill in the TL learning, most TL learners claimed to be full of anxious and reluctant to while communicating with each other. It is because a feeling of embarrassment would be easily revealed while lacking of communicative interaction with each other in the TL, which sentimentally affect their perceptions, such as WTC [3, 6–8]. The definition of WTC refers to an intention to start and get into a conversation with a particular time and space [9, 10]. As a result, it would be influenced by where the environment is to proceed the communication. Besides, a factor in terms of confidence contains a mixed inclination of the anxiety and competence towards the TL, which turns to be as a critical factor to estimate learners' WTC in TL, such as English. Furthermore, when the learners have the opportunities to involve in different environment, their WTC and confidence might be differ by the influence of the settings correspondingly. Accordingly, a consideration of an enrichment of the TL class instruction was suggested to facilitate the development of their WTC and confidence in English [11, 12]. It not only offer more approaches for diverse the TL communication practice to the learners to make an impact on their WTC and confidence in English, but also gives the instructor to reflect and refine the TL class instruction design to promote active communication practice.

In order to further understand other conditions would affect learners' WTC in English, several features of WTC behaviors [3, 13] were addressed as the conditions influencing their WTC in the TL. The WTC behaviors were mostly identified from interview data of the previous study [3]. For example, group size, familiarity with interlocutor, interlocutor participation, degree of topic preparation, cultural backgrounds, and medium of communication. So, not only the supplement of environment might make an impact their WTC in the TL, but also these WTC behaviors in terms of conditions should also be concerned to understand of how their WTC in the TL might be influenced accordingly.

2.2 Oral Communication with TL Teaching and Learning

The use of synchronous communication (SC) has been identified in several prior studies that to benefit the TL learning [14–17], specifically for communication skill. The synchronous communication refers to a computer-mediated communication which support and close to a real-time interaction [18]. Accordingly, the more timely interactive means as a familiar way of chatty receiving-and-responding to enrich the communication practice in the TL, English. Additionally, SC allows two modes of demonstrations in terms of a text or audio way of communication takes place [19]. The current study tries to understand and investigate whether the supplement of either text or audio SC would make a difference on learners' WTC in English.

3   Methodology

3.1   Participants

The current study recruited the first year college students as participants. All the participants were neither majoring in English subject nor in English related majors. The study took place in a General English class as a required course for the freshmen in the college. Apart from the weekly class instruction, they did not take any other English subject classes at the college.

3.2   Instruments

Questionnaires with open-ended questions were the instruments used in the current study. The first one was the WTC behaviors questionnaire adopted from [13], to examine the learners' perceptions on which WTC behaviors would influence their WTC in English generally. It ranked by a Five Likert scale with a follow-up open-ended question asking the reason they picked the item for their perceptions. The second one was the WTC questionnaire adopted from [20], to investigate their WTC in English with the supplement of SC for communicative practice in English. Since there were two modes of SC were conducted, the WTC questionnaires were implemented concerning text and audio SCs respectively.

3.3   Procedure and Data Analysis

The current study was conducted in a General English class at college for seven weeks. The first year General English class at college contained various daily topics, such as entertainment, traveling, culture, food, and so on. In addition, the class usually taught for a passive way to mainly practice the listening and reading skills. For example, the vocabulary, phrase, and sentence learning On the other hand, the current study tries to come up an alternative means to encourage learners to have productive communication practice by engaging with the SC for supplemental practice in the classroom. There were English topics selected from the textbook used in the General English class for the communicative practice class design. The communicative practice class design included three steps which the first step was warm up of today's topic instruction for approximately 20 min. Then the second step was pair work for about 30 min. At last, the third step was discussion which gave a short time about 10 min of checking feedback with the teacher and other learners.

The data analysis of the current study was investigated with quantitative and qualitative analysis. Descriptive analysis of mean scores and standard deviation would be presented to have an initial view on which WTC behavior learners perceived most and least to make an impact on their WTC in English generally. Their open-ended feedback would be collected and generalized to supplement the data interpretation. Then, Pearson correlation was applied to investigate whether the different modes of SC would influence learners' WTC in English respectively or not.

4 Results and Discussion

To understand and react to the two research questions, *do the features of WTC behaviors influence learners' WTC in English respectively?* And *do the different modes of synchronous communications (SC) influence learners' WTC in English respectively?* The section of results and discussion would be showed by tables with explanations.

4.1 WTC Behaviors

This study investigated how the features of WTC behaviors might affect English learners' WTC in English, and how the modes of SC might influence their WTC in English. Quantitative and qualitative results of learners' feedback on the influence of WTC behaviors would be presented as follows. Table 1 demonstrates the results of descriptive analysis on the mean scores and standard deviation of the WTC behavior factors. The WTC behavior of familiarity with the interlocutor (M = 4.00, SD = .67) obtained the highest mean score comparing to other WTC behaviors. Meanwhile, the WTC behavior of interlocutor participation (M = 3.66, SD = .65) gained a higher mean score to other WTC behaviors. Regarding the open-ended feedback, the learners replied as talking to the partner who knows each other, made them feel more stress-free than to those they did not know. At the same time, the familiarity offered an air of comfort to have an interaction while the unknown resulted in a discomfort to communicate with each other. Some learners also mentioned that to communicate with unacquainted partner, made them worried about making any mistakes. The result rebounded the study that acknowledged the perceived WTC behavior in terms of the

Table 1. The Mean and SD of learners' perceptions on WTC behaviors.

WTC behaviors	Mean (M)	Standard deviation (SD)
Group size	3.56	0.62
Confidence	3.47	0.67
Familiarity with the interlocutor	4.00	0.67
Interlocutor participation	3.66	0.65
Topic	3.44	0.67
Vocabulary capacity	3.56	0.91
Conversational context	2.94	.098
Communication strategy	3.22	0.91
Medium of communication	3.53	0.80

role of interlocutor [3], and it is interesting to indicate the importance of the interlocutor role to make an impact on the learners' WTC in English. Moreover, it tended to be the most prominent WTC behavior on their WTC in English among other WTC behaviors. Furthermore, the attitude of the interlocutor in the communication would further make a difference on interaction. They said that more actively participant in the communication the interlocutor has, a mutual feeling of the other reacted as well. Oppositely, if the interlocutor were not willing to work together, the air would grow into awkward and embarrassing.

In relation to other WTC behaviors responses, the group size (M = 3.56, SD = .62) and the vocabulary capacity (M = 3.56, SD = .91) are inclined to be great factors influencing learners' WTC in English. Concerning the group size, learners were pairing for the communicative activity practice. Most of them explained the familiarity of the interlocutor seemed to be the essential condition of the grouping. Some of them found it was interesting to have random pair grouping, which made them look forward to the new partner for discussion. Regarding the vocabulary capacity, they described it weighted fundamentally for a smooth communication. Although the WTC behavior of vocabulary capacity did not expose as much crucial as the mentioned factors statistically, the learners perceived it would directly affect whether a smooth communication would be conducted. They explained that the more terminology they understood, the more help it can accomplish the task. As a result, once you have larger vocabulary capacity, you might be more willing and capable to communicate to others. However, most of them admitted that they had limited vocabulary knowledge which would become a problem to continue the communication even if they were willing to fulfill the task. Besides, WTC behaviors in terms of medium of communication (M = 3.53, SD = .80), confidence (M = 3.47, SD = .67), topic (M = 3.44, SD = .67), and communication strategy (M = 3.22, SD = .91) revealed different influences on the learners' WTC in English. They showed the experiences of coping with different modes of SCs to do the tasks with their partners. They further explained perceived less pressure via modes of SC while the in person circumstance remained lots of tense to interact with each other. Also, whether they perceived confidence in communicating in English would be affecting their WTC in English. Be afraid of making mistakes which resulted in the insufficient confidence they hold, and a reluctance to communicate in English was observed. The WTC behaviors of topic and communication strategy did not appear to be as an initial factor affecting their WTC in English. It seemed to be a external factor to justify only if they were satisfied with other factors. What is more that the WTC behavior of conversational context (M = 2.94, SD = .98) was rated as the lowest factor. The possible reason can be that it was alike to the topic and communication strategy which tended to be a peripheral condition for accomplishing the task. Once the learners were content with the WTC behavior factors directly affect their insights, the external factors might be seen as critical to make an impact on their WTC in English.

4.2 The Correlation of WTC in the Text and Audio SCs

Then, a follow-up investigation on the results of the different modes of SC in terms of text or audio representation would influence learners' WTC in English. The results of

Table 2. The results of the different modes of SC on learners' WTC in English.

	Confidence	Modes of SC
WTC	0.58*	Text SC
	0.63*	Audio SC

Pearson correlation were displayed within the following table illustrations. Table 2 demonstrates the results of learners' WTC and confidence in the text SC. An affirmative correlation was identified between their WTC and confidence in English in the text SC ($r = .58$, $p < .05$). Accordingly, the results might refer the text SC environment setting to offer a benefit on the development of their WTC and confidence. In addition, Table 2 also shows the results of learners' WTC and confidence the audio SC, which also an affirmative association was verified between their WTC and confidence in English in the audio SC ($r = .63$, $p < .05$). So, the results might explain the audio SC environment setting formed a similar atmosphere of the text SC, which also enriched learners' WTC and confidence while lowered their affective filter to communicate in English in these environment settings. In sum, the above results were likely to suggest that the engagement of SC effectively provide the alternative to the English as TL learners on encouraging their WTC and confidence in English in the supplement classroom setting for practice.

5 Conclusions

The study attempts to investigate what features of WTC behaviors would influence English learners' WTC in English, and whether an engagement of SC would influence to their WTC respectively. The purpose of understanding their WTC behaviors in English was to recognize how they experienced the different factors might be crucially influencing their WTC in English accordingly. The results showed that a number of WTC behaviors factors would be able to affect the learners' WTC in English. Particularly, they concerned the role of interlocutor influenced their WTC in English mostly. Then, the vocabulary capacity they have held would also be an essential factor to cause WTC as well as a smooth of communication. On the other hand, though the factor of communication medium was not rated as high as other WTC behaviors, they mentioned by the medium for communication, it did reduced tightness and pressure during the communication. Furthermore, the results also revealed positive correlations between their WTC and confidence in both modes of SCs. The finding confirmed that the supplement of SC tool as facilitation for TL communication practice, which the engagement might further play an enhanced role to the development of their WTC and confidence in English. In sum, the finding of the study not only indicated [9, 14] the supplement of SC benefited communication practice in TL but also in favor of its support for the learners' affective features for TL communicative practice.

References

1. Liu, M., Zhang, W., Lu, Z.: Reticence and anxiety in Chinese university ESP poetry class: a case study. J. Lang. Cult. **2**(2), 20–33 (2011)
2. Sun, Y.C., Yang, F.Y.: I help, therefore, i learn: service learning on Web 2.0 in an EFL speaking class. Comput. Assist. Lang. Learn. **28**(3), 202–219 (2015)
3. Cao, Y., Philp, J.: Interactional context and willingness to communicate: a comparison of behavior in whole class, group, and dyadic interaction. System **34**, 480–493 (2006)
4. MacIntyre, P.D.: Willingness to communicate in the second language: understanding the decision to speak as a volitional process. Modern Lang. J. **91**(4), 564–576 (2007)
5. Mak, B.: An exploration of speaking-in-class anxiety with Chinese ESL learners. System **39** (2), 202–214 (2011)
6. Baker, S., Philp, J.: The role of gender and immersion in communication and second language orientation. Lang. Learn. **50**(2), 311–341 (2006)
7. Clement, R., Baker, S., MacIntyre, P.: Willingness to communicate in a second language: the effects of context, norms, and vitality. J. Lang. Soc. Psychol. **22**(2), 190–209 (2003)
8. Yashima, T.: Willingness to communicate in a second language: the Japanese EFL context. Modern Lang. J. **86**(1), 54–66 (2002)
9. Ko, C.J.: Can synchronous computer-mediated communication (CMC) help beginning-level foreign language learner speak? Comput. Assist. Lang. Learn. **25**(3), 217–236 (2012)
10. MacIntyre, P., Baker, S., Clement, R., Conrad, S.: Willingness to communicate, social support, and language-learning orientations of immersion students. Stud. Second Lang. Acquis. **23**, 369–388 (2001)
11. Clement, R.: Second langauge proficiency and acculturation: an investigation of the effects of language status and individual characteristics. J. Lang. Soc. Psychol. **5**, 271–290 (1986)
12. Léger, D., Storch, N.: Learners' perceptions and attitudes: implications for willingness to communicate in an L2 classroom. System **37**(2), 269–285 (2009)
13. Cao, Y.: A sociocognitive perspective on second language classroom willingness to communicate. TESOL Q. **48**(4), 789–814 (2014)
14. Alastuey, M.C.B.: Perceived benefits and drawbacks of synchronous voice-based computer-mediated communication in the foreign language classroom. Comput. Assist. Lang. Learn. **24**(5), 419–443 (2011)
15. Johnson, G.: The relative learning benefits of synchronous and asynchronous text-based discussion. Br. J. Educ. Technol. **39**(1), 166–169 (2008)
16. Zou, B.: Teachers' support in using computers for developing students' listening and speaking skills in pre-sessional English courses. Comput. Assist. Lang. Learn. **26**(1), 83–99 (2013)
17. Stockwell, G.: A review of technology choice for teaching language skills in the CALL literature. ReCALL **19**(2), 105–120 (2007)
18. Sykes, J.M.: Synchronous CMC and pragmatic development: effects of oral and written chat. CALICO J. **22**(3), 399–431 (2005)
19. Yanguas, Í.: Task-based oral computer-mediated communication and L2 vocabulary acquisition. CALICO J. **29**(3), 507–531 (2012)
20. Reinders, H., Wattana, S.: Can I say something? The effects of digital game play on willingness to communicate. Lang. Learn. Technol. **18**(2), 101–123 (2014)

Effects of Flipped Jigsaw Collaborative Learning on English as a Foreign Language Learning Anxiety

Yoshiko Goda[1(✉)], Masanori Yamada[2], Kojiro Hata[3], Hideya Matsukawa[4], and Seisuke Yasunami[5]

[1] Graduate School of Instructional Systems, Kumamoto University, 2-39-1, Kurokami, Chuo-ku, Kumamoto 8608555, Japan
ygoda@kumamoto-u.ac.jp
[2] Faculty of Arts and Science, Kyushu University, 744, Motooka, Nishi-ku, Fukuoka 8190395, Japan
mark@mark-lab.net
[3] Faculty of Modern Social Studies, Otemae University, 6-42, Ochayashocho, Nishinomiya, Hyogo 6620961, Japan
k-hata@otemae.ac.jp
[4] Center for Institutional Research, Institute of Excellence in Higher Education, Tohoku University, 2-1-1 Katahira, Aoba-ku, Sendai, Miyagi 9808577, Japan
matukawahideya@tohoku.ac.jp
[5] Faculty of Advanced Science and Technology, Kumamoto University, 2-39-1, Kurokami, Chuo-ku, Kumamoto 8608555, Japan
yasunami@kumamoto-u.ac.jp

Abstract. This research aims to investigate the effects of a blended learning approach that combines flipped learning with the jigsaw method of open educational resources for collaborative learning on English as a foreign language (EFL)-related learning anxiety (hereinafter referred to as flipped jigsaw). EFL learning anxiety was measured via the Foreign Language Classroom Anxiety Survey (FLCAS) prior to and following flipped jigsaw collaborative learning activities. Eighty-nine sophomores enrolled in Computer Assisted Language Learning participated in this study, and the data of the seventy-four participants who completed both pre- and post-FLCAS assessments were analyzed via a paired-t test. The results show that EFL learning anxiety items related to course preparation demonstrated significant changes following the flipped jigsaw activities. This implies that flipped jigsaw collaborative learning activities may promote learners' outside-the-classroom preparation, and that such preparation may lead to better performance and learning anxiety reduction.

Keywords: Flipped learning · Jigsaw approach · Flipped jigsaw · Collaborative learning · Open educational resources

© Springer International Publishing AG 2017
T.-T. Wu et al. (Eds.): SETE 2016, LNCS 10108, pp. 654–664, 2017.
DOI: 10.1007/978-3-319-52836-6_69

1   Introduction

Flipped learning has been employed in English as a Foreign Language (EFL) learning settings and has gradually risen in popularity, though Engin (2014) stated that few classrooms have adopted this practice [5]. The jigsaw method is often used in an attempt to activate learners' interactions and to facilitate collaborative learning in EFL education settings [2]. To maximize the benefits associated with both instructional strategies, a combination of flipped learning and the jigsaw approach (hereinafter referred to as flipped jigsaw) was designed and introduced [8]. In their related study, they reported that students perceived the practice as positive and useful for EFL learning. This research focused on EFL learning anxiety, and thus the effects of flipped jigsaw collaborative learning on anxiety were investigated.

The advancement of technology urges practitioners and researchers to reorganize approaches and processes in order to address new learning needs, learning styles, and emerging literacies [9]. In this research, a computer supported collaborative learning (CSCL) support system, C^4 (C-quad), served as an online discussion platform [16], and YouTube materials acted as open educational resources; these tools were employed in the design and implementation of the flipped jigsaw. The C^4 was developed based on a community of inquiry [6] and its applications for CSCL design [7]. Thus, the flipped jigsaw demonstrates an ingenious integration of available pedagogical approaches and information communication technology (ICT) and creates a synergistic effect on learning.

2   Related Literature

2.1   Flipped Learning

The concept of the flipped classroom was described as follows: "that which is traditionally done in class is now done at home, and that which is traditionally done as homework is now completed in class" [3]. Sams and Bergmann (2013) described that flipped learning concerns how best to use in-class-time with students [14]. Flipped learning emphasizes student preparation prior to class and focuses on learner-centered active learning; this is beneficial for EFL learners and allows them to reduce their language learning anxiety.

Some research has been conducted on flipped learning in EFL education settings. Hung (2012) reported on the effectiveness of the flipped class in EFL learning as compared to the non-flipped class. Regarding the advantages of flipped learning [12], Homma (2015) reported that pre-class tasks provide opportunities for students to build their autonomy; additionally, higher value teacher-led discussion practice inside the classroom leads to greater English fluency and competence. Student-created videos as flipped learning lessons were utilized in the research of Engin (2014) [5], who reported that they served to improve student awareness of focus-on-form and accuracy.

2.2   Collaborative Learning and the Jigsaw Approach

The jigsaw method was originally designed by Eliot Aronson as an instructional method to reduce racial prejudice at the elementary school level, to promote inter-group cohesion, and to increase enjoyment relating to cooperation with group members [1]. In current research into CSCL, the jigsaw method has been utilized to activate students' interactions and to improve their quality of learning. The approach provides students with the opportunity to learn new things in an expert group and to then teach those learned lessons as an expert in a jigsaw group. This method encourages students to depend on one another in order to achieve success as a group.

2.3   Flipped Jigsaw in EFL Learning

Goda, et al. (2015) reported on the practice of applying flipped jigsaw collaborative learning activities in EFL education [8]. Researchers investigated students' perceptions of the activities, focusing on four items via a researcher-made 6-point-Likert questionnaire. These four items were: (1) interest in the topic, (2) the load of English practice compared with CALL, (3) the expectation of English skill improvement, and (4) satisfaction. The data of 163 university students were organized in a descriptive manner. The results showed that many students experienced a high study load of English practice with the flipped jigsaw collaborative learning approach, though expectations of English skill improvement averaged relatively high as well. The authors proposed that the flipped jigsaw method may force students to exert more time and effort on English learning. Additionally, this method might increase students' learning ownership due to the jigsaw approach's emphasis on social pressure; for example, each student is assigned one piece of material, and that student acts as the only expert in that area for his or her small group. Thus, the student may feel peer pressure to perform well. In this study, changes in EFL learning anxiety focused on flipped jigsaw collaborative learning.

2.4   EFL Learning Anxiety

Anxiety is viewed as an important factor that affects second language acquisition (SLA). Anxiety may serve different functions; such feelings may be facilitating in a low-anxiety state or debilitating in a high-anxiety state [15] There are three types of anxiety: (1) trait anxiety, (2) state anxiety, and (3) situation-specific anxiety [4]. In a study of SLA, examinations of situational anxiety gained more attention and were most highly considered [11]. In many works of research on anxiety and its relationship to SLA, the Foreign Language Classroom Anxiety Scale (FLCAS) [10] is generally used. This research study targeted sophomores who were beginning to study EFL. The research of MacIntyre and Gardner (1989) [13], however, focused on students in the later stages of EFL learning and found that some students who demonstrated poor performance in EFL learning experienced increased anxiety due to continued bad learning experiences. Students facing a high-anxiety state should concentrate on better learning practices and strive to decrease their EFL-related anxiety. Horwitz et al. (1986) suggested two options to allow educators to better handle student anxiety: "(1) they can help them learn to cope with the existing anxiety-provoking situation; or (2) they can make the learning context less stressful" [10].

This research, which aimed to study anxiety relating to EFL learning, focused on an investigation of the benefits and effects of flipped jigsaw in order to foster EFL learning initiatives and support the research findings of Goda et al. (2015) [8].

3 Research Method

3.1 Participants

One hundred and one sophomores enrolled in Computer Assisted Language Learning at a national university in Japan participated in this study. Ninety-three participants joined in all activities of the flipped jigsaw; however, only the data of the seventy-four participants who completed both the pre- and post-questionnaires were analyzed via a paired-t test in order to measure their anxiety levels. Participants were majoring in mechanical engineering and most were male (Male: 67, Female: 7). The average TOEIC scores of the participants were as follows: Listing = 245, Reading = 180, and Total = 425, which was slightly lower than the averages of other sophomores at the university. Based on arguments regarding the relationship between anxiety and learning experience [13], participants' anxiety levels might be higher than those of other students at the university with a lower language proficiency.

3.2 The Design and Implementation of Flipped Jigsaw Collaborative Learning Activities

The design and implementation of the flipped jigsaw approach followed the former research of Goda, et al. (2015) [8]. The flow of the learning activities is described in Fig. 1. Three classes and two out-of-class activities were embedded in the design for three weeks. In the first week, students received instruction regarding the procedures and the purpose of the activities. One of three video clips was randomly assigned to each student, and students would then act as experts in their assigned content. Students were required to submit Assignment 1, wherein they answered four open-ended questions regarding the video through Moodle, a learning management system prepared at the university; assignments were due the day before the following class. This forced each student to prepare for expert discussion—and, further, for jigsaw discussion—during the next class session.

The final discussion topic was as follows: "What skills, knowledge, and attitudes should be acquired in the 21st century? How can we effectively and efficiently learn new things in our modern society? Compare and contrast the traditional and new education methods." The video clips had been selected by researchers according to the following criteria from open educational resources such as YouTube: videos must be approximately four minutes in duration, demonstrate focused content relating to the final jigsaw discussion, and contain relatively plain English. The content of the three selected videos involved (A) games, (B) interviews of experts, information about digital content, and descriptions of skills that would be needed by future generations, and (C) data on ICT use in the education initiatives of various countries.

In an expert group discussion, three to four students who watched the same video were gathered and their understanding of the video content was analyzed for twenty minutes. Following the expert activity, students were asked to revise their answers to Assignment 1. Then, three members from different expert groups were organized into jigsaw groups. The students were instructed to share their findings and understandings of the assigned video content with their jigsaw group and were asked to discuss the final topic for forty minutes. Following the jigsaw discussion, students reflected upon what they had learned and organized their opinions and thoughts on the final topic for ten minutes. Students were then instructed to submit Assignment 2, a report of the final topic, via Moodle by the next class session. Students enriched their reflected notes in the second class during the flipped jigsaw session.

During the final class in the third week, reports submitted as Assignment 2 were peer reviewed, and the students presented their thoughts on the final topic to the class.

As for ICT use in this research, links to the open educational resources were provided on the website connection function of Moodle, and the expert discussions and jigsaw discussions were completed via the CSCL support system, C^4. Instruction regarding how to complete the flipped jigsaw was displayed on the bulletin board system (BBS) of Moodle.

3.3   Instrument and Data Analyses

The Foreign Language Classroom Anxiety Survey (FLCAS) was employed as an instrument to collect data regarding EFL learning anxiety. FLCAS consists of 33 five-point Likert scales with internal reliability (Cronbach $alpha$ = .93) and test-retest reliability (r = .83, p < .001). Appendix A describes the items included in the questionnaire. The items included in the scales were related to three general sources of anxiety: (1) communication apprehension, (2) tests, and (3) fear of negative evaluation.

FLCAS was conducted at the end of the first class, to serve as a pre-questionnaire, and again during the third class, to serve as a post-questionnaire. Students completed both questionnaires via the questionnaire function of Moodle.

The scores for each item of the pre- and post-FLCAS were organized as descriptive results. Then, the correlations between pre- and post-questionnaire responses were calculated. In order to investigate any significant changes, paired t-tests for each item and total scores of pre- and post-FLACS responses were conducted.

4   Results

4.1   Descriptive Statistics and Correlations of Pre-and Post-FLCAS Items

Table 1 provides the results of descriptive statistics and correlations of pre- and post-FLCAS assessments. The mean, standard deviation, standard error, correlational r, and its significance are organized in the table. Though the means of FLCAS items for both pre- and post-questionnaires are relatively constant, the means of pre-questionnaire items are slightly higher than those of most post-questionnaire items. In the pre-questionnaire, Q1, Q3, Q9, and Q10 average higher than 3.5. However, there are no items with an average higher than 3.5 in the post-questionnaire assessments.

As for the correlations, a lower correlation indicates a change between pre- and post- questionnaire responses. Conversely, a higher correlation indicates a consistency between pre- and post- questionnaire answers. The items with lower (less than .30) correlations were Q12 ($r = .10$), Q6 ($r = .19$), Q23 ($r = .27$), and Q24 ($r = .29$). Thus, the flipped jigsaw approach may affect students' anxiety in those areas.

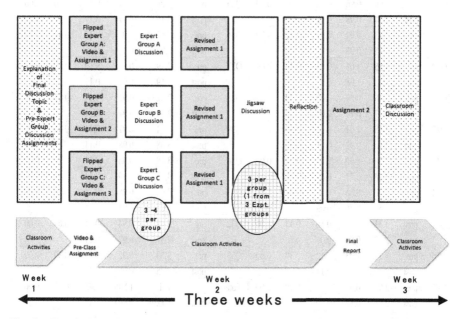

Fig. 1. The design of a flipped jigsaw collaborative learning project *Note*. Dotted pattern: classroom activity; gray: individual activity; white: group activity; checked: group size.

4.2   Significant Changes in EFL Learning Anxiety

The results of paired t-tests are summarized in Appendix A. Significant differences between pre- and post-questionnaire responses were found on Q9 ($t = 2.03$) and Q22 ($t = -2.82$), with a pre-set alpha of .05. Additionally, a significant tendency was observed on Q3 ($t = 1.89$, $p = .08$).

Table 1. Descriptive statistics and correlation of Pre- and Post-FLCAS responses

		M	SD	SE	r	sig.			M	SD	SE	r	sig.
Q1	pre	3.53	1.05	0.12	0.42	0.00	Q18	pre	2.27	0.94	0.11	0.36	0.00
	post	3.37	1.09	0.13				post	2.38	0.82	0.10		
Q2	pre	2.80	0.91	0.11	0.41	0.00	Q19	pre	2.93	1.00	0.12	0.33	0.01
	post	2.72	1.01	0.12				post	3.03	0.98	0.11		
Q3	pre	3.60	0.95	0.11	0.38	0.00	Q20	pre	3.31	0.96	0.11	0.51	0.00
	post	3.37	1.01	0.12				post	3.20	0.95	0.11		
Q4	pre	3.26	0.91	0.11	0.40	0.00	Q21	pre	2.87	0.94	0.11	0.58	0.00
	post	3.42	0.98	0.11				post	2.89	0.90	0.10		
Q5	pre	2.89	0.88	0.10	0.34	0.00	Q22	pre	2.85	0.92	0.11	0.46	0.00
	post	2.95	0.91	0.11				post	3.16	0.91	0.11		
Q6	pre	3.31	0.95	0.11	0.19	0.12	Q23	pre	3.01	1.07	0.12	0.27	0.02
	post	3.14	0.85	0.10				post	2.97	1.13	0.13		
Q7	pre	3.45	1.06	0.12	0.31	0.01	Q24	pre	3.31	0.99	0.12	0.29	0.01
	post	3.42	1.02	0.12				post	3.43	0.92	0.11		
Q8	pre	2.88	0.96	0.11	0.36	0.00	Q25	pre	3.08	0.96	0.11	0.50	0.00
	post	2.74	0.98	0.11				post	3.16	0.97	0.11		
Q9	pre	3.65	0.94	0.11	0.41	0.00	Q26	pre	3.07	1.02	0.12	0.44	0.00
	post	3.41	0.95	0.11				post	2.92	0.96	0.11		
Q10	pre	3.55	1.05	0.12	0.40	0.00	Q27	pre	3.19	0.89	0.10	0.47	0.00
	post	3.41	1.08	0.13				post	3.19	0.97	0.11		
Q11	pre	2.46	0.89	0.10	0.30	0.01	Q28	pre	2.62	0.92	0.11	0.47	0.00
	post	2.37	0.79	0.09				post	2.69	0.94	0.11		
Q12	pre	3.18	1.01	0.12	0.10	0.39	Q29	pre	3.14	0.97	0.11	0.44	0.00
	post	3.16	0.92	0.11				post	3.08	0.98	0.11		
Q13	pre	3.38	0.90	0.10	0.34	0.00	Q30	pre	3.18	0.96	0.11	0.50	0.00
	post	3.28	0.77	0.09				post	3.24	0.99	0.12		
Q14	pre	2.58	0.86	0.10	0.44	0.00	Q31	pre	2.93	0.98	0.11	0.66	0.00
	post	2.55	0.76	0.09				post	3.07	0.94	0.11		
Q15	pre	3.31	0.86	0.10	0.43	0.00	Q32	pre	2.49	0.94	0.11	0.61	0.00
	post	3.27	0.82	0.09				post	2.57	0.97	0.11		
Q16	pre	3.28	1.03	0.12	0.39	0.00	Q33	pre	3.38	0.92	0.11	0.39	0.00
	post	3.19	0.92	0.11				post	3.35	0.90	0.10		
Q17	pre	2.95	0.99	0.12	0.40	0.00	Total	pre	101.66	12.49	1.45	0.41	0.00
	post	2.88	0.88	0.10				post	100.96	12.67	1.47		

5 Discussion and Future Implications

Most items of the post-FLCAS had scores that were slightly lower than those of the pre-FLCAS. In particular, three (Q1, 3, 9) out of four items with an average higher than 3.5 are related to "speaking." This implies that the flipped jigsaw approach may marginally reduce students' anxiety in this area. The inferential statistics and t-tests demonstrated that significances were found for the items related to preparation (Q9 and 22). To join the flipped jigsaw group, students had to show engagement and needed to form a learning-ownership connection. The flipped approach functions to allow students to become responsible for their learning and teaches them to prepare outside the classroom. As Homma (2015) suggested, the flipped EFL approach leads to autonomous control and prepared learning at home. Furthermore, the jigsaw approach functions to harness peer pressure in order to encourage at-home preparation due to its application of social psychology to the establishment of inter-dependence in a jigsaw group, as mentioned in Benson (2003). The correlation results indicate that some changes following the application of the flipped jigsaw approach may also affect students' self-perception, thought, and consciousness (Q6, 12, 23, 24).

The results of this research study indicate that the flipped jigsaw approach might have the potential to reduce students' EFL learning anxiety related to speaking due to its emphasis on learning ownership and sufficient at-home preparation. This method might also affect students' self-consciousness regarding English learning, which might imply that the flipped jigsaw approach allows students to reflect on their learning experiences. These findings are consistent with the benefits associated with flipped learning and the jigsaw method as instructional strategies. As such, a combination of these two strategies may maximize their learning benefits.

In this study, weak designs in both pre-test and post-test experiments were utilized. There was no control group against which changes in EFL learning anxiety could be compared. Thus, more rigorously designed research is necessary to examine the true effects of flipped jigsaw collaborative learning.

The design and implementation of the flipped jigsaw approach should be evaluated and improved to reduce learners' anxiety. It must be noted, however, that the design and implication of the flipped jigsaw method may affect the research results. Technology and various open educational resources were employed as teaching materials in this study of the flipped jigsaw approach; such resources are critical to a proper understanding of the effects of the flipped jigsaw method. Thus, a variety of practices relating to different topics, situations, participants, and blended learning methods should be investigated, and solid practices should be accumulated.

While this research study focused on EFL-related learning anxiety, the effects of the flipped jigsaw approach on other psychological factors, such as quality of collaboration and EFL proficiency, should also be investigated in future research.

Acknowledgement. This work was supported by the Japan Society for the Promotion of Science (JSPS) Grants-in-Aid for Scientific Research (KAKENHI) under Grant Number 26282056.

Appendix A. FLCAS Items and Results of Paired-*T* Tests for Pre- and Post-FLCAS Assessment

#	Items	Paired Differences (Pre - Post)			*t*	Sig.
		M	*SD*	*SE*		
1	I never feel quite sure of myself when I am speaking in my foreign language class.	0.16	1.16	0.13	1.20	0.23
2	I don't worry about making mistakes in language class.	0.08	1.04	0.12	0.67	0.51
3	I tremble when I know that I'm going to be called on in language class.	0.23	1.09	0.13	1.81	0.08†
4	It frightens me when I don't understand what the teacher is saying in the foreign language.	−0.16	1.03	0.12	−1.35	0.18
5	It would not bother me at all to take more foreign language classes.	−0.05	1.03	0.12	−0.45	0.65
6	During language class, I find myself thinking about things that have nothing to do with the course.	0.18	1.15	0.13	1.31	0.19
7	I keep thinking that the other students are better at languages than I am.	0.03	1.23	0.14	0.19	0.85
8	I am usually at ease during tests in my language class.	0.14	1.10	0.13	1.06	0.30
9	I start to panic when I have to speak without preparation in language class.	0.24	1.03	0.12	2.03	0.05*
10	I worry about the consequences of failing my foreign language class.	0.15	1.17	0.14	1.10	0.28
11	I don't understand why some people get so upset over foreign language classes.	0.09	1.00	0.12	0.82	0.42
12	In language class, I can get so nervous that I forget things I know.	0.01	1.30	0.15	0.09	0.93
13	It embarrasses me to volunteer answers in my language class.	0.09	0.97	0.11	0.84	0.40
14	I would not be nervous if I were speaking the foreign language with native speakers.	0.03	0.86	0.10	0.27	0.79
15	I get upset when I don't understand what the teacher is correcting.	0.04	0.90	0.10	0.39	0.70
16	Even if I am well prepared for language class, I feel anxious about it.	0.09	1.07	0.12	0.76	0.45
17	I often feel like not going to my language class.	0.07	1.02	0.12	0.57	0.57
18	I feel confident when I speak in foreign language class.	−0.11	1.00	0.12	−0.93	0.36
19	I am afraid that my language teacher is ready to correct every mistake I make.	−0.09	1.15	0.13	−0.71	0.48

(*continued*)

(continued)

#	Items	Paired Differences (Pre - Post)			t	Sig.
		M	SD	SE		
20	I can feel my heart pounding when I'm going to be called on in language class.	0.11	0.94	0.11	0.99	0.33
21	The more I study for a language test, the more confused I get.	−0.03	0.84	0.10	−0.28	0.78
22	I don't feel pressure to prepare very well for language class.	−0.31	0.95	0.11	−2.82	0.01**
23	I always feel that the other students speak the foreign language better than I do.	0.04	1.33	0.15	0.26	0.79
24	I feel very self-conscious about speaking the foreign language in front of other students.	−0.12	1.15	0.13	−0.91	0.36
25	Language class moves so quickly that I worry about being left behind.	−0.08	0.96	0.11	−0.73	0.47
26	I feel more tense and nervous in my language class than in my other classes.	0.15	1.06	0.12	1.21	0.23
27	I get nervous and confused when I am speaking in my language class.	0.00	0.97	0.11	0.00	1.00
28	When I'm on my way to language class, I feel very sure and relaxed.	−0.07	0.96	0.11	−0.61	0.55
29	I get nervous when I don't understand every word the language teacher says.	0.05	1.03	0.12	0.45	0.65
30	I feel overwhelmed by the number of rules you have to learn to speak the foreign language.	−0.07	0.97	0.11	−0.60	0.55
31	I am afraid that other students will laugh at me when I speak the foreign language.	−0.14	0.80	0.09	−1.45	0.15
32	I would probably feel comfortable around native speakers of the foreign language.	−0.08	0.84	0.10	−0.83	0.41
33	I get nervous when the language teacher asks questions that I haven't prepared in advance.	0.03	1.01	0.12	0.23	0.82
	FLCAS_total_pre - FLCAS_Total_post	0.70	13.71	1.59	0.44	0.66

Note. $N = 74$, $df = 73$. † $< .1$, * $<= .05$, ** $<= .01$.

References

1. Aronson, E., Patnoe, S.: Cooperation in the Classroom: The Jigsaw Method, 3rd edn. Pinter & Martin Ltd., London (2011)
2. Benson, M.P.: Learner autonomy in classroom. In: Nunan, D. (ed.) Practical English Language Teaching, pp. 289–308. McGraw Hill, New York (2003)
3. Bergmann, J., Sams, A.: Flip your classroom: reach every student in every class every day. ISTE, Eugene, ASCD, Alexandria (2012)

4. Ellis, R.: The Study of Second Language Acquisition. Oxford University Press, Oxford (1994)
5. Engin, M.: Extending the flipped classroom model: developing second language writing skills through student-created digital videos. J. Sch. Teach. Learn. **14**(5), 12–26 (2014)
6. Garrison, D.R.: E-learning in the 21st Century: A Framework for Research and Practice, 2nd edn. Routledge, New York (2011)
7. Goda, Y., Yamada, M.: Application of CoI to design CSCL for EFL online asynchronous discussion. In: Akyol, Z., Garrison, D.R. (eds.) Educational Community of Inquiry: Theoretical Framework, Research and Practice, pp. 295–316. IGI Global, Hershey (2012)
8. Goda, Y., Yamada, M., Matsukawa, H., Hata, K., Yasunami, S.: Practical report on flipped jigsaw collaborative learning of English as a foreign language. In: The 23th International Conference on Computers in Education, pp. 591–595 (2015)
9. Homma, J.E.B.: Chiba Univ. Commer. Rev. **52**(2), 253–275 (2015)
10. Horwitz, E., Horwitz, M., Cope, J.: Foreign language classroom anxiety. Modern Lang. J. **70**, 125–132 (1986)
11. Horwitz, E., Young, D.: Language Learning Anxiety: From Theory and Research to Classroom Implications. Prentice Hall, Englewood Cliffs (1991)
12. Hung, H.T.: Flipping the classroom for English language learners to foster active learning. Comput. Assist. Lang. Learn. **28**(1), 81–96 (2014)
13. MacIntyre, P., Gardner, R.: Language anxiety: its relationship to other anxieties and to processing in native and second languages. Lang. Learn. **41**, 513–534 (1991)
14. Sams, A., Bergmann, J.: Flip your students' learning. In: Educational Leadership, March 2013, pp. 16–20 (2013)
15. Williams, K.: Anxiety and formal/foreign language learning. RELC J. **22**, 19–28 (1991)
16. Yamada, M., Goda, Y., Matsukawa, H., Hata, K., Yasunami, S.: C4 (C quad): development of the application for language learning based on social and cognitive presences. In: Bradley, L., Thousny, S. (eds.) 20 years of EUROCALL: Learning from the Past, Looking to the Future. Proceedings of the 2013 EUROCALL Conference, pp. 258–264, Évora, Portugal

Application of Facebook Platform Assists Taiwanese Students to Learn Vietnamese

Thi Thanh Tuyen Mai and Eric Zhi-Feng Liu[(✉)]

Graduate Institute of Learning and Instruction, National Central University,
Taoyuan City, Taiwan
vinhan268@gmail.com, totem.ncu@gmail.com

Abstract. Facebook is the most popular social networking site among people. It is also a most popular online discussion platform among students. Our research includes two stages, the first stage of this study includes the result of data analyzed from interviews of 23 Taiwanese learners assigned to experiment group in which they were using Facebook as platform to learn Vietnamese. The second stage that comprised control group in which they learned through traditional class room teaching, their data is still not analyzed yet. The result of interview from experimental group showed that, Taiwanese learners were interested in Facebook group to learn Vietnamese. The result suggested that Facebook platform can help boosting up their motivation and confidence, improve Vietnamese languages skills in grammatical, vocabulary, reading and writing.

Keywords: Facebook · Online learning · Vietnamese language · Learn Vietnamese

1 Introduction

Technology has been used for learning language and teaching in several years. Several studies have investigated the role of technology in language learning. Dunkel (1990) found that the possibilities of computer technology could increase learners' self-esteem, vocational preparedness, language proficiency and overall academic skill. In other hand, technological innovations could increase learner's interest and motivation, this provide students with increased access to target language input, interaction opportunities, and feedback (Golonka et al. 2014). In the past, the application of technology in language classroom included the use of audio/video, voice, television, computer and so forth. As the technology advanced, online discussion platforms, such as Facebook, Instagram, Linkedin, Twitter and others, have been popular in recent years. According to The Statistics Portal (2016), as of the first quarter of 2016, Facebook had 1.65 billion monthly active users; this platform is also one of the most famous popular social networks worldwide.

In fact, Facebook can be used for research in education, where educators are recognizing the possibilities of tapping into the already popular social networking site to reach students with learning material. Several research have indicated that Facebook can positively affect classroom practices and student involvement (Aydin 2012). According to Mazer et al. (2007), Facebook is widely used. First, Facebook is a highly interactive

© Springer International Publishing AG 2017
T.-T. Wu et al. (Eds.): SETE 2016, LNCS 10108, pp. 665–670, 2017.
DOI: 10.1007/978-3-319-52836-6_70

virtual social network; any Facebook user can easily search and view others Facebook page through the Facebook network. Second, Facebook offers an alternative site designed to enhance the relational exchanges between a teacher and a student. Similarly, Aydin (2012) noted that, the main reasons why students participate on Facebook is maintaining communication between their friends and family members, but Facebook also contributes to an easier flow of communication among teachers and students.

Various studies in the past have investigated the role of Facebook platform in language learning. Shih (2011) found that, Facebook provided the Taiwanese students with opportunities to access others' writing and improve their grammar, structure and content, organization and vocabulary in English learning. The interaction via Facebook includes providing feedback and discussing about the contents which were posted in English language learning classroom, promoting the use of language learning strategies (Alias et al. 2012). Blattner and Fiori (2009) emphasized the group application available on Facebook and highlighted the benefits of authentic language interaction and the development of language awareness, they found that Facebook has unique features to offer constructional experiences while maintaining privacy and safety, increase motivation and improve performance in language classes. In the study of Kabilan et al. (2010), they reported that, Facebook as an online environment that facilitates English language learning, which can help learners improve language skills, increase their confidence and motivation, and have more positive attitude towards learning English.

Hence, the purpose of this study is to examine Facebook platform, if it used as a tool that could support Taiwanese learners to learn Vietnamese language.

2 Method

2.1 Participants

The three classes for Vietnamese learning comprised of 23 participants from the Center for Continuing Education in northern Taiwan. All participants spoke Mandarin Chinese or Taiwanese as a first language.

This study was conducted from spring of 2015 until spring of 2016. The sample group was composed of 8 men and 15 women who were aged between 18 to 62 years. The total duration of the Vietnamese course is 24 h.

2.2 Research Process

Background of the study. This study aims at investigating the use of Facebook platform in assisting Taiwanese students in Vietnamese learning. This study includes two stages, the first stage is an experiment of participants using the Facebook to submit and comment a series of assignments designed by the researcher. The second stage is an experiment of participants without using the Facebook to accomplish the tasks given by the researcher. The same series of tasks was given for those both groups designed by the researcher. Thus, the second stages is continuing, this paper only presents the result of the first stages.

Using Facebook as a training tool. Facebook has been regarded as one of the most popular social networking tool of this decade. In other words, Facebook can be an interesting tool for research in language. In the study of Kabilan et al. (2010), Malaysian learners perceived Facebook could be an educational environments that enhancing their English language skills and motivation, confidence, attitude towards learning the language. Thus, the feature of Facebook that student who has a Facebook account to browse and feedback or comments that takes place during their online discussions. Furthermore, this study focused on how Taiwanese learners develop Vietnamese language via Facebook platform.

Research Objectives. In this study, the researcher aimed to investigate the issues related to the application of use of Facebook in Vietnamese language. For this purpose, the researcher analyzed the following points:

- The effect of use of Facebook platform to assist Taiwanese students learning Vietnamese language.
- The type of issues that students have encountered while using Facebook.
- The type of communication and feedback among learners.

Research procedure. In this study, the students' tasks were: Initially, the students were asked to add a private Vietnamese learning group in Facebook. After that, seven assignments were given for students, included: two listening assignments, two reading assignments, two writing assignments and one presentation assignments. All assignments were posted on the Facebook group, the students were requested to post their assignments and give comments on peers' assignments. At the beginning of the study period, a pre-test was requested. At the end of the study period, a post-test was requested and a questionnaire were administered to get their feedback on the effectiveness of use of Facebook platform on enhancing their Vietnamese language skills and the difficulties the students have faced, while using the Facebook group as well as suggestions to improve their language skills. For getting more deeply information about the use of Facebook group, one by one interview was carried out as well.

3   Findings

The findings only revealed the results of interviews employed by the learners in this paper. To obtain more in-depth information about affective of use of Facebook in Vietnamese learning, all of students were required to have an interview with the researcher after the end of study period. The responses of interviews were carefully recorded and coded by the researcher. The interview questions included students' motivation, effectiveness of use of Facebook, improvement of language skills, advantages and disadvantages of using Facebook and some type of issues that students have encountered while posting assignment and commenting peers' assignment. To summarize the interview of students, their feedbacks excerpts are as follows:

3.1 Motivation

Most of students responded that Facebook could be an online environment for enhancing their motivation in learning Vietnamese skills:

"I am expecting for the assignments of other classmates because some of them who are excellent in Vietnamese can present some new words in the right context". (S3).

"When a classmate posts an assignment on the Facebook, I feel quite motivated to understand what they have written and if I do not understand, I l check the online dictionary or ask them" (S6).

3.2 Confidence

In the students' opinion, their confidence level has increased in Vietnamese skills:

"I think I can post my assignment as soon as I can, because I know that the teacher will help me to correct my error as soon as she can" (S5).

"Using Facebook to complete my assignment is a new challenge for me, because I am very scared of sharing my assignment to my classmates. I think there are lots of errors in my assignment, so I can share only with the teacher. But now it is different, my classmatse can do it. So, I think I can do it. It is really hard for the first time, but gets better at the second and third times. The most important thing is that the teacher always encourages me to learn better Vietnamese" (S15).

3.3 Effectiveness of Using Facebook

Most of the interviewees regarded that Facebook as an effective tool for learning Vietnamese. Twenty one (21) students responded that they never had same experience in using social networking to learn language before. Only two students did not use Facebook as much, because normally they did not spend much time on Facebook except posting the assignments that were required. However, use of Facebook group allowed students having more discussions than traditional classroom; students could ask the teacher and classmate in Vietnamese grammar as much as they wanted. After having more discussions and flowing classmates' assignments, students found that their Vietnamese grammar and vocabulary were much better. In other aspect, Facebook allowed students to follow classmates' assignments anywhere and anytime. By this way students could easily memorize the vocabulary and grammar. In addition, using Facebook to post students' assignment allowed them immediately refer internet resources to complete the assignments.

3.4 Advantages and Disadvantages of Using Facebook

As numerous reports of students in this study, Facebook is very easy and useful tool to learn language. Several students indicated that they can discover new words, look up the meaning of new words or use of grammar from classmate via Facebook group. Additionally, Facebook can be a free, instant, private tool for asking some advice from teacher and peers. Finally, some students pointed out that, they have encountered several issues in using word or grammar while learning Vietnamese at time of outside the class, by doing so, posting question on Facebook group is the best way to get the answer of those issues.

In other aspect, besides of some advantages of using Facebook, several disadvantages of Facebook were reported. First of all, students mentioned that when the teacher would write the post and required students to post assignment on Facebook, in fact the teacher could know anyone who had read the post. In the students' opinion, it is a pressure for them to accomplish the assignment. Second, some students explained that, click the "like" button on peers' assignment could help them follow the post as well, but some of them felt sick with the notifications of leave comments, expressed by some students that they did not use the Facebook as much. Third, some students liked to share in the Facebook, but some time they showed less attention to learn language, and spent much more time on Internet, as there are various kinds of distractive things on Facebook.

3.5 Type of Issues that Students Have Encountered While Posting Assignment and Commenting Peers' Assignment

When posting a comment or replying to peers' comments, the students took an opportunity to practice their language skills. As the response of some students, they had to adjust on psychological state to post and comment peers' assignment. One of the main reasons is students were afraid of making mistakes and did not dare other classmates to know. Second, in most of the time, students did not know how to response peers' assignment, that they might make wrong comment in the process of correction. Some students also argued that they did not have enough time to skim peers' assignments after hard working day, because students always posted their assignments as late as they could before the deadline date. It is worth noting that, the comment of peers' assignment not only took place on Facebook group, privacy happened between student and student who posted the assignment or who were excellent in Vietnamese language class.

In general, through the posting and commenting, the students made a conscious effort to understand and learn the language. By sharing more of feelings and ideas and commenting on other's opinion, students were able to learn vocabulary, grammar, content and structure of the context as well.

4 Conclusion and Discussion

Facebook as an online discussions that were an effective tool to learn Vietnamese language. Students in this study indicated that they joined a specified Facebook group that enabled them to share ideas and some interesting topics. Results of the interviews suggested that students' grammatical, vocabulary, reading and writing skill were gained better after the study period, when they were given opportunities to use Facebook group for discussions. A larger number of students also had positive attitudes towards this online tool to continue to learn Vietnamese in next study period, keep sharing and talking with each other after the completion of study period. The findings of this study not only discuss about the effectiveness of using Facebook to assist students to learn Vietnamese language better, understanding about students' thinking while using online tool to learn language, helping students to solve any issue they had faced to improve their target language skills is an important factor in building healthy communication.

Hence, this study is only the first stage in our research process. Future research should examine the difference in control group and experimental group through analysis of pre-test and post-test, questionnaire, interview of both groups, and how learners interactive with each other to obtain knowledge.

References

Alias, A.A., Ab Manan, N.A., Yusof, J., Pandian, A.: The use of Facebook as language learning strategy (LLS) training tool on college students' LLS use and academic writing performance. Procedia Soc. Behav. Sci. **67**, 36–48 (2012)

Aydin, S.: A review of research on Facebook as an educational environment. Educ. Technol. Res. Dev. **60**(6), 1093–1106 (2012)

Blattner, G., Fiori, M.: Facebook in the language classroom: promises and possibilities. IJITDL **6**(1), 17–28 (2009)

Dunkel, P.: Implications of the CAI effectiveness research for limited English proficient learners. CITS **7**(1–2), 31–52 (1990)

Golonka, E.M., Bowles, A.R., Frank, V.M., Richardson, D.L., Freynik, S.: Technologies for foreign language learning: a review of technology types and their effectiveness. CALL **27**(1), 70–105 (2014)

Kabilan, M.K., Ahmad, N., Abidin, M.J.Z.: Facebook: an online environment for learning of English in institutions of higher education? Internet High Educ. **13**(4), 179–187 (2010)

Mazer, J.P., Murphy, R.E., Simonds, C.J.: I'll see you on "Facebook": the effects of computer-mediated teacher self-disclosure on student motivation, affective learning, and classroom climate. Commun. Educ. **56**(1), 1–17 (2007)

Shih, R.C.: Can Web 2.0 technology assist college students in learning English writing? Integrating Facebook and peer assessment with blended learning. Australas J. Educ. Tec. **27**(5), 829–845 (2011)

The Statistics Portal. http://www.statista.com/

Developing a Speaking Practice Website by Using Automatic Speech Recognition Technology

Howard Hao-Jan Chen[✉]

Department of English, National Taiwan Normal University,
Taipei, Taiwan
hjchen@ntnu.edu.tw

Abstract. English oral communication ability has become increasingly important for many EFL learners. This paper introduces how we use a new automatic speech recognition technology to develop a website for EFL students. This website offers several different types of exercises which allow students to practice speaking and obtain immediate feedback. A group of 30 EFL students were invited to use the website. A survey was conducted to investigate students' perceptions of this site. The results indicated that most students enjoyed using this website; they also felt the site could help improve their English oral skills. Students, however, also pointed out that the website content and design can be further improved.

Keywords: EFL · Speaking · Automatic speech recognition · Errors · Feedback

1 Introduction

The importance of effective English oral communication ability has been widely recognized at the global level. Educational institutes have already begun to explore different methods to help individuals achieve improved oral skills. For example, some schools and universities have hired more native English speakers and also reduced class sizes and expect that these changes will lead to more teacher-student interactions.

1.1 Improving Speaking Skills with Automatic Speech Recognition (ASR) Technologies

Based on the suggestions made by various researchers, ASR-based software programs might be able to provide benefits such as interactions and feedback [1]. [2] have developed a web-based conversation environment called CandleTalk. CandleTalk is equipped with an ASR engine that judges the accuracy of the input. This system was developed to help EFL learners receive explicit speech act training that leads to better oral competence. The results of an experimental study on CandleTalk showed that the application of ASR was helpful for college freshmen in the learning of the speech acts.

© Springer International Publishing AG 2017
T.-T. Wu et al. (Eds.): SETE 2016, LNCS 10108, pp. 671–676, 2017.
DOI: 10.1007/978-3-319-52836-6_71

Although these web-based ASR program seem promising, the corrective feedback provided by most ASR-based system was still limited. [3] indicated that users were often not satisfied with the feedback provided by TellMeMore, one of the most well-known commercial software programs based on ASR technologies. [3] suggested that a good ASR system should be able to provide clearer feedback to learners.

1.2   Research Questions

As previous research has shown, there are several advantages of using ASR programs, but studies also address problems of ASR programs, such as erroneous and limited feedback [4, 5] and lack of interaction [6]. If a new and improved web ASR-based training system can be developed, then second language learners can benefit more. This study aimed to develop a unique ASR-based language learning site based on the new Kaldi Speech Recognition Toolkit and further investigate EFL students' perceptions of this innovative site. Two major research questions were proposed:

1. What are young EFL learners' perceptions of the ASR-based language learning site?
2. What are the strengths and limitations of the ASR-based learning site from young EFL learners' perspective?

2   Methodology

2.1   Subjects

To better understand young EFL students' perceptions of the ASR-based web system, thirty junior high school students was invited to participate in this study. These students were 9th graders taking an English course and they were invited to use the ASR website in a computer lab.

2.2   Instrument: The Speaking Practice Site Based on ASR Technologies

The ASR-based oral skills training website was developed with funding from the Ministry of Education, Taiwan. The development team used Kaldi, a well-known open-source toolkit designed by [7] for building speech recognition systems. Given that there are some technical restrictions and browser compatibility issues, students are asked to use Firefox as the browser for using the ASR technologies.

There are three different types of interactive exercises based on ASR technologies. The first type of exercise is one of the most commonly used exercises in various commercial ASR-based programs. This conversational exercise, as shown below in Fig. 1, asks students to read/listen to a sentence and then choose the most appropriate response from three options by saying the answer via the microphone.

In the first type of interactive exercise, after students say the answer, the ASR system will provide immediate feedback. If the students' answer is correct, the system

Ordering food
為點餐 停止.唯發音

1. A: Excuse me, I'm ready to order. B: Okay. What would
you like to order? A:_____

A. I'll have a cheeseburger and an   B. Three people, please.   c. I don't want a cheese
apple pie.   cake. Sorry.

2. A: Hello, madam, would you like to order now? B: Yes,
what do you have? A: _____

A. We have steak and pork.   B. What do you like to   c. I will have a cup of
                              drink?   coffee, please.

3. A: Can I make a reservation for dinner? B: _____

Fig. 1. Choose an appropriate response

will highlight the answer and give students a positive feedback. Then students can move on to the next question. If the chosen answer is not appropriate, then the system shows "the answer is not quite right". The learner can then try again. One example of the first type of interactive exercises is shown in Fig. 2. In this type of exercises, students are not given specific feedback on each individual word.

2. A: Hello, madam, would you like to order now? B: Yes,
what do you have? A: _____

A. We have steak and pork.   B. What do you like to   c. I will have a cup of
                              drink?   coffee, please.
                              恭喜你答對了!!

3. A: Can I make a reservation for dinner? B: _____

A. Sure, how many people are   B. Well, how long do we   c. What's your address?
there?   have to wait?
                                好像不太正確喔~

4. A: We want to book a table by the window. B: Sorry!
_____

A. We are a group of five.   B. We are busy.   c. We're all booked up.

Fig. 2. The feedback from the website (Color figure online)

The second type of exercise, "Useful Expressions in Daily Life", is a simper exercise. In this section, some useful English expressions with Chinese translations are provided. Students just need to say the English sentence out loud, and the ASR system determines if the sentence produced by students is acceptable. If students' pronunciation is correct, then the system simply shows the original sentence again. If students have minor difficulties with some word in the sentence, the problematic word was highlighted in orange color. If students have major difficulties with some word, the word was highlighted in red color. These highlighting helps to remind students that they need to pay more attention to these problematic words. An example is shown in Fig. 3.

The last type of exercise combines animated videos and automatic speech recognition technologies. Students first view animated videos, and then they are asked to play different roles and to practice the sentences. For each sentence, students just need to say the sentence out loud, and the ASR system determines if the sentence produced by students is acceptable. If students' pronunciation is correct, then the system simply shows the original sentence again. If students have minor difficulties with some word in the sentence, the problematic word was highlighted in orange color. If students have

Fig. 3. Colored feedback on students' pronunciations (Color figure online)

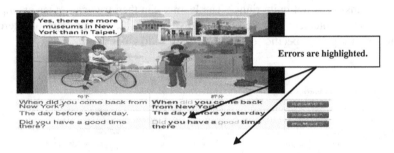

Fig. 4. Animated video and conversation practice(Color figure online)

major difficulties with a certain word, the word was highlighted in red color. An example is shown in Fig. 4.

In addition to the learning content and tools, a tracking device was also developed to help students monitor their own participation and progress, given that this system is mainly designed to encourage students to do these pronunciation exercises after classes. The learning record also offers school language teachers an effective way of monitoring student performance.

2.3   The Procedure for Collecting User Feedback

To obtain user feedback from students, a group of 30 EFL students were asked to use the website and then commented on the content and design of the website. These junior high school students were asked to use the site in a computer lab over a 4-week period. Each week they were assigned to use the website, and each weekly session lasted for approximately 45 min. At the end of the last meeting, a questionnaire was distributed to solicit their feedback. The questionnaire consisted of 3 open-ended questions asking students if they like the website and about the strengths and weaknesses of the website and suggestions for improvement.

3 Survey Results from the Students

Based on the responses to the three open-ended questions, the following positive feedback was provided by students.

1. This website is good for students who need to improve their pronunciation and listening skills. The website is also useful for vocabulary learning and listening
2. The site has a wide range of options from very easy items to more difficult items.
3. The site is easy to use and can provide useful feedback on pronunciation.
4. For students who do not dare to speak, this is a good tool for them to practice conversation.

In addition to the strengths, students also provided specific suggestions to further improve the content and design of this website. Students first suggested that the user interface should be more attractive. Second, the website could be designed as an online interactive game. Third, the ASR evaluation standard might be too low for some exercises.

4 Discussion

4.1 Students' Attitudes Toward the ASR-Based Oral Training Site

Based on the user surveys, the ASR-based system can provide learners with more opportunities for producing target language output. Most students indicated that they liked the rich content and the convenience of accessing the website. They felt that this site could be helpful for their speaking and listening skills and vocabulary knowledge. In summary, students regard this website as a very useful learning tool, and their overall reaction to the website was positive.

The findings of this study are similar to those of previous studies about users' positive attitudes toward other ASR systems for language learning [2, 8]. Students enjoyed using this site mainly because it allowed them to practice speaking skills and get immediate corrective feedback. Although most students showed very positive attitudes toward the ASR-based website, they also identified several weaknesses and limitations. These included user interface design, learning content, and evaluation standards.

4.2 Possible Directions to Improve the ASR-Based Oral Skills Training Site

A problem noted by some students is that the standard set by this speech recognition engine is sometimes too low for some words. In fact, how to determine a proper standard has been an important issue in building up any ASR system for second or foreign language learning. [8] pointed out that some commercial ASR systems (CNN Interactive, TellMeMore, and Microsoft Encarta) actually allowed learners to adjust the sensitivity settings (i.e., the standard of acceptance). There were advantages and disadvantages to this practice. If a student can adjust the settings, then he/she might feel less frustrated. However, it is also likely that students might set the threshold level too low and the system could thus not detect any deviations from the students' speech input.

In addition to the aforementioned problem, students further made some suggestions. They expected that the interface would be more interesting and that the whole site would be designed like an online game. It is obvious that young students like more entertaining learning content. The team might need to develop more interesting learning content and activities to attract these young learners.

References

1. Neri, A., Cucchiarini, C., Strik, H., Boves, L.: The pedagogy-technology interface in computer assisted pronunciation training. Comput. Assist. Lang. Learn. **15**(5), 441–467 (2002)
2. Chiu, T., Liou, H., Yeh, Y.: A study of web-based oral activities enhanced by automatic speech recognition for efl college learning. Comput. Assist. Lang. Learn. **20**(3), 209–233 (2007)
3. Chun, D.M.: Come ride the wave: but where is it taking us? CALICO J. **24**(2), 239–252 (2007)
4. Neri, A., Cucchiarini, C., Strik, H.: The effectiveness of computer-based speech corrective feedback for improving segmental quality in L2 dutch. ReCALL **20**(02), 225–243 (2008)
5. Wang, Y.H., Young, S.S.C.: A study of the design and implementation of the ASR-based iCASL system with corrective feedback to facilitate english learning. Educ. Technol. Soc. **17**(2), 219–233 (2014)
6. Kwon, O.W., Lee, K., Kim, Y.: GenieTutor: a computer assisted second-language learning system based on semantic and grammar correctness evaluations. In: Proceedings of the 2015 EUROCALL Conference, pp. 330–335. Padova, Italy (2015)
7. Povey, D., Ghoshal, A., Boulianne, G., Burget, L., Glembek, O., Goel, N., Hannemann, M., Motlicek, P., Qian, Y., Schwarz, P., Silovsky, J., Stemmer, G., Vesely, K.: The kaldi speech recognition toolkit. Paper Presented at IEEE 2011 Workshop on Automatic Speech Recognition and Understanding. IEEE Signal Processing Society, Hawaii (2011)
8. Chen, H.-J.H.: Evaluating Five Speech Recognition Programs for ESL Learners. Paper Presented at the ITMELT 2001 Conference, Hong Kong. http://elc.polyu.edu.hk/conference/papers2001/chen.htm (2001)

Classification of Speaking Proficiency Level by Machine Learning and Feature Selection

Brendan Flanagan[1]([⊠]), Sachio Hirokawa[2], Emiko Kaneko[3],
and Emi Izumi[4]

[1] Graduate School of Information Science and Electrical Engineering,
Kyushu University, Fukuoka, Japan
b.flanagan.885@s.kyushu-u.ac.jp
[2] Research Institute for Information Technology,
Kyushu University, Fukuoka, Japan
[3] Center for Language Research, Aizu University, Aizuwakamatsu, Japan
[4] Center for General and Liberal Education, Doshisha University, Kyoto, Japan

Abstract. Analysis of publicly available language learning corpora can be useful for extracting characteristic features of learners from different proficiency levels. This can then be used to support language learning research and the creation of educational resources. In this paper, we classify the words and parts of speech of transcripts from different speaking proficiency levels found in the NICT-JLE corpus. The characteristic features of learners who have the equivalent spoken proficiency of CEFR levels A1 through to B2 were extracted by analyzing the data with the support vector machine method. In particular, we apply feature selection to find a set of characteristic features that achieve optimal classification performance, which can be used to predict spoken learner proficiency.

Keywords: Foreign language proficiency · Machine learning · Feature selection · SVM

1 Introduction

At present there are many machine readable data that are publicly available, and this has increased the application of machine learning to the task of supporting language learning. In this paper, we analyze the NICT-JLE corpus[1] to investigate which words describe and discriminate different speaking proficiency levels by applying a method of machine learning called SVM (Support Vector Machine) to the classification task. The corpus consists of 1280 transcribed recordings of the Standard Speaking Test [1–3] (herein referred to as SST) English language learner exam. Each exam contains 3 different tasks and the transcriptions are made up of the dialogue between the examiner and examinee. The proficiency level for each examinee was determined by an expert examiner and ranked on a scale from 1 to 9, from beginner to advanced respectively. In this paper, the focus of the classification analysis will be on the Common European Framework of Reference for Languages: Learning, teaching, assessment (CEFR)

---

[1] http://alaginrc.nict.go.jp/nict_jle/indexE.html.

© Springer International Publishing AG 2017
T.-T. Wu et al. (Eds.): SETE 2016, LNCS 10108, pp. 677–682, 2017.
DOI: 10.1007/978-3-319-52836-6_72

(Council of Europe, 2001) [4] which is utilized internationally, rather than the SST proficiency levels that are applicable only within Japan.

The equivalent proficiency levels of SST, CEFR, and CEFR-J (a version of the CEFR that has been tailored to the needs of Japanese learning English) as defined by Tono et al. [5] are shown in Table 1. It should be noted that SST level 4 can be assigned to either CEFR level A1 and A2, and we will refer to these as CEFR1 and CEFR2 respectively. In this paper, the evaluation of the classification method was performed with SST level 4 included in the CEFR level A2. The classification of SST level 4 included in the CEFR level A1 should be investigated in future work. SST level 9 is included only in CEFR level B2.

Table 1. Equivalent levels of CEFR, CEFR-J, and SST.

CEFR	–	A1			A2		B1		B2		C1	C2
CEFR-J	Pre A1	A1.1	A1.2	A1.3	A2.1	A2.2	B1.1	B1.2	B2.1	B2.2	C1	C2
SST	1	2/3	3	4	4	5	6/7	8	9	9	9	9

For each of the 1280 examinee's in the SST data there are 5 stages of the interview that have been transcribed. In this paper, the results for each examinee were represented as one document, and there were 1280 sample documents for which the proficiency level classification problem was analyzed. Examinees who have an SST proficiency level of 1 were excluded as it would be equivalent to Pre A1 CEFR level. A total of 9,626 words were analyzed along with 11 parts of speech (POS) from Lancaster University's CLAWS5 and CLAWS7 tag sets[2].

Automated language scoring using a computer was first proposed by Page in 1968 [6]. Since then research into the prediction of foreign language proficiency has focused on a number of different approaches. Supnithi et al. [7], analyzed the vocabulary, grammatical accuracy and fluency features of the NICT-JLE corpus. SVM and Maximum Entropy classifiers were trained to automatically predict the proficiency level of the learner, with SVM achieving the best prediction accuracy of 65.57%. There has also been research into extracting features that can be useful in classifying proficiency levels in the NICT-JLE corpus [8, 9]. In this paper, analysis by SVM and feature selection is used to not only improve the accuracy of proficiency classification, but also identify optimal sets of characteristic features that can describe learners from different proficiency levels.

2 Proficiency Level Classification by SVM and Feature Selection

The occurrence frequency (tf) of each word was used to vectorize each of the transcripts. This was realized by creating a term document matrix of the exam transcripts using GETA[3].

---

[2] http://ucrel.lancs.ac.uk/claws5tags.html, http://ucrel.lancs.ac.uk/claws7tags.html.

[3] http://geta.ex.nii.ac.jp.

To evaluate the performance of classifying documents into two classes of proficiency levels, the documents of level X were represented as positive examples, while the documents of level Y were represented as negative examples to train a machine learning model. SVM^{perf} [10] was use to train and test models on the data of the corpus. The experiment process can be broken down into 3 main steps. All features (words, POS tags) are used to train a model in step 1. The ranking $weight(wi)$ scores for each feature are then extracted from the model in step 2. These feature weights are then ranked in step 3 were the classification performance of models trained and evaluated using feature selections of increasingly larger sets of $N = 1, 2,... 10, 20,.., 100$ is analyzed. The optimal feature selection is the best performing model trained on N features. The classification performance of each model was evaluated using 5-fold cross validation.

The feature $weight(wi)$ score extracted in Step 2 represents the distance from the SVM hyperplane that separates the positive and negative classes on which the model was trained. Models were trained with the upper proficiency level learner data as the positive class, and the lower level learner data as the negative class. Features that have positive $weight(wi)$ are characteristic of upper level learners, and a negative feature $weight(wi)$ are characteristic of lower level learners.

2.1 Feature Selection Measures

The classification performance of a model trained using all features for A1 and A2 were: Precision 0.8923, Recall 0.8117, F-measure 0.8491, and Accuracy 0.7830. Although the classification performance is quite high, we do not know which grammar items are effective for discriminating between different proficiency levels. In this paper, we apply the method from Sakai and Hirokawa [11] to the problem of feature selection to find a set of optimal discriminating features.

The feature score $weight(wi)$ extracted in Step 2 was calculated using 6 different evaluation measures as shown in Table 2. $df(w)$ is the number of documents in which the word w occurs, and abs returns the absolute value of the enclosed value.

Table 2. Measures used for Feature Selection.

Symbol	Measure	Symbol	Measure
w.o	$weight(wi)$	w.a	$abs(weight(wi))$
d.o	$weight(wi) * df(wi)$	d.a	$abs(weight(wi) * df(wi))$
l.o	$weight(wi) * log(df(wi))$	l.a	$abs(weight(wi) * log(df(wi)))$

In the case of measures that do not take the absolute value of the score: the top N positive $weight$ features are selected along with the top N negative $weight$ features for vectorization. For measures that do take the absolute value of the score the top $2N$ positive $weight$ features are selected for vectorization.

3 Proficiency Classification Performance

This section explains the results of the proficiency classification performance by accuracy that are shown in Table 3, and plots of feature selection results for all measures shown in Fig. 1. The x-axis in these plots represents 2 N number of features selected. The results for A2 vs B1, shown on the left of Fig. 1, and B1 vs B2 show that as the number of selected features increases, the accuracy increases following a curved line, suggesting that as the number of features increases the accuracy will steadily get higher. In other words, it is not possible to classify these classes with few features. Conversely, in the results of A1 vs A2, A1 vs B2, and A2 vs B2, shown on the right of Fig. 1, the accuracy rises quickly at around $N = 10$. This indicates that a decent level of classification performance can be achieved using a small number of features.

Table 3. Classification performance when using all feature words.

Acc	A2	B1	B2
A1	All 0.8188	All 0.9675	All 0.9966
	N = 20 0.7607	N = 20 0.8099	N = 20 0.7763
	N = 50 0.7837	N = 50 0.8615	N = 50 0.9333
	N = 100 0.8171	N = 100 0.9269	N = 100 0.9760
A2		All 0.8673	All 0.9879
		N = 20 0.6292	N = 20 0.8774
		N = 50 0.7750	N = 50 0.9657
		N = 100 0.8393	N = 100 0.9846
B1			all 0.8512
			N = 20 0.4493
			N = 50 0.6809
			N = 100 0.8405

The baseline classification performance of a model that was trained using all of the features is shown in Table 3. It can be seen that the classification performance of adjacent proficiency levels is low. The classification accuracy of feature selection is shown in Fig. 1, where for the plot on the left A1 is the positive class and A2 is the negative class, and the x-axis is 2 N top ranking features selected. When N = 200 of greater the accuracy of the model is slightly better than a model trained using all features. The two measures: l.o and d.o outperform the baseline at N = 9 which indicates that classification can be achieved with a small number of features.

4 Proficiency Classification Performance

The top 10 characteristic features of level A1 are compared to other levels in Table 4. The feature "jp" represents a Japanese word that was said in the exam and has been replaced during transcription. Regardless of which level A1 is compared to, the nouns: cat, theater, boy, zoo, lion, and monkey are frequent. This is most likely effected by the contents of picture cards on which conversations are based in certain SST tasks. On the other hand, other levels have higher numbers of verbs, adverbs, and adjectives. However, more high level parts of speech features such as VERB and ADJ are not seen as characteristic features. Therefore, discrimination between levels is not possible using simple parts of speech. Even though the POS tag information was analyzed, looking at the top ranking features when comparing A2 and B1, only 3 POS tags appear as characteristic features: C7 = RGQ (adverb expressing a degree) for A1, and C7 = RRR (comparative adverb) and C7 = DA (adjective used as pronoun) for B1. Also in Table 4 is can be seen that different characteristic features are chosen when comparing A1 to different levels. An unexpected result is that classification can be achieved with just 20 features.

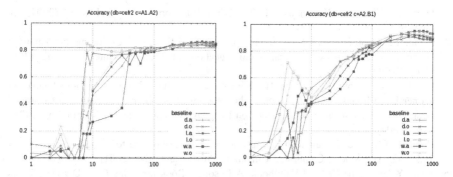

Fig. 1. Performance accuracy of feature selection.

Table 4. Characteristic features of A1 and other comparative levels.

Characteristic features of level A1	Comparative level characteristics
look, please, jp, first, work, just, picture, what, friend, cat	(A2) home, find, when now, will, ask, other eat, think, if
ten, c7 = RGQ, story, speak, theater, boy our, bring, anonym., favorite	(B1) really, also, ask call, actually, different c7 = RRR, your, stay c7 = DA
theater, pardon, cold color, zoo, lion, monkey shinjuku, recently, tv	(B2) an, into, drive brother, anything, club fun, once, teacher explain

5 Conclusion and Future Work

In this paper, we analyzed the transcripts of a speaking test corpus by applying SVM machine learning to the problem of classifying the differences between CEFR proficiency levels. Feature selection was used to find an optimal feature set by evaluating the model accuracy. It was found that a set of about 20 features produced the same performance as a model trained using all words and an accuracy of greater than 90%. For adjacent levels the classification accuracy was around 10% less. Classification of levels A1 vs B1 and B1 vs B2 were difficult and decent accuracy could not be achieved using small numbers of features. The characteristic features of level A1 contained numerous Japanese words, proper nouns, and simple nouns. In this paper, when assigning the equivalent levels of SST and CEFR we made the assumption that SST level 4 was contained within CEFR level A2. The analysis of SST Level 4 as CEFR A1 should be carried out in future work. Also the analysis of CEFR-J levels which are more detailed than CEFR level should be undertaken in future work.

Acknowledgment. This work was supported by JSPS KAKENHI Grant Number 15H02778, 24242017, and 15J04830.

References

1. Izumi, E., Uchimoto, K., Isahara, H.: The NICT JLE Corpus. ACL Publishing (2004). (in Japanese)
2. Izumi, E., Uchimoto, K., Isahara, H.: The NICT JLE corpus: exploiting the language learner's speech database for research and education. Int. J. Comput. Internet Manag. **12**(2), 119–125 (2004)
3. Izumi, E., Uchimoto, K., Isahara, H.: The overview of the SST speech corpus of Japanese learner English and evaluation through the experiment on automatic detection of learners' errors. In: 4th International Conference on Language Resources and Evaluation, pp. 1435–1438 (2004)
4. Council of Europe: Common European Framework of Reference for Languages: Learning, Teaching, Assessment. Cambridge University Press, Cambridge (2001)
5. Tono, Y. (ed.): The CEFR-J Handbook: A Resource Book for Using CAN-DO Descriptors for English Language Teaching. Taishukan Publishing (2013). (in Japanese)
6. Page, E.B.: The use of the computer in analyzing student essays. Int. Rev. Educ. **14**(2), 210–225 (1968)
7. Supnithi, T., Uchimoto, K., Saiga, T., Izumi, E., Virach, S., Isahara, H.: Automatic proficiency level checking based on SST corpus. In: Proceedings of the RANLP, pp. 29–33 (2003)
8. Abe, M.: Frequency change patterns across proficiency levels in Japanese EFL learner speech. Apples: J. Appl. Lang. Stud. **8**(3), 85–96 (2014)
9. Flanagan, B., Hirokawa, S.: The relationship of English foreign language learner proficiency and an entropy based measure. IEE **1**(3), 29–38 (2015)
10. Joachims, T.: Training linear SVMs in linear time. In: Proceedings of the ACM-KDD, pp. 217–226 (2006)
11. Sakai, T., Hirokawa, S.: Feature words that classify problem sentence in scientific article. In: Proceedings of the 14th International Conference on Information Integration and Web-based Applications & Services, pp. 360–367 (2012)

Integrating Mind Tools and Peer Assessment for Assisting Students in Foreign Language Learning

Ting-Chia Hsu[✉]

Department of Technology Application and Human Resource Development,
National Taiwan Normal University, 162, Section 1, Heping East Road,
Daan Block, Taipei 10610, Taiwan
ckhsu@ntnu.edu.tw

Abstract. This study compared the learning effectiveness, speaking time length, communication competence, foreign language speaking anxiety, and cognitive loads of high and low English proficiency students playing the roles of both assessors and practitioners in a mobile-assisted language learning activity. This study integrated a concept-mapping application as a mind tool with an oral recorder application on tablets to support EFL learners speaking English. The system, named CMAS (i.e., the Concept Mapping-Assisted Speaking system), includes peer assessment and evaluation of concept maps at the end of each round of activities. After three rounds, the results indicated that the overall speaking effectiveness including appropriateness of vocabulary, pronunciation, intonation, fluency, grammar, and accuracy of the high proficiency students was significantly higher than that of the low proficiency students. The cognitive loads of the low proficiency students were higher than those of the high proficiency students. However, there was no significant difference between the length of speaking time of the two groups. There was no remarkable difference between the speaking anxieties of the two groups after the experiment. The CMAS benefited not only the high-proficiency students but also the low-proficiency students, especially in terms of the speaking time length and the speaking anxieties of the low-proficiency students so future research directions were identified based on the results.

Keywords: EFL · Concept mapping · Speaking · Peer assessment · Speaking anxiety · Cognitive load

1 Introduction

It is of vital importance for EFL learners to perform English speaking well and to regard speaking as a learnable skill (Sun 2008). As Nunan (2003) indicated, one of the chief reasons for learning English is to learn how to speak English and communicate with others in English. English speaking is the ability to employ the language to achieve the aim of managing communication well (Ockey et al. 2015). Mastery of English speaking for communication can provide career benefits, such as job and promotion opportunities (Duan and Gu 2004). Developing one's English speaking

© Springer International Publishing AG 2017
T.-T. Wu et al. (Eds.): SETE 2016, LNCS 10108, pp. 683–690, 2017.
DOI: 10.1007/978-3-319-52836-6_73

capability is likely to not only offer career benefits, but also to achieve academic requirements (Tsou and Huang 2012). In terms of the difficulties of teaching speaking in Taiwan, the time for teaching English is limited, so instructors should employ methods and media to enhance the students' learning opportunities (Harmer 2013; Swan 2005). In a week, there are three to four English classes in most junior high schools. In this time, not only the contents of the textbook should be covered, but also adequately exercising the four skills in class is necessary. Therefore, time for teaching speaking is limited, and more efforts should thus be made to teach speaking in class in Taiwan.

Many well-known foreign language tests, such as TOEFL and GEPT (i.e., the General English Proficiency Test). These English certification tests usually provide a topic or a figure, and ask the examinees to speak based on it. Therefore, teachers train students to see a picture and describe it, a task similar to the abovementioned oral proficiency tests. Therefore, this study trained students to use a mobile-assisted concept mapping learning strategy to organize their thinking for a given speaking topic. After drawing the concept map, they see it and speak English to discuss the topic, rather than merely reading aloud.

A previous study pointed out that the computer-assisted concept mapping learning strategy had a positive impact on the use of listing, enforcing, and reviewing when students were learning English as a Foreign Language (EFL), and it especially had greater benefit for low-level than high-level students (Liu et al. 2010). With the advance of handheld devices, the computer-assisted concept map application is now able to be developed on mobile devices to help individuals organize their thoughts or opinions effectively anytime and anywhere, so as to achieve meaningful learning (Kukulska-Hulme et al. 2009). For example, Chen (2014) integrated concept mapping instruction with the Short Message Service (SMS) on mobile phones, and found that the method strengthened EFL learners' vocabulary learning. Prior to oral proficiency development, language output production is expected to profitably link to the concepts originating from the learners' cognition. Therefore, this study integrated a concept map application with an oral recorder application on handheld devices to help English as foreign language learners train their speaking.

Towler and Broadfoot (1992) reported that students would reflect on their own work and learning performance when they take the roles of both learners (practitioners) and reviewers (assessors), while another study indicated that peer assessment contributes to learners' development of domain-specific skills via the evaluation and reflection cycle (Van Zundert et al. 2010). In addition, a previous study has proved the validity of peer assessment, finding a positive correlation between the ratings given by teachers and peers (de Grez et al. 2012). In sum, in this study, the students drew their own concept map for self-reflection and cognitive organization, and reviewed their peers' work for reflecting on or emulating each other's work. The students used their tablet PCs installed with the application which included both the concept map application and the oral recording application. Moreover, they could use their tablet PCs to see their peer's concept map and listen to their speaking so that they could grade their peers and inspect others' work at the same time. The research questions proposed in this study are as follows.

1. Was there any difference between the learning effectiveness and length of speaking time of the students with high and low English proficiency using the proposed approach?
2. Was there any difference between the foreign language speaking anxiety of the students with high and low English proficiency using the proposed approach?
3. Was there any difference between the cognitive loads of the students with high and low English proficiency using the proposed approach?

2 Method

2.1 Participants

The participants of this study included 29 9th-grade students (15-year-olds) in a junior high school in Taiwan, who learned English as a Foreign Language. Of these, 15 had high and 14 had low English proficiency. There were 14 groups (13 pairs and one group of three) conducting oral speaking peer assessment using mobile devices which stored their peer's concept map and oral output. Each pair included one high and one low English proficiency student, while the group of three had two high proficiency and one low proficiency student.

2.2 Research Tools

Every student was equipped with a tablet PC installed with concept mapping applications and notebook applications which were used to store the concept map and the oral recording. The grading of speaking included the appropriateness of vocabulary, pronunciation, intonation, fluency, grammar, and accuracy, as shown in Table 1.

Table 1. Speaking criteria

Grading	Criteria
5	Can pronounce English words correctly and naturally Can speak English fluently and make good use of it to communicate The English content meets the requirements of the questions Can deal with the grammar and vocabulary of English well
4	Can pronounce English words approximately correctly and naturally Can speak English approximately fluently but makes some mistakes The English content approximately meets the requirements of the questions Can deal with the grammar and vocabulary of English sentences but is not able to make good use of it
3	May pronounce English words incorrectly sometimes but can still be understood Speaks English slowly but can use it to communicate The English content mostly cannot be understood There are some errors in the use of grammar and vocabulary

(continued)

Table 1. (*continued*)

Grading	Criteria
2	Often pronounces English words incorrectly Speaks English very slowly and cannot use it to communicate The English content is hard to understand There are many errors in the use of grammar and vocabulary
1	Always pronounces English words incorrectly The English content is very hard to understand The use of grammar and vocabulary is mostly incorrect
0	Does not answer the questions

2.3   Experimental Procedure

This study integrated a concept map application with an oral recorder application on handheld devices for helping English as foreign language learners train their speaking. The system is named CMAS (i.e., the Concept Mapping-Assisted Speaking system). In other words, this study used the concept map strategy to assist students in organizing their thinking before performing an oral task. Each lesson was based on one topic. After the students had studied the lesson, they manipulated the concept map application to organize and generate a graphic showing their reflections and meaningful structure. After completing the concept map for the speaking topic, they could only see the concept figure, and then had to start speaking. The application on the tablet PC stored their speaking record and the concept map together. They then uploaded it to the online drive so that their peers could evaluate their speaking quality no matter where they were. To ensure that the thinking of the students was close to the speaking topic, the teachers also evaluated each student's concept map. The procedure of CMAS is shown in Fig. 1.

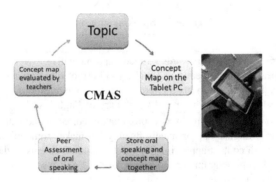

Fig. 1. The steps of the CMAS application

After three rounds of CMAS treatment, a total of 87 concept map outcomes were generated. The overall experimental procedure is shown in Fig. 2.

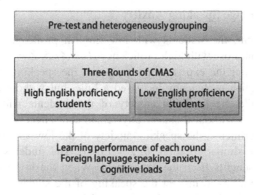

Fig. 2. The experimental procedure.

3 Result

3.1 Learning Effectiveness and Speaking Time Length

The concept maps the students generated not only showed their comprehension of the topic, but also helped the low proficiency students organize their thinking and achieve the required speaking length. There was no significant difference between the evaluation results of the concept maps generated by the students with high and low English proficiency ($U = 84.5$, $Z = 0.896$). Therefore, it was confirmed that the students had similar comprehension and preparation of the topics. The next step was to use English to speak according to the concept map they had developed on their tablet PC. Their speaking content was recorded. As a result, this study found that length of the foreign language speaking time of the high and low proficiency students had no significant difference ($U = 85$, $Z = 0.873$). In other words, the low English proficiency students could speak for as long as the high English proficiency students with the support of the concept map. However, it is not easy to make progress in speaking proficiency in several rounds of CMAS. Based on the speaking assessment rubrics, the oral speaking score of the high proficiency students still remarkably outperformed that of the low proficiency students ($U = 36$, $Z = 3.081^{**}$), as shown in Table 2.

Table 2. Independent Mann-Whitney U test of learning effectiveness and Time Length

Evaluation	Speakers	N	Mean	SD	Mean rank	Rank total	U	W	Z
Oral speaking score	High-proficiency	15	4.69	0.08	19.60	294.00	36.00	141.00	3.081**
	Low-proficiency	14	4.07	0.15	10.07	141.00			
Time length (seconds)	High-proficiency	15	44.18	3.64	16.33	245.00	85.00	190.00	0.873
	Low-proficiency	14	39.40	2.40	13.57	190.00			

*$p<.05$

3.2 Foreign Language Speaking Anxiety

Before the experiment, the students with low English proficiency had much more speaking anxiety than those with high proficiency ($U = 47.5$, $Z = 2.511^*$), as shown in Table 3. However, after the experimental treatment, the speaking anxiety of the students with high English proficiency increased a little, but without a statistically significant impact, while the speaking anxiety of the students with low proficiency decreased a little, also without a statistically remarkable effect. As a result, after the three rounds of experiments, the speaking anxiety of the low and high English proficiency students were similar ($U = 80.50$, $Z = 1.070$). The students with low English proficiency gained benefits from the experiment. When the low English proficiency students had opportunities to inspect the speaking of the students with high English proficiency, they would learn from their successful work and self-reflect on certain orally failed pronunciation.

Table 3. Independent Mann-Whitney U test of speaking anxiety

Test	Assessor	N	Mean	SD	Mean Rank	Rank total	U	W	Z
Pre-test	High-proficiency	15	2.05	0.18	11.17	167.50	47.50	167.50	-2.511^*
	Low-proficiency	14	2.85	0.17	19.11	267.50			
Post-test	High-proficiency	15	2.08	0.18	13.37	200.50	80.50	200.50	-1.070
	Low-proficiency	14	2.52	0.25	16.75	234.50			

$^*p<.05$

3.3 Cognitive Loads

Although the CMAS rounds contributed to the learning anxiety of the low English proficiency students, their cognitive loads were still higher than those of the high English proficiency students ($U = 26.00$, $Z = 3.469^{**}$), regardless of the intrinsic ($U = 29.00$, $Z = 3.337^{**}$) or extrinsic cognitive load ($U = 25.50$, $Z = 3.506^{***}$), as shown in Table 4. The prior proficiency of the students had great impacts on how they performed in the speaking activities. The students tried their best to perform better when their output was recorded on the tablet PC to give to their peers to assess their oral practice.

Table 4. Independent Mann-Whitney U test of cognitive loads

Variance	Speaker level	N	Mean	SD	Mean rank	Rank total	U	W	Z
Mental load (Intrinsic cognition load)	High-proficiency	15	1.65	0.17	9.93	149.00	29.00	149.00	-3.337^{**}
	Low-proficiency	14	2.70	0.19	20.43	286.00			

(*continued*)

Table 4. (*continued*)

Variance	Speaker level	N	Mean	SD	Mean rank	Rank total	U	W	Z
Mental effort (Extrinsic cognition load)	High-proficiency	15	1.64	0.16	9.70	145.50	25.50	145.50	−3.506[***]
	Low-proficiency	14	2.64	0.18	20.68	289.50			
Cognitive load (Overall)	High-proficiency	15	1.65	0.16	9.73	146.00	26.00	146.00	−3.469[**]
	Low-proficiency	14	2.68	0.18	20.64	289.00			

**p<.01; ***p<.001

4 Conclusions

This study conducted CMAS cycles in a junior high school and compared the impacts of the CMAS approach on high and low proficiency students. Due to the assistance of the concept mapping to the low proficiency students, the speaking length of those students was as long as that of their high proficiency peers, resulting in no significant difference between the speaking anxieties of the student with high and low English proficiency. However, it is not easy for students with low performance to make improvements in their use of appropriate vocabulary, pronunciation, intonation, fluency, grammar, or accuracy in a short time. As a result, the low proficiency students still represented higher intrinsic and extrinsic cognition loadings in foreign language speaking, and thus could not create the effect of communicating with others. In contrast, students with high English proficiency could communicate well. While the researchers did not employ instant computer-mediated communication in this study, future studies will consider employing a peer-tutoring instrument instead of the peer-assessment instrument for oral practice, and will then compare the variation or differences in students' speaking anxiety or any dimension mentioned in the results of this study.

Acknowledgement. This study is supported in part by the Ministry of Science and Technology in Taiwan under contract numbers: NSC 102-2511-S-003-055-MY2 and MOST 105-2628-S-003-002-MY3. This study was conducted in a junior high school and the author is grateful to Miss Chia-Lin Lu for carrying out the experiment in her English class.

References

Chen, C.J.: Using concept mapping instruction in mobile phone to learning English vocabulary. Creative Educ. **5**(1), 4–6 (2014)

De Grez, L., Valcke, M., Roozen, I.: How effective are self-and peer assessment of oral presentation skills compared with teachers' assessments? Act. Learn. High Educ. **13**(2), 129–142 (2012)

Duan, P., Gu, W.: Teaching trial and analysis of English for technical communication. Asian EFL J. 6(1), 1–9 (2004). http://citeseerx.ist.psu.edu/viewdoc/download?doi=10.1.1.196.9251&rep=rep1&type=pdf

Harmer, J.: Thinking about language teaching: selected articles 1982–2011. ELT J. 67(2), 250–253 (2013)

Kukulska-Hulme, A., Sharples, M., Milrad, M., Arnedillo-Sánchez, I., Vavoula, G.: Innovation in mobile learning: a European perspective. Int. J. Mob. Blended Learn. (IJMBL) 1(1), 13–35 (2009)

Liu, P.L., Chen, C.J., Chang, Y.J.: Effects of a computer-assisted concept mapping learning strategy on EFL college students' English reading comprehension. Comput. Educ. 54(2), 436–445 (2010)

Nunan, D.: The impact of English as a global language on educational policies and practices in the Asia-Pacific region. TESOL Q. 37(4), 589–613 (2003)

Ockey, G.J., Koyama, D., Setoguchi, E., Sun, A.: The extent to which TOEFL iBT speaking scores are associated with performance on oral language tasks and oral ability components for Japanese university students. Lang. Test. 32(1), 39–62 (2015)

Sun, Y.-C.: The toastmasters approach: an innovative way to teach public speaking to EFL learners in Taiwan. Reg. Lang. Cent. J. 39(1), 113–130 (2008)

Swan, M.: Legislation by hypothesis: the case of task-based instruction. Appl. Linguist. 26(3), 376–401 (2005)

Tsou, W., Huang, Y.: The effect of explicit instruction in formulaic sequences on academic speech fluency. Taiwan Int. ESP J. 4(2), 57–80 (2012)

Towler, L., Broadfoot, P.: Self-assessment in the primary school. Educ. Rev. 44(2), 137–151 (1992)

Van Zundert, M., Sluijsmans, D., Van Merriënboer, J.: Effective peer assessment processes: research findings and future directions. Learn. Instr. 20(4), 270–279 (2010)

Game-Based Educational Application
for Informal Learning of English Using FLEG

Boyu Wang[1(✉)], Feier Tang[2], Kousuke Kaneko[3], Masanori Yamada[4],
and Yoshihiro Okada[5]

[1] Faculty of Information Science and Electrical Engineering,
Kyushu University, Fukuoka, Japan
boyu.kyudai@gmail.com
[2] Graduate School of Human-Environment Studies,
Kyushu University, Fukuoka, Japan
[3] Cyber Security Center in Kyushu University, Fukuoka, Japan
[4] Faculty of Arts and Science, Kyushu University, Fukuoka, Japan
[5] Innovation Center for Educational Resource,
Kyushu University, Fukuoka, Japan

Abstract. With the development of Information and Communication Technology (ICT), various types of educational applications have emerged to enhance learning. Informal learning using a mobile device or an ICT tool is one among them. The problem with an educational application is that an educator has to possess the required programming skills and knowledge of ICT skills to develop the application. Educators can hardly be expected to develop their own educational application. Therefore, this paper introduces an educational framework called FLEG (Framework for Location-based Educational Game Application) to help educators develop their gamification-based application using geolocation information without needing any programming skills, and it offers an explanation of the design and development of this framework. A sample game-based educational application is also presented with results to evaluate the application.

Keywords: Informal learning · Gamification · Educational framework · GPS information

1 Introduction

The developments in the field of Information and Communication Technologies (ICT) in recent years have led to their immense use in the field of education. Many educational applications have been developed based on the functional use and convenience of mobile devices. These ICT tools are suitable for "informal learning," that is, active learning in a non-organized educational environment. Gamification-based approaches are sometimes used in informal learning to enhance learner motivation. On game-based applications, Robert (2014) lists the different kinds of games and their purposes, such as commercial games, educational games, and mobile games. Educational games are expected be highly used in future research [4].

© Springer International Publishing AG 2017
T.-T. Wu et al. (Eds.): SETE 2016, LNCS 10108, pp. 691–700, 2017.
DOI: 10.1007/978-3-319-52836-6_74

Evaluation methods to measure learning effectiveness of an educational application are important in educational technology research fields. The ARCS model suggested by Keller and Suzuki (1988) is effective in terms of learning motivation [6]. The ARCS model has four scales to evaluate the following: Attention, Relevance, Confidence, and Satisfaction. Attention refers to factors that a learner may consider attractive (e.g., role-playing or hands-on experiences); relevance is about factors that a learner may require (e.g., immediate or future usefulness); confidence entails factors that can increase chances of succeeding (e.g., self-growth); and satisfaction involves feedback factors (e.g., rewards or benefits). This paper introduces an educational application developed using our framework known as FLEG (Framework for Location-based Educational Game Application). The application was designed using the ARCS model, and its effectiveness was investigated using a questionnaire.

FLEG is aimed at developing a location-based educational application. There have been remarkable results from research on the effectiveness of location-based learning [1, 5]. Peacock (1997) and Gilmore (2011) show that a context-awareness-based learning connecting to the learner's context such as social situation has proven to enhance learning effectiveness [3, 7]. These types of location-based applications for learning are suitable for informal learning using ICT tools or mobile devices.

Since mobile devices are high-performance tools, a single device is enough to help students in their learning instead of complex systems; therefore, mobile devices are extremely useful in the educational field.

This paper begins with a short review of related works in Sect. 2. The design and development details of FLEG are described in Sect. 3. Section 4 introduces an example application developed using FLEG. Section 5 explains the procedure of an experiment using the application. Section 6 shows the results of a questionnaire survey about users' experience after playing the gamification-based application. Last, the paper concludes by explaining several related plans for future research.

2   Related Works

In this section, we introduce two tools: ARIS and Unity. Our system is designed to look similar to and is based on the model of ARIS. Unity is an important tool used in our system to develop and install our application in both iOS and Android devices.

2.1   ARIS (Augmented Reality and Interactive Storytelling)

ARIS, a Web tool to design Interactive storytelling Augmented Reality games, can be easily used to develop mobile games even if one does not have programming skills. Developed by Gagnon et al. in the University of Wisconsin-Madison, it has been used by various educators, and several game applications have been developed using ARIS [2]. ARIS can be used in learning storytelling, but learners cannot communicate with each other using the application. In our framework, as a game-based learning application, we considered adding a communication system to help users communicate with each other online.

2.2 Unity

Unity, a game engine, is used to develop mobile applications and games. With the official API provided by Unity, one can easily develop applications using information from the gyroscope, digital compass, and GPS systems of mobile devices. Unity's target users are professional developers, as educators cannot develop educational applications without programming skills.

3 Design and Development of the FLEG System

Considering the missing elements of ARIS, we designed and developed a new framework. The main game genre supported by the framework is for an encampment games like Ingress developed by Google. Using the framework, educators can develop educational applications using geolocation information.

We called our new system FLEG (Framework for Location-based Educational Game Application), that is, a framework to develop a location-based educational game application for educators and learners [10], educators can develop their own game with this system, and then use their own game to improve their students' motivation to study, by this way, we wish to help students learn English better.

FLEG is aimed at helping to develop educational material using geolocation information without requiring any programming skills. With this concept, we designed and developed a prototype system. First, for educators who do not have programming skills, this system provides a no-programming environment; using tools provided by this system, educators can create their own games easily by uploading files and images. For professional programmers, this system provides a basic communication system and function to edit code and expand it for developing games that are more complex.

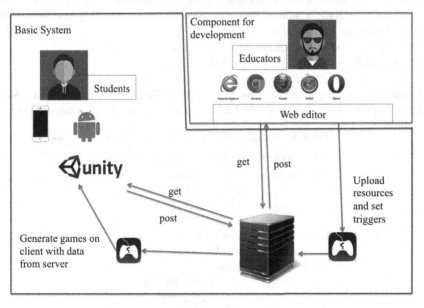

Fig. 1. System architecture of FLEG (based on ARIS)

The framework comprises (1) the basic system comprising two parts and (2) the component for development (Fig. 1). The two parts of the basic system help in communication between the Web editor and the server and the mobile devices, and implements the location-based augmented reality function. The component for development helps in the function of editing content for the educational application; it also offers the function of uploading educational resources and provides an interface to analyze the game data.

3.1 Users and Detailed Functions of FLEG

Within this system, the educators use the component for development to develop educational contents, while learners use the client part of the basic system to learn. When developing the application, educators upload questions using the component for development. After inserting and, then, editing information, such as geographical information, or the characters in the game, or the triggers of events, the application can be developed. When playing the game application, learners choose the application developed by the educators in the client part of the system. They start their study activation with the augmented reality function provided by the client part of the system.

3.2 Architecture of FLEG

This system contains the server, the client part, and the Web editor part just like the ARIS model. The server operates data between the three parts. The client part contains functions to access the games created by Web editor.

The Web application and client application were published in the server at the Innovation Center for Educational Resource, Kyushu University. They can be accessed from the following URLs.

Web Application: http://edusys.icer.kyushu-u.ac.jp.

Client Application: http://auth.icer.kyushu-u.ac.jp.

Table 1 shows the implementation environment of FLEG.

Figure 2 shows the demonstration image of the Web application of FLEG. Since the Client Application can access only ItoSramble now, it will be introduced in Sect. 4.

Table 1. Implementation environment of FLEG

Part of System	Implementation environment
Web Application	Ubuntu 14.04.1 Unicorn 5.1.0 Ruby 2.1.2p95 Sinatra 1.4.6
Database	Ubuntu 14.04.1 MySQL 5.6.26
Client	Unity 5.2.3 Google Map for Unity Google Map Static API iOS, Android

Fig. 2. Web application demonstration

4   A Game Called "ItoScramble" Developed Using FLEG

As a research target, our research team successfully designed a game application called "ItoScramble."

4.1   Details of ItoScramble

This game application ideally contains three elements: first, an educational environment that is location-based; second, an immersive virtual environment; and third, the game elements.

To make it more educationally effective, this game application needs to meet the psychological structural framework of a game. Table 2 shows how our team designed ItoScramble and the design elements were added into ItoScramble to achieve the main categories of its characteristics.

Table 2. Main categories of characteristics and ItoScramble game design [8, 9]

Categories	Elements in ItoSramble
Background and setting	Fiction as Game story
	Game stages really exist in universities
Game dynamics	Bases can be occupied with accuracy
	Encampment, support tools
Winning and losing features	Get point, get bonus
Character development	Collect point to level up
Multiplayer features	Team with multiple players,
	Visualizing Player's information

Based on the psychological structural framework of a game, we designed the fiction for ItoScramble and determined the concrete rules for playing the game. Students are first divided into two groups called human and crystal. They are then required to undergo a rank test to determine their rank. After getting their rank, the game starts; they then play this encampment game with their own mobile devices in a confined district and within a prescribed time. (These limits are explained to the students at the beginning of the class.) When a student accesses one base, the system will give the student 10 questions based on his rank. After solving the 10 questions, based on the accuracy of the answers and the time taken to solve the 10 questions, the student can occupy this base. Apart from these rules, ItoScramble also provides three tools to students: an attack tool, to fight for a base for a companion aggressively if it is occupied an enemy group; a self-help tool, to delete one option from four options in a question if the student does not know the right answer; and finally, a defense tool, to make one's base occupied by a companion inaccessible to the enemy group.

4.2   Development of ItoScramble

As FLEG is not yet designed completely to develop a game with no programing skills, we developed ItoScramble with FLEG by expanding the functions of FLEG, similar to the way professional programmers do. With these expanded functions, we can perform data transportation using JSON with the communication functions of FLEG, set bases, and create the question set and user set using the existing functions of FLEG. Then, to develop ItoScramble, we set a trigger and developed GUI within the client application developed by Unity and added several functions to operate the database in the server. Thus, we were able to successfully develop ItoScramble. Figure 3 shows the sample interface of ItoScramble.

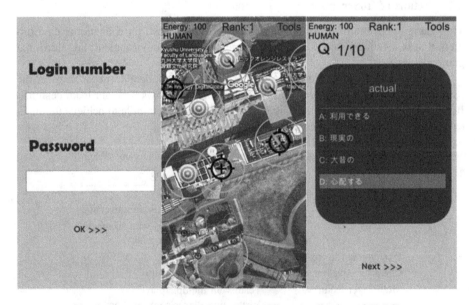

Fig. 3. Sample interface of ItoSramble (Client Application of FLEG)

5 Formative Evaluation of Usability and Instructional Design

Our team conducted an experiment in a class held on the Hakozaki Campus, Kyushu University. Thirteen students participated in the experiment on formative evaluation. They played ItoScramble for 40 min and learned English vocabulary using the game-based application. We provided a questionnaire on improving our framework and evaluating its usability and instructional design. Each question was to be rated on a Likert scale of 1 to 5, with 1 referring to poor feedback and 5 referring to appreciation. The questionnaire also asked the students to write something in the free description space to help improve ItoScramble.

6 Results of Formative Evaluation

In this experiment, our purpose was to find out how we can improve ItoScramble to get the expected result, and whether the FLEG had successfully developed ItoScramble as expected. Therefore, the most important mission was to find the defects in the game design or system bugs and to know the differences in the design of ItoScramble and a reality game application. Before we evaluate the framework, we must evaluate the game ItoScramble developed using this framework.

Table 3. Formative evaluation results

Items	Average	SD
1: I was interested in the settings and the story of this game	3.42	1.26
2: The game plot was very clear to me	3.92	1.11
3: The information in the story was enough for me to understand the game	3.67	1.03
4: The context of the game story motivated me to play the game	3.92	1.04
5: I paid attention to the game settings and story construction	3.75	0.92
6: I understand the relevance of the game story	2.58	1.19
7: The game construction and story raised my interest	2.67	1.03
8: It was easy to play this game	2.83	0.99
9: I certainly learned English vocabulary using this game	3.08	0.95
10: The interface of this game was very clear	2.75	1.09
11: The information on the interface was enough for me to play the game	3.58	0.76
12: This game was easy to control	2.75	1.16
13: The game was effective in helping me learn English vocabulary using the geolocation data	3.33	1.03
14: This method gives me more opportunities to learn in daily life	3.50	0.65
15: This method of learning has increased my awareness of the game's relevance to me	3.25	1.09
16: This method of learning by playing the game has motivated me to learn better	3.67	1.25
17: This game can be played intuitively	3.50	0.76
18: I enjoyed playing the game	4.67	0.47
19: I am satisfied with the game	3.67	0.62

Table 3 shows the results of our questionnaire survey after the students played ItoScramble. The data are the responses to 19 items from 13 students. The items were set carefully to ensure that students could give concrete answers (Point 1 represents "I do not think so at all, Point 5 represents "I strongly agree with that"). Items 5 to 9 among the 19 items were about the ARCS model. These values determined whether the game had enhanced students' motivation or not. Item 5 got a score of 3.75 points, indicating that this game actually attracted students' attention. Items 6 and 7 got 2.58 and 2.67 points, respectively, indicating that the students did not understand the "Relevance" between the game story and themselves; so, the game story needs be changed in future research. Finally, item 8 got 2.8 points indicating that the students did not consider that the items in the game were too easy, implying that the game can actually challenge them to study.

The game story and construction were rated highly by the learners, for example, item 2, "The game story was very clear to me" (3.92), and item 4, "The context of the game story motivated me to play this game" (3.92). The interface design was appreciated by the learners (Item 11 and 17). Overall, the learners enjoyed this game and were satisfied with it.

7   Conclusion and Future Works

7.1   Conclusion

This paper presented FLEG, a framework for a location-based educational game application, and introduced an example of a gamification-based educational application developed using the framework. A questionnaire based on the experiment rated on a Likert scale revealed user experiences of the application. The findings showed that the educational application is effective in promoting informal learning of English from the viewpoint of the ARCS model.

7.2   Future Works

In future research, we need to add functions to help educators who do not have programming skills to develop their own game application.

Web editor uses Google Maps to show map information on it. Educators can set triggers into the map with this Web editor. Educators can also set elements (like NPC, items, dialog, GUI) using the Web editor. Finally, educators can set rules for their game (start time, end time, single player or multi player, and to find item or to obtain all bases). By setting these triggers, they can easily develop their own game.

Another part, the client application, should not only be to access ItoSramble, but also to other games created by the Web editor. Therefore, client application should provide an interface to check all games that have been created so that learners can access all the games.

However, since these functions have already been implemented by ARIS, our system needs to incorporate more complex functions to remove the defects found in ARIS.

First, ARIS supports only iOS devices; we resolved this using Unity as a development tool. Second, ARIS does not offer an online communication system, but merely provides the game on a student's mobile device. Our team decided to add an online communication system in our new system so that students can easily communicate with each other; this can enable them to get help from other learners or offer help to others and understand their learning state.

Finally, using this easy-to-expand framework, instead of the one provided by ARIS, we want to provide an easy model for developers based on the internet communication function of FLEG. They will not need to use or expand our client application when they want to design their own system. They can easily expand the server part to whatever they need to. Our server is simple because we developed it with the Sinatra Framework, and therefore the source code of the server part contains only several hundreds lines of code and is easy to understand.

7.3   Concrete Target of FLEG

Although the targets have been previously described, we need to define them in more concrete terms and explain the functions used to develop FLEG continually and continue work in the future. The Web API and detailed functions used by professional programmers should be defined and made easy to understand in future work; therefore, we want to create documentation and publish it on our Web editor. This would be another way for educators who do not have programming skills to develop game applications after our system has resolved the defects in ARIS.

7.4   Evaluation of FLEG and ItoSramble

After adding essential functions to FLEG, we plan to evaluate its usability by conducting an experiment on students and educators who do not have programing skills by explaining to them how to use this system and then let them create their own game application. After the experiment, we could use a questionnaire to know whether they understood the functions of the system and whether they were able to develop game application using FLEG. ItoScramble is one of the mock-up application by FLEG. The effects of ItoScramble should be evaluated as comparative research, in order to improve the validity and reliability of system implemented by FLEG.

Acknowledgment. This research project is supported by Grant-in-aid for Challenging Exploratory Research (Number: 15K12415) sponsored by Japan Society for the Promotion of Science (JSPS).

References

1. Connolly, T.M., Boyle, E.A., MacArthur, E., Hainey, T., Boyle, J.M.: A systematic literature review of empirical evidence on computer games and serious games. Comput. Educ. **59**(2), 661–686 (2012)
2. Gagnon, D.: ARIS [Open-source augmented reality authoring tool and game engine software]. Unpublished Master's thesis from University of Wisconsin-Madison (2008). http://arisgames.org/wp-content/uploads/2011/04/ARIS-Gagnon-MS-Project.pdf

3. Gilmore, A.: "I Prefer Not Text": developing Japanese learners' communicative competence with authentic materials. Lang. Learn. **61**(3), 786–819 (2011)
4. Godwin-Jones, R.: Games in language learning: opportunities and challenges. Emerging technologies. Lang. Learn. Technol. **18**(2), 9–19 (2014)
5. Hainey, T., Connolly, T., Stansfield, M., Boyle, E.: The differences in motivations of online game players and offline game players: a combined analysis of three studies at higher education level. Comput. Educ. **57**(4), 2197–2211 (2011)
6. Keller, J.M., Suzuki, K.: Use of the ARCS Motivation Model in Courseware Design. Lawrence Erlbaum Associates Inc., Publishers, New Jersey (1998)
7. Peacock, M.: The effect of authentic materials on the motivation of EFL learners. ELT J. **51** (2), 144–156 (1997)
8. Tang, F., Wang, B., Kaneko, K., Goda, Y., Okada, Y., Yamada, M.: Design of Location-Based Game to Support English Vocabulary Learning in University, Research Report of JSET Conferences, vol. 16-1, pp. 573–580 (2016)
9. Wood, R.T., Griffiths, M.D., Chappell, D., Davies, M.N.: The structural characteristics of video games: a psycho-structural analysis. CyberPsychol. Behav. **7**(1), 1–10 (2004)
10. Wang, B., Tang, F., Kaneko, K., Yamada, M., Okada, Y.: Design and Implementation of Educational Application Framework Supporting Gamification-Based Informal Learning Using Geolocation Information, Research Report of JSET Conferences, vol. 16-1, pp. 569–572 (2016)

Timeline Wiki: Reflections on the Use of an Innovative Teaching Strategy

Aubrey Neil Leveridge(✉)

Vantage College, University of British Columbia, Vancouver, BC, Canada
neil.leveridge@ubc.ca

Abstract. The present paper reflects on a project that investigated the use of an alternative presentation form of a wiki: a timeline wiki. The timeline wiki presents relations and/or linking within the learning content more saliently, possibly reducing the amount of cognitive load, while providing the learner with an overview of the learning content. The curriculum was formed around a CLIL approach through an SFL lens. A learning attitude survey was employed to gather student perceptions on the usability, effectiveness, and satisfaction with the tool. The results suggest that this alternative presentation mode enhanced learner autonomy.

Keywords: Collaboration · Timeline wiki · Learner autonomy · SFL · CLIL

1 Introduction

Collaborative learning, the grouping of students for the purpose of attaining academic goals, has been widely valued in education; however, the integration of collaborative tasks in the classroom remains a struggle for many instructors [1]. Web2.0 tools such as blogs, shared document creation platforms, and wikis have enhanced the classroom integration of collaborative learning. Blogs support the sharing of ideas in collaborative workspaces [2, 3]; shared document creation platforms focus on the updating, modifying and/or replicating of a document [4]; and wikis enable the creation of knowledge content through social collaboration [5]. This development of encyclopedia-like repositories of content knowledge makes wikis a unique tool amongst the three. When learners attend to the collaborative creation of content knowledge, this creative process can facilitate the building of autonomous language learning abilities [6].

Wikis allow for the collaborative construction of repositories of content knowledge. The content knowledge is presented to the reader in the form of articles. To create connections between the articles and to define relationships, hyperlinks are used [7]. Although hyperlinks provide a connection between related materials, the relationship itself remains somewhat abstract. Through hyperlinks, relationships become evident serially, as learners progress through the content. However, this serialism view tends to be less representative of relationship constructs in the real world, which are often more complex and consisting of various elements. As such, over-arching views of multiple relations between various elements may remain elusive when presented serially. In particular, chronological relationships of historical events are generally depicted either

© Springer International Publishing AG 2017
T.-T. Wu et al. (Eds.): SETE 2016, LNCS 10108, pp. 701–711, 2017.
DOI: 10.1007/978-3-319-52836-6_75

through hyperlinks one event at a time or in static timeline graphics limiting the amount of learner control. This type of linking tends to be too abstract for some learners to notice and a cognitive burden to others [8]. In addition, hyperlinks and static timeline graphics may prevent learners from forming a well-defined concept of the scope of the overall learning content [9]. Hence, there is a need for studies that focus on alternative presentation of wikis in which relations within the learning content appear more salient and are less of a cognitive burden. This would allow students to visualize the scope of learning content and making it easier for students to see interrelations/connections, in a multidimensional or dynamic view, thus resulting in greater control of their learning, thus promoting learner autonomy.

The present paper reports on the implementation of a project that investigated the deployment of an alternative presentation form of a wiki: a timeline wiki. Student perceptions following their use of the timeline wiki were collected. This project attempted to discover if the timeline wiki facilitated learner autonomy by: (1) presenting relationships more saliently through multimodal links i.e. the interactive timeline, topic page, and traditional hyperlinks (see Fig. 1); and (2) providing an over-arching view of the wiki content allowing for a better visualization of the course content scope. The remainder of this paper will provide a description of the timeline wiki, the educational setting, the methods of data collection employed, the results and discussion. The paper will end with concluding remarks.

The Timeline Wiki. The timeline wiki proposed by the author, allows for wiki content information to be presented along an interactive timeline with topic pages. This interactive timeline presents content in a more visual and versatile manner allowing the learner to scroll through the content chronologically or by using the more traditional hyperlinks provided (see Fig. 1). Presenting information along an interactive timeline may also have the effect of lessening cognitive load as learners can progress through the timeline seamlessly, at their own pace, controlling their individual progression through the learning content. Learners are not forced to trace their steps back through the wiki, as with the more traditional style of hyperlinks, but can scroll through the content displayed on the timeline.

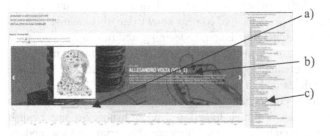

a) Interactive timeline which can be scrolled chronologically

b) topic page

c) hyperlinks

Fig. 1. Timeline wiki with (a) the interactive timeline, (b) topic page, and (c) traditional hyperlinks

The students were first provided with a link to a Google Sheet (a collaborative online spreadsheet) with subject headers and placeholders. Student groups were formed and then each group chose a topic related to major discoveries in Physics and then required to research the topic and upload the content to the appropriate placeholders on a Google Sheet. Google Sheets was chosen because it automatically updates and publishes input by multiple users, in this case, seventy-three users and one course administrator. Also, as a precautionary measure, all the data entered is recorded by Google Sheets and saved on Google Drive, in this way the spreadsheet is backed up and can be reverted to any one of its iterations. As each group uploaded content, they were also required to indicate the date of that the physics discovery occurred. The content, including the date of discovery, was automatically compiled and updated live by Knightlabs (an open-source internet-based tool), ordered chronologically and then automatically published using a Blackboard learning management system (UBC Connect), as seen in Fig. 1. UBC Connect was used as a gateway (see Fig. 2) so the wiki content could be shared with the students while preventing unauthorized access.

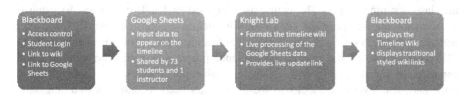

Fig. 2. Timeline wiki access and processing flowchart

The timeline wiki was an ongoing student-centered task in which groups of students were required to research, gather, and build content based on major physics discoveries and then related to experiments they had performed in the physics class or lab. The students are situated as the experts of the content knowledge. As information is posted, it is made public to other students in the course. As such, all students in the course can witness the progression and development of the timeline wiki, the collection of links, and the amount of interactions by other students and/or groups. Witnessing the progression and development of learning content make the course requirements more transparent as students are able to judge individual course involvement comparatively. This may be most beneficial to students who are unsure of the quality of engagement required of them and have not produced an acceptable amount of content or have produced content that is of lower quality. Students are better able to gauge the amount and quality of input required and can proceed on their own.

2 Background and Methodology

In this section, an overview of the current project is provided. This overview includes a description of the courses involved, the language instruction pedagogy, the integration of the timeline wiki, the participants, and the instruments employed.

2.1 Background

The present study is underway at Vantage College (VC) at the University of British Columbia (UBC). VC is a first year program for international students with a strong foundation in English but whose English proficiency is slightly lower than the UBC direct entry requirements. These students are provided with innovative interdisciplinary first-year programs that link core content courses (such as Physics 118) to language instruction and support courses (such as Vant 140). While taking all first year program courses with their Vantage cohort, students are able to improve their academic language proficiency. Upon successful completion of the VC program, students continue into the second year of their chosen programs [9, 10].

2.2 Description of Linked Courses

Physics 118 (PHYS 118) is a first-year introductory physics course focusing on electricity, light and radiation. The course is taught over one accelerated summer semester that lasts for nine weeks. The course is composed of hands-on classes focusing on problem-solving and practical exercises, with demonstrations of electricity and magnetism, electric circuits, and radioactivity applications. This course is analogous to the PHYS118 course offered by the UBC science program as it has the same academic expectations for all assignments, exams and lab reports. The course is taught at the same pace and level of difficulty as the direct-entry sections, albeit with a heightened sensitivity to students' language needs.

Vantage 140 (VANT 140) is the language oriented course associated with PHYS 118. One of the aims of VANT 140 is to help students develop strategies for self-directed learning. This language course is designed to support students as they learn the technical material from the content courses (such as PHYS 118), raising their communication skills to a level that will allow them to succeed in the direct-entry program starting in second year. The assignments and exams in these language courses focus solely on language skills, but in a discipline-specific context, and are evaluated completely independently of the content courses.

This course has been designed to reinforce student learning and advance students' disciplinary literacy through heightened understanding of the links between language and the construction of disciplinary knowledge. By the end of the course, students are able to:

1. identify key features of organization and language use in physics genres typically found in physics texts while using the knowledge of these features to produce effective annotation; for example, students, from their annotations, will be able to explain relevant Physics concepts clearly; describe links to known/related content; present, question, and comment upon conceptual links effectively
2. better understand the language of science (including technical and non-technical vocabulary items and organization and grammar features) and demonstrate their understanding of major physics discoveries and concepts through oral debates

3. deliver a brief oral presentation in which they demonstrate not only a good understanding of key PHYS118 concepts but also an ability to negotiate and communicate effectively with group members.

Students are required to successfully pass both content and language courses in order to complete the program and proceed to the second year of their studies.

2.3 Language Instruction Pedagogy

Vantage College's (VC) approach to curriculum was formed around content and language integrated learning (CLIL). The specific approach to CLIL maintained by the VC Academic English Program utilizes the links between language choices and meanings made in academic contexts. The approach is chiefly informed by Systemic Functional Linguistics (SFL). Through an SFL lens, the relationship between language form and functional meaning becomes evident [11]. In other words, SFL facilitates understanding of how vocabulary and grammar choices that communicators make contribute to the achievement of given communication functions in context, such as how experience is represented, how interpersonal relations are enacted and how texts are organized as described in Hyland's [12] work on disciplinary genre. Examples of common genres in a physics course are a final project report and a lab report. While the elements of a final report may include a descriptive summary of the background and motivation of the project along with analysis and conclusions, a lab report would consist of procedural descriptions and observations. Although both examples are within a discipline-specific genre, each has a generic form which help the genre achieve its specific functions. Successful learners will be able to better understand and participate in academic cultures, by meeting the expectations of peers and professors in their discipline-specific genre.

2.4 The Timeline Wiki and Pedagogical Approaches

The timeline wiki is a collaborative project designed for first-year international students' learning experience. The successful completion of the collaborative project requires social interaction in the target language. Social interaction is essential for language learning as language learning can be described as the outcome of a co-construction of knowledge, rather than individually constructed knowledge [13–15]. The co-creation of the timeline wiki requires students to engage in the target language within the discipline-specific genre. Moreover, the timeline wiki provides students with a forum to: (1) communicate co-constructed knowledge using genre-specific language; (2) create meaning using language choices specific to the genre, and (3) position themselves as experts while participating in an academic culture. Such provisions may facilitate autonomous language learning.

2.5   Integration of Online Wiki Timeline Component

This subsection outlines the integration of the timeline wiki into the VANT 140 course. The students were required to engage with the learning content from the associated PHYS 118 and re-contextualize the material to co-construct wiki articles. The students then relied on these articles as constructs of knowledge from which to base in-class debates.

1. Annotation Skills: students were required to annotate specific readings from the physics textbook. The readings annotated were explanations of the concepts related to either the lab work or in-class experiments in PHYS 118. These experiments are derivatives from substantial research contributions made by pioneering physicists.
2. Introduction to the Timeline Wiki project: Small groups consisting of four or five students were assigned and topics chosen. Topics were based on pioneering physicists who made substantial research contributions in the realm of electricity, light and radiation.
3. Timeline creation: Groups published the first draft of wiki content based on the annotations made in their textbook, research on their assigned physicist with links to current-day applications of their discoveries.
4. Introduction to Commenting, i.e. Errors/Missing information/Enhancement: Wiki readers provided comments in regards to wiki content and language use from which the wiki writers could revise their wiki article.
5. Revision of wiki content and further research of topic.
6. Introduction to Debate: Students prepared debates based on the content groups provided in the timeline wiki on background and links between physicists, physics concepts and current day applications.
7. In-class debates: Students remained in assigned groups and debated the merits of their chosen physicist's contributions to current-day applications. Students were only able to use information that had been posted on the timeline wiki.
8. In-class debates: Student audience were required to participate as judges and critiques of the debates.
9. In-class debates: Student audience were required to ask debaters pertinent questions in regards to the topic at hand.

2.6   Participants

A total of seventy-three students were registered in three VANT140 (for Physics) courses. These students were also attending the aforementioned PHYS118 course. Upon entry to VC, students had achieved an average IELTS score between 5.5–6.5.

2.7   Instruments

The two instruments employed in the current study were the aforementioned timeline wiki and a learning attitude survey.

Learning Attitude Survey. The learning attitude survey was adapted from Aydin and Yildiz's [15] questionnaire, which covers overall learning, motivation, group interaction and the use of technology on wikis. The survey was divided into three sections: usability, effectiveness, and satisfaction. A total of thirty-four questions were formed to draw out the learners' perceptions of: the saliency of presentation modes, the links and relationships; the ability to visualize the scope of content, and overall satisfaction in regards to using the timeline wiki. The level of learner autonomy that the timeline wiki affords is mirrored by the results indicated in each of the sections. In other words, responses to survey items that depict a high level of individual engagement in the target language while collaborating and/or viewing the timeline wiki, would suggest that higher levels of autonomous learning are taking place.

To avoid bias, the survey was conducted after the last class had taken place and was both voluntary and anonymous.

3 Results and Discussion

This section will detail and discuss the results from the content students produced in the wiki and the results from the adapted learning attitude survey in regards to the usability, effectiveness, and satisfaction of the timeline wiki. These three items reflect the facilitation of autonomous language learning.

3.1 The Timeline Wiki Content

As previously mentioned, the collaborative creation of content knowledge can facilitate autonomous language learning. Therefore, it is important to consider the timeline wiki in light of the collaboration that took place to produce the final iteration. The final iteration of the timeline wiki indicates that the students achieved the language-specific course goals through the collaborative creation, production, and revision, genre-specific content knowledge.

Collaborations tend to be evident in most cases, yet difficult to detect in others. Collaboration involving writing, posting, and revisions of textual content is tracked by the timeline wiki software and is thus apparent. However, evidence of collaborations involving videos or animations tend to be more elusive. The timeline wiki only records the identity of the student who uploads a video. The collaborative efforts of the group, including the initial concept, the writing of the script, and the production of the video/animation, were not recorded. As such, what may appear as an individual effort may actually involve the collaboration of the entire group.

Some groups produced videos of themselves doing physics experiments featuring a monologue of the processes involved in the experiment. These monologues included mentions of (links to) other topics or physicists within the timeline wiki. However, because these links were made verbally, they may be more easily missed by the viewer. Future considerations should be made for the provision of links within videos (or animations) so that the associations made are more salient.

3.2   The Learning Attitude Survey Results

A total of 43 responses to the survey were gathered; however, not all participants answered all questions. In terms of usability, effectiveness, and satisfaction, the timeline wiki was generally successful, which also suggests that learner autonomy was facilitated.

Usability: According to the results most of the students (67%) indicated that the timeline wiki was easy to use and did not require added mental effort (see Table 1). However, some students (18%) indicated that the timeline wiki was rigid and inflexible to work with. This result may stem from the current software limitations. For example, some students stated that the timeline wiki was rigid because images could not be directly posted. Posting images required a hyperlink for the image to appear.

Table 1. Usability

	n	Strongly disagree	Disagree	Neutral	Agree	Strongly agree
Ease of use	43	0	1	13	27	2
Flexibility of use	43	0	8	19	16	0
Cognitive load	43	2	13	15	12	1
Instability	43	2	19	11	8	3

A perception of cognitive load increase was indicated by 2 students. However, this could stem from the novelty of the timeline wiki or learning content. Eleven responses indicated that the timeline wiki was fragile or unstable. This indication may stem from the use of Google Sheets. Some students had difficulties in regards to posting content within the restrictions, boundaries, or limitations imposed by the Google Sheets template. If data was incorrectly entered on the template or the data was of the incorrect type, the timeline wiki would be displayed incorrectly or not at all.

Slightly less than half of the students (48%) indicated that the timeline wiki was effective in supporting critical aspects of their physics studies, while seventeen were neutral, and five disagreed (See Table 2). A higher number of students (62%) found that the timeline wiki increased their English language learning. This increase suggests that students were involved in producing genre-specific language which was new or novel to them. An example of this is one student-group's explanation of Gauss's Law. The genre-specific language was re-contextualized in student-created drawings that depicted the physics law in action along with supporting textual explanations. Several students provided positive comments on the addition of the drawings and how these drawings supported their understanding of Gauss's Law. Only one response (2%) indicated that intended language learning outcomes were not reached. More than half the students (62%) indicated that the collaboration required to complete the timeline wiki was effective in enhancing language and physics content knowledge.

Overall satisfaction was reported by more than 60% of the respondents while less than 10% were dissatisfied (see Table 3). There were only four indications that learning

Table 2. Effectiveness

	n	Strongly disagree	Disagree	Neutral	Agree	Strongly agree
Physics studies	42	0	5	17	19	1
English learning outcomes	42	0	1	15	26	0
Collaboration	42	0	7	9	23	3

goals were not achieved through the use of the timeline wiki. It is unclear if these findings are related to the physics or language content of the course as that was outside the scope of the current project. Collaboration was generally positive with only seven negative responses. These negative responses may be due to the demands of the tasks or due to social strains caused by individual differences or personality clashes.

Table 3. Satisfaction

	n	Strongly disagree	Disagree	Neutral	Agree	Strongly agree
General satisfaction	42	2	2	12	23	3
Learning goals	42	1	3	19	17	2
Collaboration	42	2	5	15	18	2

The findings suggest that learner autonomy is supported. The results indicate that 57% of the students (see Table 4) perceive the multimodal links afforded by the timeline wiki as creating more saliency whereas less than 10% would disagree. Some students indicated that the interactive nature and visual fluency of the timeline wiki allowed the discovery of links that might otherwise go unnoticed. The same number of students were able to recall physics concepts that were on the timeline wiki more easily. A majority of responses (62%) indicated that personal physics understanding and discoveries were made. In addition, a total of 28 students (68%) indicated an increased awareness and visualization of the course content and scope.

These results show promise but must be considered within the limitations of the study. Considerations to the small number of responses, slightly more than half of the participants, may not be generalized to entire cohort. Also, there were many neutral

Table 4. Autonomy

	n	Strongly disagree	Disagree	Neutral	Agree	Strongly agree
Saliency	42	0	4	14	21	3
Recollection of concepts	42	0	4	14	21	3
Physics understanding	42	0	3	13	26	0
Personal discovery of physics concepts	42	0	1	12	25	4
Overarching view	41	0	2	11	24	4

responses. Three survey participants were removed because all responses were recorded as neutral. Furthermore, the analysis of the quality of the language use in the timeline wiki is not within the scope of the current report and thus has not been included.

4 Conclusion

In this report, a proposed timeline wiki was introduced and results of a related survey discussed. While the timeline wiki and survey results described in this paper do indicate positive potential for educational applications which facilitate learner autonomy, one must consider that the timeline wiki is still in the creation stage. A proposal for a new software version of the timeline will be presented to fourth year computer engineering students as a final graduation group-project. This new software version will be a complete package that will not rely on external websites, will be integrated with the learning management system, i.e. Blackboard, and store all data locally, within the university's info-space. In addition to the software design, the human-computer interactions and drawbacks indicated by survey responses will also be further explored. Once these creations and adjustments have been made, further applications and empirical testing can be undertaken.

References

1. Zheng, B., Niiya, M., Warschauer, M.: Wikis and collaborative learning in higher education. Technol. Pedagogy Educ. **24**(3), 357–374 (2015)
2. Dabbagh, N., Kitsantas, A.: Personal learning environments, social media, and self-regulated learning: a natural formula for connecting formal and informal learning. Internet High. Educ. **15**(1), 3–8 (2012)
3. Yang, J.C., Quadir, B., Chen, N.S., Miao, Q.: Effects of online presence on learning performance in a blog-based online course. Internet High. Educ. **30**, 11–20 (2016)
4. Ahmad, M., Imine, A.: Decentralized collaborative editing platform. In: 2015 16th IEEE International Conference on Mobile Data Management, vol. 1, pp. 323–326. IEEE (2015)
5. Wheeler, S., Yeomans, P., Wheeler, R.D.: The good, the bad and the wiki: evaluating student-generated content for collaborative learning. Br. J. Educ. Technol. **39**(6), 987–995 (2008)
6. Kessler, G., Bikowski, D.: Developing collaborative autonomous learning abilities in computer mediated language learning: attention to meaning among students in wiki space. Comput. Assist. Lang. Learn. **23**(1), 41–58 (2010)
7. Lahti, L.: Computational method for supporting learning with cumulative vocabularies, conceptual networks and Wikipedia linkage. Int. J. Cross-Disciplinary Subj. Educ. (IJCDSE) **5**(2), 1632–1644 (2014). Shoniregun, C., Cooper, R. (eds.)
8. Hu, P., Huang, M.L., Zhu, X.Y.: Exploring the interactions of storylines from informative news events. J. Comput. Sci. Technol. **29**(3), 502–518 (2014)
9. Vantage College. https://vantagecollege.ubc.ca/

10. Murphy, M., Potvin, G.: Building bridges: an approach to the integration of English language education in first-year applied science courses for international students. In: Proceedings of the Canadian Engineering Education Association (in press)
11. Halliday, M.A.K.: The notion of "context" in language education. In: Ghadessy, M. (ed.) Text and Context in Functional Linguistics, pp. 1–24. John Benjamins, Amsterdam (1999)
12. Hyland, K.: Disciplinary Discourse, Michigan Classics Edition: Social Interactions in Academic Writing. University of Michigan Press, Ann Arbor (2004)
13. Vygotsky, L.S.: Mind in Society: The Development of Higher Psychological Processes. Harvard University Press, Cambridge (1980)
14. Lantolf, J.P.: Sociocultural Theory and Second Language Learning. Oxford University Press, Oxford (2000)
15. Aydın, Z., Yıldız, S.: Using wikis to promote collaborative EFL writing. Lang. Learn. Technol. 18(1), 160–180 (2014)

An Investigation into English Language Learners' Argumentative Writing Performance and Perceptions

Hsiu-Ting Hung[1], Hui-Chin Yeh[2($\boxtimes$)], and Chun-Hao Chou[1]

[1] National Kaohsiung First University of Science and Technology,
Kaohsiung, Taiwan
hhung@nkfust.edu.tw
[2] National Yunlin University of Science and Technology, Douliu, Taiwan
hyeh@yuntech.edu.tw

Abstract. The current study aimed to understand the feasibility of using an adapted version of a well-established model of argumentation, termed as the *Assertion, Reasoning,* and *Evidence* (ARE) model in the present study, for argumentative writing instruction in an English language classroom. Seventy-six university students were given explicit instruction on English argumentative writing using the ARE model for a semester. After the instructional intervention, two sets of data were collected, including the participants' argumentative writing passages and their responses to a post-intervention questionnaire. The results showed that although the students provided highly positive feedback on both the instructional intervention and their self-efficacy in English argumentative writing, the analysis of the students' argumentative writing performance indicated that many of the participants were unable to produce logical and reasonable arguments. This paper concludes that while the ARE model is potentially helpful, when teaching argumentative writing to second or foreign language learners, teachers should be aware of their students' difficulties in reasoning and thus place more emphasis on training logical reasoning skills in argumentation, as a means to enable its effective use by learners.

Keywords: Argumentative writing · Writing instruction · English as a foreign language

1 Introduction

Argumentation is one of the foundational academic competencies necessary for success in higher education [1]. Given that argumentation is a complex skill, many learners often fail to achieve successful outcomes without adequate training and guidance on how to think critically and make logical arguments [2]. Many educators and researchers have thus applied a well-established model of argumentation developed by Stephen Toulmin [3, 4] to promote students' learning and development of argumentation [5–10].

However, the Toulmin model contains a complex structure of six elements: *claim, warrant, data, backing, qualifier,* and *rebuttal* [3, 4], which can be challenging for students. When applied to argumentative writing instruction, the complexity of this

© Springer International Publishing AG 2017
T.-T. Wu et al. (Eds.): SETE 2016, LNCS 10108, pp. 712–720, 2017.
DOI: 10.1007/978-3-319-52836-6_76

model may even undermine its effectiveness, especially for learners who are first introduced to this writing genre. For instance, some studies have found that the elements of backing, qualifier, and rebuttal are rarely found or are poorly implemented in students' argumentative writing [11, 12]. Other studies have reported that beginners encounter difficulties in providing warrants or reasoning [13, 14].

With an understanding that the Toulmin model is often used with some difficulty and thus should be modified to accommodate learners' needs and readiness [15], we used an adapted version proposed by [16], termed as the Assertion, Reasoning, and Evidence (ARE) model in the present study. In their explication of the ARE model, [16] described *assertion* as a statement (corresponding to the Toulmin element of *claim*), *reasoning* as the contention of why the statement is valid (corresponding to the Toulmin element of *warrant*), and *evidence* as the proof of this validity (corresponding to the Toulmin element of *data*). According to the ARE model, logical reasoning is the heart of effective argumentation because it establishes the connection between an assertion and evidence. We believe that the adapted version of the Toulmin framework (i.e., the ARE model) makes the argumentation structure more comprehensible and applicable to the abilities of novice learners.

Among various practices of argumentation in education, this study focuses on argumentative writing, which refers to the writing style that requires writers to investigate a topic, gather evidence, analyze information, and then formulate an opinion concerning the topic to persuade readers. To better understand the feasibility of the proposed ARE model for argumentative writing instruction in an English as a foreign language (EFL) context, the following research questions were investigated: (1) How did students perform in argumentative writing after explicit instruction using the ARE model? (2) How did students perceive the argumentative writing instruction based on the ARE model?

2 Method

2.1 Participants

Seventy-six sophomores at a Taiwanese university, aged 19 or 20, were recruited to participate in this study. All the participants were native speakers of Mandarin Chinese, who had received formal English education for approximately eight years. They were English majors with intermediate proficiency, as determined by their self-reported scores of English proficiency tests at the time of this investigation.

The participants were enrolled in a Science and Technology in Society (STS) class, in which English was the medium of instruction. The course objective was to improve the critical thinking skills of students by discussing controversial issues in society, while simultaneously developing their argumentation skills in English, with a focus on argumentative writing. Although they had taken skill-based English courses, the participants had not previously received formal training in argumentation and so were considered novice learners of this subject.

2.2   Instructional Design

The participants received writing instruction during one 30-minute period weekly over the course of an 18-week semester; the remaining class time was spent reading and discussing STS topics. Argumentative writing instruction was based on the key principles of the ARE model. The reading material used in the course was selected from the *60-Second Science* website, which is a part of the official website of the *Scientific American* magazine. Four main topics were covered in the course: mind, technology, health, and environment. The participants were first given explicit instruction on how to form an argumentative writing passage using the triad structure of assertion, reasoning, and evidence based on the ARE model. Next, they performed four sets of guided practice, one for each of the main topics of the course. At the end of the instructional intervention, the participants were instructed to complete a summative assessment in the form of a reading-to-write task to evaluate their learning performance of English argumentative writing. The selected texts for the reading-to-write task were of a similar readability level and length to those used in the training and practice of argumentative writing in the course.

In completing the reading-to-write task, the participants had to read a 200-word text using an online learning tool, *Diigo*, and base on the reading material to compose an argumentative writing passage through the ARE model. To assist the students' reading and writing processes, *Diigo* was adopted to provide them with a range of useful functions, such as bookmarking, annotating, and editing.

2.3   Data Collection and Analysis

Two sets of data were collected in this study to answer the two research questions on student perceptions and performance of argumentative writing, respectively. One data set comprised the students' responses to an eight-item Likert-scale questionnaire, which was developed by the research team and reviewed by two English writing instructors to enhance its content validity. The questionnaire was administered to the students after their completion of the reading-to-write task. A descriptive statistical analysis was performed on the 70 returned questionnaires (92.1% response rate) to determine the students' perceptions of this instructional intervention.

The other data set contained 76 argumentative writing passages composed by the participants for the reading-to-write task, which were used for assessing their performance of argumentative writing after the instructional intervention. In analyzing the qualitative data of student work, a content analysis method was used for examining the presence and logical coherence of the desired argumentative elements (i.e., assertion, reasoning, and evidence) in the written passages for determining whether the passages were appropriate and well structured. The identification of the three focal elements mostly depended on the students' explicit use of discourse markers, such as "I believe," "we should," "because," and "according to research." When the student writers only implied their opinions, their semantic structures were examined for logical thought. It should be noted that grammar was not evaluated because linguistic accuracy was not a focus of this study. The content analysis went through a process of double coding, in which two researchers first coded the data independently and then used the preliminary coding results for processing the second coding, in order to ensure the reliability of the analytical results (inter-rater reliability = 0.83).

3 Results

3.1 Student Performance in Argumentative Writing

Based on the structure and content of the students' argumentative writing, three major patterns emerged. In this section, we discuss representative excerpts illustrating these patterns. The student writers' use of assertion, reasoning, and evidence in argumentation is indicated in brackets immediately following the associated sentences.

- *Pattern 1: Good structure of argumentation with good quality reasoning*

Approximately 40% of the analyzed written passages were considered to be well-constructed argumentative writing, in which an assertion clearly indicated the writer's claim, reasoning clarified the writer's explanation for the assertion, and evidence supported the reasoning by presenting proof.

Excerpt 1:
I think that owners of pacemakers should consider donating their pacemakers if they don't need to use them anymore.[Assertion] The main reason is that the high price of pacemakers is not affordable for many people, particularly those from less developed countries.[Reasoning] Recent research has shown that every year one to two million people would die simply because of the fact that they don't have enough money to buy pacemakers.[Evidence] As a result, pacemaker users should donate their spare devices to those in need in order to save millions of poor people's lives.[Assertion]

Pattern 2: Good structure of argumentation with poor quality reasoning

Approximately 43% of the analyzed written passages were considered to have an effective structure of argumentation, with the three elements of assertion, reasoning, and evidence; however, the reasoning quality in these written passages was rated as weak. The most common error that the students made was not providing appropriate evidence for their reasoning. For instance, most students identified the high cost of pacemakers as the supportive reasoning for why people should donate their pacemakers after they no longer need them. However, the students did not support their reasoning by providing pertinent evidence focused on the problem of high cost; instead, most students mentioned the low infection rate in pacemaker transplant operations or the willingness of former pacemaker users to donate their unwanted devices. The following excerpt is a typical example of such an error pattern, in which the reasoning and evidence are incomplete and disconnected.

Excerpt 2:
We should support pacemaker recycling.[Assertion] It is because that many patients with heart diseases cannot afford this expensive life-saving device.[Reasoning] According to the research paper, 84% heart patients agree to donate their pacemakers

after they no longer need them. [Evidence] In addition, small humanitarian efforts at recycling proved that the infection rate is the same as new ones.[Evidence] Therefore, as long as families consent to donate pacemakers, they will be sent to people insufficient for financial help around the world to save more lives after being sterilized and wiped free of the former patient's information.[Assertion]

Another common error that the students made was not providing strong and justifiable reasoning to support their assertion. This is illustrated in the following excerpt, in which the assertion and reasoning are incoherent. Because cleanliness and safety do not imply that patients requiring a pacemaker should use a recycled pacemaker, people may still consider buying a new pacemaker if they can afford one.

Excerpt 3:
Person who needs a pacemaker should use a recycled pacemaker [Assertion] due to its cleanness and safeness.[Reasoning] Because the recycled device is sterilized and wiped free of the former patient's information by a cardiovascular center which investigated pacemaker recycling.[Reasoning] Humanitarian efforts have found that the infection rate is about 2 percent with repurposed devices, the same as for new ones.[Evidence] Therefore, people in need can use a recycled pacemaker safe and sound.[Assertion]

Pattern 3: Poor structure of argumentation with no clear reasoning

Although the majority of the written passages conformed closely to the argument structure of assertion, reasoning, and evidence, a few passages (17%) did not have the critical element of reasoning. Furthermore, not all of the presented elements in these writing passages were coherent. Excerpt 4 shows such an error pattern.

Excerpt 4:
In my opinion, pacemaker owners should donate their pacemakers after they decease, without worrying about infection.[Assertion] If pacemakers donate their devices, they can help reduce the death rate.[Assertion] According to research, the infection rates of new and recycled pacemakers are both two percent.[Evidence] So, pacemaker owners should donate their devices.[Assertion]

The initial sentence in Excerpt 4 was not considered as an acceptable assertion because it was incomprehensible to readers. According to the initial sentence, because most pacemakers are donated after the users die, the donors have no reason to worry about infection. The second sentence did not provide any reasoning or evidence for the first sentence or indicate the causal relationship between the need to donate and its impact on reducing the death rate from a lack of access to such devices. Subsequently, the writer shifted the focus to the problem of infection caused by recycled pacemakers, and the third sentence can be considered evidence of the first assertion, although these two are not presented consecutively. In the last sentence, the writer reinforces the opinion of the advisability of donating pacemakers. Although this statement corresponds to what the writer claimed in the initial sentence, it is a repetition rather than a presentation of reasoning to support the opinion. In other words, effective reasoning was missing throughout. In brief, the writer made a few assertions in this passage but provided little reasoning and evidence to support them.

3.2   Student Perceptions of the Argumentative Writing Instruction

Although the content analysis of argumentative writing revealed unsatisfactory performance of some participants, the questionnaire results suggested that the participants had high levels of satisfaction and perceived positive effects from the explicit instruction on argumentation using the ARE model. The participants were highly satisfied with every aspect of the instruction (see Table 1). The range and mean scores for each questionnaire item (as rated on a five-point Likert scale on which 5 = strongly agree and 1 = strongly disagree) were as follows.

Table 1. Descriptive statistics of the post-intervention questionnaire

Questionnaire item	Min.	Max.	Mean	SD
1. The implementation of the ARE model met the course objectives	3	5	4.49	0.55
2. This course enabled me to develop my higher-order thinking skills	3	5	4.49	0.58
3. The materials used in the course effectively explained concepts and strategies for argumentative writing	2	5	4.39	0.66
4. The instructional design of this course was innovative	3	5	4.49	0.65
5. The instructor effectively taught argumentative writing strategies in this course	3	5	4.44	0.62
6. The ARE model adopted in this course was understandable and helpful for my learning	3	5	4.46	0.63
7. This course enhanced my competence in argumentative writing	3	5	4.41	0.64
8. This course increased my interest in the study of argumentative writing	3	5	4.30	0.66

Regarding the instructional intervention, 97% of the students felt that the implementation of the ARE model met the course objective (M = 4.49, SD = 0.55), 91% indicated that the instructional design of this course was innovative (M = 4.49, SD = 0.65), and 93% considered that the ARE model was understandable and helpful for their learning (M = 4.46, SD = 0.63). In addition, the teaching performance of the instructor was well received by the majority of the students, as 93% felt that the instructor effectively taught argumentative writing strategies (M = 4.44, SD = 0.62), and 93% stated that the texts and worksheets were effectively used for explaining the various concepts and strategies for argumentative writing (M = 4.39, SD = 0.66). The questionnaire results also showed a positive impact of the instructional intervention on the students' learning motivation and self-efficacy. To be more specific, 96% of the students indicated that the course enabled them to develop their higher-order thinking skills (M = 4.49, SD = 0.58), 91% indicated that the course enhanced their competence in argumentative writing (M = 4.41, SD = 0.64), and 89% indicated that the course increased their interest in the study of argumentative writing (M = 4.30, SD = 0.66). Overall, the students reported being highly satisfied with the instructional design, instructor, and teaching material. They also considered themselves more confident and skilled in argumentative writing after taking the course.

4 Discussion

The finding that explicit instruction on argumentation was well received by the participants is similar to those of previous studies. For example, in the study of [17] the students felt that argumentative writing instruction helped them construct more organized and conceptualized arguments. In another study, [18] observed that the students responded positively to instruction on argumentation and regarded it as useful for improving their argumentative writing. However, despite the current study revealed the participants' positive perceptions of the instructional intervention, their learning outcomes were not quite satisfactory. This finding is consistent with that of [14], suggesting that warrant in the Toulmin model or reasoning in the ARE model are areas in which students improve the least or develop last. Because our participants did not receive any prior instruction on argumentation, they may have been at early stages in developing reasoning skills and may have encountered learning difficulties in this single instructional intervention. Thus, their limited achievement in the development of argumentative writing, especially with regard to reasoning, is perhaps unsurprising.

Underdeveloped logical reasoning skills were the probable main cause for the students' weak performance in argumentative writing. By analyzing the students' argumentative writing passages, it was found that problem areas were all related to reasoning, such as reasoning not justifying the assertion, reasoning not being supported by evidence, and reasoning being absent from the ARE structure. Echoing previous research [14, 19, 20], the current study suggests that mastering logical reasoning skills, which is challenging for novice learners of argumentative writing, is even more difficult for those who must express their argument in a second or foreign language.

For Taiwanese EFL writers, the stylistic influence of their first language (L1) might also undermine their English argumentative writing. Compared with the deductive and direct English style of writing, the Chinese style is more inductive and indirect. For instance, [21] observed that Taiwanese student writers tend to avoid providing what they perceive as overly detailed information in their writing because they assume that readers can interpret the meaning and intention. In a cross-cultural comparative study, [22] found that American students supported their ideas more explicitly and acknowledged the exceptions to their claims by considering different perspectives or counter arguments, whereas Taiwanese students focused on their own point and argued in an implicit manner. These stylistic differences as well as linguistic limitations may explain why many of the participants could not clearly form an opinion and follow the prescribed structure of argumentation.

5 Conclusion

We reported the use of explicit instruction in an adapted Toulmin model of argumentation for enhancing the development of argumentative writing of university EFL learners. The results showed that although the students provided highly positive feedback on both the instructional intervention and their self-efficacy in English argumentative writing, the analysis of the students' argumentative writing performance indicated that many of the participants were unable to produce logical and reasonable arguments. The overall research findings have led us to the conclusion that while the proposed ARE model is potentially helpful, when teaching argumentative writing to second or foreign language learners, teachers should be aware of their students' difficulties in reasoning and thus place more emphasis on training logical reasoning skills in argumentation, as a means to enable its effective use by learners.

References

1. Andrews, R.: Argumentation in higher education: improving practice through theory and research. Routledge, New York (2010)
2. Faigley, L., Selzer, J.: Good Reasons with Contemporary Arguments. Allyn & Bacon, Boston (2000)
3. Toulmin, S.: The Uses of Argument. Cambridge University Press, Cambridge (1958)
4. Toulmin, S.: The Uses of Argument, 2nd edn. Cambridge University Press, Cambridge (2003)
5. Bacha, N.N.: Teaching the academic argument in a university EFL environment. J. Engl. Acad. Purp. 9(3), 229–241 (2010)
6. Berland, L.K., Reiser, B.J.: How classroom communities make sense of the practice of scientific argumentation. Sci. Educ. 95(2), 191–216 (2011)
7. Cavagnetto, A.R.: Argument to foster scientific literacy: a review of argument interventions in K-12 science contexts. Rev. Educ. Res. 80(3), 336–371 (2010)
8. Driver, R., Newton, P., Osborne, J.: Establishing the norms of scientific argumentation in classrooms. Sci. Educ. 84(3), 287–312 (2000)
9. Erduran, S., Simon, S., Osborne, J.: TAPping into argumentation: Developments in the application of Toulmin's Argument Pattern for studying science discourse. Sci. Educ. 88(6), 915–933 (2004)
10. Lunsford, K.J.: Contextualizing Toulmin's model in the writing classroom: a case study. Writ. Commun. 19(1), 109–174 (2002)
11. Crammond, J.: The uses and complexity of argument structures in expert and student persuasive writing. Writ. Commun. 15(2), 230–268 (1998)
12. Qin, J., Karabacak, E.: The analysis of Toulmin elements in Chinese EFL university argumentative writing. System 38(3), 444–456 (2010)
13. Sadler, T.D.: Informal reasoning regarding socioscientific issues: a critical review of research. J. Res. Sci. Teach. 41(5), 513–536 (2004)
14. Stapleton, P., Wu, Y.A.: Assessing the quality of arguments in students' persuasive writing: a case study analyzing the relationship between surface structure and substance. J. Engl. Acad. Purp. 17(1), 12–23 (2015)
15. Fulkerson, R.: The Toulmin model of argument and the teaching of composition. In: Emmel, B., Resch, P., Tenney, D. (eds.) Argument Revisited, Argument Redefined: Negotiating Meaning in the Composition Classroom, pp. 45–72. Sage, Thousand Oaks (1996)
16. Meany, J., Shuster, K.: On that Point!: An Introduction to Parliamentary Debate. International Debate Education Association, New York (2003)
17. Yeh, S.S.: Empowering education: teaching argumentative writing to cultural minority middle-school students. Res. Teach. Engl. 33(1), 49–83 (1998)
18. Cheng, F.W.: A socio-cognitive modeling approach to teaching English argumentation. Asian ESP J. 6(1), 120–146 (2010)

19. Hirose, K.: Comparing L1 and L2 organizational patterns in the argumentative writing of Japanese EFL students. J. Second Lang. Writ. **12**(2), 181–209 (2003)
20. Kobayashi, H., Rinnert, C.: Task response and text construction across L1 and L2 writing. J. Second Lang. Writ. **17**(1), 7–29 (2008)
21. Chien, S.C.: Discourse organization in high school students' writing and their teachers' writing instruction: the case of Taiwan. Foreign Lang. Ann. **44**(2), 417–435 (2011)
22. Cheng, F.W., Chen, Y.M.: Taiwanese argumentation skills: contrastive rhetoric perspective. Taiwan Int. ESP J. **1**(1), 23–50 (2009)

Lessons from Six Years of Online Proficiency Testing Associated with the Freshman and Sophomore English Course in a Technology University

Gloria Shu Mei Chwo[✉]

Department of Applied English, Hungkuang University,
Taichung, Taiwan
schwo@hk.edu.tw

Abstract. Since 2010, HungKuang university in Taiwan, which teaches almost entirely through the medium of Chinese, has undertaken an increasingly intensive program of twice yearly online English testing of freshman and sophomore students, using both the Bridge and Full Test of English for International Communication (TOEIC) in mock and real versions. The purpose is to inform the institution, English staff, and students themselves about the developing English proficiency of the students and plan future policies accordingly, so as to not only meet ever increasing external demands for graduates with good English but also to propose potential innovating plan for future English course. A preliminary analysis of more than 4000 students' online assessment results found the overall mean proficiency is well below the institutional target of minimum total score 350. Pedagogical implication was proposed to innovate the online learning and testing platform in order to meet the challenge of future course planning.

Keywords: Freshman and sophomore english course · TOEIC test · Online testing · Listening and reading

1 Introduction

This paper reports on six years of English language online proficiency testing of students at a technological university in central Taiwan, and the thinking that it prompts about how best to use English testing at tertiary level in such a context. Since the testing was undertaken for pedagogical and institutional rather than pure research purposes, much of what the tests show naturally has prime significance for stakeholders at the university where the testing was done. However, we aim here to highlight points which we feel have some interest for a wider international audience of those involved in English language testing. In particular we feel that the context, described next, is similar to contexts in many countries round the world where English is a foreign rather than second language, yet is taught to students of all majors at university, and that the test we adopted, TOEIC, is also one widely used. We have not however found any other accounts of extended use of TOEIC in such contexts, in relation to the real issues that are important there.

© Springer International Publishing AG 2017
T.-T. Wu et al. (Eds.): SETE 2016, LNCS 10108, pp. 721–726, 2017.
DOI: 10.1007/978-3-319-52836-6_77

2 English Testing at HungKuang

Prior to 2010, English proficiency was tested using mock versions of the locally accepted Taiwanese General English Proficiency Test (GEPT), and indeed this sort of testing also continues now. The TOEIC program of testing began in 2010 because it was felt that an internationally valid test was required to serve as a convincing indicator of the university's capacity to compete in the globalized world arena, and because TOEIC was better targeted on the type of English that the students need. This matches the trend towards taking TOEIC in Taiwan in general, where numbers of takers of the full TOEIC have risen from around 68,000 in 2005 to nearly 344,000 in 2014. Again, in line with an increasing world trend, online testing was implemented.

The main purposes of the testing could be summed up as:

- to provide information to the institution, English teachers and students about what proficiency levels are currently attained,
- in the freshman and sophomore years, to provide test taking practice for the students, who are required to take an official full TOEIC from ETS later, to demonstrate achievement of the score required of university graduates,
- to guide decision making about where to invest resources in future to improve proficiency cost effectively, with respect to:
  - English teaching (how well is the current system performing? how many hours are needed? of the current sort or more ESP? with what sort of grouping of learners into classes (by proficiency level or by major...)? etc.)
  - English language testing (how often? what test?),
- consequently to improve the standing of the university, which is partly judged against other universities from its published student TOEIC scores, which are used as an international quality indicator,
- to be able to offer a subsidy to students who attain a certain target TOEIC score before graduation and thus increase the percentage of those who do this, which will assist the university in obtaining MOE grants to further promote English proficiency,
- to enable the internationalization of the campus so as to be able attract students from English speaking countries,
- and to equip the students better to function in a globally competitive world, given the TOEIC score requirements of major businesses in Taiwan.

The university in fact currently sets a full TOEIC target to be achieved by graduation from the university of 550 for English major students and 350 for non-English majors. 550 equates with B1 in the CEFR, as described above, and is quite a modest target for English majors given that, for example, the average mainland China score, and the average requirement of major employers in Taiwan, is over 100 points higher and so closer to B2 or upper intermediate. 350 is between A2 and B1 - in fact closer to A2 (officially corresponding to a full TOEIC score of 225) than to B1 (550). A2 is the upper end of 'basic user') and is characterised for listening and reading as: "Can understand sentences and frequently used expressions related to areas of most immediate relevance (e.g. very basic personal and family information, shopping, local geography, employment). Can communicate in simple and routine tasks requiring a simple and direct exchange of information on familiar and routine matters.". Clearly this is also quite a modest target for non-English major students given the general Taiwan average for technological universities of full TOEIC 415 in 2014, and the world average of 450 in that year, together with the likely level of English needed in many future jobs the students might do. However, in fact it represents an increase on an earlier 2014 target of 250, which was raised following external reviewer comments.

In the freshman and sophomore years, tests of both Full and Bridge TOEIC have been used, together with mock versions of both (only with full time students). The university subscribes to the American Magazine Center (AMC) website which supplies TOEIC tests online especially to the Chinese speaking market: AMC purchases back TOEIC tests from ETS and makes them available together with mock tests and other TOEIC practice resources. Mock Bridge TOEIC lasts 50 min, fitting the English lesson at HungKuang University. It includes 25 multiple choice items on listening comprehension and 25 on reading comprehension. The number of correct responses in each part is converted so that adding the two section scores together gives a total score on a scale ranging 0 to 100. The aim is for students to obtain practice from using these online resources in the freshman and sophomore years. Due to the limited space in computer rooms, the plan is to give students a mock TOEIC Bridge on a semester basis. There are 12 rounds of mock tests on the AMC e-learning site, where students have access to practicing online. We hope that through this, students can become familiar with the online mock versions of TOEIC and take either real Bridge or full TOEIC by graduation. Students have to take real TOEIC tests officially from ETS, at their own decided time and at their own expense, by the year of their graduation. If they achieve the required score before graduation, the university will reward them financially or waive their freshman or sophomore English credits (only for full time students). If not, they have to retake a free course, English grammar and writing, or else they will not be allowed to graduate, which is a serious penalty for non-English major students.

Most tests during the freshman and sophomore years were delivered online and taken by students in university computer laboratories. The mock tests were however not always taken in controlled conditions. Some teachers let students take the test at home, so unknown sources of help may have been used, and they are not scored on the official TOEIC scales. Table 1 shows the numbers of TOEIC test takers that we have stored record for, from 2010 onwards. On the most recent four testing occasions, where most of the data comes from, we can see that there has been a policy of mainly using a mock test in the autumn, as a warm up for a real Bridge TOEIC test in the spring.

The online testing is integrated into the English course as a once per semester formative assessment usually arranged in week 13 or 15 of the 18 week semester to see how proficiency has changed as a result of the teaching. No test preparation work is especially done for it and the tests are of course independent of the textbook material: i.e. the tests are not seen as summative measures of achievement in the English course. It is up to the teacher whether he/she wants to use the results to guide what they teach. The results crucially are examined by the university authorities, e g Academic Affairs, to check whether students outperformed the previous year and whether they are good enough for the university to be able to apply for a MOE grant, since the MOE often

Table 1. Numbers of tests of four types taken in each semester over the period 2010–2016

		Real full TOEIC	Real Bridge TOEIC	Mock full TOEIC	Mock Bridge TOEIC
		Count	Count	Count	Count
Test period	2010 autumn	2	0	9	0
	2011 spring	6	0	8	0
	2011 autumn	6	0	95	0
	2012 spring	1	2	81	0
	2012 autumn	31	14	292	1
	2013 spring	1	6	0	275
	2013 autumn	56	86	0	1919
	2014 spring	165	1935	20	0
	2014 autumn	471	215	3581	0
	2015 spring	492	5251	233	0
	2015 autumn	0	0	0	0
	2016 spring	0	0	0	2704

evaluates the university based on whether its existing policies have been effective in upgrading student English proficiency.

3 Current Questions

Has student general proficiency increased over the 5 years of testing?

4 Findings

In Table 2 we can see some overall upward trend in the mock tests. In the real tests, however, although there is an upward trend since spring 2014, there was a high before then. The pattern is similar if freshmen and sophomores are plotted separately, except that the recent slight rise in the mock tests is due to the former not the latter. We may set this against the background that in Taiwan as a whole, average scores for the full TOEIC rose by only 7 points from 529 in 2005 to 536 in 2014.

Table 2. Score progression over test occasions 2010–2016 (where data is available).

		2010 autumn to 2013 spring	2013 autumn	2014 spring	2014 autumn	2015 spring	2016 spring
		Mean	Mean	Mean	Mean	Mean	Mean
Real full TOEIC	Listening	101.27	77.56	55.37	105.63	136.69	
	Reading	80.47	57.61	41.24	77.14	84.43	
	Total	190.07	133.77	89.86	181.35	221.62	
Real Bridge TOEIC	Listening	34.07	62.12	33.61	34.96	47.72	
	Reading	24.86	56.40	25.29	27.04	44.56	
	Total	55.08	118.16	58.91	61.93	92.31	
Mock full TOEIC	Listening	25.43	.	34.80	28.57	63.58	
	Reading	16.35	.	27.20	29.45	58.46	
	Total	41.62	.	62.00	58.03	122.34	
Mock Bridge TOEIC	Listening	25.44	29.55	.	.	.	29.34
	Reading	17.10	29.54	.	.	.	25.03
	Total	42.54	59.09	.	.	.	54.28

A tentative conclusion could be that, whether due to the students' effort or the teaching quality, there is at least evidence of improvement regardless of test type over the last three testing occasions.

5 Discussion and Conclusion

We may argue for the following implications which may extend to contexts similar to ours.

The main finding is the generally low average proficiency level in the area of CEFR A1 or at best A2, compared with the B1 or B2 needed to meet local employer or international competitor standards. Apart from a minority of individuals, our students may well be typical of freshmen in EFL contexts way beyond our own, struggling with the same issues. Anecdotally we are aware of a similar situation in many universities in Thailand, and in Saudi Arabia, an EFL context where the authorities have nevertheless taken the additional bold step of implementing the delivery of a number of key majors (e.g. medicine and engineering) entirely through English medium in many universities. Some public universities in Taiwan are also moving this way, towards English medium instruction (EMI), and sooner or later HungKuang may need to do the same. Thus it remains a pressing challenge how to get student English rapidly up to a level to be able to cope with this.

The lack of clear progress between freshman and sophomore years draws attention to the need for reconsideration of the focus and effectiveness of the teaching, as well as of the motivation of the students. As one teacher remarked, "My students know to take TOEIC is a gateway to global enterprises but most of them consider it too tough for them. Although I gave them online assignments to practice TOEIC, they felt frustrated in the process. The test took 2 h and the items were too long for them to comprehend.

They prefer TOEIC Bridge or CSEPT but still could not pass our school English graduation threshold so they turned to the alternative course—English Grammar and Writing. I saw students dozing in class, swiping their cell phones, or eating. I felt sympathy for them because they spent tuition and didn't feel motivated in learning English. They began studying English since 6 years old but preferred professional fields to English. The duration of learning English does not take root in them."

This problem has been recognised in Taiwan way beyond HungKuang. Although colleges and universities have established English test score graduation thresholds, without also setting clear and persuasive English learning goals and better planning of teaching, the effect on elevating students' motivation is limited and students' English ability does not improve. Such a course may work for a minority of students but cannot improve overall English ability effectively. Thus, quite a few scholars, including Prof. C.M. Chen, have already proposed that a revolution needs to occur in freshman English. For example, Prof. Cheng-Chin Lee, former director of the Ministry of Education, Cultural and Education International, proposed that it requires a "learning-goal-oriented" learning strategy to promote college students' English ability, which also means triggering students' perception of English speaking and writing fluently as an "expected goal" by activating teaching to construct and strengthen students' self-access motivation. Prof. Chang,Vincent Wu-Chang, former professor of the National Normal University, English Department, also suggests that, in order to promote the effect of college English education, one should begin with "multiple but intertwining aspects of curriculum revolution, testing evaluation planning, internet multimedia use and teachers' professional growth". Such a curriculum revolution aims to promote students' workplace or academic competitiveness, as described earlier and could involve new English courses that are not only practical and professional but also academic, so as to strengthen the applicability of what is taught.

At HungKuang, therefore, on the teaching side, maybe consideration needs to be given to dividing the students by major and doing work part of the time at least which connects more directly with the occupations associated with a particular major, i.e. ESOP rather than EGOP. After all, can one argue that the workplace language of a nurse and a food caterer would in reality have that much in common? This might also help the learner side by making the English feel more relevant to their future employment needs, and so providing more incentive to learn. Students themselves have in fact from time to time asked for this, but at present the Language Centre budget does not allow for more than a small amount of this.

In short, our analysis of recent English tests in our university suggests important lessons for all stakeholders, in the areas of the English teaching syllabus, motivation of the learners, and the future regime of testing to be adopted.

Applying MOOCs to Standard Courses: Some Facts

Hsing-chin Lee[(⊠)]

Department of Applied Foreign Languages,
National Taipei University of Busienss,
Taipei City, Taiwan
hsingchinlee@ntub.edu.tw

Abstract. The study aims to uncover some facts regarding the availability of courses of an online platform, Coursera and the comparison of MOOCs to a standard curriculum. Two questionnaires were designed and conducted for the pilot and the main study. Specific questions such as: (1) What other online learning platforms have students used before? (2) What are the top three courses which are not provided in their curriculum but are demanded? And (3) How popular might English-taught Coursera courses be to students of Applied Foreign Languages? are asked.

1 Introduction

This study was conducted in the hopes of further understanding how MOOCS, and in this particular case, Coursera, can positively impact students' academic performance when used in conjunction with university courses. Coursera is a classic example of a MOOCS platform where students are able to sign up for college-level courses in a variety of subjects at their convenience. Coursera is an international platform and collaborates with 43 institutes worldwide. The courses are provided in more than ten languages. Prior to the commencement of the course, you may choose whether or not to apply for a certificate. If you wish to receive a certificate upon completion of the course, it will come at a fee of US$49 however all courses are free of charge.

The target group of this study was focused on all junior college students at the National Taipei University of Business (hereafter NTUB) but was later narrowed down to junior college students of the Department of Applied Foreign Languages due to certain difficulties. Coursera courses favored by NTUB students shall also be discussed as well as details of the course content and material. Two questionnaires were designed and conducted for the pilot and the main study. The first questionnaire was given out to all fifth grade junior college students at NTUB. Unfortunately, the ill-designed questionnaire contained too many questions that were too general. Furthermore, very few students had heard of Coursera prior to filling in the questionnaire so the first attempt sadly did not bear much fruit for harvest. After some period of discernment and correction, the second questionnaire was designed. It contained more specific questions such as: (1) What other online learning platforms have students used before? (2) What are the top three courses which are not provided in their curriculum but are demanded?

© Springer International Publishing AG 2017
T.-T. Wu et al. (Eds.): SETE 2016, LNCS 10108, pp. 727–732, 2017.
DOI: 10.1007/978-3-319-52836-6_78

And (3) How popular might English-taught Coursera courses be to students of Applied Foreign Languages? Moreover, reasons why students take Coursera courses are discussed as well as whether the result of the second questionnaire is valid and meets the intended objectives. We also venture into the realms of face to face instruction versus online instruction according to student preference and whether native English teachers are of more interest. Finally, comparison between content of the top three Coursera courses mentioned previously and those provided by the university are discussed.

2   Design of the Questionnaires

The objectives are to promote the use of MOOCS and to encourage self-learning. We also hope to encourage students to take full advantage of such platforms as they are able to take courses within their interests but which are, unfortunately, not available in their university curriculum. The purpose of this study is also to show that there is a demand for more current, internationalized courses so that our future graduates may effortlessly into the competitive world of business. The original target group were all fifth-grade students from every department of NTUB and it was later exclusive to only those of Applied Foreign Languages in the second questionnaire.

The reason for this change is the fact that the majority of the students had not heard of Coursera. However, most of our questions were related to the platform itself. Adding to this inconvenience, most students did not fill in the questions meticulously and were instead, more concerned about the numerous questions presented. As a result, the first questionnaire was a failure. Perseveringly, the researcher reviewed the mistakes practically and designed the second questionnaire.

The second questionnaire was more systematically designed than the first one. Additionally, the target group was narrowed down to only fifth grade junior college students of the Department of Applied Foreign Languages (AFL hereafter). Due to the fact that most Coursera courses are delivered in English, the AFL students were made suitable target group for this study as English is their main focus of study.

Since the range of the first questionnaire asked was not focused enough, the researcher decided to lessen the ambiguity of the questions posed by restricting the number of questions and the scope of the research, in order to obtain and focus on the necessary data needed in this paper.

In a nutshell, the researcher aimed to discover what other online platforms (MOOCs) have students used before, what are the possible top three courses which are not provided in their curriculum but are demanded, the content of the top three courses and how popular might English-taught Coursera courses be to students of Applied Foreign Languages be are compared? Moreover, the reasons why students take Coursera courses are discussed in charts. It is equally stressed how many students prefer "face to face" instruction to online instruction. Moreover, the questionnaire provides an insightful fact how many students are more interested in the courses taught by native English teachers.

3 Discussion

The design of the study was conducted via questionnaire. Two hundred and four questionnaires were collected (81.6%). A total of 204 students participated in the research. As shown on Pie 1, there are more female students than male students percentage being 86.76% to 13.24%.

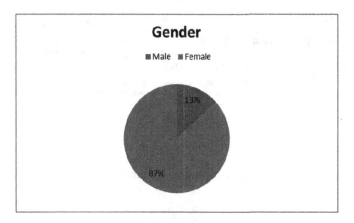

Pie. 1.

The result was not satisfactory as only 15% of students had heard about Coursera, while a large majority of the students, approximately 85%, were not familiar with the online platform. As the chart below shows, among 15% of students who had knowledge of the aforementioned MOOCs, 44.4% of them learnt about Coursera from instructors at NTUB, 24.4% from family and friends, 20% from the Internet, 4.4% from news media, 4.4% from newspaper and magazines and the remaining 2.2% from lectures related to online-open-source learning materials (Fig 1).

Most students heard of Voice Tube and Tutor ABC but only half of them have ever used either of them. Tutor ABC is the most famous online learning platform known by the most students participating in this study, but only 10% of students have accessed to it. The following pie chart indicates what other online learning platforms are possible (Pie 2).

76% of students prefer "face to face" teaching and 24% of students prefer online teaching. Up to 80% of students think they are more interested in the courses taught by foreign teachers.

According to the first questionnaire, only one-fourth of the students heard of Coursera. Among these students, the majority have heard of it from teachers in school and 16% from families and friends, 15% from the internet, 8% from newspaper and magazine, 4% from news media.

A number of advantages of taking Coursera courses include its courses being from verified institutions. There are nine categories courses in Coursera, including Data Science, Personal Development, Arts and Humanity, Business, Computer Science, Life

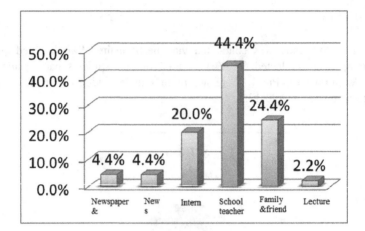

Fig. 1.

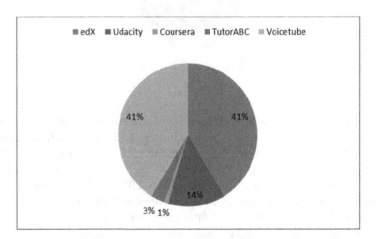

Pie. 2.

Science, Math and Logic, Physical Science and End Engineering and Social Science are open for selections. These credentials can later help students improve their level of expertise.

Art and Humanity (30%), Personal Development (22%) and Social Science (14%) are the top three categories among the students of AFL in NTUB. Other than that, Business accounts for 12% and Life Science, 11%. Data Science, Math and Logic and Physical Science and End Engineering and Social Science account for 2%.

Art and Humanity includes history, philosophy, music and art, language and literature. Personal Development is to make people understand how to learn and discover their creativity and speech introduction. Social Science is about economy, education, government and society, law and psychology.

77% of the students know that Course courses are all taught by famous universities lecturers and colleges' professors around the world. The reputation of colleges is the biggest factor that draws students to sign up for the courses.

Moreover, the study shows that 57% of students take these courses based on their interest of study. But then why do students choose those courses in particular? The following pie chart indicates 36% of the learners expect to learn professional skills on the courses because it is more and more important to get promoted in jobs by having extra Coursera learning experience. Apart from professional knowledge, English, Extending worldview and overseas teaching methods are what students expect to learn from Coursera courses (Pie 3).

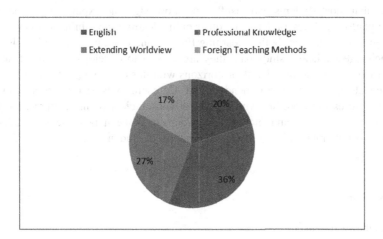

Pie. 3.

The purpose of this study is to help students improve their employability, learn more about this online learning platform and how they can make good use of their time by selecting their favorite subjects outside the classroom. Moreover, the fact that the credits taken after finishing Coursera courses can be waved at the NTUB is not learned among students. So, when asked whether they know that the credits taken from Coursera can be waved? Only 10% of the students reply positively. This indicates that the university needs to find more ways to get more students familiar with the platform. Besides, 90% of students are willing to take courses on Coursera if the university issues a policy, that is: to those who have completed all the courses and want to apply for a certificate can gain US$ 50 subsidy.

When asked whether they would be willing to take Coursera courses if the courser course fee can be reimbursed by the university, 90% of the students confirm a YES.

When asked how students think about the academic course credits provided at the university, they think the studyload demanded by the university is not too heavy and most of them are willing to take other courses on their own time.

There are of course, constraints regarding the scope of the research and more samples are needed for a more well-rounded analysis. In terms of various levels of

English in different departments, there might be more interesting findings when further study is carried out.

4 Conclusion

The nature of this study was to provide some facts regarding the availability of courses of Coursera and the comparison of the online courses to a standard curriculum to student preference. By providing the facts, it is hoped that students understand what Coursera is and to give them the motivation to take courses online by showing them the advantages of applying Coursera to standard curriculum. The result of the study indicates that most students had insufficient knowledge and experience of the online learning platform, Coursera, let alone other online learning possibilities. They are well motivated to use Coursera both in learning English and other professional skills. Apart from their already heavy studyload, they are willing to develop some other skills in different fields and also broaden their horizons with this convenient means of learning.

In conclusion, it is recommended that Coursera provided courses taught by renowned professors from all over the world with efficient online lectures, handouts, interactive assignments, and most of all, Coursera make it possible for students in Taiwan to collaborate with the global community of students.

References

1. https://zh-tw.coursera.org/
2. https://en.wikipedia.org/wiki/Coursera
3. http://findonlineeducation.com/tools/how-to-use-coursera-for-online-education/
4. http://blog.coursera.org/post/88309220917/four-proven-advantages-of-online-learning-that
5. https://www.facebook.com/Coursera/info/?tab=page_info
6. http://libir.tmu.edu.tw/bitstream/987654321/5345/2/%E6%91%98%E8%A6%81.pdf
7. https://en.m.wikipedia.org/wiki/Coursera
8. https://en.m.wikipedia.org/wiki/Massive_open_online_course

Assessment in the eLearning Course on Academic Writing – A Case Study

Blanka Klimova[✉]

University of Hradec Kralove, Rokitanskeho 62,
Hradec Kralove, Czech Republic
blanka.klimova@uhk.cz

Abstract. Evaluation is an inseparable part of any learning process. It is of high importance because it can either motivate or demotivate students in their studies. The purpose of this article is to discuss assessment as part of the overall evaluation in one eLearning course run at the Faculty of Informatics and Management in Hradec Kralove, Czech Republic. Firstly, the difference between the evaluation and assessment concept is clarified, and the assessment concept is specified. Secondly, the author of this article discusses the content of the Course of Academic Writing, describes the assessment and its feedback in this course, and shows how students work on their assignments. Finally, she highlights benefits and limitations of such assessment.

Keywords: eLearning course · Academic writing · Assessment · Evaluation · Feedback

1 Introduction

One of the key steps in any learning process is its evaluation because students want to know how they succeed in their learning and the result of this evaluation undoubtedly motivates or demotivates them in their further studies. Therefore the evaluation plays a crucial role in both teaching and learning. The evaluation is usually performed at the very end of any course, when a mark is assigned after a completion of a task, test, quiz, lesson or learning activity [1]. On the contrary, assessment requires the collection of evidence as to a student's performance over a period of time to measure her/his learning and understanding. It is aimed at student's on-going improvement throughout the course. Watson [2] states that people could understand assessment as the journey, while evaluation as the snapshot.

In writing classes formative and summative assessments are used. However, with respect to learning and acquiring writing skills, formative assessment should prevail since one of the major purposes of writing assessment is to provide feedback to students. The reasons are as follows [3]:

- Formative assessment provides students with a reason to read and understand the teacher's comments on their writing.
- Formative assessment helps learners use the teacher's comments in the following assignments and thus to improve their writing.

© Springer International Publishing AG 2017
T.-T. Wu et al. (Eds.): SETE 2016, LNCS 10108, pp. 733–738, 2017.
DOI: 10.1007/978-3-319-52836-6_79

- Formative assessment provides students with more time for thinking and writing about assigned topics and thus contributes to better thinking and writing.
- Formative assessment makes students be more critical of their own writing and revise their writing.

The purpose of this article is to discuss assessment as part of the overall evaluation in the eLearning course on Academic Writing, which is taught at the Faculty of Informatics and Management in Hradec Kralove, Czech Republic.

2 Methods

The method used for the analysis of the topic of assessment in the eLearning Course on Academic Writing is a case study [4] in order to demonstrate how this assessment can be conducted and how students experience it. In addition, the sample of participants is not that large due to the focus of the explored eLearning course.

3 Assessment in the Course of Academic Writing and Its Findings

One of the most common teaching approaches used at the Faculty of Informatics and Management (FIM) in Hradec Kralove is blended learning [5–7] since it combines both traditional teaching and online learning and the eLearning course of Academic Writing is then part of it. The Course of Academic Writing is an optional, one semester course. Students meet a teacher once every two weeks in the period of 13 weeks, i.e., one semester. The course has been taught at the faculty already for ten years in the course of both semester. It is especially offered to the students of the first year, but it can be also attended by students of higher classes who go and study abroad. The course deals with the whole process of writing and features that are strikingly different in English and Czech language such as making references or use of formality. The content of this course consists of six modules, which are run face-to-face for 90 min and their content is also implemented into the eLearning Course on Academic Writing [1].

The modules are as follows:

1. Paragraphing and summarizing
2. Writing an argumentative essay
3. Writing a research article, including bibliography and references I
4. Writing a research article, including bibliography and references II
5. Writing an article for the English version of Wikipedia
6. Writing a self-reflective essay

Each module is then followed by home written assignment, for which students usually have one week at minimum and they submit it online through the eLearning course. Altogether students have to write five assignments since the last one – Writing a self-reflective essay is done in class and not included in final evaluation because it is students' reflection on their writing, the whole course, but it should also make them think what they have achieved. The topics of the essay vary according to the form of the essay. Figure 1 below then illustrates the evaluation scale used for the assessment of each assignment.

Writing Components	Criteria/ Traits	Score
Content	*extent, relevance, subject knowledge*	30%
Organization	*coherence, fluency, clarity, logical sequencing*	20%
Vocabulary	*richness, appropriate register, word form mastery*	20%
Language use	*accuracy (a use of articles, word order, countable versus uncountable nouns, prepositions, sentence constructions)*	25%
Mechanics	*paragraphing, spelling, capitalization, punctuation*	5%

Fig. 1. The evaluation scale used in the Course of Academic Writing (author's own processing, based on [8, 9])

After submitting each assignment, students obtain written online feedback on the assignment from their teacher, which should make them think of their writing and help them improve in their following assignment. The feedback is usually done within three days after the submission. Furthermore, sometimes students are asked to rewrite, revamp and revise their assignment it if it is not comprehensible and there are many grammar mistakes. The pass mark for their assignment is 50%. In addition, students get another, this time, oral feedback during the following face-to-face lesson. This feedback is provided by the teacher with a special focus on the most serious writing errors, which are discussed. Moreover, each face-to-face lesson students have a chance to practice writing in class by writing short texts connected with their next assignment. These are done in pairs or individually, but they are also assessed by students themselves. In this way, students learn how to provide feedback and it makes them think of their own writing.

In the winter term of 2015, 11 students participated in the course. This number might seem small but correcting every second week their essays which are usually 350–500 words long on average imposes a significant burden on the teacher. Out of these 11 students, two were male students and nine were female students. In the end only ten students completed the course. The reason was the topic of the fourth essay on Cognitive decline and dementia which most of the students found difficult because it was not related to their field of study as in other cases. This was also confirmed by students in their self-reflective essays. The easiest was probably Assignment 1, which was only 1–2 paragraphs on the description of a lecture/seminar they had that week (without writing any bibliography) and Assignment 5 on which students work in pairs and they thoroughly enjoyed it although they had to use also their computer skills in order to edit and upload it into the English version of Wikipedia according to their requirements.

The worst grades were given for Assignment 3, in which students were learning how to write bibliography and references. These skills were new for students, and thus, they made mistakes.

As far as the students' work on the assignments is concerned, the evaluation tools in the course revealed that students spent most of the time on studying and uploading their assignments into the eLearning course on Mondays and Tuesdays. The reason is that Tuesdays were the days of submitting their assignments and also the days of contact classes. Consult Fig. 2 below.

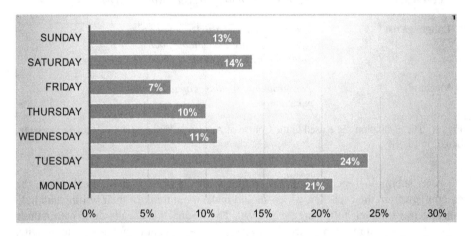

Fig. 2. Days of students' activity in the eLearning course, author's own processing based on the data from the e-learning course [10]

In addition, students were most active in the eLearning course between 12 and 1 in the afternoon and then 5 and 10 in the evening.

4   Discussion

The findings show that the writing course is not easy and students need an instant and continuous support from their teacher in order to complete it successfully. Therefore even more attention should be paid to the continuous assessments (as part of the whole evaluation), their feedback and encouragement of students to learn. The teacher may also ask students to write diaries on their writing improvements, difficulties and progress [11].

In addition, the findings reveal that students mainly learn and work when the deadline of their assignment is approaching. For example, student 10 confessed in his/her essay, s/he had had to persuade herself/himself to write the essay in the chosen time. The time period of their learning, however, indicates that students prefer to study between five and ten in the evening, i.e., when they finish their daily activities, calm down and have a more extended period for their academic work. In this sense, the blended learning approach seems to be an ideal solution to their studies [12]. However, the findings of this case study indicate that in the Course of Academic Writing more emphasis should be also put on social and relational aspects, not only on the course delivery. Students should be encouraged to collaborate both in class and in the eLearning course, as well as to provide mutual feedback on each other's writing. This can be also improved by choosing better essay topics which should be more related to students' field of study and thus be of interest to most of the students. In addition, more in class writing practice, such as writing references or bibliography, should be conducted.

5 Conclusion

In conclusion, effective assessments can satisfy both students and their teacher. They can motivate students and provide them with confidence in their further studies [13]. And it is the teacher who is especially responsible for the whole success of the course delivery and its methodology.

Apart from some difficulties, students' feedback on the whole course from their self-reflected essays revealed that they were satisfied with the assessment and its feedback and they admitted learning a lot of new things which they could use in their further studies at the faculty.

Acknowledgments. The paper is supported by the SPEV project 2017 run at the Faculty of Informatics and Management of the University of Hradec Kralove, Czech Republic.

References

1. Klimova, B.: Assessment in smart learning environment – a case study approach. In: Uskov, V.L., Howlett, R.J., Jain, L.C. (eds.) Smart Education and Smart e-Learning. SIST, vol. 41, pp. 15–24. Springer, Heidelberg (2015). doi:10.1007/978-3-319-19875-0_2
2. Watson, S.: Assessment, evaluation and final marks (2014). http://specialed.about.com/od/assessment/a/AandE.htm
3. Klimova, B.: The role of feedback in EFL classes. Procedia – Soc. Behav. Sci. **199**, 172–177 (2015)
4. Yin, R.K.: Case Study Research: Design and Methods. Sage, Newbury Park (1984)
5. Frydrychova Klimova, B.: Blended learning. In: Mendez Vilas, A., et al. (eds.) Research, Reflections and Innovations in Integrating ICT in Education, vol. 2, pp. 705–708. FORMATEX, Spain (2009)
6. Frydrychova Klimova, B., Hubackova, S., Semradova, I.: Blended learning in a foreign language learning. Procedia – Soc. Behav. Sci. **28**, 281–285 (2011)
7. Frydrychova Klimova, B., Poulova, P.: Forms of instruction and students' preferences - a comparative study. In: Cheung, S.K.S., Fong, J., Zhang, J., Kwan, R., Kwok, L.F. (eds.) ICHL 2014. LNCS, vol. 8595, pp. 220–231. Springer, Heidelberg (2014). doi:10.1007/978-3-319-08961-4_21

8. Bacha, N.: Writing evaluation: what can analytic versus holistic essay scoring tell us? System **29**, 371–383 (2001)
9. Jacobs, H.J., et al.: Testing ESL Composition: a Practical Approach. Newbury House, Rowley (1981)
10. Evaluation (2016). http://bboard.uhk.cz/webapps/portal/frameset.jsp?tab_tab_group_id=_2_1&url=%2Fwebapps%2Fblackboard%2Fexecute%2Flauncher%3Ftype%3DCourse%26id%3D_299_1%26url%3D
11. Horvathova, B.: Diary studies as a research tool in investigating language learning. In: Research in Foreign Language Education, Brno, MSD, pp. 108–143 (2012)
12. Vesela, K.: Teaching ESP in New Environments. CA-CLIL. ASPA, Veľké Zálužie (2012)
13. Laskaris, J.: Planning assessments for your eLearning course (2015). http://www.talentlms.com/blog/planning-assessments-for-your-elearning-course/

Workshop on the Applications of Information and Communication Technologies in Adult and Continuing Education

How Solid Learning Model Influence Learners' Creativity?—An Empirical Study to Explore the Relationships Between Personalization, Interdisciplinary Capability and Creativity

Xuesong Zhai[1], Jing Zhang[2(✉)], Huifu Xu[3], Yan Dong[4],
Qiaoqiao Zhan[5], Yuee Chen[1], Huimin Zhang[1], and Jing Yuan[6]

[1] School of Foreign Studies, Anhui Jianzhu University,
Hefei, Mainland China, China
zhxs@mail.ustc.edu.cn, {343850447,1031606202}@qq.com
[2] Institute of Higher Education Study, Anhui University,
Hefei, Mainland China, China
13705516631@163.com
[3] Shanghai Open University, Shanghai, Mainland China, China
hfxu@shtvu.edu.cn
[4] School of Educational Technology, Beijing Normal University,
Beijing, Mainland China, China
Dongy@bnu.edu.cn
[5] School of Architecture and Urban Design, Anhui Jianzhu University,
Hefei, Mainland China, China
Migao0526@163.com
[6] School of Foreign Studies, Anhui Sanlian University,
Hefei, Mainland China, China
1210279581@qq.com

Abstract. With growing promotion of 3D technology, Solid Learning (SL) model, featured by construction of individualized context and integration of multidisciplinary knowledge, is increasingly attracting educators' attention. Although previous research indicated that SL is helpful for improving learners' innovation, few studies were conducted to examine the driving mechanism, which warrants the further exploration. A total of 58 students were selected to participate in 12-week SL Introductory Landscape Design classes in an university located in the middle of Mainland China. The results of the survey indicated that personalization and interdisciplinary have positive relationship to learners' creativity in the solid learning settings. Additionally, learners' interdisciplinary capacity was a partial mediator rather than complete mediator of personalization and learners' creativity. This research theoretically contributes to explore the driving mechanism of students' innovation in SL context, and practically many referable values were offered for promoting learners' creativity.

Keywords: Solid learning · Personalization · Interdisciplinary · Capability · Creativity

© Springer International Publishing AG 2017
T.-T. Wu et al. (Eds.): SETE 2016, LNCS 10108, pp. 741–748, 2017.
DOI: 10.1007/978-3-319-52836-6_80

1 Introduction

With profound integration of 3D technology into education, Solid Learning (SL) model, employing the technology of instant prototyping and digital manufacture into courses design, has been increasingly attracting educators' attention [8]. Previous research has indicated that SL had great positive influence on motivating learners' creativity and innovation compared with traditional learning model [17]. However, few studies were conducted to investigate the mattering factors and driving mechanism for promote learners' creativity in the context of solid learning model, which warrants theoretical ground as well as practical reference for cultivating learners' creativity in the future.

Distinct from traditional learning model, SL provides a platform for learners to perform personalized project in a 3D context, in which the individualized study model was ensured in the whole process from idea creation, 3D model design to solid printing. Furthermore, in contrast to the traditional 2D settings, learners are required to apply multidisciplinary knowledge, when studying in the context of SL. From the perspective of the characteristic of solid learning, personalizational design was proposed as an main antecedence to students' creativity. Besides, learners' interdisciplinary ability was employed as a mediator to further explore the inner mechanism between the personalized design and students' creativity. In the current study, A total of 58 undergraduates and postgraduates majoring in Landscape Design participated in the Introductory Landscape Design sample classes with 3D pens in an university located in the middle of Mainland Chinese. After the 12-week experimental classes, students' creativity questionnaire and interview data were collected to investigate the proposed model.

2 Research Background and Hypotheses

2.1 Solid Learning Model

Solid learning model, featuring in design of personalization and integration of multi-disciplinary, motivates learner's explosive desire as well as innovation capability. Different from traditional learning model, SL embeds the 3D technique of instant prototyping and digital manufacture into education, which makes learning process "touchable" and visualized. Since traditional 2D learning model restrains the peers' interaction in the process of learning, more learners are in favor of expressing their ideas freely in the SL context. Some researchers suggested that SL could make knowledge visualized which help instructors to evaluate the students learning performance, and in turn offer related personalized instructions to them [11]. Moreover, SL also integrate learners' interdisciplinary capacity into learning that can broaden students' analytical perspectives [18]. It was thus proposed that in the SL settings learners' interdisciplinary capacity could enhance students to access to multidisciplinary knowledge, and expand their cognitive space.

2.2 Personalization and Creativity

SL effectively stimulated learners' desire of exploration and met their personal learning demand. Some researcher found that in the Robotics experimental classes students were absorbed in personalized design of solid learning [9]. Thereafter, educators have been encouraging students to create their own personalized designs and works in SL context [3, 7], and students are encouraged to visualize their thoughts, which promote them access to expressing their minds. Hong and Baker [5] supposed that students' spacial conception, such as design scheme, clarity of concept expression can be achieved by adopting 3D printers, which offered students a personalized environment to acquire knowledge flexibly, where learners' inspiration is stimulated. Synthesizing these findings lead to the following hypothesis:

H1: Personalized design of SL is positively associated with students' creativity.

2.3 Mediator Role of Interdisciplinary

SL help students with completion of multidisciplinary works from diverse channels, and it could be beneficial to students for the sake of acquirement of related knowledge in return. SL is applicable to STEM concept, which encourage students integrate the knowledge of science, technology, engineering and mathematics [16]. Besides, innovation and interdisciplinary methodology are closely related [13]. Marxist philosophy defined interdisciplinary methodology as adopting multiple disciplinary collaboration to address one certain problem beyond the restraint of disciplines boundary. Interdisciplinary capacity can be defined as an ability to integrate knowledge of distinctive disciplines, which is one of the powerful tools triggering sparks to inspire creativity [2]. Interdisciplinary is consisted of four elements including simultaneity, collaboration, application of disciplinary knowledge, transformation of thinking pattern [4]. When solving one specified problem, learners make use of creative thinking nourished with integrated multidisciplinary knowledge, during the process their interdisciplinary capacity is trained. Moreover, the frequent transforming of diverse thinking patterns facilitates learners to associate their ideas and thoughts, which are followed by inspiration and innovation regularly.

Personalized learning model of SL offers learners opportunities with various forms to interact [11], which is an enlightening experience for students to inspire their creation. In addition, personalized learning model of SL provides learners with open space for understanding of interdisciplinary. Because interdisciplinary does not means requiring students to handle multi-disciplinary knowledge passively, but applying multidisciplinary knowledge to solve problems proactively. Synthesizing these findings lead to the following hypothesis:

H2: Interdisciplinary capacity is a partial mediator between personalization and students' creativity in SL settings.

3   Methodology

3.1   Participants and Procedure

A total of 58 undergraduates and postgraduates from one university in China participated in the SL Landscape Design experimental classes. Table 1 shows the demographics of the participants. Participants had read the product instruction of 3D pens and engaged in the landscape design with peers discussion (as shown in Fig. 1). The 3D technology with personalized design is thus utilized in this study. Compared with 3D printer, 3D pens are cheaper and portable which were compatible to be adopted in the current research for its flexibility timely and spatially [1].

Table 1. The demographics of participants

Measure	Classification	Frequency	Percent (%)
Gender	Male	29	50
	Female	29	50
Age	21–26	58	100
Education	Graduated	30	60
	Under-graduated	20	40

Fig. 1. Solid learning experimental classrooms

3.2   Instruments

To guarantee the validity and the reliability of the measurement, some satisfactory scales were adopted and modified based on the current study. The creativity scale including 3 items referred to the instrument developed by Hsu et al. [6]. Personalization scale including three items developed from Mueller et al.'s study [12]. Besides, Klein's study [10] and Piso's study [15] were employed to develop the instrument of learners' interdisciplinary capacity.

4 Results

4.1 Reliability and Validity

The reliability and validity of the instrument were examined through SPSS19.0 (shown in Table 2). Cranbach's α of all scales are over 0.73, higher than standard coefficient 0.6 proposed by Nunnally [14]. Besides, Average Variance Extracted (AVE) of each variable range from 0.47 to 0.63 (in addition to interdisciplinary capacity close to 0.5, the rest are above 0.5), which indicates that convergent validity is acceptable. Coefficients of correlation as well as mean value, standard deviation are listed in Table 3, which shows that creativity is significantly and positively correlated to the independent variables. Moreover, the square root of AVE is higher than coefficients of correlation among variables, which indicates that factors in this experiment possess high distinguish degree.

Table 2. Reliability analysis of instrument

Items	Loadings	Cronbach's α	CR	AVE
Personalization		0.67	0.77	0.53
P1 - I can achieve a personalized design in SL context.	685			
P2 - SL provides me with a personalized Learning environment	736			
P3 - I can get lasting learning motivation in SL context.	751			
Interdisciplinary capacity		0.53	0.73	0.47
IC1 - I can understand the importance better ofstructure in space design by SL model.	766			
IC2 - I can apply multidisciplinary knowledge to solve professional problems in SL context.	632			
IC3 - I can apply different thinking modes to solve the problem in SL context.	661			
Creativity		0.80	0.84	0.64
C1 - I can complete tasks creatively in SL context.	761			
C2 - I can meet various challenges in SL context.	854			
C3 - My solution to the problem is original in SL context.	780			

Table 3. Mean, SD, correlations and discriminant validity among P, IC and C.

Variable	Mean	SD	1	2	3
Personalization	4.26	0.5	1 (0.73)		
Interdisciplinary capacity	4.11	0.5	0.29**	1 (0.69)	
Creativity	4.11	0.6	0.37**	0.52**	1 (0.80)

Note: N = 58, *. p < 0.05, **. p < 0.01 ***. p < 0.001, the diagonal brackets are the square root of the AVE.

4.2 Regression Analysis

The regression analyses were conducted in three steps according to SOBEL's examination of mediation efficient. The results shown in Table 4 suggested that personalization has significant relation with creativity (p = 0.004). Besides, personalization and interdisciplinary capacity are significantly correlated (p = 0.03). Additionally, when personalization and interdisciplinary capacity were conducted as independent variables together, they both significantly related with creativity capacity (p = 0.04, p < 0.000 respectively), which suggested that interdisciplinary capability exerts partial mediating effect between personalization and creativity capacity.

Table 4. Results of regression analysis

	P → C	P → IC	P + IC → C	
			P → C	IC → C
β	0.37**	0.29*	0.24*	0.45***
R^2	0.14	0.09	0.32	
p	0.004	0.03	0.04	0.000
t	2.978	2.28	2.06	3.83

Note: P: personalization,
IC: interdisciplinary capacity, C: creativity
*. p < 0.05,**. p < 0.001, ***. p < 0.001.

5 Discussion

The purpose of this study is to investigate the driving mechanism of students' creativity in the context of solid learning. After 12-week solid learning experimental classes, the survey indicated that the personalized design of solid learning model could positively associated with learners' creativity. Students could freely design and present their mind in 3D context, thus their autonomy were inclined to be stimulated, which help to enhance their enthusiasm to exert creativity. Therefore, teaching activity in 3D should attach more importance to cultivating students' personalization with the purpose to improve students' innovation.

Moreover, Interdisciplinary is a partial mediator between personalization learning and innovation capacity. When learners perform their landscape design with 3D pens, they have to take much more elements into consideration, such as the stability of the joint, the adhesion of drawing material, which warrant learners' integration of multi-knowledge capability, and it would further promote their interdisciplinary capacity. As a new teaching model, the personalization in SL not only exert learners creativity, but also promotes learners' interdisciplinary learning model and in turn cultivate learners' creativity. It is thus suggested that SL can be applied in STEM education, Makerspace, which further consolidates learners' innovative ability.

6 Limitations and Further Study

Although this study makes certain contribution to application of solid learning to cultivate learners' innovation, it still limited by certain factors which need further research. Firstly, the 3D pens employed in this experiment, though inherited many benefits of 3D printing technique, are still not as precise as 3D printer, and the experiment instruments in the current study is compromised and more accurate 3D pens are needed in future experimental classes. Additionally, participants in this study were all college-educated students, which limited the research sample. therefore, further research is encouraged to expand sample size for the sake of robustness of current findings.

Acknowledgments. Thanks are due to for funding by the National Natural Science Foundation of China (61300060), and the Anhui provincial research projects (foundation NO.: 1508085QF131, 2015zdjy115, 2015zdjy206 & SK2015A632).

References

1. Baker, M., Hong, J., Billinghurst, M.: Wearable computing from jewels to joules [guest editors' introduction]. IEEE Pervasive Comput. 4(13), 20–22 (2014)
2. Borja, A., Bricker, S.B., Dauer, D.M., Demetriades, N.T., Ferreira, J.G., Forbes, A.T., Marques, J.C.: Overview of integrative tools and methods in assessing ecological integrity in estuarine and coastal systems worldwide. Mar. Pollut. Bull. 56(9), 1519–1537 (2008)
3. Brown, C., Hurst, A.: VizTouch: automatically generated tactile visualizations of coordinate spaces. Paper Presented at the Proceedings of the Sixth International Conference on Tangible, Embedded and Embodied Interaction (2012)
4. Eujin Pei, D., Gatto, A., Bassoli, E., Denti, L., Iuliano, L., Minetola, P.: Multi-disciplinary approach in engineering education: learning with additive manufacturing and reverse engineering. Rapid Prototyp. J. 21(5), 598–603 (2015)
5. Hong, J., Baker, M.: 3D printing, smart cities, robots, and more. IEEE Pervasive Comput. 13(1), 6–9 (2014)
6. Hsu, Y., Peng, L.P., Wang, J.H., Liang, C.: Revising the imaginative capability and creative capability scales: testing the relationship between imagination and creativity among agriculture students. Int. J. Learn. Teach. Educ. Res. 6(1), 57–70 (2014)
7. Hurst, A., Kane, S.: Making making accessible. Paper Presented at the Proceedings of the 12th International Conference on Interaction Design and Children (2013)

8. Hausman, K.K.: Solid learning files [EB/OL] (2012a). http://www.stemulate.org/2012/05/20/solid-learning-lessons/. Accessed 20 May 2012
9. Hausman, K.K.: Solid learning files [EB/OL] (2012b). http://www.stemulate.org/2012/05/29/solid-learning-files/. Accessed 29 May 2012
10. Klein, J.T.: Evaluation of interdisciplinary and transdisciplinary research: a literature review. Am. J. Prev. Med. 35(2), 116–123 (2008)
11. Manches, A., O'Malley, C.: Tangibles for learning: a representational analysis of physical manipulation. Pers. Ubiquit. Comput. 16(4), 405–419 (2012)
12. Mueller, S., Mohr, T., Guenther, K., et al.: faBrickation: fast 3D printing of functional objects by integrating construction kit building blocks. In: Proceedings of the 32nd Annual ACM Conference on Human Factors in Computing Systems, pp. 3827–3834. ACM (2014)
13. NACCCE: All Our Futures: Creativity, Culture and Education. DfEE, London (1999)
14. Nunnally, J.C.: An overview of psychological measurement. In: Wolman, B.B. (ed.) Clinical Diagnosis of Mental Disorders, pp. 97–146. Springer US, New York (1978)
15. Piso, Z., O'Rourke, M., Weathers, K.C.: Out of the fog: catalyzing integrative capacity in interdisciplinary research. Stud. History Philos. Sci. Part A 56, 84–94 (2016)
16. Schelly, C., Anzalone, G., Wijnen, B., Pearce, J.M.: Open-source 3-D printing technologies for education: bringing additive manufacturing to the classroom. J. Vis. Lang. Comput. 28, 226–237 (2015)
17. Yang, Y., Sun, Z., Zhang, K., Li, A., Sun, R., Gu, J.: Establishing solid learning new teaching mode for petroleum engineering based on CT scanning and 3D printing visualization technology. Exp. Technol. Manag. 32(09), 65–67 (2015). (in Chinese)
18. Zamora, D., Monsen, K., von Jungenfeld, R.: Crafting public space: findings from an interdisciplinary outdoor workshop on 3D printing. Paper Presented at the Moving Targets Conference Proceedings (2013)

Taiwan In-Service Teachers' Perceptions of 21st Century Learning Practice, Design Disposition, and Usage of Information and Communication Technology (ICT)

Sheng Lun[1], Tzung-Jin Lin[2(✉)], Chih-Hui Lin[3], Ching Sing Chai[4], Jyh-Chong Liang[2], and Chin-Chung Tsai[2]

[1] Graduate Institute of Architecture, National Taiwan University of Science and Technology, Taipei City, Taiwan
D10413003@mail.ntust.edu.tw
[2] Graduate Institute of Digital Learning and Education, National Taiwan University of Science and Technology, Taipei City, Taiwan
{D9822302,aljc,cctsai}@mail.ntust.edu.tw
[3] Graduate Institute of Applied Science and Technology, National Taiwan University of Science and Technology, Taipei City, Taiwan
mandy9399@yahoo.com.tw
[4] National Institute of Education, Nanyang Technological University, Singapore, Singapore
chingsing.chai@nie.edu.sg

Abstract. This study attempted to explore 157 Taiwan high school teachers' perceptions of 21st century learning practice, design disposition, and usage of ICT. To this aim, the participating teachers were surveyed by means of a questionnaire to evaluate their perceptions of 21st century learning practice, ICT usage, and design disposition. The main results indicate no significant gender differences were found among the adopted scales. Moreover, several significant correlation patterns among the four scales of perceptions of 21st century learning practice ("Critical Thinking," "Self-directed Learning," "Creative Thinking," and "Problem Solving") and "Meaningful Usage of ICT" scale in both male and female groups were found. Furthermore, in the female teacher group, "Design Disposition" was significantly positively correlated with "Self-directed Learning" as well as "Problem Solving." However, in the male teacher group, there were no significant correlations between their "Design Disposition" and the scales of perceptions 21st century learning practice.

Keywords: 21st century learning · Design disposition · ICT · In-service teacher

1 Introduction

The rapid advancement of information and communication technology (ICT) has transformed the way of teaching practice in school [1]. One of the goals of contemporary education is to prepare learners with twenty first (21st) century skills and

© Springer International Publishing AG 2017
T.-T. Wu et al. (Eds.): SETE 2016, LNCS 10108, pp. 749–755, 2017.
DOI: 10.1007/978-3-319-52836-6_81

competencies for the purpose of appropriately handling future challenges in knowledge society [2]. As indicated by several researchers [3], the essence of 21st century education has shifted its focus from mere accumulation of knowledge to creation of knowledge or artifacts. A number of international organizations have proposed different frameworks to conceptualize so-called 21st century competences [4]. Among these frameworks, several commonly advocated notions of 21st century learning practice could be identified. First, learners should take their own responsibility for learning. In other words, they should be self-directed and self-regulated to set goals, make plans, monitor progress in order to achieve meaningful learning [5]. Besides, at the same time, learners should be able to collaborate and communicate with others to comprehend and construct solutions to solve authentic real-life problems [6]. Moreover, during these learning processes, learners need to utilize not only fundamental cognitive abilities but also require a handful of higher-order thinking abilities such as creative thinking as well as critical thinking [2].

Engaging learners in the abovementioned factors of learning should, in turn, assure them to more adequately accommodate themselves in facing daily life problems or challenges and become literate citizens in the future. Although a few studies have explored learners' perceptions of 21st century learning practice in classroom [6], some other crucial issues, for example, how teachers perceive themselves to implement such practices, should not be neglected. It is argued here that school teachers should, correspondingly, be accountable to enable learners to develop 21st century capabilities. In addition, researchers [7] have advocated that the affordances of ICT could be a viable vehicle to allow teachers to flexibly meet the instructional needs in dynamic classroom contexts and different groups of learners. In order to provide learners with twenty-first-century skills, teachers are required to use various pedagogical approaches with the help of ICT applications [8].

However, successful ICT integration in a 21st century classroom should not be taken for granted. Tsai and Chai [9] argued that a third-order barrier, namely the "design thinking," may exist to hinder teachers' disposition of classroom practices with the integration of ICT applications. Generally speaking, design thinking could be viewed as individuals' reasoning processes in order to manage a variety of demands and lead to the creation or improvement of certain products, services, and experiences [7]. Teachers' design thinking and dispositions could be regarded as part of their personal beliefs [10]. It enables teachers to transform their own mode of thinking to yield practical pedagogical solutions in classrooms. Therefore, when implementing 21st century learning in classrooms, teachers' design thinking and its disposition may be needed to take into consideration.

In sum, the main purpose of this study was to explore the underlying relations between teachers' perceptions of 21st century learning practice and their design dispositions using ICT applications. Besides, the relational patterns among the targeted constructs (i.e., 21st century learning practice, ICT usage, and design disposition) may be varied in terms of demographic variables such as gender. It would be beneficial, at least in a preliminary sense, to unravel meaningful results for future research by understanding salient differences between male and female teachers.

2 Methodology

To address the research purpose of this study, 157 Taiwan in-service teachers were invited to answer a questionnaire (described below) after receiving the permission of individual teacher. All of the participating teachers completed the questionnaires within 30-minute period.

The questionnaire comprised of three main parts. To assess the teachers' perceptions of 21st century learning practice, the items in the first part were adapted from the study of Chai et al. [6]. The original version of these items were used to understand primary school students' perceptions of 21st century learning in school. In the current study, we modified the items to accommodate the teacher participants to evaluate their perceptions in this regard. That is, there are five scales with a total of 22 items, including Collaborative Learning (CL) (e.g., I guide students to actively work together with other classmates to complete tasks), Critical Thinking (CT) (e.g., I provide opportunities for students to judge the value of new information or evidences presented to them), Self-directed Learning (SL) (e.g., I guide students to set goals for their own studying), Creative Thinking (CAT) (e.g., I guide students to suggest new ways of doing things), and Authentic Problem Solving (APS) (e.g., I guide students to apply the knowledge they have to solve real-life problems). These items were shown in a five-point Likert scale from strongly disagree (1) to strongly agree (5).

Besides, a six-item scale named "Meaningful usage with ICT" from Chai et al. [6] was used in this study as the second part of the questionnaire. This scale aimed to assess the teachers' perceptions of the extent to which they use appropriate technology to support students to learn. This scale also highlights the crucial role of ICT applications in the contemporary 21st learning practice. Moreover, as aforementioned, teachers' design disposition is another central feature to implement effective practices in classrooms. Therefore, a five-item "Design Disposition" scale derived from Dong et al. [11] was also adopted to evaluate the teachers' beliefs with respect to design thinking in the third part of the questionnaire. It should be noted that each statement in the two abovementioned scales was rated in a five-point Likert mode ranging from 1-strongly disagree to 5-strongly agree.

In order to establish reliability and validity of the questionnaire with respect to 21st century learning practice, an exploratory factor analysis (EFA) was utilized after data collection. And, a series of independent t-tests were conducted to compare the male and female teachers' perceptions of 21st century learning practice, meaningful usage with ICT, and design disposition. The correlation patterns among 21st century learning practice, meaningful usage with ICT, and design disposition, revealed by Pearson correlation analysis, between the male and female teachers were also compared.

3 Results

To initially clarify the structure of this questionnaire, an exploratory factor analysis (EFA) with a varimax rotation was performed. After the validation process, a total of 19 items (shown in Table 1), grouped into five corresponding factors as hypothesized, were retained and the total variance explained is 73.24%. In addition, the reliability

Table 1. Mean, standard error, Cronbach's alpha values and rotated factor loadings for the scales of perceptions of 21st century learning practice

Item	Measure	Mean	S.D.	Cronbach's alpha	Factor loading
Collaborative Learning (CL)					
CL1	I guide students to actively work together with other classmates to complete tasks.				0.83
CL2	I guide students to actively discuss different views about things they are learning with other classmates.	4.62	0.40	0.81	0.79
CL3	I guide students to get helpful comments about their own work from other classmates.				0.73
CL4	I guide students to actively work together to learn new things with other classmates.				0.60
Critical Thinking (CT)					
CT1	I provide opportunities for students to judge the value of new information or evidences presented to them.				0.69
CT2	I guide students to think about other possible ways of understanding what they are leaning.				0.74
CT3	I guide students to evaluate different opinions to see which one makes more sense.	4.63	0.46	0.88	0.71
CT4	I guide students to decide what kind of information can be trusted.				0.78
CT5	I guide students to distinguish what are supported by evidence and what are not.				0.66
Self-directed Learning (SL)					
SL1	I guide students to set goals for their own studying.				0.68
SL2	I guide students to make plans for how they will study.				0.84
SL3	I guide students to check their own progress when they study.	4.58	0.49	0.84	0.75
SL4	I guide students to think about different ways or methods they can use to improve their study.				0.68
Creative Thinking (CAT)		4.56	0.49	0.83	
CAT1	I guide students to generate many new ideas.				0.79
CAT2	I guide students to create different solutions for a problem.				0.73
CAT3	I guide students to suggest new ways of doing things.				0.62
Authentic Problem Solving (APS)					
APS1	I guide students to apply the knowledge they have to solve real-life problems.	4.58	0.49	0.91	0.81
APS2	I guide students to practice solving real-world problems.				0.84
APS3	I guide students to think about whether their solutions to real-world problems are good.				0.81

coefficients for these scales ranged from 0.81 to 0.88 and the overall alpha was 0.93. Overall, the EFA and Cronbach's alpha results indicate that the five scales had highly satisfactory validity as well as reliability in evaluating the participants' perceptions of 21st century learning practice. In addition, the reliabilities (Cronbach's alpha) of two scales including "Meaningful usage with ICT" and "Design Disposition" also indicate satisfactory internal consistency of the measured items (Cronbach's alpha = 0.93 and 0.85, respectively).

The 157 senior high school teachers' average item scores and the standard deviations of the five scales related to 21st century learning practice as well as two other scales (i.e., "Meaningful usage with ICT" and "Design Disposition") were calculated. In turn, they showed strongest agreement on the "Critical Thinking" scale (M = 4.63, S.D. = 0.46), followed by "Collaborative Learning" scale (M = 4.62, S.D. = 0.40), "Self-directed Learning" as well as "Authentic Problem Solving" scales (M = 4.58, S. D. = 0.84, 0.91, respectively), "Creative Thinking" scale (M = 4.56, S.D. = 0.49), "Meaningful usage with ICT" scale (M = 4.19, S.D. = 0.61), and "Design Disposition" scale (M = 4.05, S.D. = 0.55).

Table 2 presents the comparison results between the male and female teachers' average item scores of the seven scales used in this study. In general, the *t*-test results indicate that no significant gender differences were found in these scales, suggesting that the male and female senior high school teachers perceived themselves as similar level regarding meaningful usage with ICT, design disposition, and 21st century learning practice in classrooms.

Table 2. Comparison of meaningful usage with ICT, design disposition and perceptions of 21st century learning practice scales between male (n = 72) and female (n = 85) senior high school teachers

Scale	Groups	Mean	SD	t value
Collaborative Learning	Male	4.60	0.38	−0.35
	Female	4.63	0.41	
Critical Thinking	Male	4.62	0.46	−0.43
	Female	4.64	0.45	
Self-directed Learning	Male	4.55	0.51	−0.81
	Female	4.61	0.47	
Creative Thinking	Male	4.55	0.49	−0.43
	Female	4.58	0.50	
Problem Solving	Male	4.57	0.47	−0.14
	Female	4.58	0.51	
Meaningful Usage with ICT	Male	4.03	0.54	−0.48
	Female	4.07	0.56	
Design Disposition	Male	4.19	0.60	−0.05
	Female	4.19	0.62	

This study further identified the correlations among the senior high school teachers' meaningful usage with ICT, design disposition and perceptions of 21st century learning practice by means of Pearson correlation analysis. As shown in Table 3, by and large, the seven scales were significantly positively interrelated ($r = 0.33 \sim 0.60$, $p < .001$) except for the "Collaborative Learning" and "Design Disposition" scales ($r = 0.24$, $p > .001$). Furthermore, the correlation patterns between the two teacher groups were examined. Some similarities and differences were revealed. First, several significant correlation patterns among the four scales of perceptions of 21st century learning practice (i.e., "Critical Thinking," "Self-directed Learning," "Creative Thinking," and

Table 3. The correlations among the senior high school teachers' meaningful usage with ICT, design disposition and perceptions of 21st century learning practice

	Collaborative Learning	Critical Thinking	Self-directed Learning	Creative Thinking	Problem Solving
Meaningful Usage with ICT	0.33***	0.56***	0.55***	0.60***	0.47***
Design Disposition	0.24	0.35***	0.38***	0.41***	0.43***

Note. *** $p < .001$, N = 157

"Problem Solving") and "Meaningful Usage of ICT" scale in both male and female groups ($r = 0.41 \sim 0.63$, $p < .001$) were found (Table 3). However, in the male teacher group, there were no significant correlations between their "Design Disposition" and the five scales of perceptions 21st century learning practice (Table 4). In contrast, in the female teacher group, some significant correlation patterns among "Design Disposition" and "Self-directed Learning" as well as "Problem Solving" ($r = 0.40$ and 0.48, respectively, $p < .001$) were unravelled (Table 5).

Table 4. The correlations among the male senior high school teachers' meaningful usage with ICT, design disposition and perceptions of 21st century learning practice

	Collaborative Learning	Critical Thinking	Self-directed Learning	Creative Thinking	Problem Solving
Meaningful Usage with ICT	0.32	0.52***	0.56***	0.63***	0.54***
Design Disposition	0.29	0.37	0.35	0.47	0.35

Note. *** $p < .001$, N = 72

Table 5. The correlations among the female senior high school teachers' meaningful usage with ICT, design disposition and perceptions of 21st century learning practice

	Collaborative learning	Critical Thinking	Self-directed Learning	Creative Thinking	Problem Solving
Meaningful Usage with ICT	0.34	0.59***	0.55***	0.57***	0.41***
Design Disposition	0.20	0.33	0.40***	0.36	0.48***

Note. *** $p < .001$, N = 85

4   Conclusions

This study initially explored the relationships among Taiwan in-service teachers' perceptions of 21st century learning practice in classrooms, design disposition and usage of ICT. Overall, the teachers' perceptions of 21st century learning practice were found to be significantly positively correlated with their meaningful usage with ICT and design disposition. Yet, in the current study, different correlation patterns are evident between the male and female teachers' 21st century learning practice and design disposition. In particular, it is unanticipated that the male teachers' design disposition was not related to their 21st century learning practice. This result suggests that, when implementing such teaching practice in classrooms, the male teachers may simply integrate ICT applications in a surface level without considering contextual factors such as learners' needs, learning materials and instructional resources. Future research could explore this issue by means of a number of qualitative approaches such as classroom observations, or interviews to gain a more refined understanding.

Besides, the quantitative results derived from this study could serve as a foundation to encourage further investigations in this line of research.

References

1. Voogt, J., Pelgrum, H.: ICT and curriculum change. Hum. Technol. Interdisc. J. Hum. ICT Environ. **1**, 157–175 (2005)
2. Voogt, J., Roblin, N.P.: A comparative analysis of international frameworks for 21st century competences: implications for national curriculum policies. J. Curriculum Stud. **44**, 299–321 (2012)
3. Tsai, C.-C., Chai, C.S., Wong, B.K.S., Hong, H.-Y., Tan, S.C.: Positioning design epistemology and its applications in education technology. Educ. Technol. Soc. **16**, 81–90 (2013)
4. Dede, C.: Comparing frameworks for 21st century skills. In: Bellanca, J., Brandt, R. (eds.) 21st Century Skills: Rethinking How Students Learn, pp. 51–75. Solution Tree Press, Bloomington (2010)
5. Zimmerman, B.J.: Investigating self-regulation and motivation: historical backgrounds, methodological developments, and future prospect. Am. Educ. Res. J. **45**, 166–183 (2008)
6. Chai, C.S., Deng, F., Tsai, P.-S., Koh, J.H.L., Tsai, C.-C.: Assessing multidimensional students' perceptions of twenty-first-century learning practices. Asia Pac. Educ. Rev. **16**, 389–398 (2015)
7. Koh, J.H.L., Chai, C.S., Wong, B., Hong, H.-Y.: Technological pedagogical content knowledge (TPACK) and design thinking: a framework to support ICT lesson design for 21st century learning. Asia-Pac. Educ. Res. **24**, 535–543 (2015)
8. Voogt, J., Erstad, O., Dede, C., Mishra, P.I.: Challenges to learning and schooling in the digital networked world of the 21st century. J. Comput. Assist. Learn. **29**, 403–413 (2013)
9. Tsai, C.-C., Chai, C.S.: The "third"-order barrier for technology-integration instruction: implications for teacher education. Australas. J. Educ. Technol. **28**, 1057–1060 (2012)
10. Chai, C.S., Koh, J.H.L., Tsai, C.-C.: A review of technological pedagogical content knowledge. Educ. Technol. Soc. **16**, 31–51 (2013)
11. Dong, Y., Chai, C.S., Sang, G.-Y., Koh, H.L., Tsai, C.-C.: Exploring the profiles and interplays of pre-service and in-service teachers' technological pedagogical content knowledge (TPACK) in China. Educ. Technol. Soc. **18**, 158–169 (2015)

Author Index